Human-Centered Built Environment Heritage Preservation

Human-Centered Built Environment Heritage Preservation addresses the question of how a human-centered conservation approach can and should change practice. For the most part, there are few answers to this question because professionals in the heritage conservation field do not use social science research methodologies to manage cultural landscapes, assess historical significance and inform the treatment of building and landscape fabric. With few exceptions, only academic theorists have explored these topics while failing to offer specific, usable guidance on how the social sciences can actually be used by heritage professionals.

In exploring the nature of a human-centered heritage conservation practice, we explicitly seek a middle ground between the academy and practice, theory and application, fabric and meanings, conventional and civil experts, and orthodox and heterodox ideas behind practice and research. We do this by positioning this book in a transdisciplinary space between these dichotomies as a way to give voice (and respect) to multiple perspectives without losing sight of our goal that heritage conservation practice should, fundamentally, benefit all people. We believe that this approach is essential for creating an emancipated built heritage conservation practice that must successfully engage very different ontological and epistemological perspectives.

Jeremy C. Wells is an assistant professor in the Historic Preservation Program at the University of Maryland, College Park and a Fulbright scholar. His research explores ways to make built heritage conservation practice more responsive to people through the use of applied social science research methods from environmental psychology, humanistic geography, anthropology, and community development/public health. Wells is a member of the Environmental Design Research Association's (EDRA's) board and past Chair. At EDRA, he created the Historic Environment Knowledge Network to engage academics and practitioners in addressing the person/place and environment/behavior aspects of heritage conservation. Wells runs the heritagestudies.org website that explores how to evolve heritage conservation practice using critical heritage studies theory to better balance meanings and power between experts and most stakeholders.

Barry L. Stiefel is an associate professor at the College of Charleston's Historic Preservation and Community Planning Program. Stiefel's research interests are in how the sum of local preservation efforts affects regional, national, and multi-national policies within the field of cultural resource management and heritage conservation. He has authored and/or edited numerous articles and books, including *Community-Built: Art, Construction, Preservation, and Place* (co-edited with Katherine Melcher and Kristin Faurest, 2017); and *Sustainable Heritage: Merging Environmental Conservation and Historic Preservation* (co-authored with Amalia Leifeste, 2018).

Human-Centered Built Environment Heritage Preservation

Theory and Evidence-Based Practice

Edited by
Jeremy C. Wells and Barry L. Stiefel

NEW YORK AND LONDON

First published 2019
by Routledge
711 Third Avenue, New York, NY 10017

and by Routledge
2 Park Square, Milton Park, Abingdon, Oxon, OX14 4RN

Routledge is an imprint of the Taylor & Francis Group, an informa business

© 2019 Taylor & Francis

The right of Jeremy C. Wells and Barry L. Stiefel to be identified as the authors of the editorial material, and of the authors for their individual chapters, has been asserted in accordance with sections 77 and 78 of the Copyright, Designs and Patents Act 1988.

All rights reserved. No part of this book may be reprinted or reproduced or utilised in any form or by any electronic, mechanical, or other means, now known or hereafter invented, including photocopying and recording, or in any information storage or retrieval system, without permission in writing from the publishers.

Trademark notice: Product or corporate names may be trademarks or registered trademarks, and are used only for identification and explanation without intent to infringe.

Library of Congress Cataloging-in-Publication Data
A catalog record for this title has been requested

ISBN: 978-1-138-58394-8 (hbk)
ISBN: 978-1-138-58395-5 (pbk)
ISBN: 978-0-429-50635-2 (ebk)

Typeset in Minion Pro
by codeMantra

To Vivie and Rosie and their bountiful future…

J.C.W.

…and to Juliet (Juju) too!

Additionally, the gratitude I have for Isaak Katz (1713–1790) and Rewecka (?–1806) of Rauschenberg, Hessen, Germany, who, two centuries before I was born, had the foresight to leave a message as to why a certain place mattered to them—inviting me into a past that became family as well as creating a purpose of motivation.

B.L.S.

Contents

Acknowledgments | xi
Foreword by Tom Mayes | xiii
Preface | xv

Introduction: Moving Past Conflicts to Foster an Evidence-Based, Human-Centric Built Heritage Conservation Practice | 1

Jeremy C. Wells and Barry L. Stiefel

Part 1
Defining a Human-Centric Built Heritage Conservation Practice | 31

1 Bridging the Gap between Built Heritage Conservation Practice and Critical Heritage Studies | 33

Jeremy C. Wells

2 The Measurement of Meaning—Psychometrics and *Sense of Place* | 45

Suzanne Elizabeth Bott

3 Meeting the Shadow: Resource Management and the McDonaldization of Heritage Stewardship | 67

Richard M. Hutchings

4 The Mystery of History and Place: Radical Preservation Revisited | 89

Jack D. Elliott, Jr.

CONTENTS

Part 2
Ways to Gather Evidence 101

5 The Perception and Preservation of Vernacular Architectural
Features in an Urban Historic District with Heritage Value:
A Case Study from Grand Rapids, Michigan 103
You Kyong Ahn

6 Image for the Future of the Historic City: Photo-Elicitation
and Architectural Preservation in Barcelona 129
AnnaMarie Bliss

7 Conservation and the People's Views: Ethnographic Perspectives
from Jones Beach State Park 143
Dana H. Taplin, Suzanne Scheld, and Setha Low

Part 3
Using Evidence to Change Practice 157

8 Tours of Critical Geography and Public Deliberation:
Applied Social Sciences as Guide 159
Jennifer Minner

9 Of Policy Lags and "Upgraded" Neighborhoods:
Historic Preservation for the Twenty-First Century 177
Ted Grevstad-Nordbrock

10 Urban Preservation: A Community and Economic
Development Perspective 195
Stephanie Ryberg-Webster

11 Using Evidence from the Community to Guide a Local
Municipality's Preservation Program 213
Kimberli Fitzgerald

12 Democratizing Conservation: Challenges to Changing the
Paradigm of Cultural Heritage Management 233
Richard A. Engelhardt, Heather A. Peters, and Montira Horayangura Unakul

viii

CONTENTS

13 Missed Opportunities: The Absence of Ethnography in America's
Cultural Heritage Programs 255
Richard Vidutis

Part 4
The Role of Higher Education in Leading Evidence-based Practice 273

14 "But Where Are the People?" Grappling with Teaching New
Approaches to Our Relationship with Place and the Past 275
Michelle Jolly, Melinda Milligan, Margaret Purser, and Laura Alice Watt

15 "The Places My Granddad Built": Using Popular Interest in
Genealogy as a Pedagogical Segue to Historic Preservation 289
Barry L. Stiefel

16 Resistance to Research: Diagnosis and Treatment
of a Disciplinary Ailment 309
Ned Kaufman

Conclusion: A Human-Centered Way Forward 317
Jeremy C. Wells and Barry L. Stiefel

*Appendix A: The Palmer House Charter: Principles for Integrating Environmental
Design and Behavior Research into Built Heritage Conservation Practice* 333
Biographies of Editors and Contributing Authors 337
Index 343

Acknowledgments

There is one person and one organization in particular that we wish to thank in framing the ideas that made *Human-Centered Built Environment Heritage Preservation* possible. Without David Lowenthal and his 1985 publication, *The Past is a Foreign Country*, our present publication would simply not exist. In May 2011, the University of Massachusetts, Amherst, hosted a conference on "Why Does the Past Matter?: Changing Visions, Media, and Rationales in the 21st Century". At the conference, David Lowenthal was recognized with a special honor for his distinguished career and gave a lecture titled "Prizing the Past for the Present and the Future." Not only was the editor, Barry L. Stiefel, in attendance at the conference and for the lecture, but also serendipitously during one of the lunch breaks, found himself sitting next to Lowenthal and enjoying a casual conversation. This personal moment and relaxed discussion provided meaningful insights pertaining to Lowenthal's philosophies on heritage as well as objectives, which planted a seed of critical thinking pertaining to how heritage preservation, best practices, and education might be reconsidered.

Without the Environmental Design Research Association (EDRA), this book could not have come to fruition. Not only is EDRA widely credited with conceptualizing and promoting the idea of evidence-based design, but it is also one of the only philanthropic organizations dedicated to bringing academics and practitioners together in a trans-disciplinary environment where the topic of practice or research matters more than one's disciplinary affiliation. This perspective is infused throughout this book and many of the chapter authors are also EDRA members and, like the editor, Jeremy C. Wells, have fully engaged EDRA's mission "to provide a collaborative, multidisciplinary community to connect theory, research, teaching, and practice to recognize, create and advocate for environments that are responsive to diverse human needs."

Foreword

In bringing together these articles for *Human-Centered Built Environment Heritage Preservation,* editors Jeremy C. Wells and Barry L. Stiefel build a bridge between the theory and practice of historic preservation that is critically important for the future of the field. When I wrote the series of essays on *Why Old Places Matter* (savingplaces.org/why-do-old-places-matter) (The essays are forthcoming as a book, Rowman and Littlefield, 2018), I drew on the many fields that study—*and often critique*—what preservationists do, from environmental psychology to architectural and aesthetic theory, critical heritage studies, and cultural geography. Yet, I noted a chasm between the work of these academic and scholarly fields and practicing preservation professionals. Many scholars analyzed what was protected as heritage, how it was protected, and for and by whom, but did not always suggest solutions to address the issues they so carefully identified and dissected. And while there were exceptions, I found that our underfunded, often embattled, and hardworking preservation professionals had neither the time nor the inclination to read, decipher, and implement the theories in scholarly work.

This volume seeks to bridge that chasm. The articles have been solicited with the express intention of proposing ideas that can be implemented to generate positive change. Coming at a crucial juncture when preservationists have tried to envision the future, this volume will not only be a welcome addition to the literature, but also should influence the practice of historic preservation in the United States, among other places abroad.

In 2017, the National Trust for Historic Preservation issued *Preservation for People: A Vision for the Future,* the culmination of nearly two years of discussions and meetings held throughout the United States in commemoration of the fiftieth anniversary of the National Historic Preservation Act of 1966. The *Vision* advocates that preservation "ground its work in human needs and aspirations, and become a prevalent, powerful, and practical force to sustain, improve, and enrich people's lives." The *Vision* signals a paradigm shift in thinking about the purposes of historic preservation. Although this idea of shifting to a people-oriented practice may not sound radical, it is a major philosophical change for historic preservation as practiced in the United States.

Moving "from fabric-centered to human-centered practice," as eloquently expressed by Michelle Jolly, Melinda Milligan, Margaret Purser, and Laura A. Watt in Chapter 14, ""But Where are the People?" Grappling with Teaching New Approaches to Our Relationship with Place and the Past," will require the re-examination of the existing tools of historic preservation, from the process of nominating properties onto the National Register of Historic Places, to application of the Secretary of the Interior's Standards for the Treatment of Historic Properties. In addition, new tools and new skill sets will be required for communities and practitioners, including new ways of engaging people in determining what places matter to them. From the use of genealogy as a gateway drug to historic

FOREWORD

preservation, to borrowing the public engagement tools of the planning profession, to traditional sociological interview tools, to the use of photographs or other visuals, the ideas suggested in this volume begin to chart a path forward to a more people-centered preservation practice.

While the overarching theme of the volume is that preservation practice should be more evidence-based, embedded in these articles is also a debate about the limits of empiricism. How much of the work of historic preservation can be studied scientifically and what can we realistically know about the many elements of people's relationship with old places? While many of the articles advocate for a scientific basis for the work of historic preservation, others note the limits of that work. In particular, the "The Mystery of History and Place: Radical Preservation Revisited," by Jack D. Elliott argues for experiencing the world "in a radically old way" and moving beyond "simply saving bricks and mortar" to evaluating historic places in terms of their symbolic potential. Yet, others lament how little the field has been studied scientifically. While I think both points of view have merit—we need both more scientific study while we must also recognize—and explore—its present-day limits, the voices, and opinions in this volume begin to shape that discussion.

In bridging that chasm between theory and practice, *Human-Centered Built Heritage Conservation* provides an important contribution to the future of historic preservation. The ideas and solutions proposed in this volume hopefully will serve as both concepts and tools to fulfill the vision that historic preservation become a "prevalent, powerful, and practical force to sustain, improve, and enrich *people's* lives."

Thompson M. Mayes, Vice President and Senior Counsel,
National Trust for Historic Preservation, Washington, D.C. 2017

Preface

The contributions for *Human-Centered Built Heritage Conservation* were largely cultivated from two significant events in 2016, the "Using Applied Social Science Methodologies to Conserve the Historic Environment: Can Evidence Change Practice?" session at the Environmental Design Research Association Conference in Raleigh, North Carolina (May 18) and the Association for Critical Heritage Studies Conference (June 3–8) in Montreal, Quebec; where the theme was "What Does Heritage Change?" Jeremy C. Wells was the organizer for the session in Raleigh, which Barry L. Stiefel and others attended, and Wells and Stiefel both attended the Montreal conference as well. Additional contributions were also recruited from outside of these events. Nonetheless, the presentations and informal conversations that took place at these conferences was the impetuous for this publication because of the desire to document not only what was done, but also to initiate a legacy of how we— all contributors—might make a positive change to the academic field and vocational profession of initiating and using evidence based on the human aspects of heritage conservation to best change practices. Only time will tell if we will have any lasting impact or success, but we hope that the reader will consider what we have done and carry forward what we believe to be a very important under- taking in the improved preservation and maintenance of cultural heritage, material artifacts of all sizes, and social-human needs.

Introduction

Moving Past Conflicts to Foster an Evidence-Based, Human-Centric Built Heritage Conservation Practice

Jeremy C. Wells and Barry L. Stiefel

This book is about building an emancipated built heritage and cultural landscape conservation practice that moves away from laws, rules, regulations, and doctrine as a basis for its required operation. In doing so, we focus on how to free conventional practice from its reliance on expert rule and disarm its authority through the use of evidence obtained through social science and participatory research methods. While there is no consensus on how this outcome can be achieved, the authors contained in this volume explore how evidence, obtained from applied social science and participatory research methods, might achieve a more democratic and grass-roots-driven conservation practice. In this chapter, we will explore the way in which the conservation of built heritage and cultural landscapes is conflicted and the form in which a human-centered, emancipated conservation practice might take, and the ways in which this goal can be put into practice using evidence. We will then summarize the papers in this book that address this goal from both theoretical and applied perspectives.

The rationale for our endeavor is supported by a growing realization that the orthodox, doctrinal foundations of building conservation have not been empirically substantiated and instead have been taken as a matter of faith (Avrami, Mason, & Torre, 2000, 10; Galindo & Hidalgo, 2005, 25; Mason, 2008, 315). To be sure, this assertion implies the dubious acceptability of conducting research to prove orthodox conservation doctrine "right" even when such work would be tainted with a confirmation bias. Indeed, as John Pendlebury (2009, 222) asserts, most research in built heritage conservation is, in fact, undertaken in this manner, with predefined outcomes. Salvador Muñoz Viñas (2005) refers to research in the field of movable and immovable object conservation as inherently tautological, where the acceptable practice is defined by the practice that came before it, and as such, meanings and values become increasingly ossified through a never-ending positive feedback loop.

In order to defeat this loop, we break a fundamental tenet in orthodox practice by assuming that heritage is in the present, not the past (c.f., Harrison, 2013, 32, 165; Silverman, Waterton, & Watson, 2017, 4, 8; Smith, 2006, 3) and that practice must address the present as well as conceivably the future too. In practical terms, this break means that "significance" is not based primarily on historical facts from an arbitrarily distant past (e.g., the "50-year rule" in the United States; similar rules are elsewhere), but on the contemporary meanings and values of everyday people (not just conventional experts). This also means that the standard practice of archival research to establish a factual past should not drive practice, but rather consulting with everyday people on the meanings and uses of heritage should be fundamental to any built heritage practitioner. (Note that this assertion does not invalidate the need for archival research; instead, we advocate for a balance in methods to inform

INTRODUCTION

practice.) Additionally, we should also consider future implications of how and why we choose, or choose not, to preserve a particular place. These assertions, therefore, provide a space to question (and more radically, dismiss) conventional conservation practice, especially as it addresses the care of old places. Indeed, if we conceptualize the professional standards that undergird built heritage conservation practice as just a manifestation of a particular cultural belief system, as Laurajane Smith (2006) posits, then the lack of empirical evidence is entirely logical because such evidence threatens to invalidate deeply held beliefs. This situation may also help to explain why built heritage conservation practice has largely failed to make the critical turn in the recognition and treatment of heritage.

How, then, should a critical turn in built heritage manifest? This question is unanswerable until "built heritage and cultural landscape conservation practice" is explicitly defined. But even before this question can be answered, it is important to ask if the care of heritage should be a professional endeavor at all. Some approaches to heritage scholarship do at least unintentionally advocate for this position, by engaging in a broad-brush dismissal of all things associated with conventional experts using a colonialist perspective, among other possibilities. To be clear, we do not take this radical position, but rather assert that a better balance needs to be found between professional practice and the needs of everyday people in how the conservation of old places is addressed. Currently, professional practice is too biased towards authority and the dismissal of local/indigenous knowledge and other ways of knowing and understanding heritage. As a field, the interest of heritage conservation is very broad, spanning activities from museums to archives and from buildings to entire landscapes. And, more recently, it has become increasingly interested in the intangible, focusing on cultural practices and marginalized communities of practice. To be clear, this book makes no attempt to broadly critique the field of heritage conservation, as its scope is far too large. It does, however, critique what we refer to as the professional care of old places, which is a less jargon-heavy term and one to which most people can easily relate. The care of old places (and even vehicles) conflates the artificial separation between the conservation of buildings, structures, and landscapes and highlights the place-centric quality of contemporary heritage work. So, in a sense, this book addresses place-centered heritage conservation.

Since this book explicitly addresses practice, it is therefore important to clearly define the specific areas of practice to which we are referring. The following list, gathered from the United States, Canada, the United Kingdom, Australia, and New Zealand, encompasses the professional areas of practice that directly address the care of old places, and is therefore the specific focus of our attention:

- Historic preservation planner
- Historic preservation officer
- Cultural resource manager/specialist
- Architectural historian
- Cultural resources program manager
- Historic site director/manager
- Preservation architect
- Historic architect
- Architectural materials conservator

INTRODUCTION

- Main Street manager

- Heritage tourism specialist

- Inspector of historic buildings and areas

- Conservation officer

- Heritage building surveyor

- Heritage planner

- Heritage policy & projects officer

- Heritage assessment officer.

Note that many of these areas overlap with other, allied interests, such as archaeology, indigenous heritage, and public history, which, although they are important, are not the focus of this book. In sum, this book is for *all* people who are interested in the professional care of old places—practitioners, students, and academics—especially as this work relates to law and policy.

To be sure, a book like this that addresses academic topics, such as empirical evidence and critical approaches, will likely largely appeal to academics and possibly alienate some practitioners. After all, as Seymour Sarason (1993, 132) acknowledges, "too many practitioners do not read what they should be reading" unless they are required to do so, such as with continuing education credit requirements; but none of the professionals who work in the care of old places have continuing education credit requirements unless they are licensed architects or certified planners. The reality is that even if easy-to-digest material on an emancipated conservation practice is made available to practitioners, most will not bother to read it. We cannot control or dictate this outcome and thus make it plain and clear. With this in mind, however, we have attempted—to the greatest extent possible—to include relevant chapters written by practitioners who work in some aspect in the care of old places because we do recognize that some practitioners take a more enlightened perspective on their work. We hope that at least some practitioners—especially policy makers—will find this material useful, and most importantly, practical for changing conservation practice within their sphere of influence.

Lastly, there is no one disciplinary tradition under which the material in the book fits. Although we rely heavily on the work of critical heritage scholars, this is not a "traditional" critical heritage studies book because we have made the bold decision to include the voices of (enlightened) practitioners as equals with scholars from critical heritage studies backgrounds. Nor is this a conventional historic preservation book that focuses on the care of fabric, such as buildings or historic districts, embedded in rules and regulations. It is certainly not a book that neatly fits in cultural resource management, which is even more driven by required rules and regulations. And it certainly is not a book that fits in the objective, factual space of history and art history or in the creative realm of design and architecture. Rather, we view this book as a transdisciplinary tool, carving out a space in between these disciplines, and more, in an effort to bridge between the chasms that separate theory and practice and between academics and practitioners. We, therefore, take the position, "in stakeholders we trust" (Wells, 2015a), which is a vulnerable perspective because of the conflicted state in which heritage conservation practice finds itself, especially in the care of old places that privileges expert rule.

INTRODUCTION

Heritage Conservation as a Practice in Conflict and the Need to Understand and Engage with the "Other"

> [T]he cultural process and performance that is heritage is about the negotiation of … conflicts.
>
> —Laurajane Smith (2006, 82)

As many researchers from critical heritage studies have observed, the meanings of heritage arise from conflict, not consensus (Breglia, 2006, 3; Daly & Chan, 2015, 492; Smith, 2006, 82; Tunbridge & Ashworth, 1996); indeed, Smith (2006) makes the claim that the goal of conventional heritage conservation practice is to perpetuate the myth that heritage is free of conflict and defined by consensus. Similarly, we argue that the meanings associated with the *practice* of heritage conservation, and specifically built heritage conservation, are also inherently conflicted with the various actors from practice and the academy engaging in mutual distrust and suspicion which leads to a lack of understanding, much less empathy. To wit, Keith Emerick (2014, 169) argues "the role of the [built] heritage specialist is now unclear" with an uncertainty if the practitioner is supposed to be an expert, a community facilitator, or some kind of contextualized hybrid. In order to achieve some level of cooperation from a wider array of heritage conservation actors, there needs to be a greater attempt at understanding the "Other." For instance, as epitomized by the original version of the Association of Critical Heritage Study's Manifesto (Campbell & Smith, 2012), heritage conservation practitioners are depicted as objects of study, which, to some degree, denies their humanity and right to be understood on terms equal with the researcher (although this does not imply that their meanings must be accepted–this is a different conversation altogether). Conversely, the nearly total failure of historic preservation in the United States and architectural and urban conservation, internationally, to engage with critical heritage studies implies a similar level of distrust and a lack of understanding of alternative perspectives, especially those that advocate for the practitioner operating primarily as a facilitator.

This conflict is not as simple as the stereotypical divide between the ivory-tower academic and the grounded practitioner; it also exists within the academy with some academics who work on built heritage fully embracing expert rule, conventional doctrine, and colonialist perspectives while other academics have taken an opposite approach, embracing more democratic, non-Western, emancipatory methods based on an ethnographic understanding of heritage that disarms expert rule. As a rule, academics originating from a fabric-based perspective (e.g., historic preservation, architectural conservation, preservation architecture) assume the former perspective while academics from social science and humanities backgrounds (e.g., anthropology, communication studies, folklore) assume the latter perspective, although there are certainly exceptions. There is probably no better example of this situation than in the academic consultants to UNESCO (especially World Heritage) and who participate in ICOMOS's scientific committees, many of which intentionally or unintentionally enforce expert rule in defense of World Heritage criteria and processes (c.f., Harrison, 2013; Pannekoek, 1998; Silverman, Waterton, & Watson, 2017; Smith, 2006; Smith and Waterton, 2012). In the United States, many academics in historic preservation also embrace and promulgate expert rule, which should not be surprising given that the historic preservation degree was created primarily to provide the staff trained in implementing environmental review laws, rules, and regulations (Tomlan, 1994)—in essence, there was a clear need to produce heritage experts to enforce the law. A difficult challenge for historic preservation and architectural conservation degree programs in the United States and

4

INTRODUCTION

abroad is what they become if they are divorced from expert rule, which, in essence, appears to invalidate a substantial reason for their existence.

An example of this kind of conflict is epitomized by a conversation that the first author had with a U.S.-based historic preservation academic, who, for the purposes of this narrative, I will refer to by the pseudonym of "John." John had recently returned from a visiting teaching opportunity located in a critical heritage studies program in the United Kingdom. While appreciative of the experience, he could not wait to return home to the United States, so he could get back to "real preservation work" that had a clear focus on buildings and their fabric. While acknowledging that people were obviously important, John clearly preferred to not have to deal with uncertainty embraced by critical approaches and he very much liked being the expert within his fabric- and design-based domain of expertise. John was adamant that critical heritage studies was *not* his focus because it had very little to do with his own work as a preservation architect. John roundly dismissed critical approaches as irrelevant to historic preservation and had little interest in teaching critical approaches to his students in the historic preservation program in which he taught. In sum, John thought that critical approaches to heritage were akin to "counting the number of angels on the head of a pin" and thus, was a waste of his time.

Before dismissing John's account as misguided at best and troglodytic at worst, it is important to recognize that his perspective must be taken into account and considered as part of the overall milieu in which many practitioners and academics, especially, those who teach in fabric-centered built heritage programs, exist. Proponents of critical heritage studies need to be more aware of this perspective and its attendant problems of engagement, because as Tim Winter (2013, 533) warns, if these researchers continue on their current path of ignoring (or marginalizing) the voice of the practitioner or fabric-centric professor/instructor, critical heritage studies researchers will further alienate themselves from practitioners and the ability to influence practice. Similarly, Witcomb and Buckley (2013, 569) advocate that critical heritage studies researchers "should … do everything we can to avoid a form of gesture that alienates a good proportion of the audience we should be engaging with or without losing our faith in the value of critique." To be sure, this is a difficult directive to actualize, but the critical heritage perspective, which gives power to the ethnographic voice and *emic* understanding/empathy, ought to be setting the example in productively engaging with the "Other," yet, we argue that there is little evidence that this discourse is occurring.

Practitioners who engage in the care of old places need to be aware, as Keith Emerick (2014, 20) explains, that "if you are trained and immersed in a system that stresses the importance of the expert view and expert values, it is not an easy or simple undertaking to reconsider yourself as just one of many interest groups." This observation also holds true for many of the academics in historic preservation and architectural conservation education programs whose authority and credibility rests not on the production of original research, which, as Ned Kaufman observes in Chapter 16 of this book, often is not produced by these individuals, but on their work as practitioners embedded in the *status quo*. This reinforces Smith's (2006) assertion that rather than being grounded in empirical evidence (which is not being generated anyway) the professional practice associated with the care of old places is just another cultural practice, among many, with no clear right to assert its values as the best and "true" way forward. But, let us be clear that the right of the built heritage expert is not just a culturally engrained value system, but one that can often manifest as the rule of law. The ramification of this situation is that where individual property rights are governed by rules and regulations meant to protect historic fabric, the conventional expert will always be in a position of power, which makes negotiation with other stakeholders consistently an inequitable process.

INTRODUCTION

Overall, for this book, we have consciously chosen one of the most difficult spaces for discourse that lies between disparate disciplines and between practitioners and different kinds of academics. These groups lack a common language and come from very different ontological and epistemological perspectives and each attempts to assert its own dominance over heritage discourse; in sum, they do not appear to want to work collaboratively. As Peter Howard (2003, 30) elucidates, "[each] discipline has controlled for very many years the conservation and preservation of the bit of heritage in which it is interested, and it will certainly not welcome your investigation into its stewardship." We accept this challenge of potentially receiving a hostile reception to our message, realizing that the transdisciplinary approach we advocate will not be welcome or accepted by many who instead advocate for very specific ways of knowing while rejecting other possibilities foreign to their discipline or field of study.

We also acknowledge that some readers will think that the work contained herein is too theoretical or too applied, or that by including the voices of practitioners, we have accepted their dominance in the heritage discourse and thus, reject the critical turn in heritage. To be clear, all authors in this volume are interested in the critical turn in heritage but do not necessarily seek the dominance of one perspective over another. We wish to promote a pluralistic and balanced idea of how a human-centered professional practice of caring for old places can manifest from both theoretical and applied perspectives and from multifarious disciplinary and field vantages. We do not prescribe to the idea that there is only one way of knowing or doing; rather, we wish to learn from as many perspectives as possible, always keeping in mind that we seek social justice from a more democratic and inclusive process of caring for old places.

To be sure, the message here is that some of the ideas explored in this book may be controversial, or too theoretical, or too applied relative to certain perspectives; they may not be easy for some individuals to accept and will represent perspectives that are normal to some disciplines, but quite unusual for others. It is far easier to engage in a discussion with people most like yourself, but the danger of an insular perspective is that it leads to a "tendency for each bit of heritage to fall into the scholarly concern of only one discipline, and therefore its presentation and interpretation to be single-faceted," as Peter Howard (2003, 140) explains. We, therefore, have undertaken an approach in this book to avoid a singular disciplinary or field perspective, and instead include many voices from many disciplines, while realizing that this approach will definitely generate conflict. And one area in which there is substantial conflict is in an understanding of both the need and the nature of "evidence" that has the ability to drive how professionals care for old places. But, it is precisely this area of study that needs to the most attention to help facilitate built heritage conservation's critical turn that is necessary to better embrace a human-centered practice.

What Is "Evidence"?

> [T]here are no sacred truths; all assumptions must be critically examined; arguments from authority are worthless. ... [W]hatever is inconsistent with the facts must be discarded or revised.
>
> —Carl Sagan (1980, 333)

> "Good" evidence is produced where there is "an openness to new ideas, no matter how bizarre or counterintuitive, and the most ruthlessly skeptical scrutiny of all ideas, old and new."
>
> —Carl Sagan (1997, 304)

INTRODUCTION

Sometime around the year 1650, at the request of a friend, a man visited a "disquieted" house in Bow, England, now a district in the eastern part of greater London. Upon arriving, he greeted the woman of the house, and she explained that the house was "extremely haunted especially above stairs, so that [the family was] forced to keep in the low rooms, there was such flinging of things up and down, of Stones and Bricks through the Windows and putting all in disorder" (Glanvill, More, & Horneck, 1681, 255). The man, thinking that this was a joke, went upstairs to investigate and was quite disturbed to see windows opening by themselves and bedding, candlesticks, and furniture flinging themselves across the room (256, 257). Realizing that something was "more than ordinary," the man ran down the stairs to escape and collect his composure. Later, while talking with the family downstairs, he saw "a Tobacco-pipe rise from a side Table ... and fly to the other side of the Room, and break itself against the wall," further confirming the haunted qualities of the house (257). Due to these disquieting events, the family soon moved and the house remained empty for many years due to its haunted reputation.

Today, we can look back at this account as superstitious nonsense, especially because of its second-hand source (as related by the storyteller). Yet, for the people of the seventeenth century, these experiences were quite real and many of these accounts were believed with an undeserved veracity; in their more extreme forms, it led to the persecution and death of innocent people as witches and sorcerers. Even in the twenty-first century, there are still people who believe in the idea of haunted houses—or, more specifically, that the "spirit" of something can be embedded in the fabric of buildings. Science, so far, has failed to find any credibility to these claims, yet they are quite real for some people in the present. There is even a contemporary field of professional practice that bases its values on these ideas that the spirit or essence of the past can somehow be contained in the fabric of buildings and other structures. It is known variously as historic preservation, built heritage conservation, architectural conservation, or monument conservation, depending on where one is located.[1]

Let us unpack this seemingly magical claim through a thought experiment. If we take a brick from Thomas Jefferson's Monticello and compare it to an identical brick made by the same person at the same time but found in a random field, which brick is more valuable? When presented with this question, most people will say that the brick from Monticello is obviously more important. Logically, this makes little sense because the material of which the brick is made is identical and the bricks look identical. One could even argue, from a scientific perspective, that the specific materials of the bricks are also identical. So, what is so different about these two bricks as to elicit such a strong, confirmatory response? The answer is that the brick from Monticello has acted as a witness to history, and in doing so, "absorbed" some of it. Or, in other words, a specific chapter in "history" that is well known with an established provenance has been imprinted somehow into the brick itself as if it is some kind of spirit, or "essence of the past," whereas this is not the case for the second brick from the field (Matzko, 2001, 8). But, where is the evidence for the phenomenon of tangible objects endowed with specific spirits of the past?

To answer this question, we need to have a clear understanding of the qualities of evidence. In simplistic terms, "evidence" is a way of substantiating a particular belief. So, the fact that people believe that the past imprints itself on the fabric of buildings is, indeed, a kind of evidence. But, is it "good" evidence? Do we want to base the practice of heritage conservation on people's feelings? Orthodox conservation practice has clearly answered this question in the negative. To be sure, orthodox practice has ample doctrine, laws, rules, and regulations that do sanction the use of historical facts as a kind of proxy for measuring the essence of history contained in fabric. Treating the built environment in this way is pseudoscience, however—overlaying a positivistic, scientific paradigm

INTRODUCTION

based on the qualities of objects onto what is clearly a social science phenomenon. In reality, there is no essence of the past in objects; instead, people *believe* it is there and base entire cultural practices on this belief, which are readily evident in the treatment of religious relics, for instance. Yet, instead of generating empirical evidence for how people feel about objects of the past, orthodox conservation practice defines its evidence through the objective qualities of fabric and facts of the past (Muñoz Viñas, 2005).

Examples of the dubious numinous evidence upon which orthodox conservation practice is based are numerous. The belief that objects contain the essence of the past is actually an ancient western tradition. During the early centuries of the Common Era, when Christianity was in its infancy, the phenomenon became prevalent through the efforts of Roman Emperor Constantine (272–337 c.e.), his mother Helena Augusta (246–330 c.e.), and mother-in-law Eutropia (d. after 325 c.e.). Most likely, this custom predates the fourth century c.e., considering that much of what Christianity was documenting at this time was often borrowed from other cultures absorbed by the Roman Empire. Helena Augusta became the patron saint of archaeology for on her trip to the Levant between 326 and 328 c.e., she not only miraculously found the True Cross and identified specific sites significant for Christianity, but also initiated the construction of churches in these locations; including the Church of the Nativity in Bethlehem, the Church of the Holy Sepulcher in Jerusalem, and St. Catherine's on Mt. Sinai (Ottaway, 1992). These churches instantly became monuments inculcated with the spirit of their respective past biblical events. By modern, scientific standards St. Helena's methodology would be considered problematic, but for the fervently faithful early Christians the process met their spiritual needs, as well as the new economy of pilgrimage tourism. According to contemporary archaeologist Gregory T. Armstrong (1967), these and other churches were symbols that established early Christianity "as an historical, this-worldly religion, a religion founded on events of a specific time and place." Moreover, it became common for churches to contain relics associated with Jesus Christ or one of the saints. The movement of preserving relics spread from the Middle East to Europe, and so forth, and became dogma in 787 c.e. when the Second Council of Nicaea declared that every church dedication should include the placing of relics, thus infusing them with holiness and a connection to a sacred event or person. During the Middle Ages, there was such a demand for relics that they were fabricated if no genuine article was to be had, or if a parish or monastery was unable to afford one. Church decrees have consistently held that what is now considered forgery is not necessarily a problem, thereby accounting for the multiplicity of limbs from the same saint as well as the great number of fragments from the True Cross (Bonser, 1962).

The importance of relic preservation and reverence within Christianity later came to influence western culture's association of ancient materials, artifacts, and sites with historic events and people. This is why a brick from Thomas Jefferson's Monticello is "holier" than another of identical age, material, size, color, and appearance without an established provenance. In a manner of speaking, the graphing of Church reverence for material objects imbedded with the spiritual essence of the past was transferred into heritage conservation's best practices during the nineteenth century, with the early theorists of Eugène Emmanuel Viollet-le-Duc, John Ruskin, Camillo Boito, among others. While early preservationists may have disagreed with one another on how to approach the restoration or conservation of a specific building, all revered buildings that were infused with the essence or spirit of a place or past events.

We see this come full circle when considering that Bethlehem's Church of the Nativity, Jerusalem's Church of the Holy Sepulcher, and St. Catherine's of Mt. Sinai are all a central focus of a UNESCO World Heritage site, a testament to both the long and continued tradition of western society's

INTRODUCTION

memorialization of these places and also the sacredness that the buildings constructed at the sites (from St. Helena's instigation) have acquired since the original biblical events.[2] Therefore, what we are proposing with this volume is both a reformation of contemporary preservation/conservation best practices as well as the custom that spans back millennia. This is not to say that the belief that objects containing the essence of the past should be completely expunged from western culture—indeed, this extreme action would be antithetical to what we are aiming to achieve. But preservation practitioners need to be made aware of this aspect of the field's heritage and be able to think critically about what may be an appropriate or inappropriate application of this cultural value that they inherited. To be sure, this exploration of the numinous quality of fabric does not necessarily represent the personal belief system of practitioners themselves, but is rather embodied in the doctrines for preservation and conservation and the laws, rules, and regulations that sprang from these doctrines.

A modern example that we will explore is the National Register of Historic Places nomination process for the United States, which fully embraces and perpetuates the idea that history imprints something in the fabric of buildings and places. Many other western countries have their own equivalents, such as the Canadian Register of Historic Places or Spain's Patrimonio Histórico Español, but our familiarity with these registers is not nearly as in-depth. Thus, our evaluation from the American perspective is due to the *weltanschauung* we have inherited. The U.S. National Park Service, who administers the National Register, directs that "[f]or a property to be significant ... the physical structure must have been there to 'witness' the event or series of events" (O'Donnell, 1998, 2). Muñoz Viñas (2005) explains that traditional theories of object conservation also embody this idea of fabric needing to absorb the essence of the past and this belief is what separates "real" or "genuine" historical objects from fake ones.

The Venice Charter (ICOMOS, 1964), whose doctrinal premises undergird all Western built heritage conservation practices, makes the assumption that people do not have the ability to differentiate original historic fabric from later additions. There is no empirical evidence for this claim, yet the Secretary of the Interior's Standards (NPS, 1995), which is based on the Venice Charter, makes the same assumption, as does the Burra Charter (Australia ICOMOS, 1999), Guiding Principles (SPAB), Principles of Repair (English Heritage, 1993), Guide to the Principles of the Conservation of Historic Buildings (British Standards Institution, 1998), and Standards and Guidelines for the Conservation of Historic Places in Canada (Parks Canada, 2003). In fact, we do not even understand *how* everyday people "read," understand, and interpret similarities and differences in age between buildings (Wells, 2015b).

Therefore, what is the nature of the evidence upon which the National Register and the Venice Charter and its derivatives are based? As was the case with early Christianity's interest in relics and holy sites, it is not as if these ideas came from thin air; in fact, they are passed on to us by philosophical European white men, such as John Ruskin, Eugene Viollet-le-Duc, and Camillo Boito. Indeed, preservation/conservation doctrine has much evidence to back up its claims, but this evidence is almost entirely rationalistic in nature, akin to canonized religious dogma. Orthodox preservation/conservation doctrine is not, by any stretch of the imagination, empirical. In other words, preservation/conservation doctrine was created through a deductive instead of an inductive process. Why does this even matter? The answer is that rationalism tends to enforce top-down, hegemonic processes because of its emphasis on certainty. Empiricism, on the other hand, is based on an assumption that we can never know the truth with absolute certainty and therefore must be open to skepticism.

INTRODUCTION

Rationalism is defined as "logical deduction (i.e., through *a priori* reasoning), from first principles to conclusions about the universe [and] eschews experience as a basis for claims to truth" (Davis, 2004, 67). In another sense, as H. Russell Bernard (1994, 3) describes, "if we just prepare our minds adequately, [truth] will become evident to us." Alternately, empiricism "begins with the study of phenomena, seeking via inductive logic (i.e., through *a posteriori* reasoning) to distill essential truths," and, as such, bases its premises on experience (Davis, 2004, 67). The Greek philosophers (e.g., Aristotle, Plato, Anaximander) rationalized the nature of the universe and inadvertently made many mistakes. It was not until the scientific method, based on empiricism, arose during the Enlightenment (which followed the Reformation) that we began to understand the truths of the universe. This example is not intended to deny the potential of a rationalistic approach to understanding the world, but it has its limitations, especially when we want to understand the minds of others.

The rationalistic basis of preservation/conservation doctrine is problematic because, as Mark Lichbach (2003, 41) explains, it is based on the "impoverished view of the self" to the exclusion of others and assumes that "[social] actors are machines that robotically calculate how external changes affect their fixed values and cognitions." A rationalistic perspective on human agency, therefore, assumes a "particularly anemic or thin version of intentionality" (ibid.). In other words, because rationalism demands an examination of reality from a perspective "inside your head," it denies the possibility of accepting evidence that is derived from the minds of others. An empirical perspective, because of its inductive method, does not presuppose an outcome, but rather theorizes an outcome from the evidence. Rationalism places a theory on the world and looks for evidence that meets this theory via the deductive method, but in the process ignores other possibilities. Rationalism, therefore, lacks a method to revise its theoretical premises based on real-world observations. To the rationalist, those that think differently are "wrong" because of flawed reasoning, not flawed observations or experiences. Thus, those who have power (e.g., the original theorists of rationalistic preservation/conservation theory) created a paradigm in which others cannot use inductive evidence to challenge authority. This characteristic alone is quite sufficient to explain the way in which contemporary preservation/conservation theory has perpetuated meanings that are now more than a century old.

Admittedly, there are many other paradigms that describe contemporary social science theory (e.g., constructivism, positivism, relativism, colonialism) beyond the relatively simplistic dichotomy of rationalism versus empiricism, but this fundamental difference in the nature of reality is essential for understanding the current divide between practice and theory in heritage conservation. The rationalistic basis for orthodox preservation/conservation doctrine means that the meanings and values of conservation are very narrow and can be interpreted as a kind of hegemonic cultural belief system (Waterton, Smith, & Campbell, 2006) based on pseudoscientific ideas (Muñoz Viñas, 2005). Orthodox doctrine is indeed based on the values of aristocratic, European, white men (Wells, 2007); this cultural belief system, therefore, excludes the values of women and people who are not from the dominant, Western cultural group of the past few centuries (Logan, 2012).

It is worth noting that the allied built environment discipline of planning turned against its rationalistic roots in the 1970s, embracing a more pluralistic, empirically guided perspective. Planners found rationalism inadequate because it resulted in the "neglect of the human side of planning," ignored too many other voices, and was inherently undemocratic (Friedmann & Hudson, 1974, 164). While rationalism still has a place in elements of urban and regional planning, it is now the standard practice in democratic countries across the globe to start a planning process by seeking and then using data from everyday people (i.e., gathering empirical evidence). In the United States, "preservation planning" is supposed to begin with the rationalistic assessment by experts to

INTRODUCTION

determine what are valid historic resources and then seek confirmation for these results from the public (Derry, Jandl, Shull, & Thorman, 1985; White & Roddewig, 1994). The valid evidence in this context is, therefore, the data that can reinforce the predetermined conclusions of the experts. Data from the public that do not meet the objective standards of the experts, as embodied in rules and regulations, are treated as if they do not exist.

Those who practice in the world of heritage conservation too often fail to pause and seriously consider how the rationalistic perspective upon which their practice is based has a negative impact on the diversity and quality of evidence. Practitioners are surrounded by evidence, but not all evidence is "good" evidence. Moreover, just because a rule or regulation requires a certain kind of evidence does not mean that this exemplifies best practice or that this is the best kind of evidence to consider. For instance, medicine has been based on evidence for millennia, but much of this evidence has been debunked in the past couple of centuries, largely because of a shift from a rationalist to an empirical basis for practice (Shryock, 1969). We now know that while leeches can be useful in narrow applications, such as reducing swelling after surgery, their broad-based use until the twentieth century was unjustified. Since the early twentieth century, the idea of sound or "good" evidence being predicated on empirical, scientific, reproducible principles has been well accepted. Yet, it was not until the early 1990s that "evidence-based medicine" introduced the idea that evidence needs to be ranked in terms of quality; evidence-based medicine, therefore, is based on high-quality evidence. And high-quality evidence is equated with the collection of data with methodological (or "scientific") rigor while low-quality evidence is synonymous with data that establishes its credibility from authority or is anecdotal. Specifically, there are four main areas that define evidence-based medicine (Solomon, 2005, 111– 112):

1 Decisions should be based on rigorous, methodologically sound research (qualitative or quantitative).

2 It is acceptable to question any existing protocol or doctrine without prejudice, even if it is currently required in practice. Problems should directly dictate the type of required evidence; doctrine or protocols should not be allowed to influence the process.

3 Arguments based on authority are not acceptable. (Authority should not dictate what is and is not evidence.)

4 There should be a continual process of gathering new empirical evidence, analyzing the data, and then using this information to influence practice; the effectiveness of this process should be monitored.

Usefully, architecture has assumed this evidence-based perspective through the practice of "evidence-based design," most significantly in healthcare facility design. It adopts the basic elements found in evidence-based medicine in which high-quality evidence informs (but does not necessarily dictate) design decisions. Typically, this evidence is gathered through research methodologies from environmental psychology, anthropology, sociology, or humanistic geography. At the core of evidence-based design is a desire to understand the relationship between people, place, and behavior (Hamilton, 2008). By understanding this relationship qualitatively through meanings or quantitatively via variables and cause/effect relationships, it is theoretically possible to design places that are better for people (Zeisel, 2006). The Environmental Design Research Association (EDRA) is widely recognized as the international authority on evidence-based design and environment/behavior research; the first author created the Historic Environment Knowledge Network at EDRA in 2008 to help explore how "evidence-based heritage conservation" might manifest. Examples of this network's activity include the creation of the Palmer House Charter in 2012 in order to define "Principles for Integrating Environmental Design and Behavior Research into Built Heritage Conservation Practice" (refer to Appendix A).

The context of these perspectives from medicine and design, therefore, raises the following query: What kind of evidence does the professional care of old places currently demand? We already know that this evidence is not likely to be empirical in nature, but what does it look like? In order to answer this question, let us use the same four elements that define evidence-based medicine and apply them to how orthodox built heritage conservation is performed. But before proceeding, it is important to further define the activities of "practice" in the care of old places. Because we are not aware of any published literature on the subject, we performed our own research on the type of work performed in this field based on seven months of US-based job postings on the Indeed.com website. Indeed.com is an efficient job aggregator and, therefore, we were guaranteed to receive the vast majority of job postings that use the phrase "historic preservation" posted anywhere in the United States. What we discovered was that three-quarters of all jobs posting during this time were in the area of regulatory compliance. In other words, the activities of the desired employee were almost completely dictated by the following federal heritage compliance laws and their associated rules and regulations from the National Historic Preservation Act of 1966:

- Section 106 (36 CFR Part 800)—"environmental review",

- Section 101 (36 CFR Part 60)—"National Register of Historic Places Criteria",

- Section 101 (36 CFR Part 68)—"Secretary of the Interior's Standards".

Jobs posted by local municipalities required compliance with design review regulations, which are codified in local preservation ordinances; overwhelmingly these regulations are based on the Secretary of the Interior's Standards (36 CFR Part 68) (Wells & Lixinski, 2016). This relationship between practice and rules and regulations is particularly important to keep in mind as we progress through our analysis.

Are Built Heritage Conservation Decisions Based on Rigorous, Methodologically Sound Research?

"Research" in the context of regulatory compliance is exclusively defined by the rules and regulations that practitioners are legally required to follow. This consists of gathering historical facts associated with buildings and places using the method of historical positivism (Tainter & Lucas, 1983), and describing the physical characteristics of buildings and places (e.g., measurements, materials lists, architectural style). Considering that the overall methodology employed fails to incorporate *any* significant research developments over the past half-century, such as post-modernism and social science techniques, it would be a far cry to say that built heritage conservation practice uses methodologically sound research. Indeed, critics are increasingly clear that the archaic research methodology used in built heritage conservation has created an environment that fosters colonialism and social oppression through hegemonic discourses and enforcement of expert rule (Green, 1998; Hutchings & La Salle, 2015; Logan, 2012; Smith, 2006; Wells, 2015a). Because of the rampant positivism prevalent in the research used in built heritage conservation, it is incapable of understanding, revealing, and

INTRODUCTION

respecting cultural differences, such as the way various indigenous and non-western peoples perceive, value, and wish to protect their heritage in a manner that is sometimes different from the western tradition (King, 2009; Milholland, 2010).

Built heritage conservation decisions are, therefore, not based on rigorous, methodologically sound research, but rather archaic techniques that are undemocratic and potentially oppressive in their application.

Can Any Existing Protocol or Doctrine in Built Heritage Conservation Be Questioned without Prejudice, Even If It Is Currently Required in Practice? To What Extent Are Arguments Based on Authority?

The rules and regulations that dictate the work of heritage conservation practitioners in the United States are based on rationalistic preservation/conservation doctrine and not empirical evidence (Glass, 1990; Rains & Henderson, 1966; Wells, 2007; Wells & Lixinski, 2016). There is a direct, linear relationship from the rationalism of John Ruskin (1907), William Morris/1877 Manifesto of the Society for the Protection of Ancient Buildings (SPAB n.d.), Camillo Boito (1884), Giovanni Carbonara (1976), Paul Philippot (1976), Cesare Brandi (1977), and Umberto Baldini (1996) to the Venice Charter (ICOMOS, 1964), the 1966 National Historic Preservation Act, and the 1977 Secretary of the Interior's Standards (Wells, 2007, 2015a). The National Park Service was similarly influenced by these authors as well as historical positivism in the development of the National Register criteria (Lee, 1950; Sprinkle, 2014). It is beyond the scope of this article to describe the exact nature of the rationalism of these authors (refer to the individual citation for specific details), but Salvador Muñoz Viñas (2005) presents a very concise summary of their ideas. As such, many of the basic assumptions of built heritage conservation practice cannot be questioned, regardless of the nature of empirical evidence presented. There are two reasons for this: (1) the rationalistic assumptions in doctrine cannot be violated; and (2) violation of doctrine is equivalent to violating the law. Considering that laws such as the National Historic Preservation Act and its subsequent amendments came about due to an "act of Congress," there is much inertia to prevent meaningful change in official government preservation policy.

As is revealed in the contributions in this book, practitioners often have to work in an environment hostile to questioning the *status quo*, including heritage rules and regulations. As Jack Elliott explains in Chapter 4, all too frequently managers tell practitioners, "you are not paid to think." As such, it is abundantly clear that all arguments must be based on authority in built heritage conservation practice, a phenomenon that Laurajane Smith calls the "authorized heritage discourse" (Smith, 2006).

In the Practice of Built Heritage Conservation Is There a Continual Process of Gathering New Empirical Evidence, Analyzing the Data, and Then Using This Information to Influence Practice?

As the majority of the processes used in the conservation of the built environment are prescribed by rules and regulations, it is not normally possible to integrate new evidence into these systems in an effort to change them. Changing the system of built heritage conservation is instead a political process that requires the creation and modification of laws, rules, and regulations (Wells & Lixinski, 2016). While some conservation doctrines, specifically the Burra Charter (Australia ICOMOS, 1999), recommend a process in which the effectiveness of conservation is monitored, in practice this is rarely

13

INTRODUCTION

defined, much less implemented. In a survey of historic preservation plans across the United States, Randall Mason (2009) did not find much evidence for attempts to monitor the effectiveness of plans. Globally, efforts to measure heritage conservation performance are in an inchoate state with few examples (Zancheti & Simila, 2012).

In sum, orthodox built heritage conservation practice is designed to reinforce its rationalist foundations and reject empirical evidence, especially when such evidence contradicts legally mandated rules and regulations. This has resulted in a practice that preferentially focuses on the tangible qualities of fabric and historical facts independently of how people perceive/value/feel about their heritage. But what would a human-centered (as opposed to a fabric-centered) conservation practice look like? To explore the answer to this question, we will now investigate the work of critical heritage studies researchers.

Informing a Human-Centered Conservation Practice Through Civil Experts

> [J]udging significance is not just an architectural or archaeological appraisal of fabric, but is also reliant upon incorporating people's experience. How place is valued in conservation terms should not, therefore, be entirely through conventional expert values; although how much this occurs in actual practice, … is [questionable].
>
> —Lisanne Gibson and John Pendlebury (2009, 8)

Since the 1990s, there has been an increasing interest in understanding heritage at large (natural and cultural) from the perspective of civil as opposed to conventional experts (Fortmann, 2008). This perspective assumes that everyone is an expert in some way about natural and cultural heritage. A civil expert, a term that originates from the tradition of participatory research, is an individual who may not be formally trained, but who, nonetheless, is an expert in local knowledge and is therefore accorded the same respect as any other expert. Conversely, a conventional expert is an individual who achieves authority and recognition through university (or other formal) training and the adoption and use of disciplinary standards. Unlike natural resource conservation, however, most research that seeks to understand cultural heritage meanings from the perspective of the civil expert does not use this term, but rather uses other terms such as the "ethnographic voice" or *emic* or insider meanings (c.f., Geertz, 1973) because of the dominance of anthropology in heritage studies. To be sure, all of these terms describe the same thing: understanding meanings and experience from the perspective of the marginalized insider in an attempt to give power and salience to these meanings in balance with researchers and (sometimes) conventional experts. For the purposes of this book, we prefer the term civil expert to describe this perspective.

Two particular movements in heritage have been influential in helping shift the perspective on the professional care of old places from a fabric-centered to a human-centered space. These are what have become known as "values-based" heritage conservation/historic preservation and critical heritage studies. Of these two movements, we think that the work in critical heritage studies, while sharing many of the perspectives from values-based conservation, makes fewer assumptions in terms of justifying existing professional practice, and as such, is more open to a blank-slate approach that balances power between civil and conventional experts. While it is beyond our scope to do a full

INTRODUCTION

review literature review on values-based conservation/preservation and critical heritage studies, it is important to do a review of the most salient ideas and their related scholars to help position the scholarship in this book within a larger conversation.

Most scholars agree that the origin of values-based preservation originated in the work of Alois Riegl (1903/1996) when he divided the values associated with built heritage into a dichotomy of "historical value" and "age value." Historical value is the objective, scientific facts associated with monuments while age value is the emotional response to these monuments. Riegl, therefore, framed arguments around the themes of quantitative vs. qualitative, objective vs. subjective, and factual vs. emotional in relation to built heritage. Later in the twentieth century, William Lipe (1984) expanded on these two values, introducing four more: associative/symbolic value, informational value, aesthetic value, and economic value. But, arguably, the most influential work in values-based preservation/conservation originates in the research of Randy Mason, Erica Avrami, and Marta de la Torre (Avrami, Mason, & Torre, 2000; Mason, 2003, 2006; Torre, 2002), which began as a Getty research project exploring "values in heritage conservation." Mason, Avrami, and Torre's research promoted the centrality of sociocultural meanings (including economic values) in informing conservation/ preservation values as a prelude to planning interventions on built heritage and cultural landscapes. Of note is that much of this research in values-based conservation/preservation is done from the disciplinary perspective of built heritage conservation and does little to disarm expert rule even though, at times, it does emphasize the important role of civil experts in planning processes. As such, there is a potentially valid concern that this work, in part, is intended to justify the *status quo* because it does not sufficiently disarm expert rule in the professional care of old places. Along these lines, Fredheim and Khalaf (2016) question the values-based paradigm altogether, concluding that the treatment of values typologies is based on a cursory, surface level understanding of the meanings of which values are made. It may very well be that a values-based approach to the professional care of old places does little to change practice as it allows practitioners to haphazardly create meaning-thin values that are then used to justify decisions that have already been made.

The rise of critical heritage studies is a more recent phenomenon than values-based conservation/ preservation, and, unlike the latter field, it is performed from a largely ethnographic perspective that emphasizes narrative, depth of meaning, and understanding marginalized voices; as such, it is nearly entirely focused on civil experts and disarming conventional heritage conservation practice across all of its sectors of engagement. Because of this focus, the voice of the practitioner—the conventional expert—is usually not considered in an effort to transfer power to civil experts. Significantly, the researchers who inform critical heritage studies do not, for the most part, originate from the discipline of built heritage conservation. Instead, most of these researchers are anthropologists or are associated with allied disciplines, such as archaeology, folklore, and public history, which employ an anthropological approach using ethnographies as their methodology of choice. While some of these researchers have a practice background in cultural resource or heritage resource management (including archaeology) and are familiar with regulatory regimes that dominate and control the conservation of the built environment, many researchers instead are grounded in practice from the field of museology, in which laws, rules, and regulations play an insignificant role in professional practice. The result is that much of the body of scholarship in critical heritage studies fails to look at the impact of the regulatory environment on the recognition and use of heritage (Wells & Lixinski, 2016). Work that overlaps law with critical heritage studies is even more rarified (Lixinski, 2015).

Most scholars place the origin of critical heritage studies at the publication of David Lowenthal's (1985) book, *The Past is a Foreign Country*, which was one of the first attempts to critique orthodox heritage conservation practice from the perspective of humanistic geography (Carman & Sørensen, 2009). In particular, it questioned long-established doctrine associated with the conservation of historic monuments and places and placed in doubt the stated reasons that experts engaged in conservation and their aims. Ideas found in *The Past is a Foreign Country* had, however, been extant in post-processual archaeology at least a decade before the book's publication. Like Lowenthal's emphasis on the subjective nature of the past, which can never be known objectively, post-processual theory also deemphasizes the objective, scientific method of conventional (or processual) archaeology, instead framing archaeological practice as a series of acts that are fundamentally interpretive in nature (Hodder & Hutson, 2003). The critical heritage studies field itself only became recognized and called as such sometime after 2009 (Winter & Waterton, 2013), but clearly these critical approaches existed decades before the name was applied to them.

Most research in critical heritage studies is based on qualitative case studies that give emphasis to the *emic* or insider perspective (or the perspective of the civil expert) on how heritage meanings are created and used. Again, this research does not usually focus on the meanings of conventional experts although the results of these case studies can certainly be used to inform practice, which is the argument we make in this book. While it is outside the scope of this brief review to summarize this large body of work, major themes that emerge is that the majority of it is focused on non-Western perspectives, how heritage is used, conflicting meanings, the use and abuse of power, and the way in which meanings survive and are sustained independently of tangible objects. In sum, these themes are very different from areas that typically inform the practice of conventional experts who are engaged in the care of old places.

Several scholars have attempted to use these qualitative case studies to inform the theoretical perspective on the creation and use of heritage, including drawing a counterpoint between civil and expert perspectives in an attempt to disarm conventional practice. This work presents evidence that heritage conservation practice is overly reliant on expert rule, emphasizes positivistic, top-down processes, and advocates for a more people-centered, ground-up approach to practice that empowers more stakeholders by giving voice to civil experts (Harrison, 2013; Gibson & Pendlebury, 2009; Lixinski, 2015; Low, 1994; Silberman, 2016; Smith, 2006; Sørensen & Carman, 2009; Sullivan, 2015; Wells, 2015a; Winter, 2013). This scholarship, however, has had little impact on the day-to-day practice of conserving the historic environment, especially in those aspects that overlap with the regulatory environment. But, more importantly, what do scholars from critical heritage studies have to say about the interface between this field and practice? Should this be the concern of critical heritage studies?

First, because of its origins as an academic pursuit, changing practice has never been the primary focus of critical heritage studies. Even post-processual archaeological theory, which formed a foundation for the field, was never intended to change practice, as academic archaeologists consistently look down upon their non-academic colleagues as second-class citizens. Significantly, in the two decades since its origin, post-processual theory has not changed the professional practice of archaeology, especially as it relates to environmental review. By 2030, will we say the same thing about built heritage conservation and critical heritage studies? If critical heritage scholars fail to engage with practice and practitioners, this outcome seems rather likely.

Second, any such claim that critical heritage studies are not intended to impact the professional practice of heritage conservation is false. Key evidence can be found in the manifesto of the Association of Critical Heritage Studies (Campbell & Smith, 2012) which clearly states that the goal of critical heritage studies is to "Increas[e] dialogue and debate between researchers, *practitioners*

INTRODUCTION

and communities" (emphasis added). Scholars are in a unique and privileged position to critique practice, which is epitomized by Tim Winter's (2013) observation that critical heritage studies "tackl[es] the thorny issues those in the conservation profession are often reluctant to acknowledge", while Keith Emerick (2014, 5) advocates that the "emerging field of critical heritage studies can offer ... alternative ways of 'doing' heritage." Clearly, Winter and Emerick believe that understanding the problems of practice through critical approaches can lead to possible solutions to change and improve practice. To be sure, focusing on changing practice does not mean that critical heritage scholars need to agree with the practitioner perspective; indeed, as Witcomb and Buckley (2013, 574) clarify, part of the work of this field is to "provoke" the practitioner as well as "engage" with practice. But—and this is very important—such an engagement needs to be productive and not alienate each side. We believe that the onus on avoiding alienation is on the side of the critical heritage studies scholar because he/she is in a unique position to understand the use, distribution, and abuse of power and to employ his/her *emic* perspective to understand and gain empathy for the "Other." Understanding the "Other" does not require an acceptance of the others' values, but respect for people as autonomous individuals capable of free, independent thought should be assumed. This perspective does not absolve the practitioner of the same level of respect or attempt to understand critical heritage studies perspectives, but there is no mechanism, organization, or tool that appears to be ready to enable this kind of discussion from the perspective of the practitioner. Simply put, it appears that it is easier for the critical heritage studies researcher to engage the practitioner than *vice versa*.

To be sure, professionals who care for old places need the kind of evidence produced by critical heritage studies scholarship, but are not getting it. For instance, practitioners do not have ready access to the generalizable/transferable knowledge about the psychological, ethnographic, and experiential dimensions of the historic environment that are required to provide a proper context for effective interpretation and communication with stakeholders (Wells, 2015b). Yet, there is no mechanism to deliver this evidence to practitioners; even in institutions of higher education, many students of historic preservation and architectural conservation degree programs do not receive this information, judged by the published courses, syllabi, and materials from these programs.

While values-based conservation/preservation and critical heritage studies provide platforms that could help to change practice, there are other ways of knowing that need to be acknowledged, but are not engaged in research that overlaps heritage studies. These include environmental psychology, humanistic geography, and, to some extent sociology. While ethnographic methods are powerful ways to understand civil experts, other methodologies, such as phenomenology, grounded theory, correlational research, behavioral science, communication theory, and experimental research could provide additional, useful insights into people, place, and heritage that are the core of the work that impacts the care of old places. Mixed-methods and quantitative designs have a significant place as well to help understand correlations and generalizable phenomena. The specific methods that appear to be underutilized include behavioral mapping, photo sorts, measurement of environmental attitudes, spatial cognition, virtual spaces and environmental simulation, content analysis, neuroscience, behavioral science, and advanced statistical methods. None of these observations is intended to mean that an anthropological perspective focused on ethnographies should be replaced; rather the argument is that this perspective needs to be joined by others.

As a result of the inherent conflicts between fabric- and human-centered approaches to conservation and perhaps because of the limited disciplinary perspectives than having borne upon the problem, there is much confusion today about what it is we are really trying to conserve. Both fabric and human-centered approaches emphasize a focus on continuity, but as opposed to the continuity of fabric, human-centered theorists (Breglia, 2006; Muñoz Viñas, 2005; Smith, 2006; Zancheti & Loretto, 2012) focus on conserving the *meanings* associated with this fabric. Taken to its logical extreme, the fabric of a heritage object can change so long as the sociocultural meanings associated with the object are conserved. A "good" decision then becomes one that conserves the sociocultural meanings of place rather than the fabric of place. It is, therefore, incumbent upon professional caretakers of old places to recognize, gather, interpret, and understand a broad array of stakeholder meanings (especially from civil experts) associated with place.

This shift in the professional care of old places to people-centered approaches means that in the future, the role of the practitioner moves from controlling meanings associated with fabric to facilitating the gathering and interpretation of meanings from many people as well as empowering communities to recognize, treat, and interpret their built heritage and cultural landscapes (Emerick, 2014; Wells, 2015a). Built heritage practitioners will need to collect and interpret these meanings with more depth and consistency than has been happening to date using efficient and pragmatic social science tools that do not currently exist. To this end, we will now examine how a human-centered focus for heritage conservation can and should change practice.

Changing the Professional Care of Old Places

[T]o understand complex issues (or even simple ones), we must try to free our minds of dogma and to guarantee the freedom to publish, to contradict, and to experiment.

—Carl Sagan (1998, 189)

To recap, the purpose of this book is to explore ways to change the professional care of old places to make it more responsive to people and human needs. The perspectives, herein, are from both academics and practitioners in an attempt to bridge the theory/practice divide with an aim of creating an emancipated practice that disarms authority. To date, the editors are not aware of any refereed publication that has attempted this important endeavor, essential for human flourishing and for the sustainability of built heritage conservation, though the cultural resource management (CRM) guru, Thomas King, has proposed some ideas in *Our Unprotected Heritage: Whitewashing the Destruction of Our Cultural and Natural Environment* (2009). Within the preface of the fourth edition of *Cultural Resource Laws & Practice*, King (2013, xii) also expresses his "hope that we may be on a verge of a paradigm shift in the whole business of CRM", and by extension, heritage conservation too.

Perhaps one of the best examples of (unpublished) work in this area is in the United States, where the National Trust for Historic Preservation has been taking a leading role in exploring what a "people-centered preservation" practice would look like, starting with the informative blogs of Tom Mayes (2016) on "Why Do Old Places Matter." At the 2016 annual National Preservation Conference, National Trust staff distributed a draft copy of a "Preservation for People: A Vision for the Future," which was based on a yearlong series of meetings with practitioners and academics across the United States. The key takeaways from this document are that (1) practitioners need to be more careful about listening to people and "honoring the full diversity of the evolving American story"; (2) heritage conservation "creates and nurtures more equitable, healthy, resilient vibrant and sustainable communities"; and (3) a successful heritage practitioner "collaborates with new and existing partners to address fundamental social issues and make the world better." This document also calls for changing preservation rules and regulations to make them more responsive to this people-centered approach.

Two themes that emerge from the Trust's work and from the papers in this book are that the laws, rules, and regulations that drive the majority of conservation practice need to change in a way that makes them more responsive to people, communities, and social justice. The second theme is that it must be acceptable for practitioners to be skeptical in their workplace and question the received wisdom of preservation doctrine and the rules and regulations that guide their practice. The field needs to create a safe space where practitioners can disagree with the status quo. The simple truth is that built heritage conservation practice cannot change without the central involvement of practitioners; and, the practitioners need to be able to disagree with authority, doctrine, and laws/rules/regulations and not jeopardize their employment.

It's All About People: Approaches to Fostering a Human-Centered Professional Care of Old Places

In our interactions with the contributing authors to this volume, we have both learned and debated multiple approaches that encourage human-centric heritage preservation/conservation practices involved in the care of old places. For these approaches we encountered four common themes, which are not necessarily exclusive (there are likely other ideas to consider that were simply not purposed from within the group of contributing authors). The underlying themes we encountered were: Defining a Human-centric Built Heritage Conservation Practice; Ways to Gather Evidence; Using Evidence to Change Practice; and The Role of Higher Education in Leading Evidence-based Practice, which form the heading for the four parts of this volume.

We begin our inquiry on Defining a Human-Centric Built Heritage Conservation Practice with the first chapter, "Bridging the Gap between Built Heritage Conservation Practice and Critical Heritage Studies," by Jeremy C. Wells. As has been commented earlier in this introduction, critical heritage studies is a nascent field that takes as its objects of attention the practice of heritage conservation and the practitioners engaged in this activity. This field has an essential role in providing evidence to substantiate conservation practice and many academics and practicing professionals ought to become more familiar with this scholarship. In this chapter, Wells investigates the "critical" stance of practitioners with the critical heritage studies perspective of scholars on the issue that they may both be engaging in the same hegemonic acts that they are simultaneously criticizing and, in the process, alienating those actors who they most need to engage. Ostensibly, there is a goal to improve how heritage conservation is done; yet there is little evidence that critical heritage studies research is actually changing conservation practice. By engaging practitioners as co-researchers, critical heritage studies researchers may find more suitable, pragmatic ways to democratize practices on the conservation of built heritage, places, and landscapes. Wells advocates that the academy needs to change how future practitioners are educated by introducing standard social science components to conservation programs that address the built environment and cultural landscapes through an emancipatory lens, with the goal of balancing human-centered versus fabric-centered approaches to the conservation of heritage.

As mentioned previously, one purpose of this volume is to reflect on the state of current social science research in supporting the practices of heritage conservation, and determine how to improve cultural heritage management goals and objectives with specific, usable tools and practices—no small feat considering the breadth and depth of tangible and intangible resources intertwined with cultural and natural resources around the world. The field of cultural resource management encompasses a multitude of resource types, from tangible archaeological artifacts such as simple pottery

INTRODUCTION

sherds and elegant cave paintings, humble workers' cottages, and soaring masterpieces of design, to intangible resources such as sacred rituals of life passages, festive seasonal traditions, and traditional lifeways unique to the people of a place. Thus, for Suzanne E. Bott's contribution on "The Measurement of Meaning—Psychometrics and Sense of Place" (Chapter 2), she explores the development of different measurement tools for evaluating heritage resources in order to provide resource managers with a formal evidence-based foundation for evaluating management alternatives *with* the involvement of the local populations. The outcomes of the evaluation process, according to Bott, can provide a variety of alternatives for planning and management decision-makers that are logically derived, thorough, and inclusive. Examples are provided from recent research in academe, government, and private practice.

Richard M. Hutchings has also found in his contribution, "Meeting the Shadow: Resource Management and the McDonaldization of Heritage Stewardship" (Chapter 3), that there is strong evidence that our most pressing heritage problems are intractable under current conditions. Hutchings believes that such discourse—deemed "truth-telling" by some and "dark" and "wicked" by others—is excluded in orthodox heritage conservation circles. According to him, not only does this show cultural resource management to be ideological, but also it suggests that practice, and thus society at-large, is ill-equipped to deal with the unfolding global heritage crisis. In the third chapter, Hutchings explores cultural resource management's "shadow" or "dark side," which he contends is a vital, powerful and routinely ignored facet of the practice. Drawing on the principles of McDonaldization—efficiency, calculability, predictability, and control—Hutchings demonstrates how resource management has become a rigid, bureaucratic, elite-driven, state-sanctioned institution and process that foregrounds capitalist interests, using the evaluation of proposed solutions to common heritage problems in Western Canada as a case study. Hutchings argues that no matter how painful, meeting the shadow is necessary because it signifies a coming-to-terms with the problems that plague us today, including the very practice of cultural resource management.

Concluding this first part on defining human-centric heritage conservation practice is Jack Elliott, Jr.'s, Chapter 4, "The Mystery of History and Place Radical Preservation Revisited". Since the historic preservation movement is specifically concerned with the symbolic dimension of historic places that we often casually refer to as their "significance," then, according to Elliott, preservation thought has primarily followed the perspective of disciplines that focus on the world as merely objective and material. These perspectives while valid in their own realms are nevertheless inadequate for dealing with the experiences at the basis of preservation that often manifest as sense of place and the sacred. Following the work of philosopher of history Eric Voegelin, Elliott suggests that symbolic dimensions require a broader understanding of the reality that encompass the interplay within human consciousness between an object on the landscape and its complex associations from which arise the symbolic potentiality of place. Such objects always have a "thing-like" character while also reflecting the mystery of the reality, which encompasses and transcends them and us. According to Elliott, this approach entails a more reflective or philosophical dimension of thought than one typically finds today among preservation professionals and bureaucracies. Additionally, it would also be truer to the mandates of the preservation movement, while recovering the vision of history as a process within which society can exist, formed by which is both concrete and specific while interfused with ambiguity and mystery. Elliott's approach also offers an alternative form of seeing the world that spans the rift between science and religion, reason and faith.

In the second part, Ways to Gather Evidence, we begin with You Kyong Ahn's, Chapter 5, "The Perception and Preservation of Vernacular Architectural Features in an Urban Historic District

INTRODUCTION

with Heritage Value: A Case Study from Grand Rapids, Michigan." Ahn investigates how architectural features should be treated in order to preserve an urban vernacular setting as a community's heritage symbol. Within her investigation, Ahn questions the larger issue of collective district identity as perceived by a place's inhabitants regarding vernacular architectural features that have been preserved for its ethnic heritage value. Ahn's employed a web survey to measure the importance of the features quantitatively. Then, a focus group with community participants was conducted to understand the underlying reasons for the importance and their relations to legitimate treatments for the architectural features. The results of Ahn's study demonstrate that preservation of an urban historic district should be thought of as a dynamic procedure involving a community's perception of architectural significance. Yet, it can be documented effectively by means of an empirical study. While Ahn's case study was conducted in Grand Rapids, Michigan, her approach could have broader applications in other communities across North America and other western countries.

AnnaMarie Bliss conduct's her case study in Spain, in "Image for the Future of the Historic City: Photoelicitation and Architectural Preservation in Barcelona," in Chapter 6. Photoelicitation uses images as a means of communication between the researcher and participants in the field. Researcher-led photoelicitation (with investigator-provided images) and participant-led photoelicitation (with participant-provided images) in architecture and design research provide the ability for both parties to engage in a deeper discussion by using relevant visual material to express impressions about the environments portrayed. According to Bliss, only one of the two types of photoelicitation is used in any given project. Her investigation asks how we may combine the two approaches to broaden the discussion between the researcher and the participant. Using data from a completed fieldwork trip to Barcelona, Spain, this project critically examines the usefulness and efficacy of combining researcher-led and participant-led photoelicitation in investigating popular architectural tourism sites. Bliss collected images from participants and participants were also shown historical and present-day reference images over the course of semi-structured interviews about their perceptions and expectations of the architecture of the Palau de la Música Catalana by Lluís Domènech i Montaner. Bliss's fieldwork assesses the role of photos in environmental design research as a tool for engaging the participant, stimulating relevant responses, and providing the researcher with solid visual evidence for concrete conclusions.

Dana H. Taplin takes a different approach to gathering evidence by simply asking people directly through ethnographic research methods in "Conservation and the People's Views: Ethnographic Perspectives from Jones Beach State Park, New York" (Chapter 7). The case study of Jones Beach is about a place that serves a diverse public—a longtime white suburban constituency, a cross-section of people of color from the boroughs of New York City, LGBTQ groups, and others. These are self-segregating constituencies, with the white users using the newer, more informal and car accessible parts of the beach, LGBTQ visitors using an area beyond easy reach of any parking lot, and the historic core of the park used increasingly by people of color. Taplin investigates how do "the people" relate to a park that is part of their history, but not everyone's history, and has hit hard times? What expectations do users have for the resources and management of the park? What do they expect in terms of preserving the park and conserving its history? Given the present use patterns and funding challenges, the newer human-centered approaches in historical conservation have much to offer in reconciling stakeholder interests at Jones Beach. Taplin's discussion is based on the data gathered in a mixed methods cultural use study of Jones Beach conducted by the Public Research Group (CUNY) in 2012, prior to Hurricane Sandy. Funded by the Alliance for New York State Parks,

INTRODUCTION

the study entailed the collection of 640 surveys for a "demographic assessment" of the park; and four days of participant observation, social activity mapping, and semi-structured interviewing for the "ethnographic assessment," which was undertaken by an interdisciplinary team of five ethnographers. Taplin's results from the study underscore how the past is both present and redefined in contemporary, routine use of the park, and how consultation with everyday users provides a valid and useful view of public history that ought to be combined with other "expert" perspectives when undertaking conservation endeavors.

Gathering evidence for the sake of evidence, though, does not bring about change. This is why within the third part the contributors delve deeper into the theme of Using Evidence to Change Practice. Many of these authors are practitioners and are thus ideally positioned to critique their own work and the overall state of practice within their specialization. We believe that this book is one of the very few examples where built heritage practitioners take this kind of critical approach, which is altogether absent in typical historic preservation, architectural conservation, and cultural resource management/heritage management literature. In Chapter 8, "Tours of Critical Geography and Public Deliberation in Texas: Applied Social Sciences as Guide," Jennifer Minner found that while there is a considerable and growing literature on mid-twentieth century buildings and landscapes, the large modern footprints of the mid-twentieth century remain largely invisible in heritage tours. These places are geographies where federal policy and local ambition converge and were realized in urban renewal and other large-scale public and private actions that massively reshaped urban space. Therefore, Minner explores the potential for community tours, offering two case studies: Austin and San Antonio. In addition to raising awareness of the importance of social history and critical geography in interpreting modernism, Minner argues for the usefulness of applied social sciences, including collaborative action theory, collaborative rationality, and phronetic social sciences, to heritage practice. Minner proposes that heritage tours can re-invigorate and give new meaning as vehicles for deliberation about power relations, urban redevelopment, and displacement, both in for appreciating the past as well as better conceptualizing the present and future planning efforts.

Ted Grevstad-Nordbrock takes a different approach than Minner, in "Understanding Preservation-Fueled Urban Revitalization: Notes from Lincoln Park, Chicago." Grevstad-Nordbrock's Chapter 9 contests the view that historic preservation programs in the United States provide an unqualified community good. According to him, conventional argument holds that many preservation programs protect historic buildings and districts from insensitive change or outright demolition, while also providing a catalyst for much-needed revitalization in de-valorized neighborhoods. Grevstad-Nordbrock challenges this rhetoric by suggesting that preservation-driven economic revitalization is not always beneficial to a local community and can, perhaps counter intuitively, work against the long-term sustainability of historic preservation efforts. Using Lincoln Park on Chicago's north side as a case study, Grevstad-Nordbrock has identified a three-stage revitalization process in historic neighborhoods: the first stage, honorific programs like the National Register of Historic Places prime neighborhoods for revitalization by anointing them as historic and therefore "special." In the second stage, Grevstad-Nordbrock observes that neighborhoods are bolstered by the availability of financial incentives for rehabilitation, and that these neighborhoods' newfound status helps attract capital reinvestment and new residents that can lead to gentrification and to the displacement of vulnerable residents. In the final stage, physical upgrading occurs that compromises the historic integrity of neighborhoods. Grevstad-Nordbrock has witnessed that historic neighborhoods can become victims of their own success as redevelopment pressures encourage additional physical change, bringing about a gradual degradation of their historic character—the very reason for historic preservation to

INTRODUCTION

begin with! Therefore, Grevstad-Nordbrock recommends that the public framework that supports historic preservation in the United States, while vitally important for protecting irreplaceable cultural heritage, needs to evolve to reflect conditions in American cities today—not those of 1960s and 1970s, when most preservation laws and incentives programs were established. Grevstad-Nordbrock thus argues for a revised framework that incorporates safeguards to minimize the potential for harmful changes in high-demand real estate markets. Moreover, attempts must be made to mitigate the negative consequences of what might be state-led, preservation-fueled gentrification.

In Chapter 10, titled "Urban Preservation: A Community and Economic Development Perspective Case Study from Cleveland," Stephanie Ryberg-Webster investigates how and why preservationists tout historic preservation's role in furthering community and economic development goals in cities around the United States. According to Ryberg-Webster, dominant arguments highlight increases in property values resulting from historic designation and positive economic impacts (including job creation and increasing tax revenue) stemming from historic tax credit projects and heritage tourism. She found that a 2011 report completed for the federal Advisory Council on Historic Preservation begins with the broad claim that "historic preservation has become a fundamental tool for strengthening American communities," contributing to core economic and community development goals including "small business incubation, affordable housing, sustainable development, neighborhood stabilization, center city revitalization, job creation, promotion of the arts and culture, small town renewal, heritage tourism, economic development, and others" (Rypkema, Cheong, & Mason, 2011). Yet, few studies address perceptions and discourses about preservation that occur external to the preservation field. To fill this void, Ryberg-Webster asks two key questions: How do community and economic development practitioners (1) view/value the historic environment? and (2) perceive the synergies/tensions between their goals and historic preservation? Ryberg-Webster's case study focuses specifically on Cleveland, Ohio—a city facing uphill economic development challenges in the face of persistent population decline and deindustrialization, while also garnering national recognition in the community development sector. The qualitative study draws on key person interviews with public-sector departments, third-sector umbrella organizations, and non-profit community development corporations. The chapter demonstrates that community and economic development practitioners strongly associate preservation with the built environment and historic fabric and that there remain significant challenges in "making the past less foreign" for community and economic development practitioners.

Kimberli Fitzgerald takes the investigation further on how to use evidence to change practice in Chapter 11, titled "Using Evidence from the Community to Guide a Local Municipality's Preservation Program: A Case Study of Salem, Oregon." In her chapter, the municipality's preservation program was suffering from a lack of community support and ineffectual attempts to designate a new historic district. In this case study, Fitzgerald demonstrates how she and the Historic Landmarks Commission used key tools grounded in communicative planning theory to identify and address problems with the historic preservation program. Through this process, Salem was able to use evidence from the community to guide positive changes to their local preservation code and program, which could have broader applications for other communities.

In Chapter 12, Richard Engelhardt, Heather Peters, and Montira Unakul, who are practitioners, use case studies in Southeast Asia to explore how ethnographic evidence can be used to democratize the traditional top-down, the expert-driven approach that often is associated with UNESCO, the World Heritage nomination and management process, and international conservation doctrines. While not necessarily rejecting these models, the authors do critique their shortcomings and point

INTRODUCTION

out that, internally, UNESCO is becoming more aware of the need to embrace bottom-up approaches driven by a greater proportion of the local community in tandem with conventional experts. While some scholars from more critical approaches would simply call for the abolishment of the World Heritage process in its entirety because of its association with expert rule, Engelhardt, Peters, and Unakul advocate for a more balanced, nuanced approach to move toward what may eventually become an emancipated practice for the care of old places. We think that this approach is important to explore.

Lastly, this section on changing practice is capped by Richard Vidutis' critique on how a social science approach is altogether absent from the world of cultural resource management and regulatory compliance. In "Missed Opportunities-The Absence of Ethnography in America's Cultural Heritage Programs" (Chapter 13), Vidutis, who is a cultural resource management professional, explains how an ethnographic approach to cultural heritage management is needed to change how professionals work with Traditional Cultural Properties (TCPs), post-disaster reconstruction, and Section 106 in ways that are critical for a more human-centric approach to compliance-based heritage conservation work. Vidutis' case studies, which explore a "humanizing, place-based model" for ethnographic practice, reinforce the larger themes in this book that focus on the need for people and place to be central to heritage conservation practice. This chapter also introduces the need for conventional practice to be informed by the work of folklorists, who have long understood the intimate relationship between intangible heritage and how people value and perceive older places, buildings, and even objects.

An irony that is rarely recognized by many heritage preservation practitioners is that the knowledge and work conducted by people is also a cultural tradition in and of itself. Since cultural knowledge is transmitted through various forms of communication—oral, body, observation of demonstration by an example, and so forth—rather than through genetics, the way we conduct preservation education is an important component to consider in reforming the field. The chapters that comprise the fourth part on The Role of Higher Education in Leading Evidence-based Practice investigate both learning between acknowledged expert and pupil, as well as scholarly research on one's own. The emphasis of the research contributed is on higher education, where skill set training is conducted most frequently for those seeking a career path within a heritage-related field, in contrast to primary education where the emphasis is on more basic levels of historical or cultural appreciation. Michelle Jolly, Melinda Milligan, Margaret Purser, and Laura A. Watt take us straight to the point in Chapter 14, '"But Where Are the People?" Grappling with Teaching New Approaches to Our Relationship with Place and the Past'. Jolly, Milligan, Purser, and Watt argue that the transformation of heritage practice into a broader, more human-centered approach requires transformation in thinking. Students and practitioners need to learn not only the logic of social science but also to see it working in practice, in an integrated, interdisciplinary fashion—which, in large part, turns out to rest in changing their "habits of mind." Jolly, Milligan, Purser, and Watt believe that students need to worry less about finding answers and more about asking questions. They define four related components of these habits of mind as particularly relevant to creating a more people-centered heritage practice, which are (1) developing an observational stance that is critical, reflexive, and questioning; (2) employing a narrativist analytical framework; (3) seeing community as a process; and (4) defining practice as collaborative, comparative, and situated. Making these habits of mind explicit and intentional, and inculcating these among themselves, students, and community partners—rather than teaching a suite of fixed methodologies—imbues heritage practice with a social science perspective that allows theory and method alike to continue to evolve.

INTRODUCTION

In Chapter 15, '"The Places My Granddad Built": Using Popular Interest in Genealogy as a Pedagogical Segue for Historic Preservation', Barry L. Stiefel takes a slightly different approach in internalizing the method of inquiry in order to facilitate deeper critical thinking and empathy in professional practice. While teaching historic preservation courses for several years, Stiefel struggled with how to respond to the demographic changes he had been observing among his students, which he attributed to the ever-evolving search in defining collective heritage in the United States. Thus, Stiefel began experimenting with an approach that he has titled, "What is Your Heritage and the State of Its Preservation?" a variation of the self-discovery-based learning pedagogical method. The premise of Stiefel's approach is that people in general, whether professional practitioners or amateurs, may become better advocates for preservation if they have undergone an experience of investigating and understanding the state of preservation of the heritage they identify with. By having had such an experience, Stiefel claims, a person can have greater empathy for when another's heritage is in peril because they would not want such negative treatment of their own. According to the projects produced by his students, this approach reflects their interest and values related to the past and contemporary historic built environment, providing an intriguing snapshot each semester of how young adults are defining their collective heritage and the national story vis-à-vis what is portrayed through the general media's message.

Ned Kaufman (Chapter 16) ends with the role of higher education in leading evidence-based practice with an investigation of "Resistance to Research: Diagnosis and Treatment of a Disciplinary Ailment." Kaufman posits that higher education does not support research into heritage conservation and has found that resistance to changing the status quo is deeply rooted in the structures of the historic preservation discipline and cannot be overcome except by alleviating three fundamental conditions. First, the highly formalized nature of preservation practice, which requires that nearly everything preservationists do be in conformance with a restricted body of law and precedent. Second, the lack of institutional capacity to absorb new knowledge reflected in the absence of think-tanks or strong university research centers and in the strong emphasis placed by academic preservation departments on teaching a rote curriculum. And third, the lack of a clear sense of purpose across the discipline, which prevents a strong research agenda from coalescing. While all three conditions will need to be addressed, according to Kaufman, the critical step towards a solution lies in the first because changing the laws will change what preservationists are allowed to do, and that will open everything up. Those who seek to generate a robust culture of preservation research should, therefore, focus on changing the laws, policies, programs, and precedents that depend on them.

Taking responsibility for the way in which we preserve and remember the past and heritage is what Lowenthal (1985) was advocating in *The Past is a Foreign Country*, and a burden we—all contributors to this volume—are attempting to undertake and address inappropriate and meaningful ways. According to Lowenthal, in his 2015 revised edition of the *The Past is a Foreign Country:*

> The rage to preserve is in part a reaction to anxieties generated by modernist amnesia. We preserve because the pace of change and development has attenuated a legacy integral to our identity and well-being. But we also preserve, I [Lowenthal] suggest, because we are no longer intimate enough with that legacy to rework it creatively. We admire its relics, but they seldom inspire our own acts and works. Past remains survive not to educate or emulate but only to be saved. Precisely because preservation has become a prime end in itself, it tends to preclude other uses of the past.
>
> Lowenthal (2015, 592)

INTRODUCTION

The common thread throughout our work is the emphasis on enhancing the quality of life for people, not the "bricks and mortar" or other physical vestiges of the past *per se*. The act of preserving, conserving, or rehabilitating the historic built environment and other material objects is a secondary agenda in order to reinforce the primary of human social or communal needs. We also want to encourage the reconnecting of an intimate relationship with the legacy of cultural heritage. In the concluding chapter, we also reflect on how the chapter examples in *Human-Centered Built Heritage Conservation* provide a basis for recommendations on future directions practitioners, academics, and those considering a prospective career in the professional care of old places might consider.

Notes

1 The activity of identifying the importance, treatment, and interpretation of the older built environment and cultural landscapes goes by many names across the English-speaking world. For the purposes of this book, we will primarily use the generic phrase "heritage conservation," which can mean the conservation of all heritage, movable and immovable, and tangible and intangible. In a more narrow sense applied to only the built environment, places, and landscapes, we use the phrase "built heritage conservation" and "the conservation of cultural landscapes." In the United States, the most common phrase for this latter activity is "historic preservation." In addition to built heritage conservation, other parts of the world use the phrases, "architectural conservation," "urban conservation," or simply "heritage conservation."

2 The UNESCO World Heritage sites where these churches can be found are the *Birthplace of Jesus: Church of the Nativity and the Pilgrimage Route, Bethlehem* (Palestine); *Old City of Jerusalem and its Walls* (Israel); and *Saint Catherine Area* (Egypt). St. Helena also initiated churches at what is now the *Baptism Site "Bethany Beyond the Jordan" (Al-Maghtas)* in Jordan, though no structures with a link to her period of significance is extant.

Works Cited

Armstrong, G. T. (1967). Imperial church building in the Holy Land in the fourth century. *The Biblical Archaeologist, 30*(3), 90–102.

Australia ICOMOS. (1999). *The burra charter*. Burwood: ICOMOS.

Avrami, E., Mason, R., & de Torre, M. L. (2000). *Values and heritage conservation*. Los Angeles: Getty Conservation Institute.

Baldini, U. (1996). Theory of restoration and methodological unity. In N. S. Price, M. K. J. Talley, & A. M. Vaccaro (Eds.), *Historical and philosophical issues on the conservation of cultural heritage* (pp. 355–357). Los Angeles: The Getty Conservation Institute.

Bernard, H. R. (1994). *Research methods in anthropology: Qualitative and quantitative approaches*. Thousand Oaks, CA: Sage.

Boito, C. (1884). *I restauratori, conferenza tenuta all'esposizione di torino, il 7 giugno 1884*. Florence: G. Barbèra.

Bonser, W. (1962). The cult of relics in the middle ages. *Folklore, 73*(4), 234–256.

Brandi, C. (1977). *Teoria del restauro*. Turin: Einaudi.

Breglia, L. (2006). *Monumental ambivalence: The politics of heritage*. Austin: University of Texas Press.

British Standards Institution. (1998). *Guide to the principles of the conservation of historic buildings. BS 7913: 1998*. London: British Standards Institution.

Campbell, G., & Smith, L. (2012). Association of Critical Heritage Studies manifesto. www.criticalheritagestud ies.org/history/

Carbonara, G. (1976). *La reintegrazione dell'immagine: Problemi di restauro di monumenti*. Rome: Bulzoni.

INTRODUCTION

Carman, J., & Sørensen, M. L. S. (2009). Heritage studies: An outline. In M. L. S. Sørensen & J. Carman (Eds.), *Heritage studies: Methods and approaches* (pp. 11–28). London; New York: Routledge.

Daly, P., & Chan, B. (2015). "Putting broken pieces back together": Reconciliation, justice, and heritage in post-conflict situations. In W. Logan, M. N. Craith, & U. Kocke (Eds.), *A companion to heritage studies* (pp. 491–506). Malden, MA: John Wiley & Sons.

Davis, B. (2004). *Inventions of teaching: A genealogy.* Mahwah, N.J.: L. Erlbaum Associates.

Derrida, J. (1973). *Speech and phenomena, and other essays on Husserl's theory of signs* (Vol. Northwestern University studies in phenomenology & existential philosophy). Evanston: Northwestern University Press.

Derry, A., Jandl, H. W., Shull, C. D., & Thorman, J. (1985). *Guidelines for local surveys; a basis for preservation planning: National register bulletin 24.* Washington, DC: National Park Service.

Emerick, K. (2014). *Conserving and managing ancient monuments: Heritage, democracy, and inclusion.* Woodbridge: Boydell & Brewer.

English Heritage. (1993). *Principles of repair (leaflet).* London: English Heritage.

Fortmann, L. (2008). Doing science together. In L. Fortmann (Ed.), *Participatory research in conservation and rural livelihoods: Doing science together* (pp. 1–17). Oxford: Blackwell Publishing.

Fredheim, L. H., & Khalaf, M. (2016). The significance of values: Heritage value typologies re-examined. *International Journal of Heritage Studies, 22*(6), 466–481.

Friedmann, J., & Hudson, B. (1974). Knowledge and action: A guide to planning theory. *Journal of the American Institute of Planners, 40*(1), 3–16.

Galindo, M. P., & Hidalgo, M. C. (2005). Aesthetic preferences and the attribution of meaning: Environmental categorization processes in the evaluation of urban scenes. *International Journal of Psychology, 40*(1), 19–26.

Geertz, C. (1973). *The interpretation of cultures: Selected essays.* New York: Basic Books.

Gibson, L., & Pendlebury, J. (2009). Introduction: Valuing historic environments. In L. Gibson & J. Pendlebury (Eds.), *Valuing historic environments* (pp. 1–16). Surrey and Burlington: Ashgate Publishing.

Glanvill, J., More, H., & Horneck, A. (1681). *Saducismus triumphatus, or, full and plain evidence concerning witches and apparitions: In two parts, the first treating of their possibility, the second of their real existence.* London: Printed for F. Collins and S. Lownds.

Glass, J. A. (1990). *The beginnings of a new national historic preservation program, 1957 to 1969* (pp. 3–27). Nashville, TN: American Association for State and Local History.

Green, H. L. (1998). The social construction of historical significance. In M. A. Tomlan (Ed.), *Preservation of what, for whom? A critical look at historical significance* (pp. 85–94). Ithaca, NY: National Council for Preservation Education.

Hamilton, K. (2008). Design based on evidence: A model for progressive practice. In D. S. Haviland (Ed.), *AIA handbook of professional practice: Student edition.* New York: John Wiley & Sons.

Harrison, R. (2013). *Heritage: Critical approaches.* New York: Routledge.

Hodder, I., & Hutson, S. (2003). *Reading the past: Current approaches to interpretation in archaeology.* Cambridge: Cambridge University Press.

Howard, P. (2003). *Heritage: Management, interpretation, identity.* London: Continuum.

Hutchings, R., & La Salle, M. (2015). Archaeology as disaster capitalism. *International Journal of Historical Archaeology, 19,* 699–720.

ICOMOS. (1964). *The Venice charter.* Paris: ICOMOS.

King, T. F. (2009). *Our unprotected heritage: Whitewashing the destruction of our cultural and natural resources.* Walnut Creek, CA: Left Coast Press.

King, T. F. (2013). *Cultural resource laws & practice.* Lanham, MD: AltaMira Press.

Lee, R. F. (1950). *Historical and architectural monuments in the United States.* Washington, DC: National Park Service.

Lichbach, M. I. (2003). *Is rational choice theory all of social science?* Ann Arbor: University of Michigan Press.

INTRODUCTION

Lipe, W. D. (1984). Value and meaning in cultural resources. In H. Cleere (Ed.), *Approaches to the archaeological heritage* (pp. 1–11). Cambridge: Cambridge University Press.

Lixinski, L. (2015). Between orthodoxy and heterodoxy: The troubled relationships between heritage studies and heritage law. *International Journal of Heritage Studies, 21*(3), 203–214.

Logan, W. (2012). Cultural diversity, cultural heritage and human rights: Towards heritage management as human rights-based cultural practice. *International Journal of Heritage Studies, 18*(3), 231–244.

Low, S. M. (1994). Cultural conservation of place. In M. Hufford (Ed.), *Conserving culture: A new discourse on heritage* (pp. 66–77). Urbana: University of Illinois Press.

Lowenthal, D. (1985). *The past is a foreign country.* Cambridge, UK: Cambridge University Press.

Lowenthal, D. (2015). *The past is a foreign country: Revised.* Cambridge, UK: Cambridge University Press.

Mason, R. (2003). Fixing historic preservation: A constructive critique of 'significance'. *Places, 16*(1), 64–71.

Mason, R. (2006). Theoretical and practical arguments for values-centered preservation. *CRM: The Journal of Heritage Stewardship, 3*(2), 21–48.

Mason, R. (2008). Be interested and beware: Joining economic valuation and heritage conservation. *International Journal of Heritage Studies, 14*(4), 303–318.

Mason, R. (2009). Preservation planning in American cities. *Forum Journal, 23*(2): 38–44.

Matzko, J. A. (2001). *Reconstructing Fort Union.* Lincoln, NB: University of Nebraska Press.

Mayes, T. (2016). Blog series: Why do old places matter? Retrieved from https://savingplaces.org/why-do-old-places-matter

Milholland, S. (2010). In the eyes of the beholder: Understanding and resolving incompatible ideologies and languages in US environmental and cultural laws in relationship to Navajo sacred lands. *American Indian Culture and Research Journal, 34*(2), 103–124.

Muñoz Viñas, S. (2005). *Contemporary theory of conservation.* Amsterdam: Elsevier.

NPS. (1995). *Secretary of the interior's standards for the treatment of historic properties.* Washington, DC: National Park Service.

O'Donnell, E. (1998). *National Register bulletin 39: Researching a historic property.* Washington, DC: National Park Service.

Ottaway, P. (1992). *Archaeology in British towns: From the Emperor Claudius to the Black Death.* London: Routledge.

Pannekoek, F. (1998). The rise of the heritage priesthood or the decline of community based heritage. *Forum Journal, 12*(3), 4–10.

Parks Canada. (2003). *Standards and guidelines for the conservation of historic places in Canada.* Gatineau, QC: Parks Canada.

Pendlebury, J. (2009). *Conservation in the age of consensus.* London and New York: Routledge.

Philippot, P. (1976). Historic preservation: Philosophy, criteria, guidelines. In S. Timmons (Ed.), *Preservation and conservation principles and practices.* Washington, DC: Preservation Press.

Rains, A., & Henderson, L. G. (1966). *With heritage so rich.* New York: Random House.

Riegl, A. (1996). The modern cult of monuments: Its essence and its development. In N. S. Price, M. K. J. Talley, & A. M. Vaccaro (Eds.), *Historical and philosophical issues on the conservation of cultural heritage* (pp. 69–83). Los Angeles: The Getty Conservation Institute. Originally published in 1903.

Ruskin, J. (1907). *The seven lamps of architecture.* Leipzig: Bernhard Tauchintz.

Rypkema, D., Cheong, C., Mason, R. (2011). *Measuring economic impacts of historic preservation: A report to the Advisory Council on Historic Preservation.* Washington, DC and Philadelphia: Place Economics and University of Pennsylvania.

Sagan, C. (1980). *Cosmos.* New York: Random House.

Sagan, C. (1997). *The demon-haunted world: Science as a candle in the dark.* New York: Ballantine Books.

INTRODUCTION

Sagan, C. (1998). *Billions and billions: Thoughts on life and death at the brink of the millennium.* New York: Random House.

Sarason, S. B. (1993). *You are thinking of teaching? Opportunities, problems, realities.* San Francisco: Jossey-Bass.

Shryock, R. H. (1969). Empiricism versus rationalism in American medicine, 1650–1950. *Proceedings of the American Antiquarian Society, April,* 99–150.

Silberman, N. (2016). Changing visions of heritage value: What role should the expert play? *Ethnologies, 36*(1–2 (special issue on Intangible cultural heritage)): 433–445.

Silverman, H., Waterton, E., & Watson, S. (2017). *Heritage in action: Making the past in the present.* Cham, Switzerland: Springer.

Smith, L. (2006). *Uses of heritage.* London and New York: Routledge.

Smith, L., & Waterton, E. (2012). Constrained by commonsense: The authorized heritage discourse in contemporary debates. In R. Skates, C. McDavid, & J. Carman (Eds.), *The Oxford handbook of public archaeology.* Oxford: Oxford University Press.

Solomon, M. (2005). *Making medical knowledge.* Oxford: Oxford University Press.

Sørensen, M. L. S., & Carman, J. (2009). *Heritage studies: Methods and approaches.* New York: Routledge.

SPAB. (n.d.). *SPAB's purpose.* London: Society for the Protection of Ancient Buildings.

Sprinkle, J. H. (2014). *Crafting preservation criteria: The national register of historic places and american historic preservation.* New York: Routledge.

Sullivan, S. (2015). Does the practice of heritage as we know it have a future? *Historic Environment, 27*(2), 110–117.

Tainter, J. A., & Lucas, G. J. (1983). Epistemology of the significance concept. *American Antiquity, 48*(4), 707–719.

Tomlan, M. (1994). Historic preservation education: Alongside architecture in academia. *Journal of Architectural Education, 47*(4), 187–196.

Torre, M. (2002). *Assessing the values of heritage conservation.* Los Angeles: Getty Conservation Institute.

Tunbridge, J. E., & Ashworth, G. J. (1996). *Dissonant heritage: The management of the past as a resource in conflict.* Chichester: John Wiley & Sons.

Waterton, E., Smith, L., & Campbell, G. (2006). The utility of discourse analysis to heritage studies: The burra charter and social inclusion. *International Journal of Heritage Studies, 12*(4), 339–355.

Wells, J. C. (2007). The plurality of truth in culture, context, and heritage: A (mostly) post-structuralist analysis of urban conservation charters. *City and Time, 3*(2:1), 1–13.

Wells, J. C. (2015a). In stakeholders we trust: Changing the ontological and epistemological orientation of built heritage assessment through participatory action research. In B. Szmygin (Ed.), *How to assess built heritage? Assumptions, methodologies, examples of heritage assessment systems.* Florence and Lublin: Romualdo Del Bianco Foundatione and Lublin University of Technology.

Wells, J. C. (2015b). Making a case for historic place conservation based on people's values. *Forum Journal, 29*(3), 44–62.

Wells, J. C., & Lixinski, L. (2016). Heritage values and legal rules: Identification and treatment of the historic environment via an adaptive regulatory framework (part 1). *Journal of Cultural Heritage Management and Sustainable Development, 6*(3), 345–364.

White, B. J., & Roddewig, R. J. (1994). *Preparing a historic preservation plan.* Washington, DC and Chicago: NTHP and American Planning Association.

Winter, T. (2013). Clarifying the critical in critical heritage studies. *International Journal of Heritage Studies, 19*(6), 532–545.

Winter, T., & Waterton, E. (2013). Editorial: Critical heritage studies. *International Journal of Heritage Studies, 19*(6), 529–531.

Witcomb, A., & Buckley K. (2013). Engaging with the future of "critical heritage studies": Looking back in order to look forward. *International Journal of Heritage Studies, 19*(6), 562–578.

INTRODUCTION

Zancheti, S. M., & Loretto, R. P. (2012). Dynamic integrity: A new concept to approach the conservation of historic urban landscape (HUL). In *Textos para discussão no. 53* (pp. 1–11). Olinda, Brazil: Centro de Estudos Avançados da Conservação Integrada.

Zancheti, S. M., & Simila, K. (2012). *6th international seminar on urban conservation: Measuring heritage conservation performance*. Recife, Brazil and Rome: CECI & ICCROM.

Zeisel, J. (2006). *Inquiry by design: Environment/behavior/neuroscience in architecture, interiors, landscape, and planning* (p. 400). New York: W.W. Norton & Company.

PART 1

Defining a Human-Centric Built Heritage Conservation Practice

CHAPTER 1

Bridging the Gap between Built Heritage Conservation Practice and Critical Heritage Studies

Jeremy C. Wells

Practitioners have long criticized higher education for its "ivory tower" perspective, in which scholars appear to be far removed from the trials and tribulations of the everyday professional. From this high vantage, it may be all too easy to critique the behavior, values, and choices of others because the scholar is removed from the messy reality of the "real" world. As David Demers (2011) summarizes, universities perpetuate a system in which scholarship is published in venues that are the least accessible to those who might benefit the most from it: Most professionals do not have ready access to the refereed journals or university-press books in which academics are required to publish and are, therefore, largely unaware of theoretical developments in their own field, especially in fields that relate to the social sciences. In addition, universities often penalize researchers for adopting topics that are too applied or close to professional practice. This situation creates an environment in which scholars who wish to change practice end up talking to themselves and not the practitioners for whom their knowledge is meant to benefit.

Cultural heritage conservation is one such field where a group of academics are increasingly studying practice with the overt goal of improving how professionals relate to, understand, and benefit the public. These "critical heritage studies" scholars closely examine the practice, policies, and limitations of heritage conservation work from museum studies to built heritage conservation. Often these scholars adopt an emancipatory goal in their work, criticizing practice through the lenses of critical theory, constructivism, post-colonialism, and post-structuralism, characterizing much of the heritage conservation practice as hegemonic, top-down, positivistic, and oppressive while espousing the goal of empowerment centered on social justice (Aaroz, 2011; Cane, 2009; Harrison, 2013;

Hutchings & La Salle, 2015; Kaufman, 2009; Lixinski, 2015; Logan, 2012; Milholland, 2010; Pendlebury, 2009; Schofield, 2009, 2014; Silberman, 2016; Smith, 2006; Smith & Campbell, 2015; Sullivan, 2015; Waterton & Smith, 2010; Wells, 2010, 2015a, b; Winter, 2013; Zancheti & Loretto, 2012). Most importantly, critical heritage studies represents the largest, most cohesive group of scholars generating empirical evidence with the overt aim to improve or change heritage conservation practice to benefit larger numbers of people. While there are academics from other areas engaging in similar work, only critical heritage studies scholars have focused their emancipatory efforts under the singular umbrella of the Association for Critical Heritage Studies (ACHS). According to the ACHS, 800 people, mostly associated with institutions of higher education, attended their 2016 conference in Montreal, Quebec, and nearly 2,000 members are represented on their website (www.heritagestudies.org).

A major caveat, however, is that there is little evidence that critical heritage studies research is actually changing practice. Moreover, in their "critical" stance of practitioners, these scholars may be engaging in the same hegemonic activities that they are simultaneously criticizing and, in the process, alienating those actors who they most need to engage. This chapter will, therefore, examine the nature of the critical heritage studies movement, how it generates empirical evidence that fails to affect practice, and the ways to bridge the gap between these scholars and practitioners.

What Is Critical Heritage Studies?

Before exploring the characteristics of critical heritage studies, it is important to define "heritage studies" and how it is different from its critical variant. In particular, in the United States, heritage studies is often synonymous with public history and has few commonalities with the social science foci inherent in critical heritage studies. In its most widely adopted use in the United States, heritage studies is the teaching of local history to primary and secondary school students facilitated by field trips to historic house museums and sites. This usage differs from its definition in Europe, Canada, and Australia, where heritage studies is associated with museum studies and cultural heritage, or the meanings associated with heritage rather than (as in the United States) the facts associated with heritage.

In a US-based context, therefore, the difference between heritage studies and critical heritage studies lies in the focus on facts versus meanings, respectively. In one of the earliest explorations of this polarity, David Lowenthal (1985) exposes the impossibility of accurately recovering the complete, tangible qualities of the past through scientific principles because of the lack of objective, factual evidence, yet built heritage conservation practice assumes the opposite. Moreover, Lowenthal is emphatic that the way in which everyday people understand, use, and experience heritage is anything but objective, and has more in common with folklore and storytelling than history (i.e., facts of the past). In this way, Lowenthal's work is very much a product of the post-modern turn in historiography that rejected the possibility of being able to objectively understand, much less to recreate or restore, the past. Realizing that knowing "history" is actually an act of interpreting *multiple possible* realities, critical approaches to historiography embraced the idea of uncertainty, especially from different cultural perspectives (Foucault, 1972; Furniss, 1999; McCullagh, 2004). Or, in more simplistic terms, history from the perspective of the conqueror is very different from history from the perspective of the conquered. Heritage studies (and its parent discipline of public history) fails to adopt this ontological perspective; however, public history remains a largely positivist endeavor that has yet to adopt the post-modern of its more theoretical peers in the academy.

One could argue that it is because the academy deprecates public history as being too applied that heritage studies in the United States retains the positivistic roots of its parent discipline's past. To be sure, public history has long focused on the collection of as many facts as possible to create simplistic, singular interpretations for mass public consumption that deny multiple interpretations of reality and extra-cultural perspectives. In the United States, one of the most public manifestations of public history is the preparation of National Register of Historic Places nominations. Keeping in mind that the goal of historical positivism is "to discover the laws ruling the temporal sequence of historical facts" (Erdmann, Kocka, Mommse, & Blänsdorf, 2005, 17), instructions for preparing a National Register nomination (National Park Service, 1997) are as follows:

> A person wishing to prepare a nomination needs a thorough knowledge of the property. By physically inspecting the property and conducting historical research, applicants can gather facts such as the physical characteristics of the property, date of construction, changes to the property over time, historic functions and activities, association with events and persons, and the role of the property in the history of the community, State, or the nation.

The applicant is then instructed to assemble these facts into an objective account, organized by temporal sequence, of what "really" happened in the past; the more accurate the account (i.e., more facts), the more significant the property can become. Other forms of public history that manifest in museums and historic sites around America share similar emphases on the objective collection of facts and typically singular interpretations.

How, then, does critical heritage studies differ from heritage studies? In the literature on heritage studies, there is a general consensus that history is "the raw facts of the past" (Aitchison, MacLeod, & Shaw, 2000, 96), while heritage "is history processed through mythology, ideology, nationalism, local pride, romantic ideas or just plain marketing" (Schouten, 1995, 21). The meanings of heritage are, therefore, subjective (often emotional) and rooted in the present and are defined by social, cultural, and individual processes. In other words, the meanings of heritage can be understood through contemporary sociocultural and experiential values, not the facts promulgated by public history and its adherents. Lowenthal (1985, 410) argues that in the realm of human experience, we create heritage; to most people, heritage is, therefore, more important than history and is a product of human invention and creativity:

> The answer is that a fixed past is not what we really need, or at any rate not all we need. We require a heritage with which we continually interact, one which fuses past with present. This heritage is not only necessary but inescapable; we cannot now avoid feeling that the past is to some extent our own creation. If today's insights can be seen as integral to the meaning of the past, rather than subversive of its truth, we may breathe new life into it.

Heritage is also intimately related to people's relationship with place as Laurajane Smith (2006, 75) alludes when claiming that "heritage is about sense of place." In the 1970s, the humanistic geographer Yi-Fu Tuan (1977, 194, 198) noted that the practice of historic preservation and public history essentially have nothing to do with how people are affected by place or attached to place. Not much has changed in practice since Tuan made this observation, primarily because the activities of historic preservation are largely dictated by rules and regulations, which, once established, are very difficult to change. The values associated with historic preservation practice have, therefore, become ossified and have not adapted to the changing values of society over the many decades since these rules and regulations were originally codified (Wells & Lixinski, 2016).

It is a revealing exercise to examine the curricula and faculty associated with "heritage studies" degree programs in the United States. Upon examining courses offered and faculty specializations, these programs differ little from self-ascribed public history programs. There is no social science-based coursework that discusses sociological, anthropological, and psychological aspects of people's relationship to heritage nor are there faculty trained in any of the social sciences. Undoubtedly, upon graduation from such a program, a student would likely have excellent skills in archival research and conventional museum interpretation but know little about the sociocultural dimensions of heritage, including stakeholders' emotional relationship to place. Largely absent in the readings and topics of these courses are literature on folklore, critical heritage studies theory, and related perspectives from the social sciences. In comparison, a look at the heritage studies degree programs in Europe, Canada, and Australia reveals a core component of social science-based coursework and an acceptance of the multivariate nature of the meanings of heritage. Typically located in departments of anthropology and museum studies rather than history departments, students learn that facts may have rather little influence on everyday people's understanding or attribution of the meanings and values of historical places and landscapes.

The core literature of heritage studies is also substantially different from critical heritage studies. In fact, it is difficult to evince any kind of theoretical basis to heritage studies in American practice beyond the positivistic view of history. In contrast, in its short existence, critical heritage studies has a rich theoretical base starting with David Lowenthal's (1985) *The Past Is a Foreign Country.* Other key authors and their relevance are as follows:

- Randall Mason (2002, 2003, 2006): Built heritage conservation practice focused on the objective qualities of fabric with ignorance of other kinds of intangible values. Practice should incorporate a "values-based" approach to conservation. Many of these values can be informed through the use of social science-based methods.

- Bagnall (2003): Everyday people's assessment of the authenticity of the historic environment is based on their ability to engage in a kind of performance with the past that generates emotionally authentic meanings.

- Laurajane Smith (2006): Introduced the concept of the "authorized heritage discourse" (AHD) in which expert practitioners control the positivistic meanings of heritage. The AHD describes a system in which the only valid way in which lay people can share meanings important to them is through the language and meanings of the expert.

- Waterton, Smith, and Campbell (2006): The values of heritage conservation experts are not more scientific, objective, or neutral than other cultural values associated with heritage. The values of experts are just another set of cultural values among many.

- Schofield (2009, 2014): Heritage consists of the "everyday" and the "ordinary" and not the monumental. Heritage is therefore not rare and unique, but rather it is ubiquitous. Because heritage is based on the meanings and experiences of everyday people, everyone is, therefore, an expert on heritage; the control of meanings should not be entirely in the hands of experts.

- Harrison (2013): Heritage conservation practice should seek to break down the artificial divide between the layperson and the expert practitioner; practice should, therefore, emphasize a bottom-up rather than a top-down approach. Authenticity is defined by the everyday experiences of people and not historical facts. The supposed divide between natural and cultural heritage is artificial; it is instead best viewed as a continuum.

In sum, critical heritage studies fully embraces the post-modern turn in the pluralistic quality of the meanings associated with heritage and seeks to understand and balance power in the relationship between various actors. It does so by using social science research methodologies to produce data that, when analyzed, provide empirical evidence that *could* influence practice.

The Relationship of Critical Heritage Studies to the Practitioner

The literature in critical heritage studies is quite clear in that its aim is to understand and change practice and it often does so by focusing on the practitioner. But, as Tim Winter (2013, 533) acknowledges, this nascent field has a tendency to alienate practitioners because it treats them as objects of study rather than as rational actors with equal standing. In this way, the emancipatory goal of critical heritage studies is subverted by subjecting practitioners to the same kind of hegemonic practice—control of meanings by experts—that its adherents promulgate.

In the inaugural 2012 meeting of the ACHS, Gary Campbell and Laurajane Smith penned a "manifesto" for the nascent organization and invited others to respond (see www.criticalheritages tudies.org/history/). This manifesto is presented as fluid and open to discussion, but as of October 2016, remains unchanged on the ACHS website with the exception that the authors' names have been removed. While acknowledging that this manifesto clearly does not represent the perspectives of all individuals associated with the ACHS or critical heritage studies in general, it is the closest document that attempts to articulate the value system of critical heritage studies. Because of the manifesto's usefully articulated perspective on the practitioner, it is worthwhile to analyze its content in this light.

The manifesto begins by explaining that it is intended to be provocative and explains that just because the preservation/conservation field has been doing things the same way for many decades does not excuse us from taking a more critical approach to practice so that it is more democratic and inclusive.

> This is a preliminary manifesto – a provocation – presaging the creation of the Association of Critical Heritage Studies and its initial conference at the University of Gothenburg in 2012. We want to challenge you to respond to this document, and question the received wisdom of what heritage is, energise heritage studies by drawing on wider intellectual sources, vigorously question the conservative cultural and economic power relations that outdated understandings of heritage seem to underpin and invite the active participation of people and communities who to date have been marginalised in the creation and management of 'heritage'.

A recurrent theme, however, in the manifesto is the use of the passive voice to describe how the meanings of heritage have been marginalized. Whether deliberate or not, it clearly makes the object of its sentences—the entity that is causing the marginalization or other deleterious activities—vague, distant, and unclear. The manifesto continues in establishing its basis for existence, with a reference to Karl Marx (1844):

> Above all, we want you to critically engage with the proposition that heritage studies needs to be rebuilt from the ground up, which requires the "ruthless criticism of everything existing".

In appropriating this language from Marx, the manifesto makes clear that the orthodox values used in heritage conservation should ultimately be destroyed and entirely rebuilt. But why is such "ruthless criticism" needed, especially in light of the possibility that some existing values/systems/ideas might potentially be compatible with this inclusive vision of heritage? To be sure, because the stated aim of the manifesto is to provoke, making such a strong argument for the destruction of the existing system of heritage conservation ought to garner many divergent perspectives. But, considering that people and not abstract entities have values, how should the people who hold these orthodox values—the practitioners—be treated? The Marxist reference implies that those with divergent values ought to be held in contempt or perhaps even ignored. In its attempts to make right the perceived wrongs of heritage practitioners, is not the manifesto engaging in the same hegemonic practices that it also condemns? In other words, egalitarian language is missing from the manifesto that would reframe the argument from one of the destruction of another cultural group's values to one of seeking balance. The next paragraph of the manifesto does explore the dichotomy of power relationships in conservation practice, however, but returns to passive language describing the way in which practitioners engage in "fetishing expert knowledge" and promote "social exclusion":

> Heritage is, as much as anything, a political act and we need to ask serious questions about the power relations that "heritage" has all too often been invoked to sustain. Nationalism, imperialism, colonialism, cultural elitism, Western triumphalism, social exclusion based on class and ethnicity, and the fetishising of expert knowledge have all exerted strong influences on how heritage is used, defined and managed.

To be sure, this paragraph is an accurate summary of a long tradition in critical heritage studies literature describing heritage as a political tool: Those who control the meanings of heritage have power. There is probably no greater example of this situation than the barbarism that ISIS and the Taliban have unleashed on Middle Eastern antiquities, which is brutally effective as a tool of political oppression. As with this example, studying aspects of the meanings and use of heritage will inevitably bring us to uncomfortable places, and the most difficult questions are the very ones that need to be asked. In fairness, the manifesto rightly indicates that we should be able to ask the question if and how practitioners are marginalizing and excluding others in their practice:

> We argue that a truly critical heritage studies will ask many uncomfortable questions of traditional ways of thinking about and doing heritage, and that the interests of the marginalised and excluded will be brought to the forefront when posing these questions.

But, it is important to note that *some* areas of preservation/conservation practice are likely to be emancipatory, especially when conducted outside the bounds of regulatory requirements. There is evidence for this claim in many of the community-based archaeological studies that have been undertaken in the past couple of decades (Wells, 2015a). While not explicitly stating so, the manifesto implies that all such practice results in marginalization and oppression. The manifesto continues, stating that the orthodox values of heritage are defined and controlled through the narrow lenses of white, Western experts and positivistic art/historical meanings. Because the traditional disciplines associated with heritage conservation lack a social science background, these disciplines, as the manifesto indicates, "sustain a limited idea of what heritage is and how it should be studied and managed." There is ample evidence for these claims in the literature (e.g., Green, 1998; Harrison, 2013;

Smith, 2006) and in the curricula of most built environment conservation degree programs, especially in the United States. Especially in built heritage, social science research methods—ostensibly, an approach quite suitable for understanding people's relationship with their heritage—are not used, taught, or considered. To be sure, public history, architecture, and art history are not particularly known for their strengths in using empirical evidence for contemporary people/place relationships or in their use of social science research methods. This observation is not intended to denigrate the role of the humanities in understanding tangible and intangible heritage, but rather to reveal that the entirety of the picture is incomplete without the social sciences.

Laurajane Smith first introduced the AHD in her book, *Uses of Heritage* (2006), and it is not surprising, as the co-author of the manifesto, that it is represented in the manifesto. The AHD is rather remarkable for efficiently encapsulating how heritage experts—e.g., historic preservationists, preservation architects, historical interpreters, preservation/conservation planners—"sideline" the values of everyday people and, instead, reinforce their own professionally taught value systems, which are often positivistic and incapable of accommodating sociocultural values. But the mention of the AHD, which is predicated on the behavior of practitioners, makes it quite clear that the target of the manifesto is not only a conservation practice but also the practitioners who are part of the system of heritage. Preservation/conservation practitioners are, in effect, the objects of study for scholars of critical heritage studies. The manifesto explains that the creation of the ACHS is to allow for a common meeting place of "critics" of heritage practice, and the implicit study of practitioners.

The manifesto then makes a list of recommendations for how to "promote existing critical innovations and interventions in heritage," focusing on the central role that the social sciences should play in research and practice and challenge positivistic approaches and quantification. It argues for a transdisciplinary approach that "integrat[es] heritage and museum studies with studies of memory, public history, community, tourism, planning and development." And, the manifesto argues for the democratization of heritage "by consciously rejecting elite cultural narratives and embracing the heritage insights of people, communities and cultures that have traditionally been marginalised in formulating heritage policy." Again, the manifesto dances around the implicit agent of this marginalizing behavior—the practitioner—without whom the ACHS would fail to have a reason to exist.

In fact, the only place in which the manifesto specifically mentions practitioners at all is in recommending a "dialogue and debate between researchers, practitioners and communities." While laudable, one wonders how effective such a dialog can be when, in essence, critical heritage studies researchers are asserting their power over practitioners by making them objects of critique and study. Out of curiosity, I have shared the ACHS manifesto with several built heritage conservation practitioners and, universally, their reaction has been one of hostility because they feel that they are being personally attacked. Admittedly, what I relate is anecdotal and I make no claim for statistical generalizability, but the fact that these hostile meanings exist is problematic. Instead of advocating for a dialog of equals in which meanings are considered from multicultural perspectives, the ACHS manifesto is arguing for the suppression of one cultural value system (that of the expert practitioner) and its replacement by another (the theories of critical heritage studies). The practitioners with whom I shared the manifesto described themselves as being motivated to help communities, not oppress them. To be sure, this response implies that these practitioners may fail to see their acceptance and promulgation of art/historical values over the values of communities as an issue, but one cannot begin to have a productive debate by marginalizing the very group of people you wish to engage.

While the ACHS manifesto fails to engage in a productive way with the practitioner, what does critical heritage studies literature have to say on this endeavor? Not surprisingly, the literature reinforces the meanings of the manifesto. Heritage conservation practitioners are consistently painted as oppressive, marginalizing entities engaging in a kind of colonizing practice that "sidelines" the values of communities (Hutchings & La Salle, 2015; King, 2009; Smith, 2006). To this end, Neil Silberman (2016, 440) makes the claim that the positivistic, art/historical system that heritage conservation practitioners perpetuate is "an instrument of top-down social engineering on a global scale." Frits Pannekoek (1998) characterizes heritage conservation professionals as a "heritage priesthood" who, in demanding fealty to the AHD, are engaging in the "misguided" psychological manipulation of people's value systems. Thomas King (2009) asserts that cultural resource management professionals purposefully use language that obfuscates meaning to frustrate and disconnect the public and engage in potentially unethical behavior that privileges a "check the box" mentality in environmental impact reviews. Lastly, Siân Jones (2009, 143) charges that professionals engage in the intentional omission of the values of communities in reports, especially when they are "compelled by professional conventions and institutional constraints to write these aspects out of conservation policy and public display."

To date, as Tim Winter (2013) alludes, critical heritage studies has largely failed to have any impact on heritage conservation practice at all. But, instead of climbing down from the proverbial ivory tower, critical heritage studies researchers—as represented in the ACHS manifesto—have instead firmly ensconced themselves in an elevated place, above the practitioner. Based on the published literature, there is little evidence that critical heritage scholars have directly engaged practitioners as equals in a dialog of change. The ACHS has not done so either and has no guidance or advice on how critical heritage studies can or should engage with practice.

Bridging the Divide

To be sure, critical heritage studies has much to offer in improving the conservation of built heritage, places, and landscapes. Because of its critical stance not only on practice but on practitioners as well, there does not appear to be an effective way to translate research into something that could usefully impact practice. To be fair, most practitioners have little or no awareness of critical heritage studies. And most students in built conservation degree programs receive little or no education in the concepts of critical heritage studies, especially the AHD, so our higher education system is complicit in perpetuating this divide. We, therefore, have an environment that is antithetical to the sharing of meanings and ideas on how practice can change. But does this necessarily have to be the case? How can this divide be bridged? I will offer several suggestions for this endeavor.

First, social scientists—especially the anthropologists who largely define critical heritage studies—need to view practitioners as allies in their mission to democratize heritage. This perspective need not require these academics to abandon critical analyses of practice, but research should be conducted in a way that respects, and ideally involves in a participatory way, professionals. The existing system of critique is inequitable in that it assumes that only critical heritage studies researchers are capable of identifying and devising solutions to the inherent problems in the current system of heritage conservation. Practitioners, therefore, need to be recognized as the primary agents of change and requires that they be attributed with value beyond mere objects of research or critique, but as active co-researchers in the overall process.

Practitioners have a responsibility as well and should seek at least a general awareness of the current state of knowledge in critical heritage studies and allied human-centered approaches to interventions in the built environment and cultural landscapes. Scholars could go a long way toward achieving this goal by making their research more easily accessible to practitioners. Notwithstanding that the academy often fails to recognize publications in professional periodicals, academics need to be publishing synopses of their research in these venues as well as open source/access scholarly journals. Many historic environment advocacy organizations have publications of this nature that reach a wide variety of practitioners. Scholars should also take advantage of sites such as academia.edu and researchgate.net as well as their university's own digital commons sites to publish their research. Where an academic journal of press holds copyright to the final, published paper, scholars can post working preprints of their research instead, directing the reader to the final, published version ensconced behind a paywall. Practitioners and academics ought to also work more closely together in reevaluating curriculum standards for educational programs that address the conservation of the built environment.

Lastly, the role of the regulatory environment in promulgating the AHD and other critiques of built heritage conservation practice has largely been ignored by both critical heritage studies researchers and practitioners as well as policymakers. The majority of work in built heritage conservation exists because of the regulatory environment. In my own (unpublished) research, which is supported by the findings of Thomas Visser (2009), I have found that over a six-month period, about three quarters of all US-based job postings for positions in historic preservation were for work that exists because of the various federal, state, and local laws that ostensibly protect heritage. These laws have remained essentially unchanged since their implementation, which, in some cases, was fifty or more years ago. We, therefore, have a heritage system based on mid-twentieth-century meanings, values, and expectations. Fundamentally, we cannot change the existing system that conserves built heritage, places, and cultural landscapes without addressing the need to change the regulatory environment. This problematic situation, however, presents a useful place for collaboration between critical heritage studies scholars, who may have little background in law, and practitioners, as well as legal scholars.

Conclusion

I began this chapter with the stereotype of the ivory tower and the role in which critical heritage studies researchers tend to perpetuate this stereotype, especially in the way heritage practitioners are treated as objects of study rather than as co-researchers or co-collaborators. The critical heritage studies movement needs to extend its emancipatory perspective to the way it treats practitioners in a more egalitarian way. This act does not require, however, the abandonment, in any way, of the critical approaches to how heritage conservation is practiced. Rather, by engaging practitioners as co-researchers, critical heritage studies researchers may find more suitable, pragmatic ways to democratize the practice of the conservation of built heritage, places, and landscapes. And, in the process, by treating practitioners in this way, they are much more likely to want to implement the changes in which they have some sense of ownership.

The academy has a large role to play here as well, in terms of how future practitioners are educated. The National Council for Preservation Education, which represents most of the historic preservation degree programs in the United States, has specific curriculum standards that all of its members must meet. These standards, which are essentially unchanged since their establishment in 1988 (Tomlan, 1988), require member programs to have courses on historic preservation theory, documentation, and the history of the built environment along with some kind of experiential activity (e.g., an internship); no other components are required. Preservation theory, as taught in most of

NCPE's member programs, is based on a nineteenth- and early to mid-twentieth-century white male, Euro-centric, art/historical perspective, taught through the publications of John Ruskin (1907/1849), Eugène-Emmanuel Viollet-le-Duc (1990/1854), Camillo Boito (1884), Alois Riegl (1996/1903), Paul Philippot (1975), and Giovanni Carbonara (1996/1976), among many others. Documentation is overtly positivistic in its aims to accurately measure and describe the visual characteristics of the built environment and to research historical facts associated with specific buildings and places. Courses in the history of the built environment reinforce a positivistic art/historical method, which focus on the ability of students to accurately describe an historical style attributed to a particular building.

We need to change how preservation theory is taught by beginning with an emancipatory approach, based on contemporary critical heritage studies literature, and then return to the past to reflect on why we have adopted this human-centered versus fabric-centered stance. This reverse historical perspective makes it clear to students that current human-centered conservation theory is a reaction to the positivism of the past and should, indeed, be the foundation of practice. Similarly, documentation should be broadened to include understanding how various communities perceive and value their historic environment, which would mandate the use of social science methods (and associated faculty trained in their use). The history of the built environment needs to shift from an outcome of identifying building styles to understanding the social and cultural origins of the environment from the distant past to the present. Lastly, students should be taught that an achievable goal of heritage conservation is the empowerment of communities and social justice. Students trained in this way will be much better equipped to engage critical heritage studies researchers as co-collaborators and would be much more effective in working with everyday people.

Works Cited

Aaroz, G. F. (2011). Preserving heritage places under a new paradigm. *Journal of Cultural Heritage Management and Sustainable Development, 1*(1), 55–60.

Aitchison, C., MacLeod, N. E., & Shaw, S. J. (2000). *Leisure and tourism landscapes: Social and cultural geographies.* London: Routledge.

Bagnall, G. (2003). Performance and performativity at heritage sites. *Museum and Society, 1*(2), 87–103.

Boito, C. (1884). *I restauratori, conferenza tenuta all'esposizione di torino, il 7 giugno 1884.* Florence.

Cane, S. (2009). Why do we conserve? Developing understanding of conservation as a cultural construct. In A. Richmond & A. Bracker (Eds.), *Conservation: Principles, dilemmas and uncomfortable truths* (pp. 163–176). Amsterdam, The Netherlands; Boston, MA: Butterworth-Heinemann.

Carbonara, G. (1996). The integration of image: Problems in the restoration of monuments. In N. S. Price, M. K. J. Talley, & A. M. Vaccaro (Eds.), *Historical and philosophical issues on the conservation of cultural heritage* (pp. 236–243). Los Angeles, CA: The Getty Conservation Institute.

Demers, D. (2011). *The ivory tower of babel: Why the social sciences are failing to live up to their promises.* New York: Algora Pub.

Erdmann, K. D., Kocka, J., Mommse, W. J., & Blänsdorf, A. (2005). *Toward a global community of historians: The international historical congresses and the international committee of historical sciences 1898–2000.* New York: Berghahn Books.

Fortman, L. (2008). Doing science together. In *Participatory research in conservation and rural livelihoods: Doing science together* (pp. 1–17). Oxford: Blackwell Publishing.

Foucault, M. (1972). *The archaeology of knowledge.* New York: Partheon Books.

Furniss, E. (1999). *The burden of history: Colonialism and the frontier myth in a rural Canadian community.* Vancouver, BC: UPC Press.

Green, H. L. (1998). The social construction of historical significance. In M. A. Tomlan (Ed.), *Preservation of what, for whom? A critical look at historical significance* (pp. 85–94). Ithaca, NY: National Council for Preservation Education.

Harrison, R. (2013). *Heritage: Critical approaches.* New York: Routledge.

Hutchings, R., & La Salle, M. (2015). Archaeology as disaster capitalism. *International Journal of Historical Archaeology, 19,* 699–720.

Jones, S. (2009). Experiencing authenticity at heritage sites: Some implications for heritage management and conservation. *Conservation and Management of Archaeological Sites, 11*(2), 133–147.

Kaufman, N. (2009). *Place, race, and story: Essays on the past and future of historic preservation.* New York: Routledge.

King, T. F. (2009). *Our unprotected heritage: Whitewashing the destruction of our cultural and natural resources.* Walnut Creek, CA: Left Coast Press.

Lixinski, L. (2015). Between orthodoxy and heterodoxy: The troubled relationships between heritage studies and heritage law. *International Journal of Heritage Studies, 21*(3), 203–214.

Logan, W. (2012). Cultural diversity, cultural heritage and human rights: Towards heritage management as human rights-based cultural practice. *International Journal of Heritage Studies, 18*(3), 231–244.

Lowenthal, D. (1985). *The past is a foreign country.* Cambridge, UK: Cambridge University Press.

Marx, K. (1844). Letter from Marx to Arnold Ruge. *Deutsch-Französische Jahrbücher.*

Mason, R. (2002). Assessing values in conservation planning: Methodological issues and choices. In M. L. de Torre (Ed.), *Assessing the values of cultural heritage* (pp. 5–30). Los Angeles, CA: The J. Paul Getty Trust.

Mason, R. (2003). Fixing historic preservation: A constructive critique of 'significance'. *Places, 16*(1), 64–71.

Mason, R. (2006). Theoretical and practical arguments for values-centered preservation. *CRM: The Journal of Heritage Stewardship, 3*(2), 21–48.

McCullagh, C. B. (2004). *The logic of history: Putting postmodernism in perspective.* Routledge.

Milholland, S. (2010). In the eyes of the beholder: Understanding and resolving incompatible ideologies and languages in US environmental and cultural laws in relationship to Navajo sacred lands. *American Indian Culture and Research Journal, 34*(2), 103–124.

National Park Service. (1997). *National register bulletin: How to apply the national register criteria for evaluation.* U.S. Department of the Interior, National Park Service.

Pannekoek, F. (1998). The rise of the heritage priesthood or the decline of community based heritage. *Forum Journal, 12*(3), 4–10.

Pendlebury, J. (2009). *Conservation in the age of consensus.* London and New York: Routledge.

Philippot, P. (1996a). Historic preservation: Philosophy, criteria, guidelines, II. In N. S. Price, M. K. J. Talley, & A. M. Vaccaro (Eds.), *Historical and philosophical issues on the conservation of cultural heritage* (pp. 358–363). Los Angeles, CA: The Getty Conservation Institute.

Philippot, P. (1996b). Historic preservation: Philosophy, criteria, guidelines, I. In N. S. Price, M. K. J. Talley, & A. M. Vaccaro (Eds.), *Historical and philosophical issues on the conservation of cultural heritage* (pp. 268–274). Los Angeles, CA: The Getty Conservation Institute.

Riegl, A. (1996). The modern cult of monuments: Its essence and its development. In N. S. Price, M. K. J. Talley, & A. M. Vaccaro (Eds.), *Historical and philosophical issues on the conservation of cultural heritage* (pp. 69–83). Los Angeles, CA: The Getty Conservation Institute.

Ruskin, J. (1907). *The seven lamps of architecture.* Leipzig: Bernhard Tauchintz. (Original work published 1849.)

Schofield, J. (2009). Being autocentric: Towards symmetry in heritage management practices. In L. Gibson & J. Pendlebury (Eds.), *Valuing historic environments* (pp. 93–113). Surrey and Burlington: Ashgate Publishing.

Schofield, J. (2014). *Who needs experts? Counter-mapping cultural heritage.* Farnham: Ashgate.

Schouten, F. F. J. (1995). Heritage as historical reality. In D. T. Herbert (Ed.), *Heritage, tourism and society*. London: Mansell.

Silberman, N. (2016). Changing visions of heritage value: What role should the expert play? *Ethnologies, 36*(1–2 (special issue on Intangible cultural heritage)).

Smith, L. (2006). *Uses of heritage*. London and New York: Routledge.

Smith, L., & Campbell, G. (2015). The elephant in the room: Heritage affect, and emotion. In W. Logan, M. N. Craith, & U. Kockel (Eds.), *A companion to heritage studies* (pp. 443–460). Chichester: Wiley-Blackwell.

Sullivan, S. (2015). Does the practice of heritage as we know it have a future? *Historic Environment, 27*(2), 110–117.

Tomlan, M. (1988, October). Preservation education. *Preservation News (supplement)*.

Tuan, Y.-F. (1977). *Space and place: The perspectives of experience*. Minneapolis, MN: University of Minnesota Press.

Viollet-le-Duc, E. (1990). *The foundations of architecture*. New York: George Braziller. (Original work published 1854.)

Visser, T. D. (2009). The status of professional career openings in historic preservation in the United States. *Preservation Education & Research, 2*, 73–84.

Waterton, E., & Smith, L. (2010). The recognition and misrecognition of community heritage. *International Journal of Heritage Studies, 16*(1), 4–15.

Waterton, E., Smith, L., & Campbell, G. (2006). The utility of discourse analysis to heritage studies: The burra charter and social inclusion. *International Journal of Heritage Studies, 12*(4), 339–355.

Wells, J. C. (2010). Our history is not false: Perspectives from the revitalisation culture. *International Journal of Heritage Studies, 16*(6), 464–485.

Wells, J. C. (2015a). In stakeholders we trust: Changing the ontological and epistemological orientation of built heritage assessment through participatory action research. In B. Szmygin (Ed.), *How to assess built heritage? Assumptions, methodologies, examples of heritage assessment systems*. Florence and Lublin: Romualdo Del Bianco Foundatione and Lublin University of Technology.

Wells, J. C. (2015b). Making a case for historic place conservation based on people's values. *Forum Journal, 29*(3), 44–62.

Wells, J. C., & Lixinski, L. (2016). Heritage values and legal rules: Identification and treatment of the historic environment via an adaptive regulatory framework (part 1). *Journal of Cultural Heritage Management and Sustainable Development, 6*(3), 345–364.

Winter, T. (2013). Clarifying the critical in critical heritage studies. *International Journal of Heritage Studies, 19*(6), 532–545.

Zancheti, S. M., & Loretto, R. P. (2012). Dynamic integrity: A new concept to approach the conservation of historic urban landscape (HUL). In *Textos para discussão no. 53* (pp. 1–11). Olinda, Brazil: Centro de Estudos Avançados da Conservação Integrada.

CHAPTER 2

The Measurement of Meaning— Psychometrics and *Sense of Place*

Suzanne Elizabeth Bott

Introduction

This purpose of this volume is to reflect on the state of current social science research in supporting the practices of heritage conservation and determine how to improve management practices. This chapter adds to the existing research with findings from an empirical study of psychological responses that were found to help measure and validate *perceptions of meaning*, or *sense of place*, in a variety of settings. The phenomenon of finding meaning in places is based on features of the place itself, both physical (natural and built) and sociocultural (affective and functional), and the psychological and physical wants and needs of the person or people in the place or setting.

Collective responses to site features and the ability of a setting to meet the expectations and needs of the user can significantly inform resource managers when determining a course of action for management and lead to higher levels of user satisfaction and stewardship. Assessing resources within the framework of a formalized, metrics-based methodology can help managers pinpoint specific areas of need and provide validated data to support decisions. The addition of focus groups, public workshops, and qualitative input can round out the framework and provide a complete analysis of resource opportunities and stakeholder interests, leading to a more successful outcome for all concerned.

This chapter offers examples from research conducted using factors determined to contribute to *creating meaning in places* based on the physical and cultural features of settings and the users' and stakeholders' wants and needs. It includes an outline of the process of developing that understanding through an analysis of published research in Geography, Environmental Design, Resource Management, and Environmental Psychology, focus groups, experimental testing, and analysis and evaluation. The results show how the research process was useful in getting to the core features of both setting attributes and user interests, which are essential in determining well-informed management strategies.

In this volume, the authors have been asked to take social science theory and methodologies and relate them to practical tools that planners and managers can use to connect people with natural and cultural resources for better management outcomes and long-term sustainability. This discourse is part of the continuous evolution of theory and methodology that helps connect those within the Ivory Towers with those in the muddy trenches, and ultimately provides an exciting opportunity to share amongst colleagues for the benefit of all involved.

Problem Statement

When resource managers set out to determine the best course of action for short- and long-term planning, they often face significant challenges considering the breadth and depth of *tangible and intangible resources* intertwined with the myriad expectations, wants and needs of locals, visitors, funding agencies and governing bodies. The field of cultural resource management encompasses a multitude of resource types, from acres of buried archaeological remains to blocks, districts, and neighborhoods of various structures in historic towns, modern cities, and sensitive rural lands. Resources range from regional environments of pristine beauty, both natural and cultural, to small, local settings that may host annual cultural festivals of hundreds or thousands of people. They may include simple, local folklife attractions on a small scale, to entire countries drawing global mass tourism on an ever-increasing level putting great strain on resource capacity. There are also indigenous cultures attempting to preserve sacred rituals and ceremonies from determined international visitors on the hunt to capture the last remaining vestiges of authenticity in an overly homogenized world.

Equally challenging are sites of profound destruction and devastation that carry the scars of trauma and their own unique *sense of place* sought by visitors in search of meaning in the most profound sense of the word. The interest in understanding the thin line separating conquest and defense, oppression and freedom, victory and defeat, has led to pilgrimages to the sites of sacred remembrance, lest we forget and mistakes be repeated. Battlefields and killing fields, regions of mass destruction, individual sites of tragedy, or those willfully destroyed in acts of blind hatred have become places where debates over commemoration vie with questions of ownership and perspective. These areas offer opportunities for bridging past divides and healing between former enemies and serve as resources for education and understanding with the intent that such events never happen again. Questions of preservation, interpretation, and perspective are sometimes not easily resolved, but an objective analysis can help identify priorities and form a framework for moving forward.

With the advent of technology, the availability of rich, diverse data is increasing rapidly, which helps lead to more responsive management, greater stakeholder satisfaction, increased stewardship, and stronger outcomes for preservation. Funding for preservation, conservation, and management has typically been low on the list of priorities when essential services and life-safety needs must be met, but the addition of robust quantitative measurements provide strength in generating and justifying management action, especially for reasons that may sometimes seem subjective on the surface. The enormity of the challenge is heightened for modern researchers and practitioners by the physical scale of the planet's resources and the magnitude of diversity of cultures and values. Despite these challenges, scientists and practitioners have managed to work together to develop useful frameworks for evaluation and management, to the point of identifying certain practices that are universally upheld as standards. Resources that suffer long-term neglect are obviously at greater risk than those that receive at least some attention; technological advances offer a greater range of tools and support to address the broad range of concerns.

Challenges and the "Shiver Effect"

The fact that cultural heritage and other areas of resource management are continuously changing with the rapid evolution of technology, and global interests bring new challenges and opportunities in resource planning, management, and conservation is clear. As evidenced at every level, challenges have grown with the ability of people to travel to foreign lands they previously 'visited' only in books and movies, or as immigrants arrive at urban centers in search of security and economic opportunity. The need for services has increased dramatically where it once evolved at a more moderate pace with communities largely able to adapt without any threat to traditional historic rural and urban fabric. The result of the increased demand and rapid pace has too often been the loss of entire neighborhoods of historic architecture and vast traditional landscapes resulting in homogenization and the loss of meaning associated with unique characteristics of historic cultures, landscapes, and other important resources.

A new era of threats from willful destruction, terrorism, war, industrial scale looting, along with the destructive effects of climate change and migration have brought about increased need for risk preparedness and emergency response management, particularly when coupled with the inadvertent losses caused by neglect. There are ever-increasing financial demands for the most pressing humanitarian and development needs and an increasing awareness that not everything can (or should) be maintained or preserved (Lowenthal 2000. Funding priorities have shifted away from preservation of places of history, arts, and culture even though they offer significant economic opportunities, and on to more urgent needs of humanitarian and environmental causes. Rather than outright willful destruction found in some locations, many resources have become victims of "demolition by neglect," a seemingly benign oversight that has resulted in significant loss. The National Park Service has an estimated backlog of maintenance approaching $12 billion dollars, half of which are for basic road maintenance and repairs (Repanshek 2017).

In addition to the economic and management challenges, the ultimate need in this age of technology and globalization is to find innovative ways to reach and inspire new generations to understand and appreciate the unique feelings of importance and meaning, the *"shiver effect,"* as described by William Dupont, AIA. These resources impart significance to the very experience that makes human existence meaningful. Dupont notes within the context of the *Abraham Lincoln and Soldiers Home National Monument*, a house where Lincoln spent considerable time during the summers of his presidency, visitors often comment on experiencing a sense of wonderment and awe when surrounded by Lincoln's personal objects:

> This shiver, this very slight alteration of the visitors' emotional state, can have tremendous positive effects:
>
> First, the visitors can realize, perhaps only unconsciously, that things built in the past are a form of evidence, a primary source that should be studied, understood, and retained for the future. This recognition fosters an appreciation of historic places as the tangible remains of history.
>
> Second, the visitors can experience a sense of wonderment and childlike discovery that momentarily suspends time and disbelief, in which past events and people are suddenly recognized in a more immediate manner, and the simple piece of wood or marble that lacked any significant meaning seconds ago transforms into a precious relic that "witnessed" great events.

Third, the accretions, or layers of time, from periods before and after Lincoln's occupancy, and the patterns of wear on those layers, can deepen visitors' appreciation of the passage of time.

And finally, the exposure of authentic material can add depth and weight to the visitors' learning experience because it fosters a direct connection to the past without mediation or interpretation.

Dupont (2003)

This experience of creating appreciation has become recognized as an important value engendered by the significant perceptions of awe, wonder, and meaning that can only be appreciated in certain unique environments. Places of this type that are so uniquely special must be protected, preserved, and celebrated, and opportunities for students to actively participate in directing the future of such special places must be provided through education on techniques to manage, interpret, and share the resources.

With the addition of "arts" to the opportunities in the "STEM" fields (science, technology, engineering, and math), the value of preservation to quality of life, health, and well-being has been heightened. Research in neuroscience, psychology, and environmental design is showing the importance of *place* in generating health and well-being, with historic sites and nature being key in creating *sense of place* and physical and mental well-being. Without the context of history, culture, community, and human achievement in equal measure to the complex intricacies of scientific systems, the education of future generations is incomplete.

Sense of Place and a Psychometric Research Case Study

"*Sense of place*," as it was termed during the research that forms the basis of this chapter, is defined as the combination of factors within a setting that provides a *perception of meaning* with the place, and, as in this case, a historic or heritage site or setting. While heritage resource managers can point to a site and explain *why* it is historically significant based on dates, people, events, or environmental features, they may have a more challenging time providing concrete data about a site's *value*. Put another way, it may be hard to explain the way people *feel* about the site and why they hold it in awe and revere its existence.

As humans with a deep innate appreciation of history, human achievement, aesthetic creation, and natural beauty, we often perceive and feel value and perceive that a certain *sense of place* is real. Indeed, if such perceptions are felt by large numbers of people or society, how can they not be "real"? Science requires that both the unseen and the physical features that inspire such perceptions be measured quantitatively and, usually to a lesser degree, qualitatively, in order to justify its existence (Mason 2002).

The significant question for resource managers and agencies relying on data to justify financial expenditures or management decisions thus becomes, "how can the construct of '*sense of place*' be *measured* and *used* as a tool to support management decisions?" The need to support the "value" of a site is relevant when it comes to making a case for budgetary decisions and, similarly, in instances where adoption of management policies that may be unpopular with users and visitors, such as site closures, access restrictions, maintenance priorities, and staffing. It is also relevant in providing data for supporting programs designed to assist psychological stress and physical well-being through access to nature and at sites of meaning (National Park Service 2011, Duvall and Kaplan 2013).

THE MEASUREMENT OF MEANING

This research, therefore, presents psychometric measurement tools for evaluating resources based on psychological perceptions and values and recommends management strategies that consider both individual and shared values. The methodology is based on literature reviews, focus groups, expert panels, and qualitative and quantitative analyses that identify factors contributing to a site's perceived value. The results allow cultural resource managers to validate and justify their short- and long-term management strategies based upon results of quantifiable data. This gives managers objective data that provide evidence-based foundations for recommending strategies to conserve, promote, fund, and implement programs based on shared values (Bott 2000). Like much of social science research into conservation, it takes a values-based approach to assessing factors that give meaning to places and evaluates, both natural and built environments and the social aspects, and includes the intangible factors (de la Torre 2002, Satterfield 2002).

Following the case study is a discussion of ways that values-based studies are contributing toward applied practice, including training programs for students to implement human-centered approaches in the practice of conserving historic environments and a brief discussion of the author's experience in the city of Mosul, Iraq during the U.S–Iraq war (2003–2010). This discussion describes innovative technology being used to help retain part of the destroyed history and offers possibilities for meeting a portion of the challenges of preservation of the region's resources destroyed during the recent warfare.

Case Study: The Development of Psychometrics to Measure *Sense of Place*

The purpose of the research undertaken in the late-1990s at Colorado State University's College of Natural Resources was to determine whether the construct of *sense of place* could be measured quantitatively and used to inform resource managers in making management decisions. The research was conducted in partial fulfillment of the requirements for a PhD in Human Dimensions of Resource Management and completed in 2000. The objectives of the study were to develop a set of psychometric domains, scales, and individual items that measure "*sense of place*" using multi-trait, multi-method techniques and test the validity of the domains and scales using two different settings and two experimental methods. The need for the study was based on interest for a more holistic approach to resource management that considered shared disciplines in both theory and application, and the diverse interests of populations, both stakeholders and management.

The literature of the late 1990s indicated a need for a shift, noting that "since the Enlightenment, aided by the dualism of mind and matter, and endorsed by the success of science, the concept of nature has been dominantly mechanistic: that is, spiritless" (Rolston 1996). The underlying sense was that there had been a significant shift in design, development, and resource management leading to a more "purposeful use of lands to maintain and renew the human spirit" (Driver et al. 1996).

The study was based on the grounded theory research involving multiple stages of review and assessment of previous research, and new data collection resulting in parsimony, precision, and ease of analysis (Creswell 1998, Patton 1980). A literature review in the *theoretical* research of Geography and Environmental Psychology and the *applied* research in Environmental Design and Resource Management was conducted with the expectation that each discipline would provide insight into conceptual factors that contribute to the construct of *sense of place* and its practical application. The conceptual insights that each of the four disciplines provided were validated by three focus groups and a Delphi review and were then used in the development of domains, scales,

49

and individual items to measure perceptions of setting experience. A survey instrument was developed, tested, revised, and administered to 398 subjects. Results were analyzed using correlation analysis and reliability analysis to evaluate strength of the scales in determining *sense of place*. Results showed that, taken together, the domains and scales were valid and reliable indicators of *sense of place*.

Phase 1: Literature Review

Perceptions of *Sense of place*. Early work by scholars in the fields of Environmental Psychology, Environmental Design, Geography, and Resource Management suggests recognition of a fundamental relationship of individuals to place. Geographer Yi-Fu Tuan (Tuan 1974) noted the presence of "*topophilia*," or the emotional connections that exist between the physical environment and human beings and identified a form of reverence called *geopiety* (Tuan 1993). Similar reflections included the Spanish notion of "*querencia*," or love of place (Sarbin 1983), and the notion of *place attachment* as the psychological bonding that develops between an individual and a place (Prohansky et al. 1983, Low 1992, Low and Altman 1992, Williams and Vaske 2003). The essence of place from a phenomenological perspective was explored (Relph 1976) to include the works of Dardel, Paassen, Hartshorne, Heidegger, and Merleau-Ponty:

- Relationships (between humans and places), such as existential, perceptual, architectural, cognitive, and abstract;

- Identity of places (insidedness, outsidedness, imagery, accessibility);

- Authenticity (fabric, alterations);

- Placelessness (kitsch, mass communication, mass culture, big business, central authority);

- Future prospects for a place (inevitability of placelessness and designing a lived world of places).

Place only became a significant focus of interest outside geography in the early 1960s because of a shift in social science attention toward issues of human-environment interaction, a cultural change in the way people related to environments, the simultaneous changes in the physical nature of environments, and the technological advancements in communication, travel, and ideological globalization (Relph 1976). *Spiritual* values of a place indicated a need for meaning in the environment (Relph 1996) and in the changing global landscape. The global village has resulted in a space-time-culture compression where a mixture of international practices and tastes is being made equally available everywhere, suggesting that a proactive citizen-driven "self-help design" is needed (ibid., p. 920).

Other descriptions noted *place as a transactive relationship* between person and setting that acts as an engaging force in a powerful, predictable manner on everybody who encounters them. "This magic, with which certain locations seem to be endowed, is certainly a force worth considering" (Steele 1981). Appleton focused on the environment's capacity to meet certain needs, including prospect and refuge (1975), while Steele focused on positive characteristics in his analysis (However, negative environments are equally powerful in creating to a less-than-positive experience at sites and places associated with immense suffering such as battlefields, concentration camps, slavery, genocide, disasters, and terrorism).

THE MEASUREMENT OF MEANING

Types of Place Experiences

- immediate feelings and thoughts
- views of the world
- occupational experiences
- intimate knowledge of one spot
- memories or fantasies
- recognition or newness
- personal identification with a "spot"
- sense of enjoyment or displeasure

Major Characteristics of Place

- identity
- history
- mystery
- joy
- surprise
- security
- vitality
- memory

The relationship of an individual to a setting can be viewed as overlapping layers of opportunities, meanings, and emotions resembling a flower with overlapping petals. The denser and more inter-related the layers, the more likely the setting develops the qualities of place *significance.*

Hull and Vigo (1990) and Hull (1992)

Those qualities lead individuals to develop attachments to place. Similarly, the basics of place are found to exist in *patterns* within the built and natural environments, patterns that, again, build upon one another (Alexander et al. 1977).

Experientially, *spirit of place*, also known as *genius loci*, is the very essence of understanding the relationship of humans in the environment, where humans can find *identification* within the world based upon the character of a place (Norberg Schulz 1979). *Sense of place* has also been described as a sometimes-overused phrase that has lost its historical meaning (Jackson 1984) regarding the physical environment and is more relevant to the *ritual associated with the time spent in places.* To maintain *sense of place*, humans must return to a more natural order that may result in a new kind of history, a new, more responsive social order, and ultimately a new landscape.

Jackson (1994)

The Use of Measurement Tools. The gap between geography and environmental psychology's perceptual evaluation was bridged with analysis of the cognitive-behavioral relationship using various techniques, including evaluation of photographs (Saarinen 1973). To better understand a person's perception of the environment and one's actions, the use of photographs and a mental mapping process called Thematic Apperception Testing (TAT) was developed that allowed individuals to respond to a stimulus (viewing photographs) and create a more elaborate product (their impressions).

Similarly, another method to measure perception compared the experiences of experts in landscape perception (as a baseline) with the experiences of individuals with increasing levels of thought and interaction within a setting (Zube et al. 1982). This method resulted in strong outcomes in satisfaction, information, and well-being, and indicated that increased interaction and cognitive evaluation by participants resulted in increased outcomes consistent with those of the trained (expert) observers. The results led to the development of design standards for national parks (Zube 1993).

A third measurement tool known as the Recreation Experience Preference (REP) model was developed to elicit motivation for recreation experiences in national parks (Driver et al. 1985). Scales were developed to clarify outcomes sought by individuals and were then used to improve planning and management of the resources. The REP model was based upon a structure of "*domains*" (large groupings of related items that represented a broad goal construct) and "*scales*" (groupings that represented smaller dimensions of the broad goal construct drawn from within the domain groupings). The REP model was used to develop the groups of characteristics for this project.

A fourth method for evaluating preferred characteristics in communities used slide-viewing and rating with a 21-point Likert-type scale called the Visual Preference Survey^{TM}. The slides focused on a range of landscape and build features. Respondents rated images on appropriateness, likeability, and potential, and the results provided an early model for eliciting responses that is still in use (Nelessen 1994).

More recent studies have focused on measuring the brain and body's activity when perceiving and experiencing settings that involve a variety of stimuli in an effort to provoke responses, both positive and negative. In general, well-being, productivity, social interactions, and emotion are being evaluated to understand how nature and design shape behavior to move beyond simple well-being and contentment into survival. The changing global landscape requires adaptation to significant external challenges as well as human mental, emotional, and physiological health (Bott et al. 2003). Significantly, nature and places of historic and cultural meaning can potentially counteract the negative effects of rapid change by providing connection to the lived world and places that contain depth and psychological richness. The use of physical sensors and smartphones can build upon early studies and traditional methods to add new insight into resource evaluation and perception and thus management (Ellard 2015).

Phase 2: Focus Groups

In order to determine the domains, factors, and individual items used to test the hypotheses that certain features contributed to creating a perception of *sense of place*, three focus groups were convened. The participants included architects, landscape architects, designers, master gardeners, and members of the general public. Each group participated in an iterative process of identifying and refining factors through a series of visualizations of settings and discussions of features. The questions were phrased to invoke memories of specific locations. Memory has been shown to be important in forming impressions leading to behaviors such as identification, attachment, and dependence because relationships to place are "time-deepened and memory-qualified" due to repeated encounters and complex associations of memory and affectation (Relph 1993). Associations with places, from the inconsequential to the profound, create lasting memories which influence all future encounters (Mitchell et al. 1991).

Transcriptions of the focus groups were analyzed using inductive coding and results indicated that 300 variables were most used to describe perceptions of place, both positive and negative. The 300 variables were separated into **four domains:** (1) Setting Domain A: *Physical* factors, (2) Setting Domain B: *Socio/Cultural* factors, (3) Individual-related Domain A: *Affective* factors, and (4) Individual-related Domain B: *Functional* factors.

The **Setting Domains** focused on (a) Physical factors of the site, both built and natural, and (b) Socio/Cultural factors focused on the people and history, along with interaction factors. The **Individual-related Domains** focused on (c) Affective factors (interests, desires), while (d) Functional factors focused on the needs a site met for a person (food, shelter, sun, shade).

The domains were evaluated by a seven-member Expert Panel with representatives from each of the four disciplines (geography, environmental psychology, resource management, and environmental design) and a survey instrument was developed. It consisted of the four domains, fifteen scales (domain sub-groups), and ninety individual factors comprising the scales and domains. A pilot test was conducted to evaluate content, technical worthiness, ordering bias, content of photograph slides, physical settings, and clarity of questions using six graduate students from the Department of Natural Resources. Modifications were made based on recommendations by the participants and the final survey instrument was circulated for review and approval by the doctoral committee and human subjects review board. Sample questions are presented in Table 2.1.

Phase 3: Survey Testing and Data Analysis

Surveys were developed to evaluate the conceptual hypothesis that two major domains comprise *sense of place*. To test the reliability of the fifteen scales and ninety individual factors that contribute to the *sense of place*, two distinctly different sites on the campus of Colorado State University were selected for evaluation. The domains, scales, and items were the dependent variables in the survey, the two different settings and two different viewing methods were the independent variables. The two settings chosen were locations on the Colorado State University campus selected based on their historic, environmental, built characteristics, and functional importance to undergraduates. The two methods of review, slide viewing and site visits, were used to compare the effects of visual perception versus multisensory perception. The question was the extent to which multisensory perception would differ from the effects of visual perception alone.

Surveys were administered to four independent groups of students ($N = 363$) using onsite assessment and viewing of slides. Individuals were the units of analysis and the subjects were undergraduate student volunteers from College of Natural Resources summer classes from within the larger student body on the campus. Volunteers from four different classes were invited to participate after an introduction and overview of the intent of the study and none of the students present in the four classes declined to participate (all appeared interested). To ensure consistency among respondents, two groups from classes on campus visited one of the two settings, while two groups from an offsite field campus viewed the slides of

Table 2.1 Domains and Sample Questions (General Examples)

Setting Domain: Physical

1. **Natural Setting**—Does the setting have a presence of nature? Is the setting barren and desolate? Is there abundant sunshine (and shade)? Is the setting dark and foreboding? Is there flowing water? Can you see or hear birds? Does it have trees and grass or flowers?

2. **Built Environment**—Are the buildings made of native materials (local stone)? Does the architecture fit the setting? Does the setting feel crowded? Can you find your way around? Are there light fixtures?

3. **Character**—Is the setting clean? Do you feel safe in the setting? Does the setting feel welcoming? Do you want to linger here?

Setting Domain: Cultural

4. **Inherent Social Relations**—Is the area historic? Does it retain authenticity? Does it have a spirit of the people? Does it fit within the larger context of the area and support the activities?

5. **Transactional Social**—Does the setting offers a sense of belonging and provide opportunities for interaction? Does it offer civility and generate respect for the individual? Does the site have a distinct energy and offer a sense of community?

Personal Domain: Affective

6. **Significance**—Is the site personally meaningful? Is it viewed as significant and valuable?

7. **Existential**—Does the site invoke a sense of connection or a sense of one's own identity? Are there feelings of attachment?

8. **Memory**—Is the setting familiar or provides a sense of connection or nostalgia?

9. **Aesthetics**—Is the setting beautiful, aesthetically pleasing, and awe inspiring? Does it generate a positive sensory experience and feelings of appreciation?

10. **Transcendental**—Is the setting inspirational, magical? Does it offer a sense of the sacred, a *spirit of place*? Does it make one feel alive, inspired, or connected to a higher power? Is there a sense of romance or strong emotions?

Personal Domain: Functional

11. **Purposive**—Does the setting meet expectations for what is needed? Does it support the role of what is intended?

12. **Informational**—Is the site or setting understandable? Is there a sense of direction, distinct landmarks, and is it easy to find one's way around in? Does it make way-finding seem intuitive, and provides information?

13. **Prospect**—Does it appear that there are options or opportunities here? Does one feel like exploring, and is there a sense of mystery?

14. **Refuge**—Is the setting non-threatening, has obvious boundaries, offers shelter and a sense of refuge? Does the setting feel safe?

15. **Well-being**—Is the area comfortable, warm, serene, reassuring? Does it allow one to feel in control, peaceful, comfortable, calm, and serene?

THE MEASUREMENT OF MEANING

one of the two settings. A set of two qualitative questions were provided to all survey participants to seek additional information on the types of sites the participants preferred and to allow for any additional thoughts or feelings elicited by the survey that the participants wanted to express.

The Statistical Package for the Social Sciences (SPSS) was used for data analysis. A minimum acceptable significance level of $p \leq .05$ was used for all analyses. Descriptive statistics were computed to explore basic characteristics of the demographics. Reliability analysis was used to evaluate the degree to which the ninety items, having been combined into fifteen summated scales and four domains, measured *sense of place* with a minimum acceptable Cronbach's alpha of $\alpha \geq .60$. All four domains were found to be reliable with a Cronbach's alpha of .85 or above (Table 2.2). Fourteen out of the fifteen scales were found to be reliable at .74 or above, and the lowest scale (Refuge) had a .61 reliability coefficient.

The capacity of the items to generate perceptions of *sense of place* between the two settings was measured using multi-mean comparison testing (Analysis of Variance) to determine the degree to which the dependent variables (domains, scales, items) differed due to settings and experimental

Table 2.2 Reliability Analysis for Four Domains and Fifteen Sense of Place Scales

Domains and Scales[1]	Cronbach's Alpha	Overall Mean Score[2]	Standard Deviation
Physical Setting Domain	**.89**	**1.02**	**1.19**
Natural Setting Scale	.74	1.04	1.33
Built Environment Scale	.85	.73	1.57
Character Scale	.89	1.28	1.02
Cultural Setting Domain	**.85**	**.87**	**1.07**
Inherent Sociocultural Scale	.82	.89	1.20
Transactional Sociocultural Scale	.86	.86	1.09
Affective Individual Domain	**.91**	**.60**	**1.15**
Significance Scale	.84	.89	1.29
Existential Scale	.87	.27	1.39
Memory Scale	.76	1.36	.97
Aesthetic Scale	.93	.65	1.55
Transcendental Scale	.93	−.16	1.39
Functional Individual Domain	**.88**	**.78**	**1.02**
Purposive Scale	.74	.95	1.48
Informational Scale	.75	1.02	.94
Prospect Scale	.82	.05	1.39
Refuge Scale	.61	1.07	.93
Well-being Scale	.95	.84	1.30

[1] Each of the Scales and Domains was summated from Individual Items.

[2] Variables were coded on a seven-point scale ranging from "Strongly Agree" (+3) to "Strongly Disagree" (−3).

viewing methods. The ANOVA mean scores showed a range of 1.52 points, from a high of 1.36 for the Memory scale to a low of −.16 for the Transcendental scale. The low score for the Transcendental scale indicates perception levels of "slight disagreement" to "neutral" for the items related to perceptions of feelings of *inspiration, magic, sacredness, a spirit of place, feeling alive, connected to a higher power, a sense of romance, and feelings of strong emotions.* Interpretation of the data based on the literature review and focus groups led the researcher to conclude that neither site on the campus lent itself to the perception of the Transcendental values. The high mean score of 1.36 for the Memory scale indicates respondent perceptions from "slight agreement" to "moderate agreement" with the items contributing to that scale: *familiar, well-known, memorable, connection, nostalgia, and knowing it well* based on the known familiarity of the settings on campus.

Mean scores for the Domains showed agreement with all four domains: Setting: Physical of 1.02; Setting: Socio/Cultural of .87; Individual: Affective of .60; and Individual: Functional of .78 (values between 0 and +1 indicate slight agreement; values between 1 and 2 indicate moderate agreement; and values above 2 indicate strong agreement). The analysis showed the campus setting chosen for featuring characteristics consistent with high *sense of place*, the historic center of the old campus, showed values between 1.14 (Individual Affective Domain) and 1.74 (Setting Physical Domain), while the mean scores for the setting predicted to exhibit low *sense of place*, the modern plaza of the science buildings, showed values between .06 (Individual Affective Domain) and .50 (Setting Cultural Domain) (Table 2.3).

Phase 4: Survey Outcomes and Implications

This study makes two main contributions to historic preservation and heritage conservation along with resource conservation in general. First, based on the research approach in the grounded theory relying on multi-stage analysis to develop and test hypotheses, the construct of *sense of place* was found to be valid and most importantly quantifiable. This provides resource managers the means to show governing agencies and decision-makers that individual and shared values contribute to the value of historic resources and provides justification for a variety of management strategies.

Second, this study shows that a common language about *sense of place* provides a starting point for interdisciplinary research and management, and outreach to stakeholders and the public. Professionals in heritage conservation, tourism planning, visitor facility management, interpretation, and other related fields will find this useful in outreach of all kinds. The most important features of a site and those that contribute to the greatest experience for different users and stakeholders need to be heard, understood, valued, and incorporated into management.

Planners and designers should invite stakeholder participation at the earliest stages of the project review process and work toward making understanding, valuing, and preserving the shared goals of the stakeholders. New forms of communication and outreach are allowing resource managers to connect with users and share issues, solicit input, and address issues associated with the significance and *sense of place*, including the more esoteric aspects of the site. The traditional methods of outreach and problem-solving can be supplemented with dynamic approaches that consider innovative solutions that were not possible until recently, and that consider user perceptions of *sense of place* and meaning beyond traditional approaches of dates and events. The process of scientifically evaluating and measuring *sense of place* and collective values is a critical step toward improving management of heritage sites and will help ensure responsive policies that will safeguard the world's irreplaceable heritage resources.

THE MEASUREMENT OF MEANING

Table 2.3 Mean Score Values and Significance Levels for Four Domains and Fifteen Sense of Place Scales for Two Campus Settings Using Two Different Experimental Methods

Mean Scores[1]

Domains and Scales[2]	Slides	Site Visit	Mean Difference	F Statistic[3]
Physical Setting Domain	**.60**	**1.41**	**.81**	**75.9**
Natural Setting Scale	.56	1.49	.93	74.9
Built Environment Scale	.29	1.15	1.22	42.1
Character Scale	.95	1.56	.61	54.3
Cultural Setting Domain	**.59**	**1.14**	**.56**	**29.3**
Inherent Sociocultural Scale	.60	1.15	.55	23.5
Transactional Sociocultural Scale	.57	1.13	.56	27.0
Affective Individual Domain	**.35**	**.84**	**.49**	**21.3**
Significance Scale	.74	1.03	.28	4.8[4]
Existential Scale	.03	.49	.45	10.4
Memory Scale	1.38	1.34	−.03	.11[4]
Aesthetic Scale	.19	1.07	.88	48.8
Transcendental Scale	−.61	.25	.86	50.6
Functional Individual Domain	**.46**	**1.09**	**.63**	**45.1**
Purposive Scale	.59	1.28	.69	23.5
Informational Scale	.92	1.11	.19	3.8[5]
Prospect Scale	−.38	.44	.82	36.0
Refuge Scale	.79	1.33	.54	37.0
Well-being Scale	.37	1.27	.90	65.9

[1] Variables were coded on a seven-point scale ranging from "Strongly Agree" (+3) to "Strongly Disagree" (−3).

[2] Each Scale and Domain was summated from individual items.

[3] All values significant at $p < .001$ except as noted.

[4] Not significant.

[5] Values significant at $p < .05$.

Conclusions: Relevance to Current Realities

This chapter was initially considered for inclusion based on the psychometric research model and outcomes, but it became clear that the opportunity to touch upon current realities of historic preservation challenges in the changing global landscape could be useful. The recent willful destruction of heritage in the Middle East, while not a new phenomenon of war, has brought about new considerations for managers. Preservation of resources in the U.S. has typically been met with a response centered around the Secretary of the Interior's four treatment approaches: rehabilitation, reconstruction, restoration, or basic preservation (Weeks and Grimmer (1995), National Park Service 1996). Today, more tools are available that offer alternatives to the traditional methods of preservation, but they also offer distinctively different consideration of the phenomenon of "being" in a place and the existence of *sense of place* (Low 2002).

In Iraq, Afghanistan, Yemen, and Syria, along with other countries around the world, the destruction of ancient sites, monuments, religious structures, and cities has caused international outrage, grief, and despair. The author worked as a reconstruction advisor for the U.S. Government in Iraq between 2007 and 2010 and worked to preserve the historic sites of the Assyrian Empire around Mosul including Nimrud, Nineveh, Khorsabad, Ashur, Hatra, and the Mosul Museum (Bott and Banning 2008).

With a team of U.S. Army Engineers and Surveyors, site surveys were made and photographs of five sites were taken, resulting in a resource of information that is proving useful to the Government of Iraq and outside agencies interested in helping preserve the historic record. Minor repairs were made at Nimrud and the Mosul Museum in accordance with representatives from UNESCO and the Iraq State Board of Antiquities and Heritage within the Ministry of Antiquities and Tourism (Figure 2.1). Representatives of each had visited key sites in and around Mosul with the help of the U.S. military and Department of State in 2008–10, and UNESCO representatives made additional visits for assessing the resources and delivering equipment to the Mosul Museum.

There was and continues to be significant support for documentation of damaged sites, international assistance to address looting and trafficking, education and training in materials conservation, and heritage cultural awareness outreach with UNESCO's #Unite4Heritage program. The Iraqi Institute for the Conservation of Antiquities and Heritage, started with funding from the Department of State in 2009, has been instrumental in training Iraqis from across the country (and from within different religious groups, ethnicities, and cultures) to manage the country's heritage resources, and other international institutions are similarly offering resources in education and training, site management, assistance in recovery of stolen artifacts, and awareness raising.

Raising awareness in any country facing destruction of its heritage may help foster a sense of shared cultural understanding and a stronger sense of identity, pride, and unity based on shared values (Figure 2.2). It may instill hope for a time when it will be possible to once again visit the

Figure 2.1 Soldiers at Nimrud, 2009 during author's work in Iraq. (Credit: Mary Prophit; used by permission.)

Figure 2.2 The Temple of Mrn from above taken during author's work at Hatra, Iraq 2010. (Photograph by the author.)

historic sites, tour the museums, and participate in cultural events, all of which help inspire the population to move ahead in daily life. These qualities are essential in post-conflict recovery of populations traumatized by occupation, destruction, and loss of control (Stanley-Price 2007).

Technology is now offering options for recreating destroyed artifacts through photogrammetry, modeling, drones, 3D printing, large-scale photography, and other exciting new developments. A program initially called Project Mosul, now Rekrei, was started by two archaeological researchers, Matthew Vincent and Chance Coughenour, in 2015 after the destruction of the Mosul Museum and the ancient Assyrian site of Nimrud in Iraq. The project crowdsourced hundreds of photos and designers were able to create models and copies of many of the destroyed objects and structures. Rekrei has grown into a larger organization and its projects are now global, including Palmyra, and sites in Belize, Kathmandu, and other locations. Rekrei was awarded the 2015 Annual Award for Innovation by digital technology conservation leader, CyArk.

CyArk was started in 2003 by Barbara and Ben Kacyra as a non-profit foundation to document sites with laser scanning and mapping and make the data available for free. Its goal is to document 500 sites by 2019 and provide that information online. In addition, CyArk provides training modules to students who have access to dozens of online lesson plans ranging from mapping Mt. Rushmore to documenting the routes of the U.S. slave trade and the history of slavery. Students at a variety of levels can create computer-aided design drawings, learn to prepare portfolios, study math, physics, and culture, and delve into conservation ethics and preservation issues with the help of online lesson plans in English and Spanish.

The Institute for Digital Archaeology (IDA), a joint venture between Harvard, Oxford, and the United Arab Emirates, formed in 2012 to similarly collect data of heritage resources from around the world to preserve and share the stewardship of those sites. IDA created a copy of the Triumphal Arch from Palmyra following its destruction and stated in part that the intent of IDA is to train local craftspeople in the techniques of construction to repair and recreate damaged structures and support local heritage, where the *sense of place* truly lives. The copy of the Triumphal Arch has been displayed in Trafalgar Square in London, Times Square in New York City, and Dubai, United Arab Emirates.

An additional example of modern technology being used to support heritage is laser displays of lost heritage. Two stone Buddha carved into the cliffs of the Bamiyan Valley of Afghanistan were destroyed by the Taliban in 2001 in one of the most dramatic displays of heritage and cultural destruction (Figure 2.3). In 2015, a laser hologram of the 150-foot tall Buddha was created by Chinese philanthropists Zhang Xinyu and Liang Hong and projected overnight for the people of the valley. Reminiscent of "sound and light" shows performed at sites since the middle of the last century using simple spotlights and recorded music, this modern, temporary installation resulted in an entirely new demonstration of restoration of lost heritage (Figure 2.4). The one-day installation resulted in universal global appreciation and helped spread awareness of the tremendous *sense of place* that the valley retains, despite the destruction of its main historical features. The installation points to future opportunities for creative recreations that provide remembrance while maintaining the destroyed landscape, an important distinction in appropriately commemorating historic events.

Italian artist and set designer Edoardo Tresoldi has recently developed a method for creating intensely beautiful architectural and archaeological artwork that promotes a significantly modern approach to the intersection of art and preservation. His work uses wire mesh to provide a permeable structure that allows clear delineation between the new and historic features of a site (Figure 2.5). Similar methods have been used successfully to recreate the sense of history in a place, for example, the Benjamin Franklin Ghost House in Philadelphia designed by Robert Venturi and Louise Scott Brown in 1976. The lower cost of construction and maintenance makes Tresoldi's structures and sculptures a particularly elegant design solution that resonates with new methods of computer modeling and mesh design to create clearly modern representations of the historic construction (Figure 2.6).

Similarly, educational programs that take the youth of today and train them to be the experts of tomorrow ensures that the legacy of heritage conservation will continue. It is clear that outreach to youth must be done in ways that excite them—in the field and the lab, with computers and minds fully engaged in global connectivity. This is the way to inspire international interest and foster greater understanding that will lead to both an ethic of shared caring and responsibility, and a universal desire to delve deeper into the field of heritage conservation and management.

Figure 2.3 Sketch of Buddha in Bamiyan Valley, Afghanistan, prior to 2001 demolition by Taliban. (Credit: © Haley K. Bott; used by permission.)

Figure 2.4 Watercolor of hologram projection in 2015 of Bamiyan Buddha. (Credit: © Haley K. Bott; used by permission.)

Figure 2.5 Wire Mesh Structure "Basilica of Siponto"—Manfredonia, Italy—2015. Blind Eye Factory. (Credit: © Blind Eye Factory/Edoardo Tresoldi; used by permission.)

Figure 2.6 Wire Mesh Sculpture "Incipit" for Meeting del Mare festival—Marina di Camerota, Italy—2015. © Fabiano Caputo. (Credit: © Blind Eye Factory/Edoardo Tresoldi; used by permission.)

Efforts such as the U.S. Department of the Interior's "Every Kid in a Park" program, part of the National Park Service's 2016 Centennial, was a strategy to bring Fourth Graders and their families into the outdoors with programs developed to excite and inspire children. In ten years, there will be a spike in students entering universities and colleges to study cultural and natural resources, from the impacts of climate change on international heritage sites to mapping previously "invisible" cultural routes with new methods satellite technologies, because of this innovative program (US DOI 2016). The National Park Service also funds field training for staff and field crews in traditional conservation methods through the Vanishing Treasures program and the Missions Initiative (NCPTT 2016). Various universities offer joint workshops with the National Park Service and international partners. This training shares traditional knowledge, taught by local elders and experts in a field setting, where the goal is to primarily train and assist National Park Service staff, but also university students and other interested professionals, while providing a service to the park or heritage site by conducting work that's needed.

Similarly, another joint university project is the "Warriors Project" where students from Howard University, a historically African-American college, and Haskell Indian Nations University, a historically Native-American college, partnered with the Mescalero Apache Nation to explore their shared histories. Projects included an archaeological field school for students in New Mexico and a project with the Institute of Oral History at the University of Texas at El Paso (CESU 2016). Historic American Building Surveys and Historic American Landscape Studies have been conducted with the University of Montana, the University of Wyoming, and the University of Colorado-Denver and Boulder (O'Brien 2009).

Numerous other opportunities to gain practical experience are offered through universities and colleges throughout the world, and students may participate in study abroad programs, internships, practicums, and internships at firms, state and local government, heritage conservation organizations such as the International Council on Monuments and Sites (ICOMOS), the National Trust for Historic Preservation (NTHP), and tribal, state and local historical preservation offices.

In the meantime, higher education needs to continue to bridge the gap for students who choose higher education to undertake a theoretical study along with applied practice and make it interesting and relevant. Many students who have not received the benefit of advanced technology in school, and graduate students interested in deeper understanding of the foundations of heritage conservation theory, will choose programs that offer the newest technology with internships and fieldwork as a central part of the program. In the interim, as higher educational programs quickly evolve and adapt to technological advances, there are many supplemental programs available through online courses, field schools, community colleges, and technology camps.

The applied skills are only part of the education—the *sense of place*, reverence, awe, and interpersonal exchange are where the greatest values are formed. In the era of technology and globalization, opportunities to share between youth and masters of the trade, particularly in the field—the deserts, mountains, forests, plains, and coastal areas are needed to feed the passion of preservation. With limited federal funding, new opportunities for outreach to impart the sublime qualities that make historic, cultural, and natural places alive will have to be provided by industry foundations, the private sector, and non-governmental organizations. Sharing fieldwork and solving problems in the lab create shared values and respect among people. Children and young people are particularly open and without preconceived biases, and it is up to educators and resource managers to promote opportunities for shared learning and relationship-building that will lead to trust and confidence for the future stewardship and preservation of our shared global heritage.

As noted by philosopher Alain de Botton,

> Although we belong to a species that spends an alarming amount of time blowing things up, every now and then we are moved to add gargoyles or garlands, stars or wreaths, to our buildings for no practical reason whatever. In the finest of these flourishes, we can read signs of goodness in a material register, a form of frozen benevolence. We see in them evidence of those sides of human nature which enable us to thrive rather than simply survive. These elegant touches remind us that we are not exclusively pragmatic or sensible: we are also creatures who, with no possibility of profit or power, occasionally carve friars out of stone and mould angels onto walls. In order not to mock such details, we need a culture confident enough about its pragmatism and aggression that it can also acknowledge the contrary demands of vulnerability and play – a culture, that is, sufficiently unthreatened by weakness and decadence as to allow for visible celebrations of tenderness.

de Botton (2006)

Acknowledgments

I wish to express my sincere thanks to the editors of this volume, Drs. Jeremy Wells and Barry Stiefel, for their gracious support and the opportunity to present this research. I would like to thank my colleagues on the executive bureau of the International Scientific Committee for Cultural Tourism at

THE MEASUREMENT OF MEANING

ICOMOS—Sue Millar, the late- Augusto Villalon, Murray Brown, and Graham Brooks, for helping formulate ideas on conservation that added to this chapter; Sami al-Khoja and Tamar Teneishvili of UNESCO for assistance with our work in Iraq; Dr. Nancy Odegaard, Atifa Rawan, Dr. Pat O'Brien, and Brooks Jeffery for our work together in Afghanistan; and Haley Katherine Bott for images of the Bamiyan Buddha.

Dedication

This work is dedicated to my late father, Colonel Donald H. Bott, for his passion for life and his encouragement to seize every opportunity for education, adventure, and doing important work for others.

References

Alexander, C., Ishikana, S., Silverstein, M., Jacobsen, M., Fiksdahl-King, I., & Angel, S. (1977). *A Pattern Language*. New York, NY: Oxford University Press.

Appleton, J. (1975). *The experience of landscape*. London: John Wiley.

Bott, S. E. (2000). *The development of psychometric measurement tools to measure sense of place* (Doctoral Dissertation, Colorado State University).

Bott, S. E., & Banning, J. H. (2008). *The use of psychometric scales to measure spirit of place relevance to heritage conservation efforts from Ninewa Province, Iraq*. International Council on Monuments and Sites. Retrieved October 12, 2016, from www.icomos.org/quebec2008/cd/toindex/77_pdf/77-RrEt-92.pdf

Bott, S., Cantrill, J. G., & Myers, O. E. Jr. (2003). Place and the promise of conservation psychology. *Human Ecology Review, 10*(2), 100–112.

CESU: Cooperative Ecosystem Studies Units (CESU) Network Federal Program. Retrieved October 12, 2016, from www.cesu.psu.edu/default.htm

Creswell, J. (1998). *Qualitative inquiry and research design*. Thousand Oaks, CA: Sage Publications.

CyArk. Retrieved October 12, 2016, from www.cyark.org/education/

de Botton, A. (2006). *The architecture of happiness*. New York, NY: Random House, Inc.

de la Torre, M. (2002). *Assessing the value of cultural heritage*. Los Angeles, CA: Getty Conservation Institute.

Driver, B., Dustin, D., Baltic, T., Elsner, G., & Peterson, G. (1996). Nature and the human spirit: Overview. *Nature and the human spirit: Toward an Expanded Land Management Ethic* (pp. 3–8). Venture, State College, PA.

Driver, B., Nash, R., & Haas, G. (1985). Wilderness benefits. *Proceedings of the National Wilderness Research Conference*, USDA Forest Service Intermountain Research Station, Ogden, UT, 294–319.

Dupont, W. A. (2003). A place for authenticity at Lincoln Cottage. *Forum Journal of the National Trust for Historic Preservation, 18*(1), 6–17.

Duvall, J., & Kaplan, R. (2013). *Exploring the benefits of outdoor experiences on veterans*. Ann Arbor, MI.

Ellard, C. (2015). *Places of the heart*. New York, NY: Bellevue Literary Press.

Hull, R. B., IV. (1992). Image congruity, place attachment and community design. *Journal of Architectural and Planning Research, 9*(3), 181–192.

Hull, R. B. IV., & Vigo, G. (1990). Urban nature, place attachment, health, and well-being. In D. Relf (Ed.), *The role of horticulture in human well-being and social development* (pp. 149–152). Portland, OR: Timber Press.

Jackson, J. B. (1984). *A sense of place, a sense of time*. New Haven, CT: Yale University Press.

Jackson, J. B. (1994). *Discovering the vernacular landscape*. New Haven, CT: Yale University Press.

Low, S. M. (2002). Anthropological-ethnographic methods for the assessment of cultural values in heritage conservation. In M. de la Torre (Ed.), *Values and heritage conservation research report* (pp. 5–30). Los Angeles, CA: Getty Conservation Institute.

Low, S. M. & Altman, I. (1992) Symbolic ties that bind. In Altman & S. M. Low (Eds.), *Place attachment* (pp. 165–185). New York, NY: Plenum Press.

Lowenthal, D. (2000). Stewarding the Past in a Perplexing Present. In E. Avrami, R. Mason, R., & M.de la Torre, (Eds.), *Values and Heritage conservation research report* (pp. 18–25). Los Angeles, CA: Getty Conservation Institute.

Mason, R. (2002). Assessing values in conservation planning: Methodological issues and choices. In M. de la Torre (Ed.), *Values and heritage conservation research report* (pp. 5–30). Los Angeles, CA: Getty Conservation Institute.

Mitchell, M. Y., Force, J. E., Carroll, M. S., & McLaughlin, W. J. (1991). *Forest places of the heart.* Journal of Forestry, 92 (4), 32–37.

National Center for Preservation Technology and Training (NCPTT), National Park Service. (1996). *Youth Training Program in Vernacular earthen architecture and associated cultural traditions|1996–1931.* Cornerstones Community Partnerships, Inc. Retrieved October 12, 2016, from www.ncptt.nps.gov/blog/youth-training-program-in-vernacular-earthen-architecture-and-associated-cultural-traditions-1996-31

National Park Service. (2011). *Healthy parks, healthy people: US strategic action plan.* www.nps.gov/public_health/hp/hphp/pres/1012-955-WASO.pdf

Nelessen, A. C. (1994). *Visions for a New American dream.* Chicago, IL: APA Planners Press.

Norberg-Schulz, C. (1979). *Genius Loci.* New York, NY: Rizzoli International Publishers.

O'Brien, W. P. (2009). *A decade of progressive partnerships: CESUs and cultural resources in the NPS. CRM: The Journal of Heritage Stewardship, National Park Service, 6*(2), 82–89. Retrieved October 12, 2016, from www.nps.gov/CRMjournal/Summer2009/research4.html

Patton, M. Q. (1990). *Qualitative evaluation and research methods.* Newbury Park, CA: Sage Publications.

Prohansky, H. M., Fabian, A. K., & Kaminoff, R. (1983). Place-identity. *Journal of Environmental Psychology, 3,* 57–83.

Rekrei (formerly Project Mosul). Retrieved from https://projectmosul.org (June 21, 2017)

Relph, E. (1976). *Place and placelessness.* London: Pion.

Relph, E. (1993). Modernity and the reclamation of place. In D. Seamon (Ed.), *Dwelling, Seeing and Designing.* (pp. 25–40). Albany, NY: State University of New York Press.

Relph, E. (1996). Place. In I. Douglas, R. Huggett, & M. Robinson, (Eds.), *Companion encyclopedia of geography* (pp. 906–922). New York, NY: Routledge.

Repanshek, K. (2017). GAO: National Park Service needs to evaluate its approach to tackling deferred maintenance. National Parks Traveler. Retrieved June 2017, from www.nationalparkstraveler.org /2017/01/gao-national-park-service-needs-evaluate-its-approach-tackling-deferred-maintenance

Rolston, H. (1996). Nature, spirit and landscape management. In B. L. Driver, et al. (Eds.), *Nature and the human spirit.* (pp. 17-24). State College, PA: Venture Publishing.

Sarbin, T. R. (1983). Place identity as a component of self. *Journal of Environmental Psychology, 3,* 337–342.

Saarinen, T. (1973). The use of projective techniques in geographic research. In W. Ittelson (Ed.) *Environment and cognition* (pp. 29–52). New York, NY: Seminar Press.

Satterfield, T. (2002). Numbness and sensitivity in the elicitation of environmental values. In de la Torre (Ed.), *Values and heritage conservation research report* (pp. 77–99). Los Angeles, CA: Getty Conservation Institute.

Stanley-Price, N. (2007). Cultural heritage in postwar recovery. *Papers from the ICCROM Forum held on* October 4–6, 2005, ICCROM, Rome.

Steele, F. (1981). *The sense of place.* Boston, MA: CBI Publishing.

Tresoldi, E. www.edoarotresoldi.com (June 21, 2017).

Tuan, Y. F. (1974). *Topophilia.* Englewood Cliffs, NJ: Prentice-Hall.

Tuan, Y. F. (1993). *Passing strange and wonderful.* Washington, DC: Island Press/Shearwater Books.

US DOI. (2016). *Every Kid in a Park Federal Program.* Washington, DC: U.S. Department of the Interior, National Park Service. Retrieved October 12, 2016, from https://everykidinapark.gov.

Weeks, K. D., & Grimmer, A. E. (1995). *The secretary of the interior's standards for the treatment of historic properties: With guidelines for preserving, rehabilitation, restoring & reconstructing historic buildings.* Collingdale, PA: Diane Publishing.

Williams, D. R., & Vaske, J. J. (2003). The measurement of place attachment: Validity and generalizability of a psychometric approach. *Forest Science, 49*(6), 830–840.

Zube, E. H. (1993). The search for harmony in park developments. In *visual quality of built environments in National Parks* (pp. 3–10, NPS D-903). U. S. Department of the Interior National Park Service, Denver Service Center.

CHAPTER 3

Meeting the Shadow

Resource Management and the McDonaldization of Heritage Stewardship

Richard M. Hutchings

> We have in all naiveté forgotten that beneath our world of reason another lies buried. I do not know what humanity will still have to undergo before it dares to admit this.
>
> — Carl G. Jung

There is strong evidence that our most pressing heritage problems are intractable under current conditions (Balint et al. 2011; Foster 2009; Hutchings 2017; Lazarus 2009; Lewicki et al. 2002; Rogers 1998; The Club of Rome 1970). Yet, such discourse—deemed "truth-telling" by some and "dark," "stark," "wicked," "fatalist," and "cynical" by others—is excluded in orthodox cultural resource management circles.[1] Not only does this show the project to be ideological, it suggests the practice, thus society at large, is ill-equipped to deal with the unfolding global heritage crisis.

It is in this context that I explore resource management's "shadow" or "dark side," a vital, powerful and routinely ignored facet of the institution.[2] Focusing on the core assumptions that define cultural resource management (CRM), I consider the benefits and implications of "meeting the shadow" (Zweig and Abrams 1991).

The shadow of concern here is resource management's "rationality," defined and discussed in terms of George Ritzer's McDonaldization thesis (1983, 1993, 1996) and its theoretical precursor, Max Weber's Iron Cage (1930; see also Alexander 2013). McDonaldization is an extension of Weber's theory of *rationalization* (Ritzer 1993:18–19):

> Weber believed…the modern Western world had produced a distinctive kind of rationality that was unknown not only in its own history, but also in the history and current reality of every other part of the world. Rationality of one type or another had existed in all societies at one time or another, but none had produced the type of rationality distinctive to the modern West.

Weber called this Western way of knowing "formal" rationality (1993:19):

> To Weber, *formal rationality* means that the search by peoples for the optimum means to a given end is shaped by rules, regulations, and larger social structures. Thus, individuals are not left to their own devices in searching for the best means of attaining a given objective. Rather, there exist rules that either predetermine or help them discover the optimum methods.

The *bureaucracy* was the paradigm case of formal rationality for Weber (Ritzer 1993:20), generally understood to be a formally rationalized structure or organization "characterized by a hierarchical chain of command and precisely delimited roles and responsibilities governed by written rules" (Hale 1990:560). Constituting the "scientific organization of inequality through which people are dominated and oppressed," Weber conceived of bureaucracy as an *iron cage*, an "all-powerful system of organization that would regulate all aspects of individual life" (Hale 1990:560, 569), including heritage.

According to George Ritzer, the fast-food restaurant has usurped bureaucracy as the model of Western rationality. Constructed atop Weber's theory of rationalization, Ritzer's *McDonaldization thesis* states that the five principles of the fast-food industry—efficiency (increased optimization), predictability (increased certainty), calculability (increased quantifiability), control (increased via science and technology), and irrational outcomes (e.g., increased dehumanization)—have come to dominate more and more sectors of society. My point here is that resource management is one of those dominated sectors.

No matter how painful, meeting the shadow is necessary as it signifies a coming-to-terms with the problems that plague us today. This includes seeing resource management as an iron cage where resource managers—locked into a bureaucratic program of efficiency, calculability, predictability, and control—have *no choice* but to extinguish unorthodox (non-Western, non-capitalist) heritage landscapes and stewardship practices on behalf of the power elite directing the resource management project.[3]

From this vantage, cultural resource management might not so much be "broken"—a view that implies it is "fixable"—as it is working as designed, a view that forces us to confront not just intractability (irresolvability) but the root causes of contemporary human problems. On the one hand, *not* considering the shadow means accepting our present situation as being predestined and natural. On the other hand, confronting resource management's "downside" offers the possibilities of new futures, what Thomas Homer-Dixon (2007) aptly calls "the upside of down." As it turns out, catastrophe (darkness) and renewal (light) are concomitant processes.

I begin my study of resource management's rationality with an overview of the shadow, where I put the concept in historical context and show how it is integral to the rationalization process. I then consider the McDonaldization of heritage stewardship in North America, demonstrating how it affects every aspect of resource management. We ignore resource management's shadow at our own peril, for only in its darkness can we see the true scope and scale of our predicament.

The Shadow

> That which we do not bring to consciousness appears in our lives as fate.
>
> Carl G. Jung

Coined a century ago by psychologist Carl Jung, the *shadow* refers to those repressed aspects of our selves that do not fit our self-image (Zweig and Abrams 1991). While Jung was primarily concerned with the personal shadow (particularly its influence on and inseparability from the ego), families, communities, societies and nations also have dark sides, what Connie Zweig and Jeremiah Abrams (1991:xix–xx) call the *collective shadow*, which "is staring back at us virtually everywhere."

Today we are confronted with the dark side of human nature each time we open a newspaper or watch the evening news. The more repugnant effects of the shadow are made visible to us in a daily prodigious media message that is broadcast globally throughout our modern electronic village. The world has become a stage for the collective shadow.

The shadow is a central theme in art and literature, appearing variously as "a monster, a dragon, a Frankenstein, a white whale, and extraterrestrial or a man so vile we cannot see ourselves in him; he is removed from us as a gorgon" (Zweig and Abrams 1991:xx). Perhaps the most recognizable and apt portrayal of the shadow-self is Robert Louis Stevenson's 1886 book *The Strange Case of Dr. Jekyll and Mr. Hyde*, where the pleasant, hard-working scientist Dr. Jekyll transforms into his shadow, the "violent and relentless Mr. Hyde" (1991:xvi). Zweig and Abrams remind us that all individuals and collections thereof—including social institutions like resource management—contain both a Jekyll and a Hyde, "a more pleasant persona for everyday wear and a hiding, nighttime self that remains hushed up much of the time."

Robert Bly (1991) describes the shadow as "the long bag we drag behind us," into which individuals and groups have deposited that which they cannot discuss openly. The bag is invisible insofar as it and its contents constitute "nondiscussables." This is problematic for a variety of reasons, notably because, as Roland Barth (2013:198) points out, a fundamental aspect of critical awareness is "attending to 'nondiscussables.'" For Barth, *nondiscussables* are those subjects "sufficiently important that they get talked about frequently but are so laden with anxiety and taboos" that—out of fear—such conversations only occur within the safe confines of a private space.

> We are fearful that open discussion of these incendiary issues in polite society…will cause a meltdown. The nondiscussable is the elephant in the room. Everyone knows this huge pachyderm is there, right next to the sofa and the fireplace, and we go on mopping and dusting and vacuuming around it as if it did not exist.
>
> (2013:198–199)

Examples of incendiary thus taboo issues include those aspects of politics, economics, race, gender, sexuality, religion and philosophy that "make us squirm" (La Salle and Hutchings 2016). While we may be quite comfortable openly discussing or even mocking someone else's beliefs or practices, the values of the dominant culture are rarely if ever open for public debate, certainly not critical public debate. This is especially true for university-trained experts and specialists—including resource management practitioners—whose income thus status and livelihood is contingent upon their "professionalism," or ability to conform to authority (Moghaddam 1997:23–51).

In resource management, conformity is produced through what Peter Berger calls "circles of social control" (1963:68–78), illustrated in Figure 3.1. Sylvia Hale describes the four control mechanisms as follows (1990:21, emphasis added):

> The innermost circle, and probably the most powerful, is guilt. We come to want to conform, to see conformity as morally proper, and nonconformity makes us feel guilty. For most of our social roles, most of our lives, this *internalized sense of guilt* may be all that is necessary to ensure conformity.
>
> Closely supporting these innermost feelings are our relations with family and friends, our primary group. Because our relationships with these people matter to us, we usually want to

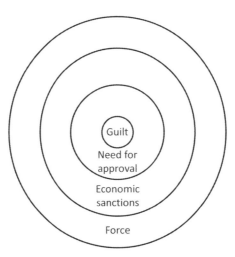

Figure 3.1 Circles of social control. After Berger (1963:68–78) and Hale (1990:21, Figure 2.1).

conform to their expectations [need for approval]. We feel unhappy if we *disappoint them by not playing our roles* in relation to them in ways that they have come to expect.

Only when these intimate processes fail, or in more impersonal aspects of our lives where friendship ties are not involved, do more formal societal sanctions come into play. These may be *economic sanctions*, in that we may risk losing our jobs or not being hired if we do not conform at least minimally to the expectation that employers have of us. Students who do not do assignments or perform in class as expected will not pass the course and will face sanctions of not being eligible for promotion or for jobs that require such courses. In such cases, we conform out of economic self-interest, meeting role demands so that other needs of our own are met.

As a last resort, *formal sanctions and laws punish* those who refuse to conform minimally to the expectations of others as to how roles must be played.

All four mechanisms affect the individual cultural resource manager's values and behaviors, as well as their desire to conform to authority, because those mechanisms define the *internalization* process—"Because we want others to approve of us, we come to want to behave in ways that earn their approval" (Hale 1990:21).[4] Internalization is a fundamental aspect of *institutionalization*, the "establishment of certain patterns of behavior as typical and expected to the point that they are taken for granted as appropriate by most members of a society" (1990:569).

An example of the effect the circles of social control have on the institution of resource management is the internalization thus replication of *authorized heritage discourse*, the self-confirming worldview of the resource management industry that "has assumed the face of commonsense," thereby becoming "an effective mechanism of social regulation, a socially regulated way of doing things" (Waterton and Smith 2009:13). I will return to authorized heritage discourse later on, as it relates directly to how resource management constitutes the McDonaldization of heritage stewardship.

Like the shadows they produce, nondiscussables are a fundamental aspect of knowledge production (Proctor and Schiebinger 2008), including the knowledge produced by resource management experts.

Sociologists speak of nondiscussables in terms of *commonsense understandings*, or "assumptions about how things work, and why, based on immediate experience" (Hale 1990:7). While "common" sense constitutes one way of knowing, another involves more coherent involves *ideologies*, "systems of values that justify certain kinds of actions or ways of life, sometimes to the detriment of the interests of other people" (1990:7). Ideologies greatly influence the way we see reality—"[t]hey tend to sensitize us in certain ways and blind us in others." Examples of ideologies include modernity (which includes the ideology of growth, development, and progress), capitalism, elitism, racism, resourcism, scientism, and positivism (Marchak 1988; Moghaddam 1997; Ritzer 1993, 1996; Thompson 1990), all of which undergird thus define the McDonaldization process, thus, arguably, resource management.

The McDonaldization of Heritage Stewardship

> We must find new lands from which we can easily obtain raw materials and at the same time exploit the cheap labor that is available from the natives of the colonies. The colonies [will] also provide a dumping ground for the surplus goods produced in our factories.
>
> Cecil Rhodes

Like the fast-food restaurant, resource management is a relatively recent cultural invention, with most of its development occurring after 1950 (King 1998; Lertzman 2009; Roberts 2004; Vig and Kraft 2000). Prior to the global spread of capitalism, small- and medium-scale societies around the world developed and maintained their own local and regional heritage stewardship strategies (Anderson 2014; Berkes 2008; Steeves 2015). Through the concomitant processes of colonization and globalization, these local or "traditional" heritage stewardship strategies were—and continue to be—extinguished, replaced by capitalist heritage regimes focused on large- or industrial-scale resource extraction, production, and consumption (Bodley 2014; Ross et al. 2011).

Ken Lertzman (2009) calls these new imperial heritage regimes Western Science Based-Management Systems (WSBMS), where the *management system* is "the sum of all the actions, the goals and objectives, the process through which they are legitimized by society, and the actors involved in carrying them out" (2009:346–347). According to Lertzman,

> There is nothing inherent in the idea of "management" that implies an objective of sustainability or conservation. If "management" embodies values and norms determined by its social context, then to the extent that they follow social norms, the goals of a management system may legitimately not include a "conservation" ethic. If a society values commodity production over conservation, then we will see management systems develop that reflect this.

In contrast to management, the term *stewardship* has a "clearly implied embedded context of values" in relation to the heritage; "While managers can 'manage' to achieve whatever objectives society has given them, stewards always have an obligation to the resources or ecosystems themselves" (2009:347). Stewardship is "always concerned with conservation and sustainability."

Lertzman's approach is important because it suggests that resource management embodies its social context. My point is that McDonald's is that context. If this is indeed the case, then contemporary resource management should be observed as being scientistically and myopically

MEETING THE SHADOW

focused on efficiency, predictability, calculability, and control, all leading to irrational outcomes (i.e., the irrationality of rationality) and "inexorable growth" (Ritzer 1996).

After a historical review of cultural resource management, I consider in the remainder of this section the different ways the four main elements of McDonaldization—efficiency, calculability, predictability, and control—are manifested in this institution, with an emphasis on cultural resource management as it is practiced in the United States and Canada. I address the paradoxical fifth element—irrationality of rationality—in the discussion section that follows. I have organized it this way because distinguishing those outcomes of the system that are expected (rational outcomes) from those deemed unexpected (irrational outcomes) is dependent upon understanding the system's underlying philosophies.

Cultural Resource Management

Before proceeding to the four elements, it will be useful to briefly reflect on how cultural resource management came to be, and how it used today. Thomas King (1998:6–7) describes how the terms "cultural resource" and "cultural resource management" were invented in the 1970s by archaeologists wanting "to equate what they did with natural resource management."

> Back in the 1970s, archaeologists in the United States faced a challenge. New laws had been enacted promoting the protection of "natural resources" on the one hand and 'historic properties' on the other. Government agencies were being required to conduct environmental impact assessments of their actions, seeking ways to protect the environment. How could archaeologists be sure that the places they were concerned about—archaeological sites—were protected by these legal requirements?

Note what King is saying here: cultural resource management is about the protection of places of interest to archaeologists and other heritage specialists, not society at large. King is clear that cultural resources should not be confused with cultural heritage: while everyone has heritage, only authorized heritage experts have "cultural resources" (Smith 2004). I will return to this important concept in the context of authorized heritage discourse.

While one might think the term "cultural resource management" refers to the management of cultural resources, it is commonly used, primarily by archaeologists, in a much narrower sense to refer to "managing historic places of archaeological, architectural, and historical interest and to considering such places in compliance with environmental and historic preservation laws" (King 1998:7).

Cultural resource management should not be mistaken for cultural heritage stewardship. Rather, cultural resource management is said to be "compliance-driven" (King 1998:11), meaning that its primary function is to ensure conformity to the state heritage regime under which the specific management system operates (Smith 2004). Cultural resource management is thus a late-modern ideological project, as is archaeology, from which cultural resource management derives much of its logic (King 1998:17–18; see also Bernbeck and McGuire 2011; Cooper 2010; Hamilakis and Duke 2007; Hutchings and La Salle 2015a; McGuire and Walker 1999; Smith 2004; Waterton and Smith 2009).

Cultural resource management's ideologies have been discussed in a variety of contexts, and many relate to capitalism, directly or indirectly (see citations above; see also *International Journal of Historical Archaeology* Volume 19, Issue 4). Randall McGuire and Mark Walker (1999:164) describe cultural resource management as a class project where the "tendency to represent middle-class interests as universal fits easily into a larger American ideology that says we are all middle class, except for a very small number of wealthy and poor individuals." Indeed, heritage experts "often represent those individuals who hold different interests in the past, or use the past in different ideological ways, as being ignorant, pernicious, or motivated solely by greed." Few appear to consider, however, that these differences in attitudes might be class-based. For example, cultural resource management's ideologies are reproduced primarily in the university (McGuire and Walker 1999:165–166; see also Hutchings and La Salle 2014).

Like McDonald's, cultural resource management is fundamentally an economic project, rooted in the ideology of capitalist development. However, just because cultural resource management is ideological does not mean it has been McDonaldized. To ascertain this, examination is needed of the four core components that define the McDonaldization process.

Efficiency

Under McDonaldization, efficiency means people choose the optimum means to a given end (Ritzer 1993:35). Although the term optimum is employed, "it is rare that the truly *optimum* means to an end is ever found. Rather, there is a striving to find and to use the *best possible* means." According to Ritzer (1993:35),

> In a McDonaldized society, people rarely search for the best means to an end on their own. Rather, the previously discovered best possible means to innumerable ends have been institutionalized in a variety of social settings. Thus, the best means may be part of a technology, written into an organization's rules or regulations, or taught to employees in an occupational socialization process.

As such, people and organizations rarely maximize. Furthermore, solutions to problems are historically situated and encumbered, the product of preexisting power structures and their institutions and bureaucracies (Acheson 2006; Coombe and Baird 2016; Homer-Dixon 2007; Hutchings 2016; King 2009; Moghaddam 1997; Plets 2016; Rogers 1998; Smith 2004).

Examples of efficiency in the fast-food industry include assembly-line production (which includes the ready-made meal) and the drive-through window. Overall, "norms, rules, regulations, procedures and structures have been put in place to ensure that *both* employees and customers act in an efficient manner" (Ritzer 1996:293).

Efficiency is a cornerstone of cultural resource management. As McGuire and Walker (1999:171) describe, "[e]conomic efficiency has become a necessity as more and more companies compete for scarce contracts." Resource management companies work "as quickly as possible." In general, those developers seeking cultural resource management services are "unconcerned with the quality of work except insofar as it gets them through various permitting 'hoops.'" As a result, government standards are not seen as minimum standards but the only standards. McGuire and Walker conclude that "[t]he need to be competitive prods CRM companies towards minimum effort, standardized research, and increased production (more contracts executed in less time for less money)."

Studies of cultural resource management and its disasters demonstrate how the efficiencies described by McGuire and Walker play out on the ground (King 2009; Mapes 2009; Stapp and Longenecker 2009; see also *International Journal of Historical Archaeology* Volume 19, Issue 4). For example, Darby Stapp and Julia Longenecker (2009:49, 53) make the following observations about a major CRM disaster in the northwestern United States involving a $19 million construction project and an Indigenous cemetery:

- "The first request [in 2003] to conduct background research and a field survey, make contact with the tribe, and prepare a report within a three-week period was unrealistic and set an unnecessary tone of urgency."

- "The budget for the initial assessment ($6,700) was too low to complete a full review. Considering the size of the project (millions of dollars and 22 acres), the sensitive location (on the waterfront in an area historically and presently occupied by Northwest Coast Indian people), and the consequences that might result from the discovery of important archaeological deposits (construction delays and cost escalation), the one-week effort to characterize the project location could only be viewed as a preliminary assessment, and designed to identify the work that would still need to be done to complete a good assessment for the project."

- "The recommendation to move ahead with the project without additional archaeological characterization was premature. … The three-day sampling effort was inadequate."

- "Basic important information about the project site…should have been generated and would have greatly improved the quality of the initial site characterization efforts. The failure of the two characterization efforts to locate the largest Native American cemetery ever found on the Northwest Coast was pivotal and speaks volumes about archaeological methodology and compliance requirements."

In this instance, the drive to be efficient or "economical" resulted in the disturbance of over 500 burials, over $8 million in cultural resource management fees, more than 400 days of project delays totaling in excess of $60 million, and the eventual termination of the construction project.[5]

Efficiency is sought in resource management because the institution works in service of development. In this regard, Thomas King (2009:14) points out that

- "The average study of a proposed project's impacts on the cultural or natural environment is done by [CRM] consultants employed by that very project's proponent, who can fire them if they don't give his project a clean bill of health."

- "The federal and state agencies responsible for overseeing the studies and keeping them honest usually view themselves—though they'll seldom admit it—as being in business of making sure projects go forward with as little impediment as possible…."

Contrary to popular opinion within the practice, resource management is *not* fundamentally about conservation or protection. Rather, the primary interest of the resource manager is "the profit margin of some companies and the jobs of some government employees" (King 2009:14).

Just as efficiency might be a government's goal, it is worthwhile to remember that government *inefficiency* can also be the product of deliberate design, as allowing inefficient institutions to exist can benefit rulers (Acheson 2006:124; see also King 2009). This is arguably the case if one considers Indigenous heritage a barrier to development (Hutchings and Lalle 2015a). Rather than being

MEETING THE SHADOW

primarily concerned with site conservation, the role of the government is to provide private companies and individuals with permits allowing them to destroy Indigenous heritage sites to make way for development. From one standpoint, this is an ineffective system when it comes to conservation; but from another, it is, in fact, highly efficient at facilitating development while offloading responsibility to private companies.

Calculability

Under McDonaldization, calculability means people emphasize things that can be counted and quantified. Involving the "tendency to use quantity as a measure of quality," calculability produces a "sense that quality is equal to certain, usually (but not always) large, quantities of things" (Ritzer 1993:62). The credo here is "quantity not quality." The goal of making things calculable is to increase efficiency, thus profits. Because of the myopic focus on quantity, a natural outcome is the decline or even absence of quality (1993:64).

Calculability in the fast-food industry is demonstrated in the focus on measuring how fast tasks take to accomplish, with the goal of speeding up rates of both production and consumption. As Ritzer (1996:293) points out,

> Various aspects of the work of employees at fast-food restaurants are timed and this emphasis on speed often serves to adversely affect the quality of work...resulting in dissatisfaction, alienation and high turnover rates. ... Similarly, customers are expected to spend as little time as possible in the fast-food restaurant. In fact, the drive-through window reduces this time to zero, but if customers decide to eat in the restaurant, the chairs are designed to impel them to leave after about twenty minutes.

While efficiency may increase, the emphasis on improving speed through calculability has a negative effect on quality.

Closely related to efficiency, calculability is manifested in resource management in its focus on the physical or material aspects of heritage, this at the expense of intangible heritage (Pocock et al. 2015). Nowhere is the emphasis on the quantifiable better illustrated than in archaeology/CRM, where the material record is given primacy insofar as it defines the field (Smith 2004; Waterton and Smith 2009).

Calculability in state-sanctioned cultural resource management is also clearly visible in the related concepts that are (1) the archaeological site (an official, authorized, or state-sanctioned heritage landscape with clear physical properties and geographic boundaries), (2) the archaeological site inventory (an official list of official sites), and (3) site numbering systems (Hutchings and La Salle 2015a:712–714). In Canada, the latter, known as the Borden Grid or *Grille Borden*, transforms the living heritage landscape into a highly calculable but entirely dehumanized space, as shown in Figure 3.2. This is because converting living Indigenous landscapes (e.g., a village named *c̓əsnaʔəm*) into archaeological "sites" by renaming them with georeferenced alphanumeric site codes (e.g., a registered site named DhRs-1) constitutes state-sanctioned heritage erasure.

Virtually all aspects of resource management today are geared towards increasing calculability. However, the idea is most prominent in cost-benefit analyses and risk assessments (Dorochoff 2007; Hutchings and La Salle 2015a; King 2009; Mazaika et al. 1995; Merrell 1995; Stapp and

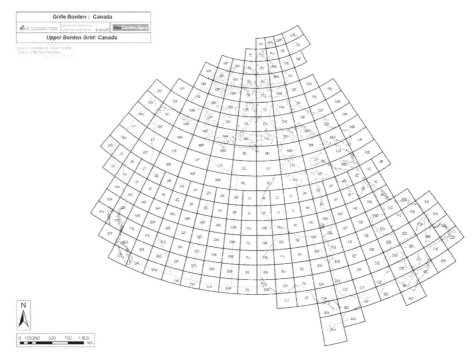

Figure 3.2 Borden grid or *Grille Borden*.
Source: Government of Canada (2007).

Longenecker 2009). Problematically, risk assessments are ideological undertakings that have been determined by some to constitute little more than heritage "triage" (Lackey 1995:343). I will return to cost-benefit analyses and risk assessments shortly.

Predictability

The third dimension of McDonaldization is predictability or the "efforts to enable people to know what to expect at all times and in all places" (Ritzer 1993:99). The goal is a world with "no surprises." To ensure predictability, a rational society emphasizes discipline, order, systemization, formalization, routine, consistency, and methodological operation (1993:83). Bureaucracies and scientific management are examples of efforts towards predictability. Examples of predictability in the fast-food industry include predictable food, made of predictable ingredients, cooked and served in a predictable (scientific, highly orchestrated) way.

Archaeological site numbering systems and risk assessments are designed to make the permitting process more predictable for developers with the goal of increasing efficiency thus profits. A similar tool is predictive modeling. Here, an equation determines the amount of time dedicated to site survey based on the expectation of what will or will not be found, which in turn affects the time and cost budgeted for a project; low-site potential means a quick and fairly inexpensive project. Where risk assessment is used as a substitute for monitoring (Merrell 1995:458), predictive modeling is used as a replacement for surveying.

Control

The fourth dimension of McDonaldization is increased control through technology (Ritzer 1993:100):

> The great sources of uncertainty and predictability in any rationalizing system are people—either the people who work within these systems or who are served by them. Hence, the efforts to increase control are usually aimed at people. McDonaldization involves the search for the means to exert increasing controls over both employees and customers. Over the years, a variety of technologies have been developed and deployed.

Technology includes not only machines and tools, but also materials, skills, knowledge, rules, regulations, procedures, and techniques, which "allows us to conceive as technologies not only obvious things such as robots, computers, and the assembly line, but also bureaucratic rules and regulations and manuals defining basic procedures and techniques" (1993:100). Ritzer sees bureaucracies as "large-scale human technologies" (1993:117–118):

> [Bureaucracies] are huge nonhuman structures with innumerable rules, regulations, guidelines, positions, lines of command, and hierarchies that are designed to dictate, as much as possible, what people do within the system and how they do it. The consummate bureaucrat thinks little about what work is to be done, but simply follows the rules, deals with incoming work, and passes it on to the next step in the hierarchy.
>
> To further limit human choice and error, paper forms are developed, and the employees need do little more than fill out the required form and pass it on, up, or across the bureaucratic hierarchy.
>
> Bureaucracies control not only the people who work in them, but also those who are served by them. Rules, regulations, prescribed paperwork, and many other aspects of bureaucratic life are designed to get the bureaucracy's clients to behave in a prescribed manner.

According to Laurajane Smith (2004:11), cultural resource management as a technology of government arose from the need "to help govern a range of social problems," especially those posed by Indigenous peoples in colonial contexts like Australia and Canada. For Smith,

> The whole process of CRM, which emphasizes the technical application of knowledge and expertise, works effectively to render wider political debates about the legitimacy of cultural and social claims on the past as non-political… This then renders "heritage" and the claims made about it, more readily "governable." The governance of heritage facilitates the de-politicization of Indigenous claims about cultural identity. This has significant consequences for Indigenous people.

While many see resource management as broken, I have come to see the technology as working as designed. Based on my study of cultural resource management in North America, I now consider non-Western, non-commercial cultural heritage an impediment to development (Hutchings 2017). In this light, the goal of the state and its cultural resource managers is to expedite the removal of such landscapes as efficiently (cost-effectively) as possible so as to allow (permit) development to continue. From this vantage, archaeologists and cultural resource managers are part of the problem, not the solution, and it seems there is very little they can do about it. I consider this to be darkest part of cultural resource management's shadow.

Meeting the Shadow

We all have a shadow. Or does our shadow have us?

Connie Zweig and Jeremiah Abrams

A Western Science Based-Management System, resource management reflects the McDonaldized society that produced it. Like the fast-food restaurant, resource management is constructed around and driven toward efficiency, with calculability, predictability and control the primary mechanisms used to achieve that end. However, resource management's shadow is not McDonaldization, per se. Rather, it is the "iron cage" McDonaldization produces, particularly as it pertains to resource management being locked into the capitalist logic of inexorable growth (Ritzer 1996).

A highly rational system, resource management largely involves urban, middle-class, state-sanctioned bureaucrats (managers) applying pro-development risk assessments and cost-benefit analyses to the stewardship of heritage, with "both costs and benefits defined primarily in narrow economic and technical terms rather than incorporating all social and emotional costs and benefits" (Hale 1990:575–576). In this context, rational systems are *unreasonable* systems—"they serve to deny the basic humanity, the human reason, of the people who work within them or are served by them" (Ritzer 1993:121). In other words, concludes Ritzer, "rational systems are dehumanizing systems."

It is this aspect of the shadow—cultural resource management as a dehumanizing system—that I have found most confounding and fascinating (Hutchings 2016; Hutchings and La Salle 2015a, 2015b; La Salle and Hutchings 2016), as it so completely undermines the institution's missionary mythos about the personal sacrifice (e.g., specialized training, student debt, low pay) archaeologists and cultural resource managers take on in order to "save" heritage that, without their expert intervention, would be lost to the ages (McGuire and Walker 1999:172). The reality is, of course, far more invidious (Hutchings 2017; King 2009; Smith 2004).

Focusing on the fifth element of McDonaldization, the paradoxical "irrationality of rationality," I elaborate here on the "negative aspects" of McDonaldized heritage regimes (Ritzer 1993:121). This involves considering "the opposite of rationality and its several dimensions," for McDonaldization can be viewed as "leading to *in*efficiency, *in*calculability, and *loss* of control." However, meeting resource management's shadow has both its "upsides" and "downsides." The latter involves dispelling the taken for granted notion that resource management is a noble cause that works in service of the common good. Seeing the institution for what it is—a destructive technology of the capitalist state—frees us to imagine new possibilities and futures.

The Downside of Up

There is much confusion today about what it is we are really trying to conserve.

Jeremy Wells and Barry Stiefel

Resource management's shadow is its "dark" or "downside." It is that which rational resource managers may ponder privately but rarely if ever discuss publicly, leading to much confusion. As discussed, the primary mechanisms driving this behavior (shadow production) are the three innermost circles of social control: guilt, need for approval, and economic sanctions. University professors are most responsible for disciplining archaeologists and cultural resource managers in the institution's values. In this regard, the toxic, "depressed," and "perverse" state of the modern academy (Berg et al. 2016; Edwards and Roy 2016) reflects perfectly the socioeconomic system it serves (Moghaddam 1997:23–76).

The shadow constitutes an existential communication crisis for humanity insofar as nondiscussables include all the important philosophical questions about heritage and heritage stewardship that we should now be asking ourselves. As Fathali Moghaddam (2010:1) points out,

> Hard times bring hard questions. Calamitous wars, international terrorism, environmental degradation and global warming, interconnected global economic depression—the twenty-first century has given birth to hard times, and we now labor under hard questions. How will we manage a world severely challenged by shrinking resources, ballooning population, huge and increasing income inequalities, terrorism, torture, and environmental collapse?

These are not questions the typical resource manager asks in the process of carrying out their duties. But they probably should.

Once imagined as the apex of scientific stewardship, state sanctioned resource management is now considered a prime driver of contemporary heritage problems, in a variety of heritage contexts (Acheson 2006; Armitage et al. 2007; Gnecco and Dias 2015; Homer-Dixon 2007; King 2009; Rogers 1998; Ross et al. 2011; Smith 2004). Fikret Berkes and colleagues (2007:308) describe the situation this way:

> Resource management is at a crossroads. Problems are complex, values are in dispute, facts are uncertain, and predictions are possible only in a limited sense. The scientific system that underlies resource management is facing a crisis of confidence in legitimacy and power. Top-down resource management does not work for a multitude of reasons, and the era of expert-knows-best decision making is all but over.

It is not helpful that resource managers and related heritage professionals react poorly when their institution is called into question (Hutchings and La Salle 2015a, 2015b; La Salle and Hutchings 2017; see also Lyons et al. 2012; Martindale et al. 2016). Consider, for example, how the following statement by Thomas King (2009:7, emphasis added) might be interpreted publicly by the typical North American resource manager:

> [W]e now have bureaucracies overseeing environmental impact assessment (EIA) and cultural resource management (CRM), and we have well-heeled private companies doing EIA and CRM work under contract. What we do not have is an orderly system for actually, honestly considering and trying to reduce impacts on our natural and cultural heritage. It's all pretty much a sham...
>
> There are good reasons to consider how something we plan may muck up [heritage], and to do so before we undertake it. And in a democracy, citizens should have real opportunities to influence what government does, or lets others do, to their heritage. It's too bad, I think, that we've let things develop in such a way that we're spending lots of money on mere public relations efforts, slathering the lipstick on the pigs of ill-considered development.

Or this from Paul Merrell (1995:457), who links ecological risk assessments (of dioxins) with homicide:

> If you feel uncomfortable with the idea of accepting risk assessment as evidence of intent to kill, I suggest it is because you, too, know that risk assessment is a sham. It is not science. Anyone who does risk assessment will admit to you that you can produce any result you want because if

we had the answers we wouldn't do risk assessments. Risk assessment is a substitution for scientific knowledge, and it is just abominable.

What Moghaddam's, Berkes and colleagues', King's, and Merrell's comments have in common is all are responses to modernity (i.e., modern society and its concomitant enlightenment philosophies) and the modernization of heritage stewardship.[6] While Moghaddam highlights the effects modernity has on the scope and scale of contemporary heritage problems, Berkes and colleagues call into question science, hierarchy, and experts. King claims resource managers actively "whitewash" heritage destruction because they are complicit in the process, which in Merrell's case is death by "the most toxic substance put together by humanity" (1995:454).

Modernity and its component parts (e.g., capitalism, rationality, individualism, science, progress) define much of resource management's shadow, and, because these are so rarely discussed openly, they constitute a major barrier to communication, resulting in significant confusion around expectations and goals. The roots of this confusion have been explored by Anthony Giddens (1990:135–137), who delineates four "adaptive reactions" to the crisis of modernity. As shown in Figure 3.3, those responses are: pragmatic acceptance, sustained optimism, cynical pessimism, and radical engagement (Hutchings 2017:113–115).

Pragmatic acceptance involves a focus on "surviving" and "the belief that much that goes on in the modern world is outside anyone's control, so that temporary gains are all that can be planned or hoped for" (Giddens 1990:136). Pragmatic acceptance is "not without psychological costs," as it implies a "numbness frequently reflecting deep underlying anxieties, which in some individuals repeatedly surface at a conscious level."

Sustained optimism is essentially the persistence of the attitudes of modernity—it is a "continued faith...in spite of whatever dangers threaten at the current time" (Giddens 1990:136).

> This is the outlook of those experts...who have criticized "doomsday" ecological scenarios in favor of the view that social and technological solutions can be found for the major global problems. For lay individuals, it is a perspective which continues to hold great resonance and emotional appeal, based as it is upon a conviction that unfettered rational thought and particularly science offer sources of long-term security that no other orientations can match.

Sustained optimism is by far the most common response in the heritage industry (e.g., King 2009:141–164; Stapp and Longenecker 2009:57–92). It is closely related to "resourcism," as discussed in the following sections.

Pragmatic acceptance	Sustained optimism
Cynical pessimism	Radical engagement

Figure 3.3 Four responses to modernity. After Giddens (1990:135–137) and Hutchings (2017:114, Figure 6.2).

Cynical pessimism represents an opposite set of attitudes to pragmatic acceptance and sustained optimism. Cynical pessimism "presumes a direct involvement with the anxieties provoked by high consequence dangers" (Giddens 1990:136):

> Cynicism is not indifference. Nor is it necessarily doom-laden, although it is hardly compatible with blunt optimism. Cynicism is a mode of dampening the emotional impact of anxieties through either a humorous or a world-weary response to them. It lends itself to parody.

Cynical pessimism is rare in heritage discourse. Thomas King (2009:166–167) provides an example in *Whitewashing* when he ponders the meaning of climate change in relation to resource management:

> What earthly point is there…in diddling about with adjustments in the way we consider environmental impacts—and impacts on things like old buildings and archaeological sites, for heaven's sake—when the atmosphere's warming, the polar ice is melting, the seas are rising? … The costs of this disaster in terms of natural and cultural heritage—including living, functioning human populations and their social systems—will be far beyond anything we can imagine measuring or mitigating.

King describes being "overcome by the feeling that I'm fiddling while Rome burns."

Radical engagement is an "attitude of practical contestation towards perceived sources of danger" (Giddens 1990:137).

> Those taking a stance of radical engagement hold that, although we are beset by major problems, we can and should mobilize [to] transcend them. This is an optimistic outlook. … Its prime vehicle is the social movement.

Constituting radical activist and revolutionary approaches, radical engagement is the least common response by heritage experts to modernity. Radical and revolutionary views are unpopular because they pose a direct threat to the power structure. As Syun Akasofu notes, "a scientific establishment is highly conservative and will attempt to preserve the power of its ruling group against any rebels" (in Wohlforth 2004:160). In the academy, radical engagement is associated with deconstructive postmodernist philosophy, discussed below.

Like Giddens, Max Oelschlaeger (1995:531) distinguishes between different responses to modernity, in this case between "resourcist" and "deconstructive postmodernist" perspectives.

> Deconstructive postmodernists believe that the modern age is based on inherently flawed Enlightenment, capitalistic, and scientific narratives that must be repudiated before culture can be reconstructed anew. In contrast the dominant stream of environmentalism, called by a variety of names, including "resourcism" and "reform environmentalism," attempts to solve problems by fine-tuning the present post-industrial paradigm. Thus, so-called modernists contend that ecological dysfunctions can be eliminated through sustainable development; deconstructionists dismiss this contention, and argue that ecocrisis reveals the contradictions structurally (and therefore permanently) in the growth dynamic of capitalistic, industrial society.

A form of sustained optimism, resourcism is resource management's governing paradigm. It is Raymond Rogers' (1995:153) "strategic, instrumental, and technical approach," which is typically science and planning oriented and "does not call the modern human project related to science, technology and capitalism into question. Instead, it focuses on monitoring activities and reforming certain practices which are deemed to have negative consequences."

Following Rogers (1998), I believe the intractability of contemporary heritage problems is related to the inaccessibility of the forces causing those problems. This inaccessibility is a product of "the increasing privatization of political power in the economy, rendering the dynamics of appropriation and domination beyond the realm of public policy or democratic processes" (1998:175). In this light, science is not the limiting factor when it comes to solving heritage problems, but political power is.

In this regard, many contemporary heritage problems can best be understood as "wicked." The term wicked builds on the notion of intractability, minimally defined as the inability to control or direct. *Wicked heritage problems*, then, are those that defy resolution "because of the enormous interdependencies, uncertainties, circularities, and conflicting stakeholders implicated by any effort to develop a solution" (Lazarus 2009:1159–1160). For Peter Balint et al. (2011:1),

> "Wicked" problems are large-scale, long-term policy dilemmas in which multiple and compounding risks and uncertainties combine with sharply divergent public values to generate contentious political stalemates; wicked problems in the environmental arena typically emerge from entrenched conflicts over natural resource management and over the prioritization of economic and conservation goals more generally.

As Richard Lazarus (2009:1160) explains, while wicked problems are synonymous with "social messes," some—including global warming—are deemed *super-wicked* because of "exacerbating features." Among those features is the fact that "time is not costless, so the longer it takes to address the problem, the harder it will be to do so." Nevertheless, inaction is the status quo (Hutchings 2017:115–116).

In his book *The Upside of Down*, Thomas Homer-Dixon (2007:214) asks why it is so difficult for people to "face reality."

> Avoiding evidence of our problems, denying their existence, displacing responsibility for dealing with them onto others, or falsely believing we can fix them when they get bad are all, in the end, rotten strategies for survival in our more dangerous world. Why do we adopt these strategies if they're so bad for us?

Homer-Dixon offers both psychological and social explanations. Psychologically, "we choose to ignore things that scare us or threaten assumptions that give our lives meaning and security." Socially,

> [p]robably the most important is the self-interest of powerful groups that have a vested interest in a particular way of doing things or viewing the world. If outside evidence doesn't fit their worldview, these groups can cajole, co-opt, or coerce other people to deny the evidence.

My work (Hutchings 2017) supports Homer-Dixon's (2007:217) finding that "modern capitalism's system of rules, institutions, and language is formidably resistant to change."

The Upside of Down

> Unalloyed and simplistic optimism about the future is really just denial in disguise.
>
> Thomas Homer-Dixon

Individuals can pay a high price for meeting, let alone embracing or "owning" the shadow (Zweig and Abrams 1991:xxiv–xxv), financially and personally. But there are also potentially significant benefits. To start, simplistic or sustained optimism—the dominant paradigm in resource management today—constitutes denial and status quo. On the other hand, taking a radically engaged deconstructive postmodernist approach where the shadow is integral to the project offers the potential for something different.

In the academy, meeting the shadow means learning the language of sociology and critical theory (e.g., Biro 2011; Foster et al. 2010; Smith 2004; Winter 2013). Owning the shadow means *activating* those ideas in daily life, a challenging undertaking under the best of circumstances. By engaging our shadow, however, we stand to "heal our relationships through more honest self-examination and direct communication" (Zweig and Abrams 1991:xxv). Meeting the shadow is an important first step in reconciliation. As Zweig and Abrams (1991:xxv) conclude, "perhaps we can…refrain from adding our personal darkness to the density of the collective shadow."

For academics, meeting the shadow means confronting the hyperpositivistic, hypercompetitive university (Berg et al. 2016; Edwards and Roy 2016; Homer-Dixon 2007; Moghaddam 1997) and telling the truth about their institution's real motivations and impacts. It means seeing the institution's underlying philosophies (e.g., modernity, neoliberalism, growth) as destructive forces, as they invariably presage and legitimize what Homer-Dixon (2007:246) calls "ruthless extraction" and "disintegration," characterized by ecological breakdown, dislocated lives, worsening poverty, and growing income gaps and violence (2007:256–264).

There is an upside to socioecological breakdown, however, what Homer-Dixon (2007:22) calls "catagenesis," a word that combines the prefix *cata* (down) with the root *genesis* (birth). Catagenesis, then, is the reinvention of the future in the face of collapse, making the "upside of down" the opportunities that emerge from a crisis—'the creative renewal of our technologies, institutions, and societies in the aftermath of breakdown" (2007:268). However,

> Our first step down this path must be to acknowledge that our global situation is urgent—that we're on the cusp of a planetary emergency—and then [we can] begin a wide-ranging and vigorous conversation…about what we can and should do.
>
> (2007:308)

Yet, truth-telling remains elusive, for "[p]eople rarely acknowledge that an accustomed way of life is unsustainable except in the face of prolonged, devastating failure" (Allen et al. 2003:150).

Conclusion

In this chapter, I set out to map the non-discussables that define cultural resource management today. I began by framing this inquiry in the core and related concepts of rationalization and McDonaldization, which are defining characteristics of modern society. It is my contention that the principles of McDonaldization—efficiency, calculability, predictability, and control—have transformed heritage stewardship into a rigid, bureaucratic, elite-driven, state-sanctioned institution that foregrounds capitalist interests. These features constitute cultural resource management's shadow, which heritage managers routinely ignore as a matter of daily practice.

The shadow constitutes those parts of resource management that resource managers rarely, if ever, discuss in professional settings. This includes their institution's integral role in state-sanctioned heritage destruction. Engaging the shadow means critically engaging with resource management's underlying philosophies, notably "resourcism" and "management." It means recognizing that management is not stewardship and that resources are not heritage. It means full consideration of intractability and all things "wicked."

Although not without personal and professional costs, owning the shadow can lead to increased truth-telling thus more meaningful communication. Above all, engaging the shadow means the freedom and ability to imagine the "upside of down" (Homer-Dixon 2007:265–266), for

> No matter whether our future brings disintegration, renewal, or something in between, we can be sure the that the road in front of us won't be straight and that our grandchildren's world will look starkly different from ours today. The famous claim that we have reached the end of history—that capitalist democracy will become the universal and final form of social order—will look silly in retrospect. We in the West, anesthetized by materialism and egged on by a self-satisfied intelligentsia, may have convinced ourselves that our way of life is the apex of economic and political achievement and that, within its bosom, we can sustain some kind of endless plateau of hedonistic satisfaction. In reality, though, history isn't close to ending. It has barely begun.

Notes

1   A prominent example of this exclusion is Thomas F. King's (2009) *Our Unprotected Heritage: Whitewashing the Destruction of Our Cultural and Natural Environment*, a book that has received little scholarly attention in North America, despite its accurate and detailed portrayal of the late modern heritage environment. I believe its unpopularity is in part a result of what some see as King's "negative" and "cynical" portrayal of the resource management industry (see King 2009:169–170). Another prominent example is Laurajane Smith's (2004) *Archaeological Theory and the Politics of Cultural Heritage*. Ignorance of these works says a lot about the state of contemporary North American heritage discourse (Proctor and Schiebinger 2008).

2   A key premise here is that archaeology and cultural resource management constitute a singular *institution*—"a unique structure and set of imperatives that direct the actions of people within it" (Bakan 2004:1). Specifically, archaeology/CRM is a legal institution, whose existence and capacity to operate depends upon state law (King 1998; Smith 2004).

3   C. Wright Mills (1956) uses the term *power elite* to describe those who occupy dominant positions in dominant institutions (military, political, economic). Highlighting their interwoven interests, Mills shows the typical citizen or group to be relatively powerless when it comes to making meaningful structural change.

4   The term *internalization* refers to "the process of learning group values and behavioral expectations and wanting to conform to them from an inner sense that they are morally right" (Hale 1990:569).

5   See Lynda Mapes (2009) for a detailed account of the Tse-Whit-Zen disaster.

6   See John Barry (2007:43–50) for an overview of the heritage–modernity nexus. For more detailed analyses, see Michael Zimmerman (1994), Ørnulf Seippel (2002), John Bellamy Foster (2009), and Andrew Biro (2011).

References

Acheson, James M. (2006). Institutional Failure in Resource Management. *Annual Review of Anthropology* 35:117–134.

Alexander, Jeffery C. (2013). *The Dark Side of Modernity*. Polity, Cambridge and Malden.

Allen, Timothy F. H., Joseph Tainter, and Thomas Hoekstra. (2003). *Supply-Side Sustainability*. Columbia University Press, New York.

Anderson, Eugene N. (2014). *Caring for Place: Ecology, Ideology, and Emotion in Traditional Landscape Management*. Left Coast Press, Walnut Creek.

Armitage, Derek, Fikret Berkes, and Nancy Doubleday, eds. (2007). *Adaptive Co-Management: Collaboration, Learning, and Multi-Level Governance*. UBC Press, Vancouver.

Bakan, Joel. (2004). *The Corporation: The Pathological Pursuit of Profit and Power*. Penguin Canada, Toronto.

Balint, Peter J., Ronald E. Stewart, Anand Desai, and Lawrence C. Walters. (2011). *Wicked Environmental Problems: Managing Uncertainty and Conflict*. Island Press, Washington, D.C.

Barry, John. (2007). *Environment and Social Theory*. Second Edition. Routledge, London.

Barth, Roland. (2013). Culture in Question. In *The Jossey-Bass Reader on Educational Leadership*, edited by M. Grogan, pp. 197–206. Jossey-Bass, San Francisco.

Berg, Lawrence D., Edward H. Huijbens, and Henrik Gutzon Larsen. (2016). Producing Anxiety in the Neoliberal University. *The Canadian Geographer* 60(2):168–180.

Berger, Peter L. (1963). *Invitation to Sociology: A Humanistic Perspective*. Doubleday, New York.

Berkes, Fikret. (2008). *Sacred Ecology*. Second Edition. Routledge, London.

Bernbeck, Reinhard, and Randall H. McGuire. (2011). A Conceptual History of Ideology and Its Place in Archaeology. In *Ideologies in Archaeology*, edited by R. Bernbeck and R.H. McGuire, pp. 15–59. University of Arizona Press, Tucson.

Biro, Andrew, ed. (2011). *Critical Ecologies: The Frankfurt School and Contemporary Environmental Crises*. University of Toronto Press, Toronto and London.

Bly, Robert. (1991). The Long Bag We Drag Behind Us. In *Meeting the Shadow*, edited by C. Zweig and J. Abrams, pp. 6–12. Tarcher/Penguin, New York.

Bodley, John H. (2014). *Victims of Progress*. Sixth Edition. Rowman and Littlefield, Lanham and New York.

Coombe, Rosemary J., and Melissa F. Baird. (2016). The Limits of Heritage: Corporate Interests and Cultural Rights on Resource Frontiers. In *A Companion to Heritage Studies*, edited by W. Logan, M.N. Craith, and U. Kockel, pp. 337–354. Wiley-Blackwell, New York.

Cooper, Malcolm A. (2010). Protecting Our Past: Political Philosophy, Regulation, and Heritage Management in England and Scotland. *The Historic Environment: Policy and Practice* 1(2): 143–159.

Dorochoff, Nicholas. (2007). *Negotiation Basics for Cultural Resource Managers*. Left Coast Press, Walnut Creek.

Edwards Marc A., and Roy Siddhartha. (2016). Academic Research in the 21st Century: Maintaining Scientific Integrity in a Climate of Perverse Incentives and Hypercompetition. *Environmental Engineering Science* Preprint, doi:10.1089/ees.2016.0223.

Foster, John Bellamy. (2009). *The Ecological Revolution: Making Peace with the Planet*. Monthly Review Press, New York.

Foster, John Bellamy, Brett Clark, and Richard York. (2010). *The Ecological Rift: Capitalism's War on the Earth*. Monthly Review Press, New York.

Giddens, Anthony. (1990). *The Consequences of Modernity*. Polity Press, Cambridge.

Gnecco, Cristóbal, and Adriana Schmidt Dias. (2015). On Contract Archaeology. *International Journal of Historical Archaeology* 19(4):687–698.

Hale, Sylvia M. (1990). *Controversies in Sociology*. Copp Clark Pitman, Toronto.

Hamilakis, Yannis, and Philip Duke, eds. (2007). *Archaeology and Capitalism: From Ethics to Politics*. Left Coast Press, Walnut Creek.

Homer-Dixon, Thomas. (2007). *The Upside of Down: Catastrophe, Creativity, and the Renewal of Civilization.* Vintage Canada, Toronto.

Hutchings, Richard M. (2017). *Maritime Heritage in Crisis: Indigenous Landscapes and Global Ecological Breakdown.* Routledge, London.

Hutchings, Richard M., and Marina La Salle. (2014). Teaching Anti-Colonial Archaeology. *Archaeologies* 10(1):27–69.

———. (2015a). Archaeology as Disaster Capitalism. *International Journal of Historical Archaeology* 19(4):699–720.

———. (2015b). Why Archaeologists Misrepresent Their Practice: A North American Perspective. *Journal of Contemporary Archaeology* 2(2):S11–S17.

King, Thomas F. (1998). *Cultural Resource Laws and Practice.* AltaMira, Lanham.

———. (2009). *Our Unprotected Heritage: Whitewashing the Destruction of Our Cultural and Natural Environment.* Left Coast Press, Walnut Creek.

La Salle, Marina, and Richard M. Hutchings. (2016). What Makes Us Squirm—A Critical Response to Community-Oriented Archaeology. *Canadian Journal of Archaeology* 40(1):164–180.

Lackey, Robert T. (1995). The Future of Ecological Risk Assessment. *Human and Ecological Risk Assessment* 1(4):339–343.

Lazarus, Richard James. (2009). Super Wicked Problems and Climate Change: Restraining the Present to Liberate the Future. *Cornell Law Review* 5:1153–1233.

Lertzman, Ken. (2009). The Paradigm of Management, Management Systems, and Resource Stewardship. *Journal of Ethnobiology* 29(2):339–358.

Lewicki, Roy, Barbara Gray, and Michael Elliott, eds. (2002). *Making Sense of Intractable Environmental Conflicts: Concepts and Cases.* Island Press, Washington, D.C.

Lyons, Natasha, Ian Cameron, Tanya Hoffmann, and Debbie Miller. (2012). Many Shades of Grey: Dispelling Some Myths About the Nature and Status of CRM in British Columbia, a Response to La Salle and Hutchings. *The Midden* 44(3/4):6–8.

Mapes, Lynda V. (2009). *Breaking Ground: The Lower Elwha Klallam Tribe and the Unearthing of Tse-Whit-Zen Village.* University of Washington Press, Seattle and London.

Marchak, M. Patricia. (1988). *Ideological Perspectives on Canada.* Third Edition. McGraw Hill Ryerson, Toronto and New York.

Martindale, Andrew, Natasha Lyons, George Nicholas, Bill Angelbeck, Sean P. Connaughton, Colin Grier, James Herbert, Mike Leon, Yvonne Marshall, Angela Piccini, David M. Schaepe, Kisha Supernant, and Gary Warrick. (2016). Archaeology as Partnerships in Practice: A Reply to La Salle and Hutchings. *Canadian Journal of Archaeology* 40:181–204.

Mazaika, Rosemary, Robert T. Lackey, and Stephen L. Friant, eds. (1995). *Ecological Risk Assessment: Use, Abuse, and Alternatives.* Amherst Scientific Publishers, Amherst.

McGuire, Randall, and Mark Walker. (1999). Class Confrontations in Archaeology. *Historical Archaeology* 33(1):159–183.

Merrell, Paul. (1995). Legal Issues of Ecological Risk Assessment. *Human and Ecological Risk Assessment* 1(4):454–458.

Mills, C. Wright. (1956). *The Power Elite.* Oxford University Press, Oxford.

Moghaddam, Fathali. (1997). *The Specialized Society: The Plight of the Individual in the Age of Individualism.* Praeger, Westport and London.

———. (2010). *The New Global Insecurity: How Terrorism, Environmental Collapse, Economic Inequalities, and Resource Shortages Are Changing Our World.* Praeger Security International, Santa Barbara.

Oelschlaeger, Max. (1995). Postmodernism and the Environment. In *Conservation and Environmentalism,* edited by R. Paehlke, pp. 530–532. Garland, New York and London.

Plets, Gertjan. (2016). Heritage Bureaucracies and the Modern Nation State. Towards an Ethnography of Archaeological Systems of Government. *Archaeological Dialogues* 23(2):193–213.

Pocock, Celmara, David Collett, and Linda Baulch. (2015). Assessing Stories Before Sites: Identifying the Tangible from the Intangible. *International Journal of Heritage Studies* 21(10):962–982.

Proctor, Robert N., and Londa Schiebinger. (2008). *Agnotology: The Making and Unmaking of Ignorance*. Stanford University Press, Stanford.

Ritzer, George. (1983). The McDonaldization of Society. *Journal of American Culture* 6:100–107.

———. (1993). *The McDonaldization of Society: An Investigation into the Changing Character of American Life*. Pine Forge Press, Thousand Oaks and London.

———. (1996). The McDonaldization Thesis: Is Expansion Inevitable? *International Sociology* 11(3):291–308.

Roberts, Jane. (2004). *Environmental Policy*. Routledge, London.

Rogers, Raymond A. (1995). *The Oceans Are Emptying: Fish Wars and Sustainability*. Black Rose Books, Montreal, New York, and London.

———. (1998). *Solving History: The Challenge of Environmental Activism*. Black Rose Books, Montreal, New York, and London.

Ross, Anne, Kathleen Pickering Sherman, Jeffery G. Snodgrass, Henry D. Delcore, and Richard Sherman. (2011). *Indigenous Peoples and the Collaborative Stewardship of Nature: Knowledge Binds and Institutional Conflicts*. Left Coast Press, Walnut Creek.

Seippel, Ørnulf. (2002). Modernity, Politics, and the Environment: A Theoretical Perspective. In *Sociological Theory and the Environment*, edited by R.E. Dunlap et al., pp. 197–229. Rowman and Littlefield, Lanham and Oxford.

Smith, Laurajane. (2004). *Archaeological Theory and the Politics of Cultural Heritage*. Routledge, London.

Stapp, Darby C., and Julia G. Longenecker. (2009). *Avoiding Archaeological Disasters: A Risk Management Approach*. Left Coast Press, Walnut Creek.

Steeves, Paulette. (2015). Academia, Archaeology, CRM, and Tribal Historic Preservation. *Archaeologies* 11(1):121–141.

The Club of Rome. (1970). *The Predicament of Mankind: Quest for Structured Response to Growing World-Wide Complexities and Uncertainties*. The Club of Rome, Rome.

Thompson, John B. (1990). *Ideology and Modern Culture*. Stanford University Press, Stanford.

Vig, Norman J., and Michael E. Kraft. (2000). *Environmental Policy*. Fourth Edition. CQ Press, Washington, D.C.

Waterton, Emma, and Laurajane Smith, eds. (2009). *Taking Archaeology Out of Heritage*. Cambridge Scholars Publishing, Cambridge.

Weber, Max. (1930 [1992]). *The Protestant Ethic and the Spirit of Capitalism*. Translated by Talcott Parsons. Routledge, London.

Winter, Tim. (2013). Clarifying the Critical in Critical Heritage Studies. *International Journal of Heritage Studies* 19(6):532–545.

Wohlforth, Charles. (2004). *The Whale and the Supercomputer: On the Northern Front of Climate Change*. North Point Press, New York.

Zimmerman, Michael E. (1994). *Contesting Earth's Future: Radical Ecology and Postmodernity*. University of California Press, Berkeley.

Zweig, Connie, and Jeremiah Abrams, eds. (1991). *Meeting the Shadow: The Hidden Power of the Dark Side of Human Nature*. Tarcher/Penguin, New York.

CHAPTER 4

The Mystery of History and Place

Radical Preservation Revisited

Jack D. Elliott, Jr.

> We forget... that there is a natural history of souls, nay, even of man himself, which can be learned only from the symbolism inherent in the world about him.
>
> It is the natural history that led Hudson to glimpse eternity in some old men's faces at Land's End, that led Thoreau to see human civilizations as toadstools sprung up in the night by solitary roads, or that provoked Melville to experience in the sight of a sperm whale some colossal alien existence without which man himself would be incomplete.
>
> Loren Eiseley
> "Strangeness in the Proportion" (Eiseley, 1971, p. 148)

> For the essence of life is presentness, and only in a mythical sense does its mystery appear in the time-forms of past and future. They are the way, so to speak, in which life reveals itself to the folk.... For it is, always is, however much we may say It was. Thus speaks the myth, which is only the garment of the mystery.
>
> Thomas Mann
> *Joseph and His Brothers* (Mann, 1945, pp. 32–33)

Historic preservation refers to the activities and the organizations—both private and governmental—that are concerned with preserving remnants of past human activity—artifacts, buildings, and places—based upon their possessing the quality of significance. This quality recalls the fact that historic preservation ostensibly goes beyond (but without rejecting) academic history's concern with reconstructing objective history to a broader philosophical focus on what these places mean in relation to questions such as "who we are, where we came from, and what is the legacy that shapes and enriches us" (Moe, 2002, p. 14). Like as not though, these questions, lying at the very roots of historic preservation and human existence, are seldom mentioned in practice. In lieu of this, justification often moves to arenas of thought that are more comprehensible by the public such as the generation of "tourist dollars." While this might gain currency in a world devoted to production and financial success, it doesn't mean that it actually grapples with or even comprehends the nature of its concern.

THE MYSTERY OF HISTORY AND PLACE

Human history is in part a chain of objectively lived and reconstructed persons and events. However, as the philosopher of history Eric Voegelin often pointed out, it also includes the dimension of consciousness through which history is "illuminated with meaning from within by the human beings who continuously create and bear it as the mode and condition of their self-realization." This illumination manifests through an "elaborate symbolism" that includes rites, myths, laws, sacred places, and theory that serve to make sense of human life and the cosmos within which they live making it "an integral part of social reality." Furthermore, the symbols "express the experience that man is fully man by virtue of his participation in a whole that transcends his particular existence," effectively serving as pointers, or reminders, that make life "transparent for the mystery of human existence" (Voegelin, 2000, p. 109). By the mystery of human existence, or the mystery of being, Voegelin alludes to a dimension of existence that transcends human concepts, a quality that we can only point to when we ask "Why do we exist rather than not exist?" (Hughes, 1993, pp. 1–3). Here, we intuit that there is more to existence than what is given through our senses. Furthermore, to know that past societies interpreted their existences in a multi-dimensional manner leads to the corollary that we too, being part of the same historical process also view the world through similar symbolic structures. Our appropriation of the past involves in part images which are enmeshed in symbolic overtones that we are not readily aware of, especially when we are focused only on the objects.

The holistic nature of human experience was truncated by the rise of positivism, or scientism, which excluded from knowledge that which does not conform to scientific methods. Knowledge in this view refers only to the facts pertaining to empirical objects. All else falls into the realm of value amounting to little more than opinion or subjective prejudice. Acceptable knowledge, therefore, is reduced from the totality of human experience—in its range from the concrete to the apperception of mystery—to the delimitations of methodology. Such a positivistic knowledge would, of course, prove most receptive in the realm of technology, production, and job-training, where knowledge produces power and power dominates public dialogue (Trepanier, 2016). Given the modern mind's ability to deal with the objective and the technical yet coming up short when dealing with the nature of human experience and symbolization, Walker Percy referred in his 1989 NEH Jefferson lecture to a radical incoherence, a "Fateful Rift"—the "San Andreas Fault in the Modern Mind"—represented by the dominance of empirical science to the exclusion of complementary means of knowing (Percy, 1991).

The historic preservation movement is devoted to the preservation of "significant," or symbolic, components of the landscape. Over the last century, it has become institutionally ensconced in the form of private organizations, university departments, and governmental bureaucracies in the form of agencies and regulations. Through these, the movement has acquired a large public voice strongly affecting the public perception of history. Despite its being mandated to deal with symbolic dimensions of history, the voice of the movement has—with a few exceptions—been primarily positivistic.

In 2002, my article "Radical Preservation: Toward a New and More Ancient Paradigm" sounded a call to recover the roots of meaning that are foundational to the historic preservation movement (Elliott, 2002). "Radical"—from the Latin *radicalis*—refers to roots, to a time of origins, and to fundamental principles, and a concern for such first principles (or basic axioms) is in the Aristotelian sense the basis of philosophy. For Voegelin, the root of history is essentially philosophical, an inquiry into the nature of human existence that ranges from the concrete upward to the ineffable mystery (Webb, 1981, pp. 17–18). The term radical refers to a convergence of those elements in an endeavor basic to the human condition.

90

Radical Preservation called for the recovery of an older way of grasping the world. We must cultivate, as E.V. Walter stated in his treatise on the experience of landscape, "some old perspectives to grasp things whole and entire. We need to recover a way of thinking that ancient people took for granted... We need to experience the world in a radically old way" (Walter, 1988, p. 3).

In calling for a recovery of roots, I was not and am not calling for a new methodological insight relevant only to the preservation movement but to a recovery of all that is implied when we speak of history and place as significant, or meaningful. This calls for broader insights that are seldom if ever encountered in the reigning positivistic focus on the material. These insights will by virtue of the nature of human experience have to span the San Andreas Fault of the modern mind separating fact and value, science and religion, the concrete and the mysterious.

Glimmers of Transcendence

The experience of history and its symbolization are multidimensional. Far more than a detached object of study consisting of material entities and their relations, it is a process that we stand within where we see it from a limited perspective like tadpoles within the world of a mud puddle and certainly not from a detached perspective outside and above the process. While it is possible to discern entities and causal processes, yet everything is nevertheless suffused with a penumbra of mystery like light seen by tadpoles filtering in from above.

Symbolization is at the heart of preservation concerns. The word "significance"—the foundation of preservation activities—is derived from the word "sign," practically a synonym for symbol. With significance, we are delving into the heart of symbolization, and this entails more than a focus on merely historical objects but on the conscious experience of them. It is here that the object (historical and otherwise) in all of its dimensions of meaning is to be found. No objects are intrinsically significant; they are only significant to the degree that they enter into conscious experience at the nexus of the past, present, and future (McMahon, 1999).

During a field trip in Europe, the founders of quantum physics Niels Bohr and Werner Heisenberg visited Kronborg Castle in Denmark, once the home of the historical Prince Hamlet, the prototype of the central character in the Shakespearean play. While there Bohr reflected on the experience, remarking:

> Isn't it strange how this castle changes as soon as one imagines that Hamlet lived here? As scientists, we believe that a castle consists only of stones and admire the way the architect puts them together. The stone, the green roof with its patina, the wood carvings in the church, constitute the whole castle. None of this should be changed by the fact that Hamlet lived here, and yet it is changed completely. Suddenly the walls and the ramparts speak a different language. The courtyard becomes an entire world, a dark corner reminds us of the darkness in the human soul, we hear Hamlet's "To be or not to be".... everyone knows the questions Shakespeare had him ask, the human depths he was made to reveal.... And once we know that, Kronberg becomes quite a different castle for us.
>
> (Quoted in Tuan, 1977, p. 4)

The castle is in part an empirical object that can be examined scientifically. Yet, as Bohr observes in light of Hamlet it is changed. But what is changed? Certainly not the empirical castle. Here, we must consider the fact that the castle is a part within a much larger experiential whole. The "objective" image of the castle is only part of the experience of it. Behind it lie the remembered historical associations: Who built it? When was it built? Who was associated with it? Then there are associations with Shakespeare's play which raise broader, more philosophical associations in "the human depths he was made to reveal." All contribute to a symbolic potency leading through a web of associations onto endless horizons eventually pointing to the mystery of being itself. Why is there something rather than nothing?

There is no distinct experience of the castle as a separate object to which one then attaches feelings or speculations. Instead, the place as experienced appears as an object, or a focal point, embedded in a web of associations, some concrete, some much less so. The place as experienced as the nexus of historical and narratological associations and potentially to echoes of the beautiful, even pointing to that which cannot be captured by words, the ineffable. It "gathers world" a Heideggerean term aptly used by Christian Norberg-Schulz (1980) in his phenomenology of place and building, indicating that what a place or building is, is based on its context within its world of historical and geographical associations and meanings, many lying latent and subliminal.

My own experience with history and place goes back to my own origins at an extinct townsite, Palo Alto located in rural Mississippi, which has been connected through family and community back to 1846 when my great-great-grandparents settled there and opened the first store and post office. Digging into the history of the area, I early intuited, was more than procuring and interpreting facts. For every artifact, site, and fact encountered evoked linkages that were both personal, yet, gave rise to larger and larger contexts with each standing for the interconnectedness of personal experience, community life, history, and existence itself along with the associated philosophical questions. Further, the history of Palo Alto beginning in 1846 had no distinct ending leading as it did up through time to me, the teller of the tale. Thus, while the history was about something objective, yet it also took place as an analogical story in my head, which was in turn inside the objective world.

In his thoughtful book *A Place to Remember: Using History to Build Community*, Robert R. Archibald recalled how his quest for a more adequate understanding of his work in historic preservation forced him to read widely and to meditatively explore his own memories of history and place. From this endeavor, came the insight that public history exceeds the usual concerns of scholarship to include the interplay between history, culture, and human life. In effect, it concerns not just facts about material phenomena but more broadly and more inclusively, it concerns *meaning* and *values*. Of all these, the most important is transcendence, the intimation of something beyond, of a reality that transcends and encompasses our very existence. As Archibald observed,

> [Transcendence] is fundamental to humanity and without it we are diminished in capacity and potential, removed from sources of inspiration and the wellsprings of creativity, deprived of tranquility. In these experiences the human spirit soars, insights gleam, and wisdom abounds. And we all seek and require the respite and relief that these experiences provide. Good places, good communities offer people opportunities for inspiration, crucibles for creativity, and realization of potential. The necessity of such places must inform all that we do. This we can know from the past.
>
> (Archibald, 1999, p. 129)

Regarding the experience of place and evocations of transcendence, the French philosopher Paul Ricoeur rhetorically asked,

THE MYSTERY OF HISTORY AND PLACE

Is it simply a residual phenomenon, or an existential protest arising out of the depths of our being, that sends us in search of privileged places, be they our birthplace, the scene of our first love, or the theater of some important historical occurrence—a battle, a revolution, the execution ground of patriots? We return to such places because there a more than everyday reality erupted and because the memory attached to what took place there preserves us from being simply errant vagrants in the world.

(Ricoeur, 1978, p. 31)

This calls to mind a wide range of places such as churches, memorial shrines, temples, and places deemed sacred by American Indian tribes. The terms "sacred" and "holy" are often used in reference to battlefields, realms where reenactors "seek imaginative entry into the heroic past" (Linenthal, 1993, p. 5). If interrogated they might reply that they didn't mean "sacred" in a "religious sense." Regardless of what their definition of a religious sense might be, they do appear to be inchoately expressing the sense of experiencing something that transcends the everydayness of life. Scholars often refer to the work of Rudolf Otto in his seminal work *The Idea of the Holy* (Otto, 1958, originally published 1917) which proposed that the basis of religious traditions was the experience of the holy or sacred which is encountered as the *mysterium tremendum et fascinans*, an ineffable mystery that is both terrifying and tremendous. Another scholar of comparative religion, Mircea Eliade often noted that in a world preoccupied with the material the experience of the sacred still occurs, but is often not recognized behind the "camouflage of the sacred" (Eliade, 1959, pp. 204–208), an experience probably behind many of the references to "sacred" or "holy ground" whether in traditional properties or the majesty experienced by John Muir in the Yosemite Valley. The awareness of this can help give one a sense of place in the world (Elliott, 1994, pp. 33–34).

Such intimations are fundamental as motivations for preserving places and buildings. However, it is often forgotten that the origin of preservation does not derive from sites and buildings per se but from the sites *with* their symbolic associations—"the memory attached to what took place there." The movement originated with attempts to symbolize an inchoately apprehended transcendental order as perceived in a quasi-mythical past and as part of a growing national civil religion (Bellah, 1967), such as the commemorative activities of erecting monuments to historical events and heroes and the preservation of places such as Mount Vernon and Plymouth Rock. In this regard, geographer Lester Rowntree and anthropologist Margaret Conkey observed that preservation movements tended to arise as a process whereby "landscape symbols are promoted to alleviate stress through creation of shared symbolic structures" in which the landscape emerges as a "cosmological symbol" (Rowntree & Conkey, 1980, pp. 459, 468). Similarly, in her study of historic preservation in Charleston, South Carolina, geographer Robin Datel saw the movement offering Charlestonians "the reassurance of a familiar place" a symbol of permanence amidst the flux of change (cf. Datel, 1985; Datel, 1990; Carmichael et al., 1994). In a larger context, this can be seen as part of the Charleston Renaissance in which a body of architects, artists, authors, poets, and preservationists rallied in support of "the betterment of the city" by tapping into the heritage of the area (Florence County Museum).

Similar experiences underlie the National Historic Preservation Act of 1966 (NHPA) which provides the legislative basis of many preservation activities. The spirit of this legislation is articulated in the report, *With Heritage So Rich*, which observed that mobility and change had left Americans with "a feeling of rootlessness combined with a longing for those landmarks of the past which give us a sense of stability and belonging." The report then prophetically stated that

THE MYSTERY OF HISTORY AND PLACE

If the preservation movement is to be successful, it must go beyond saving bricks and mortar. It must go beyond saving occasional historic houses and opening museums. It must be more than a cult of antiquarians. It must do more than revere a few precious national shrines. It must attempt to give a sense of orientation to our society, using structures and objects of the past to establish values of time and place.

(Special Committee on Historic Preservation, 1983, p. 193)

The originating forces were, therefore, not simply concerned with the material that is with saving "old things." Instead, they recognized, however inchoately, that they concerned symbols that expressed a sense of meaning, purpose, and identity, in essence the experience of transcendence. In doing so preservation opposed, albeit unconsciously, two of the ideals of secularism: the hegemony of scientism and the rejection of an exemplary history. However, few grasped the problems that would be incurred by institutionalizing its concerns within a social and intellectual milieu that had abandoned the requisite standards of understanding. As legislation was written and organizations created, few, if any, had the ability to rise above the limitations of modern thought dominated as it is by empirical methods. Subsequently, inherently flawed understandings were institutionalized and promulgated by a flurry of activity focused on technical and regulatory matters.

The Closure of Horizons

Human experience and symbolization take place within social contexts. Social mechanisms serve to promote and disseminate symbols as the means of communication. The establishment of preservation societies and agencies was intended, however inchoately, to promote the dissemination of meanings associated with artifacts and places. However, what is being promoted, and what meaning has been lost?

After I began working for the Historic Preservation Division of the Mississippi Department of Archives and History in December 1985, I intuitively recognized the potential offered for recovering the full range of experience and symbolization. Because my own professional training provided little help in understanding, I began to read widely in matters pertaining to phenomenology of place and comparative religion and eventually began to write and publish articles. Despite these efforts my colleagues were largely uninterested, and my continued efforts were for the most part ignored as if they were rocking the bureaucratic boat. I composed an introduction to our comprehensive plan for historic preservation, designed to recover the importance of these matters. There was no response, and the manuscript soon disappeared.

In an in-house memorandum in 1999, I suggested that the historic preservation movement has a responsibility to go beyond intellectual provincialism to a recovery of the fundamental principles involved in interpreting the symbolic dimension of place. After all, preservation purports to be concerned with the preservation and dissemination of symbols from the past which have implications for bettering the public's horizons of understanding and moral concern. It seems obvious that preservationists should have an understanding of the matters with which they are concerned. Unfortunately, this is not always the case. My memorandum was not well received, and I was called into the office of the Deputy SHPO. His major concern was that calling the preservation profession to reflection upon the spirit of its mission was overstepping the bounds, bounds apparently defined by an uncritical adherence to the letter of the law and the regulations. To make his point, he told a story:

> There are millions of automobiles in use every day. Every morning people get up and go to work in them. Cars throng the highways. Inside each car is a complex mechanism that permits it to move. Yet very, very few drivers have any understanding of the mechanics involved in the automobiles. Nor do they need to. Preservationists are like the drivers, and preservation is like the cars. Preservationists work with preservation on a day to day basis. They are paid to do this. Yet do they need to understand what preservation is about? Of course not!

Then came the concluding line: "Preservationists are *not* paid to think!"

I could only think that this "parable" was askew, but in a manner that was insightful into the problem. By comparing preservationists to drivers, they were clearly perceived as being passive users of a product rather than active designers. I was informed that I must uncritically adhere to bureaucratic mandates. If they were flawed and even self-defeating, the problems were outside our purview to critique and we must plod on obediently. The broader implications exemplify an institutional setting in which (1) professionals are trained in a positivistic tradition based on "objective" knowledge with little ability to deal with the attendant depths of meaning, and (2) the bureaucracies to coordinate professional activities actively discourage and suppress the questioning of flawed concepts. In other words, the institutional background of historic preservation effectively suppresses the very thought that is required to understand and communicate its concerns.

Nor was I alone to recognize such problems. Robert Archibald reflected his growing awareness of a discrepancy between history as a scholarly discipline and history as a dimension of human life. Upon beginning a career as museum curator, he discovered that his scholarly training was inadequate for understanding the multidimensionality of the lived experience of history primarily because the "mantle of objective distance" associated with his training equated "the search [for truth]…with the use of scientific methodology"(Archibald, 1999, pp. 20–31, 117–118, 155–158). Similarly, William J. Murtagh, the National Park Service's first Keeper of the National Register, has observed: "Inexplicably, many preservation leaders seem to have lost sight of the motives which once fueled their movement and have become preoccupied with *how* to preserve…with little or no discrimination as to *what* they are preserving and *why*" (Lewis, 1975; cf. Buttimer, 1980; French, 1980; Percy, 1996; Murtagh, 1997, p. 167; Pannekoek, 1998, p. 30). While these methods might be appropriate for positivistic scholarship, they provided little understanding of his principal concerns.

In simple, if historic preservation has been assigned the task of dealing with an elusive quality of experience such as symbolism, then the practitioners who provide the primary interface with the public should be able to interpret significance in a manner that does it justice. The recognition of the dimension of meaning involved has led some to searching for what is perceived to be meaningful, an approach that has much to offer. However, it does offer the possibility of reifying the experience, by elevating what may be little more than nostalgia or a fleeting fixation, which could thereby be transformed into a matter of great public concern.

The originating forces were, therefore, not simply concerned with the material, i.e. saving "old things." Instead, they recognized, however inchoately, that they concerned symbols that expressed a sense of meaning, purpose, and identity, in essence the experience of transcendence. In doing so, preservation opposed, albeit unconsciously, two of the ideals of secularism: the hegemony of scientism and the rejection of an exemplary history. However, few grasped the problems that would be incurred by institutionalizing its concerns within a social and intellectual milieu that had abandoned the requisite standards of understanding. As legislation was written and organizations created, few, if any, had the ability to rise above the limitations of modernistic thought. Subsequently, inherently flawed understandings were institutionalized and promulgated by a flurry of activity focused on technical and regulatory matters.

These are exemplified by the use of the term "significance," which plays a critical role in preservation legislation and regulations from as early as the Historic Sites Act of 1935 through the 1966 NHPA, among others. At a conference devoted to examining the concept, Katherine H. Stevenson observed that it is "the central, defining core of our programs because it specifies the universe of properties that we recognize, protect, provide assistance to, and interpret" (Stevenson, 1998, p. 16). Yet the notion of significance was based upon an erroneous assumption—that it is a characteristic inherent in a property, that is to say, that it exists in a property and has little relation to more comprehensive considerations of meaning. For example, the NHPA states that "[t]he quality of significance…is *present in* districts, sites, buildings, structures, and objects [emphasis added]" which possess integrity and meet at least one of the four National Register criteria of significance. All of these criteria are based upon objective and associative characteristics, effectively separating them in thought and practice from the traditional concerns with symbolic qualities that to expand our horizons of understanding and moral concern (Tainter & Lucas, 1983). Historical properties could then be effectively placed under the purview of various scholarly disciplines, whose practitioners, trained only in studying objective phenomena, were unable to comprehend that the concept was "illogical, unworkable, and [did] not entirely suit the purpose for which it was intended" (Tainter & Lucas, 1983, p. 715). By implication, history is no more than a material process affording things to study and collect as pastimes for antiquarians and aesthetes.

These concerns have become institutionalized, so that incentives are locked into place for endless continuation, while there are disincentives for the few who question the status quo. The most pervasive disincentive is the entrenched incomprehension of that which falls outside of effectively methodological purviews creating an intellectual/social milieu which isolates those who would recall the movement to a broader vision. For persistent gadflies, social pressures can be more direct. With its institutional and financial basis and its public visibility, the preservation movement serves to legitimize the notion that culture and heritage are little more than old stuff. The reduction of meaning to material terms has two direct implications. First, it indicates that thinking based upon positivistic assumptions is so deeply engrained that few notice that culture and significance have been reduced to little more than the sum total of material objects that exist in a given space. Second, it provides the basis for endless bureaucratic activity that would disseminate these flawed notions to the public.

The ramifications are readily apparent. Mandated by the NHPA with the task of identifying and preserving "significant" properties, the federal government placed the National Park Service in charge of the agenda and state historic preservation offices were created to assist. Additionally, the federal agencies involved with lands such as the U.S. Army Corps of Engineers, the National Forest Service, and the Bureau of Land Management all created divisions or departments with "heritage managers" to oversee "cultural resources" as one manages coal, petroleum, timber, and wildlife. Preservationists in their employ had no trouble finding endless numbers of artifacts, buildings, and sites that fit within the broadly defined criteria of significance, all of which had to be surveyed, inventoried, nominated to the National Register, or archaeologically excavated. Additionally, the availability of vast sums of money for archaeological work to "preserve cultural heritage" endangered by projects using the federal funds launched a new industry in which companies have been created to excavate sites and, in general, engage in Cultural Resources Management (CRM). While the modern world has largely forgotten its cultural heritage, in one sense of the term, government entities and CRM firms now retrieve masses of artifacts and arcane information, all dutifully stored in climate-controlled environments for the edification of posterity. The availability of grants for National Register properties and other cultural projects has spawned the growth of museums and conferences, while the marketability of cultural projects has fostered "heritage tourism" initiatives for attracting tourist business—heritage as a commodity.

We are now seemingly drowning in "heritage," a term often used but seldom commented on despite its seeming importance. We "celebrate" it at cultural festivals and cultural museums. We turn the homes of musicians, artists, and entertainers into shrines to these gurus and saints of the new age. Experts wait in the wings ready to provide lectures on arcane cultural and historical topics. Hardly anything that humanity has ever created is beneath being treated like sacred relics. Not surprisingly, there is virtually no understanding as to what it means. One would be hard pressed to find any serious discussion of the spiritual dimensions of life in this frenzy of activity. Instead we are surrounded by the propagandistic usage of terms such as "multiculturalism" and "cultural diversity" that forgo the search for meaning for facile celebrations of "many truths" that glibly abandon the pursuit of any truth common to all. As Jacques Barzun observed, although there is

> more and more cultural stuff to house, classify, docket, consult, and teach...in the qualitative, honorific sense, culture...is declining. It is doing so virtually in proportion as the various cultural endeavors—all this collecting and exhibiting and performing and encouraging—grow and spread with well-meant public and private support.
>
> (Barzun, 1989, pp. 4–5)

David Lowenthal has also commented on this state of affairs:

> Preservation has deepened our knowledge of the past but dampened creative use of it. Specialists learn more than ever about our central biblical and classical traditions, but most people now lack an informed appreciation of them. Our precursors identified with a unitary antiquity whose fragmented vestiges became models for their own creations. Our own more numerous and exotic pasts, prized as vestiges, are divested of the iconographic meanings they once embodied. It is no longer the presence of the past that speaks to us, but its pastness. Now a foreign country with a booming tourist trade, the past has undergone the usual consequences of popularity. The more it is appreciated for its own sake, the less real or relevant it becomes.
>
> (Lowenthal, 1985, p. xvii)

Spanning the San Andreas Fault

Human existence finds itself in an immeasurably small present located between a remembered past and an anticipated future. All human knowing and action take place within this framework despite naïve and polarizing claims that champion either the return to a Golden Age and the rejection of the future or the rejection of a dark past in favor of an enlightened future. With a dominance of empirical science, the past has often been reduced to little more than a source of information rather than the basis of self-understanding a with symbolism spanning facts and values enmeshed in an awareness of the transcendent mystery.

Radical Preservation was conceived to serve as a gadfly to raise questions and critique the preservation movement calling it to recover the holistic experiential base lying beneath the call to preserve symbolic elements of the landscape. The primary goal is to establish the foundational role of preservation as a radical hermeneutic, an interpretation that aims to recover a more comprehensive understanding and to disseminate it to its public through recovering the symbolism inherent—not in the landscape per se—but in our experience of the landscape.

There is no permanent meaning to material things, that is meaning is not "inherent" in them. Instead, they have primarily the *potential* of being meaningful, a potential that is actualized in the present experience and upon reflection. This potentiality can vary based upon the physical nature of places and their symbolic linkages (e.g. Kronborg Castle and its linkage to Hamlet). Furthermore, experiences of place are not unique and idiosyncratic. The search for unity, or commonalities, is critical for understanding this and communicating it to the public. If everything is idiosyncratic then there is no common basis for recognizing communicating anything.

Consciousness of history and place spans a range of what Voegelin termed the complex of experience and symbolization with the two going hand-in-hand. Without conscious experience of reality, there is no symbolization, just as there are no symbols without experience; to forget the experience behind the symbolization is to render the latter meaningless. Because experience and symbolization occur within the same reality, we see equivalences between similar experiences and symbolizations that appear cross-culturally from perceptible objects and the facts that describe them to the experience of mystery and the multivalent symbols that point to it (Voegelin, 1990). In these equivalences we find commonalities.

Because history is a process in which we exist, it plays a formative role in our personal existence whether we recognize it or not. This realization is behind the traditional concerns with personal formation (whether they be Confucian learning or Greek *paideia*) that promote the cultivation of virtues such as wisdom and *pietas* through exposure to insights and symbols from the past. Because historic preservation is concerned with the symbolism of history and questions pertaining to basic principles, it would not be far off mark to say that it has a stake in encouraging these virtues. This would necessarily involve raising horizons of understanding and moral concern, effecting personal transformation through exposure to symbols from the past. Closely related to wisdom is the virtue of *pietas*, or piety, which, despite its popular meaning today, refers to a respect for nature, other people, and the past, respect growing out of the knowledge that they represent a larger community of being to which we owe our existence and our responsibility. Richard Weaver described *pietas* as a "lost power or lost capacity for wonder and enchantment" (Weaver, 1995, p. 28).

Wisdom and *pietas* are concerned with transcendental values—the True, the Good, and the Beautiful. According to Freeman Tilden in his wise little book, *Interpreting Our Heritage*, Beauty is the key to understanding the need to preserve because Beauty is the call of wonder, the call toward something beyond, the guide toward the True and the Good. He wrote that it is "the path along which our quest for understanding must go. Surely we deal with an essence that is beyond our powers of expression. But we can, and we do, feel its reality" (Tilden, 1977). Beauty is represented in part in those places which despite their imperfections possess a *genius loci*, a sense of place, that call us to wonder at that which transcends the empirical.

Radical Preservation is a call to recover, not just the roots of the preservation movement but the roots of human experience and that which has been forgotten in the modern world with its positivistic focus on the empirical. Beyond simply saving bricks and mortar it is also a call to a broader, more inclusive hermeneutic that also evaluates historic places in terms of their symbolic potential.

Furthermore, preservationists must be able to communicate this to the public and instill within it an understanding that goes beyond seeing preservation as a matter of saving old stuff. Such a hermeneutic is demanded by the very nature of a field that invokes the aura of mystery found at privileged places. In doing so, Radical Preservation lays out an approach that spans Percy's San Andreas Fault of the modern mind.

Bibliography

Archibald, R.R. (1999). *A place to remember: Using history to build community.* Walnut Creek, CA: AltaMira.

Barzun, J. (1989). *The culture we deserve.* Middletown, CT: Wesleyan University Press.

Bellah, R.N. (1967). Civil religion in America. *Daedalus*, 96, 1–21.

Buttimer, A. (1980). Home, reach, and the sense of place. In Buttimer, A., & Seamon, D., (Eds.), *The human experience of space and place,* New York, NY: St. Martin's Press, 166–187.

Carmichael, D.L., Hubert, J., Reeves, B., & Schanche, A. (Eds.). (1994). *Sacred sites, sacred places.* London: Routledge.

Datel, R.E. (1985). Preservation and a sense of orientation for American cities. *Geographical Review*, 75, 125–141.

Datel, R.E. (1990). Southern regionalism and historic preservation in Charleston, South Carolina, 1920–1940. *Journal of Historical Geography*, 16, 197–215.

Eiseley, L.C. (1971). *The night country: Reflections of a bone hunting man.* New York, NY: Charles Scribner's Sons.

Eliade, M. (1959). *The sacred and the profane: The nature of religion.* New York, NY: Harcourt Brace Jovanovich.

Elliott, J.D., Jr. (1994). Drinking from the well of the past: Historic preservation and the sacred. *Historic Preservation Forum*, 8(3), 26–35.

Elliott, J.D., Jr. (2002). Radical preservation: Toward a new and more ancient paradigm. *Forum Journal*, 16(3), 50–56.

Florence County Museum. The Charleston Renaissance, Florence, SC. Retrieved from www.flocomuseum.org/charleston-renaissance/the-charleston-renaissance/

French, R.S. (1980). On preserving America: Some philosophical observations. In the National Trust for Historic Preservation (Ed.), *Preservation: Toward an ethic in the 1980s,* Washington, DC: The Preservation Press, 182–192.

Hughes, G. (1993). *Mystery and myth in the philosophy of Eric Voegelin.* Columbia, MO: University of Missouri Press.

Lewis, P.F. (1975). The future of the past: Our clouded vision of historic preservation. *Pioneer America*, 7(1), 1–20.

Linenthal, E.T. (1993). *Sacred ground: Americans and their battlefields.* Urbana, IL: University of Illinois Press.

Lowenthal, D. (1985). *The past is a foreign country.* Cambridge, UK: Cambridge University Press.

Mann, T. (1945). *Joseph and his brothers.* New York, NY: Alfred A. Knopf.

McMahon, R. (1999). Eric Voegelin's paradoxes of consciousness and participation. *Review of Politics*, 61, 117–139.

Moe, R. (2002). President's report: The power of place. *Forum Journal*, 16(2), 9–14.

Murtagh, W.J. (1997). *Keeping time: The history and theory of preservation in America.* New York, NY: John Wiley & Sons.

Norberg-Schulz, C. (1980). *Genius loci: Towards a phenomenology of architecture.* New York, NY: Rizzoli.

Otto, R. (1958). *The idea of the holy: An inquiry into the non-rational factor in the idea of the divine and its relation to the rational.* London: Oxford University Press.

Pannekoek, F. (1998). The Rise of a heritage priesthood." In M.A. Tomlan (Ed.), *Preservation: Of What, for Whom?* Ithaca, NY: National Council for Preservation Education, 29–36.

Percy, G. (1996). Preservation at a crossroads. *Historic Preservation Forum*, 10(3), 30–35.

Percy, W. (1991). The fateful rift: The San Andreas Fault in the modern mind. In P. Samway (Ed.), *Walker Percy: Signposts in a strange land.* New York, NY: Farrar, Straus, and Giroux, 271–291.

Ricoeur, P. (1978). Manifestation and proclamation. *The Journal of the Blaisdell Institute*, 12, 13–35.

Rowntree, L.B., & Conkey, M.W. (1980). Symbolism and the cultural landscape. *Annals of the Association of American Geographers*, 70, 459–474.

Special Committee on Historic Preservation. (1983). *With heritage so rich*. Washington, DC: The Preservation Press.

Stevenson, K.H. (1998). Opening comments. In M.A. Tomlan (Ed.), *Preservation: Of What, for Whom?* Ithaca, NY: The National Council for Preservation Education, 15–17.

Tainter, J.A., & Lucas, G.J. (1983). Epistemology of the significance concept. *American Antiquity*, XLVIII, 708–712.

Tilden, F. (1977). *Interpreting our heritage*. Chapel Hill: University of North Carolina Press.

Trepanier, L. (2016, September 30). The recovery of science in Eric Voegelin's thought. *Voegelinview*. Retrieved from *https://voegelinview.com/recovery-science-eric-voegelins-thought/*

Tuan, Y. (1977). *Space and place: The perspective of experience*. Minneapolis, MN: University of Minnesota Press.

Voegelin, E. (1990). Equivalences of experience and symbolization in history. In E. Sandoz (Ed.), *The collected works of Eric Voegelin*. Baton Rouge: Louisiana State University Press, Vol. 12, 115–133.

Voegelin, E. (2000). The new science of politics. In M. Henningsen (Ed.), *The collected works of Eric Voegelin*. Columbia: University of Missouri Press, Vol. 5, 75–241.

Walter, E.V. (1988). *Placeways: A theory of the human environment*. Chapel Hill: University of North Carolina Press.

Weaver, R.M. (1995). Prologue: Up from liberalism. In J.A. Scotchie (Ed.), *The vision of Richard Weaver*. New Brunswick, NJ: Transaction, 19–36.

Webb, E. (1981). *Eric Voegelin: Philosopher of history*. Seattle: University of Washington Press.

PART 2

Ways to Gather Evidence

CHAPTER 5

The Perception and Preservation of Vernacular Architectural Features in an Urban Historic District with Heritage Value

A Case Study from Grand Rapids, Michigan

You Kyong Ahn

Traditionally, historic preservation concentrated on the preservation of individually distinctive architectural traits of historic properties, such as monumental buildings. However, during the late twentieth century, historic preservation in the United States extended to include the preservation of an urban setting with little architectural distinction as a community's heritage symbol. The field's broadened scale owes to the recognitions of the unique cultural legacy of the nation (e.g., Native Indian's heritage sites), increase of minority ethnic groups and homogeneity, and loss of human dimensions in urban environments (Barthel, 1996; Cantacuzino, 1989; Diamonstein, 1978; Fitch, 2001; Jacob, 1989; Mason, 2004, 2006; Parker, 1993, 1998; Powell, 1999; Powter and Ross, 2005; Stubb, 2009; Tainter and Lucas, 1983; Wells, 2011a, 2011b).

The definition of a historic district on the National Register of Historic Places reflects this shifted mood in historic preservation. According to the National Register, a district can be historic because of the unified identity of its undistinguished buildings as well as the individual identities of its distinguished buildings (National Park Service, 1995). In this definition, preservation of the distinguished signifies the traditional preservation that identified architectural conservation with historic preservation.[1] Meanwhile, preservation of the undistinguished demonstrates the recent heritage conservation that values the sociocultural footprint of vernacular buildings (Denslagen, 1994; Hayden, 1995; Park, 1998, 2006; Parker, 1997; Powter and Ross, 2005; Stipe, 1989, 2003; Stubb, 2009).

THE PERCEPTION AND PRESERVATION

For preservation of these historic districts, historic district preservation guidelines are referred to. The guidelines were developed based on the Secretary of the Interior's Standards for Historic Preservation that were initiated in accordance with traditional preservation. For this reason, the guidelines list individual architectural features to preserve and articulate the importance of those features (Fitch, 2001; Murtagh, 1997; Park, 1998, 2006; Stipe, 1989; Weeks and Grimmer 1995; Wells, 2011a). However, the guidelines rarely clarify how these individual features are possibly linked to the collective identity of vernacular buildings as cultural/heritage symbolism. As a result, a question arises regarding how to deal with these individual features in an urban vernacular district with a heritage value. Should the vernacular architectural features be simply preserved and/or restored as in architectural conservation? If not, how should these features be thought and treated in conjunction with the preservation of such a district?

Literature Review

In an urban district preserved for its heritage value, the importance of its architectural features lies in its community's reciprocal relationship with the features (Alderson, 2006; Barthel, 1996; Day, 2002; Handler, 2014; Mason, 2004, 2006; Spenneman, 2006; Stubbs, 2009; Wells, 2011a, 2011b). Reciprocity is generated by how community people interplay with the physical/architectural features. Through individual and social activities, such as daily meetings, frequent visits, and community events in the environment, community people embody their feelings in the architectural features and subsequently impart important meanings to the features (Brand, 1995; Day, 2002; Dewey, 1934; Langer, 1953; Hayden, 1995; Lynch 1972; Schneekloth and Shibley 1995, 2000; Tuan, 1977).

For this reason, the meaning of architectural features originates from the decoding phase rather than the encoding – production – phase. The obtained meaning makes specific architectural features a part of a community's reality (Brand, 1995; Day, 2002; Clark, 2003; Dewey, 1934; Harmansah, 2011; Lefebvre, 1996; Rasmussen, 1964; Williams, 2007). From this perspective, Lefebvre (1996) asserts that both social and material (e.g., architectural) entities shape urban reality. The two entities are then intertwined by two different orders in a city: *near order and far order*. The former is the public value that stems from public users' interactions and connections with their buildings. In the meantime, the latter refers to the social and political ideologies of powerful institutions (e.g., Church, State) embedded in the architectural style and details of monumental building (Lefebvre, 1996:101). For instance, a monumental religious building conveys *far order* basically. However, Lefebvre (1996:101) continues to say that even such a building can only be an urban reality when the building serves the users' social practices and represents "near order."

It should be noted that a community's reciprocal relationship with architectural features involves their social and cognitive procedure in a given environment. In a community's experiential stream, specific architectural features remain meaningful in their minds through the operation of memory. Inevitably, the architectural features become mnemonic, rhetorical, and therefore, memorable. Community's memory is not simply individual, but also collective (Barthel, 1996; Day, 2002; Downing, 2000; Huyssen, 2003; Halbwachs, 1992; Langer, 1953; Lowenthal, 1985; Mason, 2004; Parker, 1997; Spenneman, 2006). Halbwachs (1992) even remarks that individuals cannot conceptualize their experiences outside of a society. The coherent pattern of experiences is coined externally. To put it simply, recollection is made and recognized meaningful only in its social context (Halbwachs, 1992). The nature of memory indicates that the importance of architecture is shared in a community's sub-consciousness. Consequently, specific architectural features serve as a source of a community's collective identity (Barthel, 1996; Halbwachs, 1992; Huyssen, 2003; Mason, 2004; Parker, 1997).

As a humanistic endeavor, contemporary historic conservation attempts to manage collective memory/identity by preserving important architectural features (Barthel, 1996; Day, 2002; Lyon, 1999; Mason, 2004; Spenneman, 2006; Stubbs, 2009). Mason (2004:64–65) says,

> Conceptually the heart of historic preservation lies in the intellectual and emotional connections we make between memory and environment. … The raison d'être of historic preservation is to be the cultivation of memory.

This contention upholds the inclusion of heritage value in present-day historic preservation and challenges the traditional view that sees historic value as firmly attached to architectural elements. A heritage value embraces community people's collective memory/identity derived from their everyday social practices. That is to say, heritage value of architectural features owes rarely to the features' innate, unchanging, and tangible attributes. Besides, during the on-going social procedure, community people constantly reinterpret their past experiences. Not all the past experiences become meaningful and develop into coherent pattern for their present memory. Meaning of the past opens to transformation in the influx of changing community's life way and visions. Thus, preservation of collective memory brings a dynamic and complex dimension to historic preservation (Alderson, 2006; Araoz, 2008; Barthel, 1996; Day, 2002; Denslagen, 1994; Handler, 2014; Hayden, 1995; Huyssen, 2003; Lowenthal, 1985; Lynch, 1972; Mitchell, 2008; Park, 2006; Spenneman, 2006; Stipe, 1989, 2003; Stubbs, 2009; Tainter and Lucas, 1983; Powter and Ross, 2005; Mason, 2004, 2006: Wells, 2011a, 2011b).

As a result, the importance of community input arose in historic preservation. For instance, in an attempt to achieve a public consensus, the Secretary of the Interior's Standards for Preservation Planning of 1983[2] and the Advisory Council on Historic Preservation Guidelines for Public Participation in Historic Preservation Review of 1988[3] were stipulated in order to promote community participation throughout preservation procedure. Still, many preservationist professionals deal with architectural features as if their value is simply tied to physical elements (Green, 1999; Mason, 2004, 2006; Milligan, 1998). Furthermore, despite the recognition of the community's role in the extended historic preservation, the process and method for quality of community input has not been discussed enough in the field. For these reasons, community's voices are often excluded even in preserving their own urban vernacular district (Hart et al., 2014; Hayden, 1995; Wells, 2011a).

Case Study Objectives and Example

In that the heritage value is in the reciprocal procedure between the community and their physical/architectural environment, preservation professionals should not simply conform to the traditional method in preserving a heritage value of an urban historic district. In this regard, this study claims that a community's dynamic relationship with their architectural features should be examined and documented in a systematic way. The document should be referred to as a fundamental resource for legitimate preservation practice in an urban historic district.

Based on this assertion, an empirical research was developed and implemented for a case study of an urban historic district characterized by vernacular buildings. The case study aimed to illustrate how vernacular architectural features should be conceived and dealt with in the urban historic district preserved for its heritage value; and how the empirical study can provide a practical resource for community-oriented preservation in such an urban historic district.

Wealthy Heights, Grand Rapids in Michigan was selected as case study example. Wealthy Heights was developed by Dutch immigrants who flocked to the area to work for a greenhouse. They built simple and cottage-style small houses in the area (Figure 5.1). The closing of this greenhouse and suburbanization in the 1960s and 1970s fostered the declination of this neighborhood. By the mid-1990s, many residential buildings were abandoned (City of East Grand Rapids, 2014; East Hills Council of Neighbors, 2005; Grand Rapids Historic Preservation Commission, 2007).

The non-profit organization South East Economic Development (SEED) was established to re-habilitate the neighborhood in 1986. The neighborhood was designated as a part of the Wealthy Theatre historic district by the city of Grand Rapids in 1997 because of its historic significance in community planning and development and ethnic heritage (Bennett et al., 1997). In 2003, the East Hills[4] Council of Neighbors and local public, private, and non-profit organizations launched the Wealthy Heights Initiative to accelerate the neighborhood redevelopment (East Hills Council of Neighbors, 2012). The principles of the initiative were affordability, neighborhood connectivity, discouragement of existing residents' displacement, social diversity, and public/private collaboration.

As subsequent efforts, the East Hills Council of Neighbors developed an Urban Forest Plan in 2009 and a Public Space Strategy in 2014 (East Hills Council of Neighbors, 2009). The latter promotes historic preservation and public space design as well (Bennett et al., 1997; East Hills Council of Neighbors, 2014). Since the announcement of the Initiative, many rehabilitation and infill construction, including the Habitat's net zero housing projects, have been conducted. The Habitat's projects intend to provide energy-efficient and affordable residences for low-income community people while coping with historic preservation guidelines (Habitat for Humanity of Kent County, 2010).

Methods

For the case study, a mixed method composed of quantitative survey and focus group was developed. These two methods were complementary in studying community participants' perceptions and preservation of vernacular building features in Wealthy Heights (Berg, 2011; Groat and Wang, 2001; Sutton, 2009). The quantitative survey was for a systematic understanding of the importance of its vernacular architectural features. Then, the focus group was for an in-depth understanding of their importance and appropriate treatments for preservation of Wealthy Heights.

A web survey using a quantitative scale was designed first to compare the preservation features of Wealthy Heights to those of Heritage Hill. Heritage Hill is the largest residential historic district of the City of Grand Rapids that contains over sixty architectural styles (e.g., Colonial Revival, Greek Revival, Italianate, and Prairie styles). It was designated as historic for the architectural significance by the National Register in 1973 (Grand Rapids Historic Preservation Commission, 2007; National Register of Historic Preservation, 2011) (Figure 5.1). This comparative study was to know where Wealthy Heights falls in the scope of urban historic districts in terms of the importance of its architectural features.

Following the web survey, the focus group with the Wealthy Heights community participants was planned. The narrative evidence from the focus group aimed to reveal the underlying reasons

THE PERCEPTION AND PRESERVATION

Figure 5.1 Residential buildings in Wealthy Heights (Top) and Heritage Hill (Bottom). Photograph by the author.

of the quantitative survey results and their relations to preservation of the vernacular architectural features. This qualitative part intended to gather information from the participants in regard to the following outcomes:

1. To understand how participants perceive integral characteristics of vernacular architectural features.

2. To understand what motivated participants' perceptions of vernacular architectural features.

3. To understand how participants' perceptions of vernacular architectural features are associated with importance and appropriate treatments of the features.

Survey Design and Implementation

Research materials were developed for a quantitative web-survey that tests the important degrees of architectural features to preserve in Wealthy Heights and Heritage Hill. First, a list of preservation features including twenty-one architectural features was determined based on the historic district preservation guidelines of various U.S. cities (Table 5.1).[5] Then, photos showcasing the determined features[6] were collected to develop typological images of the features. Categorizing, simplifying, and generalizing the photographs to test the viewers' general understanding of the importance of preservation features in urban historic districts developed the typology.

The use of typologies is underpinned by studies in architecture and cognitive science. Typology is a common method in studying, generalizing, and visualizing architectural forms and styles (McAlester and McAlester, 1984). Furthermore, many cognitive scientists accentuate the effectiveness of typological images in investigating viewers' general understanding of environmental features. They state that representative extents of images are connected with humans' general understanding of environmental images, not necessarily the similarity of the images to the real world (Abu-Obeid, 1993; Argan, 1996; Kwun, 2001; Colquhoun, 1996; Mahdjoubi and Wiltshire, 2001). Accordingly,

Table 5.1 Thirty-Six Preservation Features Listed in the Guidelines of the Sample U.S. Historic Districts

Preservation Features	U.S. Historic Districts								
Items	**A**	**B**	**C**	**D**	**E**	**F**	**G**	**H**	**I**
Shape and arrangement of building blocks		✓	✓	✓					✓
Scale of building blocks		✓	✓						✓
Orientation of site (direction of building face)		✓	✓	✓	✓	✓		✓	✓
Lot size		✓	✓	✓	✓				✓
Grass lawn			✓		✓				
Street pattern		✓	✓						✓
Walkways		✓	✓			✓	✓	✓	✓
Paving	✓		✓			✓	✓	✓	✓
Walls and fences	✓	✓	✓	✓	✓	✓	✓	✓	✓
Lighting	✓			✓			✓	✓	✓
Plantings	✓		✓		✓	✓	✓		✓
Spacing between buildings		✓		✓	✓				✓
Front yard setback		✓	✓	✓	✓	✓			✓
Driveway access			✓	✓		✓	✓		
Building scale and height		✓	✓	✓	✓	✓		✓	✓
Façade alignment patterns		✓	✓		✓			✓	✓
Ratio of solid-to-void (wall-to-opening)		✓	✓	✓					
Colors							✓	✓	✓
Formal treatment of building entrance (e.g., location, scale of entry, height of entry above street level)		✓	✓		✓	✓		✓	
Porch configuration (e.g., location and scale of entry, height of porch above street level)	✓			✓	✓	✓	✓	✓	
Garage and/or carriage houses	✓			✓	✓				
Building style	✓	✓			✓		✓	✓	✓
Exterior wall materials (e.g., brick, stone, stucco, wood siding, metal siding)	✓	✓	✓	✓	✓	✓	✓	✓	✓
Fenestration (arrangement of windows)			✓	✓					✓
Relief to building elevation	✓	✓	✓		✓			✓	✓
Roof pitch and shape	✓		✓		✓	✓	✓	✓	✓
Roof materials (e.g., shingles: wooden, asphalt, metal)	✓	✓	✓	✓	✓	✓	✓	✓	✓
Roof details (e.g., edge or sofit, and brackets)	✓				✓	✓	✓	✓	✓
Window shape and size	✓		✓			✓	✓	✓	
Window proportion	✓		✓			✓		✓	
Window materials (e.g., pane: single glass, double glass; vinyl: frame: wooden, metal, fiber glass)	✓		✓	✓	✓	✓	✓	✓	✓

Preservation Features	U.S. Historic Districts								
Items	A	B	C	D	E	F	G	H	I
Door shape and size	✓		✓						
Door proportion	✓		✓						
Door materials and finishes (e.g., door and frame: wooden, steel, aluminum)	✓		✓	✓	✓				✓
Decorative elements with functions (e.g., dormer, turret, chimney, column, guardrail, step, vent, gutter, baluster, screen)	✓			✓	✓	✓	✓	✓	✓
Decorative and aesthetic elements (e.g., pediment, pilaster, cornice, frieze, window trim and surround)	✓			✓	✓	✓	✓	✓	✓

A: Grand Rapids, MI, **B**: Salt Lake City, UT (Capitol Hill D), **C**: Norfolk, VA (Ghent HD), **D**: Bolivar, MO, **E**: Colorado Springs, CO (North End HD), **F**: San Antonio, TX, **G**: Syracuse, NY (Sedgwick-Highland-James PD), **H**: City of Monroe, WA (Borlin Park neighborhood), **I**: Ridgewood, NJ (Ridgewood Village Center HD).

typologies that convey the nature of each preservation feature (e.g., style, proportion, material, color) were created to examine how participants see the importance of preservation features in a general sense. These images were hand drawn and water colored to grab a participant's attention. Notes about specific materials and decorative details were added to help viewers understand a given image (Figure 5.2).

Along with development of the typologies, photographs of Wealthy Heights and Heritage Hill were taken and assorted according to the listed features. These photographs were engendered to check participants' perceptions of preservation features of their own historic districts. Both quantitative and qualitative values of the photographs were considered to develop these survey materials. The representative values of the typologies and photographs for the preservation features were consulted with members of the neighborhood organizations, East Hills[7] Council of Neighbors and Heritage Hill Association (Figure 5.2).

This survey consisted of four parts: demographic information, basic knowledge of historic preservation and knowledge of Wealthy Heights and Heritage Hill, rating of the importance of determined preservation features on a general basis, and rating of the importance of preservation features in Wealthy Heights and Heritage Hill. The typological images and the collage of the sorted photographs were used for the third and fourth parts, respectively. The third part intended to provide a basis for comparative measure between Wealthy Heights and Heritage Hill. In these last two parts, the system of importance ratings was set up on a scale from one to five, with one being "Not at all important" and five being "Extremely important" (Figure 5.3).

Community members of Wealthy Heights and Heritage Hill were contacted to ask for their participation in this web survey with the aid of the two neighborhood associations. The short description and web link of this survey and invitations were sent to community members primarily through emails from their respective neighborhood associations. The same things were also posted on neighborhood association websites and the neighborhood associations' Facebook pages to recruit community members.[8] Participants were anonymously and randomly assigned to the survey conditions. A total of 219 responses came in; 120 completed the survey. Ninety-one of these completed surveys

THE PERCEPTION AND PRESERVATION

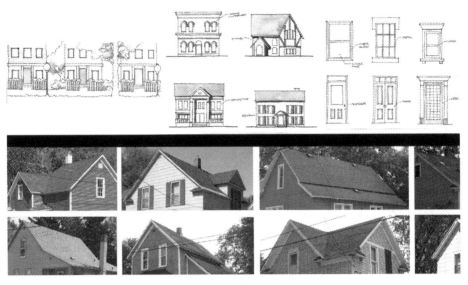

Figure 5.2 Examples of typological (Top) and photographic images of preservation features (Right). Photograph by the author.

Figure 5.3 Examples of web pages asking about important degrees of preservation features. Photography by the author.

came from current residents of the Heritage Hill district, and twenty-nine of them indicated being current East Hills residents.[9] Six out of these twenty-nine said that they were currently dwelling in Wealthy Heights.

The data were exported from Qualtrics and further analyses were done in Stata. Frequency and descriptive statistics were run for the first two parts. Two-sample t-test with unequal variance was the method of understanding the comparative nature of the study, which was used for the third and fourth parts.[10] Two sets – the typological set and the set of photographs – about a total of thirty-seven[11] preservation features were probed for differences in the mean response by the two participant groups by use of this method. An important thing to note is that this study concentrates on the test of participants' perceptions of twenty-one architectural features and discussions on the test results. The inclusion of all the listed preservation items in the survey and its data analyses, however, represents the reality that any architectural feature cannot be experienced as separated from the whole historic environment.

THE PERCEPTION AND PRESERVATION

Figure 5.4 Focus group: the group discussions (Left) and individual tour (Right). Photograph by the author.

Focus Group Design and Implementation

The focus group was composed of two parts. First, the group interview with East Hills' survey participants was made for an hour at the site of the former greenhouse. Due to the open outdoor quality of the site, this allowed participants to view the district preservation features during the interview. The survey images of the Wealthy Heights features were presented again on four presentation boards (30″ × 40″). Participants were asked to mark the acceptable degree of change to each categorical feature presented on the boards. Three-colored stickers – green, yellow, and red – were used for their markings. The three colors represented "No change," "Moderate change," and "Radical change," respectively (Figure 5.4). Afterwards, group discussions on importance and appropriate changes of each feature were conducted based on the outcomes of the marking activities.

The second part of the focus group was an individual tour of the district. This phase was intended to gather more of participants' subjective voices. Each individual participant was paired with a scribe/recorder to walk around the district for 20 to 30 minutes. During this tour, they were directed to point out desired and undesired features and reasons of their perceptions. Assistants[12] accompanied participants to facilitate their talk through each thought. Both group and individual interviews were video-recorded. Upon the completion of each tour, a small compensation[13] was made (Figure 5.4). The video-recorded data were transcribed and then, organized based on recurring ideas/comments.

The focus group participants were recruited by asking the web survey participants about their interest in a follow-up study at the end of the survey. Among the twenty-nine East Hills survey participants, eighteen expressed their interest. These eighteen participants were contacted and informed of the focus group meeting via emails. Seven out of the eighteen showed up for the focus group.

Results: Demographic Backgrounds and Association with Historic Districts

In this survey, slightly more females (East Hills [EH]: 65%; Heritage Hill [HH]: 56%) participated than males. The ages of East Hills participants were almost evenly distributed among their 20s (21%), 30s (21%), 40s (21%), 50s (21%), and 60s and over (17%). In the meantime, a little more than the half of participants from Heritage Hill were in their 50s (24%) or 60s and over (35%).[14] Almost all the participants were White (EH: 97%; HH: 93%),[15] well-educated, middle- and upper-class people.[16]

Most participants were knowledgeable of general historic preservation guidelines (EH: 76%; HH: 91%) and historic preservation guidelines for the City of Grand Rapids (EH: 65%; HH: 85%). Both participant groups thought it "Very important" to preserve historic districts (EH: Mean=4.24, SD=0.64; HH: Mean=4.41, SD=0.67). On a scale of 1 to 5, average means of each participant group's familiarity with their historic district, Wealthy Heights or, Heritage Hill were 3.93 (EH) and 4.42 (HH), respectively. In short, they were familiar with their historic districts.[17]

East Hills participants were familiar with the district because they live or lived in/near Wealthy Heights and/or had friends and/or family living in the district. Some of them also mentioned their frequent visits to the area for shopping and eating as a reason for their familiarity. In addition to being residents of the district, Heritage Hill participants were also associated with their district because of their friends and/or family living in the district and/or their jobs/or businesses in the district. Most participants thought that it was either "Very" or "Extremely" important to preserve Wealthy Heights (EH: Mean = 3.96, SD = .92; HH: Mean = 3.87, SD = .88) and Heritage Hill (EH: Mean = 4.38, SD = .62; HH: Mean = 4.60, SD = .58).

The seven East Hills participants who joined the focus group were three males and four females. Two males and one female were in their 30s. Another female was in her 50s. And rest of them were in their 60s and older. All the focus group participants were Caucasians. These participants were either past/current residents or currently worked in Wealthy Heights. They were very familiar with Wealthy Heights and knowledgeable of its history and current redevelopment projects.

The Importance and Appropriate Treatment of Architectural Features in Wealthy Heights

Among the thirty-seven typological images, both participant groups marked more than thirty images with means greater than 3.5. Both participant groups perceived most historic preservation features in a historic district as very near to 4.0, "Very important" (Table 5.2). The photographic images of Heritage Hill preservation features were perceived as important to a similar degree to these typological images, around and higher than 4.0. However, East Hills participants marked almost all the listed items including twenty-one architectural ones between 3.0 and 3.5, very near to "Somewhat important". Only "Decorative elements (both functional and non-functional)" were rated close to 4.0, "Very important". Regarding the typologies, out of thirty-seven items, twelve features including eight architectural ones were marked lower by East Hills participants. Then, more perceptual gaps between the two participant groups were found in the test of their own historic district features. East Hills participants' ratings on Wealthy Heights features were lower on all the twenty-one architectural items ($p < 0.01$) (Table 5.3).

Focus group participants marked "No change" or "Moderate change" on "Decorative elements (both functional and non-functional)" (Table 5.4). They recognized the rarity of these elements in Wealthy Heights. However, a few existing decorative features such as dormers, bay windows, a stained glass window, colorful window trims, and cornice moldings were perceived as aesthetically pleasing. This perception led to the high degree of importance. Participants indicated "No change" for preservation of these unique features. "Moderate change" manifested their desire to incorporate more of such a feature with the vernacular buildings.

Table 5.2 Means of Ratings (One Being "Not at All Important" and Five Being "Extremely Important") and *t*-Test Results of the Two Participant Groups' Perceptions of Preservation Features of Historic Districts

Historic Districts Preservation Features	Participant Groups						*t*-Test Stats			
	East Hills			Heritage Hill						
	N	Mean	SD	N	Mean	SD	dof	t	p	Stars
District Planning, Streetscape, and Landscape										
Shape and arrangement of building blocks	29	3.69	0.81	90	3.91	0.84	49.28	1.27	0.209	
Scale of building blocks	28	3.82	0.86	88	4.02	0.88	46.42	1.07	0.291	
Street pattern	28	3.75	0.80	88	3.95	0.83	46.95	1.17	0.248	
Walkways	29	4.10	0.90	90	4.24	0.78	42.54	0.76	0.454	
Paving	29	3.86	0.95	88	3.80	0.90	45.56	-0.33	0.742	
Orientation of site	28	3.96	0.69	90	3.92	0.97	63.16	-0.25	0.801	
Lot size	29	3.31	0.93	89	3.67	1.04	52.79	1.77	0.082	
Spacing between buildings	29	3.45	0.83	90	4.01	0.98	55.31	3.04	0.004	**
Front yard and/or building setback	29	3.69	0.76	90	4.21	0.83	51.10	3.14	0.003	**
Driveway access	29	3.52	0.95	89	4.09	0.79	41.48	2.93	0.005	**
Garage and/or carriage house	29	3.55	0.99	90	4.19	0.85	42.26	3.13	0.003	**
Grass lawn	29	3.21	1.15	89	3.49	1.01	43.18	1.21	0.234	
Walls and fences	29	3.69	0.81	90	3.74	0.80	47.14	0.32	0.751	
Lighting	29	4.28	0.59	90	4.30	0.77	61.28	0.18	0.860	
Plantings	29	3.62	1.08	90	3.73	1.00	44.56	0.50	0.622	
Tree canopy	29	4.59	0.57	91	4.40	0.76	62.56	-1.44	0.154	
Architecture										
Building style	29	4.10	0.67	90	4.58	0.71	49.43	2.95	0.005	**
Building scale and height	29	4.17	0.60	90	4.27	0.87	68.76	0.65	0.517	

(Continued)

Historic Districts	Participant Groups						t-Test			
Preservation Features	East Hills			Heritage Hill			Stats			
	N	Mean	SD	N	Mean	SD	dof	t	p	Stars
Porch configuration	29	3.79	0.90	90	4.08	0.95	49.66	1.46	0.151	
Formal treatment of building entrance	29	3.76	0.83	91	4.04	0.88	49.69	1.59	0.119	
Exterior wall materials	29	3.90	0.82	91	4.46	0.76	44.51	2.98	0.005	**
Ratio of solid-to-void	29	3.59	0.95	90	4.00	0.95	47.51	2.05	0.046	*
Relief to building elevation	29	3.76	0.83	89	4.29	0.86	48.88	2.29	0.026	*
Façade alignment patterns	29	3.76	1.09	90	3.93	0.99	43.94	0.77	0.447	
Fenestration	29	3.66	0.97	90	4.36	0.88	43.77	2.95	0.005	**
Window proportion	29	3.97	0.94	89	4.44	0.88	45.12	1.70	0.096	
Window shape and size	29	3.90	0.90	89	4.42	0.90	47.67	1.94	0.059	
Window materials	29	2.69	1.14	91	3.72	1.17	48.28	3.39	0.001	**
Door proportion	29	3.62	0.94	89	4.40	0.90	45.80	3.20	0.002	**
Door shape and size	29	3.66	0.86	90	4.29	0.88	48.72	3.32	0.002	**
Door materials and finishes	29	2.97	1.21	89	4.09	1.09	43.89	3.38	0.002	**
Roof pitch and shape	29	3.93	0.84	90	4.41	0.91	50.89	1.65	0.106	
Roof details	29	3.76	0.95	90	4.30	0.99	49.25	1.39	0.170	
Roof materials	29	3.21	0.90	91	3.83	1.09	56.31	1.42	0.161	
Decorative elements (functional)	29	4.07	0.75	91	4.58	0.75	47.05	2.93	0.005	**
Decorative elements (non-functional)	29	4.17	0.80	90	4.60	0.69	42.07	2.24	0.031	*
Colors	29	2.97	1.15	89	3.08	1.12	46.61	0.46	0.645	

* $p < 0.05$; **$p < 0.01$; ***$p < 0.001$.

THE PERCEPTION AND PRESERVATION

I don't know if you see the stained glass in there. I like that. It looks like it stayed there for a while. An extra feature. ... And this porch is not fancy at all, but I like the bay window and door details. These should be preserved.

So, if you look at this window element, and some of the detail at the top those are important things to preserve. The banisters and columns are important things to preserve.

We don't have decorative elements really in this neighborhood. I mean, but there is a way to add decorative elements. ... One of the reasons I like my house is that bay window in the front of it because none of the others do. It does make the front of my house stand out differently when you look down the street. It just a small change. I'll never take it down. I love it.

Look at that greenhouse over there. If you look at the above, the second story, they just added a little bit of something. It's still a regular house. It's still where a normal family would live. Nobody's trying a gingerbread up to make it look ridiculous and funky. It is in the middle of normal. ... This is just... somebody thought enough to add a little bit of something to the house.

East Hills participants recommended "Moderate change" for many architectural features. These features included "Building style," "Ratio of solid-to-void," "Façade alignment pattern, "Fenestration, "Relief to building elevation," "Window proportion," "Window shape and size, "Roof pitch and shape," "Roof details," and "Colors," which were marked between 3.0 and 3.5 (Tables 5.3 and 5.4). Basically, these features were evaluated as domineering the visual trait of Wealthy Heights. But the features were perceived as too unified, and therefore, visually less attractive and less important than the decorative features. Participants suggested moderate – visually/physically compatible – variations on these features. For instance, introductions of slightly different building colors, roof pitches and window types, and modern-style buildings similar in scale were addressed as acceptable changes. A modern town house located in a block away was pointed to as a good example (Figure 5.5).

Elliot and Rachel's house, there, had a great color on it. Just recently did that, I think. Certainly putting more windows on that dormer would make more sense. But I really like the color.

Figure 5.5 The modern town house near Wealthy Heights. Photograph by the author.

Table 5.3 Means of Ratings (One Being "Not at All Important" and Five Being "Extremely Important") and *t*-Test Results of the Two Participant Groups' Perceptions of Preservation Features of their Own Historic Districts, Heritage Hill and Wealthy Heights

Heritage Hill/Wealthy Heights				Participant Groups				*t*-Test		
Preservation Features	**East Hills**			**Heritage Hill**			**Stats**			
	N	Mean	SD	N	Mean	SD	dof	t	p	Stars
District Planning, Streetscape, and Landscape										
Shape and arrangement of building blocks	29	3.17	1.20	89	4.01	0.90	38.79	3.47	0.001	**
Scale of building blocks	29	3.48	1.18	90	3.98	0.95	40.22	2.05	0.047	*
Street pattern	29	3.28	1.25	91	4.01	0.84	36.33	2.96	0.005	**
Walkways	29	3.69	1.04	90	4.09	0.93	43.49	1.84	0.072	
Paving	29	3.10	1.11	89	4.04	0.85	39.25	4.17	0.000	***
Orientation of site	28	3.86	0.93	86	4.00	0.91	44.90	0.71	0.482	
Lot size	28	2.93	0.98	88	3.58	0.98	45.52	3.07	0.004	**
Spacing between buildings	29	3.03	0.82	89	4.01	0.83	48.08	5.53	0.000	***
Front yard and/or building setback	29	3.45	1.21	89	4.30	0.83	36.96	3.54	0.001	**
Driveway access	29	3.17	1.10	89	4.03	0.79	37.78	3.89	0.000	***
Garage and/or carriage house	28	3.25	0.84	89	4.13	0.81	43.97	4.88	0.000	***
Grass lawn	29	2.62	1.08	89	3.53	0.92	41.92	4.06	0.000	***
Walls and fences	28	3.21	0.92	86	3.77	1.04	51.31	2.68	0.010	**
Lighting	29	3.52	1.15	90	4.36	0.61	33.11	3.75	0.001	***
Plantings	29	2.90	1.11	89	3.73	0.97	42.87	3.61	0.001	***
Tree canopy	29	4.17	1.04	89	4.31	0.89	42.16	0.66	0.511	

Architecture

Building style	29	3.31	1.26	88	4.58	0.58	32.04	5.26	0.000	***
Building scale and height	29	3.31	1.23	90	4.37	0.71	34.24	4.40	0.000	***
Porch configuration	29	3.45	1.02	89	4.22	0.85	41.39	3.70	0.001	***
Formal treatment of building entrance	29	3.21	1.24	88	4.16	0.84	36.96	3.86	0.000	***
Exterior wall materials	29	3.59	1.02	87	4.46	0.73	38.00	4.27	0.000	***
Ratio of solid-to-void	29	3.34	1.14	86	4.12	0.83	38.50	3.35	0.002	**
Relief to building elevation	29	3.21	1.26	86	4.29	0.82	36.35	4.32	0.000	***
Façade alignment patterns	29	3.17	1.14	88	4.16	0.90	40.10	4.26	0.000	***
Fenestration	29	3.17	1.31	87	4.36	0.83	35.87	4.56	0.000	***
Window proportion	29	3.62	1.08	87	4.44	0.80	38.77	3.73	0.001	***
Window shape and size	29	3.38	1.15	86	4.42	0.77	36.98	4.54	0.000	***
Window materials	29	2.93	1.19	88	3.72	1.08	44.20	3.14	0.003	**
Door proportion	29	2.97	1.27	89	4.40	0.70	33.78	5.83	0.000	***
Door shape and size	29	3.41	1.24	87	4.29	0.90	38.34	3.50	0.001	**
Door materials and finishes	29	3.07	1.22	86	4.09	0.99	41.08	4.08	0.000	***
Roof pitch and shape	29	3.34	1.14	86	4.41	0.76	36.65	4.67	0.000	***
Roof details	29	3.10	1.32	86	4.30	0.77	34.62	4.64	0.000	***
Roof materials	29	2.66	1.17	88	3.83	1.13	46.23	4.72	0.000	***
Decorative elements (functional)	29	3.86	1.06	88	4.58	0.62	34.53	3.46	0.001	**
Decorative elements (non-functional)	29	3.86	1.06	87	4.60	0.62	34.58	3.54	0.001	**
Colors	29	3.31	1.23	90	4.37	0.71	34.24	4.40	0.000	***

* p<0.05; **p<0.01; ***p<0.001.

THE PERCEPTION AND PRESERVATION

Table 5.4 The Numbers of the Three Different Acceptable Degrees Marked on the Presented Images of the Wealthy Heights Architectural Features

Building Design Features to Preserve	Degree of Acceptable Change		
	No	Moderate	Radical
Building style		7	
Building scale and height	2	3	2
Porch configuration	6	1	
Formal treatment of building entrance	4	3	
Exterior wall materials	1	6	
Ratio of solid-to-void		6	1
Relief to building elevation	3	3	
Façade alignment patterns	1	6	
Fenestration	3	4	
Window proportion	1	5	
Window shape and size		6	1
Window materials		4	2
Door proportion	6	1	
Door shape and size	7		
Door materials and finishes		5	2
Roof pitch and shape	2	4	
Roof details		5	1
Roof materials		5	1
Decorative elements (functional)	4	3	
Decorative elements (non-functional)	3	4	
Colors		6	1

You have a house that was added onto twice, and chose a lower roof and then lower roof. If you want to structurally bring that up… so it matches all the way back, it actually means improvement (both aesthetically and practically). It still matches style of the neighborhood. You're not doing anything to make it worse.

I mean from a historic perspective, there is a variety. There is an enough variety to make it not ticky- tacky, you know, like a cookie cutter, but it all kinda matches.

Diamond has a very modern building with a flat roof -nearly flat roof- and a straight glass façade (Figure 5.5). It is very different than this. But I kinda like it. I don't know how to differentiate that. That two story modern building is acceptable.

The two features "Formal treatment of entrance" (Mean=3.21, SD=1.24) and "Porch configuration" (Mean=3.45, SD=1.02) were perceived as representing and facilitating community's social relationship. Many existing building entrances and porches facing the street were perceived as visually/physically open. They thought of these building entrances and porches as an inviting transition from the public to the private realms for neighborly connection. For the reason, participants marked this feature with "No change" (Tables 5.3 and 5.4).

> Whereas you can allow some variability, they (front porches) all have street facing... These two (porches) are open to the neighborhood. These should be part of community. And they are reminder to be part of a community. When you're living in this close proximity, you have to emotionally put yourself in the space. ... I think it was always built for a lot of working class families who worked in close proximity each other. They lived in close proximity each other. They helped and took care of each other. You know I kinda can imagine there were probably kids running from house to house, house to house. Nobody knew who was who and what was what, they were just all over the place... if you're moving yourself from that, the whole neighborhood changes. It really changes how they take care of each other.

Whereas, participants also recognized several building fronts with only windows and no porches that were contrastingly closed off from the neighborhood. The original porches of some of these buildings were transformed into indoor spaces by uses of glass and/or cemented walls (Figure 5.6). Participants perceived such building fronts as similar to a blunt human face. Their memory of the original and/or desirable images of these features and ambition to improve them were related to "Somewhat important" and "Moderate changes" (Table 5.4). Slightly bigger windows and restoration of the converted interior porches were suggested.

> I like the smallish front porches 'cause nothing meant to be ostentatious... You come to this one. And it's like all completely closed off. Any of them probably did it to make inside of a house little bit bigger. But it doesn't really fit.
>
> Mr. white house (Figure 5.6, the left picture) over there, brick did front porch, yes it's ugly, you know. It is extremely important to have a front porch to say, get to know your neighbors.

Except for "Exterior wall material (Mean = 3.59, SD = 1.02)", building materials such as roof, window, and door were rated as the least important (lower and close to 3.0) (Table 5.3). These materials were perceived as relatively not much critical to the visual quality of the district. Participants suggested "Moderate change" and "Radical change" (Table 5.4). Although the extents were different,

Figure 5.6 Examples of undesired building fronts. Photograph by the author.

THE PERCEPTION AND PRESERVATION

they agreed with the types of changes. Appropriate treatments of the features included the uses of cost- and/or energy-efficient and eco-friendly roofing (e.g., recycled shingles, solar panel), window (e.g., double pane glasses, vinyl) and door materials (e.g., recycled doors). Such new materials were proposed to be visually/physically compatible with the vernacular building while contributing to affordability and easy maintenance of the building. Even for "Exterior wall material" – a feature relatively important for the visual character of Wealthy Heights, they recommended "Moderate change" for a practical reason (Table 5.4). For example, participants appealed the low-income residents' difficulty with expensive preservation such as keeping the original wood siding.

> I don't wanna necessarily go and change the style of my house any way. I don't wanna change window placement and that kinda thing. But I want to be able to put maybe vinyl window in rather than have wood framed window, you know, like that kind of thing. I want to keep the look, the historic look, historic integrity, you know I mean these Habitat houses, they fit in, they bland in perfectly along my street. But they got materials (e.g., insulated sandwich panel, solar panel) that are not gonna fall apart.

> I think there is a lot of stuff out there nowadays... in materials and other things. Because of rules and regulations they cannot use. … I agree with architectural look of everything. But you gotta look at it.

> I think the material especially in this neighborhood isn't the kind of important thing in that people who live in this neighborhood as opposed to Cherry Hill or Heritage Hill…we don't make as much money as typically those people do. … They are making significantly more money than I do. …I've talked to a few people in the neighborhood and we would like to put material on our houses that lasts for a little bit more long term…than having replaced wood siding and that kind of thing.

The extent of acceptable change for "Building scale and height" (Mean=3.31, SD=1.23) was the most controversial. All the three different degrees, "Radical," "Moderate," and "No changes," were mentioned for this feature (Tables 5.3 and 5.4). This architectural feature was important in that it is visually/physically dominant and represents existing demographic characteristics (e.g., income level, family size, life style). The point led to some participants' "No change." These participants also thought that the preservation of this feature could prevent the involuntary displacement of existing low-income residents by keeping their residences still affordable. However, other participants suggested to alter this feature in order to increase visual and social diversity. They conceived of a two and half and/or three story residence as appropriate. And they thought it was not very important to keep this feature as it is. This notion impacted its degree of importance, "Somewhat important." Depending on whether they saw such an infill construction compatible with the existing two story small buildings or not, participants marked either "Moderate" or "Radical change" (Table 5.4).

> I think most buildings have the right scale and height. They show who we are. They were built much as the same… and should be preserved.

> I put a radical change being able to add a town home… style. The townhome could be tall. They would be like two and three lots wide…because they have look of a row. Maybe

THE PERCEPTION AND PRESERVATION

scale and height are relatively same though, these are two stories, yet I can see three stories or two and half.

Some of buildings on Diamond and Wealthy are three stories… I don't know if I want to see more than three stories. But I can see bigger buildings, multiple buildings, and separate buildings together. (Such buildings) can bring more diversity to the neighborhood.

Almost all the participants addressed "No change" for "Door proportion" (Mean=2.97, SD=1.27) and "Door shape and size" (Mean = 3.41, SD = 1.24) (Table 5.4). Some participants thought many front doors are important and fit perfectly the existing small residence scale.

I think changes to door shape and size especially in this neighborhood would throw off the look of homes. Well… and I think honestly one of the few things that hasn't changed is the shape and size of door.

Other participants pointed out the current use of a manufactured door, which entailed "Somewhat important" of these features in their overall ratings. Such a door was rarely historically important, yet, perceived as practical and reasonable. They found no reason for changing its standardized shape, size, or proportion.

Discussions

East Hills participants thought all the preservation features very critical to preservation of an urban historic district in general. Likewise, the preservation features of Wealthy Heights were perceived as important basically. However, all the architectural features of Wealthy Heights, the district with ethnic/heritage value, were less important than those of Heritage Hill, the district with architectural value. East Hills participants perceived most of their vernacular architectural features as open to legitimate alterations.

In this study, the difference between moderate and radical changes was subjectively determined. However, the marking activity and results accelerated participants' discussions of the given topic. In general, there was a common understanding of the importance and appropriate treatment regardless of the different degrees. In many cases, participants preferred visually/physically compatible changes to the vernacular architectural features for preservation of Wealthy Heights, which seems to have resulted in the most markings of moderate change.

Participants' concerns about the aesthetic quality of the vernacular buildings were noteworthy. Noting the connection of the aesthetic quality with community's visual identity, participants expressed their strong desire to elaborate many ordinary architectural features. In particular, in spite of the lack of quality and quantity of decorative features, the participants' aspiration to maintain and refine these few features and to have more of them ranked decorative features the most important. This perception resonates with the traditional view that aesthetics is the essential trait of architecture. According to the survey result, participants were knowledgeable about historic preservation and preservation guidelines. The high probability of participants being accustomed to architectural conservation could have affected this perception.

The other attributes of vernacular architecture influenced community participants' perceptions as well. They perceived social attributes of the architectural features as important. The appropriate treatments for building front (e.g., street facing open porch and big windows), height and scale (e.g., no change, two and a half, and/or three-story town houses) were to solidify community's demographic character and strengthen their social bond and diversity. However, this study illustrated that a controversy can arise in the pursuit of social/demographic character and diversity. For instance, the desire for protection of the existing residents from gentrification conflicted with the desire for social diversity (i.e., building height and scale). In addition, participants evaluated an acceptable change depending on how the original features were, on how they had been modified and how they have been currently serving a social function (i.e., building entrances and porches). The affordability and practicality of the features were also important issues. Wealthy Heights was historically a working-class neighborhood. Many low-income families still live in this district to this day. Such a recognition seems associated with the issues and influential to the importance and/or acceptable treatments for the building materials (e.g., more durable and less expensive materials) as well as the building scale and height (e.g., no change). Interestingly, these concerns stimulated participants' interest in construction materials and technology for a green building.

In short, the integrity of the architectural features was related to not only tangible and visual – aesthetic – but also intangible – social and practical attributes of the features, which formed the collective identity of the vernacular buildings. Community participants' desire to preserve and enhance these integral characteristics motivated their perceptions of the features and led to the important degrees and compatible changes for preservation of the vernacular architectural features. In fact, many important concepts (e.g., neighborhood connectivity, social diversity, discouragement of gentrification, affordability) that appeared concerning with social functions of the features were the principles of the Wealthy Heights Initiative. Therefore, it can be said that the importance and appropriate treatments were influenced by not only how participants experienced the features but also how they envision the features for the community.

Limitations of This Study

This study has shortcomings. The photographic images of the two district features were selectively photographed in each category. Thus, photographing views were restricted. In this sense, the developed images used for this study worked as keys to trigger participants' mental images of the features. This relied on their personal experiences, which were presumably diverse and uncontrollable.

The population sample was limited. The difference in the number of participants from the two neighborhoods seems innately associated with the difference of the neighborhood sizes.[18] However, the voices of minority community people such as Black or African American people[19] were not incorporated either. This limitation could have originated from the recruitment and survey method. Only the community members who had internet access and were on the neighborhood association mailing list were invited to this study. Many minority, low-income residents with no internet access and/or no voluntary connection with the neighborhood association were excluded consequently.

Conclusions and Future Study

Historic preservation in the United States became more broadly inclusive to celebrate the heritage values of many different ethnic/cultural groups. This shift raised an issue of how to preserve ordinary architectural features as the heritage symbol that represents community's collective memory/

identity in an urban vernacular setting. In this context, community participants' perceptions of their own vernacular architectural features in Wealthy Heights were examined by means of a mixed method. In this study, regarding preservation of Wealthy Heights, community participants' dynamic reciprocal relationship with its architectural features was well documented. Therefore, the study illustrates that an empirical method can provide community input effectively and suggests that the use of an empirical study should be encouraged in contemporary historic preservation.

The findings from this empirical study alert several things for preservation practices in an urban historic district. First, important degrees of architectural features in the preservation guidelines can be varied in urban historic districts. Second, the integral characteristics of vernacular architectural features are concerned with both physical/aesthetical and social functions of the features. Finally, the importance of vernacular architectural features and their appropriate treatments can be the outcomes of how the integral attributes were intertwined with a community's experiences and visions. And as a result, preservation of vernacular architectural features may demand various compatible changes to the features.

As mentioned previously, the limitations of the study were derived from the developed survey images and population samples. As future directions, more comprehensive representation of each categorical feature and inclusion of the minority residents are anticipated in order to enhance this study.

Acknowledgements

I am indebted to Dr. Neil Carlson, the director, and Traci Montgomery, a research associate, at the Center for Social Research of Calvin College. They have been engaged with this project from the beginning phase of developing the methodology. Their help with the survey design and implementation and data analyses were crucial to this study. Without Dr. Carlson and Ms. Montgomery's endeavor and expertise, my research idea would not have been able to be actualized and completed.

Notes

1   The importance of architectural conservation was articulated in the International Charter for the Conservation of Sites and Monuments (the Venice Charter) of 1964. The charter was developed based on European countries' desire to restore their historically monumental buildings that fell into disrepair after World War II (Denslagen, 1994; Hayden, 1995; Park, 2006; Stipe, 1989).

2   "Public involvement is most meaningful when it is used to assist in defining values of properties and preservation planning issues, rather than when it is limited to review of decisions already made. Early and continuing public participation is essential to the broad acceptance of preservation planning decisions" (National Park Service, 1996).

3   "Based on these standards and guidelines, groups that may ascribe traditional cultural values to an area's historic properties should be contacted and asked to assist in organizing information on the area" (National Park Service, 1996).

4   Wealthy Heights is one of seven neighborhoods of East Hills and belongs to Wealthy Street Historic District of the City of Grand Rapids.

5   Historic District Standards and Guidelines of City of Bolivar (MO), Design Standards for Historic Districts in Salt Lake City (UT), Ghent Historic and Cultural Conservation District Design Guidelines (Norfolk, VA), and North End Historic District Design Guidelines (the City of Colorado Springs, CO).

6   Salt Lake City, UT; Norfolk, VA; Bolivar, MO; Colorado Springs, CO; San Antonio, TX; and San Francisco, CA.

THE PERCEPTION AND PRESERVATION

7   East Hills is one of the thirty-two neighborhoods of the city of Grand Rapids. This neighborhood includes seven small neighborhoods such as Cherry Hill, Congress Park, Diamond Gate, Fairmount Square, Fitch Corners, Orchard Hill, and Wealthy Heights (Community Research Institute, 2013; East Hills Council of Neighbors, 2005).

8   Rather than conduct a random sample, it was decided that the survey would be sent out in a way that would reach all of the community members who are interested in this project. Due to the small size of the Wealthy Heights district, as our response rate was expected to be similarly small, whether recruiting a random sample or the population in general.

9   According to US Census data, the population of Heritage Hill is 3,344. The population of East Hills is 3,033. The size of the Wealthy Heights district corresponds to about one-sixth of East Hills, and it is less dense than the other districts of East Hills because of many abandoned houses under renovation. In addition, a big commercial building (1,059 Wealthy) occupies the central area of the district. (The demolition of the large building and 24,000 square feet/2,230 square meter new construction of a mixed use building are in progress.) Thus, it can be estimated that the population ratio of Heritage Hill to Wealthy Heights is a little less than 6:1 (www.city-data.com/neighborhood).

10 The two-sample t-test with unequal variance is the appropriate test due to the differences in sample size and variance between neighborhoods, but substantively equivalent results are returned by ANOVA and linear regression.

11 As shown in Table 5.1, the original feature set includes thirty-six items. But during meetings with organization members, some organization members articulated the importance of "Tree canopy," which was then added to the feature set to be tested. The community's stated interest in this specific feature seems to be related to their vision for the district (e.g., the city's Urban Forest Plan), which is expected to be investigated in the future.

12 Senior and graduate architecture students worked as their assistants.

13 A gift card of $10.00 value was given to all the participants as a compensation.

14 17% of them were in their 40s, 12% were in their 30s, and 10% were in their 20s.

15 Rest of the participants marked their races as American Indian or Alaska Native (HH: 0%; EH: 3%); Asian (HH: 0%; EH: 3%), and Other (HH: 3%; EH: 0%).

16 Household incomes of 91% participants of Heritage Hill and 89% participants of East Hill were more than $30,000; and 99% of Heritage Hill and 100% of East Hills' participants at least studied at colleges and/or have degrees higher than Bachelor's degrees.

17 Among ninety-one participants from Heritage Hill, 53% of them said that they are "Extremely familiar" with Heritage Hill and 37% of them "Very familiar"; and 10% "Somewhat familiar." Out of twenty-nine participants from East Hills, 17% of them said that they were "Extremely familiar" with Wealthy Heights; 41% "Very familiar"; 21% "Somewhat familiar"; and 17% "Not very familiar." Only 3% of them were "Not at all familiar" with Wealthy Heights.

18 See the footnote 9.

19 Whites are majority in each district (HH: 81.9% and EH: 66.6%) and black or African Americans are the second majority (HH: 9.1% and EH: 16.7%) (http://cridata.org).

References

Abu-Obeid, N.N. (1993). *Abstraction and Categorization of Architectural Forms: A Cognitive Approach Towards the Language of Architectural Form.* Unpublished doctoral dissertation, Texas A&M University, College Station, TX.

Alderson, C.R. (2006). Responding to Context: Changing Perspectives on Appropriate Change in Historic Settings. *APT Bulletin,* 37(4): 22–33.

THE PERCEPTION AND PRESERVATION

Araoz, G.F. 2008. World-Heritage Historic Urban Landscapes: Defining and Protecting Authenticity. *APT Bulletin,* 39(2/3): 33–37.

Argan, G.C. (1996). On the Typology of Architecture. In K. Nesbitt (Ed.), *Theorizing a New Agenda for Architecture: An Anthology of Architectural Theory 1965–1995.* New York, NY: Princeton Architectural Press, pp. 240–246.

Barthel, D. (1996). *Historic Preservation: Collective Memory and Historical Identity.* New Brunswick, NJ: Rutgers University Press, pp. 1–34.

Bennett, J., & Metz, J., et al. (1997, September). *Wealthy Street Historic District Study Committee Final Report.* Historic Preservation Commission of the City of the Grand Rapids.

Brand, S. (1995). *How Buildings Learn: What Happens after They're Built.* New York, NY: Viking.

Berg, B.L. (2011). *Qualitative Research Methods for the Social Sciences.* New York, NY: Pearson.

Cantacuzino, S. (1989). *Re-architecture: Old Buildings/New Uses.* New York, NY: Abbeville Press.

City of East Grand Rapids. (2014). History. Retrieved May 12, 2014, from www.eastgr.org/index.aspx?nid=96

Clark, J. (2003). Introduction: Urban Culture: Representations and Experiences in/of Urban Space and Culture. *Urban Culture,* 57: 3–10.

Colquhoun, A. (1996). Typology and Design Method. In K. Nesbitt (Ed.), *Theorizing a New Agenda for Architecture: An Anthology of Architectural Theory 1965–1995.* New York, NY: Princeton Architectural Press, pp. 248–257.

Day, C. (2002). *Spirit and Place.* Oxford; Boston, MA: Architectural Press.

Denslagen, W. (1994). *Architectural Restoration in Western Europe: Controversy and Continuity.* Amsterdam, The Netherlands: Architecture and Natura Press.

Dewey, J. (1934). *Art as Experience.* New York, NY: The Berkeley Publishing Group.

Diamonstein, B. (1978). *Buildings Reborn: New Uses, Old Places.* New York, NY: Harper & Row, pp. 13–28.

Downing, F. (2000). *Remembrance and the Design of Place.* College Station, TX: Texas A&M University Press.

East Hills Council of Neighbors. (2005). *Sustainable Affordable Housing in Wealthy Heights.*

East Hills Council of Neighbours. (2009). *Valuing Our Trees: An East Hills Urban Forest Plan.* Retrieved September 5, 2013, from www.easthillscouncil.org

East Hills Council of Neighbours. (2012). *Wealthy Heights: Moving Towards a Community Land Trust.* Retrieved March 1, 2012, from www.easthillscouncil.org

East Hills Council of Neighbours. (2014). *Public Space Strategy.* Retrieved June 8, 2016, from www.easthillscouncil.org

Fitch, J.M. (2001). *Historic Preservation: Curatorial Management of the Built World.* New York, NY: McGraw-Hill Companies, Inc.

Grand Rapids Historic Preservation Commission. (2007, November). *Historic Preservation Guidelines.* Retrieved May 12, 2014, from http://grcity.us/design-and-development-services/Planning-Department/Documents/6572_HPC%20Guidelines%20Book.pdf

Green, R. (1999). Meaning and Form in Community Perception of Town Character. *Journal of Environmental Psychology,* 19: 311–329.

Groat, L.N., & Wang, D. (2001). *Architectural Research Methods.* New York, NY: John Wiley and Sons, Inc.

Habitat for Humanity of Kent County. (2010). *Wealthy Heights Partnership Project.* Retrieved June 12, 2011, from www.habitatkent.org/BuildingGreen/WealthyHeightsPartnershipProject.aspx

Harmansah, O. (2011). Monuments and Memory: Architecture and Visual Culture in Ancient Anatolian History. In G. McMahon and S. Steadman (Ed.), *The Oxford Handbook of Ancient Anatolian.* New York, NY: Oxford University Press, pp. 623–651.

Halbwachs, M. (1992). *On Collective Memory.* Chicago, IL: University of Chicago Press.

Handler, R. (1987). Heritage and Hegemony: Recent Works on Historic Preservation and Interpretation. *Anthropological Quarterly,* 60(3): 137–141.

THE PERCEPTION AND PRESERVATION

Hart, Z.H., Halfacre, A.C., & Burke, M.K. (2004, Summer). Community Participation in Preservation of Low-country South Carolina Sweetgrass. *Economic Botany*, 58(2): 161–171.

Hayden, D. (1995). *The Power of Place: Urban Landscape as Public History*. Cambridge, MA: The MIT Press.

Huyssen, A. (2003). *Present Pasts: Urban Palimpsests and Politics of Memory*. Stanford, CA: Stanford University Press.

Jacob, J. (1989). *The Death and Life of Great American Cities*. New York, NY: Vintage Books.

Kwun, J.B. (2001). *The Application of Typology Theory in Building Design*. Unpublished doctoral dissertation, Texas A&M University, College Station, TX.

Langer, S.K. (1953). *Feeling and Form: A Theory of Art*. New York, NY: Scribners.

Lefebvre, H. (1996). *Writings on Cities*. Translated and Edited by Leleonore Kofman and Elizabeth Lebas, Hoboken, NJ: Blackwell Publishing.

Lowenthal, D. (1985). *The Past is a Foreign Country*. Cambridge, UK: Cambridge University Press.

Lynch, K. (1972). *What Time Is This Place*. Cambridge, MA: MIT Press.

Lyon, E.A. (1999, Spring). Landmark to Community: The History of Georgia's Historic Preservation Movement. *The Georgia Historical Quarterly*, 83(1): 77–97.

Mahdjoubi, L., & Wiltshire, J. (2001). Towards a Framework for Evaluation of Computer Visual Simulations in Environmental Design. *Design Studies*, 22(2): 193–209.

Mason, R. (2004). Fixing Historic Preservation: A Constructive Critique of "Significance." *Places*, 16(1): 64–71.

Mason, R. (2006, Summer). Theoretical and Practical Arguments for Values-Centered Preservation. *Cultural Resource Management: The Journal of Heritage Stewardship*, 3(2): 21–48.

McAlester, V., & McAlester, L. (1984). *A Field Guide to American Houses*. New York, NY: Alfred A. Knopf.

Milligan, M. (1998). Interactional Past and Potential: The Social Construction of Place Attachment. *Symbolic Interaction*, 21(1): 1–33.

Mitchell, N.J. (2008). Considering the Authenticity of Cultural Landscapes. *APT Bulletin*, 39(2/30): 25–31.

Murtagh, W.J. (1997 [1995]). *Keeping Time: The History and Theory of Preservation in America*. New York, NY: John Wiley & Sons. National Park Service, Chapter 8.

National Register of Historic Places. (2011). State Listings: Michigan-Kent County. Retrieved May 12, 2014, from www.nationalregisterofhistoricplaces.com/mi/kent/state.html

Park, S.C. (2006). Respecting Significance and Keeping Integrity: Approaches to Rehabilitation. *APT Bulletin*, 37(4): 13–21.

Parker, P.L. (1993). Traditional Cultural Properties: What You Do and How We Think. *CRM* 16. Retrieved February 10, 2005, from http://npshistory.com/newsletters/crm/crm-v16-special.pdf

Parker, P.L., & King, T.F. (1998) Guidelines for Evaluating and Documenting Traditional Cultural Properties. *National Register Bulletin*. Retrieved April 9, 2010, from www8.nau.edu/hcpo-p/Parker.pdf

Parker, R.D. (1997). The Architectonics of Memory: On Built Form and Built Thought. *Leonardo*, 30(2): 147–152.

Powell, K. (1999). *Architecture Reborn: Converting Old Buildings for New Uses*. New York, NY: Rizzoli.

Powter, A., & Ross, S. (2005). Integrating Environmental and Cultural Sustainability for Heritage properties. *APT Bulletin*, 36(4): 5–11.

Rasmussen, S.E. (1964). *Experiencing Architecture*. Cambridge, MA: MIT Press.

Schneekloth, L.H., & Shibley, R.G. (1995). *Placemaking: The Art and Practice of Building Communities*. New York, NY: John Wiley & Sons, Inc.

Schneekloth, L.H., & Shibley, R.G. (2000, February). Implacing Architecture into the Practice of Placemaking. *Journal of Architectural Education*, 53(3): 130–140.

Stipe, R.E. (1989). *The Venice Charter and the United States Preservation System*. Retrieved January 13, 2012, from www.icomos.org/venicecharter2004/usa.pdf

Stipe, R.E. (2003). *A Richer Heritage*. Chapel Hill, NC: The University of North Carolina Press, pp. 13–24.

Stubbs, J.H. (2009). *Time Honored: A Global View of Architectural Conservation*. New York, NY: John Wiley & Sons, Inc., Chapter 2, pp. 21–31.

Sutton, M. (2009). *Measuring Environmental Perceptions and Sense of Place in Franklin County, Florida*. Master Dissertation, Ball State University, Muncie, IN.

Tainter, J.A., & Lucas, G.J. (1983, October). Epistemology of the Significance Concept. *American Antiquity, 48*(4): 707–719.

Tuan, Y.F. (1977). *Space and Place: The Perspective of Experience*. Minneapolis: University of Minnesota Press.

Weeks, K.D., & Grimmer, A.E. (1995). *The Secretary of the Interior's Standards for the Treatment of Historic Properties with Guidelines for Preserving, Rehabilitating, Restoring and Reconstructing Historic Buildings*. Washington, D.C.: U.S. Department of the Interior. Retrieved October 25, 2014, from www.nps.gov/tps/standards/four-treatments/treatment-guidelines.pdf

Wells, J.C. (2011a, Winter). Historic Preservation, Significance, and phenomenology. *Environmental and Architectural Phenomenology, 22*(1): 13–15.

Wells, J.C. (2011b). Historical Significance Through the Lens of Contemporary Social, Cultural, and Experiential Values. *Heritage Studies and Cultural Landscapes: Research: Environmental Design and Behavior*. Retrieved July 25, 2013, from http://heritagestudies.org/research_env.shtml

Williams, R. (2007). Architecture and Visual Culture. In M. Rampley (Ed.), *Exploring Visual Culture: Definitions, Concepts, Contexts*. Edinburgh, UK: Edinburgh University Press, pp. 100–116.

CHAPTER 6

Image for the Future of the Historic City

Photo-Elicitation and Architectural Preservation in Barcelona

AnnaMarie Bliss

Human beings imbue meaning into the built environment using their experiences and perceptions of architecture and the destinations they visit as a way to understand their place in the world. Historic architecture draws tourists and travelers with the promise of forging a connection to the past (Lowenthal, 1990). Different approaches to preservation and adaptive reuse change the way visitors interact with, experience, and perceive historic spaces (Naoi, 2003). Using photo-elicitation as a primary method to understand human affinity, engagement, and imbued meaning into historic space, this chapter investigates what factors in historic building renovation and rehabilitation affect tourist reactions to the preservation and adaptive reuse efforts at the *Palau de la Música Catalana* in Barcelona, Spain. As the present built environment becomes history of the next age, civilizations will rely on architectural preservation to keep heritage alive, and in some cases, maintain it for present use. Equally, we must remember that tourists impact buildings and the historic quality of cities with overuse and abuse. Design intervention is not just for their enjoyment but also for the longevity of cultural heritage. As we enter an age of increasing building reuse, particularly in historic urban contexts, the impacts of those who visit these places to draw connections become more important to the economic, political, and social aspects of design.

Stop and think for a moment about how you would categorize yourself when you embark on journeys to new places. Are you a traveler, one who works for amazing travel experiences, or a tourist, one who passively waits for interesting things to happen to you (Boorstin, 1963)? Situate yourself in an immersive heritage environment and ask yourself in what ways architecture, experience, and your own perceptions are important. Consider how you move through historic spaces and places during your travels. What guides you? How do you see, especially in a world where there is a premium on travel photographs posted on social media?

This chapter asks: *What are the implications of architectural intervention and renovation in culturally significant buildings with respect to tourist experience of place?* To understand the impact of specific aspects of these alterations and interventions, further questions ask: *Does architectural authenticity (or a sense of the genuine and true) matter in the tourist experience? How does UNESCO World Heritage, national, or local heritage designation affect preservation efforts and potentially visitor experience of a place?* At the heart of this lies a question of how the public *sees* tourist-historic sites. With direct lines to practice, goals of the presented study are (1) to determine how these architectural interventions and renovations to the historic buildings influence tourists' experience of the place, and (2) based on the findings for this building, to create general directives for designers to address heritage preservation in architecture of touristic sites in Barcelona and globally.

In the Literature

Both architecture and tourism literature discuss broadly preservation implications; however, the consequences to context and users are less studied as the nature of the heritage site changes (Cook, 2001; Poria et al., 2012). Cultural heritage and uniqueness, or authenticity of sites, are among the most common motivations given for visiting architectural sites. Renovations of heritage physical environments affect interest and patronage as well (Barbieri, 2004; Sirefman, 1999). The context of any heritage object is important to its visitors, but more oft-studied are the changing atmospherics (i.e. color, sound, texture, service) of the place (Bonn et al., 2007). This discrepancy leaves a gap in the literature for investigations that better address the built environment surrounding historic architecture. Buildings facades also impact the observer (Askari & Dola, 2009) and several studies cite that visitors prefer the old and familiar to the new and unfamiliar (Herzog et al., 1982; Mura & Troffa, 2006). This case study looks at this opposition where old and new are juxtaposed in one building. Kevin Lynch's (1960) classic *Image of the City* discusses the idea of imageability or legibility of city environments in five distinct elements. In a US context, Nasar (1994) explains there is clearly a disparity between public and designer preferences and lays out guidelines for urban design review based on aesthetic response through meaning and perception. The limited nature and age of his study, and few comparable cases, provide an occasion for a newer, broader investigation into aesthetic preference and experience of a different kind of public, specifically historic buildings and tourists.

Additionally, personal experience and perception of the past underline the importance of the authenticity discourse in heritage studies (Chhabra et al., 2003; MacCannell, 1973; Naoi, 2003; Wang, 1999), principally on the visual quality of place. Authenticity also plays a significant role in urban World Heritage Sites (WHS), which is of particular importance to this project in Barcelona. Pendlebury et al. (2009) studied the "tension between authentic conservation and commodification" in the World Heritage setting of Edinburgh and Bath in the United Kingdom (p. 349). They find that in the urban context it is difficult to comply with conventional WHS management practices as the environment develops and changes rapidly. Further, a study in Beijing uncovered how wholesale preservation policies and clearing of the context around architectural sites had created a handicap for the city (Abramson, 2007). Visitors also seek meaningful interactions, and through careful consideration of visitor perception and behavior in response to different types of heritage, we may create better interpretations (Moscardo, 1996). To add dimension to this body of work, in Barcelona, there are opportunities to uncover how the addition of contemporary structures and the shifting context have also changed the nature of the urban environment and experience for visitors.

Theoretical Frameworks

Theories from three disciplines comprise the theoretical framework, bridging gaps, and creating a lens through which to answer questions about historic architecture in changing urban contexts. First, the architectural preservation theories of Viollet-le-Duc express the European sentiment of adaptive reuse of aging buildings, creating idealized spaces for present use, and honest expression of material and structure (Viollet-le-Duc, 1990). His work was studied by the architect of the case study, Lluís Domènech i Montaner. His structural ingenuity and sense of wonder for the organic inspired Domènech i Montaner and are likely to be attributed to the case study's prominence in structure and brilliance for the Catalan *modernisme* style, Spain's own version of the art nouveau, most famously characterized by the work of Antoni Gaudí.

Second, this study applies transactional perception, a framework that explains that man and his perception of the environment are inseparable and thus part of one system (Ittelson & Cantril, 1954). Lang (1987) writes "perception is the process of obtaining information from the environment" (p. 85). *Perceiving* is "the process by which a particular person, from his particular behavioral center, attributes significance to his immediate environmental situation" (Ittleson & Cantril, 1954, p. 26). Werner and Wapner (1952) explain that the body and the object are the two parts of the perceptual interaction where the body responds to object stimuli. Specifically, the focus here is on the transactional school of perception in which the relationship between the subject perceiving and the object of perception is key to understanding the system (Castello, 2010). Ittelson and Cantril first wrote about this theory in *Perception: A transactional approach* in 1954. They explain that within this framework, it is assumed that man and his perception of the environment are inseparable and thus part of one system. In a transaction, two implications are present: that all parts enter the encounter as active participants and they exist because of their participation in which their identity may be altered (Ittleson & Cantril, 1954). Transactionalism stresses the role of experience in the perception process (Lang, 1987).

In the environment-behavior context of architecture, this theory more aptly explains the relationship between person and environment, or place. The adoption of the phenomenological approach to studying perception highlights the importance of understanding experience to better explain the person-environment relationship. Perceptions of phenomena occurring within a space have the power to influence certain behaviors or values in visitors (Castello, 2010). Through this valuation, we may attribute meaning to places. We must understand that "experience shapes what people pay attention to in the environment and what is important to them" (Lang, 1987, p. 90). Castello (2010) says that in the built environment there are two kinds of stimuli: perceived stimuli and stimulated perception. Perceived stimuli are inherent in the environment representative of "elements comprising the environmental organization" (p. 93). Stimulated perception is created intentionally, by the architecture, in the environment to ensure a desired resultant experience. For this study, the most important parallel in this theory of perception is that past experiences, or experiences of the past, shape reactions in the present and future and thus, have the power to help us predict reactions to architectural intervention.

Finally, the study examines the theories of Ning Wang (1999) on authenticity to explain how experiences and objects are perceived by the tourist, and in this study, explain visitor senses of the physical architecture of each site, phenomenologically and visually. Authenticity as a theory and directive for practice is extremely nuanced and has footholds in many disciplines where the meanings may be nothing alike. The focus of this study will be on authenticity as it relates to tourism and historic preservation. Sharpley (1994) states, "authenticity connotes traditional culture and origin, a sense of the genuine, the real or the unique" (p. 130). Authenticity in tourism can be discussed in terms of objects and experiences. Wang (1999) further categorizes authenticity into objective, constructive, and existential subcategories to explain these experiences and reactions to objects. Each of these subcategories is something that is perceived by the tourist. The importance of authenticity

IMAGE FOR THE FUTURE OF THE HISTORIC CITY

in this study has to do with perception of the physical architecture present at each site, phenomenologically and visually. Emotional ties and personal feelings about verisimilitude also play a vital role in the nature of an authentic experience (Rickly-Boyd, 2012). However, the idea of authenticity motivates tourists to visit sites (Millar, 1989) and also influences the way in which tourists interact with and respond to heritage sites. In the auspices of cultural heritage, authenticity relates to the conservation and preservation of heritage sites in a truthful and culturally respective manner. This realm of authenticity is also contentious. The Nara Document (ICOMOS, 1994) from UNESCO states, "The understanding of authenticity plays a fundamental role in all scientific studies of the cultural heritage, in conservation and restoration planning, as well as within the inscription procedures used for the World Heritage Convention and other cultural heritage inventories." The concept of authenticity has great implications for listing sites to the World Heritage List and also for the way in which sites are preserved with respect to the Nara Document and earlier UNESCO charters. Conservation and preservation literature activates authenticity in many lights. Some of the earliest theories, those of Viollet-le-Duc, bring to light authenticity as a means by which to preserve or restore a building to an "ideal" state. UNESCO's own Venice and Athens charters bring to bear the importance of showing truth in restoration so as not to confuse the intervention with the original, using modern materials and techniques in preservation efforts, and careful attention to cultural integrity.

The Case Study

According to a Barcelona Turisme press release in 2013, Barcelona, one of the most visited cities in the world, hosted 100 million visitors between 1993 and 2013, and would host roughly ten million more each year after; many with selfie sticks and iPhones in hand. The booming industry is largely wrapped around their *modernisme* architecture. The city itself is a mash of neighborhoods and districts, but obvious by aerial map and understood underfoot by the visitor are the *Ciutat Vella*, or the old city, and the *Eixample*, or the gridded city. Many citizens of Barcelona demand reforms to manage the surge of visitors and tourist-generated income appropriated by the Spanish government. These appeals mean efforts to accommodate record visitor numbers and the booming tourism market by calling for new design interventions to major thoroughfares, museums, and other attractions. Through the adaptive reuse and preservation efforts, there is a re-interpretation of place with each new presentation of a space or facade. The *Palau de la Música Catalana* is no exception. The *Palau* is a music performance venue still active today, running guided tours during the daytime hours for roughly 400 people per day. It has expanded and renovated its historic edifice to make room for growing demand for performances and populations of visitors on the guided tours. Honest attempts at solving visitor overload have turned into an overhaul of the urban approach and historic quarter context. This chapter addresses the expectations and perceptions of the tourists who flock to a historic site with hopes of historic encounters but are greeted instead by a modern façade, a backward entry, and a confusing urban context and more confusing entry sequence.

Completed in just three years from 1905 to 1908, the *Palau de la Música Catalana* is an exemplary representation of *modernisme* architecture by Lluís Domènech i Montaner and was recognized by the UNESCO as a World Heritage site with another of the architect's building complexes in 1997. In its own right, the building is a feat of structural ingenuity, specifically its use of iron frames and

132

curtain wall type construction, the first of its kind. The *Palau* symbolizes and celebrates Catalonian imagination and cultural uniqueness through artistry and innovation. The original building boasts loud mosaics (*trencadís*), exposed red brick, stained glass, allegorical statues, and intricacy, all characteristic of its epoch. The most striking feature in the Great Hall is the stained glass lantern with its unusual shape and symbolism for the *Orfeó Català*.

For protection of the historic structure and art, modern interventions have changed the facades. From roughly 1983 to 1989 and 1999 to 2007, Catalan architect Oscar Tusquets led renovation and expansion efforts at the *Palau*. A large curtain wall of glass now adorns the west façade over what was once covered by a convent. Further, the *Petit Palau* was added as a second room for performance and rehearsal. The additions and modern renovations to the *Palau de la Música Catalana* bring visitors to the non-historic side of the building, forcing them through gift shops and a café during daily activity. The entrance is untrue to the essence of the *Palau*, not easy to find, nor symbolic of entry, facts supported by the results of this study. Interestingly, these renovations were included in the 1997 UNESCO World Heritage listing for the *Palau*, a fact that for many does not align with the qualifications or criteria for World Heritage designation. However, the glass curtain wall is suspended by its own structure separated from the original building. The case may be made for the intervention's necessity to protect and alter heritage based on use and changing cultural landscapes.

Photographs and Sociocultural Meanings

Why are photographs so important to studying preservation from a social science and tourism perspective? We have been bringing culture to people for ages. Sharing and documenting travel and leisure has become standard practice in our culture. This phenomenon goes back to the Grand Tour where wealthy individuals would venture out to see the world and bring home exotic treasures and stories of encounters with something or someone "other." Now we don't necessarily share on the wall of our homes, but we share on social media sites like Facebook, Twitter, Instagram, Tumblr, Flickr. We are an image-based society. We see the world through our own lens and the lenses of others. You are more likely to stop and read an article that has a picture associated than the one that does not. Even Twitter, a short caption social media networking site, is infusing more and more imagery because even a short 140 characters was just not capturing our attention anymore. The method presented here captures the *zeitgeist* of this age in a different way and is unique as it combines both the haptic and socio-spatial elements of design research in an unprecedented way.

Photo-elicitation is a social sciences research method that uses images to elicit responses from participants to gather data about experience, perception, and senses. In architectural research, photo-elicitation can be used to understand relationships to place. Photographs facilitate respondent-to-researcher connections and become a driver for conversation. Photographs concretize memories or at least memories of the moment. John Zeisel said in his keynote address at the 47th annual EDRA conference in Raleigh, North Carolina in May 2016 that we need the environment for memory making and recall—those two things are inseparable. Photographs are how we *consume* place but also how we communicate experience. Photographs then can *produce* data for us. They capture and allow researchers to analyze people's perceptions. Photo-elicitation employs images as a means of communication between the researcher and participants in the field. Cederholm (2012) explains that this method is a "can-opener" as photographs are an integral part of the tourist experience. Visuals are an essential component of establishing a researcher-participant connection, providing a comfortable situation, and creating an environment for sharing information (Scarles, 2012). Researcher-led photo-elicitation (with investigator-provided images) and participant-led photo-elicitation (with participant-provided images) in architecture and design research provide the ability for both parties to engage in a substantive discussion by using relevant visual material to express impressions about the environments portrayed. Generally, only one of the two types of photo-elicitation is used in any given project. However, the study here illustrates that investigators may combine the two approaches to broaden the discussion between the researcher and the participant. This chapter also examines the usefulness and efficacy of combining researcher-led and participant-led photo-elicitation in investigating popular architectural tourism sites. Images are collected from participants and participants are also shown historical and present-day reference images over the course of semi-structured interviews about their perceptions and expectations of the architecture of the *Palau de la Música Catalana*. This study of the methods used in fieldwork assesses the role of photographs in environmental design research as a tool for engaging the participant, stimulating relevant responses, and providing the researcher with solid visual evidence for concrete conclusions.

Participant-led photo-elicitation asks the participant to select photographs from his/her experience to explain feelings and perception of that experience. Photographs in this way give the participant some sense of control and have agency in the data construction process (Banks, 2001). This giving of control and power of storytelling to participants is often called photo voice (Scarles, 2012). This is how participants then may personalize their own knowledge which gives us a more holistic account of the human-environment relationship according to Garrod (2007). Photographs allow people to fashion their thoughts.

Researcher-led photo-elicitation uses researcher pre-selected images to elicit feelings and discussion from participant during interview. Here, the researcher is in control of what is viewed and the circumstances of viewing (Banks, 2001). The researcher shows images to participants and guides the discussion with questions about what the viewer sees and feels. Using photographs in environmental design research as a tool for engaging the participant, stimulating relevant responses, and providing the researcher with solid visual evidence for concrete conclusions. Awkwardness is lessened through the tangible research object. The give-and-take manner of interview takes away the tension created in interview situations by leveling the playing field.

Results and Discussion

Using both participant- and researcher-led photo-elicitation, a convenience sample of forty-two participants was used to construct the resulting data and conclusions. The goal of the convenience sample was to show a representative sample of the populations of visitors who visit the *Palau*. Interviews were conducted during tourist high-seasons over seven weeks between 2015 and 2016. Visitors were approached by the researcher following a one-hour guided tour of the *Palau de la Música Catalana*. They were told that the interviews were to assess their experience through the photographs they took while on their tours. Interviews began with participant-led photo-elicitation. Participants were asked to select their favorite or most memorable moments from the tour from their photographs, up to ten, and to use the images to describe those experiences and the feelings the images represented. For brevity, the discussion here is limited to the four most common images seen with almost every participant. The first image was generally an overall panoramic view of the Great Hall (Figure 6.1), capturing the exquisite detail of the entire room. Second, visitors showed the trencadís columns on

Figure 6.1 The overall panoramic view of the Great Hall. Photograph by the author.

the second-floor exterior balcony outside the parlor (Figure 6.2) illustrating the range of colors and variety of design represented in the mosaics. Third, the stained-glass lantern (Figure 6.3) was shown, which depicts the women of music, as the original performers were only males and Domènech wanted to include the feminine touch. Finally, images depicted close-up views of the muse sculptures (Figure 6.4) protruding from the stage wall. The muses symbolize a world united in music, each woman holding an instrument from a part of the world. With each image, participants discussed the beauty of the space or details, their own feelings of connection to the architecture because of personal interest or heritage, how much they were in awe of or liked a space, and how they preferred certain styles or portrayals of detail or imagery.

Demographically, these data represent equally a range of ages from 18 to 75. An equal percentage of six roughly ten-year age categories (18–25, 26–35, 36–45, 46–55, 56–65, 66–75) were sampled. Almost all participants were college or university educated, and several had an advanced degree or graduate-level education. Most participants, over fifty percent, were female. This statistic corresponds with the average visitors of the site confirmed through daily site observation. The *Palau* itself does not keep records of visitor genders, ages, or education levels. It does, however, keep logs of visitor nationalities. The participants in this study represent a proportionate sample of visitors in comparison to the overall nationality count of visitors to the Palau with the most visitors coming from the United States and the United Kingdom. Participants also come from Asia, Australia, and South America, again representing a comparable proportion to the Palau's visitor log. The data presented in this chapter is illustrative of a data saturation reached after forty-two interviews, but well represents the broad visitor demographics and a good sample of individual preference.

Figure 6.2 The trencadís columns on the second-floor exterior balcony outside the parlor, exhibiting the range of colors and variety of design represented in the mosaics. Photograph by the author.

Figure 6.3 The stained glass depicting the women of music. Photograph by the author.

Figure 6.4 Close-up views of the muse sculptures protruding from the stage wall. Photograph by the author.

In order to assess the data, the most common themes defined were the usage of words of affinity, preference, and aesthetics, becoming the common codes for analysis of the data. Personal preference helps to explain how visitors visually and experientially expect historic spaces and details to be displayed. Despite this code being a value judgment, it applies as a broad descriptor of the success of preservation initiatives. The code affinity refers to the degree to which participants like, love, or have warm feelings toward the architecture they are presenting through images during the course of the semi-structured interviews that lasted fifteen to forty-five minutes. A great deal of deal of affinity was shown for each of the four most common spaces or details of the *Palau*, each participant indicating that time in and seeing these architectures was important or necessary to their visit experience. Further, they indicated that the authentic experience of their visit was due to the preserved nature of these details and spaces, therefore describing existential authenticity. Preserved historic detail was preferred and shown over any modern or contemporary detailing. Participants indicated that they generally did not like to photograph new parts of the building or tour. The relative level of authenticity of the building and its associated details was relegated to the original part of the building only. Participants indicated that their images reflected what they deemed original to the building and authentic to the *Palau's* style and era. This discussion reflects the objective authenticity, as relating to the building object, perceived by the visitor. Participants also used their interviews to reflect on how the architecture related to their own lives, memories, and hopes for future travel. Many found that the *Palau* spoke to them through its own story of being a building for the people, representing the identity of the middle class and the Catalonian population. Participants were able to identify with the ambitions of the architect manifest in built form and shared through their images as reminders of each moment of their experience.

Following participant-led photo-elicitation, participants are shown images of the historic entry (Figure 6.5), which still stands but is unused during daytime tours, and the historic Great Hall. The historic entry sequence is at the front of the building under the large arches and *trencadís* facades.

Figure 6.5 The historic entry, which still stands but is unused during daytime tours. Photograph by the author.

The historic entry to contemporary entry comparison is important to understanding how the idea of procession affects visitors as it relates to an "authentic" experience of the *Palau de la Música Catalana*. The Great Hall originally had iron rails with swag that included organic lines and floral motifs, all of which are shown in the 1908 grand opening photographs used during the researcher-led photo-elicitation. With these photographs, participants were asked to what degree they liked the historic architecture and to what degree they preferred the historic entry or Great Hall. Most of the participants felt that the current entry through the glass wall (Figure 6.6) was not as authentic as if they could have entered through the original entry. There was a low degree of affinity for the glass wall as compared to the historic entry, through which visitors believed they would have felt as if they had gone back in time. The historic Great Hall garnered a high degree of affinity, but many respondents felt that the abundance of detail could have distracted from the fanciful details of the rest of the space and was, therefore, not preferred to the present aesthetic. The result here is more inconclusive about how to preserve historic detailing at such a scale. During researcher-led photo-elicitation, participants were able to more fully describe their appreciation for historic details in the Palau, often referring back to their participant-led images. These additional images helped them to also articulate how they felt about contemporary parts of the building they may not have photographed but had strong feelings toward as part of their experience. Through the addition of the researcher-selected

Figure 6.6 The current entry through the glass wall. Photograph by the author.

images, a more complete picture of the beginning, middle, and end of the tour was formed. Where participant photographs tended toward the middle part of the tour, the researcher-selected images could capture the other aspects and assess the relative engagement of the visitor at the beginning and end of their architectural experience which otherwise may have been overlooked.

Many participants were unaware of the World Heritage status of the building before visiting. Guidebooks they encountered had failed to mention the outstanding universal value of the structure and its co-listed building, the *Hospital Sant Pau*, are said to hold. Participants often remarked on the World Heritage status of the *Palau de la Música Catalana* as if to say it was an interesting fact and likely the reason for the nature or level of preservation of the historic building. Visitors then perceived the building as retaining authentic character, the UNESCO designation as a reminder. The designation was not necessarily a reason to visit, but roughly half of the participants were glad to have encountered this important World Heritage-listed historic building.

Based on these results, general directives for the future of the *Palau de la Música Catalana* can be surmised using visitor expectations and preferences that represent the world tourism population at large. The *Palau* will continue to renovate and rehabilitate as necessary to ensure the longevity of the historic structure. Currently, work is being conducted to repair tiles and other wall surfaces that have normal wear and tear from daily use. The *Palau* would be best advised to continue work that honors the integrity of the historic fabric of the building including replacing tile and mosaic with original or similar materials instead of infilling walls with plaster or gypsum board. Primary points of affinity, specifically the details and spaces in the images from the photo-elicitation interviews should be well regarded with minimal intervention that would detract from the original or authentic character. Participants, and also future visitors, would share disappointment at the covering of these historic attributes for large-scale work. A plan for preservation and work should be established to prevent distraction from key architectural features or tour highlights.

Further, using the original ticket booths near the historic entrance and using the nearby doors would enhance the experience of the visitors. Those individuals could still have access to the café space to wait but would feel as if they entered the historic building as expected. Tour participants

IMAGE FOR THE FUTURE OF THE HISTORIC CITY

then could proceed on the tour and be directed to exit through the modern glass wall and gift shop into the courtyard space and on to the city. This would eliminate confusion as to how to access the building and likely draw more visitors and, one could speculate, more ticket sales for tours and nighttime performances due to convenience and possibly spontaneous encounters. One couple indicated during their interview that they had skipped the tour the day before because they couldn't figure out how to access the building. It was only after consulting a hotel concierge that they decided to try again that day. Their story is not uncommon, many participants echoed the sentiment of confusion over the entry and could be avoided using the entrance on the main façade. The changes to the context with the addition of the courtyard space by the glass entry wall would be less of an issue with this space being more used for leisure and an exit way following the tours.

Conclusions

While this building is certainly not only a tourism venue, the most foot traffic in any given day is by visitors who seek guided tours and interaction with the architecture that makes Barcelona famous. The overall integrity of the historic building and visitor experience is due to the level of detail the building retains at present through sustained preservation efforts. Should the attention to historic detail and careful restoration be forgotten, so too would the authentic nature of the visit to this iconic place. To add to the already awe-inspiring experience and to help the arrival and entry experience, the *Palau* should consider using the original entrance and ticket spaces regularly. The data from this study illustrate the affinity and expectations people have to having an authentic experience from entry to exit.

Findings indicate that visitors indeed prefer the old aesthetic to modern facades and additions each site has completed; however, tourists are more understanding of renovation that is presented as new instead of "fake historic" style. They appreciated when tour guides pointed out changes made to the building, especially adaptations that were well camouflaged or that did not disrupt visual continuity or historic aesthetics. All participants indicate that despite renovations, the *Palau de le Música Catalana* is authentic only because architectural treatments sought to preserve historic details.

Through these data, we can see how the two types of photo-elicitation work together to give us a broader picture that may otherwise be overlooked should only researcher-led or participant-led photo-elicitation be used. In combination, we can create dialogue through which to create data rich with meaning and more content than interview alone can provide. Early analysis indicates that, in concert, the two approaches deliver a more comprehensive set of data. Where participant photographs may be lacking, researcher images provide cues for further conversation to gain a comprehensive picture of environmental perception. Through using modern technology and allowing individuals to maintain control of how they take in the experience of a tourist-historic site before the researcher comes into contact, the tourist is made an agent of the present. Letting participants guide an interview through their own photographic medium mitigates the foreignness of the historic site through the comfort of their own camera lens. The tourist feels as if they can progress through a historic space or encounter the "other" all while retaining their own present identity.

By inserting carefully selected images into the conversation, the researcher is able to strategically guide the course of interview without disturbing the agency of the participant. In navigating control over the interview experience, both researcher and participant can build a level of rapport through mediating the language and content of the interview. Each party, therefore, had the opportunity to guide the conversation to create a complete picture of the visitor experience of historic places and ultimately expectations about historic preservation.

References

Abramson, D. B. (2007). The aesthetics of city-scale preservation policy in Beijing. *Planning Perspectives, 22*(2), 129–166.

Askari, A. H., & Dola, K. B. (2009). Influence of building façade visual elements on its historical image: Case of Kuala Lumpur City, Malaysia. *Journal of Design and Built Environment, 5*, 49–59.

Banks, M. (2001). *Visual methods in social research*. London: SAGE Publications.

Barbieri, K. (2004). $63M Facelift at Brooklyn Museum set to welcome larger crowds. *Amusement Business, 116*, 5.

Bonn, M. A., Joseph-Mathews, S. M., Dai, M., Hayes, S., & Cave, J. (2007). Heritage/cultural attraction atmospherics: Creating the right environment for the heritage/cultural visitor. *Journal of Travel Research, 45*, 345–354.

Boorstin, D. J. (1963). *The image: Or, what happened to the American dream*. Harmondsworth, Middlesex: Penguin.

Castello, L. (2010). *Rethinking the meaning of place: Conceiving place in architecture urbanism*. Burlington, VT: Ashgate.

Cederholm, E. A. (2012). 6 Photo-elicitation and the construction of tourist experiences: Photographs as mediators in interviews. In T. Rakic, & D. Chambers, *Introduction to visual methods in tourism*. London: Routledge.

Chhabra D., Healy, R., & Sills, E. (2003). Staged authenticity and heritage tourism. *Annals of Tourism Research, 30*(3), 702–719.

Cook, T. (2001). Archival science and postmodernism: New formulations for old concepts. *Archival & Museum Informatics, 1*(1), 3–24.

Garrod, B. (2007). A snapshot into the past: The utility of volunteer-employed photography in planning and managing heritage tourism. *Journal of Heritage Tourism, 2*(1), 14–35.

Herzog, T. R., Kaplan, S., & Kaplan, R. (1982). The prediction of preference for unfamiliar urban places. *Journal of Population and Environment, 5*(1), 43–59.

ICOMOS. (1994). The Nara document on authenticity. *Nara Conference on Authenticity in Relation to the World Heritage Convention* (Nara, Japan, from 1–6 November 1994). Nara: Japan. Centre Documentation.

Ittleson, W. H., & Cantril, H. (1954). *Perception: A transactional approach*. Garden City, NY: Doubleday.

Lang, J. (1987). 9 Fundamental processes of human behavior. In J. Lang, *Creating architectural theory: The role of behavioral sciences in environmental design*. New York, NY: Van Nostrand Reinhold.

Lowenthal, D. (1990). *The past is a foreign country*. Cambridge: Cambridge University Press.

Lynch, K. (1960). *The image of the city*. Cambridge, MA: MIT Press.

Maccannell, D. (1973). Staged authenticity: Arrangements of social space in tourist settings. *American Journal of Sociology, 79*(3), 589–603.

Millar, S. (1989). Heritage management for heritage tourism. *Tourism Management, 10*(1), 9–14.

Moscardo, G. (1996). Mindful visitors: Heritage and tourism. *Annals of Tourism Research, 23*(2), 376–397.

Mura, M., & Troffa, R. (2006). Aesthetic perception and preference for historical and modern buildings. *Journal of Cognitive Processing, 7*(1), 66–67.

Naoi, T. (2003). Visitors' evaluation of a historical district: The roles of authenticity and manipulation. *Tourism and Hospitality Research, 5*(1), 45–63.

Nasar, J. (1994). Urban design aesthetics: The evaluative qualities of building exteriors. *Environment and Behavior, 26*, 377–401.

Pendlebury, J., Short, M., & While, A. (2009). Urban World Heritage Sites and the problem of authenticity. *Cities, 26*, 349–358.

Poria, Y., Reichel, A., & Cohen, R. (2012). Tourists perceptions of World Heritage Site and its designation. *Tourism Management, 35*, 272–274.

Rickly-Boyd, J. M. (2012). 'Through the magic of authentic reproduction': Tourists' perceptions of authenticity in a pioneer village. *Journal of Heritage Tourism, 7*(2), 127–144.

Scarles, C. (2012). 5 Eliciting embodied knowledge and response: Respondent-led photography and visual autoethnography. In T. Rakic, & D. Chambers, *Introduction to visual methods in tourism*. London: Routledge.

Sharpley, R. (1994). *Tourism, tourists, & society*. Huntington, Cambridgeshire: ELM.

Sirefman, S. (1999). Formed and forming: Contemporary museum architecture. *Daedalus, 128*, 297–321.

Viollet-le-Duc, Eugène Emmanuel. (1990). *The Architectural Theory of Viollet-le-Duc: Readings and Commentary*, ed. Millard F. Hearn. Cambridge: MIT Press.

Wang, N. (1999). Rethinking authenticity in tourism experience. *Annals of Tourism Research, 26*(2), 349–370.

Werner, H., & Wapner, S. (1952). Toward a general theory of perception. *Psychological Review, 59*(4), 324–338. doi: 10.1037/h0059673

CHAPTER 7

Conservation and the People's Views

Ethnographic Perspectives from Jones Beach State Park

Dana H. Taplin, Suzanne Scheld, and Setha Low

Built in the 1920s under the direction of the legendary urban planner and "power broker" Robert Moses, Jones Beach is a New York state park of historical significance in recalling the technocratic optimism of planning and design in the interwar period. On its fiftieth anniversary, in 1979, New York Times architectural critic Paul Goldberger called it

> an absolutely remarkable public achievement—six and a half miles [10.5 kilometers] of beachfront built out of low and shifting sandbars and filled with structures so elaborate they call to mind courthouses and college campuses, not beach buildings…Jones Beach speaks of a government dedicated to providing a truly noble public environment…a beach for the Empire City.

The state government's willingness to build and maintain so large and complex a park shaped its reputation as a "people's palace." In recent years, however, visitation has dropped. The state park agency was in discussions with the Trump Organization to privatize a key node as a business opportunity for Trump and income-generating strategy for the park. Hurricane Sandy interrupted the already fraught negotiations as it damaged many of the park's structures and illuminated the hazards of building a structure as large as that proposed by Trump in a flood zone. At the same time, the state's emergency response to hurricane damage brought a new interest in revitalizing the park and the appropriation of sizable capital funds for that purpose.

Jones Beach serves diverse publics—a longtime white, largely suburban constituency, a cross section of people of color from the boroughs of New York City and from Long Island, LGBTQ groups and others. These are variably self-segregating constituencies, with the white users drawn to the newer, more informal and car accessible parts of the beach, particularly parking Field 6, LGBTQ visitors using an area beyond easy reach of any parking lot, and the historic core of the park used increasingly by people of color. How do "the people" relate to a park that is part of their history—but not everyone's history—and that has hit hard times? What expectations do users have for the expenditure of resources toward the preservation of the park's built environment?

Space and History

In conventional historic preservation practice, buildings and districts are deemed significant for their association with historical events—signing of the Declaration, Paul Revere hanging lanterns in the North Church belfry—or for their artistic value as architectural works. Preservation practice employs the building crafts to restore the fabric of certain buildings to their period of significance, and, more generally, imposes codified protection to regulate future maintenance and alteration. There are underlying assumptions that historic preservation will enhance public edification, aesthetic satisfaction, and historical consciousness. The human-centered approaches to preservation, alternatively, seek to find what is valuable in historic environments to people in the present and future. What do the people who pass through and use specific buildings or larger built contexts make of the environment's historical associations and artistic values? In the case of the built environment of Jones Beach, we wonder what, from a cultural and psychological perspective, is valuable about its structures to people today and tomorrow.

Like any public environment that is amenable to walking, the beach offers a range of potentialities, from orchestrating a daily cultural scene of mass recreation to affording visitors a nice day of relaxation. De Certeau (2011) wrote of walking in the city as an everyday spatial practice, one where walkers weave and write an urban text. Walkers, he noted, being within the urban text, cannot read the whole. De Certeau (2011) begins his account of walking in the city with a view from the 110th floor. The view from high up meets the urge to apprehend the whole fabric which, until the advent of tall buildings, could not be satisfied except through the vicarious pleasure of the mapmaker's bird's-eye view. Visually and topographically open spaces within the city allow the walkers to grasp larger passages of the text they write, and at the beach, the visual field is so wide open that everyone can enjoy the view of the great body ballet to which each visitor contributes through their bodily activity.

Low (2003) uses the term "embodied space" to mean spatial experience, knowledge, and memory gained through physical bodily activity. The term would appear to suit de Certeau's (2011) concept of urban walking as a spatial practice that, like putting language to speech, "enunciates" urban social space. Bodily movement at the beach similarly enunciates a sociocultural text that forms and dissolves daily through the summer season. A park like this, with beach, boardwalk, and recreational facilities, invites and affords freer, more varied bodily activity than sidewalks and squares in the city. Here people swim, run, walk, play games on the sand. It is an embodied space in that one relates to the space through movement and sensation. Unlike de Certeau's (2011) walkers, the beach goers can apprehend the whole scene. Having done some park visitor research at Jones Beach, we think the embodied space experience and the "visibility' of the social scene the visitors create is informative for historic preservation purposes.

Amid the predominant emphasis on "period of significance" and building craft practices that restore structures thereto, historic preservation has embraced alternative philosophies. John Ruskin and his followers detested the practice of restoration, specifically of restoring historic buildings as to strict form; rather advocating preserving them in their decay. It was not so much the form that has true historical meaning, Ruskin thought, as the materials themselves, which, in the case of buildings from the Middle Ages, were lovingly made and put in place by past generations. The act of restoration destroys much of this material continuity in the quest to refashion the original form. The contemporaneous French theorist Viollet-le-Duc, and many others, articulated what became the mainstream approach, which emphasizes restoration as to form. In the case of Jones Beach, nothing is truly old, but historic preservation practices and protection is widely applied in North America to buildings no older than these (Ruskin, 1849; White, 1962; Lowenthal, 1985).

CONSERVATION AND THE PEOPLE'S VIEWS

Recent thought in historic preservation derives in part from Ruskin's emphasis on memory. David Lowenthal's (1985) work has been credited as having moved the focus on heritage conservation from fabric to people. Mason (2004) crystalizes the issue as a tension between fabric and memory. Concerns over fabric focus on practices that *fix* the fabric, relegating memory to a static conception of significance. Mason argues for a more flexible understanding of preservation as a connection between fabric and memory where the core benefit of preservation is to cultivate society's collective memory. Historic preservation at Jones Beach is surely framed from the fabric-centered perspective (Wolfe, 2004; Moroney, 2013). Given the present use patterns and funding challenges, human-centered approaches in historical conservation have much to offer in reconciling stakeholder interests at Jones Beach. Further, a more nuanced perspective on Moses's purposes at Jones Beach is complementary with a flexible approach to managing the park's resources in ways that recognize the values visitors attach to them as well as the challenges of maintaining a fixed built environment on a fragile barrier island.

Jones Beach: From Robert Moses to Corporate Sponsorship

According to Robert Caro's highly critical biography of Moses, *The Power Broker* (1974), Jones Beach was an international sensation when it opened in 1929. The spacious layout, extravagant architecture, and numerous diversions and amenities received ecstatic press and attracted design and public official visitors from Europe and elsewhere in North America to view what Moses had wrought from the shoals and sandbars of Hempstead Bay. The design includes a parkway along the length of the newly built up barrier island, giant but masked parking lots (Fields 4 and 5), and a wide boardwalk linking two elegant bathhouse and pool structures. A Central Mall, perpendicular to the boardwalk and landscaped with flower beds, lawn, and boxwood hedges, is anchored by a "campanile" in Art Deco-Collegiate Gothic hybrid style containing a water storage tank to serve the park's facilities. The bathhouses offered locker, pool, changing room, and shower facilities to thousands of visitors; a formal, high-ceilinged dining room, loggias, and terraces, rendered in a mix of art deco and streamline modern styles. Goldberger (1979) calls West Bathhouse "Neo-Collegiate Gothic WPA Art Deco."

In the 1920s, people would come to and depart the beach dressed in street clothes, and, in many cases, spend some of their time at the beach dressed. The shift to public informality began after World War II, yet, many continued to use the bathhouses after the war and spend some of their time at the beach dressed. In some of the postwar photographs presented here, such as the scene above in front of the West Bathhouse, most of the users in sight are dressed. The visitor experience might include dining, swimming, playing games, and attending an exhibit or a concert. Both everyday attire and swimming attire was more elaborate and cumbersome in the 1920s and 1930s than clothing today and there was no driving to the beach in a swimsuit or a quick change in the car. The bathhouse facilities served the need of most visitors to change into and out of swimming attire at their convenience (Moroney, 2013).

From Lefebvre (1991), we take the idea of space as socially produced, that is, built with specific socially normative ends and understood from within a particular sociocultural context. Here, Moses and his design team repudiated the cluttered design vocabulary of public beaches, produced up to that time within a laissez-faire profit system by multiple actors, often for specific class and ethnic groups. Seeking to transcend the particular class and ethnic associations of many commercially produced beaches, which were subject to rapid decline in social status, Jones beach reworked the Progressive Era architectural vocabulary of children's playgrounds on a grand scale. The enormous bathhouses and water tower set in an axial Beaux-Arts ground plan is an exercise in creating new monuments to a technocratic, prosperous, future-oriented society. The vigorously hybrid architectural vocabulary uses forms that resonate particularly in New York, where the short-lived Art Deco style reached its height, and whose architects made over campuses in nearby New Haven and Princeton in Collegiate Gothic. Moses wielded a power that is associated with the social production of space, employing monumental architecture and a formal beaux-arts ground plan to underscore the civic respectability of the place and reify automatic respect for national institutions. The nautical flags, water tower, Central Mall, and monumental bathhouses remain and contribute to the retention of these values decades later.

The park was a showcase for modernism, not only in its structures, landscapes, and technics of mobility but also in its vision of a uniform middle-class leisure society. The park was to have an equalizing effect on visitors: people would be uplifted by the elegant surroundings and high standards of service. There would be no billboards, hot dog vendors, or other crass elements. The expectation of mass conformity was reinforced at first by extreme measures. It is said that to keep the place spic-and-span, the abundant uniformed staff would immediately pick up a gum wrapper or anything else dropped by a careless visitor, communicating to all that Jones Beach tolerated only the highest standards of conduct.

Its suburban location allowed Jones Beach to maintain the veneer of middle-class respectability through the turbulent 1960s, a time when parks in New York City were showing the conflicts and strains of the era's social divisions. More recently, funding and visitation declined, leading to the closure of three of six recreation complexes added after 1945. One of the postwar beach areas closed in 1999, another in 2006, and a third in 2009. A fourth area, the smallest one, was undone by beach erosion in the 1980s. Budget cuts brought the closure of the East Bathhouse and its pool in 2009. Visitation in 1977 was 14.5 million. By 1991 visitation was still 14 million, according to a New York Times account, but only six million by 2005, where it remains today (Saslow, 2009).

While a latter-day Robert Moses might choose to level eighty-year-old structures built to serve needs that in part no longer exist, and build something up-to-date in their place, the contemporary discourse is about preserving the Moses design and, through historic preservation and "corporate sponsorship opportunities," to rejuvenate its once bustling social nodes. The state parks office placed Jones Beach State Park and its related parkways on the State Register of Historic Places in 2005. It was later added to the National Register of Historic Places. An historic preservation group on Long Island released a report at about the same time criticizing the management of the park in the 1970s and 1980s for making "crucial decisions" without sufficient regard for the original design. These measures included "cheap" replacement outdoor lighting fixtures, "featureless" aluminum frame replacement windows on the West Bathhouse and eliminating the reflecting pools beside the Jones Beach tower. The Friendly's restaurant sign at the West Bathhouse was singled out as a "jarring" example of the kind of commercialism that Moses would have never allowed (Wolfe, 2004).

Apparently, Moses allowed no franchises at Jones Beach. The food service and other retail offerings were provided directly by the park. In recent times, the park contracts with a restaurant service which can bring franchises in. The former Marine Dining Room at the West Bathhouse was partly occupied by the offending Friendly's in 2012, although not since Hurricane Sandy struck later that year. The Boardwalk Restaurant, built with New Deal funds in 1936–1937, occupied a location opposite the snack bar where the Central Mall meets the boardwalk. This building was demolished after a fire in the 1960s and replaced in 1966 by a squat glass and stone structure designed by a prominent

CONSERVATION AND THE PEOPLE'S VIEWS

modernist architecture firm, Skidmore, Owings and Merrill. At that time, we guess no one thought of the original buildings, then only 30–35 years old, as historic, and the architect was free to provide a contemporary design. The state park system introduced corporate sponsorship opportunities in 2001 (Saslow, 2009). Five years later, the 1966 Skidmore building was demolished, to be replaced by a new structure built along the lines of the original building. But this time, the state would not build the building; the state sought a "private partner" to build and operate the restaurant and pay rent to the state. Donald Trump was the only bidder.

The larger and higher building Trump proposed brought immediate controversy. Soon the state parks office became embroiled in litigation with the Trump interests over floodplain issues. A Wall Street Journal article in 2012 reports parks Commissioner Rose Harvey announcing a new agreement with Trump, after five years of stalemate, that settles the lawsuits and allows the stalled project to proceed. The state would collect $74 million in rent over 40 years. Mr. Trump claimed that Robert Moses would be proud of "Trump on the Ocean," although as the 2005 historic preservation report notes, Moses banned concessions and any form of commercialism at the park. The Trump project was opposed by some Nassau County residents: One quoted in the Journal article opposed the scale of Trump's facility. "This is the people's historical beach, not Trump's beach."

A group sympathetic to Trump calling itself the "Alliance to Revitalize Jones Beach" claimed the opponents were imagining a casino or high rise coming from Trump, whereas "this is a three-story building, really beautiful, in keeping with the neighborhood" (Alliance, 2017). The Trump project died later in 2012 after Hurricane Sandy damaged the park, flooded the site, and substantiated the state's concern over building a large structure having kitchens in the basement within a floodplain.

Although the Trump project would not have involved historic preservation, per se, it was put forward with clear reference to the prevailing architectural context at Jones Beach. Other than being too large, the proposed building was consistent with its surroundings, having similar facade material, massing, and scale. The restaurant use was as before although larger and geared to private parties and events as much as to public dining. The public debate pro and con also took historic preservation values into account, as with the comment quoted above about the "peoples' historical beach."

While such marriages between the state and private interests have transformed public spaces in the heart of New York City they have so far not progressed at public spaces like this that lie far from the city center. At Jones Beach, the state managers, having stepped back from the edge of privatization, have succeeded in finding more public funds, at least for capital expenses. A press release in March 2014 announces $65 million in new capital funding for the "Jones Beach Revitalization Plan" to restore buildings, plantings, and irrigation systems. A set of renderings accompanying the press release promises a reopened East Bathhouse and various new and rebuilt recreational facilities. The press release alludes to "expanded concession services" involving "public-private partnerships."

We base our discussion here on data gathered in a mixed methods cultural use study of Jones Beach conducted by the Public Research Group (CUNY) in 2012 (prior to Hurricane Sandy). Funded by the Alliance for New York State Parks, the study entailed the collection of 640 surveys for a "demographic assessment" of the park; and four days of participant observation, social activity mapping, and semi-structured interviewing for the "ethnographic assessment," which was undertaken by an interdisciplinary team of five ethnographers. Results from the study underscore how the past is both present and redefined in contemporary, routine use of the park, and how consultation with everyday users provides a valid and useful view of public history that ought to be combined with other "expert" perspectives when undertaking conservation endeavors.

Methodology

The research was organized in two phases, a survey phase to establish a statistically accurate snapshot of the composition of park visitors and their activities, then an ethnographic phase to investigate the users' cultural associations with the park. Phase One involved 640 surveys completed over the three days of work with a research team of five field workers and one or sometimes two supervisors. Four days of fieldwork were allotted for Phase Two, with four field workers and one supervisor.

Having some statistically valid and reliable data on park usership would be valuable to park managers and advocates. While ethnographic research is an essential tool for understanding social organization, cultural associations, and other dimensions of how people use and attribute value to public resources, the data it yields lacks the advantage of being statistically representative of the whole population of park users. We used the survey method to establish basic parameters and the ethnographic method to delve more deeply into the place-making context. The survey phase provided simple, reliable facts about the visitors and the ethnographic phase explored questions raised by the survey data.

Phase I: Assessing Demographics

The survey phase assessed the demographic composition of park visitors in terms of the following characteristics: sex, age, race/ethnicity, area of residence, structure of group (i.e., with whom and how many people is one visiting the park), activities one expects to participate in while visiting the park and expected areas to visit while in the park.

The 11-question survey was collected from respondents with hand-held electronic devices—iPads—using an online survey software, Quicktap. The survey software reported out the data in Excel-compatible spreadsheet form, which was then imported into SPSS, a statistics software program, to report the results.

The sampling plan assumed that summer visitation varies consistently within weeks (different weekday and weekend populations) but not across weeks, and that sampling the visitor population of any given fair weather week will provide a very serviceable characterization of high season usage. The sampling approach outlined at the outset of the project anticipated reaching visitors as they entered the park. In consultation with the park staff, we chose the parking lot approach. After some preliminary observation of the patterns in parking lots, we saw an opportunity in Parking Fields 4 and 5 to approach visitors as they walked from the parking lots through the passageways leading to the beach. Nearly everyone using those lots uses one of the two passageways connecting each with the beach. The walk was long enough to take the survey and the flow of visitors into and through a channel gave us a workable control point at which to apply a random selection procedure.

To get a random sample, the field workers sought to approach every fourth person or group to take the survey. If that person declined, they would then ask the next person or group to participate, and after that survey completion, wait for the fourth next person/group, and so on. Random sampling was also obtained by covering all the entry points to the park in proportion to their usage, by sampling people very early in the morning one day, into the evening another day, and otherwise throughout the day; and by dividing our time proportionally between weekends and weekdays. We conducted the survey on Saturday July 8, Sunday July 9, and Tuesday July 11, 2012.

Later in the day, we sampled people on the central beach and boardwalk and in certain peripheral spots: West End Field 1 and the gay-lesbian beach east of Field 6. In the peripheral locations, on the boardwalk, and on the beach, the approach was markedly different from the original idea of reaching people on their way to the park. The approach at these locations—of finding people where they are— was like the approach in the ethnographic portion of the study, except that the fieldworkers continued to be systematic in choosing people to take the survey. Smaller numbers of visitors were sampled at other locations: Zach's Bay, a calm-water beach for families, and Field 10, a bayside fishing facility.

Phase II: Ethnography

The ethnographic assessment involved semi-structured interviewing of visitors where we found them, "participant observation," a basic ethnographic research approach, and behavioral mapping, as inter-related methods for collecting ethnographic data. The purpose of the fieldwork is to develop knowledge of the social ecology of the park: who is there, what they do, relations and/or conflicts among users or between users and the park and its managers, staff, and concessionaires; how people use park resources, user expectations of the park, meanings, preferences, visitors' knowledge of the park and its features and programs, and visitors' ideas for improvement. The ethnographic research would include the services—and facilities—rating questions the state park agency had formerly used in its visitor surveys.

We conducted four days of field research at Jones Beach. We used data from some of the survey variables to inform our selection of areas and populations. We used zip code data to determine which parts of the park had proportionately larger use by New York City residents, as the question of city resident use of state parks in suburban jurisdictions was of particular interest to Open Space Institute, the research funder. We used data from the race/ethnicity variable to set targets for interviews across basic race/ethnicity categories so as to reflect the park's diversity proportionally.

The individual interviews all followed an interview instrument prepared and reviewed with co-operation of the Open Space Institute and state parks staff. Field workers collected 25–30 individual (and key-informant) interviews per ethnographic site.

Park User Perspectives

Like much work in historic preservation, the issues at Jones Beach focus on the treatment of built form—how to maintain it and to what level of authenticity, how and whether to introduce new elements within the historic fabric, and so on. We turn to the cultural use study data for indication of the meanings typical Jones Beach visitors attach to the park's material landscape. How do issues of preservation and new development figure in the values visitors attribute to the park?

Some visitors, when asked whether the park had any special meaning for them, volunteered details about the park's architectural landmarks—for example, a middle-aged couple who had grown up coming to Jones Beach in the 1980s. Now they live elsewhere but this visit brought back many memories. When asked about special places, the man said, "…the tower is something we always remember. My wife's grandfather worked on it." Asked how Jones Beach has changed over time he recalled

> …there was a sense of elegance. The railing was made of mahogany, you know. I think the benches were made of teak. I understand that these materials don't last but I do miss it. Also,

the flagpole at the Central Mall used to have all these flags on the ropes that came down—it was not Morse code, but it was something nautical. I miss that maritime theme of the Central Mall.

Noticeable in this discussion is the focus on materials—mahogany, teak—rather than forms. The tower is memorable because his wife's grandfather worked on it, presumably on its construction. This recalls Ruskin's ideas about the value of old buildings—not their correctness of form, either in decay or following restoration, but the connection they make with past generations through their substance. The wooden railing—probably teak rather than mahogany—was replaced by some more practical synthetic material. What is wrong with the replacement? He does not say, only that he misses the original wood material. From one user's fleeting comments we cannot know whether the practical solution was the right one. Still, materials make a difference. People experience the built and natural elements of the park as a material reality, especially on the beach itself where the shoes come off and sand, sun, and surf are intensely felt. A wooden ship rail can be felt too: someone might run their hand along a teak railing sooner than its alloy metal replacement. The wooden railing echoes the wooden surface of the boardwalk. Even with shoes on, people notice and appreciate the smooth wooden planks and notice too when the surface seems to need renewal. Boardwalks continue to be largely surfaced in wood rather than cheaper and more durable synthetics because the materiality of wood is important. Other beach visitors talk about specific structures or designed landscapes too, but many refer more generally to the place in bodily experience and memory.

A park like this with beach, boardwalk, and recreational facilities invites and affords bodily activity and sensation. Bodily sensation can be intense in this space: sunbathing, the feel of hot sand under bare feet, playing volleyball, negotiating the surf, and many other experiences. This may be one reason why materials in the built environment have resonance—less so than feeling the sun, sand, and water, but the sight and touch of the teak railing, the kinetic sensation of walking on the boardwalk, the sight of the sandstone and "Barbizon brick" of the building façades in the sunlight are all part of the felt materiality of memories produced through embodied space.

Space at the beach is reified through bodily sensation. People comment on the amount of space, the ease of finding one's own spot even among the crowds, or by walking away from the more populous locations. For one respondent, the meaning of being here is in "…just looking out to the horizon and enjoying the view of the sea." Another participant at Field 6 spoke of the timelessness and continuity of the beach. He described getting "lost out of time" while being here along the long shoreline and the broad horizon. From this viewpoint, this expansive space and its horizon and the seeming stability of its constituent parts—sea, sand, sky—affords refuge from the constant change people experience generally. The material features of the park's built environment belong to that continuity even if they recede in significance behind the natural landscape of sand, water, sky, and horizon. Perhaps the jazzy Art Deco East and West Bathhouses, once so up-to-date, now belong to the "timeless" natural scene.

Memory and Belonging

Memories built through embodied space at the beach, as described by study participants, often relate to the sense of belonging. For example, a patron of the gay beach says the special meaning of

CONSERVATION AND THE PEOPLE'S VIEWS

the park to him is all his memories that include "hanging out with all my friends and partying here: The togetherness, the unity." A middle-aged woman who grew up in the area recalled one time when

> ...the entire neighborhood came down when we were kids—I mean the whole neighborhood. It was like the adults just got to talking and everybody decided in one perfect moment that they, we, would all go down to Jones. As a kid you have to understand how special that was. It was like a block party at the beach. You and all your closest friends.

This woman's husband, joining into the interview, remembered being there for all night bonfires. He talked about friendships with people who he would only see at Jones Beach in the summertime. They disappeared at the end of August and then they reappeared in June. "You didn't know where they went. In retrospect, I suppose many of them were city kids, but we were all together in the summer and then poof! They were gone."

Memories of visiting the beach with any sort of group can reinforce the sense of belonging. A man interviewed at the gay beach remembered visiting with a large group two years earlier, which he said made him feel as if he and his friends owned the beach. Many visitors are immigrants and making a home-away-from-home territory at Jones Beach can recall a sense of a homeland. As one man at the gay beach told an interviewer, being at the beach "reminds me of my country. It helps keep me stay alive here [in the US]." Other people interviewed on the beach especially those with memories from their youth or childhood, expressed similar sentiments, of associating Jones Beach with belonging to something memorable. One woman talked about being stuck during the blackout and bonding with all the other people at the beach as the usual schedules and obligations were suspended: "The NYC blackout when we were stuck here. Eventually, we had to make our way back home in the dark. There was a feeling of being a part of something with a bunch of strangers." A young man on the beach opposite to Central Mall feels that everyone gets along and says this is a byproduct of their all being New Yorkers. In these narratives of the beach as a welcoming social space, the particular features of the landscape and built environment disappear.

The ample space at Jones Beach facilitates a self-sorting process among regular visitors, as some user constituencies claim certain territories within the park. People self-segregate themselves at the beach: some associate or identify with the family area, some with the party scene at Field 4, some with the gay beach east of Field 6, some with the natural areas at the West End, some with the children's beach at Zachs Bay, and so on. These informal appropriations of space constitute an important element of that sense of belonging. The ability of such constituency groups to make their own places within the park facilitates the perceptions among many participants in our ethnographic study that people get along at Jones Beach *because* there is plenty of space. A black male visitor interviewed east of the Field 6 guarded beach thought everyone gets along here and reasoned this was a function of the size of the park: "There's so much space so it's all okay." The Field 6 area, he observed, is "full of couples and families—people who want peace and quiet [and older people] who don't want a ra-ra time." Other visitors at Field 6 informed us approvingly that the park not long ago instituted a radio ban at Field 6.

Self-sorting into constituencies can also be a vehicle for making invidious distinctions. One woman describes the social scene at Field 4 (i.e., by the Central Mall, which is between and equally accessible from Fields 4 and 5) as wild and youth-oriented, and the interviewer notes, "...the marijuana smoke blowing through our conversation highlighted this." He describes the scene as extremely crowded and lively: "Nearby drinking and hookah smoking combined with three or four competing radios

Public Memory, Public Space

Beach users participate in the telling of a public history that combines nostalgia, personal experience, and folk legend. A retired male schoolteacher from Jackson Heights, in Queens, who said he had been coming to Jones Beach for 60 years—i.e., since 1952, and who comes at least 20 times in the summer season—showed his knowledge of the park, its features and history. He described the role of Robert Moses in building the park as a white, middle-class space. He seemed saddened by the park's decline, citing the closure of the Boardwalk Restaurant and of the East Bathhouse, decay of the shuffleboard court and the golf course. He said the state "has no money" and saw the intrusion of the Donald Trump project as a sign of decline. Nevertheless, he considered Jones Beach among the "best in the world" and "nicer than the beach at Waikiki. The state should bring it back to what it was twenty years ago" by reopening the East Bathhouse and its pool and adding more personnel. He approved of the present cultural diversity of the users: the park had now become "what it should be: a park for everyone." There are other beaches closer to his residence, but "there's something about Jones Beach."

In this rich narrative by someone with many memories who seems to visit now by himself, Jones Beach is a union of built and natural environment, the natural part almost without parallel, in his judgment, and the built part memorable, even ennobling; in decline but deserving of restored funding. From this perspective, it is important to preserve the grand conception and its major components that have served the public so well over many decades. The likes of Trump should not sully the atmosphere; instead the state should honor the park's legacy by funding it properly. Whether architectural details and or original materials can be compromised in refurbishing and restoring may not be as important as keeping the elements of the composition intact.

Other older visitors expressed similar ideas, on the one hand longing to restore the park to full operation and high standards, and, on the other, approving of the present cultural and class diversity among visitors. Many visitors remember the park's postwar heyday of enormous popularity among a mainly white, middle-class clientele, genteel restaurants as well as snack bars, and nautical flags snapping smartly from the ship masts that decorate the formal lawn. This is the nostalgic lore of Jones Beach, comprising history, symbolic cultural references, and values which some users nostalgically long to reinstate. Some wish the park would reopen its mothballed facilities—East Bathhouse, the West End, and the Boardwalk Restaurant. People did not necessarily realize the restaurant building was gone, both the original one and its 1960s replacement, as some said they felt it should be reopened. One woman likened the restaurant to Howard Johnson's—popular, reasonably priced, with good food. The mass-consumer, universalizing middle-class atmosphere of Howard Johnson's thrived in the 1950s and 1960s when Jones Beach was still operating at full throttle in much the same manner—a full-service day resort for Greater New York's huge, prosperous and mostly white middle class. Often research participants who expressed such sentiments, like having a nice restaurant like Howard Johnson's again, also expressed approval of the diverse publics that Jones Beach serves today. This poses one of challenges park managers face: how to revive the non-commercial vitality of the park's services in a way that satisfies the more varied tastes and identities of today's park visitors.

A few respondents commented on mothballed facilities. A Latina interviewed on the beach near Central Mall said she would like to have the park reopen the unused West End parking fields and reopen the East Bathhouse—in her words, "...the large unused changing stations behind the wall at Field 4." A young man at the gay beach offered, as a suggested improvement, fixing the buildings "... in a more modern way. Make it look like you want to come."

The reduced footprint of the park's services and oversight enhances belonging for some users. At the gay beach, many participants said they did not want lifeguards or changing facilities bathrooms for fear that these services would attract more users and dispel the privacy gay visitors enjoy now. Others saw this as a trade-off: they would benefit from bathrooms and feel some injustice and not having lifeguards in their stretch of beach, yet they concede the counter-argument that having these things risks the privacy of the gay beach. Similarly, at the West End, where large parking fields and bathhouses were built in the 1960s and subsequently abandoned, those who go out there like the absence of crowds and describe a particular sense of ownership.

Our ethnographic interviews included a question asking people whether it mattered that Jones Beach is a public space—a question beyond comprehension forty or fifty years ago but pertinent today as the park seeks support to maintain its facilities from within and outside the government. Almost every participant directly answered that question in the affirmative. People felt that it being fully public was part of its very essence that everyone can come to make it their own place, and that full access is crucial. Many people spoke in terms of affordability, that the rich have plenty of nice places but ordinary people can't survive without places like this to come. Several offered the observation that people in New York City typically live in apartments and do not have access to an expansive natural environment without the state providing a place like Jones Beach. An African-American man described the scene as "...a friendly crowd, people are out with family and friends. It's a diverse crowd over here. Just look at this place. This is America."

This enthusiasm for Jones Beach as public space relates inversely to the persistence of an urban legend that asserts a deliberate technological exclusion of poorer people and people of color from the park. As Caro (1974) has it, Moses deliberately made the overpasses on the Southern State, Meadowbrook and Wantagh Parkways leading to Jones Beach from New York City too low to accommodate buses, specifically to keep poorer visitors, especially blacks, who in the 1920s would have lacked private automobiles, away from Jones Beach. One female participant, a professional here from Brooklyn with her husband, said she had looked up Robert Moses online and had been "ticked off" to learn that the beach had been originally designed to limit access to the white middle class. Another patron similarly associated the Robert Moses legacy with exclusionary efforts and thought this particular history justifies redoubled efforts to keep the beach "one-hundred percent accessible." Caro's massive biography was widely read and highly influential. Scholars took up the theme when Langdon Winner (1980) told the same story as an example of artifacts having a politics. Jeorges (1999) refutes the myth with several explanations. Parkways go back to the nineteenth century. As elongated parks with roads, they generally permitted only carriages and buggies for recreational drives, not heavy wagons and commercial teams. Parkways excluded commercial traffic because they were meant to be retreats from the noisy city streets. Commercial traffic was excluded from parkways by custom over many decades, and buses would not have been ordinarily allowed on the new Long Island parkways in the 1920s and 1930s no matter how high the bridges were. As designed, the bridges carry local roads over the parkways without additional elevation. Given the generally good transport network on Long Island in the twenties, which would have allowed people to get around by various routes and modes of travel, there would have been no justification for the considerable additional cost of making the bridges higher than they needed to be to carry local roads over the parkways.

CONSERVATION AND THE PEOPLE'S VIEWS

Additionally, Joerges cites Robert Fitch (1996) who attributes the New York City area's parkway designs not to Moses but to the Regional Plan Association's 1929 plan for New York and environs. According to Fitch, "Just about every highway and bridge credited to Robert Moses was conceived and planned by the RPA. Moses simply poured the concrete on the dotted lines indicated on the plan" (Quoted in Joerges, 1999: 427): Woolgar and Cooper (1999), also explicitly refuting Winner's (1980) thesis that the Long Island parkway bridges have political qualities, offer evidence that the bridges are not, in fact, too low for buses. They quote a student attending a lecture explicating Winner's thesis, the student having interrupted the professor to object:

'That's totally wrong!'
'Yes, well, wait, not yet, we're coming to the criticisms.'
'No, no, I mean it's not true. I ride the buses on the damn parkway all the time.'
'What?!'
'I mean, the bridges don't prevent buses going down the parkway.'

A brief period of pedagogic turmoil ensues. The iconic exemplar is being challenged at first base. Forget about Winner's argumentative structure, his questionable ascription of motive, the inconsistencies in his critiques of technological determinism. The interpolating New Yorker is claiming that the basic material premise of the example is wrong...

(Woolgar and Cooper 1999: 433–434)

Certainly, buses are part of the main public transport from New York City to the beach: Long Island Railroad from Manhattan or Brooklyn to Freeport and then bus from Freeport down the Meadowbrook Parkway to Jones Beach. In the 1970s and 1980s, the Long Island Railroad advertised a package ticket: round-trip transportation to the beach by train and connecting bus plus bathhouse and locker privileges. The idea of an autocratic villain causing the bridges to be low to keep blacks away from Jones Beach has popular appeal. However apocryphal in respect to the politics of artifacts, the picture it paints is consistent with the broad historical record of subtle and overt discrimination against blacks at public beaches and many other sites well into the post-World War II period (see Kahrl, 2012). Jones Beach indeed attracted a white, middle-class clientele for many years, for reasons more varied and complex than this tale of intrigue.

Conclusion

The past is both present and redefined in contemporary use of the park. From visitors' awareness of and membership in the sociocultural "scene," their concerns for full public access, and from the various ways of visiting and using the park gives access to feelings of belonging, what emerges is Jones Beach as a public space that connects people with the social past and present. Like any other nice beach, its natural features allow all the recreational activities that attract people to beaches. The roads and parking fields, boardwalk, buildings, and other built features give this particular park a social structure that visitors as well as critics observe as being related to New York City, an out-of-town adjunct to the city comparable in its reach and scale and diversity of places and people. Results from the study underscore how consultation with everyday users provides a valid and useful view of public history that can be combined with other "expert" perspectives when undertaking conservation endeavors. Speaking with visitors in systematic research fashion satisfies the need to involve more voices than the professionals in historic preservation decisions and an additional authoritative view of the public history that is desirable to preserve and foster. Jones Beach is historical in representing an era of trust in government and the political will to carry out a grand gesture for the public good. The park's history also carries the more ambiguous legacy of the autocratic ways of a "power broker" including forceful social control and race and class discrimination. It is clear from our research that the social control of mass conformity built into the landscape has dissipated and that the social relations of the park have been reinterpreted as a place welcoming of diversity and belonging. The landscape and built environment have similarly been reinterpreted as a place of possibility and personal and social freedom.

What continues to attract most users to the park is the chance to be part of an animated urban scene. Participating in the scene—seeing oneself in it as well as the whole scene—remains one of the pleasures of Jones Beach. One inference from our data is that even in decline the original, central area of the park with its bathhouses, boardwalk, and central mall facilitates this highly varied yet visible social scene. Repurposing and renewal of the historic structures in ways that add to the possibilities of pleasurable experience of being amid an urban scene will be welcome to many visitors. Yet, as a park, Jones Beach is large enough to offer more private spaces for visitors who prefer to be away from the throng, and that too is a desirable feature.

References

Alliance to Revitalize Jones Beach (website). Accessed Feb. 3, 2017. http://jonesbeachalliance.org/faqs/

Caro, R. (1974). *The power broker: Robert Moses and the Fall of New York*. New York: Vintage.

De Certeau, M. (2011). *The practice of everyday life*. 3rd Ed. Berkeley, University of California Press.

Fitch, R. (1996). *The assassination of New York*. New York: Verso.

Goldberger, P. (1979). Design notebook: After 50 years, the design of Jones Beach still inspires awe. *New York Times*, July 12.p. C12.

Jeorges, B. (1999). Do politics have artefacts? *Social Studies of Science* 29(3), June, pp. 411–431.

Lefebvre, H. (1991). *The production of space*. Trans. Nicholson-Smith, D. Malden, MA: Oxford University Press.

Low, S. (2003). Embodied spaces: anthropological series of body, space, and culture. *Space and culture* 6(1), February, pp. 9–18.

Lowenthal, D. (1985). *The past is a foreign country*. Malden, MA: Cambridge University Press.

Mason, R. (2004). Fixing historic preservation: A constructive critique of "Significance". *Places* 16(1), pp. 64–71.

Moroney, E. (2013). *Jones beach and storage structures and cultural landscape report*. Albany, NY: New York State Office of Parks, Recreation and Historic Preservation. https://parks.ny.gov/inside-our-agency/documents/JonesBeachHistoricStructuresandCulturalLandscapeReport.pdf

Ruskin, J. (1859). *The seven lamps of architecture*. New York: John Wiley & Sons.

Saslow, L. (2009). Jones beach hit hard by budget cuts to parks. *New York Times*, April 15.

White, J. (1962). *The Cambridge movement: The ecclesiologists and the Gothic revival*. Cambridge: Cambridge University Press.

Winner, L. (1980). Do artifacts have politics? *Daedalus* 109(1), Winter, pp. 121–36.

Wolfe, A. P. (2004). Jones Beach State Park. *Society for the Preservation of Long Island Antiquities*. http://splia.org/wp-content/uploads/2012/12/Jones-Beach-Report-2004-sm.pdf

Woolgar, S., & Cooper, G. (1999). Do artefacts have ambivalence? Moses' bridges, Winner's bridges and other urban legends in S&TS. *Social Studies of Science* 29(3), June, pp. 433–449.

PART 3

Using Evidence to Change Practice

CHAPTER 8

Tours of Critical Geography and Public Deliberation

Applied Social Sciences as Guide

Jennifer Minner

In the past decade, the aesthetics of mid-twentieth-century modernism have regained popularity, raising the profile of the modern design and contributing to efforts to preserve modern architecture. This is reflected within the pages of magazines such as *Dwell* and *Atomic Ranch,* which promote modern aesthetics from its origins in early to mid-twentieth-century architecture to its expression in contemporary design (Boddy, 2009). Representations of modernism in print and online media are joined by the growing availability of architectural tours. These are efforts of non-profit groups such as DOCOMOMO-US, which are dedicated to raising public awareness about modern design.[1]

What often remains left out of popular magazines and heritage tours are the much trickier aspects of modern landscapes to interpret. Beyond Palm Springs Modernism Week or tours of mid-century modern *Streets of Dreams* are the remains of the Modern Movement associated with urban renewal, public housing, and other large-scale interventions to redesign urban space. There are numerous reasons these modern buildings and landscapes are not often featured in tours. Former urban renewal districts often do not have the abundance of interested homeowners or the congregation of merchants likely to support architectural tours compared to urban districts of older vintage. Tenants in public housing may not wish their homes to be put on display (Chan, 2014) and local heritage groups may not see them as historic either (although that is beginning to change). Furthermore, sites associated with modernism may be viewed with ambivalence, mixed emotion, or disdain by those who remember firsthand controversial acts of urban renewal and redevelopment. Despite the importance of modern landscapes to local history, they often remain sizeable urban memories disconnected from either heritage tours or deliberation about urban change.

In Central Texas, the large urban footprints of modern architecture and modernist planning reflect the explosive growth and transformation that happened at mid-twentieth century. These modern footprints include HemisFair, a public space carved out of an urban neighborhood for the 1968 World's Fair in San Antonio. In Austin, experiments in segregated public housing, integrated

159

CRITICAL GEOGRAPHY AND PUBLIC DELIBERATION

single-family housing, and urban renewal were precursors to contemporary issues of displacement and change in the historically African-American and Hispanic neighborhoods of East Austin. While these histories are well known to some, they have not commonly been included or interpreted in public heritage tours. This article describes tours that engaged community members with interpretation and discussion of the large-scale redevelopment of urban space – including its political geography, social history, and the legacy of modernist design and planning.

Tours that encourage public appreciation for modernism should do more than promoting an acquired aesthetic appreciation. Tours are important social and educational practices that have the power to either narrow or broaden understandings of the past. They also have the capacity to encourage open dialogue and deliberation and to reveal and address power relations, the main thrust of three important theories of applied social sciences – communicative action theory, collaborative rationality, and phronetic social sciences. The incorporation of these social science theories and associated practices has the capacity to enrich the connection between material and social aspects of heritage, and to broaden heritage to a wider set of values and experiences. These theoretical frameworks could enable heritage to become more relevant to contemporary deliberations over the future of urban neighborhoods and public space. This chapter contributes to a central tenant of this book, that applied social sciences can be transformative for heritage practice. I further argue that tours and other similar mobile events can provide an essential opportunity for critical interpretation and two-way dialogue that can lend more depth and inclusivity to heritage conservation.

In the following section, I discuss the rifts between the aesthetic and social approaches to heritage tours. The following section describes applied social science theories and their relevance to heritage. The fourth section describes a tour of a former world's fair site in San Antonio, relating heritage tactics and the tours to communicative action theory, collaborative rationality, and phronesis. In the fifth section, I discuss community tours in Austin, Texas, providing additional observations about the relevance of these theories in planning community tours. A concluding section proposes the use of theories of applied social sciences in professional practice and heritage, education, and to encourage public dialogue about the past, present, and future.

Disjunctures between the Aesthetic and the Academic

At the 67th Annual Conference of the Society of Architectural Historians, Phil Gruen described a growing disjunction between academic approaches to the built environment and tours designed for a popular audience:

> As I see it, the disjunction is between tourism (and its conventional focus on individual architects, styles, and aesthetics) and *current* academic scholarship and teaching in architectural history (and its investigation of context, stories, and the vernacular). To broadly oversimplify, one might say that academia today is far more interested in telling stories about buildings that reads them as part of the social, political, and economic fabric, thereby rendering them more ordinary and—intentionally or not—stripping buildings of their alleged greatness. Meanwhile, the tourist industry seems unconcerned with such scholarship, continuing on its merry way to promote beauty, grandeur, styles, and notable architects. Yet architectural tourism— superficial though it may be—remains popular and largely an economic success; academia,

160

CRITICAL GEOGRAPHY AND PUBLIC DELIBERATION

meanwhile, remains smug in its claims to intellectual rigor and is satisfied to retreat into its journals and lectures that—while interesting, illuminating, and important—are often rather arcane.

(Gruen, 2014)

In this quote, Gruen grapples with academia's emphasis on the social, and often critical history of place, contrasting it with the much more prevalent focus in heritage tourism on aesthetics and appreciation of place rather than complex narratives. In Gruen's dichotomy, architectural tourism and scholarship are becoming mutually exclusive and the joy of looking, comprehending, and appreciating places cannot mix with themes of social, economic, and political history.

Lending some credence to his argument, it is common for architectural tours of modernism to focus on single family homes of middle-class and well-to-do to the public. These home tours most often concentrate on aesthetics and the history of the house as an art object. The residential emphasis is unsurprising; the historic homes tour is a common format, in which homeowners showcase their individual efforts to preserve and remodel their homes. Andrew Hurley points out that home tours often feature newly remodeled interiors with limited interpretation related to social history or geographical context (Hurley, 2010). He notes that the emphasis of home tours is often on sharing contemporary home remodeling tips, rather than the faithful representation of a particular era or movement within architecture. Residential real estate and building products promoted in popular magazines reinforce the appreciation of modern architecture as a private act of connoisseurship. Here, interpretation of modernism becomes synonymous with the consumption of modern-era furnishings and real estate. On the other hand, Kitson (2015) calls domestic historic preservation tours "a social practice demonstrative of urban hospitality, an opening of self and neighborhood toward strangers, critical in the making of ethical urban communities" (p. 2).

Even given the social value of home tours, they most often represent only a narrow spectrum of residential architecture. This leaves out an enormous amount of mid-twentieth-century buildings and landscapes—namely the government and institutional buildings, public housing, and parks associated with federal government experiments such as urban renewal and public housing. If architectural tours help to define the boundaries of modern design in the public imagination, then an emphasis on private residences creates blind spots that influence popular perceptions of modernism, simplifying it into visions of sublime domesticity. This, in turn, may mean missed opportunities at conversations about the institutional and commercial landscapes, and other public spaces people experience.

In contrast to Gruen's characterization of tours, the emphasis on aesthetics should not be understood as simply an outcome of architectural tourism or the popular architectural press. Ned Kaufman has pointed toward a bias toward architectural design rather than social history in historic preservation practice (Kaufman, 2009). Longstreth (1999) has critiqued preservationists' "style fetish," which is a reliance on categories that reinforces the idea that historic preservation should be tied to a building's purity as exemplar of a particular architectural style. Thus, efforts to identify and interpret "pure examples" of architectural styles may turn to orthodoxy and overshadow the social and political significance of places.

The following case studies are useful illustrations of the potential not only to focus on the social history and critical geography of modernism and urban renewal, but to increase public deliberation about contemporary issues that relate to choices in urban planning, redevelopment, and preservation. "Social history" refers an emphasis on interpreting collective histories, including those of women's organizations, racial and ethnic associations, and other collective community organizations and identities (Hurley, 2010). "Critical geography" refers broadly to scholarship within geography and the social sciences that is rooted in critical theory (Blomley, 2006).

In the following section, I introduce social theories that can be used to invigorate heritage tours so that they not only celebrate social history and tend to critical geography, but also so that they relate more broadly to the present and future of urban spaces. These applied theories of social science include first, tending to communication from the perspective of communitive action theory and collaborative rationality, areas of social science that have transformed urban planning practices in the late twentieth century. Second, I discuss phronetic social science, as a means of inquiry into power relations and its relationship to public dialogue and debate. I then argue for tours that aid in deliberation over contemporary issues of power, redevelopment, and displacement by encouraging public discussion and raising awareness about power relations and urban space.

Applied Social Sciences: Collaborative Rationality and Phronetic Social Sciences

Communicative action theory has been called a dominant paradigm in urban planning, an area with shared evolution and concerns in managing urban change as heritage and historic preservation (Birch & Roby, 1984; Holleran, 1998; Mason, 2009; Page & Mason, 2004). Communicative action theory was originally rooted in critical theory, a diverse set of theories in pursuit of emancipation from the oppressive structures of society. Jurgen Habermas originated communicative action theory focusing on the pursuit of consensus based on rationality and a focus on intersubjectivity, or the capacity for people to communicate despite differences (Habermas, 1984). Through attending to the means and veracity of communication, Habermas describes striving for ideal speech conditions through which rational consensus about action may be discovered. John Forester re-articulated and extended Habermasian theories of communicative action, preparing a framework to guide the democratic deliberation within planning processes (Forester, 1989). This framework, as laid out in *Planning in the Face of Power*, provides a diagnostic tool in which planners may locate the sources of distorted communication that prevent effective communicative action. Forester has operationalized Habermasian ideal speech principles in a way that makes it comprehensible to urban planners, creating a framework that planners can use to seek the conditions by which consensus may be reached.

Judith Innes and David Booher have developed a related, yet distinct concept of collaborative rationality, which is a set of practices based on conflict negotiation and mediation, and aimed at joint fact-finding and decision-making in urban and environmental planning (Innes and Booher, 2010; Innes, 2004). This has also been called "collaborative learning and co-management" in which stakeholders in a planning process self-organize into communities of co-learners aimed at jointly defining problems and solutions for management of environmental resources (Randolph, 2012). In this model,

> Expert knowledge as well as community knowledge are both part of the dialogue. Information plays a central role in collaborative dialogue and working through discrepancies and differences among knowledge sources can produce more accurate and meaningful information than can a lone expert or a single study.

> (Innes, 2016, 1)

CRITICAL GEOGRAPHY AND PUBLIC DELIBERATION

For heritage studies, these areas of social science theory and associated practices offer potential means to address differences in how people value places and bridge the gulf between preservation practice as a relatively narrow set of expert practices and the varied ways in which people understand heritage (Wells, 2015). This area of social science theory melded with consensus building connects to Wells' (2015) discussion of conservation social science and grassroots, bottom-up efforts of environmental conservation groups.

A second area of applied social sciences is called "phronesis" or "phronetic social sciences" (Flyvbjerg, 1998; Flyvbjerg, 2001; Flyvbjerg, Landman, and Schram, 2012). In *Making Social Science Matter*, Flyvbjerg traces the origins of phronesis from an interpretation of the writings of Aristotle through the social and political theories of Niccolo Machiavelli, Friedrich Nietzsche, and Michel Foucault. Flyvbjerg describes methodological guidelines for a phronesis-based social science, which are intended to make social science a more fruitful endeavor with the capacity to uncover and critique power relations as they are manifested in society. Phronesis is one of three Aristotelian intellectual virtues, which can be understood as "practical knowledge and ethics" and "deliberation about values and its relation to praxis" (Basu, 2009, 484). The other two virtues include "episteme," which is closest to scientific knowledge or "know-why," and "techne" or "know-how" associated with knowledge and skill associated with craft and production (Basu, 2009, 484; Flyvbjerg, 2001). Flyvbjerg advises social science researchers to focus on value questions such as "Where are we going? Is it desirable? What should be done?" The researcher is advised to place power at the core of his or her research. The primary concern of phronetic social sciences is *how* power is exercised, rather than settling on an analysis of *who* has power.

Phronetic inquiry explores and challenges the actions and motivations as described by actors in urban development, deeply analyzing these in comparison to what actors actually do. The gap between discourse and action are then used to reveal power relations. Phronesis-based research builds from the "polyphony of voices" (Flyvbjerg, 2001, 139), where the social science researcher should assume no single rationality nor should she listen only to one authoritative voice. By extension, the researcher cannot claim final authority. This means that a researcher must carefully sort through multiple interpretations from many sources. It also means that the test of the validity of one's own research is not tied to a single definitive source, instead, the judgment of validity is tied to the extent to which the researcher has illustrated that she has listened to multiple voices and small details and have accurately incorporated them. Deep case studies are not only accepted as central to the practice of social sciences, but they become essential resources for open and transparent public debate. They are considered not less valid or empirical than other forms of quantitative and qualitative research (Flyvbjerg, 2001).

While these applied social scientific theories and areas of practice have been repeatedly applied to urban planning, there has been little application within historic preservation or heritage. Two following case studies provide opportunities to reflect on tours as a means of communication and support for public deliberation on the one hand, and as an opportunity to publicly interpret and explore research related to power relations on the other. Applying these frameworks to the organization of tours may transform tours of aesthetics and historical description to richer acts of public deliberation and dialogue.

Here, it is important to acknowledge that these applied theories of social sciences were not explicitly discussed by tour organizers beforehand. Rather, the tours make for convenient illustrations of these applied social scientific concepts, which could and I argue *should* be used with intentionality in future tours. I also describe the limits to case study examples and ways in which future tours could have more impact.

163

Touring HemisFair '68: Modern Design, Cultural History

The history of international expositions or world's fairs, offer a particularly rich arena to modernism and the geography of city shaping. HemisFair '68 is one such event. Although understudied in comparison to other international expos, it was a watershed event in the history of San Antonio. The fair helped thrust San Antonio from a sleepy military town onto the global stage, or at least a national one, with the help of prominent business and community leaders and Texan politicians, including US President Lyndon Baines Johnson. The effort to stage the fair brought together a multitude of community organizations that made significant contributions to this site and to city building efforts (Holmesly, 2003).

Much like other fairs of the period, HemisFair '68 blended celebratory images of cultural and ethnic groups both international and domestic, with images of modern progress, technology, and commercial prowess. Reflecting the fair's theme, "the Confluence of the Civilizations of the Americas," the *HemisFair '68 Official Souvenir Guidebook* proclaimed: "Bilingual and cosmopolitan, San Antonio lays claim to the lustrous heritage spun from the colorful threads of many cultures. On that foundation, HemisFair'68, in the truest sense, is the outcome of visionary, twentieth century pioneering" (San Antonio, Fair, Inc. 1968). Despite the language of racial acceptance, the fair site was a product of urban renewal; federal funds and local initiative were used to raze a once vital, multi-ethnic neighborhood.

The fair site was repurposed as HemisFair Park after the world's fair. The park now includes tourist attractions and a convention center, as well as a federal courthouse and non-profit offices. Despite the ongoing uses of the former site, the district has struggled for vitality over the years; some of the former pavilions have remained in use, while others have fallen into disuse and disrepair. In recent years, HemisFair Park Redevelopment Corporation (HPARC), which manages and operates the site, led a master planning effort, the most recent of several prior revitalization efforts since the fair.

Recent plans call for the development of a new mixed use community at HemisFair Park (Hemisfair Park Area Redevelopment Corporation, 2012). While extolling the virtues of a restoration planned for one of the nineteenth-century buildings, it depicted remaining pavilions left over from the fair as future sites for mixed-use development. The plan appeared to erase mid-twentieth-century buildings and landscapes on site to be redeveloped as new mixed use development via public-private partnerships. These transformations were not viewed as wholly negative by local preservationists, especially with some aspects of the plan that would restore some former pavilions. However, the quiet erasure of world's fair pavilions in the plan, without public deliberation over the value of these buildings raised the concern of Mid Tex Mod, the Central Texas Chapter of Docomomo US. In collaboration with the San Antonio Conservation Society, tour organizers sought to open a conversation about preserving former fair pavilions whose building footprints disappeared in the master plan's future land use map.

The HemisFair '68 tour was a means of promoting public awareness while asking representatives from HPARC, the City of San Antonio, and other community members and academics to come together to present various vantage points on the history of the site. By extension, this was an opportunity for encouraging public talk about the value of the remaining architecture and artwork of the fair (see Figures 8.1 and 8.2). Tour organizers thought of the event as a potentially powerful method of elevating the mid-twentieth-century history on site and giving visibility to places that offered important symbolic landmarks of the history of urban renewal, migration, and attempts at uniting Texas as a place of Hispanic, Anglo, and Pan-American identities.

Figure 8.1 Image depicts 92.6 area that would be cleared for HemisFair '68.

Source: University of Texas at San Antonio Libraries, Archives and Special Collections, San Antonio Fair, Inc., Records, 1962–1995.

Figure 8.2 Aerial view from a helicopter of HemisFair '68 taken a few weeks before opening day.

Source: University of Texas at San Antonio Libraries, Archives and Special Collections, San Antonio Fair, Inc., Records, 1962–1995.

William Sinkin, the first President of the San Antonio Fair, Inc., was invited as a featured speaker on the tour. He had overseen the process of urban renewal for the creation of the fair, a formidable accomplishment given what at the time seemed an impossible timeline for securing federal urban renewal funds.[2] Despite local resistance to urban renewal, Sinkin's story was one of success, and he remained a civic leader and local celebrity after the fair.[3] On the tour, he spoke about the triumphs of the fair and its legacy. A local historian provided a contrasting vantage point, focusing on a group of 23 nineteenth-century buildings and one early twentieth-century building that were the last remaining architectural specimens from the neighborhood cleared for the fair.[4] She also described the heroic efforts of the San Antonio Conservation Society and O'Neil Ford, a regionally known and admired architect in Central Texas, to save some of the neighborhood's historic buildings and how they were incorporated into the fair. Her critical narrative emphasized the loss of the neighborhood (Figure 8.3), while also describing how Ford recognized the value of traditional urban fabric and in so doing, contributed to the evolution of regional variants of modernism.

Tour guides underscored former pavilions that appeared to be threatened with demolition in plans for the park. Land use maps in the master plan coded the former Federal and Texas Pavilions as mixed-use or open space, but the plan did not explicitly mention demolition. HPARC officials had been ambiguous and evasive in response to direct questions as to whether these pavilions would remain when the master plan was implemented, but the land use map seemed to clearly depict the pavilions as missing from the future vision. Two of these buildings comprised the former Federal Pavilion—the former Confluence Theater and an exhibition hall connected by a formal outdoor plaza. The Confluence Theater originally housed a 1,200-seat theater where visitors could watch the Confluence movie, directed by Francis Thompson (San Antonio, Fair, Inc. 1968, 40). At the dramatic conclusion

Figure 8.3 Photograph from survey of buildings prior to demolition. This is one of 1,349 structures demolished in the urban renewal area.

Source: University of Texas at San Antonio Libraries, Archives and Special Collections, San Antonio Fair, Inc., Records, 1962–1995.

of the documentary, "the legacy" of the confluence of civilizations was described as bring about "the harvest" of cultural benefits and "the promise of the future" (San Antonio Fair, Inc. 1968, 40). A central theme of the outdoor plaza was that of "migration," a theme that still resonates today.[5]

The former Texas Pavilion was also designed to be permanent and remained after the Fair as the Institute of Texan Cultures, a museum dedicated to cultural heritage in Texas. The Texas pavilion was conceived as an opportunity to emphasize the contributions of many ethnic and racial groups in the development of the state. Within a central dome that is two stories high and 60×80 feet (18.28×24.38 meters) in diameter an "ultramodern film and slide presentation using 36 screens and 42 projectors" (San Antonio, Fair, Inc. 1968, 44) created a spectacle meant to instill a sense of awe and appreciation for Texas' racial and ethnic diversity.

The tour also visited pavilions that appeared secure in the HemisFair Park master plan. This included the Tower of the Americas. During the fair, the Tower of the Americas served as a beacon expressing pan-Americanist ambitions to align political and economic interests between the US and Latin America (González, 2011). A tour of the Women's Pavilion provided interpretation and access to the interior of the still extant, but empty and underutilized building. Designed by Cyrus Wagner, the exterior of the building features the handprints of many prominent San Antonio women who collaborated in planning and raising money for the pavilion. Representatives of the Women's Pavilion at HemisFair, Inc. described how its legacy was honored through charity work that continues to be carried out by the organization in the pavilion's name.

Tour organizers emphasized that the time period associated with HemisFair '68 was one temporal layer in a much longer history and with many overlapping community attachments. The tour stopped at the site of the Acequia Madre, a series of ditches that was integral to Spanish settlement in the region. Reaching toward interpretation of the possible future of the site, an HPARC board member shared information about management of the park and plans for revitalization. Stuart Johnson, a key organizer and tour guide, recalled:

> There were certainly multiple ways to interpret a lot of these sites and for me, one of the important aspects of HemisFair is the layers of culture and timelines. So as much as I think the focus on the importance of the mid-century structures, when you're doing an actual, physical walking tour of the site, I think it's a disservice to focus strictly on that at the expense of relating how those buildings tie in to their landscape and everything that has come before or after that.
>
> (Johnson, 2013)

The tour presented modernism "in situ" and with a sense of complexity by relating materiality and design to urban context and by incorporating speakers to participate from multiple perspectives. The embrace of cultural heritage in the artwork and exhibits of the fair were discussed in their contrast with the actual history of the fair, which disproportionately impacted minority residents and business owners who were forced to move in clearing the site for the fair (Holmesly, 2003). Appreciation for the aesthetics of modernism or its uplifting messages of equality and international cooperation contrasted with the inequalities and displacement in the production of HemisFair '68. The lofty discourse of government and business groups, even as their actions furthered segregation and displacement, either implicitly or by design, was a powerful leitmotif.

Participation in the HemisFair tour appeared to solidify the commitment of the San Antonio Conservation Society to once again organize against demolitions as it had during the days of urban renewal, this time to defend remaining modern architecture that replaced the former neighborhood.

The year following the tour, the San Antonio Conservation Society issued a statement in favor of preservation of the former Confluence Theater and the Institute of Texan Cultures (Olivio, 2012). The first tour was followed by additional tours. These tours provided further opportunities to accentuate the material aspects of the fair and their leftover buildings as valuable assets. Since then, the Texas Historical Commission determined a large portion of the site eligible as a national historic district, a decision opposite from an earlier assessment that it did not retain historic integrity (Wolfe, 2013).

The tours illustrated how advocates could openly interpret the site's complex history, encouraging not only an appreciative, but also a critical look. The tour encouraged further dialogue about the value of the buildings and landscapes created during the fair, a layer of history had been downplayed during the master planning process. However, the history of the fair was not "candy-coated" as merely an opportunity to celebrate modernism, but to open up multiple interpretations of it. The tour organizers also aimed at sharing information they had gathered through multiple voices and reveal missing or distorted information, acts which related to both the practices of collaborative rationality and of phronetic social science.

Jane Jacob's "Walk and Talks" in East Austin

The second set of tours in Austin, Texas, provides another case study at the juncture of critical geography and social history. They also speak to the potential to inform contemporary deliberation over gentrification and the role of local, state, and federal government agencies in exacerbating or attempting to address issues of affordable housing, displacement, and racial relations. The tours were held in East Austin, an area east of Interstate-35, which bisects the city near to Austin's downtown. The tours emphasized the geography and history of African American and Hispanic neighborhoods, businesses, and community institutions.

A series of three annual tours in East Austin were organized as part of an annual international Jane's Walk event in which organizers across the US and Canada produce free tours to encourage the public to explore and appreciate their neighborhoods.[6] The Jane's Walk tours are held in honor of urbanist Jane Jacobs, who wrote the seminal critique of modernist planning, *The Death and the Life of Great American Cities* (Jacobs, 1961). The namesake for the tours provided a not-so-subtle dissonance to the interpretation of mid-twentieth-century sites in East Austin. The East Austin Jane's Walk tours alternately reinforced Jane Jacob's critiques of mid-century planning and urban renewal, while featuring public housing projects and other public works left in the wake of modernism that had become important community assets in their own right. The tours included a broad range of sites, including a substantial number related to public housing, urban renewal, and public experimentation with integration at mid-twentieth century (see Figure 8.4).

Eliot Tretter, then a lecturer within the University of Texas at Austin's geography department, was a key tour guide and organizer of Jane's Walk tours of East Austin. The tours emphasized Tretter's scholarship on the geography of segregation, urban politics, and public works from early twentieth century through the period of urban renewal.[7] Tretter described how the concentration of African-American and Hispanic populations within the neighborhoods in East Austin was largely a result of public policy as well as the action of private deed restrictions (Tretter, 2013a). A 1928 city plan promoted segregationist policies and, as a result, African Americans were refused infrastructure and city services outside of East Austin (Koch and Fowler, 1957). The construction of Interstate-35 in the 1950s reinforced the division between Austin's more affluent and ethnically White West side and African American and Hispanic neighborhoods in East Austin.[8]

Figure 8.4 Map depicting sites from the 2012 Jane's Walk tour. Key: 1 = Metz Elementary School; 2 = 1500 Robert Weaver Avenue and LBJ's Historic Oak Grove; 3 = Chalmers Court; 4 = Blackshear Urban Renewal, 5 = Our Lady Guadalupe Catholic Church; 6 = Victory Grill; 7 = Ebenezer Baptist Church; 8 = French Legation; 9 = Zavala Elementary School. Map by Joshua Conrad.

Tretter's interpretation not only focused on the geography of race, class, and urban politics, it included critiques of neoliberal policies of the present.[9] Like HemisFair Park, East Austin is subject to looming questions about preservation and redevelopment; controversies abound, from questions about demolition of public housing to the City of Austin's redevelopment initiatives, which have been critiqued by local community leaders for promoting gentrification. In a post-tour interview, Tretter commented,

> I find it fascinating how little is understood about this history by the general public... and how little is taught about the history of urban renewal. Both its positive sides, like the production of parks and all kinds of interesting infrastructural innovations and developments that happened under the regime of state-backed urban renewal, but also how incredibly horrible it was for so many of the affected communities. Now that's not to say that urban renewal was not well documented within scholarship, but if you were to kind of walk around in the city and you were to try to talk to people, they would talk about gentrification and there would be little appreciation or knowledge of previous attempts to remake urban space through state-backed programs.
>
> (Tretter, 2013c, December 11)

The tour included sites associated with efforts at racial integration. This included Austin Oaks Subdivision, a housing subdivision dedicated by President Lyndon Baines Johnson in 1968 (Figure 8.4, site #2). Funded through a grant from the US Department of Housing and Urban Development, faculty at the University of Texas at Austin contracted with multiple builders to construct an experimental subdivision consisting of ten model affordable homes (Structural Mechanics Research Laboratory, 1971).[10] University researchers involved in the design of the subdivision tested the preferences of ten White, Hispanic, and African-American families who purchased the single-family dwellings, as well as surveying the needs and preferences of these demographic groups in the surrounding area. The study also focused on energy performance and durability of building materials, which employed experimental techniques and pre-fabricated components.

The tours featured the scholarship of historical anthropologist, Dr. Fred McGhee, who shared the history of public housing. In one tour, McGhee recounted the history of Chalmers House, which was built for White residents and Santa Rita Courts, constructed for Mexican-American families. In another tour, McGhee focused on Rosewood Courts, which was built to house African-Americans. The three racially segregated public housing developments were constructed in the late 1930s. Santa Rita Courts was the first of the three public housing developments and the first housing project in the nation to be completed under the Housing Authority Act of 1937 (Figure 8.5) (Housing Authority of the City of Austin, n.d.). At the time of the second tour, Rosewood Courts was threatened with demolition and McGhee sought very specifically to raise awareness about both the historical value of public housing and the continued function that it served as affordable housing in a rapidly gentrifying community.

Figure 8.5 Residents sitting outside of public housing development. Image no. ND-41–145-02, Austin History Center, Austin Public Library.

CRITICAL GEOGRAPHY AND PUBLIC DELIBERATION

The Jane's Walk tour in 2013 emphasized African-American history from Antebellum Austin to the recent past and contemporary issues, and like the HemisFair tour, modernism was presented in situ. The tour included interpretation of the lives of enslaved workers at the French Legation, a private home established in 1841 by Alphonse Dubois, who had been sent by the French Monarch to establish relations between Texas and France.[11] Another local historian and community leader spoke about the significance of commercial corridors in East Austin, home to many African American businesses, and also about a subsequent period of disinvestment during the 1980s attributed to the War on Drugs and continued racial discrimination.[12] The tours in East Austin sought to uncover what might otherwise be hidden or easily overlooked. The tours provided expansive views of the politics of change and of modernism's impacts, positive and negative, on residents of East Austin, past and present.

Informal discussions also took place about present-day displacement through gentrification. In the recent past, there had been high profile battles about the role of historic preservation in East Austin's gentrification (Chusid, 2006). This set of tour guides included preservationists, academics, and community members with intimate knowledge not only of history and historic resources but who were immediately knowledgeable about the needs and struggles of the people of color in East Austin. A member of the local preservation board for the City of Austin, and a tour organizer noted the lasting impacts of the tour. She explained that Preservation Austin, a nonprofit heritage advocacy group, shifted the way it related to preservation and urban development issues in East Austin. In an interview, she commented:

> I think that participating in the tours was part of a number of efforts of Preservation Austin's East Austin Working Group... So you had a few people who attended the first tour... as a result, I did see [the people who participated] as very proactive, in my capacity as a landmark commissioner. I saw them come before us on East Austin issues associated with people of color or sites of significance to people of color in a strong way. Not, 'Hey, here's an endorsement letter, but a, 'We're here to talk about this.'

> (Roberts, Andrea, 2013, November 6)

In the set of East Austin tours, new opportunities for joint learning are made possible, which encouraged additional dialogue between the local heritage society and communities of color, two sets of groups that in the past had found limited common ground.

Conclusions

The tours in San Antonio and Austin did not present a monolithic Modern Movement, nor did they focus primarily on aesthetic aspects of modernism. They presented modern architecture and urban design as complex, multifaceted, and situated within a broader social context and longer temporal trajectory. The tours traced history and geography in ways that can unite place attachment and interest in material legacies with discourse and action that addresses power. The content of the tours revealed the power of government agencies and business groups that could either displace or assist, celebrate or oppress low-income residents and communities of color at mid-twentieth century. They also addressed present-day power relations, for instance, by sharing new or different information than what was represented in HemisFair Park's master planning process and by connecting current day issues of gentrification in East Austin with racism and segregation during the twentieth century.

CRITICAL GEOGRAPHY AND PUBLIC DELIBERATION

Here, it is important to point out limitations of the case study tours. The tours, although multivocal and facilitating informal dialogue, were organized around sharing expert knowledge that included preservation professionals and advocates, academics and community leaders. Although the tours were very open-ended, they could have been more specifically organized to facilitate co-learning and joint fact-finding and to open more two-way communication between experts and interested laypeople who could share other forms of local knowledge. In addition, tour organizers could have been done to systematically gauge the perceptions of participants, through pre- and post-surveys and other forms of active engagement. After all, tours are both opportunities for empirical data collection and sharing and they are potentially powerful ways of continual exploration of the multiple meanings and perceptions people make out of the built environment.

Power, whether interpersonal, institutional, or structural, is important in the practice of heritage and preservation planning. Heritage professionals operate in a complex context that requires a deep and nuanced understandings of power in order to be effective and to equitably serve multiple and often divided publics. Applied social sciences can be useful in both heritage practice, and especially in graduate education to train professionals. Knowledge of applied social sciences can increase heritage professionals' ability to find small create acts of agency or expansive opportunities for leadership that can support change. Tours are just one means that both professionals and community residents can consider in seeking new forms of dialogue about urban change.

Community tours should aspire to make visible not only the designed and material patterns in the built environment but also the patterns and structures of discrimination and oppression, cooperation and coalition. Tours provide a significant opportunity to add complexity to perceptions of urban space that serve not only to satisfy the public's appetite, but to whet it. Tours offer the ability not only to give voice to history, but to support the public's ability to participate in deliberations over the future of modernism's myriad manifestations in the urban landscape. In the process of touring the complexities of the past and present, the dynamics of power may be revealed and new forms of consensus and collaboration about the future may emerge.

Notes

1   As an example, DOCOMOMO-US is an organization dedicated to the documentation and conservation of buildings, sites, and neighborhoods of the Modern Movement. In 2016, it offered more than fifty tours in twenty states and more than thirty cities across the US on its annual tour day. Docomomo US. "Docomomo US Tour Day | Docomomo United States." 2016. www.docomomo-us.org/tourday. (Last Accessed October 8, 2016)

2   This is also highlighted in an excerpt from his memoir reprinted in the *San Antonio Express-News*: Sinkin, Bill. 2014, February 3. "Bill Sinkin: My Life and Times, Part 2 - San Antonio Express-News." *San Antonio Express-News*, Online edition, sec. Local. Accessed January 10, 2017. www.expressnews.com/news/local/article/Bill-Sinkin-My-Life-and-Times-Part-2-5187369.php.

3   One might see some limited parallels in his role to that of Robert Moses for the 1964 World's Fair. William Sinkin was politically different from Robert Moses, a Democrat versus a Republican. Sinkin's professional contributions did not include the breadth of urban renewal sites, parks, and roads that Moses legacy included in New York. HemisFair '68 also differed from the 1964 World's Fair in that demolition of a neighborhood was required for the site in San Antonio, whereas the site of the 1964 New York World's Fair was built on a former ash dump that had already been repurposed as a World's Fair site in 1939. Although lesser known outside of San Antonio, William Sinkin's contributions locally were celebrated in multiple articles about him after his death in February 2014.

4　Jennifer Speed. Modern Design, Cultural History tour. October 8, 2011.

5　After the fair, the Confluence Theater has been converted to a federal courthouse and is presently the John S. Woods Federal Courthouse Building. The Exhibit Hall was converted to the Adrian Spears Judicial Training Center.

6　The tours in Austin took place annually from 2011 to 2013, although this article focuses on the two most recent tours.

7　The tours also drew from the research of Andrew Busch on urban renewal and segregation (see Bush, 2013).

8　The section of Interstate 35 that runs east of Austin's downtown opened in 1962.

9　His interpretation reflected his published scholarship as well as research underway, but published later. See: Tretter, 2011; Tretter, 2013a; Tretter, 2013b; Tretter, 2016.

10　The Austin Oaks subdivision is also featured on a walking tour brochure paid for by the City of Austin. See: Gutierrez, 2010.

11　Tour speakers include Stephanie Jarvais, a local historian and former director of the French Legation Museum and Noel Harris Freeze, who was director of the museum at that time.

12　This was Bertram Allen, leader of the community organization The Passon Society, and author of: Allen, B. (1989). *Blacks in Austin*. Austin, TX: Self-published.

References

Allen, Bertram. (1989). *Blacks in Austin*. Austin, TX: Self-Published.

Basu, Ranu. (2009). Phronesis through GIS: Exploring political spaces of education. *The Professional Geographer* 61(4): 481–492. doi: 10.1080/00330120903103106

Birch, E. L., & Roby, D. (1984). The planner and the preservationist: An uneasy alliance. *Journal of the American Planning Association* 50(2): 194–207. doi:10.1080/01944368408977175

Blomley, Nicholas. (2006). Uncritical critical geography? *Progress in Human Geography* 30(1): 87–94.

Boddy, Trevor. (2009). The Conundrums of Architectural Criticism. *Journal of Architectural Education* 62(3): 8–96. doi: 10.1111/j.1531-314X.2008.00254.x

Busch, A. (2013). Building 'A City of Upper-Middle-Class Citizens': Labor markets, segregation, and growth in Austin, Texas, 1950–1973. *Journal of Urban History* 39(5): 975–996.

Chan, Melissa. Queensbridge Houses Tenants Fear Upcoming Walking Tour Will Bring Stream of Gawkers. *New York Daily News*, May 1, 2014.

Chusid, J. (2006). Preservation in the progressive city: Debating history and gentrification in Austin. *The Next American City* (12): 23–27.

Flyvbjerg, Bent. (2001). *Making Social Science Matter: Why Social Inquiry Fails and How It Can Succeed* Again. Cambridge, UK: Cambridge University Press.

Flyvbjerg, Bent. (1998). *Rationality and Power*. Chicago: University of Chicago Press.

Flyvbjerg, Bent, Landman, Todd, and Schram, Sanford. (Eds.). (2012). *Real Social Science: Applied Phronesis*. New York: Cambridge University Press.

Forester, John. (1989). *Planning in the Face of Power*. Berkeley: University of California Press.

Gruen, Phil. Unpublished "Introduction" for "'And on Your Left': Taking the Architectural Tour Seriously". Panel presented at the 67th Annual Conference of the Society of Architectural Historians, Austin, Texas, April 10, 2014. Text from e-mail circulated April 7, 2014.

González, Robert Alexander. (2011). *Designing Pan-America: U.S. Architectural Visions for the Western Hemisphere*. 1st ed. Roger Fullington Series in Architecture. Austin, TX: University of Texas Press.

Gutierrez, Diana. (2010). "The Tejano Walking Trail (Walking Tour Brochure)". Paid for by the Neighborhood Enhancement Fund administered by the City of Austin Planning and Development Review Department. www.americantrails.org/NRTDatabase/trailDocuments/3795_70_Tejano_Trail.pdf

Habermas, Jurgen. (1984). *The Theory of Communicative Action: Reason and the Rationalization of Society, Vol. 1.* Boston, MA: Beacon Press.

Hemisfair Park Area Redevelopment Corporation. (2012, February). *HemisFair: Framework and Master Plan.* Hemisfair Park Area Redevelopment Corporation. Retrieved from www.hemisfair.org/pdfs/2012-06-18_Hemisfair_Framework_and_Master_Plan.pdf

Holleran, Michael. (1998). *Boston's "Changeful Times": Origins of Preservation & Planning in America.* Baltimore, MD: Johns Hopkins University Press.

Holmesly, Sterlin. (2003). *HemisFair '68 and the Transformation of San Antonio.* San Antonio, TX: Maverick Publishing Company.

Housing Authority of the City of Austin. (n.d.). "Report of the Housing Authority of the City of Austin for the Years 1938–1939". City of Austin.

Hurley, Andrew. (2010). *Beyond Preservation: Using Public History to Revitalize Inner Cities. Urban Life, Landscape and Policy.* Philadelphia, PA: Temple University Press.

Innes, Judith E. (2004). Consensus building: Clarifications for the critics. *Planning Theory* 3(1): 5–20. doi: 10.1177/1473095204042315

Innes, Judith E. (2016). Viewpoint Collaborative rationality for planning practice. *Town Planning Review* 87(1): 1.

Innes, Judith E. and David E. Booher. (2010). *Planning with Complexity: An Introduction to Collaborative Rationality for Public Policy.* London and New York: Routledge.

Jacobs, Jane. (1961). *Death and the Life of Great American Cities.* New York: Random House, Inc.

Johnson, Stuart. (2013, December 16.) Telephone Interview.

Kaufman, Ned. (2009). *Place, Race and Story.* New York: Routledge.

Koch & Fowler, consulting engineers. (1957). A City Plan for Austin, Texas (1928). Reprinted by City of Austin, Department of Planning.

Kitson, Jennifer. (2015). Home touring as hospitable urbanism. *Journal of Urbanism: International Research on Placemaking and Urban Sustainability.* doi:10.1080/17549175.2015.1111924

Longstreth, Richard. (1999). Architectural history and the practice of historic preservation in the United States. *Journal of the Society of Architectural Historians* 58(3): 326–333.

Mason, Randall. (2009). *Once and Future New York: Historic Preservation and the Modern City.* Minneapolis: University of Minnesota Press.

Olivio, Benjamin. (2012, April 18). Conservation Society opposes demolition of Institute of Texan Cultures, Wood Courthouse—The Downtown Blog. *San Antonio Express-News.* San Antonio, TX. Retrieved from http://blog.mysanantonio.com/downtown/2012/04/conservation-society-takes-stand-on-institute-of-texan-cultures-wood-courthouse-demolition/

Page, M., & Mason, R. (Eds.). (2004). *Giving Preservation a History: Histories of Historic Preservation in the United States.* New York, NY: Routledge.

Randolph, J. (2012). *Environmental Land Use Planning and Management* (2 ed.). Washington, DC: Island press.

Roberts, Andrea. (2013, November 6). Telephone interview.

San Antonio, Fair, Inc. (1968). *HemisFair 1968 Official Souvenir Guidebook.* Dallas: A.H. Belo Corp. P. 21.

Structural Mechanics Research Laboratory, Center for Building Research at the University of Texas at Austin. (1971, December.) *HUD Austin Oaks Project.* Volumes I–VI. Prepared for USA Department of Housing and Urban Development. Office of the Secretary Low-Income Housing Demonstration Contract No. H-1038, LIHD-2.

Tretter, Eliot. (2013a). *Austin Restricted: Progressivism, Zoning, Private Racial Covenants, and the Making of a Segregated City.* Final Report to the Institute for Urban Policy Research and Analysis. Austin, TX: University of Texas at Austin. www.academia.edu/1888949/Austin_Restricted_Progressivism_Zoning_Private_Racial_Covenants_and_the_Making_of_a_Segregated_City.

CRITICAL GEOGRAPHY AND PUBLIC DELIBERATION

Tretter, Eliot M. (2013b). Contesting sustainability: 'SMART Growth' and the redevelopment of Austin's Eastside: 'SMART Growth' and the redevelopment of Austin's Eastside. *International Journal of Urban and Regional Research* 37(1): 297–310.

Tretter, Eliot. (2013c, December 11). Skype interview with author.

Tretter, Eliot. (2016). *Shadows of a Sunbelt City: The Environment, Racism, and the Knowledge Economy in Austin* (Geographies of Justice and Social Transformation Series). Athens, Georgia: University of Georgia Press.

Tretter, Eliot. (2011). "The Privilege of Staying Dry: The Impact of Flooding and Racism on the Emergence of the 'Mexican' Ghetto in Austin's Low-Eastside, 1880–1935." In *Cities, Nature and Development: The Politics and Production of Urban Vulnerabilities*, edited by Sarah Dooling and Gregory Simon. Farnham, Surrey, England; Burlington, VT: Ashgate Publishing Company.

Wells, Jeremy. (2015). Making a case for historic place conservation based on people's values. *Forum Journal* 29(3): 44–62.

Wolfe, Mark. (2013). "Letter to Amy E. Dase, Prewitt & Associates, Inc. Boundaries for the HemisFair Park Historic District, San Antonio, Bexar County, Texas (Prewitt Report No. 867, Revised July 2013)". Texas Historical Commission.

CHAPTER 9

Of Policy Lags and "Upgraded" Neighborhoods

Historic Preservation for the Twenty-First Century

Ted Grevstad-Nordbrock

> The Congress finds and declares that... in the face of ever-increasing extensions of urban centers, highways, and residential, commercial, and industrial developments, the present governmental and nongovernmental historic preservation programs and activities are inadequate to insure future generations a genuine opportunity to appreciate and enjoy the rich heritage of our Nation...
>
> (National Historic Preservation Act of 1966, as Amended)

In this declaration from the preamble to the National Historic Preservation Act (NHPA), the federal government justifies its need for a heightened engagement with the protection of historic places. It argues that new legislation is required to protect the "rich heritage" of the United States from imminent threats—from suburban sprawl, highway-building, and new development. The NHPA was enacted in 1966 and amended several times over the decades that followed. Yet it is still, today, a document very much grounded in the era in which it was written. This begs several important questions. Since the NHPA is the foundation for much historic preservation activity in the United States today, does it fairly and appropriately respond to current threats to the nation's heritage? Does legislation (and its associated policies and programs) crafted as a bulwark against the ravages of urban disinvestment and renewal now offer relevant guidance in a country that has embraced cities and urban living in ways that would have been unimaginable in the suburbs- and auto-oriented 1960s? Should the NHPA undergo further amendments to better respond to the current threats to historic places?

This essay explores the idea that federal historic preservation policies and programs have indeed failed to keep pace with the changing social and economic realities of American cities. It suggests the existence of a problematic policy lag. Policies that were designed to raise public awareness of, and appreciation for, threatened historic places have been so successful in this effort that they have created a new set of problems and challenges. This lag in public policy has produced unintended outcomes that at times work against the role of government to ensure socially just and economically equitable solutions to societal problems.

Perhaps the most troubling of these outcomes is gentrification: the social and physical "upgrading" of neighborhoods and the accompanying displacement of vulnerable residents. The connection between preservation and gentrification has fueled impassioned arguments (e.g. Listokin et al. 1998; Smith 1998). Critics note preservation's propensity for carving out exclusive spaces of affluence in cities—"gilded ghettos"—while simultaneously depleting the pool of affordable housing. Supporters counter this in their recognition that preservation has not only protected irreplaceable historic sites, but it has also been a stabilizing influence in struggling urban neighborhoods and provided a platform for inducing not only revitalization but community pride.

With a focus on federal preservation programs like the National Register of Historic Places, this essay suggests that the process of revitalization in historic neighborhoods is often punctuated by a tipping point. Before this point is reached, preservation serves in its conventional role as a protector and promoter of historic places and agent of stabilization. Once a neighborhood is stabilized, however, and that tipping point is reached, preservation then transforms into a vehicle for gentrification that can alter the neighborhood's population and—counterintuitively, perhaps—compromise its historic integrity. The Lincoln Park neighborhood of Chicago, locus of much historic preservation activity and gentrification, provides a useful case study in support of this argument. No attempt is made in this essay to "prove" that preservation causes gentrification. Rather, it merely calls attention to the social and physical changes that accompany historic preservation activity and suggests that additional research in this area is warranted—as are policy updates to address any lags.

Neighborhood Change in Chicago

Chicago, like many cities of the American rustbelt, experienced profound physical and social decline in the decades following World War II. The decentralization of population at the metropolitan scale was driven, in large measure, by the demand for new housing in the suburbs and the governmental policies that favored development there (Hirsch 1983; Katz 1989; Teaford 1990). White flight and the attendant decamping of businesses and jobs left Chicago with an infrastructure larger than what could be supported by its diminished population and tax base. Disinvestment and abandonment came to characterize many of the city's older neighborhoods, as did the familiar social problems of unemployment, poverty, and crime.

Yet, against the centrifugal flow of population and investment to the suburbs, small but noteworthy pockets of urban repopulation and reinvestment were observable beginning in the 1960s. This was described as "gentrification": the return of the gentry, with its middle-class predilections and financial resources, to urban neighborhoods that were affordable, amenity-rich, distinguished by handcrafted historic architecture, and within commuting distance of downtown and its employment base (Lees et al. 2008). This unexpected return of the middle class—this "return to the city" as it was called—was heralded as a sign of central city revival.

It became obvious to observers that this process of gentrification impacted existing lower-income residents in less than favorable ways (Smith 1982; Lyons 1996; Atkinson 2000; Newman and Wyly 2006; Podagrosi and Vojnovic 2008). The arrival of wealthier residents was often accompanied by the economic revaluation of a neighborhood. As costs of living increased, residents were forced

OF POLICY LAGS AND "UPGRADED" NEIGHBORHOODS

out as landlords raised rents, affordable apartments were converted into more lucrative condominiums, and smaller residential units in multi-family buildings were consolidated into fewer, larger ones (Hamnett and Randolph 1986). In Chicago, Lincoln Park was the early epicenter of this change.

Lincoln Park is a large municipally designated Chicago Community Area, or neighborhood,[1] situated approximately four miles north of the Loop, the city's central business district. Its eastern border hugs Lake Michigan and its namesake public park. The neighborhood is considered one of Chicago's most historically significant areas (Foerstner 1986) and is renowned for the vernacular architecture that defines its dense residential streets and commercial arteries. Its historic buildings date from the decades between the Chicago fire in 1871 and World War II, with a noteworthy exception found in the string of post-war high-rises that stretch along the lakefront.

Lincoln Park developed as a working class, ethnic European enclave in the last quarter of the nineteenth century (Pacyga and Skerrett 1986). Its physical character today—blocks of well-maintained buildings, many handcrafted and architecturally unique—belies the humble origins of the area's original residents. The neighborhood remained a stable enclave until the Great Depression, at which time delayed building maintenance and the subdividing of housing into multiple units began to alter the neighborhood's character. In the years that followed World War II, local manufacturing, once dependent on proximity to the Chicago River, was freed by new modes of transportation and relocated to more favorable sites in the suburbs. Newer residential neighborhoods at the city's periphery and the burgeoning suburbs beyond drew population from older quarters like Lincoln Park. In this shifting environment, the neighborhood's desirability plummeted and the 1950s and 1960s saw increasing poverty. African-American and Latino residents filled the void left through white flight.

Yet the passage of time has shown these physical and social changes to be transitory. Lincoln Park emerged in the last quarter of the twentieth century as a revitalized postindustrial neighborhood that is one of the most desirable in Chicago (Betancur, Domeyko and Wright 2001; Grevstad-Nordbrock 2015). In the popular press and in scholarly literature on urban revitalization, the area is frequently mentioned as the city's first, best-articulated, and most traditional example of gentrification (Fidel 1992; DeBaise 1998; Hudspeth 2003; Rast 2005; Weber, Doussard, Bhatta and McGrath 2006; Betancur 2011). A 1980 *Chicago Tribune* article captures this in its unequivocal description of Lincoln Park as "one of the clearest examples of gentrification in the city today," a neighborhood characterized by highly visible signs of property upkeep and improvement, rapidly increasing property values, and changing local demographics (Sebastian 1980, p. B1B). The author of the article notes a palpable decline in the number of poor residents living in the neighborhood.

Gentrification began modestly in the 1960s in Lincoln Park's southeast corner, in the Old Town Triangle district (Cohen 1980; Bennett 1990; Suttles 1990; Fidel 1992; Bennett 2010). Early gentrifiers here practiced what became known as "sweat equity": the low-cost, do-it-yourself approach to the rehabilitation of one's own home (Old Town Triangle Association 2013). Residents were drawn to Old Town Triangle by the presence of affordable, batch-produced architecture that stood in stark contrast to the mass-produced tract homes of the suburbs. Proximity to the Loop and its diversifying service sector jobs provided the economic means to make settlement in Old Town Triangle viable.

From this beachhead, gentrification was described as spreading into adjacent areas to the north and west over the next twenty years. By the 1980s, most of Lincoln Park was gentrified or in the process of becoming so. In 1984, the *Chicago Tribune* extolled the positive changes in Lincoln Park over the previous twenty years, noting how the area "contains some of Chicago's real estate hot spots as many older buildings are rehabilitated and resold for many times their 1960s prices" (Myers 1984, p. G3). By the late 1990s, gentrification in Lincoln Park had ceased to be the newsworthy topic it once was: the neighborhood had become indelibly associated with the process. The magnitude of upgrading in Lincoln Park is evident in the demographic and housing census data[2] from that era (Table 9.1). While signs of gentrification could be found across the entirety of Lincoln Park by 2000, the process proceeded unevenly and at different rates. A single census tract (718) provides a particularly striking view of the upgrading at work during this period.

Table 9.1 Upgrading Indicators at Three Geographic Scales: Census Tract 718, Lincoln Park Neighborhood, and City of Chicago. Dollars Adjusted for Inflation to Year 2000 Values. All Census Tracts Standardized to Year 2000 Geography to Allow Inter-Decadal Comparisons

	Lincoln Park census tract 718 (% of total)	Lincoln Park neighborhood (% of total)	City of Chicago, excluding tracts with missing data (% of total)
Race and Ethnicity			
White (1970)	3,008 (70.78%)	59,759 (88.13%)	2,202,211 (65.52%)
White (2000)	2,267 (80.25%)	56,140 (87.28%)	1,201,384 (41.76%)
White (#change)	–741	–3,619	–1,000,827
Black (1970)	1,028 (24.19%)	4,904 (7.23%)	1,102,560 (32.80%)
Black (2000)	437 (15.47%)	3,394 (5.28%)	1,063,959 (36.98%)
Black (#change)	–591	–1,510	–38,601
Hispanic (1970)	1,141 (26.85%)	9,880 (14.57%)	247,278 (7.36%)
Hispanic (2000)	61 (2.16%)	3,254 (5.06%)	749,224 (26.04%)
Hispanic (#change)	–1,080	–6,626	501,946
Income and Poverty			
Per Capita Income (1970)	$9,624	$18,279	$14,804
Per Capita Income (2000)	$86,174	$64,527	$19,912
Per Capita Income (%change)	795.37%	253.01%	34.51%
Family Income (1970)	$33,123	$45,808	$44,907
Family Income (2000)	$156,551	$137,030	$46,221
Family Income (%change)	372.62%	199.19%	2.92%
Families in Poverty (1970)	228	2,297	128,257
Families in Poverty (2000)	34	449	105,509
Families in Poverty (%change)	–85.09%	–80.45%	–17.73%
Welfare Households (1970)	105	821	49,517
Welfare Households (2000)	0	434	72,877
Welfare Households (%change)	–100%	–47.13%	47.17%
Employment and Education			
Professionals (1970)	149	11,142	246,725
Professionals (2000)	1,210	29,681	404,192
Professionals (%change)	712.08%	166.38%	68.82%

	Lincoln Park census tract 718 (% of total)	Lincoln Park neighborhood (% of total)	City of Chicago, excluding tracts with missing data (% of total)
Manufacturers (1970)	324	8,303	397,593
Manufacturers (2000)	104	2,610	158,254
Manufacturers (%change)	−67.9%	−68.56%	−60.19%
College Graduates (1970)	144	8,977	153,138
College Graduates (2000)	1,607	37,612	459,365
College Graduates (%change)	1,015.97%	318.98%	199.96%
Housing			
Owner-Occupied Units (1970)	200	4,001	396,104
Owner-Occupied Units (2000)	734	14,342	460,755
Owner-Occupied Units (%change)	267%	258.46%	16.32%
Median Value Units (1970)	$59,020	$107,643	$86,021
Median Value Units (2000)	$448,200	$393,280	$164,525
Median Value Units (% change)	659.40%	265.36%	91.26%
Median Gross Rent (1970)	$468	$536	$545
Median Gross Rent (2000)	$1,102	$970	$612
Median Gross Rent (% change)	135.66%	80.97%	13.08%

Source: U.S. Census Bureau decennial data (1970, 2000).

The National Register and Historic Preservation's Economic Turn

The passage of the NHPA in 1966 was by all accounts a watershed event. Its goals were nothing less than to formalize government's role in historic preservation and establish a broad framework for its practice across the United States. It provided the federal government with a means to address policies and programs that were unintentionally detrimental to historic resources (Murtagh 1997; Tomlan 2015). To this point, the NHPA was described as a tool for transforming the federal government "from an agent of indifference, frequently responsible for needless loss of historic resources, to a facilitator, an agent of thoughtful change, and a responsible steward for future generations" (Advisory Council on Historic Preservation 2002). The cornerstone of the NHPA is the National Register of Historic Places. A simple inventory, the National Register is the "official list of the Nation's historic places worthy of preservation... [and] part of a national program to coordinate and support public and private efforts to identify, evaluate, and protect our historic and archeological resources" (National Park Service n.d., p. 1). National Register-listing is an honorific designation.[3] The distinction of owning an officially designated property is expected to instill a sense of stewardship and commitment to that historic property.

To help make preservation of existing structures more attractive than new construction, the Congress introduced financial incentives in the 1970s. This injected an economic imperative into historic preservation that enticed the private sector to participate in this public-private enterprise (Advisory Council on Historic Preservation 1979). The Tax Reform Act of 1976 was the first of these. This legislation removed incentives for developers to demolish certified historic structures by prohibiting demolition as a deductible business expense (Tyler, Ligibel and Tyler 2009). The act also allowed for the charitable contribution of easements to protect historic building façades and allowed taxpayers "to treat for depreciation purposes 'substantially rehabilitated historic property' as if they were the original users of the property"—in essence, providing owners of historic income-producing properties with a tax break to support the rehabilitation of their buildings (Joint Committee on Taxation 1976, p. 102). The Revenue Act of 1978 solidified government's commitment to private sector preservation with the establishment of the Investment Tax Credit to support the rehabilitation of historic properties. The Economic Reform Act of 1981 expanded these incentives. Finally, the passage of the Tax Reform Act of 1986 rolled back the generous incentives established in 1981 but left the tax credit at twenty percent. The credit established in 1986 remains virtually unchanged today.[4] These incentives helped offset the added costs of rehabilitating historic buildings and thus, made preservation competitive with new construction. In this way, preservation functioned as a de facto urban revitalization tool (Ryberg-Webster 2015).

Revitalizing Lincoln Park

Lincoln Park's post-war revitalization was in no small measure the result of community organizations actively promoting the neighborhood. Numerous volunteer groups were established in the 1950s to champion individual sections of Lincoln Park and counter the perception that the neighborhood was becoming a slum. Boosterism took many forms: tours of rehabilitated homes, neighborhood walking tours, garden tours, and other events designed to help build community spirit. The goal of these activities was not simply to encourage an appreciation of the neighborhood's unique attributes and local history. Rather, there was a normative component to such activity, an underlying call to residents to upkeep or improve their properties in ways that would strengthen the neighborhood and its housing values (Hurley 2010).

As early as 1961, residents of Lincoln Park were promoting their neighborhood as a "potential Georgetown," an urban enclave poised for revival (Anonymous 1961). Like the Georgetown neighborhood of Washington, DC, or other east coast and southern cities famous for their historic fabric (Figure 9.1), historic preservation was seen as the appropriate catalyst for revitalization. An article in the *Chicago Daily Tribune* from 1961 captured this sentiment. Titled "Rehabilitation Is Key to Lincoln Park Plan," the author highlighted a recent house rehabilitation project that involved "modernizing yet retaining charming features of the building such as exterior ornamental stone carvings, interior oak floors, marble fireplaces, window shutters, high ceilings, and curving banisters" (Avery 1961, p. 4). These early rehabbers laid the foundation for historic preservation in Lincoln Park and helped create an ethos that would later drive the establishment of National Register districts in the neighborhood.

Revitalization in Lincoln Park entered a new phase in 1966 with the enactment of the NHPA.[5] The listing, or designation, of National Register sites in Chicago, began shortly thereafter. Lincoln Park's first listings occurred in 1973 with the houses of two local luminaries: the Francis J. Dewes House at 503 West Wrightwood Avenue and the Ann Halsted House at 440 Belden Street. Three large historic districts were also listed in Lincoln Park during the 1980s. Two sit completely within Lincoln Park and one straddles it and the adjacent Lake View neighborhood to the north. The Sheffield Historic District (listed in 1976; expanded in 1983, 1985, and 1986) and the Old Town Triangle Historic District (listed in 1984) occupy the neighborhood's center and southeast corner, respectively. A third historic district, the Lakeview Historic District (listed in 1977), sits primarily in its namesake neighborhood to the north.

The Sheffield Historic District extends over much of the center of Lincoln Park. Approximately three hundred "contributing" (that is, historically significant) buildings are included in this district,

OF POLICY LAGS AND "UPGRADED" NEIGHBORHOODS

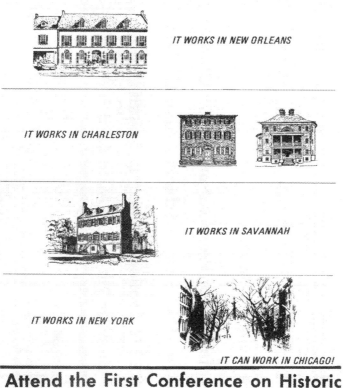

Figure 9.1 "Preservation for Tomorrow" conference (1972).
Source: DePaul University Special Collections and Archives.

which is large by the National Register standards. The National Register nomination tied the district's historic significance to its ensemble of turn-of-the-century buildings and its ability to evoke the neighborhood's middle-class roots:

> Its character as a residential neighborhood is interlaced with well-defined shopping streets has come down to us in a relatively pristine condition compared to similar neighborhoods elsewhere in the city… What these factors add up to is a district that is easily interpreted and enjoyed by the average person who can still identify with its century-old middle class urbanistic values. Few other neighborhoods in Chicago have architectural heritage that is so pleasing because it is so consistent in scale, materials, textures, and other spatial relationships. In short, Sheffield is a distinctive historic district because its original middle class urban character has survived with sufficient impact to enable most of us to find through it a sense of our time and place in history.
>
> (National Register of Historic Places 1975, 1983, 1985, 1986, n.p.)

The listing of the Sheffield Historic District in the National Register was noted with fanfare in a *Chicago Tribune* article that linked its newfound historic status with Lincoln Park's ongoing revitalization. The colloquially titled "Old Neighborhood Gets a People Lift: There Goes the Neighborhood... Revitalized!" attributed the district's unprecedented rebirth to its architecture, now formally recognized as historic (Eshbach 1975). A fertile mix of new, young professionals and residual old-timers was deemed responsible for "saving" a neighborhood that had been destabilized by the redlining activities of local banks in the 1950s. Unmentioned in the *Chicago Tribune* article were the local African-American and Hispanic populations that would be the first to be displaced from Lincoln Park as revitalization picked up pace (Betancur 1996). This was typical of newspaper reports on Lincoln Park at this time.

The introduction of tax incentives to support the rehabilitation of National Register-listed properties renewed support for preservation in the 1980s. Neighborhood groups and individual residents were no longer the most vocal advocates, however. Rather, local banks, architectural firms, and in particular, developers, lent their support (Gaspar 1977; Anonymous 1982a, b). Richard N. Holtzman, a particularly outspoken developer with the real estate firm Preservation Chicago, Inc., specialized in tax credit-assisted rehabilitation work and openly called on property owners and community leaders to work together to create additional historic districts—new sites for tax credit-fueled revitalization (Wiezorek 1984; Anonymous 1987). By 1988, the *Chicago Sun-Times* noted an "insatiable" demand among Chicago's developers, both "big-time" and "small-time," for historic preservation tax credits to defray the costs of rehabilitation work and minimize investment risks in parts of the neighborhood that had yet to be "pacified" (Cotton 1988).

Physical Upgrading in Lincoln Park

In assessing the changes to Lincoln Park and its housing stock over the last half-century, a three-stage transformation cycle is evident (Suchar 2006). This cycle begins with the rehabilitation of residential buildings, continues as owners expand their properties within zoning-determined limits, and culminates with tear-downs and new construction as market demands dictate the construction of new buildings. In Lincoln Park, this process began with rehabilitation and stabilization projects that rendered older buildings livable by contemporary standards. The restoration of decorative elements, both interior and exterior, followed essential stabilization efforts. As several scholars have noted, such restoration work becomes the primary means by which gentrifiers symbolically express their wealth and middle-class tastes (Jager 1986; Suchar 1992).

A process of building out and up follows this first stage. This involves the densification of lots so as to maximize the usable space allowable under zoning and other land use controls. This stage makes for a variety of unconventional and decidedly un-historical architectural forms that are anathema to historic preservation purists (Figures 9.2 and 9.3). The additions and alterations that occur in this stage would be subjected to municipal controls in a local landmark district and, if not prohibited outright, an attempt would be made to mitigate negative impacts to the building's historic fabric and its context. However, in the National Register-listed Sheffield Historic District, city approval of proposed alterations is not required.

In the third and final stage, tear-downs and new infill construction reshape the neighborhood in more fundamental ways (Cleaver 1990; Lurz 1999). The economic rationale for tear-downs in older, historic neighborhoods is clear:

> In a bullish market, that is one in which land values are high and rising and where developers are actively searching out new building sites, it is almost inevitable that as soon as the value of

Figure 9.2 1959 North Howe Street, located in the Sheffield Historic District (National Register of Historic Places, listed 1976; expanded in 1983, 1985, and 1986). An example of "façadectomy": the building's original 1890s façade preserved with new construction to the rear. Photograph by the author.

any given site equals or exceeds the value of the structure on it, there will be inexorable pressures on the owner to tear the building down and replace it with a more profitable use.

(Stipe and Lee 1987, p. 5)

In the Sheffield Historic District, new construction is often executed in contemporary architectural styles that make little effort to fit in with the historic character of the neighborhood (Figure 9.4). Other newly constructed buildings attempt to mesh with the existing fabric by adopting faux historicizing forms that may seem to the casual observer suitably urban and historic. Often, however, these forms are historically inappropriate to the age of the neighborhood or the local architectural idiom (Figure 9.5).

Infill construction in historic neighborhoods like Lincoln Park reflects the tastes of affluent residents who at once desire density, walkability, and an architecturally rich and diverse environment,

Figure 9.3 1934 North Bissell Street, located in the Sheffield Historic District (National Register of Historic Places, listed 1976; expanded 1983, 1985, 1986). Example of maximizing floor-space in an existing historic building through the addition of an additional story. Photograph by the author.

Figure 9.4 1947 North Howe Street (built c. 1995), located in the Sheffield Historic District (National Register of Historic Places, listed 1976; expanded 1983, 1985, 1986). New construction in a contemporary style. Photograph by the author.

Figure 9.5 New-build house at 1862 North Dayton Street, in the Mediterranean Revival style (built c. 1990). Photograph by the author.

Figure 9.6 1863 North Howe Street, located in the Sheffield Historic District (National Register of Historic Places, listed 1976; expanded in 1983, 1985, and 1986). Marketed by developers as a teardown in May 2014. Photograph by the author.

yet at the same time demand space and amenities allowed through new construction. The *Chicago Reader* described this as "sneak development," a means of reworking an historic urban neighborhood into something palatable to suburban consumers: "People are moving back to the city, but they're not moving into the city on the city's own terms. They're manipulating the environment so they can have the city on their own terms" (Osran and Reimann 1989, n.p.).

Redevelopment activity in Lincoln Park resulted in steadily escalating property values and the removal of what was once affordable housing. Displacement accompanied these changes. Reporting on a 1980 survey published by Advance Mortgage Corporation of Detroit, the *New York Times* noted that Lincoln Park, much like Capitol Hill in Washington, DC, and various gentrifying enclaves in New York City, was steadily losing its poor population through the forces of gentrification-fueled displacement. The article described how reinvestment in Lincoln Park's building stock was differentially impacting neighborhood residents. Citing restored single-family homes that were selling for $500,000, the article noted how reinvestment "also meant replacement of low-income residents, who are often members of minority groups" (Horsley 1980, p. 8).

Rehabilitation projects, building expansions, and tear-downs are all prevalent in Lincoln Park's historic areas and are emblematic of ongoing gentrification. Developers actively promoted demolition and new construction during the 2010s (Figure 9.6). The reshaping of the cityscape has occurred across Lincoln Park, and the honorific National Register-listed districts within the neighborhood— the Sheffield Historic District in particular—are no exceptions.

Preservation at the Crossroads

Historic preservation's role in revaluing neighborhoods and its relationship to gentrification— although difficult as it is to definitively tease out—was acknowledged even before financial incentives were injected into the process (Newsom 1971). In 1979, the National Commission on Neighborhoods offered an early cautionary note in its report to the Congress, *People, Building Neighborhoods*, that the "return to the city" movement (as gentrification was described at the time), while in many respects beneficial to struggling neighborhoods, stood a real chance of replicating the mistakes of urban renewal and by inadvertently stimulating displacement (National Commission on Neighborhoods 1979). The report implicates historic preservation—and tax credit-subsidized rehabilitation projects specifically—as an unintended driver of gentrification and displacement in urban neighborhoods. It goes on to note how federal tax provisions for historic rehabilitation "often come at the expense of low and moderate income residents of those newly discovered historic neighborhoods, many of whom have been displaced by more affluent homeowners" (Ibid., p. 191). Yet, in the years since this report was written, relatively little effort has been made to better understand the nature of this relationship, let alone to mitigate the negative effects that accompany historic preservation programs. This silence is surprising given the steady growth in the use of federal incentives (and their state equivalents) and their active marketing as tools for urban revitalization (National Park Service 2013).

In 2005, the local non-profit organization Preservation Chicago called attention to the physical degradation of Lincoln Park's gentrified National Register-listed historic districts. After years of "atrocious, disfiguring alterations" to the neighborhood's architectural fabric (Mary C. Means, National Trust for Historic Preservation-Midwest Office, cited in Gapp 1980), the Sheffield Historic District was singled out as one of "Chicago's Seven Most Threatened" historic sites (Preservation Chicago 2005). In spite of its listing on the National Register (and being expanded three times in the years following), the district was being altered through a process of piecemeal alteration, demolition, and new construction that had already, by 2005, severely compromised the neighborhood's historic integrity.

Preservation Chicago placed the blame for the district's woes squarely on the area's two long-standing neighborhood groups and their refusal to advocate on behalf of preservation. The failure of these groups to sustain their advocacy work beyond the first wave of revitalization that began in the 1950s reveals an important insight into historic preservation in areas experiencing gentrification and skyrocketing demands for housing. Preservation garners greatest support when a neighborhood is deemed transitional or at a perceived tipping point between revitalization and decline. However, over time, this support either dwindles among residents, as threats to the neighborhood diminish, or a change in preference occurs: in a stable neighborhood with untapped real estate potential, increasing capital reinvestment and redevelopment trump the more conservative concerns for preservation. In other words, the preservation of historic buildings may simply begin to matter less to residents with the passage of time.[6] In the case of Lincoln Park, demolition and new construction began almost as soon as the neighborhood was "pacified" by pioneering gentrifiers. These changes have gradually but inexorably compromised the historic integrity of the neighborhood.

Recommendations

Two published works provide an apt starting point for a discussion of recommendations to address preservation's policy lag and the need for updates. The first is the previously discussed *People, Building Neighborhoods*. This government report from 1979 was one of the first to acknowledge preservation's likely role in gentrification and displacement and provided a set of prescient recommendations for how to mitigate the impacts of preservation-fueled displacement. Many of these are still relevant today. The report recommended that historic preservation be a part of a devolved program of urban revitalization whereby locals would exert greater control over the process:

> [A]ll levels of government must develop strong policies which insure that historic preservation programs do not contribute to displacement of low and moderate income and minority residents in [historic] designated areas. These policies must include a monitoring system which consistently and effectively reviews preservation programs throughout their implementation phase
>
> National Commission on Neighborhoods (1979, p. 55).

To address this issue, the report recommends a mixture of program and policy changes that would empower local leaders and residents and calls for the provision of technical and financial support to help urban communities cope with displacement brought about by preservation. A policy that formally acknowledges the relationship between preservation, gentrification, and displacement would help raise awareness and spur productive conversations on this contentious topic. At present, these conversations rarely occur in productive settings. Furthering the recommendation for a monitoring system, an impact statement might be required as supporting documentation for a National Register nomination. This statement would ideally draw attention to the potential cost of living increases and reductions in affordable housing that could result from listing. This would allow city officials to better plan for change and aid neighborhood residents who might be adversely impacted by historic designation.[7]

Of the recommendations made in *People, Building Neighborhoods*, few have been carried out in whole or in part. A notable exception is the suggestion that financial incentives be "stacked" to concurrently meet the goals of historic preservation and other urban revitalization initiatives. The report recommends that "historic preservation funds should be able to be combined with other federal funds [for use by] non-profit organizations for projects that benefit low income people, minorities and the elderly" (Ibid., pp. 55–56). The stacking of incentives has indeed become a standard practice among both private and non-profit developers. In particular, low-income housing tax credits have successfully been used to incorporate below-market-rate housing units in rehabilitated historic buildings. As noted in the *Annual Report on the Economic Impact of the Federal Historic Tax Credit for FY 2015*, between 1978 and 2015, nearly twenty-eight percent of all housing units produced through the historic rehabilitation tax credit program were for affordable to low- and/or moderate-income families. In 2015, the number stood at thirty-four percent (Center for Policy Research 2016, p. 4). Government agencies would do well to more aggressively encourage such mixed-income projects and perhaps even require the inclusion of low-income units as a condition of the availability of historic rehabilitation tax credits. This is, particularly, a timely issue given recent calls to promote the use of the tax credit program in the very types of neighborhoods most vulnerable to gentrification:

> The Secretary called for the greater promotion and utilization of the Federal Historic Preservation Tax Incentives Program in economically depressed areas, and asked that the [National Park Service] conduct an internal review focused on additional opportunities to improve the program and help revitalize these areas

> (National Park Service 2016, p. 2).

The second relevant source of recommendations is a 1998 article in *Housing Policy Debate* by David and Barbara Listokin and Michael Lahr (Listokin et al. 1998). Titled "The Contributions of Historic Preservation to Housing and Economic Development," this thoughtful essay traces historic preservation's role in urban revitalization and in so doing broaches the issue of preservation-fueled gentrification and displacement. The authors offer several recommendations for minimizing such outcomes. Among their recommendations are creation of preservation-friendly zoning and building codes and the removal of the income-producing requirement for federal rehabilitation tax credits. Perhaps most significantly, they also suggest the creation of a tiered system for historic designation to allow more flexibility in how properties are adaptively reused. This, coupled with a scalable system of tax credits, would allow for targeted preservation efforts that respond to the specific conditions of a community.

A final recommendation specifically related to the National Register is warranted, one that is straightforward in principle yet potentially costly to the federal and state agencies that oversee the program. This involves the accuracy and currency of data. Very simply, the National Register program would benefit greatly from the requirement of periodic updates on the status of individually listed properties and properties within historic districts—their physical condition, current use, and so on. Updates to National Register nominations currently occur on an irregular and piecemeal basis, if at all, and as the Lincoln Park example above suggests, a significant change to listed properties often goes without notice. Mandated updates would provide a richer and far more accurate dataset for analysis, in particular, spatial analysis, given the widespread use of GIS and the availability of georeferenced data. This would facilitate research into preservation's role in reshaping communities and provide a continuous stream of feedback to the agencies that manage the National Register.

Concluding Thoughts

As a way of breathing new life into urban neighborhoods during an era when the suburbs commanded most of the growth in metropolitan areas, historic preservation seemed an unconditional success. A neighborhood like Lincoln Park was repeatedly described in the press from the 1970s onward as the gold standard among historic neighborhoods—an enclave where the presence of historic buildings could drive revitalization and succeed where governmental urban renewal projects with similar objectives had failed. Lincoln Park was promoted locally as a model for other neighborhoods that might similarly gentrify. A subtle but critical part of this process was the historic imprimatur that National Register status conferred on a neighborhood. The official recognition of a district like the Sheffield Historic District differentiated it from other areas, rendering the area as "special." The availability of federal and state financial incentives to historic property owners within the district reinforced this distinction and ultimately helped to solidify the affluent and exclusive character of the neighborhood that exists today.

This exploratory essay concludes by asking several questions about the role of historic preservation in urban neighborhoods and its relationship to gentrification. If honorific programs like the National Register of Historic Places focus attention on neighborhoods and spur their revitalization, which in turn creates pressures to redevelop these neighborhoods so as to maximize real estate profits, is this policy doing what it was designed to do, namely to preserve historic resources? Is it a good public policy to support programs that may cause displacement of vulnerable populations? Moreover, is it a good public policy to invest in the private rehabilitation of historic buildings when many of these buildings, as those of Lincoln Park exemplify, may eventually succumb to redevelopment pressure and be significantly altered or demolished anyway? No facile answers are offered, just the observation that the public policy targeting rapidly changing historic environments needs to evolve to remain relevant. The current lag in policy begs attention and clarifying research is long overdue.

Notes

1 It bears mentioning that "Lincoln Park" is a loosely defined and fluid label used to describe the neighborhood immediately around the namesake public park. However, the official Chicago Community Area of Lincoln Park is expansive and encompasses no fewer than eight unofficial and amorphous neighborhoods, one of which is also referred to as "Lincoln Park." See DeBaise, C. (1998), Bennett, L. (2010).

2 The 2000 census is used as a cut-off date here. Changes in data collection methodology that began with the implementation of the American Community Survey in 2005 render comparisons between pre- and post-2000 decennial data problematic.

3 In contrast to the honorific National Register, the designation of local landmarks typically—but not always—imposes restraints on property owners. Local landmarking is a regulatory process.

4 The State of Illinois piggybacked off the federal government's efforts and, in 1982, introduced a property tax assessment freeze program. Like the federal tax credit program, this state initiative subsidizes private investment in historic buildings but focused on historic owner-occupied residences instead of income-producing properties. Although the value of the program was debated in the newspapers as a potential drain on local tax revenues (Storch 1979), it eventually garnered support among its targeted beneficiaries—homeowners—and entered the toolbox of financial instruments that support preservation work in Illinois (Guarino 1991).

5 This was bolstered locally by the establishment of Chicago's own preservation ordinance two years later, which empowered the city's Commission on Chicago Landmarks to recommend to City Council individual buildings and historic districts for recognition and protection. Like similar entities across the United States, the Commission was given authority to approve proposed alterations and demolitions of landmarks and the right to refuse a building or demolition permit if the proposed changes would negatively impact the landmark.

6 Weber et al. noted in their 2006 study of Chicago's gentrifying neighborhoods that "escalating land values... provide a central impetus to replace old—and in the eyes of many, 'vintage'—buildings with newer housing stock" (Weber, Doussard, Bhatta and McGrath 2006, p. 23).

7 Precedents for this already exist. Federal environmental regulations under 40 CFR 1508.8 discuss both the direct and indirect effects of projects on the environment. The effects are broadly defined as "ecological, aesthetic, historic, cultural, economic, social, or health, whether direct, indirect, or cumulative... [and] may also include those resulting from actions which may have both beneficial and detrimental effects, even if on balance the agency believes that the effect will be beneficial."

References

Advisory Council on Historic Preservation. (1979). *The Contribution of Historic Preservation to Urban Revitalization*. Advisory Council on Historic Preservation. Washington, D.C., Government Printing Office.

———. (2002). The National Historic Preservation Program: Overview. Accessed on August 9, 2017 from http://www.achp.gov/overview.html

Anonymous. (1961). *Househunter's New Target: Midtown Manors. Preservation News*. Washington, DC: National Trust for Historic Preservation 1: 4.

———. (1982a). Tax Breaks on Historic Buildings Explained in Upcoming Seminars. *Chicago Tribune*, March 20: A11.

———. (1982b). Rehab Tax Law Conference Set. *Chicago Tribune*, March 14: B2B.

———. (1987). Preservation Chicago Restores Old Buildings. *Chicago Sun-Times*. March 6: n.pag.

Atkinson, R. (2000). Measuring Gentrification and Displacement in Greater London. *Urban Studies* 37(1):149–165.

Avery, S. (1961). Rehabilitation Is Key to Lincoln Park Plan. *Chicago Daily Tribune*, August 31: S1.

Bennett, L. (1990). *Fragments of Cities: The New American Downtowns and Neighborhoods*. Columbus: The Ohio State University Press.

———. (2010). *The Third City: Chicago and American Urbanism*. Chicago: The University of Chicago Press.

Betancur, J. J. (1996). The Settlement Experience of Latinos in Chicago: Segregation, Speculation, and the Ecology Model. *Social Forces* 74(4):1299–1324.

———. (2011). Gentrification and Community Fabric in Chicago. *Urban Studies* 48(2):383–406.

Betancur, J. J., I. Domeyko, and P. A. Wright. (2001). *Gentrification in West Town: Contested Ground, 52*. Chicago: University of Illinois at Chicago, Voorhees Center for Neighborhood and Community Improvement.

Center for Policy Research, Rutgers University. (2016). *Annual Report on the Economic Impact of the Federal Historic Tax Credit for FY 2015*. New Brunswick, NJ: Rutgers University.

Cleaver, J. (1990). Teardowns Build in Popularity in Older, Historic Communities. *Crain's Chicago Business* 13(27): n.pag.

Cohen, M. (1980). Historic Preservation and Public Policy: The Case of Chicago. *The Urban Interest* 2(2):3–11.

Cotton, R. (1988). Tax Breaks Can Offer Restoration Incentive. *Chicago Sun-Times*. October 21: 35.

DeBaise, C. (1998). It's Hard to Tell Today, but Lincoln Park Once Was an... *Chicago Tribune*, January 20: n.pag.

Eshbach, E. (1975). Old Neighborhood Gets a People Lift: There Goes the Neighborhood... Revitalized! *Chicago Tribune*, July 10: B1.

Fidel, K. (1992). End of Diversity: The Long-Term Effects of Gentrification in Lincoln Park. In *Gentrification and Urban Change*, ed. R. Hutchison, 145–164. Greenwich, CT: JAI Press Inc.

Foerstner, A. (1986). Birth of the Neighborhoods: Farms, Brickyards Built Lake View, Lincoln Park. *Chicago Tribune*, June 4: F17.

Gapp, P. (1980). Landmark Foundations are Shaky. *Chicago Tribune*, October 4: n.pag.

Gaspar, M. (1977). Tax Break Available for Historic Commercial Properties. *Chicago Tribune*, July 3: A2.

Grevstad-Nordbrock, T. (2015). "An Analysis of Diverse Gentrification Processes and Their Relationship to Historic Preservation Activity in Three Chicago Neighborhoods." Unpublished Ph.D. dissertation, Department of Geography, Michigan State University.

Guarino, J. (1991). For Some, Tax Freeze is an Historic Event. *Chicago Tribune*, September 8: n.pag.

Hamnett, C., and B. Randolph. (1986). Tenurial Transformation and the Flat Break-up Market in London: The British Condo Experience. In *Gentrification of the City*, eds. N. Smith and P. Williams, 121–152. Winchester, MA: Allen & Unwin, Inc.

Hirsch, A. R. (1983). *Making the Second Ghetto: Race and Housing in Chicago, 1940–1960*. Cambridge: Cambridge University Press.

Horsley, C. B. (1980). "Revitalization" Held to Be Spotty. *New York Times*, June 1:1, 8.

Hudspeth, N. (2003). Gentrification and Decline in Chicago: Defining Neighborhood Change with Census Data. Accessed on August 9, 2017 from https://www.voorheescenter.com/publications.

Hurley, A. (2010). *Beyond Preservation: Using Public History to Revitalize Inner Cities*. Philadelphia: Temple University Press.

Jager, M. (1986). Class Definition and the Aesthetics of Gentrification: Victoriana in Melbourne. In *Gentrification of the City*, eds. N. Smith and P. Williams, 78–91. Winchester, MA: Allen & Unwin, Inc.

Joint Committee on Taxation. (1976). *Summary of the Tax Reform Act of 1976 (H.R. 10612, 94th Congress, Public Law 94-455)*. Washington, D.C., U.S. Government Printing Office.

Katz, M. B. (1989). *The Undeserving Poor: From the War of Poverty to the Ware on Welfare*. New York: Pantheon Books.

Lees, L. et al., eds. (2008). *Gentrification*. New York: Routledge.

Listokin, D. et al. (1998). The Contributions of Historic Preservation to Housing and Economic Development. *Housing Policy Debate* 9(3):431–478.

Lurz, B. (1999). Interesting Infill. *Professional Builder* 64(9):50–56.

Lyons, M. (1996). Gentrification, Socioeconomic Change, and the Geography of Displacement. *Journal of Urban Affairs* 18(1):39–62.

Murtagh, W. J. (1997). *Keeping Time: The Theory and History of Preservation in America*. Revised ed. New York: Preservation Press/John Wiley & Sons, Inc.

Myers, L. (1984). Community of Personalities: Lincoln Park/Lake View East Runs Gamut. *Chicago Tribune*, June 6: G3.

National Park Service, U.S. Department of the Interior, Technical Preservation Services. 2013. *Federal Tax Incentives for Rehabilitating Historic Buildings: 35th Anniversary*. Washington, DC.

———. (2016). Report to the Secretary of the Interior on the Federal Historic Preservation Tax Incentives Program. Washington, DC.

National Register of Historic Places. (1975) (rev. 1983, 1985, 1986). *Sheffield Historic District and Boundary Increases*. Department of the Interior. Washington, D.C., National Park Service.

Neighborhoods, N. C. o. (1979). *People, Building Neighborhoods*. Washington, D.C.: United States Government Printing Office.

Newman, K., and E. Wyly. (2006). The Right to Stay Put, Revisited: Gentrification and Resistance to Displacement in New York City. *Urban Studies* 43(1):23–57.

Newsom, M. D. (1971). Blacks and Historic Preservation. *Law and Contemporary Problems* 36(3):423–431.

Old Town Triangle Association. (2013). *Old Town Triangle Newsletter*, March/April: n.pag.

Osran, T., and C. Reimann. (1989). Sneak Development: Old Town Preservationist Fight the Attack of the Incredible Expanding Buildings. *Chicago Reader*, July 27: n.pag.

Pacyga, D. A., and E. Skerrett. (1986). *Chicago, City of Neighborhoods: Histories and Tours*. Chicago: Loyola University Press.

Podagrosi, A., and I. Vojnovic. (2008). Tearing Down Freedman's Town and African American Displacement in Houston: The Good, The Bad, and the Ugly of Urban Renewal. *Urban Geography* 29(4):371–401.

Preservation Chicago. (2014). Sheffield Historic District - 2005 Chicago 7. Preservation Chicago 2005. Accessed on August 9, 2017 from http://preservationchicago.org/chicago07/?cat=15

Rast, J. (2005). *Curbing Industrial Decline or Thwarting Redevelopment? An Evaluation of Chicago's Clybourn Corridor, Goose Island, and Elston Corridor Planned Manufacturing Districts.* Milwaukee, WI: The University of Wisconsin-Milwaukee, Center for Economic Development.

Ryberg-Webster, S. (2015). Urban Policy in Disguise: A History of the Federal Historic Rehabilitation Tax Credit. *Journal of Planning History* 14(3):204–223.

Sebastian, P. (1980). Culture, High Property Values in Lincoln. *Chicago Tribune*, November 2: B1B.

Smith, N. (1982). Gentrification and Uneven Development. *Economic Geography* 58(2): 139–155.

———. (1998). Comment on David Listokin, Barbara Listokin, and Michael Lahr's 'The Contributions of Historic Preservation to Housing and Economic Development: Historic Preservation in a Neoliberal Age. *Housing Policy Debate* 9(3): 479–485.

Stipe, R. E., and A. J. Lee eds. (1987). *The American Mosaic: Preserving a Nation's Heritage.* Washington, DC: US/ICOMOS.

Storch, C. (1979). Landmark Home Tax Freeze Blasted. *Chicago Tribune*, July 1: B2D.

Suchar, C. S. (1992). Icons and Images of Gentrification: The Changed Material Culture of an Urban Community. In *Gentrification and Urban Change*, ed. R. Hutchison, 165–192. Greenwich, CT: JAI Press, Inc.

———. (2006). Chicago's Central Area. In *New Chicago: A Social and Cultural Analysis*, eds. J. P. Koval, L. Bennett and M. I. J. Bennett, 56–76. Philadelphia: Temple University Press.

Suttles, G. D. (1990). *The Man-Made City: The Land-Use Confidence Game in Chicago.* Chicago: The University of Chicago Press.

Teaford, J. C. (1990). *The Rough Road to Renaissance: Urban Revitalization in America, 1940–1985.* Baltimore, MD: The Johns Hopkins University Press.

Tomlan, Michael. (2015). *Historic Preservation: Caring for Our Expanding Legacy.* New York: Springer.

Tyler, N., T. J. Ligibel, and I. R. Tyler. (2009). *Historic Preservation: An Introduction to Its History, Principles, and Practice.* 2nd ed. New York: W.W. Norton & Company, Inc.

Weber, R., M. Doussard, S. D. Bhatta, and D. McGrath. (2006). Tearing the City Down: Understanding Demolition Activity in Gentrifying Neighborhoods. *Journal of Urban Affairs* 28(1):19–41.

Wiezorek, J. (1984). Homes of the Past Give Birth to Homes of Future. *Chicago Tribune*, June 6: G12.

CHAPTER 10

Urban Preservation

A Community and Economic Development Perspective

Stephanie Ryberg-Webster

Preserving urban historic resources has a long history within preservation practice, dating to early efforts in Boston (Holleran, 2001), New York (Mason, 2004, 2009), Charleston (Weyeneth, 2000; Yuhl, 2005), and beyond. Over the course of the twentieth century, urban preservation initiatives at times found synergies with broader urban planning efforts (Greenfield, 2004; Ryberg, 2013a), while also functioning as a counter-narrative in the face of large-scale demolition typically associated with urban renewal and mid-century highway building. By the end of the twentieth century, cities across the country were engaging in local community and economic development (CED) efforts to build, strengthen, and revitalize neighborhoods and downtown districts in the wake of ongoing federal devolution and shifting urban development and planning theories that prioritize grassroots processes, citizen engagement, and tailored strategies responding to micro-conditions. At the same time, municipal preservation practice grew exponentially after the passage of the 1966 National Historic Preservation Act and the creation of the National Register of Historic Places, which established a federal precedent for designating both individual buildings and entire historic districts. Cities across the country, including Cleveland, formed local preservation commissions to identify, designate, and regulate the change of important historic resources.

Today, these two broad areas of practice – urban preservation and community/economic development – co-exist within the space of older and historic neighborhoods. While the intersections of preservation with CED practice in the field are nuanced, vary place-by-place, and shift over time, recent literature emanating from both scholarly research and preservation practice argues that preservation can and should play a prominent role in furthering CED goals in neighborhoods and cities around the United States. The most prominent arguments highlight positive economic outcomes including job creation, increased tax revenue, and stabilized or improved property values, an important goal for legacy cities such as Cleveland and a cautionary note for high-growth cities facing rapid price increases and gentrification pressure. The purported benefits of preservation from within the field can be broad and lofty at times. For instance, a 2011 report completed for the Advisory Council on Historic Preservation begins with the broad claim: "historic preservation has become a fundamental tool for strengthening American communities" (Rypkema, Cheong & Mason, 2011). Specifically, the report states, preservation contributes to core economic and community development goals including "small business incubation, affordable housing, sustainable development, neighborhood stabilization, center city revitalization, job creation, promotion of the arts and culture, small town renewal, heritage tourism, economic development, and others" (Rypkema, Cheong & Mason, 2011).

Yet, there is little to no research about the on-the-ground synergies, tensions, and perceptions that shape CED practitioners' interaction (or lack thereof) with preservation. This chapter begins to fill that void through a qualitative analysis of CED practitioners' perceptions about urban heritage, historic preservation, and the future of the urban built environment. The research intentionally focuses on perceptions and discourses about preservation occurring *external* to the preservation field with an explicit goal of providing reflexive critique and insight into the preservation profession and opening the doors to a broader dialogue between these allied areas of practice that often operate in silos. Through greater understanding about the perspective of CED practitioners, we can shape a more productive, inclusive, relevant, and influential preservation practice in legacy cities and beyond. Recognizing that CED is an expansive and diverse area of practice, the perspective of these non-preservationists is crucial as they often work to stabilize and improve older and historic neighborhoods and make decisions about the future of (both designated and undesignated) historic buildings.

The research focuses on CED practice in Cleveland, Ohio, which is an ideal setting for untangling this complex interaction. Cleveland is a shrinking, rust-belt, "legacy city" rich in history that faces an uphill battle in the face of entrenched decline, resulting from more than six decades of continuous population loss and ongoing economic restructuring in the wake of deindustrialization. The city has a robust CED sector (Yin, 1998; Lowe, 2008), with individual Community Development and Economic Development Departments within the city government (in addition to the city's planning commission), a number of city-wide, non-profit CED organizations, and over twenty-five neighborhood-based community development corporations (CDCs). Cleveland also has a robust preservation sector. The Cleveland Landmarks Commission, formed in 1971, was the first local historic preservation commission in the State of Ohio, while the Cleveland Restoration Society is an active and nationally-recognized non-profit advocacy group working throughout Northeast Ohio. As a legacy city that boomed in the early twentieth century, but has lost more than fifty-five percent of its population since 1949, Cleveland has a rich architectural and cultural heritage combined with an extreme oversupply of buildings. Short-term needs to reduce vacancy and abandonment have resulted in demolition rising to the top as a key stabilization mechanism, yet the future of the city's irreplaceable built heritage hangs in the balance and there is minimal research on the role of preservation in shaping the future of legacy cities (Baumann, Hurley & Allen, 2008; Bertron & Rypkema, 2012; Ryan & Campo, 2013; Ryberg-Webster & Kinahan, 2014; Kinahan, 2016; Ryberg-Webster & Kinahan, 2016).

Two overarching questions guide this research: (1) How do CED practitioners view and value the historic built environment? And, (2) How do CED practitioners perceive the synergies and/ or tensions between their goals and historic preservation? In other words, is the past foreign to CED practitioners? As a qualitative study, the primary data sources include interviews with public-sector departments (Community Development and Economic Development) and city-wide and neighborhood-based non-profits (Cleveland Neighborhood Progress, Neighborhood Housing Services, and fourteen neighborhood CDCs), as well as archival sources including neighborhood and organization plans, internal organization documents, media accounts, websites, and other ephemera.[1] These varied data sources provide a rich basis for untangling the multiple, complicated, complex and even – at times – contradictory values that CED professionals place on tangible (i.e. buildings) and intangible (i.e. memory, traditions) heritage. The findings discuss how CED professionals define, use and perceive preservation and how their perceptions align and/or differ from contemporary practices and theories within the preservation field. CED practitioners strongly associate preservation with the built environment and historic fabric, yet there remain significant challenges to bridging the gap between on-the-ground CED practice and historic preservation.

The View from Two Silos

Although often operating in the same physical spaces of cities, urban preservation and CED practice are not universally in sync and, in fact, often operate within professional silos, which can make the two at odds with each other in some instances. While there may be exceptions of cities with highly integrated preservation and CED efforts, in most cases these two practices take place within distinct offices, without a high degree of coordination, and with varying goals and strategies. Differing arguments about the role of preservation in CED within existing literature mimic this disconnect in practice. On one hand, preservationists promote CED benefits stemming from recognizing and promoting community heritage and designating and rehabilitating historic resources. At the same time, preservation entities realize that "historic preservation has not been recognized as a gauge regarding the quality of the community, and the value of historic buildings to economic recovery and community identity has not been universally acknowledged" (ACHP, 2014, p. vi). Scholars have also noted that "preservation research and advocacy largely exist in a silo that is disconnected from the dominant urban policy discourses" (Ryberg-Webster & Kinahan, 2014, 120). On the other hand, the vast literature on CED rarely mentions historic preservation or gives it anecdotal treatment at best.

The View from Preservationists

From the vantage point of preservation-oriented literature, historic preservation can and should play a prominent role in CED practice (Figure 10.1). There are three general arguments put forth supporting a preservation-based CED practice: (1) physical improvements, (2) economic benefits, and (3) engagement and empowerment opportunities. Collectively, these form the basis for a larger claim that preservationists should have a so-called "seat at the table" in urban decision-making (Evans, 2011; Evans, 2014; Patterson, 2016). First, preservation brings specific expertise, resources, and tools for improving the physical landscape of places. This is the most traditional aspect of preservation and, in all likelihood, what most people think of when they think of historic preservation practice. Focusing on restoring or adaptively reusing the tangible built environment is at the core of historic preservation and the highly visible, physical upgrading of historic buildings can serve as a symbol of revitalization. The physicality of preservation resonates with efforts to improve buildings, districts, and neighborhoods and is codified in practice via local and national historic designation and review processes and key incentives such as federal and state rehabilitation tax credits.

In the late twentieth century, the literature began evaluating and promoting the economic benefits of preservation – a trend that has escalated in recent years. Although the economic value of historic resources has a long history within the preservation field, these arguments have gained heightened prominence recently in a culture of policy-making wherein elected officials and other leaders equate

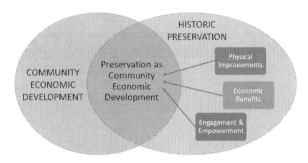

Figure 10.1 The contributions of preservation to community and economic development, from the perspective of historic preservation. Illustration by the author.

positive economic outcomes with successful programs. Scholarship has documented that historic district designation stabilizes or improves property values, which is a particularly pressing concern for CED practice in distressed legacy cities (Leichenko, Coulson & Listokin, 2001; Mason, 2005; Coulson & Lahr, 2005; Gilderbloom, Hanka & Ambrosius, 2009; Ijla et al., 2011; Shipley, Jonas & Kovacs, 2011; Thompson, Rosenbaum & Schmitz, 2011; Zahirovic-Herbert & Chatterjee, 2012; Kovacs, Galvin & Shipley, 2015; Koster, van Ommeren & Rietveld, 2016). A wealth of policy studies explore the economic impact of preservation, particularly historic tax credit investments and heritage tourism, finding positive outcomes in terms of job creation, local tax revenue and other economic stimuli (e.g. Mason, 2005; Cronyn & Paull, 2009; Lendel et al., 2015; CUPR, 2016). Scholarly research on the role of preservation in urban economies is less robust, although a few studies explore this relationship. Wonjo (1991) reviewed the intersection of preservation with economic development, while Listokin, Listokin, and Lahr (1998) provide a well-rounded overview of the intersections between preservation and CED. More recently, Ryberg-Webster (2013b) found that federal rehabilitation tax credits helped reshape and restore vibrancy to downtown districts in a number of cities and Ryberg-Webster and Kinahan (2016) concluded that historic tax credit investments occurred across the diverse landscape of legacy cities bringing housing and other essential uses to even the most distressed areas. Providing a counter to the dominant narratives that preservation can be a boon for cities and neighborhoods, Kinahan (2016) found no evidence of either revitalization benefits or gentrification markers in legacy city neighborhoods experiencing high levels of rehabilitation tax credit investment.

Much more recently, preservationists have considered the potential for their practice to empower communities through engagement (e.g. Brown, 2016; Dubrow, 2016; Minner, 2016). As of this writing, this line of thinking is more theoretical than embraced in practice, although there are a few real-world examples of engaged and inclusive preservation efforts (e.g. Hayden, 1995). A human-focused, values-based preservation practice would involve processes and outcomes that differ from the traditional, expert-oriented practice that dominates the field today. Rather, preservation would be more grassroots, participatory, inclusive, and open to diverse views of heritage and significance, particularly for traditionally disenfranchised groups such as racial minorities, immigrants, women, and/or low-income populations (e.g. Avrami, Mason & de Toree, 2000; Mason, 2006; Wells, 2015).

Preservation practice, though, largely still operates by utilizing experts to define what "counts" as historic, what has enough "integrity" to merit recognition, and controlling (again by experts) material changes to worthy properties. While scholars have explored ways to expand preservationists' understanding of historic significance (Mason, 2006; Page & Miller, 2016), the field has not rigorously dealt with the structural bias that material integrity creates against historic resources in traditionally disadvantaged communities. Furthermore, preservation rarely embraces the tools of civic engagement that are imperfect, yet significantly further advanced, in allied fields such as urban planning. Thus, while there is an emergent model of a more connected, relevant, and dynamic preservation profession, it is not widespread in practice.

The potential relevance of this emergent approach to preservation for inner-city neighborhoods that are often the focus of CED efforts is vast, as these are often (although certainly not universally) communities with majority minority populations that are low-income, sometimes in extreme poverty, with high percentages of female-headed households. In other words, cities such as Cleveland have large swaths of neighborhoods that are nearly completely African American, poor, and occupied by women with children. In Cleveland's Hough neighborhood, for instance, ninety-six percent of residents are African American, forty percent are in poverty, and seventy-seven percent are female-headed households with children. As recent writing suggests, "social justice was not an overt aim of the preservation community in 1966. But today…it is a priority for many practitioners, who desperately hope to connect preservation practice with the broader work of building a more just society" (Page & Miller, 2016, 4).

The View from Community and Economic Development

The discourse about preservation's role in CED looks quite different from the CED perspective. In practice, CED is a complex profession involving a myriad of actors from the sub-local to national scale including neighborhood-based CDCs, municipal agencies, city planners, local housing agencies, land banks, non-profit intermediaries and umbrella organizations, funders, state housing agencies, federal entities such as the Department of Housing and Urban Development (HUD) and the Economic Development Administration (EDA), and other urban policymaking entities. In general, writing associated with CED practice portrays preservation as a niche profession that is relatively small and mostly tangential to larger CED goals, although there is a small area of overlap that is largely project-specific (i.e. restoring a particular building) (Figure 10.2).

There is a vast literature focused on CED, with entire peer-reviewed journals dedicated to the subject (i.e. *Community Development, Economic Development Quarterly*). While a comprehensive

Figure 10.2 The contributions of preservation to community and economic development, from the perspective of community and economic development. Illustration by the author.

review of this massive body of writing is not possible in the space of one chapter, a summary review of key research reveals the lack of attention or value placed on preservation. For instance, in the early twenty-first century, economic development scholars addressed the value of urban amenities as an attractive force underpinning economic growth, with historic resources, architecture or cultural heritage rarely given more than a casual mention (Glaeser, Kolko & Saiz, 2001; Clark et al., 2002; Clark, 2004; Silver, Clark & Yanez, 2010). In community development, the asset-building approach has gained prominence, based on the idea of improving communities by capitalizing on physical, human, social, financial, environmental, cultural, political and other assets (Green & Haines, 2007; Phillips & Pittman, 2009; Boehlke, 2012). Despite defining a physical asset as a fixed resource that "endures over a long period of time and is rooted in place" (Haines, 2009, 41), there is a dearth of research on the role of preservation within community development (Filion et al., 2004; Carr & Servon, 2009; Ryberg, 2010; Ryberg-Webster, 2016). In their comprehensive review of the literature, Ryberg-Webster and Kinahan (2014, 128) concluded that "the asset-building framework suggests the need for grounded inquiries about the synergies and tensions between preservation and community development, including if and how community developers use historic resources." Recognizing the narrow view of preservation with CED literature on amenities and assets, Ryberg-Webster and Kinahan (2014, 128) also called for expanding these definitions "to include less tangible elements of place such as cultural heritage, tradition, and memory."

The CED literature addressing legacy cities emphasizes rightsizing via demolition, vacant building and land reuse, municipal financial management in the wake of diminished resources, and continued post-industrial economic restructuring (Vey, 2008; Mallach, 2010; Pallagst, 2010; Mallach, 2011; Mallach & Vey, 2011; Brophy & Mallach, 2012; Dewar & Thomas, 2012; Hummel, 2015). Calls for demolition dominate the legacy city policy discourse, a reasonable response to the oversupply of buildings that depresses the real estate market (Mallach, 2012). Mallach (2012, 227), for example, argues that "no number of heartwarming anecdotes of small victories, of artists buying and fixing up hold houses...should divert attention from the overarching reality that these cities have a vast oversupply of housing and other buildings."

At the same time, legacy cities have rich histories of national significance, with this heritage and associated legacy so prominent that it fulfills a definitional role. According to the American Assembly (2011, 1), "Legacy – a word that invokes thoughts of both extraordinary inheritances and obsolete relics – is a suitable descriptor for a group of American cities that have *rich histories and assets*, and yet have struggled to stay relevant in an ever-changing global economy." Yet, even in writing that seemingly has a natural affinity for preservation such as Mallach's (2010) text, *Bringing Buildings Back*, there is minimal treatment of the subject. Ryberg-Webster and Kinahan (2014, 130) thus conclude that "it is imperative, particularly given the urgency associated with demolition policies, to question...what benefits and impediments exist to integrating preservation into community and economic development...and who makes decisions about what we save and what we destroy."

Community and Economic Development and Historic Preservation in Cleveland

Cleveland, Ohio, situated on the south shore of Lake Erie, rose to prominence at the turn of the twentieth century as an industrial powerhouse first associated with oil and gas production via John

D. Rockefeller's Standard Oil Company, and later as a center of steel and auto production. In 1840, Cleveland had a mere 6,071 residents, making it the forty-fifth largest city in the U.S. By 1920, the city had grown to 796,841 residents and claimed a spot as the nation's fifth largest city, a rank it held for at least twenty years. After reaching its peak population (914,808) in 1949, Cleveland began a decades-long decline stemming from economic restructuring, deindustrialization, and population loss. Today, the city is once again the forty-fifth largest in the nation (396,815) and has experienced more than a fifty-five percent decline from its peak population (ECH, 2016).

This history of rapid growth and continued contraction has left a built landscape reminiscent of the industrial era and scarred by painful decline. Cleveland has a rich working-class and immigrant heritage, with a legacy of housing, neighborhood business districts, churches, and social halls that in many cases retain their ethnic affiliations. The industrial legacy persists in both vacant and continuously operating manufacturing facilities, warehouses, and infrastructure. Downtown Cleveland has recently experienced a resurgence, largely spurred by historic tax credit supported adaptive reuse projects (Ryberg-Webster, 2013b). Across the city's east side, neighborhoods are African-American communities that typically formed in former Jewish enclaves, yet have gained historic prominence in their own right. Across the city, there are twenty-six local historic districts, more than 300 local landmarks, at least thirty-six National Register historic districts and more than 160 individually designated resources on the National Register.

Historic preservation in Cleveland is largely affiliated with two entities: the public-sector Cleveland Landmarks Commission (CLC) and the non-profit Cleveland Restoration Society (CRS). The city established the former in 1971 and it was the first such commission in the State of Ohio. The CLC is a fairly typical local preservation commission, designating local landmarks and historic districts and reviewing applications for alterations. The Cleveland Restoration Society is a nationally-recognized non-profit preservation organization, which advocates on behalf of preservation interests, conducts fee-for-service work, and operates the innovative Heritage Home program – a low-interest loan program available in most of Cleveland's neighborhoods and in many surrounding suburban communities for owners of homes more than fifty years old.[2]

At the same time, Cleveland faces an uphill battle to overcome depressed housing values that were exacerbated by the recent foreclosure crisis, widespread deferred maintenance, and excess infrastructure. Vacancy and abandonment plague neighborhoods, homes, industrial plants, warehouses, offices, and neighborhood retail and mixed-use buildings. Around twenty percent of the city's housing stock sits vacant and nearly fifteen percent of the city's residential units were demolished between 1980 and 2010. Concentrated poverty in many neighborhoods further precludes home maintenance, much less rehabilitation. The city's median household income is around $26,000 and about thirty-five percent of the city's residents live in poverty (CCPC, 2016).

A network of CED entities work to stabilize and improve Cleveland's neighborhoods and the lives of its residents. These include more than twenty-five neighborhood-based community development corporations, which have existed in various forms since the late 1960s in Cleveland. At the city level, Cleveland has distinct Community Development and Economic Development Departments. The Economic Development Department's mission is "to provide assistance to businesses expanding within or relocating to the City of Cleveland: including financing, workforce solutions and technical assistance that will encourage investment in the community to enhance the lives of our citizens" (CCDED, 2016). This department also works on neighborhood retail, developing the Heath-Tech Corridor that connects downtown Cleveland to the University Circle cluster of educational, cultural, and medical institutions, including the Cleveland Clinic. The Community Development Department is the primary agency in charge of funds flowing from HUD and supports a variety of programs to "conserve and expand the housing stock; revitalize commercial areas; acquire, maintain, and market vacant land; improve the quality of human services; and develop small area or neighborhood strategies" (CCDCD, 2016). The department has initiatives focused on home improvements, lead hazards, residential tax abatements, and storefront renovations. To comply with federal preservation laws, namely Section 106 of the National Historic Preservation Act, the Community Development Department employs two full-time historic preservation officers.

Community Economic Development Perspectives on Preservation in Cleveland

In general, CED practitioners in Cleveland do not self-identify as preservationists, yet they recognize that their work takes place in older and historic communities throughout the city. In Cleveland, as elsewhere, CED encompasses a diverse array of activities and foci, while CED practitioners have a spectrum of personal perspectives, professional experiences, and work responsibilities. Furthermore, CED occurs in a range of neighborhoods with highly varied building stocks, market conditions, and needs, while the range of organizations and agencies undertaking CED work have their own unique missions and approaches. Within this complex landscape of local CED practice in Cleveland, there is not a universal view about the value of heritage, the definition of preservation, or the applicability of preservation to CED activities. Rather, there are a spectrum of perspectives ranging from rather neutral or apathetic to fairly strong support and appreciation for preservation. For instance, at one end of the spectrum, a local economic developer stated: "I haven't tried to destroy any landmarks, I try to avoid that," while another presented the view: "I wouldn't lay in front of a bulldozer to stop [demolition of] some of those old... warehouse buildings. They are nondescript. They don't function for business and they don't add value." On the other hand, other CED practitioners expressed fairly strong support for historic resources and preservation stating things like "When I saw the building I fell in love with it. It's gorgeous" and, even more emphatically "preservation is important. It gives neighborhoods their character and authenticity."

Over time, preservation activities of some form have occurred throughout the Cleveland area and the practice, in general, is fairly common in cities today. As such, every interviewee had some preconceived idea about what preservation is, what it means and why it happens. Despite their own views about preservation's benefits or drawbacks, Cleveland's CED practitioners believe that preservation mostly occurs because it is required, using phrases such as "they force you to" or "they have to" to explain why preservation occurs in various situations. Further articulating this viewpoint, one public sector professional explained, "I think there's very few developers or entities out there that are doing [preservation] because they think it's important," while another stated, "I can't say for sure what they'd do if they weren't obligated to do historic restorations." At the same time, CED practitioners recognize that in some (rare) cases, preservation is preferred and chosen, rather than compulsory. This generally occurs in one of two situations: (1) tax credits and incentives facilitate isolated projects and/or (2) select neighborhoods "are just more historically-minded" and "see their history as more of an asset than other neighborhoods."

An Alliance in Brick and Mortar

The built environment provides the strongest link between preservation and community economic development and a logical starting point for exploring synergies and thinking through future partnerships. Quality urban places remain a crucial element within CED practice, although debates remain about whether or not community and economic developers should focus more on improving place (i.e. neighborhood improvement) or people (i.e. education, workforce training) strategies (Bolton, 1992; Crane & Manville, 2008; Davidson, 2009; Barca, McCann & Rodrıguez-Pose, 2012). The focus on restoring and rehabilitating the built environment is at the core of historic preservation and CED practitioners recognize this synergy, describing the importance of the historic physical fabric as such:

> The nature of historic buildings are everything that an urban community needs for walkability. Restoring historic structures increases our walkability score...and then that makes them more attractive for people who want to move into the city.
>
> One of the things that makes Cleveland a great place to visit is that we have maintained so much of our historic stock. People like looking at historic buildings. People enjoy looking at the architecture, it helps us with tourism.

And, perhaps most succinctly: "The schools aren't going to sell the city, it's our built environment."

Digging beneath the surface, though, reveals potentially divergent views about what makes for a high-quality urban environment, the standards and materials that should be used, and how to proceed in severely depressed urban markets. While historic architecture is generally touted as an asset for neighborhoods, no interviewees could clearly articulate what is necessary to preserve and/or when to enforce strict standards for rehabilitation. "Historic" remains an ambiguous term that CED practitioners have difficulty defining. In many cases, CED organizations take a "know it when you see it" approach, as it is easier to visually identify architecturally significant buildings. The limited focus that historic preservation is only applicable or relevant to high-architecture structures, results in CED practitioners questioning the relevance of preservation for large swaths of working-class neighborhood housing, frame housing, non-descript industrial buildings, or other vernacular resources. In practice, buildings are often isolated from their context in decision-making. While CED practitioners may recognize that a particular neighborhood or portion of a neighborhood is historically significant, there is little support for preserving every structure in such an area to a high preservation standard.

Economic Benefits and Trade-Offs

In recent years, preservationists, supported by a number of policy and scholarly studies, have promoted the economic benefits of historic preservation – ranging from creating jobs to boosting property values to increasing local tax revenues. On the surface, these arguments align with many of the goals of CED, yet in practice CED professionals have a narrow view of preservation's economic benefits, focusing mostly on state and federal tax incentives. In many cases, projects using the federal and/or state historic rehabilitation tax credits are the primary touchpoint between CED and preservation. Reflecting a common sentiment across organizations, one practitioner noted that tax credits are often "the life or death of a project."

Only a few interviewees touched on some of the arguments that preservationists promote, noting that "the cost of new construction is so much higher than the cost of renovating historic that it just makes common sense to do it." In another case, a community developer focused on the local nature of preservation work:

> Preservation is heavily labor intensive. If you want to talk about improving the local economy, there's no better place to start talking about it than historic preservation. You can't repair a railing in China. It's got to be a carpenter who lives on Lorain Avenue.

These views are not pervasive though, with most CED entities expressing the perception that preservation will come with excessive costs. The concern about the price of preservation is particularly emphasized when discussing severely depressed markets, which are pervasive in legacy cities such as Cleveland. A community developer who works in a neighborhood where nearly forty percent of residents live in poverty and fifty percent of households have an annual income of *less than* $20,000 described the financial burden of preservation: "It cost us a lot of money. I guess we lost our shirt on it. The outcome is good, but we lost a lot of money doing that." Another described the financial challenges as such:

> We can love the way a building looks, but if it doesn't pencil out and if we applied all the historic tax credits to it and any other incentive we have and it still can't work financially then no one is going to do it.

The struggle to spur neighborhood market recovery, a prominent issue in legacy city CED practice, adds complexity to thinking about the economics of preservation. Much more so than typically occurs in preservation practice, CED professionals highlighted the opportunity costs of preservation and expressed concern that preventing demolition would impede market recovery. In other words, demolition removes excess buildings from an oversaturated market, reducing vacancies, and stabilizing the value of remaining properties. CED practitioners perceive a direct conflict between the need for demolition and preservation goals, as one interviewee summarized: "there are neighborhoods where we are a long way away from the market recovering and mothballing a house or a structure could be an impediment to market recovery."

Furthermore, CED organizations face extremely limited resources and work in areas with high need, creating an environment rife with trade-offs and difficult decisions. Out of the nearly thirty neighborhood-based CDCs in Cleveland, there are about five that mention preservation in their mission, vision or values, although this is just one among many priorities even for these organizations. For example, the Detroit Shoreway Community Development Organization, which works in one of the city's stronger west-side neighborhoods, identifies "historic preservation and our neighborhood heritage" as one of ten core values (DSCDO, 2016). The majority of CDCs, though, make no explicit mention of preservation in their mission or programming. Working in the Lee-Harvard neighborhood, the Harvard Community Services Center's programming includes community gardening, safe routes to school, "Mom's First" (an initiative to reduce infant mortality), code enforcement, commercial revitalization, environmental preservation, community outreach, food pantry, before and after-school programming, summer child care, suspension programs, and senior services, among others (HCSC, 2016). Although the organization has recently partnered with the Cleveland Restoration Society, a non-profit preservation advocacy group, to research and document significant local history and possible new historic districts, other priorities of neighborhood stabilization, social services, and community health take precedence. Many interviewees articulated this tension, noting that "CDCs really struggle with the preservation of buildings and have to go above and beyond fundraising that could be going towards other programs that their organizations run." Reflecting a common sentiment, CED practitioners view preservation as a "hurdle" and think of their organizations as "at odds with historic preservation because they [CED entities] are trying to assist the residents."

Community Heritage in Community (Re)Building

The belief that community heritage manifests within the built fabric of places is a core value within preservation, and a well-established concept for determining historical significance. Yet, the profession has not fully embraced methods of engaging communities in preservation practice, nor has it explored the potential benefits of a more community-driven process. Cleveland's CED practitioners perceive preservation as a non-inclusive practice, with a few exceptions. For example, one interviewee noted that preservation "builds a sense of community," while another expressed that "historic preservation allows for people to look with pride" at their neighborhood. More common, though, is an assumption that CED constituents (residents and other community members) are not supportive of or engaged with preservation. This suggests the need for preservationists to build a larger, popular base of support to overcome the perception that "there might not be the will of the community to actually preserve."

From the analysis of CED in Cleveland, it remains clear that longstanding perceptions of preservation are deep and persistent. CED practitioners reveal a dominant and telling thread of descriptors that run counter to their efforts to rebuild communities, strengthen neighborhoods, and improve the lives of residents. According to various interviewees, preservation is:

- Very specialized,

- An all or nothing game,

- An ancillary issue,

- A means to an end,

- Not inviting or understandable,

- A very high standard,

- Unattainable,

- Onerous,

- Not worth the time, and

- Obstructionist.

One of the consistent descriptors for preservation, mentioned at some point in nearly every interview is simple: "elitist." Given that CED efforts often focus on stabilizing and improving marginalized, distressed and lower-income communities, the perception of continued elitism creates a very real barrier to integrating preservation thinking and approaches within CED. These sentiments reinforce the idea that non-preservationists (or "outsiders") view preservation as a "Movement of No" (Meeks, 2016, 170).

Conclusions: Envisioning an Engaged Preservation

While this research shows some alignment and synergy with CED practice in Cleveland, there is also strong evidence of real and perceived barriers, raising a fundamental question for the future of preservation: How can the preservation profession overcome these perceptions, a necessary precondition for becoming an engaged partner in CED in Cleveland and beyond? The exploration of preservation within Cleveland's CED efforts confirms that preservation operates largely in its own silo. Recent work has pushed the field to expand its purview, adopt flexible tools, and become an engaged partner in broader urban planning and revitalization efforts, but it remains an uphill battle to bring this message to CED professionals and/or to change perceptions of practitioners who do not identify or read preservation literature. The dominant perceptions of preservation are that the field narrowly focuses on architecture, strictly adheres to stringent rules, relies on experts to define significant history, and offers limited benefits beyond tax credit financing. To move beyond (and reverse) these perceptions, preservationists must take *action*, including changing policy, reframing the dialogue, investing in engagement, and other bold steps that will redefine what preservation means for people and neighborhoods.

Preservationists have developed a fairly robust body of professional writing that assists in navigating existing policies, promotes the benefits of existing tools – particularly tax incentives, and offers technical guidance in "proper" methods of rehabilitation. This sharing of information is useful for anyone undertaking traditional preservation work but does little to move more engaged notions of preservation forward. It is essential for the field to document, publicize, and critically reflect (in the interest of continuous improvement) any on-the-ground projects and collaborations take place which may illustrate preservation's ability to be inclusive, to provide benefits for low-income and disadvantaged communities, to offer flexible tools to meet community needs, and so forth. In this way, preservationists can begin to reframe the profession from one of rules and enforcement to one that fosters broader goals of empowerment, social justice, sustainability, and inclusive and equitable revitalization. One major challenge that preservationists must directly address, particularly in legacy cities, is the issue of demolition. Amongst the CED community in Cleveland, where demolition is a leading neighborhood stabilization strategy, there was zero recognition that preservationists might support or even participate in decision-making about demolition. Yet, many preservation entities have explicitly recognized the need for a balanced approach (Bertron & Rypkema, 2012; PRN, 2015).

To become a more relevant partner in CED, preservationists can embark on two key changes: (1) increasing flexibility and (2) becoming participatory. Preservation scholars have already called for more flexibility within preservation standards and regulations, particularly, within the legacy city context. For instance, Bluestone (2016, 53) argues that "in the name of stewardship, we preservationists have abided by too many inane, overwrought, curatorial, highly regulated approaches to adapting old buildings to new uses," while Hurley (2016, 114) calls for the field to "consider a more flexible, holistic approach, responsive to the redevelopment needs and historical sensibilities of local communities." This push for flexibility resonates with the CED practitioners who are working under extreme resource constraints and are eager for middle-ground approaches achievable in the short term. There is a desire in CED practice to improve the appearance and physical quality of spaces. One interviewee highlighted the need to just paint wood homes: "you've got chipping and peeling paint. Who is going to want to go in there? Do you pick places that look run down?" Another described efforts at commercial district improvement: "we try to help improve the facades but these businesses are hanging on by a shoestring. My thing is to stabilize them, improve the look. Then, maybe later we could really do it up." Thus, there is a synergy in sentiment about the possibility and need for flexible strategies. The common interest in the built environment is common ground for preservationists and CED practice and would provide an ideal space for preservation to experiment with moderate rehabilitation strategies, phased approaches, and other middle-ground methods that contribute in a meaningful way to the shared goal of improving communities and neighborhood space.

Second, preservation must become engaged and participatory. This idea follows Brown's (2016, 59) call for "democratizing preservation" in which the field develops "new tools that give every person a voice in determining what is worth preserving in their community" and Minner's (2016, 80) call for an "equity preservation agenda" that is inclusive, diverse, participatory, and redistributive. For preservationists to contribute to the future of older and historic communities the field must become inclusive of people from an array of socioeconomic, racial, and cultural backgrounds. It will be insufficient to simply build partnerships with CED practitioners, as worthwhile as it may be, if CED and other local leaders assume that there is little to no support for preservation amongst their constituents. An essential step is to open the preservation process, following the lead of urban planning practice which has made great strides in the area of civic engagement and participation since the late 1960s. This is a costly and time-consuming practice that will require the preservation field and its supporters to deeply commit to communities, invest in engaged processes, and ensure that tangible results directly flow from those processes.

Looking forward, there is much at stake for preservation and for communities around the country. Whether cities are facing severe contraction, as in Cleveland, or extreme growth pressure, tough choices will always be made about the future of the built environment. Our built heritage embodies a cultural, social, and architectural legacy of countless individuals and communities over time and its future hangs in the balance. The preservation profession has much to offer in thinking about the future of older communities including, but certainly not limited to, researching and documenting histories, telling stories in meaningful and visible ways, financing physical improvements, honoring history and heritage, supporting the compatible design, and understanding the importance of continuity in place over time. Yet, self-identified outsiders, who do not view themselves as preservationists (despite working on a daily basis in older neighborhoods) view preservation as narrow, siloed, and elitist. While a few neighborhoods embrace preservation, in many, it is simply a penalty system to be avoided rather than a helpful partner. As Mason (2016, 157) summarizes, "one could fairly say that preservationists…have become obsessed with regulation." At this crucial moment, preservation is at a crossroads. To become a truly collaborative partner in CED, preservationists must embrace what Stephanie Meeks, President of the National Trust for Historic Preservation, has labeled a "Movement of Yes" (Meeks, 2016a; Meeks & Murphy, 2016b). Preservationists should also choose the dynamic path of inclusivity, engagement, and flexibility, to ensure that our built environment embodies the past while accommodating the future.

Notes

1 To protect the anonymity of interviewees, all quotes are generally attributed to CED practitioners in Cleveland. At times, I provide some additional layer of detail (i.e. a public sector employee, a director of a neighborhood-based non-profit) when it enhances the meaning and context of the quote.

2 For more information on the Cleveland Restoration Society's Heritage Home Program, see: www. heritagehomeprogram.org/.

References

Advisory Council on Historic Preservation (ACHP). (2014). *Managing Change: Preservation and Rightsizing in America*. Washington, DC: Advisory Council on Historic Preservation.

American Assembly. (2011). *Reinventing America's Legacy Cities: Strategies for Cities Losing Population*. New York: American Assembly.

Avrami, E., Mason, R., & de Torre, M. L. (2000). *Values and Heritage Conservation*. Los Angeles: Getty Conservation Institute.

Barca, F., McCann, P., & Rodrıguez-Pose, A. (2012). The Case for Regional Development Intervention: Place-Based Versus Place-Neutral Approaches. *Journal of Regional Science* 52(1): 134–152.

Baumann, T., Hurley, A., & Allen, L. (2008). Economic Stability and Social Identity: Historic Preservation in Old North St. Louis. *Historical Archaeology*, 42(1): 70–87.

Bertron, C., & Rypkema, D. (2012). *Historic Preservation and Rightsizing: Current Practices and Resources Survey*. Washington, DC: Advisory Council on Historic Preservation.

Bluestone, D. (2016). Disloding the Curatorial. In M. Page & M. Miller (Eds.), *Bending the Future: 50 Ideas for the Next 50 Years of Historic Preservation in the United States* (53–56). Amherst: University of Massachusetts Press.

Boehlke, D. (2012). Preserving Healthy Neighborhoods: Market-Based Strategies for Housing and Neighborhood Revitalization. In A. Mallach (Ed.), *Defining a Future for American Cities Experiencing Severe Population Loss* (151–175). New York: American Assembly.

Bolton, R. (1992). "Place Prosperity vs. People Prosperity" Revisited: An Old Issue with a New Angle. *Urban Studies* 29(2): 185–203.

Brophy, P. C., & Mallach, A. (2012). Reforming Local Practice in Governance, Fiscal Policy and Land Reclamation. In A. Mallach (Ed.), *Rebuilding America's Legacy Cities* (243–263). New York: American Assembly.

Brown, D. (2016). A Preservation Movement for All Americans. In M. Page & M. Miller (Eds.), *Bending the Future: 50 Ideas for the Next 50 Years of Historic Preservation in the United States* (57–61). Amherst: University of Massachusetts Press.

Carr, J. H., & Servon, L. J. (2009). Vernacular Culture and Urban Economic Development: Thinking Outside the (Big) Box. *Journal of the American Planning Association* 75(1): 28–40.

Center for Urban Policy Research (CUPR). (2016). *Annual Report on the Economic Impact of the Federal Historic Tax Credit for FY 2015*. New Brunswick, NJ/Washington, DC: Center for Urban Policy Research/National Park Service.

City of Cleveland, Department of Community Development (CCDCD). (2016). Retrieved from www.city. cleveland.oh.us/CityofCleveland/Home/Government/CityAgencies/CommunityDevelopment

City of Cleveland, Department of Economic Development (CCDED). (2016). Retrieved from www. rethinkcleveland.org/About-Us.aspx

City of Cleveland Planning Commission (CCPC). (2016). Retrieved from http://planning.city.cleveland.oh.us/

Clark, T. N. (2004). *The City as an Entertainment Machine*. Oxford: Elsevier.

Clark, T. N., Lloyd, R., Wong, K. K., & Jain, P. (2002). Amenities Drive Urban Growth. *Journal of Urban Affairs* 24(5): 493–515.

Coulson, N. E., & Lahr, M. L. (2005). Gracing the Land of Elvis and Beale Street: Historic Designation and Property Values in Memphis. *Real Estate Economics* 33(3): 487–507.

Crane, R., & Manville, M. (2008). People or Place? Revisiting the Who Versus the Where of Urban Development. *Land Lines* 20(3): 2–7.

Cronyn, J., & Paull, E. (2009). Heritage Tax Credits: Maryland's Own Stimulus to Renovate Buildings for Productive Use and Create Jobs. *The Abell Report* 22(1): 1–8.

Davidson, N. M. (2009). Reconciling People and Place in Housing and Community Development Policy. *Geo Journal on Poverty Law & Policy* 16(1): 1–10.

Detroit Shoreway Community Development Organization (DSCDO). (2016). Retrieved from www.detroitshoreway.org/our_mission.aspx

Dewar, M., & Thomas, J. M. (Eds.). (2012). *The City after Abandonment.* Philadelphia: University of Pennsylvania Press.

Dubrow, G. (2016). From Minority to Majority: Building on and Moving Beyond the Politics of Identity in Historic Preservation. In M. Page & M. Miller (Eds.), *Bending the Future: 50 Ideas for the Next 50 Years of Historic Preservation in the United States* (72–75). Amherst: University of Massachusetts Press.

Encyclopedia of Cleveland History (ECH). (2016). Retrieved from https://ech.cwru.edu/timeline.html

Evans, E. (2014). A Seat at the Table: Preservation and Rightsizing in Legacy Cities. Keynote address at the 2014 Missouri Preservation Conference, Excelsior Springs, Missouri.

Evans, E. C. (2011). *Historic Preservation in Shrinking Cities: Neighborhood Strategies for Buffalo and Cleveland* (Masters thesis). Columbia University, New York.

Filion, P., Hoernig, H., Bunting, T., & Sands, G. (2004). The Successful Few: Healthy Downtowns of Small Metropolitan Regions. *Journal of the American Planning Association* 70(3): 328–343.

Gilderbloom, J. I., Hanka, M. J., & Ambrosius, J. D. (2009). Historic Preservation's Impact on Job Creation, Property Values and Environmental Sustainability. *Journal of Urbanism* 2(2): 83–101.

Glaeser, E. L., Kolko, J., & Saiz, A. (2001). Consumer City. *Journal of Economic Geography* 1(1): 27–50.

Green, G. P., & Haines, A. (2007). *Asset Building and Community Development.* 2nd ed. Thousand Oaks, CA: Sage.

Greenfield, B. (2004). Marketing the Past: Historic Preservation in Providence, Rhode Island. In M. Page & R. Mason (Eds.), *Giving Preservation a History: Histories of Historic Preservation in the United States* (163–194). New York: Routledge.

Haines, A. (2009). Asset-Based Community Development. In R. Phillips & R. H. Pittman (Eds.), *An Introduction to Community Development* (38–48). New York: Routledge.

Harvard Community Services Center (HCSC). (2016). Retrieved from www.harvardcommunitycenter.org/programs

Hayden, D. (1995). *The Power of Place: Urban Landscapes as Public History.* Cambridge, MA: The MIT Press.

Holleran, M. (2001). *Boston's "Changeful Times": Origins of Preservation & Planning in America.* Baltimore: Johns Hopkins University Press.

Hummel, D. (2015). Right-sizing Cities in the United States: Defining Its Strategies. *Journal of Urban Affairs* 37(4): 397–409.

Hurley, A. (2016). Making Preservation Work for Struggling Communities: A Plea to Loosen National Historic District Guidelines. In M. Page & M. Miller (Eds.), *Bending the Future: 50 Ideas for the Next 50 Years of Historic Preservation in the United States* (114–118). Amherst: University of Massachusetts Press.

Ijla, A., Ryberg, S., Rosentraub, M. S., & Bowen, W. (2011). Historic Designation and the Rebuilding of Neighborhoods: New Evidence of the Value of an Old Policy Tool. *Journal of Urbanism* 4(3): 263–284.

Kinahan, K. L. (2016). *Neighborhood Revitalization and Historic Preservation in US Legacy Cities* (Doctoral dissertation), Cleveland State University, Cleveland.

Koster, H. R., van Ommeren, J. N., & Rietveld, P. (2016). Historic Amenities, Income and Sorting of Households. *Journal of Economic Geography* 16(1): 203–236.

Kovacs, J. F., Galvin, K. J., & Shipley, R. (2015). Assessing the Success of Heritage Conservation Districts: Insights from Ontario, Canada. *Cities* 45: 123–132.

Leichenko, R. M., Coulson, N. E., & Listokin, D. (2001). Historic Preservation and Residential Property Values: An Analysis of Texas Cities. *Urban Studies* 38(11): 1973–1987.

Lendel, I., Clouse, C., Cyran, E., Guzman, T., Piazza, M., Ryberg-Webster, S., Post, C., & Kalynchuk, K. (2015). *Ohio Historic Preservation Tax Credit Economic Impact Study.* Cleveland: Maxine Goodman Levin College of Urban Affairs. Retrieved from http://engagedscholarship.csuohio.edu/urban_facpub/1334

Listokin, D., Listokin, B., & Lahr, M. (1998). The Contributions of Historic Preservation to Housing and Economic Development. *Housing Policy Debate* 9(3): 431–478.

Lowe, J. S. (2008). Limitations of Community Development Partnerships: Cleveland Ohio and Neighborhood Progress Inc. *Cities* 25(1): 37–44.

Mallach, A. (2010). *Bringing Buildings Back: From Abandoned Properties to Community Assets.* 2nd ed. Montclair, NJ: National Housing Institute.

Mallach, A. (2011). Demolition and Preservation in Shrinking U.S. Industrial Cities. *Building Research & Information* 39(4): 380–394.

Mallach, A. (2012). Depopulation, Market Collapse and Property Abandonment: Surplus Land and Buildings in Legacy Cities. In A. Mallach (Ed.), *Rebuilding America's Legacy Cities* (85–109). New York: American Assembly.

Mallach, A., & Vey, J. S. (2011). *Recapturing Land for Economic and Fiscal Growth.* Washington, DC: Brookings Institution.

Mason, R. (2004). Historic Preservation, Public Memory, and the Making of Modern New York City. In M. Page & R. Mason (Eds.), *Giving Preservation a History: Histories of Historic Preservation in the United States* (131–162). New York: Routledge.

Mason, R. (2005). *Economics and Historic Preservation: A Guide and Review of the Literature.* Washington, DC: Brookings Institution, Metropolitan Policy Program.

Mason, R. (2006). Theoretical and Practical Arguments for Values-Centered Preservation. *CRM: The Journal of Heritage Stewardship* 3(Summer, 2): 21–46.

Mason, R. (2009). *The Once and Future New York: Historic Preservation and the Modern City.* Minneapolis: University of Minnesota Press.

Mason, R. (2016). A New Ownership Culture: Concepts, Policies, and Institutions for the Future of Preservation. In M. Page & M. Miller (Eds.), *Bending the Future: 50 Ideas for the Next 50 Years of Historic Preservation in the United States* (157–161). Amherst: University of Massachusetts Press.

Meeks, S. (2016a). Become a "Movement of Yes." In M. Page & M. Miller (Eds.), *Bending the Future: 50 Ideas for the Next 50 Years of Historic Preservation in the United States* (170–173). Amherst: University of Massachusetts Press.

Meeks, S., & Murphy, K. C. (2016b). *The Past and Future City: How Historic Preservation is Reviving America's Communities.* Washington, DC: Island Press.

Minner, J. (2016). Revealing Synergies, Tensions, and Silences between Preservation and Planning. *Journal of the American Planning Association* 82(2): 72–87.

Page, M., & Miller, M. (Eds.). (2016). *Bending the Future: 50 Ideas for the Next 50 Years of Historic Preservation in the United States.* Amherst: University of Massachusetts Press.

Pallagst, K. (2010). Viewpoint: The Planning Research Agenda: Shrinking Cities–a Challenge for Planning Cultures. *Town Planning Review* 81(5): i–vi.

Patterson, J. (2016). Dispatch from Seattle. Retrieved from https://rightsizeplace.org/category/commentary/

Phillips, R., & Pittman, R. H. (2009). A Framework for Community and Economic Development. In R. Phillips & R. H. Pittman (Eds.), *An Introduction to Community Development* (3–19). New York: Routledge.

Preservation Rightsizing Network (PRN). (2015). *Action Agenda for Historic Preservation in Legacy Cities.* Retrieved from https://rightsizeplace.org/actionagenda/

Ryan, B. D., & Campo, D. (2013). Autopia's End: The Decline and Fall of Detroit's Automotive Manufacturing Landscape. *Journal of Planning History* 12(2): 95–132.

Ryberg, S. R. (2010). Neighborhood Stabilization through Historic Preservation: An Analysis of Preservation and Community Development in Cleveland, Houston, Providence & Seattle (Doctoral dissertation), University of Pennsylvania, Philadelphia.

Ryberg, S. R. (2013a). Historic Preservation's Urban Renewal Roots: Preservation and Planning in Midcentury Philadelphia. *Journal of Urban History* 39(2): 193–213.

Ryberg-Webster, S. (2013b). Preserving Downtown America: Federal Rehabilitation Tax Credits and the Transformation of US Cities. *Journal of the American Planning Association* 79(4): 266–279.

Ryberg-Webster, S. (2016). Heritage Amid an Urban Crisis: Historic Preservation in Cleveland, Ohio's Slavic Village Neighborhood. *Cities* 58, 10–25.

Ryberg-Webster, S., & Kinahan, K. (2014). Historic Preservation and Urban Revitalization in the Twenty-First Century. *Journal of Planning Literature* 29(2): 119–139.

Ryberg-Webster, S., & Kinahan, K. L. (2016). Historic Preservation in Declining City Neighbourhoods: Analysing Rehabilitation Tax Credit Investments in Six US Cities. *Urban Studies* [forthcoming].

Rypkema, D., Cheong, C., & Mason, R. (2011). *Measuring the Economic Impacts of Historic Preservation: A Report to the Advisory Council on Historic Preservation.* Washington, DC: Advisory Council on Historic Preservation.

Shipley, R., Jonas, K., & Kovacs, J. F. (2011). Heritage Conservation Districts Work: Evidence from the Province of Ontario, Canada. *Urban Affairs Review* 47(5): 611–664.

Silver, D., Clark, T. N., & Yanez, C. J. N. (2010). Scenes: Social Context in an Age of Contingency. *Social Forces* 88(5): 2293–2324.

Thompson, E., Rosenbaum, D., & Schmitz, B. (2011). Property Values on the Plains: The Impact of Historic Preservation. *The Annals of Regional Science* 47(2): 477–491.

Vey, J. S. (Ed.). (2008). *Retooling for Growth: Building a 21st Century Economy in America's Older Industrial Areas.* Washington, DC: Brookings Institution Press.

Wells, J. (2015). Making a Case for Historic Place Conservation Based on People's Values. *Forum Journal of the National Trust for Historic Preservation* 29(3): 44–62.

Weyeneth, R. R. (2000). *Historic Preservation for a Living City: Historic Charleston Foundation, 1947–1997.* Columbia: University of South Carolina Press.

Wonjo, C. T. (1991). Historic Preservation and Economic Development. *Journal of Planning Literature* 5(3): 296–306.

Yin, J. S. (1998). The Community Development Industry System: A Case Study of Politics and Institutions in Cleveland, 1967–1997. *Journal of Urban Affairs* 20(2): 137–157.

Yuhl, S. E. (2005). *A Golden Haze of Memory: The Making of Historic Charleston.* Chapel Hill: University of North Carolina Press.

Zahirovic-Herbert, V., & Chatterjee, S. (2012). Historic Preservation and Residential Property Values: Evidence from Quantile Regression. *Urban Studies* 49(2): 369–382.

CHAPTER 11

Using Evidence from the Community to Guide a Local Municipality's Preservation Program

Kimberli Fitzgerald

Effective preservation planning successfully addresses the needs and reflects the values of the community; however, these needs and values are always changing. I have written this chapter from my own, personal perspective as a preservation planner and realize that many of the ideas I am discussing are likely to exist in scholarly literature, primarily in relation to communicative planning theory. But I am a practicing professional, first and foremost, and not a university professor. I think the ideas that I discuss here are very important for other practitioners to learn about because they are examples of how evidence from a community can be used to guide a local municipality's preservation planning program. I have worked in the field of preservation planning in Oregon for almost twenty years and my background is in city planning and historic preservation consulting for local jurisdictions.

This chapter focuses on a problem that became quickly apparent when I first started as a historic planner at the City of Salem in February 2009: the community was not particularly happy with how the City was managing its preservation program. The City submitted a National Register District nomination for the Fairmount neighborhood to the State Historic Preservation Office, and then withdrew it due to the angry outcry and concerns about unfair regulation from property owners within the potential district. In particular, in January 2009, the City of Salem mailed a notice to property owners within the District notifying them that they were already subject to local design review regulations even though the State Advisory Committee on Historic Preservation (SACHP) was not scheduled to review the proposed district until February, and official designation would not have been effective for months. A bad winter storm in the middle of January had resulted in property damage throughout the proposed district, requiring some to attempt to obtain building permits for required repairs, only to be told their building permits could not be issued until the required historic design review had been completed, which would take at least a month. Angry property owners were appalled that Salem's local code allowed regulation even for resources that were only being considered for designation. My task was to understand why there was such a strong backlash to designation by the neighbors of the Fairmount neighborhood. As I could see initially from the issues resulting from the storm, I knew that the current preservation program did not allow for expedited staff review. I anticipated that the program was not aligning with the needs of the community in other areas as well and that I needed to chart a new course. This chapter is my attempt to describe how I used evidence gathered from the local community to influence the City preservation program.

Even though the overall method that I used was very much in the tradition of communicative planning, I am a process-oriented planner and was trained to address problems using the rational planning process. I, therefore, combined these two approaches to best serve the needs of the community using the planning model established by Edward Banfield (1959). Banfield's five-step approach to planning is as follows:

1. Current conditions and needs assessment,

2. Design of courses of action,

3. Comparative evaluation of consequences,

4. Choice among alternatives,

5. Implementation of the chosen alternative.

I used this process along with the already established public participation framework already used by the City's Historic Landmark Commission (HLC) to assess the problems with their historic preservation program and move forward with an implementation plan. This public participation framework was originally created in order to comply with requirements of Oregon's Land Conservation and Development Commission's Goal 1, relating to citizen involvement. Goal 1 was adopted in 1973 as part of Oregon's statewide planning goals, which set policy on land use and related issues, including citizen involvement and historic preservation. Goal 1 (OAR 660-015-0000(1)) requires that local jurisdictions develop a citizen involvement program that ensures that citizens can be involved in all phases of the planning process. It requires that local jurisdictions *(1) provide for widespread citizen involvement, (2) assure effective two-way communication with citizens, (3) provide the opportunity for citizens to be involved in all phases of the planning process, (4) assure that technical information is available in understandable form, (5) assure that citizens receive a timely response from policymakers, and (6) adequate funding is included for citizen involvement.* I will start with an assessment of current conditions and how the problem was defined followed by the ways in which the community was engaged, the data were collected, and how this information led to changes in the City's preservation program.

Assessing Current Conditions and Clearly Defining the Problem

I applied for a Certified Local Government (CLG) grant to hire a consultant team, NW History Matters, who had experience in both historic preservation and meaningful public participation to help me and the Historic Landmarks Commission (HLC) determine what the problems were, and to develop a historic preservation plan to begin to change the course of the program, and, finally, to solve these problems. I had worked with these consultants before on various projects in both Oregon and Washington, and I knew that they were effective.

We began with the first step of the Banfield's planning process by documenting the City's current processes and codes. This process was straightforward, establishing who does what, when and how, and included a general assessment of the effectiveness of the existing processes. This assessment included an evaluation of the design review application processes. As I had anticipated, all applicants were required to go before the HLC to receive design review approval, regardless of whether their work was a major alteration or a minor repair. There was a clear need to streamline these processes to accommodate staff review and approval. In 2009, in Salem we had a well-established HLC, which appeared to be thriving according to the Oregon State Historic Preservation Office (SHPO). Salem had been a CLG since 1989, and was in good standing with the SHPO, after recently being audited for compliance with CLG requirements. However, the program was in trouble. In addition to the public outcry and concerns about unfair regulation expressed within the Fairmount neighborhood, which derailed the establishment of a new historic district after the snowstorm in January, two disgruntled applicants had recently appealed HLC design review cases to the City Council citing unfair treatment by the HLC. One HLC member was in the process of being personally sued for liable, for statements that were made against an applicant during a design review public hearing. Even more challenging to address were the number of historic property owners that were violating the code by not going through the historic design review process at all. Our enforcement officers were receiving at least one complaint a week. It was clear that the program was not achieving its desired outcome which is stated in Salem's code (SRC 230.001):

> Purpose: ...to identify, designate and preserve significant properties related to the community's prehistory and history; encourage the rehabilitation and ongoing viability of historic buildings and structures; strengthen public support for historic preservation efforts within the community; foster civic pride; encourage cultural heritage tourism; and promote the continued productive use of recognized resources, and to implement the policies contained in the Salem Area Comprehensive Plan for the preservation of historic resources.

The question was why. We couldn't easily see why, so we decided to ask the community itself.

The consultant team from NW History Matters began work on the project in January 2010. One of their first jobs was to add information to the City's website about the project and send out a media release to inform the public of the grant we received. The very first step in this project was a public workshop with the consultant team and the HLC. The HLC defined for the consultant team how they wanted the public outreach to be managed, and what questions they were looking to answer from the community. The HLC was interested in establishing a technical advisory committee (TAC) with experts and community stakeholders to manage and assess the feedback from the public. The HLC's initial questions for the community were focused on its codes and processes for historic design review. The HLC's primary goal of this initial outreach was to determine what was working well with the historic design review process, and what needed improvement.

Public Outreach Process

The interactive process to develop Salem's new Historic Preservation Plan involved and incorporated feedback from a variety of groups including neighborhood associations (CANDO, NEN, SCAN), Travel Salem, Heritage Organizations (Deepwood, Bush House, the Willamette Heritage Center), the Chamber of Commerce and the Homebuilders Association. In addition to continuing and ongoing communication with planning staff, public participation in the planning was overseen by a TAC, which was established by the HLC. This TAC was comprised of fifteen (15) members appointed by

LOCAL MUNICIPALITY'S PRESERVATION PROGRAM

the HLC including preservation architects, historians, contractors, heritage tourism specialists, contractors, neighborhood representatives, and building division staff.

At the first TAC meeting, the Committee established their public outreach plan. Their first goal was to host a Historic Preservation Round-Table to get direct input from historic property owners and stakeholders. The goal of this meeting was to identify initial topics of interest and concern, which would inform the survey and to ask attendees for ideas about how to distribute the survey to historic property owners and the larger community. At this meeting, the TAC directed City staff to create a webpage to provide current information regarding the project, with links to historic code, maps, and resource guides. A flier was mailed to stakeholders and historic property owners inviting them to attend (Figure 11.1).

Approximately, thirty-five people attended the Round-Table. During this public workshop, our consultant team asked participants to separate into smaller focus groups in order to provide detailed feedback within their most significant area of interest. The TAC had chosen these areas ahead of time. The focus groups included: Preservation Code; Education and Outreach; Financial Incentives; and Heritage Tourism. A member from the consultant team, who wrote down their feedback on large

Figure 11.1 Round-table flier. Photograph by the author.

LOCAL MUNICIPALITY'S PRESERVATION PROGRAM

paper tablets, facilitated discussion within each focus group. This feedback was then shared with the larger group.

At this workshop, attendees were also asked how best to gather input from historic property owners and the larger community. Suggestions included development and distribution of surveys using Surveymonkey. Attendees suggested sending a postcard with a link to complete the survey digitally but also suggested having paper copies available at central locations like the library for those who didn't have computers or didn't feel comfortable with a digital survey. It was pointed out that at least forty percent of historic property owners are above the age of fifty-five, so they may not be comfortable with digital tools. Another idea that came out of this meeting was to ask the newspaper to help get the word out about the project and using other media tools, such as the local public radio station.

Based on the results from the Round-Table, the TAC determined that two surveys were to be developed, one for historic property owners and one for Historic Landmarks Commissioners. The survey for the Landmarks Commissioners would be focused on their perception of the historic preservation code, the protection of historic resources, and the historic design review process. Postcards inviting residents and stakeholders to participate in the survey were mailed to every historic property owner. In 2009, Salem had four National Register Historic Districts comprising 400 resources and 100 individually listed properties. Stakeholders included representatives from neighborhood associations (CANDO, NEN, SCAN), Travel Salem, Heritage Organizations (Deepwood, Bush House, the Willamette Heritage Center), the Chamber of Commerce and the Homebuilders Association. The TAC determined that no representatives outside of the city would be included, except from the Oregon SHPO.

It was determined by the TAC and the consultants that newer methods of outreach through social media and the web would not effectively reach older residents who either did not own a computer or were not comfortable with this method of communication. Representatives from the TAC worked with a local reporter who wrote an article that appeared on the front page of Salem's Statesman Journal that provided information about the HLC's current project and the outreach. The three-page article also included information about Salem's current program, maps of our historic districts as well as a link to the city's webpage. We had great feedback on this method of outreach through the newspaper, especially from the older residents. Since older residents were more likely to subscribe to the newspaper, compared to younger residents, they were able to learn more about program and the survey from this newspaper article, because they were not accessing the online outreach materials. Many of the older residents were also able to take the survey online with assistance by city staff either at the planning office or at the library, however, some still preferred complete only a paper copy of the survey. To accommodate the younger, more digitally savvy population, and at the suggestion of our consultants, we held an online chat. The staff at the *Statesman Journal* estimated about twenty percent of their readers were getting all of their news online. We held an online chat with the consultants for the project the day after the article came out to respond to questions about the project and the program.

This was the first time that the staff and the HLC had worked with the paper in this way, and it was a really interesting and new way to receive input and questions from the public. Up until this point, the HLC was used to receiving input and feedback in more traditional ways, through written surveys or testimony at public hearings or at public workshops. Through this online method, held during the day, the consultants were able to "virtually" talk with people who had not been able to attend the public workshops held in the evening. Approximately, twenty people "signed" in and participated in an online chat, which was hosted on the Statesman Journal website. The discussion questions and input were compiled and organized by topics of interest and concern (Table 11.1).

Table 11.1 Summary of Online Chat Comments

Topic	Rank	Comments (online chat):	Comments Compared to Survey Results
Notification:		Potential owners are not made aware of the strict restrictions that will be placed on them when purchasing a historic home. They are often blindsided when they try to make updates to their homes. In addition, if you already own a home or property before it is placed on a historic register, you are suddenly plagued with fees and denials to make changes to your own property. • When purchasing a historical home, the guidelines should be included in the disclosures statement I liked the Landmarks information newsletter.	56.5% felt they knew what kind of projects require review. However, 44.8% either didn't know or weren't sure.
Workshops Energy Efficiency, Windows Technical Assistance:		Workshops on making your historic home energy efficient without changing the character of the home and not breaking the bank. Wood windows are too much money and do not provide the efficiency needed. I'd love to see more resources dedicated to energy efficiency and historic preservation. They are at odds with each other right now, it appears. I live in a historic home and because of the limits on what is available and what I can afford the home in question is NOT very energy efficient. Windows are a big heat sink, not to mention there is no REAL insulation in this place. The siding will need to be replaced soon, as there is water that somehow gets behind the siding and blisters the (NEW) paint. I am the owner that must replace the leaking roof, because each previous owner found it cheaper to shingle over the leak... short term fix at best. I need help if you want to keep this house HISTORIC. Or, we can do what has been done in the past... Hide the defects and sell. • I think we should be proud of our heritage and strive to preserve it for future generations. It would also be helpful to be able to have a consultant we could go to for historic paint colors, and even landscaping.	Second to providing grants, education through workshops was the highest answer on the survey.
HLC Role:		I wish the group could be more proactive • More HLC newsletters	81.7% felt it would be useful to develop partnerships
Archaeology:		Archaeology is an important issue that has long been neglected and misunderstood. Let's get something going!	Most people weren't sure about having an archaeology program; 41% not sure, 41% yes, 18% no

Historic Property Owner Survey Methodology and Results

The consultant team and the TAC created the survey. The survey included less than ten questions phrased as questions using a Likert scale with a range of five options to answer (from Strongly agree to Strongly Disagree). It was decided by the TAC that since the HLC was only interested in receiving feedback from historic property owners about their experience with the design review process and the code, since these owners are the only individuals subject to historic design review, the survey itself would be limited to just these owners, but the questions themselves would include more topics than just historic design review and code. The questions focused on the four key areas identified at the Round Table Workshop: Preservation Code; Education and Outreach; Financial Incentives; and Heritage Tourism. At the Round-Table workshop, the consultants developed ideas about how to encourage property owners to take the survey solicited from the group. It was suggested that a postcard be mailed with a link to an online survey. A phone number for one of our consultants was given on the postcard and paper copies were made available for those who weren't comfortable taking the online survey. Survey results were compiled by the consultant team and presented to the TAC and the HLC.

The survey was "open" for two weeks and 100 property owners responded to the survey through Surveymonkey, and twenty-five residents responded with written paper surveys. The goal of the HLC and the TAC was to get at least a ten percent response from historic property owners. Salem has 500 historic properties. The response of 125 individuals reflected twenty percent of this population exceeding our goal. Findings showed that respondents, in general, did not feel that the city had adequate programs for educating residents and visitors about the history of Salem and that the review process is difficult to understand. When the surveys were tallied, the responses indicated that primary areas of concern were a lack of flexibility in the code, overregulation, and long complicated application reviews (Table 11.2).

Historic property owners expressed serious concerns about the HLC's lack of understanding about the financial hardships caused by owning historically designated properties. There appeared to be no understanding in the community of the significance of Salem's history and its built environment, and why historic resources were being regulated in the first place. Many complained that they had never been notified before they purchased their designated property, and wished they had been told what their responsibilities would be before they bought. Other responders indicated that while Salem did have a number of worthwhile heritage sites within the community that deserved recognition, the HLC was not recognizing these resources or promoting them either to local residents or visitors. Historic property owners felt overregulated and didn't understand the basis for this regulation or the fundamental purpose of Salem's historic preservation program. The code was based upon the Secretary of the Interior's Standards in a way that didn't make sense to property owners, so there was a clear need to create a code that was more suited to Salem.

I think that for both the HLC and TAC, since so many complaints were heard about overregulation, the biggest surprise from this survey was that the respondents believed that the City should develop requirements for property owners to maintain their historic buildings, and that there was a need to develop a code to address the demolition by neglect. In addition to multiple choice questions, a "free-form" response option was offered. We received input regarding the need for educational workshops that educate both residents and visitors about Salem's heritage, as well as the need for financial incentives and notification to buyers regarding historic designation. Other respondents were concerned about the cost of retaining and repairing wood

Table 11.2 Survey Response Summary. The Responses to the Survey Questions Have Been Summarized with those Responding Positively (Either a Strongly Agree or Somewhat Agree), Negatively (Either a Strongly Disagree or Somewhat Disagree) and "Not Sure"

Questions	Positive Response (%)	Negative Response (%)	Not Sure (%)
1. Do you feel that the current Historic Preservation Ordinance and Design Guidelines adequately address the protection of historic resources?	37.4	**39.4**	23.2
2. Do you know what kind of projects require review?	**56.5**	17.7	27.1
3. Do you think the review process reasonable and easy to understand?	28.2	**44.6**	27.2
4. Do you think the City should develop requirements for property owners to maintain their buildings to prevent demolition by neglect?	**77.8**	16.2	6.1
5. Do you think the city has adequate programs for educating residents and visitors about the history of Salem?	25.7	**44.3**	30.9
6. What are some additional programs or services you would like to see to promote historic preservation and the city of Salem? (Free Response)	79.1-Grants or Loans to Historic Property owners 68.1-Educational Workshops	N/A	N/A
7. Do you think that preservation interests compete against other city goals like economic development and housing?	**48**	33	19
8. Do you think that Salem should develop an archaeology program?	**40.4**	20.2	39.4
9. Do you think the city should complete historic inventory other areas of Salem? Please note the area that needs more historic survey/inventory work. (Free Response)	Highland-27.9 NEN-20.9 SCAN-30.2 SESNA-25.6 West Salem-37.2	N/A	N/A
10. Given limited resources available for historic preservation, would it be useful for the City to develop partnerships with other groups, such as museums, visitor's association, schools, libraries, and/or historic societies?	**81.7**	6.1	13.3
Free form: What groups would you recommend?	Marion County Historical Society/Mission Mill-92.2 Bush House-71.4 Deepwood-68.8 Travel Salem-67.5 Salem Library Polk County Historical-57.1	N/A	N/A

windows. One respondent wrote that *"Wood windows are to[sic] much money and do not provide the efficiency needed."* Quite a few respondents were upset about the recent demolition of four houses at Mission and Liberty Streets and expressed interest in amending the code to prevent this in the future. One respondent wrote, *"I am upset that the owner of the property at Mission and Liberty Streets was allowed to let his property deteriorate to a point where it had to be demolished."*

HLC Surveys and Interviews Methodology and Results

The TAC and the consultants for the nine Historic Landmarks Commissioners developed the second survey. This survey was conducted initially online utilizing Surveymonkey, but was supplemented by one-on-one (hour long) interviews with HLC members, which were held at the Community Development Department over a one-week period. A total of twenty questions were asked of the Commissioners, and focused on the same four key areas of the first survey (Preservation Code; Education and Outreach; Financial Incentives; and Heritage Tourism), using a Likert scale with a range of five options to answer (from Strongly agree to Strongly Disagree). The HLC survey also included additional questions regarding their level of training and understanding of the code and their assessment of city policies as they relate to preservation, and the TAC decided that the consultants should ask these supplemental questions in one-on-one interviews. In these interviews, the Commissioners were asked more specific questions to better define issues relating to the code, education, financial incentives, and potential partners for development of a heritage tourism program.

Findings from the Landmarks Commission survey generally mirrored those from the general public, in that they felt that fixing the code should be the first priority, since it was not "clear and objective" to administer, and they felt that they needed additional training, especially in the area of ethics and the appropriate procedures for running a quasi-judicial land use hearing. The Commission also felt unsupported and disconnected from the Planning Commission and City Council, and that it was often perceived that the HLC was at odds with other city priorities.

In particular, understanding the issues around the code was a priority of the HLC and the TAC, and so through both the HLC survey and follow-up interviews, additional information was gathered to help clarify the concerns. At the time of the survey, the code was based upon the Secretary of the Interior's Standards for Rehabilitation. Any exterior changes to either historic contributing or non-contributing properties within Salem's four historic districts required review before the HLC. Since the Commission only meets once a month, the time required for design review typically took an average of six weeks, which was a hardship for some owners. One of the most confusing aspects for both Commissioners and residents appeared to be why an alteration to a non-historic, non-contributing resource within a district would require the same type of review and approval by the HLC as a clearly significant historic landmark. Another concern was the required review for repair. As noted earlier, in January 2009, there had been a severe winter storm, where a number of resources were damaged and required repair. Many residents felt it was unreasonable to require a lengthy review and approval process simply to repair their buildings. In general, especially for Commissioners, the guidelines were felt to be open to interpretation and did not provide a clear measure of predictability for owners. For example, in Standard #9, where it states that new additions: *"shall be differentiated from the old and shall be compatible with the massing, size, scale and architectural features to protect the historic integrity of the property and its environment."* The word "compatible" is vague and requires interpretation. This word meant different things from one Commissioner to another. For example, one Commissioner, an architect, felt that a compatible addition would be required to have the same type of siding and trim as the original resource and that it should be designed so it would not be possible to tell that it was new. This Commissioner felt that this differentiation could be accomplished through documentation. Another Commissioner, a historic preservation professional, believed that a compatible new addition should have a different (modern) material, but replicate the design of the siding and the trim, so that it is clear that it is new (even without documentation).

Addressing the Issues Identified in the Round-Tables, Surveys, and Interviews

After receiving input from the round-table workshops and surveys, the TAC met several times to analyze the results and start developing goals to address the issues identified. Members of the TAC were divided into teams and asked to focus on goal development within the areas of significant interest. Each team was asked to develop a table/matrix, which aligned a topic or a goal in the form of a question with the feedback received (Table 11.3).

The TAC team discussions were then able to focus on weighing the "pro's and con's" and determining how to address each problem through development of a specific goal within each significant area defined. Out of the four initial areas, five TAC teams emerged, with a new, additional one for communication and outreach. It was clear that communication and effective public participation and outreach was an area that needed special attention. Each team was responsible for clearly stating their goal in a positive way, including specific actions and strategies as well as defining participants and a timeline for implementation (Table 11.4).

The TAC developed an implementation matrix based upon the recommendation of the consultant team for all five goals, with specific actions and strategies for each goal. Once this Matrix had been fully developed, a second postcard was mailed to historic property owners with an invitation to attend an Open House to discuss the goals, and indicate their priorities. A total of twenty-five people attended this meeting, which was held in Council Chambers, after a regular HLC meeting. Participants indicated their preferences by placing different colored dots on the goals that were printed out on large paper and hung on the walls of Council Chambers (Figure 11.2).

While the TAC had organized the five goals in order of their priority, the consensus from the participants at this meeting resulted in a reorganization of the goals. Goal 1 was still ranked as the first priority (fix the code), the second priority was survey and protect new resources, the third priority was development of a heritage tourism program, the fourth priority was improving education and outreach, and the fifth priority was development of economic incentives. The public outreach for the Preservation Plan culminated with a joint public work session with the HLC, the Planning Commission, and City Council to discuss the Plan and finalize prioritization of the goals. The Planning Commissioners and City Council performed the same "dot" exercise that the public had completed at the Open House, and the Goals were reorganized by priority once more. The City Council and Planning Commission retained a rewrite of the code as the first priority but moved Goal 4 (Education and Outreach) to the second priority. Goal 5 was prioritized as Goal 3 (Economic Incentives), Goal 2 prioritized as fourth (survey and protect new resources); and Goal 3 was prioritized as the fifth priority (development of a heritage tourism program).

Table 11.3 Neighborhood Resources Feedback Table

Neighborhood Resources – Roger and Nadine Heusser, and Chris and Lola Hackett

Topic	Rank	Pro	Con
Historic Districts: Are they are valuable tools for maintaining our neighborhoods, or is it a too onerous?		Preserving Salem's historic districts enhances the City's economic development goals by creating a link from Salem's residential neighborhoods to downtown businesses and prevents Salem from becoming just another commuter community. Preserving the historic districts as viable family neighborhoods is important to recruiting and retaining skilled professionals who work at Salem Hospital, Willamette Univ. SAIF, and the Capitol. • Recognized that "thriving neighborhoods" are essential to the preservation of our city. Otherwise, Salem will become one long strip mall. In terms of City goals, maintaining historic neighborhoods makes the city a more desirable place to visit and move to. When we take pride in our city, it shows and makes it far more attractive to others.	The process is not fair because of the way those opposed to the designation must register opposition. It's an imposition of those who don't want the district to have to go through the review process. If the number of districts continues to grow, the number of properties to regulate will break the city. Stop trying to force things. Spend money on infrastructure instead. • Give property owners more voice in what happens.
Allowing Other Uses: How do we provide opportunities for low-impact businesses in historic buildings without degrading the residential qualities of the neighborhoods?		The purpose of Specific Conditional Uses is to encourage the preservation of historic buildings that otherwise might be demolished for commercial building due to location on busy streets; so there are instances when providing additional uses keeps the building from being demolished (JO opinion)	Specific Conditional Uses and Rezoning – impacts the residential qualities of the neighborhood; there are more than enough commercial buildings available. • Please help PRESERVE our Gaiety Hill neighborhood by NOT allowing for any zone changes

Neighborhood Resources – Roger and Nadine Heusser, and Chris and Lola Hackett

Topic	Rank	Pro	Con
Maintenance - Demolition Regulations: This issue is of high profile in light of the houses on Liberty and Mission. How do we balance requirements for maintenance so that "demolition through neglect" can't occur?		The city should be ashamed about allowing the demolition of historic properties. I'm disappointed to see how prohibitive the guidelines are for me to make simple improvements to my historic home, while the guidelines don't do enough to protect some unscrupulous individuals from tearing down homes that contribute to the historic district. I think the City should enforce the existing Historic Guidelines and requirements so that property owners can't demolish their homes due to neglect. Littering is a problem—need to make requirements and requests and reminders, engage schools and business owners. • Most respondents on the survey indicated a need for stronger demolition requirements.	Putting any more rules on the backs of homeowners that live in historic districts may cause potential buyers to think twice about purchasing a home in the historic district, and thus, lower the value of our homes. • There are already huge hurdles in place (some of them reasonable, but huge none the less) that historic homeowners have to climb over to make changes and updates to our homes.
Inventory/Survey: How important is it to determine, on a city-wide basis, where our most valuable historic resources are located?		As an owner of a non-historic house but old one, I am surrounded by people who buy the houses for future apartment complexes. More inventory on the homes needs to be done so that historic houses don't go away. • Highland, SCAN, and West Salem neighborhoods are considered to be the areas that need more survey.	None noted.
Misc.			

Table 11.4 Implementation Matrix-Goal 1 (Code)

Steps	Participants	Timeline				
		Ongoing	2011	2012–2014	2015–2017	2018–2021
Goal 1. Improve the process and revise the historic preservation code and design guidelines.						
A. Strategy: Improve Design Review Process						
Action 1: Provide faster service and reduce review time						
Gather examples of COA's and develop process and form	Planning, Building, HLC		1/2011–3/2011			
Develop process for determining effect at time of application submittal	Planning, HLC, Building		1/2011–3/2011			
Develop process for emergency repair review	Planning, HLC, Building		1/2011–3/2011			
Prepare language that can be incorporated into code revisions	Planning, Building, HLC		4/2011–6/2011			
Action 2: Provide technical and design assistance prior to application						
Develop architectural-subcommittee process	Planning, Building, HLC		3/2011–6/2011			
Establish members of group to meet on-site	Planning, Building, Urban Dev., SHPO		4/2011			
Prepare draft language for code revisions	Planning, Building, HLC		4/2011–6/2011			
Conduct architectural sub-committee meeting	Architectural Sub-committee	✓	6/2011	✓	✓	✓

Steps	Participants	Timeline				
		Ongoing	2011	2012–2014	2015–2017	2018–2021
Conduct on-site meetings	Planning, Building, Urban Dev., SHPO	✓	6/2011	✓	✓	✓

Action 3: Develop options for mitigating adverse effects

Steps	Participants	Timeline				
Identify legal and logistical issues	Planning and Legal staff		3/2011			
Prepare process for considering mitigation	Consultant w/Planning Staff support		4/2011			
Prepare draft language for code revisions	Consultant and Staff		3/2011–6/2011			

Action 4: Address demolition by neglect

Steps	Participants	Timeline				
Identify legal and logistical issues	Planning and Legal staff		3/2011			
Develop process for demolition by neglect	Planning, HLC, Building, Compliance Services		4/2011			
Prepare draft language for code revisions	Consultant and Staff		3/2011–6/2011			

B. Strategy: Revise Regulations

Action 1: Revise historic preservation chapter

Steps	Participants	Timeline				
Draft code language	Consultant w/Planning Staff support		3/2011–6/2011			
Conduct public meetings	Consultant and Staff		7/2011–9/2011			
Review proposed language	Legal Staff		9/2011			
Present to City Council	Planning Staff		10/2011			
Adopt Revisions	Planning Staff		12/2011			

LOCAL MUNICIPALITY'S PRESERVATION PROGRAM

Figure 11.2 Open house. Photograph by the author.

Final Goals and Implementation

The HLC recommended five goals with associated strategies and action items in their 2010–2020 Preservation Plan to address issues and concerns that had been brought up through their extensive public outreach process:

Goal 1: Revise the historic preservation code and design guidelines

Goal 2: Develop a public outreach and education program

Goal 3: Develop Economic and Recognition Incentives program

Goal 4: Survey and recognize Salem's Historic Resources

Goal 5: Promote Heritage Tourism and Local History

While each of the goals was established independently to address specific problems identified in the outreach, they were all meant to address two overarching themes: (1) preservation of Salem's historic resources in order to educate the community about Salem's unique past, and (2) private property owners who own and maintain historic properties provide a community benefit and deserve both incentives and recognition for this service. Additionally, improving communication with historic property owners and the community had to be a priority for the HLC in order to ensure the success of the overall program.

These five goals were presented to the HLC for their review and discussion and were prioritized and an implementation plan developed. At the end of the summer 2010, a draft Historic Preservation Plan was presented to a joint meeting of the HLC, Planning Commission and City Council, who recommended that the Plan be adopted. In response to public concern about the complexity of the code, the TAC, HLC, Planning Commission, and City Council all identified revision to the code as the first priority. Throughout the fall of 2010, I worked with the HLC to draft a new streamlined historic code. The feedback we received from the public outreach indicated that historic property owners wanted two primary code revisions. First, they were interested in shorter, simpler application reviews. Second, they were interested in more clear and objective design standards in order to make the process more predictable, with different standards for historic contributing resources and historic non-contributing resources. We developed criteria for simple exterior alterations like roof replacements, in-kind window and door replacements, and rear additions that had clear standards for materials and design. In general, in kind replacement material is preferred, but material from the period of significance of the resource is allowed provided the appearance is substantially the same. Design requirements require preservation of character-defining features.

If property owners adhered to these design standards, they did not have to go before the HLC, instead, they could take advantage of a quicker, more streamlined administrative design review approval process for these types of alterations. Property owners were also interested in additional exemptions for ordinary maintenance and repair, or work that is done on a rear or secondary façade that is not visible from the right of way. These changes were made, and the revised code was adopted in December 2010. New criteria were written for demolition approval. A new criterion was added to the demolition review, requiring the applicant to demonstrate that their proposed new use would be of a higher benefit to the community than retaining the existing resource. The HLC felt strongly that this should be added in order to end speculative demolition and ensure the community value of the resource was evaluated. The code was also written to address the demolition by neglect and ensure property owners were maintaining their property. Specifically, SRC 230.095 states that

> No owner of a historic contributing building or an individually listed resource shall maintain and keep such building or resource in a manner that promotes or allows deterioration, dilapidation and decay of any portion of the building or resource, or that would, if the building or resource is vacant, allow open entry by unauthorized persons. Violation of this subsection is hereby declared to be a public nuisance which may be abated.

In 2011, the first year the Plan became effective, we completed the work identified as the number one priority. The following year, the effectiveness of the revised code was evident. The City had twice as many historic design review applications as the year before, and code enforcement cases went down by half. Work on the second and third goals began, including the development of our first residential grant program, which was created to offer small grants to historic property owners for exterior maintenance and restoration projects for the first time.

Progress toward Completing the Goals

Now it has been seven years since the public outreach resulting in the adoption of Salem's first Historic Preservation Plan, and the initial revision of the historic code. Of the five adopted goals, we are on track to have all five completed within the next year. We have completed one additional round of revisions to our historic code, adding a new section for public historic resources. This section is very unique, in that it offers Public Agencies (State of Oregon) an alternative process. We worked closely with the Oregon State Historic Preservation Office to ask state agencies what was working well and what wasn't in both the local historic design review processes and the Section 106/State ORS 358.653 review and compliance processes. The feedback we received was that there was a lot of duplication of work, and the direction received from the Salem HLC was oftentimes at odds with that of the Oregon State Historic Preservation Office. So we developed an alternative, more streamlined process.

LOCAL MUNICIPALITY'S PRESERVATION PROGRAM

Oregon State Agencies in Salem who own designated resources now have a choice. They can choose to go through the City of Salem's historic design review process, and receive a Decision that will serve to satisfy the requirements of SHPO's review and compliance, or they can choose to go through the Oregon SHPO's review and compliance process in lieu of design review before the HLC. Several agencies have taken advantage of this process since it has been adopted, and it is very successful.

The proposed demolition of a local landmark recently brought out very powerful feelings in the community regarding the value of this particular landmark. In this case, the HLC used our newly adopted demolition criteria for the first time and required the applicant to submit full development plans for the reuse of the site at the time of the demolition application and explain why their proposed use had more community value than the existing resource. The new demolition criteria: "Does the proposed use have a higher benefit to the community than retaining the existing historic resource?" caused a lot of healthy debate first at the HLC where the demolition request was denied, and then later at the City Council who heard the request on appeal and overturned the HLC decision, allowing the demolition. In both public hearings, the core issue that was discussed was the community value of the local landmark as compared to the proposed new use. Therefore, it is clear that this new criterion is an excellent one, which helps our community get to the heart of the issue of what it really values. In this case, the process worked. The question we are left to consider moving forward is whether or not the code is continuing to produce the community's desired outcome or whether it needs to be redrafted to ensure a different outcome?

The HLC established a subcommittee to work on addressing Goal 2, development of an Education and Outreach program. The first priority was the creation of a notification process to notify homebuyers of the historic designation of a property. We decided to work with the City's Finance Department to notify prospective buyers through the City's lien program. This notification works in the form of a fake 'lien' on the property and triggers a notification letter that is sent to the Title Company when they check for any outstanding city liens prior to the sale.

This method of notification does not cost the city anything, and has been a very successful method of notification. The HLC's education and outreach subcommittee then worked to create and more fully develop a multi-faceted program for education and outreach. They established a speaker's bureau, inviting interesting speakers to talk about Salem's history. They hosted workshops for historic homeowners about how to maintain historic windows, and more recently hosted a workshop on how to seismically retrofit a historic house. In addition to a paper and digital newsletter, the HLC established a blog, Facebook, and Twitter account. With the help of an intern, the HLC now posts content about Salem history regularly on Facebook and Twitter. A challenge for the HLC has been that it is very time consuming to maintain a social media presence, so the maintenance of this program is an issue they hope to address.

Another very successful facet of the outreach program is the HLC photo contest. This contest was first established in 2015 and was modeled after the National Trust "This Place Matters" campaign. Participants have been invited to submit photos of significant Salem buildings, neighborhoods, and places. The HLC selects three to four winners, and all the photos are displayed at the State Capitol during the historic preservation month (May). Winners of this contest are also given fun prizes. One of the more surprising activities we embarked on was a new radio show, called "Salem History Matters". The show airs once a week on Salem's public radio station, KMUZ, and invites guests with interesting stories to share about Salem's history.

We had a very surprising success while we were working on the third goal, the establishment of economic and recognition incentives. As with the Education and Outreach goal, the HLC established a sub-committee to help develop economic and recognition incentives.

LOCAL MUNICIPALITY'S PRESERVATION PROGRAM

While city staff had applied for a CLG grant to initiate a pilot program for a Residential Toolbox grant, a very generous donor came forward who was willing to donate funds toward this program. In Salem, as with many states, the only financial incentives for historically designated properties were limited to income-producing properties on the National Register. A majority of people the HLC heard from were residential property owners, or those locally designated, who had no access to any help or support to maintain their properties. In response to this donor's generosity, the City established a new trust and agency account for historic resources, which allows those who are interested to donate funds toward the historic preservation programs. This donor also gave a generous donation of $96,000 to help fund the restoration of a depot building near Salem's main train station that is dear to many people in the community. The HLC chose to establish a robust awards program, giving awards to people like this generous donor in recognition of his service to preservation in Salem, during the historic preservation month of May. The most difficult work has been in the area of identification (survey) and designation of historic resources. This upcoming year, we will continue our work on Goal 4, survey and recognition of Salem's Historic Resources, which has been challenging because of the lack of support for new survey and designation of historic resources in Salem.

As with the other priority areas, the HLC established a sub-committee to develop alternatives and decide how to address this goal. It was initially quite frustrating because we had received feedback from the surveys and outreach that survey and designation was a need. However, it wasn't clear how to address this issue. Here, in Oregon, we have a state law that mandates private property owners' consent to the designation of their historic resources (ORS 197.772), which in Salem has extended to include the survey as well. A citizen might believe a historic building is worthy of designation as a historic resource, but when it's owned privately it is not up to the HLC to designate it. It must be the owner's choice. Our biggest challenge continues to be the tension between the rights of private historic property owners and the responsibility the HLC has to ensure the preservation of Salem's cultural landmarks. What the HLC decided to do is to implement a new program, called the Salem Heritage Neighborhood Program. It does not involve designation or regulation. This Program is intended to accomplish two things: educate neighborhoods about their history and heritage, and also work with existing neighborhood associations to accomplish positive projects, building relationships and a better understanding of historic preservation and do some historic building survey in the process.

The first neighborhood the HLC worked with was the Grant Neighborhood. In this neighborhood, we helped the neighborhood produce a calendar featuring pictures of their neighborhood, as well as an architectural guidebook and walking tour. These two items were then used as fundraisers to help raise money for the neighborhood that they could use to accomplish other preservation projects. In order to develop architectural guidebook and calendar, we enlisted the help of several interns from Willamette University, who were able to complete a Reconnaissance Level Survey (RLS) of the buildings fifty years old or older within the neighborhood. We were then able to use the data from this survey to recommend a smaller portion of their neighborhood for historic designation, as it has the historic integrity to be eligible for listing on the National Register. However, it is up to the neighborhood to decide whether or not they will be interested in pursuing National Register listing. There still has been no significant movement on the part of private property owners to list their properties either on the Local Historic Resource List or on the National Register of Historic Places in Salem, however, we are now working with another neighborhood in Salem on similar projects. This Spring, in fact, we are training a number of neighborhood volunteers to help with the RLS survey using ArcGIS Collector on their smartphone. It is hoped that with more participation from the neighborhood and property owners, there may be more incentive to work towards designation.

230

LOCAL MUNICIPALITY'S PRESERVATION PROGRAM

Probably the biggest surprise was how quickly the HLC worked to accomplish Goal 5. While the City Council and Planning Commission identified it as the last priority, in recognition of the efforts of the HLC and other cultural non-profits, Salem received the Heritage All-Star Designation from the Oregon Heritage Commission in 2012, prompting the creation of the Salem Heritage All-Star Forum. The Forum established a community-wide advocacy group dedicated to increasing heritage tourism, and defining Salem as a heritage destination. Salem is one of just six communities in Oregon with this designation. This group has worked on some exciting projects together, including a collaboration and communication guide and the development of several short videos which promote Salem's cultural and Heritage sites. The first video is a trailer that features a broad view of Salem. The second video is a longer one, which provides a more in-depth history of Oregon's State Capitol Building. The group is on track to complete two more videos in 2017 featuring other cultural and heritage organizations in Salem. Their biggest challenge in the near future is becoming their own independent non-profit, separate from the City and the direct support of the HLC. The HLC's Historic Preservation Plan accomplishments and challenges over the last six years can be seen in the following table:

Goal	Primary Work Completed	Follow-Up Work	Problem Solved?
Goal 1: Revise Code	Major Code Revision, Adopted, 2011	New Public Code Adopted, 2013	Exemptions Allowed for Repair/Work on secondary facades Separate Criteria for HC/NC More Administrative Review Streamlined Process
Goal 2: Education and Outreach	Historic Designation Owner notification, 2010	Newsletter; Radio show; Workshops; Social Media Program; Heritage Neighborhood Program. Forum videos. Photo Contest, 2011–2016	Owner's notified at time of sale; Salem's History needs to be Shared and Celebrated through a variety of multimedia venues Educational Workshops needed
Goal 3: Economic and Recognition Program	Residential Toolbox Grant; Historic Preservation Month Awards, 2011–2016	Seismic Retrofit Grants, 2016; Heritage Neighborhood Recognition Program	Homeowners need help maintaining historic properties; Incentive program needed; Owners need to be acknowledged and recognized for their work
Goal 4: Survey and Designation	Survey of Heritage Neighborhoods, ArcGIS Collector, 2016		Political support needed for survey and designation; Salem's unprotected resources need to be identified and designated.
Goal 5: Heritage Tourism	Heritage All-Star Designation; 2012–2016	Establishment of Heritage All-Star Forum	Leadership needed and independent Heritage Tourism organization developed apart from City

Lessons for Other Communities

In Salem, the HLC set out on a project seven years ago to determine what the problems were with their historic preservation program, with a goal of developing a ten-year historic preservation plan to begin to change the course of the program, and, finally, to solve these problems and improve the

231

success of the program in the community. We are close to the end of the term of this plan, with just three years remaining. There have been some surprising successes and some surprising challenges, but overall, the goals identified within the plan have been accomplished, key problems addressed, and the perception of the HLC and the historic preservation program has improved. Challenges still remain, however, and it is not certain when we may ever have another historic district designated in our community. Our program has changed significantly, where before it was primarily regulatory, now it is currently incentive-based, with a heavy emphasis on education. The HLC has stated on more than one occasion that it is now critical to communicate in an ongoing way with historic property owners and other stakeholders in the community. For example, they never initially intended to develop a new program like the Heritage Neighborhood Program. However, it was born out of necessity, in response to what they were hearing from the community and they are finding some surprising benefits through this program. While no additional resources have been designated yet, the relationships and communication between the HLC and the community have been transformed. The HLC has now become more than just a "regulator." They are a resource and an ally to neighborhoods, helping them develop products that both celebrate their history and raise funds for projects neighbors care about.

The HLC recognizes that the initial public outreach at the beginning of the Plan was the first step in transforming their relationship with the community. Many plans completed within the world of city planning require public outreach. It can be done in many different ways. In this particular case, the public outreach process defined the Plan and guided the work that came after, not the other way around. This method of public participation was a key piece to it being accepted by the community, especially since stakeholders not only felt heard through this process but saw their concerns addressed and resolved. Too often HLCs unfortunately make their plans and their goals in a vacuum, without meaningful public participation. Their public outreach is a matter of simply "informing" their community what they will be doing after they have already decided. Especially, if what they are doing involves additional regulation of a person's private property "for their own good," or "for the good of the community," this is especially difficult to digest.

Other key success factors included the development of a small number of goals that were designed to address clear problems within a limited timeframe. For staff, it was so important that this plan included a small number of achievable goals, with clearly defined tasks and participants. The implementation of this plan has been easy in a large part because of this implementation matrix. The HLC adopts an annual work-plan every year, which is based upon the Preservation Plan and the implementation matrix, which is very clear and easy to follow. I believe that my example of Salem's historic preservation program is a good one that other jurisdictions can look to in order to see that the communicative planning process works. Evidence in the form of public input from a community can be used to guide a local municipality's preservation planning program. It is important to remember that regardless of federal legislation and national trends, historic preservation operates at a local level, one community at a time. Building a successful preservation program today can happen through an effective combination of meaningful community participation and implementation of a historic preservation plan that has a clear vision and results in a concrete public benefit.

Reference

Banfield, Edward C. 1959. "Ends and Means in Planning," *International Social Science Journal*, 11(3), 361–368.

CHAPTER 12

Democratizing Conservation

Challenges to Changing the Paradigm of Cultural Heritage Management

Richard A. Engelhardt, Heather A. Peters, and Montira Horayangura Unakul[1]

Heritage management, both cultural and natural, was conceived as the province of elites: governments and professionals preserving grand landmarks deemed significant by the privileged and empowered inheritors of past structures of wealth and power. Yet, during the past twenty years, as definitions of cultural heritage have been challenged and become more encompassing, the paradigm of cultural heritage management has shifted away from statist, technocratic approaches to one of broad-based consensus-building, particularly at the local level, a shift which reflects the political framework of the period and global trends in the dialectic between culture and development.[2]

In exploring the shift towards more consensual approaches in the paradigm of cultural heritage management which recognize multiple claims and sources of authority, this chapter will investigate not only the key threats to cultural heritage protection and management, but also, importantly, the tension between international treaty-inspired government processes and meaningful community participation. It will raise and analyze the role the United Nations Educational, Scientific and Cultural Organization (UNESCO) has played at the forefront of this discussion, and the challenges UNESCO has encountered. These are namely the challenges encountered in negotiating a balance between top-down statist models of conservation, which reflect UNESCO's nature as an intergovernmental organization and form part of the international politics of prestige, and models driven by more local concerns. The latter often focus on the role heritage has to play in sustainable development in all its dimensions, encompassing dimensions of identity and social well-being in addition to more narrowly defined economic goals.

It is in this light that this chapter will investigate how the statist, elitist model originally developed and promoted by UNESCO is changing as UNESCO itself responds, globally, to an increasingly broader base of power with more diverse views of heritage and its significance. The paradigm is changing, albeit slowly, to one in which the communities themselves have active voices in defining what is and is not their heritage, and how their past should be managed and conserved. UNESCO is unique within the UN family because it addresses culture directly. Founded in November 1945, UNESCO's purpose, as stated in its Constitution is:

> to contribute to peace and security by promoting collaboration among nations through education, science and culture in order to further universal respect for the rule of law and for human rights and fundamental freedoms which are affirmed for the peoples of the world, without distinction of race, sex, language or religion, by the Charter of the United Nations.

> (UNESCO 2011)

Within this far-reaching mandate, the organization has become the leading arbiter of international normative standards and practices for the safeguarding of cultural heritage, especially World Heritage. UNESCO not only safeguards and promotes culture with a capital "C" – such as masterpieces of art and architecture – but also culture in the anthropological sense – culture with a small "c". This is the culture of the people, expressed in an endless diversity of local expressions, and nourished through the generations by tradition and practice, and without which the landmark cultural achievements of societies and civilizations could not be achieved.

In order to explore the prevailing trends in heritage management and the evolution that has occurred, particularly from the middle of the 1990s onwards, the first section of this chapter will review key international standard-setting documents that have engendered or reflected shifts in the cultural heritage management paradigm. The analysis will be anchored by the principal UNESCO conventions and declarations guiding the conservation of cultural heritage sites, especially, those protected under the 1972 Convention Concerning the Protection of the World Cultural and Natural Heritage. It will also take into account other documents and charters adopted by professional conservation bodies which either foreshadow or, more typically, build on the UNESCO conventions. Against the backdrop of these developments in global heritage conservation and management philosophy and practice, the authors will examine the dialectic within UNESCO's attempts to reflect this paradigm shift to more consensus-based processes in its normative standards and mechanisms, while operating within the constraints of the inter-governmental processes of the conventions that positions the state as the primary interlocutor.

The chapter will then scrutinize how this paradigm shift is translated from the normative to the operational level by analyzing the successes and challenges of selected case studies from the heritage management programs and projects developed and implemented by the Office of the UNESCO Regional Advisor for Culture in Asia and the Pacific (RACAP) beginning in 1997. These are initiatives that aimed to tap into and valorize traditional community-based heritage management frameworks and to promote community-based participation in heritage protection and management within the Asia-Pacific region. The authors illustrate how the participation of communities[3] can meaningfully change the dynamics of heritage management and protection, and how it can become an integral part of sustainable development strategy and practice.

The Cultural Heritage Conservation Imperative: New Challenges, New Responses and a Paradigm Shift

The challenges that face cultural heritage conservation today are more complex and far-reaching than the issues that the cultural heritage profession grappled with fifty years ago. Whereas the restoration and reconstruction efforts of post-World War Two, Europe grappled with technical issues of material authenticity and historical accuracy, today's issues regarding culture and cultural heritage are now implicated in very fundamental ways in contemporary discourse and policy debates on sustainable development. The conservation of the material artifacts of cultural heritage is no longer seen as an end unto itself. The protection of cultural heritage is seen as a means to safeguard diverse cultural values and particularistic knowledge that is embodied in the full panoply of the world's cultural heritage, both in its material and immaterial manifestations. As such, safeguarding cultural heritage is fundamental to safeguarding cultural rights, which is in turn an inalienable part of the rights-based approach to sustainable development. Increasingly, the recognition of the importance of culture and the good management of cultural heritage resources is extending beyond the remit of UNESCO, and is now integrated into the Sustainable Development Goals (SDGs), the overarching global strategy adopted on 15 September 2015 by the United Nations and the development community at large. In a public address given at the Global Colloquium of University Presidents hosted at Yale University on 11 April 2016, Irina Bokova, Director-General of UNESCO, reflected upon the significance of cultural heritage within the context of conflict, and emphasized the importance of culture not only to the very survival of a people but also to the entire world. As an example, she noted the joy felt by the people when UNESCO provided support to the people of Timbuktu, Mali to rebuild their heritage destroyed by Muslim extremists. She stressed that "heritage can really lift up a population of people, of communities, and mobilize and unite them" (Gonzalez 2016). This paper argues that community involvement is the central fulcrum that enables cultural heritage to be leveraged as a driver of sustainable development in its fullest, most diverse and most democratic sense. It does so by re-asserting the active agency of heritage bearers, in all their manifestations and within all corners of society, to create a multitude of development pathways that reach beyond the heritage of the state to valorize and mobilize the heritage of the people in a self-reaffirming and productive manner.

Although it is not the purpose of this chapter to provide a history and analysis of the ongoing debate within the development world regarding the role of communities and other stakeholders within the broad spectrum of development projects, it is important to refer to the considerable literature surrounding this debate (for example, Chambers 1983, 1994; Ferguson 1990, 1994; Freund 1990; Mansuri and Rao 2013; Olivier de Sardan 2005; Ramalingam 2013). In short, the modern history of the participatory approach to development which meant involving local communities within the development framework, coupled with the shift of the role of government stakeholders from central to local (decentralization), began post World War Two. During the 1950s and early 1960s, USAID and the Ford Foundation guided the development model for small-scale projects by promoting and championing community participation and decentralization. Critics of community involvement and decentralization argued that not only was this approach marked by serious failures, but also was especially less successful with large-scale development projects aimed at industrial and agricultural growth. Consequently, during the rest of the 1960s into the 1980s the development model's focus shifted to more top-down models (Mansuri and Rao 2013).

Nonetheless, the proponents of local participation continued their struggle against the top-down, elitist model, raising many examples of where funders adopting the plans of macro-economists wasted time and funding. An excellent example is found in James Ferguson's study of peasants in Lesotho (1990, 1994). Trained as an anthropologist, Ferguson carried out an in-depth ethnographic study on the economy of local Lesotho villages, including agriculture, out-migration, and cattle-raising. Through this study, he clearly established that assumptions adopted by the developers were not only wrong but also that they led to misguided, erroneous development plans that were doomed to failure. Robert Chambers, creator and champion of the Participatory Rural Appraisal (PRA) approach (1983, 1994), attacked the elitist, top-down approach as one which would fail because it included neither the knowledge nor needs of the local communities, and offered a tool to assess this knowledge and these needs. Although many anthropologists disagreed with his PRA tool, criticizing it for being too shallow and "rapid," they did applaud the returned spotlight on the communities' needs themselves. From the 1990s to the present, many of the large donor institutions – World Bank (WB), Asian Development Bank (ADB), and government aid agencies – have continued to include the participatory approach to various degrees.

Stepping outside the framework of the development field, the concept of involving the participation of local communities in the re-discovery and documentation of their own heritage was also explored by archaeologists (Silliman 2008) and by ethnographic filmmakers who developed "participatory video," by which indigenous peoples, equipped with cameras and taught the technical skills of their use, documented and explored their view of their lives and cultures (Lunch and Lunch 2006; Steinfield et al. 2016). The discussion was further probed by academics within the discourse of heritage, especially built heritage, for example, Kemmis and McTaggert (2005) and Wells (2015).

United Nations agencies, including UNESCO, participated in this debate and catalyzed a collective response by the international community. In a prescient move, the 1972 Convention Concerning the Protection of the World Cultural and Natural Heritage – popularly known as the World Heritage Convention (UNESCO 1972) – foreshadows this connection between heritage, communities, and sustainable development. It is worth bearing in mind that the World Heritage Convention was born during the same era as the sustainability movement, emerging from the 1972 United Nations Conference on Human Environment in Stockholm, Sweden. Since its formal adoption by the UNESCO General Conference in 1972, a total of 193 Member States of UNESCO have become States Parties to the World Heritage Convention (as of July 2018). This makes it the most universal of all international conservation instruments.

The World Heritage Convention calls on each State Party to ensure effective measures for the "protection, conservation and presentation of the cultural and natural heritage situated on its territory" (Article 5), especially when the heritage becomes vulnerable due to the growing pressures stemming from both natural and human causes. In particular, the Convention encourages States Parties to "adopt a general policy which aims to give the cultural and natural heritage a function in the life of the community and to integrate the protection of that heritage into comprehensive planning programmes" (Article 5a). By doing so, this article opened the door to something new, and raised awareness about the need for community involvement in the heritage management process, albeit in a toothless way. Critics note that this provision merely requires the adoption of a policy that would *aim* at involving the community, but not requiring it (Tuensmeyer 2014:49). Moreover, it does not specify an active role for the community but rather positions the community as a passive recipient of government policy. Nonetheless, the nod to communities within signatory State Parties in the World Heritage Convention was already notable within the context of the conservation profession of that era.

The notion of community involvement was largely absent in earlier international conservation charters that proposed universal standards for the protection of monuments and sites and put an emphasis on top-down management. One of the earliest of these is the Venice Charter, drawn up in 1964 and adopted by ICOMOS in 1965.[4] Groundbreaking for its time, the Venice Charter strove to define "the principles guiding the preservation and restoration of ancient buildings" which are seen as part of the "unity of human values" and "common heritage" (Venice Charter 1964, paragraph one).

DEMOCRATIZING CONSERVATION

The Venice Charter established a privileged role for the "expert" in undertaking conservation work at all stages: from ascribing value to the heritage resource to the selection of conservation actions aimed at preserving those values (Venice Charter; Article 9). Not mentioned or considered in the Venice Charter is the role of communities living in or around these monuments and sites, who were excluded from all phases of the conservation process from identification to protection, as well as conservation to evaluation, and adaptation to use.

Throughout the rest of the 1970s and 1980s, the top-down heritage management paradigm remained largely intact. For instance, UNESCO International Safeguarding Campaigns required the governments to identify heritage to be protected, and "experts" to carry this out. The majority of declarations, resolutions, and charters drafted during these decades still reflected the concerns of cultural experts and authorities as how to best carry out conservation of archaeological and historic sites. Communities, when mentioned, are noted primarily as needing heritage education and having their "awareness raised," presumably in order to sustain the work of the conservation specialists. The work of planning and safeguarding remained in the hands of the cultural authorities and technical specialists. These documents included the Declaration of Amsterdam (1975), the Resolution of the International Symposium on the Conservation of Smaller Historic Towns (1975), the Florence Charter on Historic Gardens (1982), and the Convention for the Protection of the Architectural Heritage of Europe (1985), among others.[5]

The Nara Document on Authenticity (1994) was one of the seminal documents to give momentum to the paradigm shift to community involvement in the conservation and management process. For the first time, in an international instrument intended to influence the future of conservation practice, a consensus of professionals recognized that "responsibility for cultural heritage and the management of it belongs, in the first place, to the cultural community that has generated it, and subsequently to that which cares for it" (Nara Document on Authenticity 1994, Article 8). This was a radical and revolutionary position for the time, and created impetus for community engagement with and stewardship over local heritage resources. The Burra Charter, drafted by ICOMOS Australia in 1979 and substantially revised in 1999, reflecting twenty years of accumulated experience working with communities, is particularly noteworthy for its emphasis on the need to define cultural significance through a broad-based process of consultation as the starting point for the conservation process. Acknowledging the different notions of heritage between its settler and indigenous populations, the Burra Charter marked a dramatic shift from the Euro-centric concept of heritage monuments and sites to the concept of heritage places that encompass landscapes and other non-built features that resonates more strongly with its indigenous peoples. The Burra Charter introduces that heritage should be understood and managed in the specific local socio-cultural contexts to which it belongs, and by engaging with a diversity of stakeholders to which the heritage is significant (Burra Charter 1999, Articles 11–12).

The developments during the 1990s reach fuller maturity during the early years of the twenty-first century. In 2002, the Budapest Declaration on World Heritage (2002) emphasized the need to "seek to ensure the active *involvement of our local communities at all levels in the identification, protection and management of our World Heritage properties* (Budapest Declaration, paragraph 3, sub-paragraph 5). For the first time, the language is clear and strong. The declaration is not simply advocating, but calls for "ensuring" the involvement of communities and their participation in all aspects of the heritage process: identification, protection, and management. Indeed, in other UNESCO circles, it had become increasingly axiomatic to assert the centrality of the local community in the heritage enterprise.[6] The key role of communities was enshrined in two more recent UNESCO conventions, also dating to the early years of the twenty-first century, namely the Convention for the Safeguarding of the Intangible Cultural Heritage (ICH) (UNESCO 2003) and the Convention on the Protection and Promotion of the Diversity of Cultural Expressions (UNESCO 2005). The 2003 Convention states that: "Each State Party shall…identify and define the various elements of the intangible cultural heritage present in its territory, *with the participation of communities, groups and relevant non-government organizations*" (Article 11, item [b]). The emphasis on the participation of communities is further underscored in Article 15 titled "Participation of communities, groups and individuals." This article states, "each State Party shall endeavor to ensure the widest possible participation of communities, groups and, where appropriate, individuals that create, maintain and transmit such heritage, and *to involve them actively in its management.*" The Convention requires the explicit involvement and agreement of the communities in all activities safeguarding ICH, including the nomination of ICH elements to the two Lists associated with the 2003 Convention and the inventory of ICH elements. The 2005 Convention upholds the importance of cultural diversity of all humankind, and calls upon States Parties to do all they can to foster, support, and encourage the freedom of cultural diversity and expression. It underscores the primacy of the rights of civil society and the private individual to have this freedom. It states that by signing the Convention: "Parties acknowledge the fundamental role of society in protecting and promoting the diversity of cultural expressions. Parties shall encourage the active participation of civil society in their efforts to achieve the objectives of this Convention" (Article 11). The Yamato Declaration on Integrated Approaches for Safeguarding Tangible and Intangible Cultural Heritage (2004), drawn up on the occasion of the tenth anniversary of the Nara Document, demonstrated the crossover of certain approaches from the 2003 Convention into the realm of tangible heritage. In particular, it explicitly called for the "close collaboration and agreement with the communities and groups concerned" in integrating the safeguarding of tangible and intangible heritage, where appropriate. With reference to development, the Declaration promotes "economically rewarding heritage-related activities without compromising the integrity of communities and the viability of their heritage."

Although the language regarding communities found in the text of the World Heritage Convention itself has not been revised, this groundswell within the heritage profession quickly developed into a tsunami of practice, so much so that the World Heritage Committee formally incorporated the key recommendations of Nara Document, *in extenso*, into the Operational Guidelines of the World Heritage Convention in 2005. In 2007, "community" was formally added as the fifth "C" of World Heritage Committee's strategic objectives.[7] This strategic engagement with communities reflected a shift in the approach of the World Heritage Committee away from merely listing new heritage sites, to ensuring their sustainable management. The Periodic Reporting process, which was only introduced into the World Heritage procedures in 1998, found that, across the board, the state of conservation of World Heritage properties was deteriorating at an alarming and ever-increasing rate. Furthermore, it found that this deterioration was due in large part to an inadequate response to the threats posed by development processes, and the lack of the integration of heritage conservation into community planning frameworks. This was in direct contradiction to Article 5 of the World Heritage Convention itself. Armed with this data, it was only then that the norms and mechanisms of elitist, statist models of heritage conservation could be effectively challenged. Not only had the prevailing government-led approach to cultural heritage conservation proved inadequate to protect the most iconic of World Heritage sites, but also it did little to involve those communities that generated the heritage in the first place, nor did it enable them to participate in its management, and enjoy the results of heritage protection.

The on-going shift from statist to community-based models of management was also undergirded by the reality that private entities or communities claim an overwhelming percentage of the historic environment in some capacity, either through use or through ownership. As such, the meaningful involvement of a broader group of stakeholders at the local level in the identification, preservation, restoration, and reuse of heritage becomes inevitable. These communities have become the crucible for forging creative, new strategies for heritage conservation, such as those based on living traditions of cultural practice and community stewardship of material cultural assets. At the same time, these heritage resources also constitute the resource base to power local development strategies designed to uplift local people's lives, thus, strengthening the case for community involvement in heritage conservation as part of the larger sustainable development paradigm.

Towards Operationalizing the New Vision of Heritage Management

While this "new vision" of the role of heritage conservation within the development paradigm resonates with both the public lobby and the conservation profession, the operationalization of the vision is not a straightforward path. Because heritage sites are considered to be public goods and the state is the de facto protector of public goods in the legal context of the modern nation-state, the reality in most countries is that heritage site management continues to be the domain of the state. The responsibility for such sites continues to be enshrined in legal and regulatory frameworks that provide punitive measures, and sometimes incentives, to protect heritage. National and local government agencies are empowered to wield these regulatory instruments to protect heritage sites, sometimes from the very inhabitants who make up the social fabric of the site.

The mainstream practice of heritage conservation is still dominated by a small corps of educated elites who style themselves as heritage management "experts." Trained at elitist institutions, these "experts" have acquired the skills needed to implement technical interventions intended to conserve historic monuments, archaeological sites, urban districts, and landscapes. Even in those countries that acknowledge the importance of civil society and grassroots participation in heritage management, educated heritage experts retain strong authority and control over heritage management.

Given the entrenched nature of top-down approaches to scientific heritage conservation, in what ways, then, can more space be created for communities? The authors question whether it is sufficient simply to operationalize the World Heritage Convention's call for the state to give the heritage a "function in the life of the community," or whether the engagement with communities needs to be deeper, more extensive and more meaningful. Critics have pointed out that, in contrast to the 2003 Convention which requires the documented consent of communities in nominating an ICH element, "officially, there is no World Heritage mechanism to ensure community involvement in the nominations and inscription process" (Poulios 2011:145).

Beyond the actual inscription process, for many, participation requires inclusion in the entire heritage conservation and management process, beginning with identification of the heritage assets all the way to site monitoring. Moreover, it is one in which the local community is not merely consulted, but plays an active role in decision-making processes, much like arguments made for the involvement of communities in community-based tourism (Kontogeorgopoulos et al. 2014). Others argue that as long as communities benefit economically, and are satisfied with these benefits, then, they are "participating" in the process (Li 2006; Xu et al. 2009). The authors of this chapter understand meaningful community involvement to be the former. It is one in which communities living in or around heritage sites are consulted about, and participate in the heritage management process in some way which satisfies their aspirations. They should also benefit from the entire heritage management process from identification through to sustainable management. This includes integrating heritage protection into long-term development planning for the community.

In contrast to national or international "experts" who are often parachuted in, members of the local community know themselves and their heritage better than any outsider, and can offer a great deal of useful knowledge to the conservation and management process. Harper (1997:147) notes that "it is important to realize that local influencers have much to offer as they have probably thought about the problems to be tackled far longer than any of the 'professionals' that are often imposed on the community from the outside" (quoted in Gould 2009:10). As noted above the increasing attention paid to the role of communities in heritage management is an issue that was mirrored in the development field as a whole. As such, the main actors, for example, agencies and experts, serving within this field, began exploring ways to reconfigure not only their own role, but also that of the states. In concert with the states, ways were sought to restructure the traditional development frameworks in order to permit a more consensus-based strategy with regard to communities.

Against the backdrop of this evolving institutional landscape, UNESCO has had to re-evaluate traditional heritage management frameworks, seeking different strategies which would foster the inclusions of a stronger community voice. By periodically revising the Operational Guidelines of the World Heritage Convention to reflect – or indeed catalyze – evolving thinking in the heritage field, UNESCO's standard-setting function continues to be of relevance.[8] In the best cases, it has been able to serve as a laboratory of ideas or a clearinghouse in developing and disseminating new models for multi-party involvement in heritage management. In some instances, through operational activities on the ground, the organization has been able to deploy its convening power in order to facilitate a process of consultation which extends beyond the narrow group of institutions and agents normally involved in site management. At the end of the day, however, as the organization operates through the primary channel of national governments, the ability to engage with local stakeholders, and the pace of change are ultimately dependent on the level of readiness and openness in each locale. In many cases, it should be noted that the adoption of the rhetoric of community-based and consensual approaches has gained more traction than the actual translation into practice. Top-down technocratic processes, which have taken root over decades of bureaucratic-led heritage management, have proven difficult to displace entirely. It is not unusual to find that consultation is often carried out only in a token way – for instance, by convening public reviews for policies or plans, which have already been drafted completely by expert consultant firms, simply for the sake of checking off the "required consultation" tick, box in the to-do list. Even in more genuine attempts to carry out consultation, professional heritage managers, experts or state agencies tend to have an out-sized voice, overpowering or sidelining other opinions or viewpoints from smaller players and actors in the room.

However, despite these bumpy beginnings, the very fact that consultation is now a *de jure* part of many heritage policy-making and planning processes at least opens the door for a more participatory approach to heritage management. The global standard setting function of UNESCO in this regard, which stipulates the importance and mandatory nature of community involvement in various aspects and steps of the heritage management process, has helped to raise both the bar in both the rhetoric and practice – sometimes in quantum leaps, but more often in an incremental manner. So, for instance, countries in the process of nominating the World Heritage sites now have to clearly explain the role of communities in the nomination process itself and in the proposed management of the site. In some cases, this requirement has led to genuinely transformative effects. In Myanmar, as part of the process of nominating the Pyu Ancient Cities to the World Heritage List, a series of local heritage trusts were set up in each of the three proposed towns with the support of the Ministry of Culture. The heritage trusts – which bring together local leaders, business people, youth representatives, etc. – were active participants in the nomination process and, following inscription of the site in 2014, continue to act as champions for site protection, heritage education, and local community development. It can only be surmised that World Heritage nomination has given impetus to this initiative, in a governance context where engagement with civil society is still nascent.

Putting the New Paradigm into Action: Models from the Asia-Pacific Region

In seeking to test and refine this new conceptual framework, the Office of the UNESCO RACAP initiated a series of programs starting in the late 1990s. The main thrust of the programs was to institutionalize the role of community and other stakeholders in heritage management in the Asia-Pacific region as a means of acknowledging that without their support, preserving heritage would be a losing struggle and an empty exercise. Over the course of a decade, with successes and failures along the way, the following lessons were learned about heritage practice in the region:

- The need to *build broad-based coalitions* that includes customary heritage guardians, the government at national and local levels, cultural heritage management experts, the private sector, civil society and ordinary citizens (as demonstrated in the LEAP program).

- The need to link heritage conservation with development goals, with direct involvement and benefits for local people (as piloted in the Nam Ha Ecotourism project).

- The need to *valorize traditional modes of heritage conservation and management* that are often embodied in local agents and knowledge bearers and to marry them to scientific conservation know-how (as codified in the homeowner's manuals series and the Cultural Survival and Revival in the Buddhist Sangha project).

- The need to *transfer heritage conservation knowledge and capacity to younger generations* in a long-term institutional manner through the commitment of local educational institutions (as carried out through the Asian Academy for Heritage Management network).

The Local Effort and Community Preservation in Asia and the Pacific (LEAP) program modeled a new approach to cultural heritage conservation and management for the region. It was one led by public consensus, enabled by local government, and supported by private sector financing. The LEAP program aimed to mobilize and empower local communities to identify, advocate, conserve, manage, and utilize their culture and local heritage within a developmental context. The objective was for communities to retain and strengthen their cultural identity while benefiting economically and socially from their cultural capital.

One of the primary projects that was developed under the LEAP concept was "Cultural Heritage Management and Tourism: Models for Co-operation among Stakeholders". The five-year project began in 1999 and finished in 2003 with a workshop held in Penang to evaluate and mainstream project results. Initially, five historic towns were identified to participate, all of which were already inscribed on the World Heritage list. They were: Bhaktapur (Nepal), Hoi An (Viet Nam), Lijiang (China), Luang Prabang (Lao PDR), and Vigan (Philippines). The pilot sites were later expanded to include other sites, including sites that were not yet listed: the Rice Terraces of the Philippine Cordilleras, Kandy (Sri Lanka), Kokana (Nepal), Levuka (Fiji), and Penang and Melaka (Malaysia). The project aimed to develop not only models of cooperation among the various stakeholders at each pilot site, but also to create networks among the pilot sites. It was hoped that these networks would facilitate exchanges that would, in turn, enable stakeholders at the pilot sites to resolve many of the common issues plaguing historic towns together.

Community teams were identified at each of the pilot sites which were expected to be a representative of all stakeholders: government officials, cultural heritage management experts, the private sector, civil society, and ordinary citizens. These teams were meant to initially serve as a proxy and eventually as a basis for building actual long-term coalitions on the ground. In many cases, participating in the project gave team members a rare chance to communicate laterally across existing silos and to cooperate in concrete terms. These teams were guided through a multi-step process that started with mapping local cultural assets, followed by carrying out in-depth studies of the impact of tourism on heritage preservation at their sites, and finally drawing up action plans for sustainable tourism. At each step, each team presented their findings to an audience that included not only the teams from the other pilot sites, but also a wide range of heritage management and tourism experts from the region. The teams were then tasked with implementing the action plans at each site, drawing upon the cooperation of various stakeholders already included in each local team. The experiences from each team were then synthesized into a set of models called the Lijiang Models.

One noteworthy success emerging from this process of stakeholder consultation, joint planning, and action was the scheme for the capture and reinvestment of tourism revenue back into local heritage conservation in Hoi An, Viet Nam. The local heritage authorities, politicians, and heritage homeowners were able to negotiate an innovative mechanism to split revenue from entry tickets among the owners of various heritage attractions, the heritage office, and the local and provincial governments. In so doing, tourism revenue in Hoi An is able to directly support conservation of the most-visited heritage assets, other heritage buildings under the remit of the heritage office as well as other public services administered by the government, respectively. Building such coalitions did not always prove to be so straightforward or effective, however. In participating countries with weak civil societies, the project had to consider carefully how to best include grassroots participation. The concept of "community" was left intentionally broad, in order for the teams to include not only people from the grassroots level of the heritage property, but also government authorities and expert heritage managers who exercised a significant role. Defining "community" in this way enabled the project to guarantee the involvement of a grassroots constituency even at those sites where communities were less vocal and in which the government assumed the leading role in every aspect of local life. Although implementation of the LEAP program could not reverse this structure, it nonetheless brought the role of a broader group of often-overlooked local stakeholders into the framework, and their partial role in the management and development of their heritage site was acknowledged and accepted. Despite the positive gains in coalition building through the project, it still proved difficult to override entrenched power structures and interests, particularly economic ones. As the profits from heritage tourism increased at some sites, so did the reluctance of the government to relinquish its control over heritage management and economic development, while local enterprises and residents were crowded out by outside investors.

DEMOCRATIZING CONSERVATION

Figure 12.1 Typical view of the World Heritage Town, Lijiang, Yunnan, China. Photograph by Heather Peters.

In Lijiang (Figure 12.1), the tourism industry has become dominated by larger and better-financed business concerns from elsewhere in China (Kunming, Beijing, and Shanghai, for example), as well as by international hotel consortiums and travel franchises. The local government benefited through these outside contracts, but local businesses and the communities did not. In Lao PDR, the government policy decreed that all locally generated revenue had to be sent to the central government after which only a certain percentage was re-allocated back to the local authorities at the heritage site. Only part of this could be given to the heritage management office for use in conservation activities, and there was no mechanism for sharing the monies with the local community that had, in the first place, generated this revenue.

Given the lack of financial resources and policy support mechanisms in many countries, the project teams noted the importance of having strong private sector involvement in heritage conservation and management; access to credit including micro-credit; and local policy makers who are willing to set up required legal frameworks for heritage protection. Implementation strategies should aim at sustainability and replicability of activities that can result in multiplier-effect or spin-off projects. To complete this strategic scenario, incentives and other forms of recognition should be put in place in order to encourage local community participation and to counteract the perceived negative effects of conservation vis-à-vis economic development. The contrasting experiences above suggest that building coalitions, even ad hoc ones in this case within the context of a UNESCO-initiated project, can be successful if their energies are directed towards a particular well-defined problem, in this case, the development of a sustainable tourism framework that generates funds for local people and the heritage site. It is worth noting that in Hoi An, with active facilitation from the heritage office, the stakeholders taking part in the process were generally representatives of the range of actual key stakeholders on the ground. Furthermore, as the case of Hoi An shows, the solution that was generated proved to be long-lasting as it answered to the needs of all stakeholders involved in the process. Within the context of decentralized authority at the provincial and local levels, Hoi An was able to find a solution driven by local stakeholders that was not beholden to national-level political or fiscal control. Moreover, at the time of the project, outside investment was still at a nascent stage, and therefore, it was possible to pre-emptively establish a framework that privileged the role of local enterprises and residents. Finally, the revenue-sharing mechanism was translated into an institutionalized mechanism that was formally adopted in the regulatory framework for managing the site in a manner that continues to reflect this broad coalition of interests. While the public and private sector variables have continued to evolve in Hoi An, the essential elements of this system are still in place and functioning.

Linking Heritage Conservation with Development Goals and Benefits for Local People

While experimenting with projects seeking to integrate local communities into the safeguarding and management of cultural heritage, RACAP expanded the LEAP concept into the area of natural heritage as well. Similar to the management paradigm for cultural heritage, the management of national parks, reserves, and protected areas all over the world traditionally relied on an elitist top-down structure overseen by experts. This model has a long history that can be traced back to the first national park in the United States, namely, Yellowstone National Park listed in 1872.[9] The management plan created by authorities for environmental protection focused on the concept of "uninhabited wilderness" devoid of people. This model meant ejecting the people who traditionally lived in the park's area. Yellowstone, regretfully, became the global model for park management, especially considering that it was also among the first cohort of twelve places designated on the World Heritage List in 1978. It was not until the 1950s and 1960s that park managers in protected areas in other parts of the world began to question this model. They not only realized the rights-based issues resulting from the removal of local populations from their land, but also began to understand the significance of the traditional knowledge held by these populations over the centuries – knowledge that often served to protect, not destroy, the park's natural values (Stevens 1997a, b, c).

Recognizing that people are part of landscapes also impacted on the very foundation of the World Heritage Convention. By initially separating cultural from natural heritage, the Convention created a false dichotomy. By re-inserting people back into their proper environment, the Convention could work with these populations for realistic and more effective management. During the 1990s, this newfound understanding was reflected in the adoption of the category of "cultural landscapes," sites which integrated the natural biodiversity and cultural values of a landscape, including the intangible knowledge of the people who lived within the boundaries of the site (Mitchell, Rossler and Tricaud 2009). The Nam Ha Ecotourism Project was set up in and around the Nam Ha National Biodiversity Conservation Area in Luang Namtha Province, Lao PDR. The project was implemented in two phases from 1999 to 2002 and 2005 to 2007. The area contains a culturally diverse population of over twenty ethnic groups who are largely dependent on non-timber forest products, hunting, harvesting of timber, and shifting cultivation. The project aimed to test if community-based tourism could provide alternative livelihoods, in order to help protect the environment while bringing needed benefits to local populations and safeguarding their cultural heritage. Building upon the LEAP framework, a team of stakeholders was formed that brought together different government departments at the local and national levels (forestry, culture, and tourism), academic institutions, and local communities.

The project directly engaged with villagers in the protected area to identify nature-hiking trails and to guide visitors along the trails, with the eco-guides sharing their extensive knowledge about the local ecology and wildlife. The project was designed so that the eco-guides, some of which were drawn from the provincial Department of Forestry, were also expected to monitor wildlife species while conducting hikers along the trails, thus, taking on an adjunct conservation function as well. The villagers constructed and operated eco-lodges which provided meals and housing to the visitors. As part of the package, visitors also received souvenirs produced by local artisans. A village revolving fund was set up to manage and distribute the proceeds from the eco-tourism activities. In this way, a viable alternative system of income generation was established for the participating local villages.

The Nam Ha project was anchored by a dedicated team of young Lao officials who worked with the communities under the initial guidance of an international technical advisor. The project was designed so that the communities would eventually assume control and management over time. The project, despite its successes, was not without its challenges. Because of the low capacity of the staff in the provincial Department of Forestry, coupled with lack of department funds to provide any support for the work of the guides, the plan to utilize the eco-guides as conservation monitors proved difficult to operationalize fully. Total autonomy also proved difficult because the authorities did not fully buy into the basic premise of community-based management. Part of the reason for this is the very nature of the highly centralized government of the Lao PDR, which is reluctant to relinquish control. In the end, a hybrid approach with joint involvement of local villages and the district tourism office was worked out. Nonetheless, during its implementation, the management framework created by the Nam Ha project was held up by the Lao National Tourism Administration as the model for eco-tourism in their country. The ultimate success was seen in the many replicas and spin-offs of the community-based model in later, private sector enterprises that gradually entered the province.

Valorizing Traditional Modes of Heritage Conservation and Management

The approaches piloted by UNESCO in the Asia-Pacific region were not only predicated on the involvement of local people in the heritage management process as such, but also on the acknowledgment of their knowledge concerning heritage and heritage resource management. In opposition to the model of external experts having the most authoritative voice in decision-making, a more holistic model of heritage management and sustainable development requires the valorization of the complete human ecology, including the embodied knowledge and practices needed to sustain the local culture and cultural resources not simply as assets, but as intrinsic sources of value and identity. By putting this knowledge at the center of the management process, the role of the knowledge-bearers themselves is consequently reaffirmed as well.

Notwithstanding this philosophical stand, within the reality of modern socioeconomic and governance regimes, a number of other factors had to be acknowledged in project design. Given the primacy of globalized norms of heritage conservation, in many cases, the above premise was not easily accepted; there was an onus to actually prove that the traditional techniques were "scientifically" valid. Given the role of the technocrats and experts layered over customary modes of production and conservation, it would not be possible to completely sideline modern conservation standards, techniques, and requirements, including those required by the World Heritage Convention such as site monitoring. Another issue was that not everyone within a heritage locale had the breadth or depth of knowledge regarding traditional heritage practices as their forebears, while the corps of specialized artisans was also dwindling. And yet by a dint of ownership patterns, the majority of heritage resources – historic houses, temples and other religious buildings, community buildings and landscapes – continued to be in the hands of private or communal entities, who increasingly lacked the know-how to maintain or restore their properties. In response to these issues, RACAP initiated a process to capture and codify knowledge about traditional approaches to heritage conservation, drawing upon the remaining, often elderly, knowledge-bearers. This body of knowledge was then married to modern conservation techniques where appropriate, resulting in localized frameworks for heritage management which combined deep knowledge of the site with complementary methods practiced by the international heritage profession. The various case studies below will shed light on how this was operationalized in practice.

With a view to "democratizing" conservation beyond the hands of experts and technocrats, it was important to then disseminate this body of knowledge to the owners and users of the heritage resources. While encouraging local stewardship and participation in the conservation and management of local cultural resources, it was understood that for community-based actions to have lasting, widespread, and sustainable impact, it was important to ensure that conservation work was conducted using the highest technical standards. Adhering to these standards was not only necessary for the integrity and authenticity of the heritage site (per World Heritage requirements), but also precluded the possibility of critiques that local people were ill equipped to carry out "proper" conservation work. UNESCO Bangkok initiated the "Homeowners' Manuals" series to shift the focus away from expert-led conservation to resident-led conservation in several sites around the region: Hoi An (Viet Nam), Jogjakarta (Indonesia), Kathmandu Valley (Nepal), Lijiang (China), and Vigan (Philippines). Written by heritage experts in consultation with local communities and heritage offices, they served as practical guidelines for the individuals and families living in the heritage towns. They provided information in the care, renovation and possible adaptive reuse of the families' historic houses. They outlined the "dos and don'ts" of heritage repairs and emphasized the relevance of local knowledge regarding building materials and techniques. Through these manuals, homeowners were equipped to play a more active and informed role in maintaining and preserving their houses. The role of the heritage managers, in this process, was re-defined as that of a mentor, i.e. someone who provided oversight and technical skills when homeowners' were lacking.

Nonetheless, the tension between the stakeholders with an entrenched interest in the status quo and those newly empowered members of the community was inevitable. For example, in some places, the "elite" heritage managers resented the challenge that these manuals posed to their all-powerful role and authority. In one case, the chief architect of the heritage office explained that the manual would only confuse homeowners who had limited technical understanding and it would be best for them to consult directly and in person with the heritage site managers if they had a question

DEMOCRATIZING CONSERVATION

about conserving their houses. In another context, the community itself interpreted the homeowner's manual to be another mechanism of control, acting as a proxy of state and international regulations that restricted their rights to freely renovate or upgrade their houses. Instead of being welcomed as a mechanism of self-empowerment, the manuals were seen as insidious instruments of dis-empowerment.

Another factor was that in most cases, homeowners were themselves not carrying out the actual construction work, but merely guiding contractors and builders. If the contractor proved recalcitrant to the techniques advocated in the manual – for reasons of cost, expedience, or lack of skilled traditional artisans or building materials – then, the homeowner would be in a difficult negotiating position and many times would lack the depth of technical knowledge to adequately inspect and verify the quality of construction work. In an attempt to address the role of traditional stewards in a more holistic sense, and to equip them with actual practical skills, RACAP developed another project, The Cultural Survival and Revival in the Buddhist Sangha Project. This project aimed to revive the role of the "*sangha*" (communities of Buddhist monks) in the hands-on conservation of monasteries and the practice of a wide range of traditional arts, crafts, and intangible cultural traditions that were central to the life of the monastery and the community at large. Whereas monks in many Buddhist traditions were once the builders of temples and practitioners of temple-based arts, social upheavals, together with the political and economic transformations of the twentieth century, had largely disenfranchised this group of traditional knowledge bearers. While many *sangha* communities retained their role as moral beacons in the community, their auxiliary functions as teachers, doctors, and artisans dwindled with the emergence of the modern nation-state, its takeover of public services such as education and its regulation of activities in the interest of public safety such as construction. While still the residents, and ostensibly the guardians of Buddhist temples, monks were increasingly sidelined from maintenance and restoration processes. This was, in part, due to the lack of transmission of knowledge within the monkhood about Buddhist arts, crafts, and associated rituals.

The project sought to strengthen the teaching institutions and mechanisms needed to pass down this endangered knowledge within the *sangha*. It produced training curricula and materials covering a range of Buddhist arts and rituals spanning south, southeast and east Asia, from Nepalese stone chaitya carving to Cambodian mural painting, and from playing ritual instruments in Arunachal Pradesh to sand mandala construction in Sikkim, India. "Style books" about Buddhist artistic motifs in each site were printed to ensure that the unique artistic character of each temple community will remain distinctive. Manuals and instructional videos were developed about the production process of building and decorative arts associated with temples. These training materials were tested and deployed through training activities and programs targeting Buddhist monks and local craftspersons. The project focused on developing long-term training platforms rather than ad hoc training activities. The authorities included monastic bodies and government training institutions, certified many of the training curricula. The project involved monk and lay craftspeople, numbering over 1,700 in total, who were equipped with the knowledge and skills needed to maintain Buddhist temples, artifacts, and rituals in the long term.

The strategy of engaging with a local institution with strong roots and social relevance ended up being largely successful. Engaging with the *sangha* proved to be an inspired platform to interface with society at large in the cause of safeguarding Buddhist heritage. Not only the *sangha*, but also the lay communities which supported the *sangha,* already had a strong desire to support their Buddhist traditions. The project did not have to convince the community of the importance of continuing the traditional Buddhist culture and artisan skills, particularly those that were dying out. Even in the context of socialist countries where the *sangha* had experienced the worst upheavals during the 1960s and 1970s, the *sangha* demonstrated its resilience as self-contained institutions in themselves, with nearly all of the *sangha* bodies at the greatly diverse pilot sites asserting effective control and managing an array of heritage preservation activities. As they will continue to anchor their larger communities in the long-term, the *sangha's* capacity to function more effectively as stewards of cultural heritage and as models of appropriate practice for other stakeholders, including local authorities, has been reinforced through these project activities.

Transferring Heritage Conservation Knowledge and Capacity to Younger Generations

The experiences of the various case studies above show that, even with an expanding role for local communities, there is still a function for professional heritage managers. While they may no longer be the sole source of authority in conservation and management within the expanded institutional landscapes created by this new paradigm, they nonetheless continue to serve as sources of specialized technical inputs, facilitators, and mentors. Whatever their new roles, it is now acknowledged that these heritage managers have to be sensitive to communities, and the interplay between tangible heritage and ICH that is particularly important in the context of the Asia-Pacific region. However, within the region, there is a dearth of heritage managers equipped with these new skill sets and, more worryingly, few educational institutions producing such heritage managers. In the meanwhile, the enthusiasm for nominating World Heritage sites and ICH elements from Asia and the Pacific continues to grow unabated, alongside the unstoppable momentum for other national and local heritage initiatives. This means that the volume of heritage work is now quickly outstripping the capacity of the homegrown heritage profession to engage.

The Asian Academy for Heritage Management was the response conceived by UNESCO, ICCROM, and leading heritage practitioners in the region to meet this need in a professional, systematic, sustainable, and cost-effective way. The academy was set up as a network of institutes of higher learning that are engaged in the research and teaching of some aspect of heritage conservation and/or cultural resource management. The range of institutional members grew to encompass a wide range of universities spread both geographically and in terms of disciplines. This included institutions offering courses in architecture and architecture conservation; archaeological and protected site management; sustainable tourism management; culture industry management; culture institution management (museums, theatres, art galleries, dance companies, music groups, etc.); and human settlement planning, among other subjects. With a view to bridging from heritage conservation and management theory into practice, and to reflect real-life challenges faced by heritage sites across the region, the Asian Academy encouraged the review and reform of existing heritage curricula as well as convening field schools at actual heritage sites. To encourage this dialogue, the field schools brought together academics with heritage site managers and other professionals as well as local stakeholders, both as trainers as well as trainees. In this manner, a dialogue was fostered between the academy, practitioners, and local stakeholders, which in many cases was previously lacking. The field schools also provided a platform to push the conceptual envelope as well as the skill sets of participants into emerging areas of heritage conservation, for instance, dealing with themes such as urban archaeology, underwater archaeology, and ICH.

By working through the platform of educational institutions, UNESCO was able to mainstream the new approaches to heritage management that are being piloted in the field into academia and the heritage profession. Not only did this field-based body of knowledge – working with communities, reifying traditional conservation modes and know-how, structuring meaningful stakeholder interactions, and mobilizing heritage towards sustainable development outcomes – influence the way a new generation of heritage practitioners work, it also infuses into the theory, philosophy, and standards of heritage practice across different disciplines. In this way, these up-and-coming heritage practitioners became better positioned to work in the most symbiotic manner with communities, traditional custodians, local authorities, experts, and other agents who are now increasingly involved with the heritage management enterprise. While the Asian Academy has provided one model of innovating heritage education, the larger exercise of refashioning the role of experts and preparing experts to take on their new role of facilitator (rather than as primary drivers in heritage conservation) still remains a challenge. Whereas urban planning schools have been offering courses in facilitation as part of the rise of Habermasian-influenced communicative and participatory planning approaches over the past two decades, for heritage practitioners, this set of knowledge and skills remains underdeveloped in many curricula. Therefore, many heritage practitioners are required to come to grips with their new role through learning-by-doing, as participatory approaches are increasingly required, if not by regulation, then by demands from increasingly pro-active interlocutors among local stakeholders and the public.

Conclusions: Reflections on Democratizing Conservation

The first objective of this chapter was to illuminate the shifting paradigm in heritage management from one which emphasized the role of governments and elite experts to one that included the voice of the communities living in and around heritage sites, and to situate it within the more general debate that took place in the field of development during the past fifty to sixty years. With a particular focus on World Heritage, this was done through a review of selected international standard setting documents and conventions covering a span of more than forty years. The second objective was to determine whether or not this shift had any impact on the realities of heritage management in general, and specifically to analyze UNESCO's response to the shift both in normative and operational terms. In terms of the latter, the chapter analyzes a series of innovative programs and projects developed by the Office of the UNESCO RACAP.

The case studies presented here each highlighted a specific condition for community-based heritage conservation: (1) building broad-based coalitions; (2) linking heritage conservation with development goals, with direct involvement and benefits for local people; (3) valorizing traditional modes of heritage conservation and management, and marrying them to scientific conservation know-how; and (4) transferring heritage conservation knowledge and capacity to younger generations in a long-term institutional manner through educational institutions. In reality, the real key to "democratizing conservation" requires most, if not all, of these components to be in place. Despite occasional criticism from the scholarly community (e.g. Smith 2006a, 2006b, 2015) of UNESCO's perceived role in perpetrating hegemonic heritage practices, particularly, through its conventions and related statutory processes, notably the World Heritage Convention, the experiences chronicled above demonstrate that UNESCO has a meaningful role to play in negotiating this transition to more people-centered models of heritage management. The sway that the organization exercises in global, national, and local heritage circles should be seen as a powerful lever that reshapes normative standards, retools policy, influences professional guidelines, catalyzes debate and ultimately informs practice in the field. This influence can be seen in the emerging global recognition of culture and heritage as undeniable pillars of sustainable development, and an inalienable part of a rights-based approach to ensuring well-being for all.

In spite of the acknowledged importance of UNESCO-led inter-government action to champion the conservation of heritage assets worldwide, the essential role of communities living in and around heritage sites for managing and ensuring the long-term safeguarding of these sites cannot be ignored. International resolve must be translated into site-based practice that is accomplished through community-based action. The purpose of community-based heritage conservation is not to encourage people to return to some nostalgic past, but rather to use heritage as the divining rod for determining the direction each community wishes to take in its future development. This will help to ensure that the end result of development efforts will be acceptable and appropriate to each community's economic needs, and respectful of each community's social and cultural values.

Notes

1   The authors collectively, and Richard Engelhardt specifically, were part of the design and implementation of the programs outlined in this chapter. With time, they feel that they are well situated to assess the successes, challenges, and failures of these programs and projects.

2   Although the focus of this chapter, and indeed much of the work of the authors, is on cultural heritage management, it is important to note that the UNESCO 1972 convention addressing world heritage addresses both cultural and natural heritage. In 1994, a category for cultural landscapes, sites which combine both cultural and natural values was adopted. Interestingly, a shift in the model for natural heritage management, from an "exclusive", top-down framework in which local populations were evicted from park areas to an "inclusive, shared community approach, officially appeared in a resolution issued by IUCN at their 1975 General Assembly held in Zaire" (Stevens 1997c: 38). The paradigmic shift in cultural heritage management followed about a decade later.

3   An exhaustive sociological discourse of what is meant by "community" is outside the scope of this chapter. For our purposes, and within the context of the heritage conservation process, we adopt a definition that focuses on geography, is inclusive and is not reductionist in historical, ethnographic, or sociological contexts. Some link communities with indigenous groups (Gould 2009; Tuensmeyer 2014). Others categorize different kinds of possible communities (see Poulios 2011) in relation to heritage sites. For example, does a community still have to live at the site in order for it to be considered part of a heritage property? Can it still maintain a special association with the site despite the people having moved away? We can cite, for example, the Jigalong in Western Australia who have moved away from their ancestral lands, but still retain spiritual claims. Can the community be a group with special claims to the site, but which does not and never did use the site as it was in the past (for example, the contemporary Buddhist communities living in and around the Angkor Wat complex)? Does the community have to be a single-source, or ethnographically homogenous community? Although the Old Town of Lijiang is characterized as a Naxi historical town, this is a historically and ethnographically reductionist definition of the community. From its founding, the town has been home to Tibetans, Han, and other ethnic groups in addition to the Naxi.

4   ICOMOS, the International Council on Monuments and Sites, is a non-governmental professional body and a statutory Advisory Body to the World Heritage Committee in the implementation of the World Heritage Convention.

DEMOCRATIZING CONSERVATION

5 It should be noted that there is a growing body of literature reviewing the various charters discussed in the above paragraphs and critiquing their implementation. For example, Hardy (2008), Jokilehto (1999), Kulikauskas (2007), and Wells (2007).

6 See for example, those discussions that led to the Report of the World Commission on Culture and Development, *Our Creative Diversity*, published by the UN in 1996.

7 The other four Cs of the strategy are: Strengthen the Credibility (of the representative character of the World Heritage List); ensure the effective Conservation (of properties inscribed on the World Heritage List); promote the development of effective Capacity-building (of professionals and others in order to ensure adequate conservation of inscribes properties); and increase public awareness through Communication (to the public of the outstanding universal values of the properties inscribed on the List and thus the imperative for their safeguarding (Budapest Declaration 2002).

8 It should be noted that the 2015 Operational Guidelines request that communities linked with proposed World Heritage properties be involved in the World Heritage nomination process and require that they give their "free, prior and informed consent." See, paragraphs 12, 23, and 119 of the 2015 Operational Guidelines.

9 Yellowstone National Park is located mostly in the state of Wyoming with some land extending into Montana and Idaho.

References

Budapest Declaration on World Heritage. (2002). http://whc.unesco.org/archive/2003/whc-02-conf202-5e.pdf

Burra Charter. (1999). http://australia.icomos.org/publications/charters

Chambers, Robert. (1983). *Rural Development: Putting the Last First*. Harlow, UK: Pearson Education.

———. (1994). The Origins and Practice of Participatory Rural Appraisal. *World Development* 22.7:953–969.

Ferguson, James. (1990). *The Anti-Politics Machine: "Development, Depoliticization and Brueaucratic State Power in Lesotho"*. Cape Town: David Philip.

———. (1994). The Anti-Politics Machine – "Development" and Bureaucratic Power in Lesotho. *The Ecologist* 24.5:176–181.

Freund, Bill. (1990). The Ironies of Development. A Review of James Ferguson the Anti-Politics Machine: "Development, depoliticization and bureaucratic state power in Lesotho". *Transformation* 13:104–107.

Gonzalez, Susan. (2016). "We all have a stake in protecting cultural heritage says UNESCO Director-General", *Yale News*, 16 April 2016.

Gould, Peter G. (2009). The Role of Communities in Sustainable Heritage Preservation. Paper downloaded from www.sustainablepreservation.org

Hardy, N. (2008). *The Venice Charter Revisited: Modernism, Conservation and Tradition in the 21st Century*. Newcastle: Cambridge Scholars.

Harper, P. (1997). The Importance of community involvement in sustainable tourism development. In M. Stabler (ed.), *Toursim and Sustainability: Principles to Practice*. Wallingford, UK: CAB International, pp. 143–149.

Jokilehto, J. (1999). *A History of Architectural Conservation*. Oxford: Butterworth Heinemann.

Kemmis, S. and McTaggert, R. (2005). Participatory action research: Communicative action and the public sphere. In N.K. Denzin & Y.S. Lincoln (eds.), *The Sage Handbook of Qualitative Research*. Thousand Oaks, CA: Sage Publications.

Kontogeorgopoulos, Nick, Anuwat Churyen and Varaphorn Duangsaeng. (2014). Success Factors in Community-Based Tourism in Thailand: The Role of Luck, External Support and Local Leadership. *Tourism Planning & Development* 11.1:106–124.

Kulikauskas, Paulius. (2007). International Charters on Conservation: The Lost c(l)auses. *City and Time* 3(3):5. www.ct.ceci-br.org

Li, Wen Jun. (2006). Community Decision-making – Participation in Development. *Annals of Tourism Research* 33.1:132–143.

Lunch, Nick and Chris Lunch. (2006). Insights into Participatory Video: A Handbook for the Field. Downloaded from www.insightshare.org

Mansuri, Ghazala and Vijayendra Rao. (2013). *Localizing Development – Does Participation Work?* Washington, DC: The World Bank.

———. (2015). Transacting UNESCO World Heritage: Gifts and Exchanges on a Global Stage. *Social Anthropology/Anthropologie Sociale* 23.1:3–21.

Mitchell, Nora, Mechtild Rossler and Pierre-Marie Tricaud (eds.). (2009). *World Heritage Cultural Landscapes: A Handbook for Conservation and Management.* World Heritage Papers 26. UNESCO, World Heritage Centre: Paris.

Nara Document on Authenticity. (1994). www.icomos.org/charters/nara-e.pdf

Nara + 20 www.japan-icomos.org/pdf/nara20_en.pdf

Olivier de Sardan, Jean-Pierre. (2005). *Anthropology and Development: Understanding Contemporary Social Change.* London & New York: Zed Books. Translated by Antoinette Tidjani Alou.

Poulios, Ioannis. (2011). Is every Heritage Site a 'Living' One? Linking Conservation to Communities' Association with Sites. *The Historic Environment* 2.2:144–156.

Ramalingam, Ben. (2013). *Aid on the Edge of Chaos: Rethinking International Cooperation in a Complex World.* London: Oxford University Press.

Silliman, S.W. ed.. (2008). *Collaborating at the Trowel's Edge: Teaching and Learning in Indigenous Archaeology.* Tuscon: University of Arizona Press.

Smith, Laurajane. (2006a). *The Uses of Heritage.* Routledge: London and New York.

———. (2006b). Uses of Heritage, Heritage as Identity. Downloaded from https://courseworks2.columbia.edu/courses/10532

———. (2015). Intangible Heritage: A challenge to the authorised heritage discourse? In Revista d'Ethnologia de Catalunya. June, Num. 40.

Steinfield, Charles, Susan Whche, Hastings Chiwasa, Tian Cai and Japher Mchakulu. (2016). Using Participatory Video for Smallholder Farmer Training in Malawi. Global Center for Food Systems Innovation Publication Series, Michagan State University, USAID.

Stevens, Stan, ed. (1997a). *Conservation through Cultural Survival: Indigenous Peoples and Protected Areas.* Washington, DC: Island Press.

———. (1997b). The Legacy of Yellowstone. In *Conservation through Cultural Survival: Indigenous Peoples and Protected Areas.* Washington, DC: Island Press, pp. 13–32.

———. (1997c). New Alliances or Conservation. In *Conservation through Cultural Survival: Indigenous Peoples and Protected Areas.* Washington, DC: Island Press, pp. 33–62.

Tuensmeyer, Vanessa. (2014). The UNESCO World Heritage System: An additional impetus or obstacle for indigenous activism? In H. Holleland and S. Solheim (eds.), *Between Dream and Reality: Debating the Impact of World Heritage Listing.* Primitiv Tider special edition 2014, Oslo: Represokalem, pp. 49–59.

UNESCO. (1972). Convention Concerning the Protection of the World Cultural and Natural Heritage. http://whc.unesco.org/archive/convention-en.pdf

———. (2003). Convention on the Safeguarding of the Intangible Cultural Heritage. www.unesco.org/culture/ich/index.php?lg+en&pg+00006.

———. (2005). Convention on the Protection and Promotion of the Diversity of Cultural Expressions. http://en-unesco.org/creativity/convention/what-is/convention-text

DEMOCRATIZING CONSERVATION

————. (2011). "UNESCO past and present", *UNESCO Archives*, www.unesco.org/archives/new2010/en/history_of_unesco.html

Venice Charter. (1964). www.icomos/charters/venice_e.pdf

Wells, J.C. (2007). The plurality of truth in culture, context and heritage: A (mostly) post-structuralist analysis of urban conservation charters. *City and Time* 3(2:1):1–13.

————. (2015). In stakeholders we trust: Changing the ontological and espistimological orientation of build heritage assessment through participatory action research. In B. Szmygin (ed.), *How to Assess Built Heritage? Assumptions, Methodologies, Examples of Heritage Systems.* Florence and Lublin: Romualdo Del Bianco foundation and Lublin University of Technology.

Xu, Honggang, Trevor Sofield, and Bao Jigang. (2009). Community tourism in Asia: An introduction. In BAO Jiagang (ed.), *Tourism and Community Development, Asian Practices*, pp. 1–17. Madrid: World Trade Organization.

Yamato Declaration on Integrated Approaches for Safeguarding Tangible and Intangible Cultural Heritage. (2004). http://portal.uneco.org/culture/en/files/238631/10988742499Yamato_Declaration.pdf. Yamato_Declaration.pdf

CHAPTER 13

Missed Opportunities

The Absence of Ethnography in America's Cultural Heritage Programs

Richard Vidutis

The Cultural Resources Management (CRM) industry is the main driver of historical and cultural research in America following the National Historic Preservation Act (NHPA) of 1966 and its regulations required by Section 106 review (36 CFR 800) and Criteria of Evaluation (36 CFR 60.4). About 1,300 CRM firms across America employ some 10,000 archaeologists, architectural historians, historians, architects, and an occasional ethnographer generating $1 billion in gross revenues each year (Marion 2013). The Section 106 process is national in scope documenting the nation's heritage while proclaiming that it covers the whole spectrum of cultural and historical expression. Theoretically, the Section *106 review* provides the public with an opportunity to influence how projects with federal involvement affect historic properties. In practice, though it restricts itself to historical and archaeological data collected, analyzed, and determined by degreed specialists with rarely any ethnographic input from the inhabitants of the community in which the heritage sites are located.

It is time to explicate the whole scope of what "culture" means in the fields of CRM and historic preservation, where the basic working assumptions of integrity, significance, and the fifty-year threshold for significance limit what is observed and what is ignored in documenting heritage. Arguing for the incorporation of community knowledge as part of standard operating procedures will be a challenge. For those seeking change in Section 106's governance of historical and cultural documentation, Critical Heritage Studies (CHS) has much to offer CRM conceptually. CHS employs a community-based approach to heritage management that can benefit the Section 106 regulation framework. David Lowenthal, considered the founder of the field of Heritage Studies, formulated his central idea in *The Past is a Foreign Country* (1985) that people create heritage through human experience and that it is a product of human creativity. This premise is at the heart of ethnographic research.

Using projects, I have carried out for private firms, the National Park Service, and Federal Emergency Management Administration (FEMA), I will present examples of phenomena of cultural displays, social rituals, and historical artifacts that appear at sites that do not fit into the current *modus operandi* Section 106 review, yet, are vital cultural statements by the community. I will also show how oral interviewing can add interpretive elements to a site's function, and add historical data that are not available in repositories. The simple technique of querying people can lead to discoveries that increase the effectiveness of field teams seeking to unlock cultural and historical layers of a site. Data collecting should be more than just a processual activity, which clients and agencies might prefer for compliance ease but often leaves out the human interpretive elements that deepen the understanding of the heritage artifact.

Finally, ethnographers—folklife specialists, folklorists, cultural anthropologists, and others—are seeking ways to engage CRM to include ethnographic narratives. After decades of absence from CRM, how feasible is their contribution in view of their lack of training in the Section 106 process, and resistance by historians and archaeologists to change CRM *modus operandi* developed through the years now firmly in place. But the solution for their participation must be found, perhaps beginning with access to Traditional Cultural Property (TCP) projects of non-indigenous groups that require ethnographic documentation.

The Foundations of CRM

The history of the present system of site evaluation dominated by archaeologists and architectural historians goes back to the 1940s, beginning with the post-war reservoir developments that motivated salvage archaeology. It was later expanded to other river systems known as the River Basin Surveys (RBS). RBS projects took place in the United States after the flood control act of 1944 and were a major step in the development of CRM archeology. Originally created by the Smithsonian Institution, it was turned over to the National Park Service in 1969. The RBS did not ignore historic sites being the first to investigate non-Native sites (Govaerts and Mulkerin 2014). Along with the Interagency Archeological Salvage Program, these were the most ambitious archaeological projects ever undertaken in the United States. Administered by the National Park Service from 1945 to 1969, the programs had profound effects—methodological, theoretical, and historical—on American archaeology stimulating the public's interest in preserving their heritage.

In the 1960s, the expansion of the Interstate Highway system combined with urban renewal resulted in the destruction of archaeological sites and urban neighborhoods. That led to new federal legislation, specifically the National Historic Preservation Act in 1966 and the requirements of Section 106, the National Register of Historic Places, State Historic Preservation Offices (SHPOs), etc. This movement was dominated by historians who grudgingly acknowledged archaeology. But by the 1970s, archaeologists fought back and achieved passage of the Moss-Bennett Act of 1974. It was implemented by the National Park Service and heralded the need for other agencies to hire archaeologists or do contract work, resulting in the term "Cultural Resource Management" (King 2011, personal communication).

The Early Hopeful History of Ethnography-Folklore

After an absence of decades, ethnographers and folklorists have recently shown an interest in re-entering the CRM arena especially in the evaluations of TCPs for non-indigenous groups.[1] Until now, TCPs have been written mainly for indigenous populations using ethnographic sources and methods. In a desire to level the field, ethnographers and folklorists want to apply those same approaches to other ethnic or non-indigenous populations, especially focusing on intangible data such as beliefs and expressive arts. So, where has ethnography been all this time? Ethnography, particularly in the form of Folklore, was once poised to take on the work of participating with archaeology and history in documenting cultural resources. For a while, it seemed that folklore would be significantly involved in the preservation movement. In 1979, the National Park Service approached the American Folklife Center to contribute an ethnographic section to a project that was recovering

MISSED OPPORTUNITIES

cultural data along the Tennessee-Tombigbee Waterway being constructed by the U.S. Army Corps of Engineers. But unfortunately, the Center withdrew from the project ostensibly because it did not want to be associated with the culturally destructive aspects of the project.

Perhaps, feeling it had made a mistake, in 1980, Alan Jabbour, Director of the American Folklife Center, began working with the House of Representatives on an amendment to the National Historic Preservation Act known as Section 502. It directed the National Park Service and the American Folklife Center to prepare a report "on preserving and conserving the intangible elements of our cultural heritage such as arts, skills, folklife and folkways" (NHPA 1996, Sec. 502). In support, the House of Representatives Report 96–1457 (1980) made it clear that the intangible should be on equal footing with the tangible and: "…such as those protections now accorded tangible historical resources." In the United States, at that time there were forty-six states with state folklorists along with folklorist holding public positions throughout the country at city, county, and regional levels.

The momentum from folklore continued with two publications. In 1983, a report appeared entitled *Cultural Conservation: The Protection of Cultural Heritage,* prepared by Ormond Loomis of the Florida State Folklife Center, who coordinated the study and report. It appealed for serious sustained efforts to document at the local level not just culture but its related history as well. It follows a mandate contained in 1980 amendments to the 1966 National Historic Preservation Act for the Secretary of the Interior, in cooperation with the American Folklife Center, to prepare and submit to the president and Congress a report addressing strategies for "preserving and conserving the intangible elements of our cultural heritage such as arts, skills, folklife, and folkway" (Loomis 1983, 1). In 1988, Burt Feintuch brought together essays in *The Conservation of Culture: Folklorists and the Public Sector* on issues relevant to folklorists in the public sector: record, present, and preserve forms, both intangible and tangible such as music, custom, festival, storytelling, dance, art, and architecture. The publication is a collection of conference papers held at the University of Kentucky in 1985 entitled "Folklife and the Public Sector: Assessment and Prognosis," which raised questions concerning public sector efforts by folklorists. The impetus for the publication and conference came from Loomis's *Cultural Conservation.* When the Regan administration had come to an end, the recommendations of the *Cultural Conservation* report were forgotten. Nevertheless, a certain momentum continued as the National Park Service and the American Folklife Center collaborated on projects to document certain cultural resources. It seemed like it would be the start of ethnography's positioning itself within the preservation movement, and there were a couple of groundbreaking projects that provided examples for future like-minded approaches, had folklore continued the path of cooperation with other cultural disciplines.

One was the New Jersey Pinelands study in 1986, Mary Hufford's *One Space, Many Places: Folklife and Land Use in New Jersey's Pinelands National Reserve,* where local inhabitants, the Pineys, were consulted regarding conflicts and resolutions of their traditional life. Here was a premier TCP study where people understood themselves to be linked to special places such as marshes, cranberry bogs, and forests that were fundamental to their identities. The other study prepared in 1988 by cooperation between the American Folklife Center, the National Park Service, and the Utah State Historic Preservation Office was *The Grouse Creek Cultural Study: Integrating Folklife and Historic Preservation Field Research* (Carter and Fleischhauer 1988). A Mormon cowboy community, Grouse Creek, was evaluated as a historic property consisting of a cluster of working cattle ranches, where the relationship analyzed was the way people lived on the landscape.

Twenty-nine years ago, the publication of *The Grouse Creek Cultural Survey* was the first project to offer a model for combining folklore and preservation in a cultural resource survey. In the book's

MISSED OPPORTUNITIES

forward, Jerry L. Rogers writes, "One of the lessons of the Grouse Creek Cultural Survey is that America's heritage lives on in people's activities as well as in their material objects." And because of it, "Historic preservation in the Grouse Creek Cultural Survey becomes a broader, richer field: it moves toward cultural preservation--a union of past and present, of architecture and community life." Unfortunately, as a co-author, Tom Carter put it: the Grouse Creek model

> appears to have had little impact on either preservation or folklore methodology. After the project was finished, the historians went back to doing history; the folklorists forgot about the rewards of a comprehensive approach and went back to seeking out and celebrating exceptional folk artists.

An important opportunity to build on this integrative model was lost.

Or as Peggy Bulger, former Director of the American Folklife Center at the Library of Congress, in her American Folklore Society Presidential Plenary Address, put it in 2002:

> By demonizing powerful institutions such as the Army Corps of Engineers and refusing to deal with their agendas, our outraged sensibilities have kept us on the fringes of this important work, rather than in a central position with our colleagues from related disciplines.

> (Bulger 2002)

Both the Pinelands and Grouse Creek folklife studies show relationships between people and place and of their perceptions. The people's perceptions deal with values such as how to live appropriately, how to interact with others, important environmental issues, what constitutes valuable tools or dwellings, how to hunt, etc. It all talks about people's perceptions of how place creates and fosters tradition and in turn how tradition values the places it thrives in or on. In the long historical view, the rejection of the Tennessee-Tombigbee was an unfortunate decision because it might have been the doorway to large-scale involvement by ethnography in federal projects across the country that would have raised ethnography to a level equal to history and archaeology in preservation and CRM, a level it does not enjoy today. Since then archaeologists took the reins of historic preservation. And so, CRM today defines cultural resources primarily as archaeological and historical, and rarely as ethnographic.

Thomas King, public sector archaeologist and well-known critic of the Section 106 process, believes that the field has shortsighted itself by relegating TCPs only to Native American societies.

> TCPs aren't just for tribes, and they aren't found only in the country. Nor are they only for so-called "ethnic" communities. An urban neighborhood, for example, may be valued by people who are not necessarily of minority ethnicity; it's their TCP, and if it meets the National Register's criteria, it's eligible for the Register as such.

> T. King (comments on National Register Bulletin 38)

The reason for folklore's/folklife's reluctance to participate in national preservation programs is due to typology. Exterior features, such as orientation and function, are viewed with reduced interest as being distant and secondary. The folkloric approach, according to the folklorist Henry Glassie (1975), does not analyze the uses or function of a house or its physical surroundings in making

258

typological classifications. This proclivity of folk researchers towards collecting variants led Richard Dorson, Director of the Folklore Institute, Indiana University, to describe them as: "...more hortatory rather than theoretical, ethnographic rather than philosophical" (Dorson 1973, 40). In their own way, folklorists, like historians and archaeologists, also focused on the tradition bearer and practitioner as an artifact with scant regard for the context. TCP work, on the other hand, requires data from the perspective of the occupant and user. Ethnography withdrew its potential contribution of information gathered on traditions, artifacts, folk architecture, rituals, displays, and beliefs. All of which are primary data in arguing for cultural significance.

Tangible and Intangible Cultural Heritage

The concept of cultural heritage as object is shifting. Cultural heritage recalls artifacts (paintings, drawings, prints, mosaics, sculptures), historical monuments, and buildings, as well as archaeological sites. But the concept of cultural heritage is even wider than that and has gradually grown to include all evidence of human creativity and expression: photographs, documents, books and manuscripts, and instruments, etc. either as individual objects or as collections. Today, towns, underwater heritage, and the natural environment are also considered part of cultural heritage since communities identify themselves with the natural landscape as well as with cultural artifacts. Moreover, cultural heritage is not limited to material objects that we can see and touch. It also consists of immaterial elements: traditions, oral history, performing arts, social practices, traditional craftsmanship, representations, rituals, displays, knowledge and skills sometimes transmitted from one generation to the next, and occasionally ad hoc creations to express one's feelings about a situation, for example, in response to disasters.

Conservation can no longer be based on the object's intrinsic quality. It must be founded on the ability to recognize aesthetic, historic, scientific, social values, etc., upon which society's cultural identity can be built. Attempts at constructing acceptable TCPs for the National Register highlight certain problems with the major one being that "Trying to make such determinations, as required by the National Register program standards, can often lead to artificial constructs in conflict with traditional perspectives" (Lusignan 2009, 42), especially, in the realm of intangible cultural values. Interestingly, both indigenous and non-indigenous traditional communities provide cultural specialists with similar problems when determinations are argued based on intangible values associated with places that are not limited by boundaries or even exhibit visible shapes. The quandary for cultural professionals is whether to accept local knowledge as evidence for determinations. Insisting determination be based on physically observable assets is a biased Western approach to history demanding physical evidence, the artifacts of architecture and archeology, while sidelining its own rich Western traditions of ethnographic observation that cites intangible traditions related to the place.

> The act of reconstructing history through excavation and interpretation of material remains creates a concept of history as that which is artefactual....this logic has led to a narrow interpretation of culture as history....quantified according to archaeological standards of artefactual integrity, it becomes impossible to recognize culture as anything that is not artefactual in nature.
>
> (Wilkerson 2010, 145)

Paul Lusignan lays out NPS's rules of TCP engagement:

> Properties such as Native American spiritual places, culturally valued landscapes, and traditional neighborhoods were often given short shrift because of their perceived incompatibility with established methodologies for identifying, surveying, and nominating more common "historic" properties such as houses, bridges, dams, and archaeological sites. *It was never intended that the National Register change into a vehicle for recognizing cultural values that were purely intangible, but rather to provide mechanisms for identifying and documenting those physical places that might be associated with less tangible aspects of cultural identity* [emphasis mine].

> (Lusignan 2009, 42)

Standard Operating Procedures of CRM and the Use of TCPs

CRM has decades of accepted preservation research procedures, where surveyors simply are not used to consulting with local inhabitants about the significance of their cultures. Under constraints of budget, time, and staff, surveyors quickly make judgment calls during windshield and walking reconnaissance surveys without the presence of ethnographers and call it standard operating procedures. Alanen and Melnick (2000) made a critical observation about the usual "windshield surveys" administered during resource documentation especially of buildings, which fail to identify significant cultural resources located within. For example, a documentation project in Seattle's International District overlooked the oldest intact example of a Japanese bathhouse, the Hashidate-Yu, in the basement of the Panama Hotel, simply because no one thought to look inside nor ask what the item was.

One possible reason why so few "non-indigenous" TCPs have been developed is that the term—Traditional Cultural Property—is not codified anywhere in federal law or regulation, which means the federal agencies are not compelled to pursue them. The 1992 amendment to NHPA, Section 101, only mentions properties as being significant to "Indian Tribes and Native Hawaiians" and does not mention by name any other ethnic or traditional group. For some managers of preservation projects this means that areas of significance to Tribes and Native Hawaiian organizations are the only areas that have ever been recognized by the Congress and, thus, the federal agencies are mandated to recognize by law. This point was driven home by a regional historic preservation officer in Albuquerque: "The NPS/NR can publish all of the 'TCP' Bulletins they want. The SHPOs can talk about all the non-indigenous 'TCPs' they want. They cannot change existing law, or invent new ones, try though they might" (Siegel, Regional HP Officer. U.S. Fish and Wildlife Service—SW Region, 2011, personal communication). The problem of representation is not limited to TCP projects but is the norm for all recording projects. The result is, as Thomas King stated: "It's hard to escape the conclusion that a centrally defined and maintained register is a rather undemocratic... institution" (King 2002, 19–20).

With current interest to humanize CRM, I was curious to learn what the attitudes towards the concept were with SHPOs across the country. I contacted all sixty State and Territorial State Historic Preservation Offices through the American Cultural Resources Association forum in 2011 and 2014. Responses came back from SHPOs, state historical societies, historic preservation departments, and individuals. Only about half replied but the responses provided a snapshot regarding attitudes and problems pursuing ethnographies of non-indigenous TCPs. Expressed were issues of funding, staff

MISSED OPPORTUNITIES

size, conceptualization, nomination rejections, priorities, active pursuit of TCPs, and preference for Native American TCPs. The responses are grouped according to the following categories:

Prepared to Accept TCP Nominations from Any Group

Colorado

Pursuant to the "2020 Colorado Statewide Preservation Plan. The Power of Heritage and Place: A 2020 Action Plan to Advance Preservation in Colorado" (2010), Colorado has posted a list of select needed historic contexts and threatened and underrepresented resource types, some of which include non-indigenous traditional cultural places. The *Selected Historic Contexts Priorities* aims to steer researchers and surveyors to identify needed themes and to be dynamic and evolve through public and stakeholder input.

> Liverman (Nat. and State Register Coordinator, 2014, personal communication)

Indiana

Rather than have special studies, Indiana uses a survey program to try to identify vernacular rural landscapes and districts considering designed places can be traditional cultural places such as traditional Euro-American places of recreation. Indiana houses its information on historic resources in State Historic Architectural and Archaeological Research Database (SHAARD), which contains, among other subjects, data from previously conducted cultural resource inventories, research projects, CRM project reports, NPHP listings, including 250,000 paper records from past surveys.

> (Unsigned, Indiana, 2011, personal communication)

Louisiana

As a part of regular historic preservation work under Section 106, TCP's have rarely been addressed in Louisiana up until the time of the BP oil spill. Our office does not have any records of identified TCP's across the state, nor am I aware of any work that has specifically been done to identify them within the context of Section 106 efforts.[2] However, as part of the oil spill response, there has been an extensive ethnographic project, one of their goals being the identification of TCP's for indigenous and non-indigenous communities.

> (Lee 2015, personal communication)

And regarding employing ethnographers,

My feeling is that both folklorists and ethnographers are capable of conducting TCP research and should be called upon to do so, rather than those whose training does not include working with traditional people and communities.

> (Lee 2015, personal communication)

No Preference for TCPs

Idaho

Idaho SHPO has not made a decision not to seek nonindigenous TCPs and we would welcome submissions from interested parties.

(Reid, State Archaeologist, Deputy SHPO, 2014, personal communication)

California

We would never make a "blanket" decision to not process a non-indigenous TCP. If a property meets National Register Criteria for Evaluation, and the criteria for TCPs, we would process it without hesitation.

(Correia, Supervisor, Registration Unit, 2014, personal communication)

Conceptualizing TCPs

California

One of the problems with this endeavor is to get people to view things more as landscapes and holistically rather than as just 'sites' – archaeological or otherwise.

(Lindahl, Senior State Archaeologist, 2011, personal communication)

Guam

It is also possible that the War in the Pacific National Park (Asian Invasion Beach Unit) might also meet the criteria as a traditional cultural property as survivors from the invasion of Guam (and their offspring) continue to visit it for its role during WWII. That is if you do not apply the restriction of the use having to remain the same as the property is now a place of homage to the invasion.

Olmo (Dept. Parks and Recreation, 2014, personal communication)

TCP Attempted but Not Accepted

Delaware

We did try to nominate one some years ago, in The Ardens Historic District...In the end, the National Register decided it did not fit the definition of a TCP. There were problems with the desire of the Ardens to bring the period of significance up to the present, there were problems with so many of the buildings being altered or relatively modern, and there were problems with the definitions of traditional and cultural.

Guerrant (Research Manager, DE Div. Historical & Cultural Affairs, 2011, personal communication)

Idaho

Several years ago, the College of Idaho in Caldwell did attempt to nominate an on-campus property of traditional significance to several generations of students, but it was not accepted by the National Park Service on the grounds that the student body didn't qualify.

Reid (State Archaeologist, Deputy SHPO, 2014,
personal communication)

Indigenous TCPs Are a Priority

Alaska

Most of our conversations about TCPs are about indigenous subsistence and lifestyle practices and places.

(Antonson, State Historian, 2014,
personal communication)

Maine

The Maine Historic Preservation Commission has not prepared reports (or other documentation) for any non-indigenous Traditional Cultural Properties. This is not a priority for our office.

(Mitchell, Nat. Register Coordinator, HP Commission, 2014,
personal communication)

Minnesota

While I appreciate the desire to investigate "non-indigenous" TCPs, my staff does not differentiate our priorities related to TCPs in that way. We feel that American Indian properties are underrepresented in the National Register as it is and we would welcome TCPs of any type submitted for review.

Howard (HP Dept., MN Hist. Soc., 2014,
personal communication)

Staff and Funding Shortage for Non-Indigenous TCPs

Alabama

Like most states, we are suffering severe budget cuts, staff retirements, and layoffs. While the thought of pursuing such studies is intriguing, we have not yet had the opportunity to do so.

(Wofford, Deputy SHPO, 2014,
personal communication)

Alaska

The Alaska Office of History & Archaeology has not undertaken preparing non-indigenous traditional cultural property reports. The reason why is that the office has not had funds for general research studies or available staff to undertake such projects...

(Antonson, State Historian, 2014, personal communication)

Colorado

Our efforts are restricted by the fact that these nominations are in addition to regular staff duties.

(Liverman, National and State Register Coordinator, 2014, personal communication)

Minnesota

Although we have discussed several properties deserving of TCP investigation, we are not in a position to investigate them currently. Our office has very little funding for survey and nomination work. Most of the survey work and nominations are initiated from outside our office walls.

Howard (HP Dept., Hist. Soc., 2014, personal communication)

Disaster Ethnography—Challenges to Evaluation Criteria

The increase in climate change has brought into focus the inadequacies of the Section 106 review and CRM practices in mitigating damaged heritage resources. This was especially true of FEMA's efforts in rebuilding devastated communities after hurricanes Katrina and Rita deluged the Gulf Coast. As a contract historian and ethnographer, I worked for FEMA on three natural disaster events: Hurricane Katrina (2005–2006), Hurricane Sandy (2012–2013), and Missouri Floods (2016). All three events presented documentary situations to collect ethnographic data beyond the stipulations of Section 106 and Criteria of Evaluation.

Natural and manmade disasters present conditions for cultural discoveries. ICOMOS[3] notes that destruction can be an opportunity for discovery and identifying potential new attributes, both tangible and intangible, establishing their post-trauma status in support of a property's value, and under various criteria, they can be integral to the property. The NHPA does not mention subsidiary cultural attributes that appear in disaster situations, nor does CRM consider them in its Section 106 review reports. But they are vital if people display them in post-disaster events. Confronting devastated landscapes presents unfathomable choices as to where to start all over again, what is important to save, and who decides what is kept (Figure 13.1)?

Ethnography will have to play a major proactive role in disaster events in the widest possible sense: analyze the social, economic, historical, legal, and political context within which disasters develop; and, finally, explain how the restoration of "normal" life conditions are to be pursued by different private and institutional actors. Reconstruction based on current concepts of integrity and

Figure 13.1 A warning to potential looters copying FEMA's X search codes ("Katrina crosses") to suggest four looters have been shot already. New Orleans, LA, Hurricane Katrina, 2005. Photograph by the author.

Figure 13.2 Warning drivers to fear voodoo in the aftermath. Plaquemines Parish, LA, Hurricane Katrina, 2005. Photograph by the author.

the fifty-year rule is inadequate to safeguard places that are labeled as significant according to local community definitions. The site and its structure are central to visualizing a community's heritage. Whatever intangible aspects are related are expressed in relation to the specific site or affected area. Post-disaster displays of resilience in Louisiana after Hurricane Katrina and Hurricane Sandy in New Jersey consisted of teddy bears, dolls, flags, and collections of salvaged items, and, especially, written communications (Figure 13.2).

Mixed into the array of physical and verbal displays at shattered sites were FEMA's first responders' uses of X-codes on houses to designate conditions of the structures and of the people within them (Figure 13.3). FEMA first responders were communicating to rescue teams that came later but the owners' displays of objects and verbal pronouncements and their interpretations are not always obvious in meaning. Since everyone had fled to other parts of the country it was not possible to interview the authors of the displays and communications. But, certainly, residents constructed memories and narratives of their unique experiences out of the Hurricane Katrina X's and verbal and physical displays (Miller 2011, 54; Moye 2010).

Figure 13.3 Christmas crèche in front of St. Thomas Church as symbol of rebirth. Plaquemines Parish, LA, Hurricane Katrina, 2005. Photograph by the author.

Truncating Heritage in Favor of High Culture Forms

The situation regarding architectural mitigation across Louisiana after Hurricane Katrina ravaged the state "provides a good example of the failure of agencies to recognize the utility of TCPs as a way of understanding the significance of the human–space relationship," so concluded Morgan et al., in an analysis of the US government's attempts at preservation in the central Gulf Coast (Morgan et al. 2006, 716). Furthermore,

> When local, state, and federal officials and the nonprofit preservation sector first sought to calculate the hurricane's impact on heritage resources, they initially turned to the inventories of historic properties maintained by the states and the federal government. It quickly became apparent that most places the hurricane damaged or destroyed were not included in such inventories and, in fact, had never been considered for placement in them. There simply was no record of many of the common places whose loss people mourned, whose loss threatened that most intangible and critical sense of place tying people to their community and to the landscape.
>
> (Morgan et al. 2006, 716)

Many towns were not adequately documented with preference given to so-called "significant architecture" that maintained integrity. Very few of such "insignificant houses" ever gained NRHP stature, meaning that most of them never entered any comprehensive architectural inventory. This

Figure 13.4 During my six-month FEMA assignment, this teddy bear by Raritan Bay was well looked after and never taken away. Front Street, Union Beach, NJ, Hurricane Sandy, 2012. Photograph by the author.

created two problems: "first, gaining direct assistance to recover from the impact of the hurricane, and second, having their community places recognized in the recovery efforts as locales of special significance to the people that lived there" (Morgan et al. 2006, 713).

Hired as an ethnographer by FEMA, I was tasked with researching churches in New Orleans's Lower 9th Ward. It quickly became obvious that identification of the churches was a difficult prospect: few are listed in the phonebook or the Internet; there are no complete membership records; some churches are not members of any church association; some homes are regular places of worship but do not have outside signs; and some are reluctant to use the name Spiritual in the name of their church because of negative association some people hold with the group and its voodoo rituals (Figure 13.4). One source says there may be as many as 200 Spiritualist churches in New Orleans. Interviewing its inhabitants surely would have been the only way to identify them as even FEMA's "Action Plan for the Lower 9th Ward" had suggested to do but likely never did (Dawdy 2005). FEMA was aware that in order to accurately pinpoint significant structures access to the refugees was needed, which would have required reaching out to countless cities across the country where they had resettled. But that did not happen.

In the case of post-Katrina New Orleans, where tens of thousands of homes were destroyed, focusing research on folk forms alone has become very difficult as so few have survived. In Louisiana, whole areas have disappeared that the state had not previously inventoried. Yet, people live in other types of housing that architectural historians dismissed as not significant and folklorists ignored because they lacked folk forms. What is left in many areas is the so-called "insignificant architecture" of mass production housing with no obvious visible relation to the past. The norm for both folklorists and historians in their respective ways was to focus their documentation on select architectural forms—"significant because of integrity" specimens for architectural historians, and vernacular or folk for folklife specialists such as shotgun houses. Both were not interested in function. To safeguard architecture lacking proper qualities for inclusion on the National Register, governmental agencies providing monies for reconstructions must accept new interpretations of significance from the victim's perspective and not impose regulations that have no bearing on how and what a community wants reconstructed:

> How communities identity themselves is fluid and situational, as is the way in which community constituents define the relationship between themselves and the places they inhabit. Seemingly ordinary places underrepresented in the federal documentation process can be as important to the people who live in them as the properties that outside preservationists deem worthy of the National Register. As people began to assess the toll of the hurricane on their communities, residents, government officials, and preservation professionals grappled with the issue of how to mitigate hurricane damage in coastal and urban regions never before even considered for recognition in the federal system. This lacuna reflects an institutional misunderstanding of what makes the places we inhabit important.
>
> (Morgan et al. 2006, 715)

Oral History: Integrating Everyday Life

Oral history records the perspectives of individuals who might not otherwise appear in the historical record. Often it is insufficient to reconstruct a historical site from the written record alone. Informants can enrich our understanding of history by telling their version of events and interpret the traditional uses of particular objects and structures of specific landscapes or locate demolished buildings and their functions. "By giving voice to people not included in the usual historical sources, oral history can provide a fuller, more honest picture of the past by answering the how's and why's of human action" (Mercier and Buckendorf 1992, ii).

A Phase II archaeological investigation at the abandoned nineteenth-century Kalke Farmstead (Striker and Vidutis 1997) in preparation for the construction of gas storage facilities is a good example of the important role oral history plays in detailing the bits and pieces of a heritage site when working in teams. In this case, my use of oral history potentially prevented serious legal troubles for a company whose archaeologists misidentified vandalized grave markers for fieldstones during a walking survey of a field in the winter time that was part of the area of potential effect. My interview with a Kalke Farmstead neighbor about the history of the area identified the surveyed field as a cemetery that was not recorded on any historical maps.

Future Strategies: An Ethnography of Advocacy

Historic preservation and CRM approaches already perform intensive documentations that include physical descriptions, architectural and engineering drawings, and photographs. But ethnographic approaches do not just add to the architectural, and more broadly to landscape description, but actually show how place-based descriptions are the bases for chronological and social change—the form is defined in terms of function through time, its uses and meaning to inhabitants. The power of ethnography is in its ability to document through individual examination—interviews, observation, participation, recordings, collections.

In the last few years, there has been a growing desire by folklorists to actively participate in CRM work. The venue chosen is the concept of the TCP to fill out the spectrum of ethnicities that up until now have been almost exclusively used in documenting indigenous traditional places. TCPs have the

MISSED OPPORTUNITIES

potential to highlight people's voices from any community to mark what is significant to them personally. But there is more to CRM than just TCPs. Although folklorists are seeking entry into CRM to "better position folklorists and folklore methodologies as central forces in historic preservation" (Summers 2013, 1), how will they play a role in the industry? How are folklife specialists going to insert themselves into mindsets that prepare CRM reports without feeling the need to employ ethnographers? Are ethnographers willing to develop working relationships with other disciplines and differing perspectives on history and culture?

After Hurricane Katrina hit the Gulf Coast ethnographers stayed out and, in the case of folklorists, only recorded refugee escape stories. There should have been a serious effort at "urgent ethnography" to quickly deal with the disaster zone, interview refugees about the makeup of their devastated communities, about both tangible and intangible values associated with significant social places. Instead, there was the slow science of scholarly inaction to publish much later erudite analyses that function more as memorials instead of providing people with an immediate voice. For example, *Second Line Rescue: Improvised Responses to Katrina and Rita* (Ancelot et al. 2013), a project based in Houston, interviewed numerous escapees from New Orleans, where a large population fled especially from the Lower 9th Ward. Remarkably, questions for refugees about important cultural and social locations of the lost homeland were not developed. At the moment of such deep crisis as losing one's home and even family members, the fate of the community and how to resurrect it must be foremost in the escapee's mind. Yet, the interviewers were interested only in stories about how people escaped, lived through the hurricane, and devised survival skills in the face of governmental ineptitude in providing help to hurricane victims. A remarkable moment for remembrance was lost.

But along with the ethnographic methods that folklorists want to bring to the table, they will also need to develop a savvy understanding of Section 106, which is a procedural law. During the Section 106 review, the ethnographer would have to commit his expertise and methodology in the dialogue between interested parties such as the federal agency, the community, the State Historic Preservation Officer, and local consulting parties. As Thomas King has put it, it is more "action anthropology" than ethnography and requires the ethnographer to help the people engage and make the preservation system work for them. This may become the major role that the ethnographer will play in CRM. The passage of amendments to NHPA to demand more ethnography in CRM products would be a major step in strengthening the community's input and recognizing their perceptions in determining significance. But of even greater possible impact on the humanization of CRM work is the cooperative work that occurs in teams of different disciplines and foci. Will CRM allow for such destabilizing changes?

Conclusion

It seems clear that Cultural Resources Management as practiced today across the country is inadequate to faithfully mitigate the cultural landscape to suit all of its inhabitants. Section 106 and the Criteria of Evaluation are simply out of date having been developed at a quieter time when the climate and humans were less destructive and society was less demanding in what should be saved in its name by vested cultural specialists who come from outside and only see artifacts and categories. Times are changing and to leave the definition of culture solely in the hands of historians and archaeologists cuts off the people's demanding voice to decide the definitions for their communities. Heritage Studies, which considers significant any object, site, or feeling expressed by people has a great potential to democratize preservation at every level of the social scale. Ethnographers may be the only ones who can fix the problem in preservation through the simple act of talking with people about who they are, what they want, and observing their activities. But ethnographers have to be prepared to work alongside others in the field if they are to spot those areas that cry out for recognition. That is just one half of the problem. The other half is whether CRM will allow community definitions to decide criteria of evaluation when it is ethnographers who cite them for inclusion. But ethnographers have to be trained to work within CRM in teams on every project that comes along and not just on the more glamorous TCP tickets. Holistic ethnography is more than just documentation of expressive culture and is about all forms of human activity. Under Heritage Studies, cultural disciplines have the potential to learn from each other's perspectives and create a community-based approach to heritage management in the service of all members of society.

Notes

1 A traditional cultural property, then, can be defined generally as one that is eligible for inclusion in the National Register because of its association with cultural practices or beliefs of a living community that (a) are rooted in that community's history, and (b) are important in maintaining the continuing cultural identity of the community (National Register Bulletin 38: *Guidelines for Evaluating and Documenting Traditional Cultural Properties*, Parker and King 1990). Bulletin 38 broadened the range of properties possible for eligibility and listing in the National Register of Historic Places that up to then were being overlooked "by preservationist and/or the government despite their significance to contemporary peoples" (Lusignan 2009, 37).
2 The lack of TCPs in Louisiana is remarkable when considering the state is one of the richest locations of folk cultures in the country. Yet, a working relationship between SHPO and Louisiana arts councils has never been developed until now.
3 ICOMOS (International Council on Monuments and Sites) is an advisory body to the World Heritage Committee on cultural heritage issues regarding world heritage sites.

References

2020 Colorado Statewide Preservation Plan. (2010). "The Power of Heritage and Place: A 2020 Action Plan to Advance Preservation in Colorado." www.historycolorado.org/sites/default/files/files/OAHP/Programs/StatePlan.pdf

Alanen, Arnold R., and Robert Z. Melnick. (2000). *Preserving Cultural Landscapes in America*. Baltimore: Johns Hopkins University Press.

Ancelot, Barry J. et al., eds. (2013). *Second Line Rescue. Improvised Responses to Katrina and Rita*. Jackson: University of Mississippi Press.

Antonson, Jo. (2014). Deputy SHPO, Alaska State Historian. December 9. Personal communication.

Bates, Diane C. (2016). *Superstorm Sandy. The Inevitable Destruction and Reconstruction of the Jersey Shore*. New Brunswick, NJ: Rutgers University Press.

Bulger, Peggy. (2002). "Looking Back, Moving Forward: The Development of Folklore as a Public Profession." *Presidential Plenary Address*. American Folklore Society (AFS) meeting, Rochester, NY.

Carter, Thomas, and Carl Fleischhauer. (1988). *Grouse Creek Cultural Survey: Integrating Folklife and Historic Preservation Field Research*. Library of Congress, Washington, DC.

Correia, Jay. (2014). State Historian III, Supervisor, Registration Unit. California SHPO. December 11. Personal communication.

Dawdy, Shannon Lee. (2005). FEMA/SHPO Liaison. "Action Plan for the Lower Ninth Ward. FEMA Historic Preservation." November 26.

Dorson, Richard M. (1973). "Concepts of Folklore and Folklife Studies." In *Folklore and Folklife, an Introduction*, edited by A.M. Dorson. Chicago and London: The University of Chicago Press.

"Eureka Fire Museum." (2017). Milltown Fire Department. www.milltownfire.org/page/view/3715

Feintuch, Burt, ed. (1988). *The Conservation of Culture: Folklorists and the Public Sector.* Publication of the American Folklore Society, New Series, edited by Larry Danielson, Vol. 5. Lexington: University Press of Kentucky.

Glassie, Henry. (1975). *Folk Housing in Middle Virginia.* Knoxville: University of Tennessee Press.

Govaerts, Lotte, and Meghan Mulkerin. (2014). "How the River Basin Surveys Shaped Historical Archaeology." September 10. www.nmnh.typepad.com/rogers_archaeology_lab/2014/09/rbsshapedhistoricalarchaeology.html

Guerrant, Alice H. (2011). Research Center Manager. Delaware Division of Historical and Cultural Affairs. June 30. Personal communication.

House of Representatives. (1980). Report No. 96–1457 (Commission on Interior and Insular Affairs), Title III, Section 502. (96th Cong., 2d Sess., 1980)

Howard, Barbara. (2014). Director, Historic Preservation Department, Minnesota Historical Society. December 15. Personal communication.

Hufford, Mary. (1986). *One Space, Many Places: Folklife and Land Use in New Jersey's Pinelands.* Washington, DC: American Folklife Center, Library of Congress.

"ICOMOS. (2017). Guidance on Post Trauma Recovery and Reconstruction for World Heritage Cultural Properties." International Council on Monuments and Sites. Paris.

King, Thomas F. (2002). *Thinking about Cultural Resource Management: Essays from the Edge.* Walnut Creek, CA: AltaMira Press.

King, Thomas F. (2011). Archaeologist. Silver Spring, Maryland. Personal communication. Oct 8.

King, Thomas F. (2013). Comments on National Register Bulletin 38. www.nps.gov/nr/publications/guidance/TCP_PublicComments/Tom_King_NRB_38_Reading_text.pdf

Lee, Dayna Bowker. (2015). Senior Historian and Ethnographer. Earth Search, Inc. New Orleans, LA. November 5. Personal communication.

Lindahl, Kathleen. (2011). Senior State Archaeologist. Archaeology, History & Museums Division. California State Parks. October 31. Personal communication.

Liverman, Astrid. (2014). National and State Register Coordinator, History Colorado. December 10. Personal communication.

Loomis, Ormond. (1983). *Cultural Conservation: The Protection of Cultural Heritage in the United States.* Washington, DC: Library of Congress.

Lowenthal, David. (1985). *The Past is a Foreign Country.* Cambridge: Cambridge University Press.

Lusignan, Paul R. (2009). Historian, National Register of Historic Places. "Traditional Cultural Places and the National Register." *Traditional Cultural Properties: Putting Concept into Practice*, 26(1):37–44. The George Wright Forum. www.georgewright.org/261lusignan.pdf

Marion. (2013). "Cultural Resources Management: A $1 Billion Industry." Cultural Heritage Partners. Law-Policy-Strategy. www.culturalheritagepartners.com/cultural-resources-management-a-1-billion-industry/

Mercier, Lauie, and Madeline Buckendorf. (1992). *Using Oral History in Community History Projects.* Oral History Association Pamphlet, Series #4. Oral History Association.

Miller, Charles Alan. (2011). *X Marks the Spot: Decoding the Hurricane Katrina 'X' through Urban Memory of New Orleans Residents.* Tulane University, A Thesis Submitted to the Graduate Faculty of the University of Georgia (Master of Arts). www.getd.libs.uga.edu/pdfs/miller_charles_a_201308_ma.pdf

Mitchell, Christi. (2014). National Register Coordinator, Maine Historic Preservation Commission. December 16. Personal communication.

Morgan, David W., Nancy I. M. Morgan, and Brenda Barrett. (2006). "Finding a Place for the Commonplace: Hurricane Katrina, Communities, and Preservation Law." *American Anthropologist*, 108(4):711–715. www.sonoma.edu/users/p/purser/Anth590/katrinacommon.pdf

Moye, Dorthy. (2010). "Katrina + 5: An X-Code Exhibition." Photo Essay. August 26. www.southernspaces.org/2010/katrina-5-x-code-exhibition#footnote3_ztzc2pf

The National Historic Preservation Act (NHPA) of 1966, as amended. Section 502 (16 U.S.C. 470a note) www.gsa.gov/graphics/pbs/nhpa.pdf

Olmo, Richard. (2014). Guam Department of Parks and Recreation. December 15. Personal communication.

Parker, Patricia L. and Thomas F. King. (1990). National Register Bulletin 38: *Guidelines for Evaluating and Documenting Traditional Cultural Properties*. Washington, DC: U.S. Department of the Interior, National Park Service, Interagency Resources Division.

Reid, Kenneth C. (2014). State Archaeologist and Deputy Idaho SHPO. December 12. Personal communication.

Siegel, David. (2011). Regional Historic Preservation Officer. U.S. Fish and Wildlife Service - Southwest Region. August 11. Personal communication.

Striker, Michael, and Richard Vidutis, Historian. (1997). "The Kalke Farmstead: A Two-Part Report on the History and Architecture of the Kalke Farmstead and Phase I and Phase II Archaeological Investigations at Site 36-Ti-109 and 36-Ti-110, Tioga County, Pennsylvania." 3D/International, Environmental Group, Cincinnati, Ohio. Submitted to Market Hub Partners, LLP, Houston, Texas.

Summers, Laurie Kay. (2016). "Integrating Folklore and Historic Preservation Policy: Toward a Richer Sense of Place." American Folklore Society. www.afsnet.org/?page=FHPPolicyPaper#

Unsigned, Indiana. (2011). Response to use of TCP's.

Vidutis, Richard, Historian. (1993). "Desert Queen Ranch (William F. Keys Ranch)." Joshua Tree National Monument, 29 Palms, CA. Report: HABS CA-2347. Historic American Buildings Survey, National Park Service, Washington, DC. www.cdn.loc.gov/master/pnp/habshaer/ca/ca1700/ca1799/data/ca1799data.pdf

Vidutis, Richard, Historian. (2002). "Roaring Creek Bridge, State Road 2005 Spanning Roaring Creek in Locust Township, Slabtown, Columbia County, PA." Report: HAER PA-631. Historic American Engineering Record, National Park Service, Washington, DC. www.cdn.loc.gov/master/pnp/habshaer/pa/pa3900/pa3999/data/pa3999data.pdf

Vidutis, Richard, Historian. (2013). Site Visit Notes. FEMA-DR-4086-MJ [Hurricane Sandy]. Willow Grove Cemetery, Cheesman Cemetery, and Presbyterian Cemetery, New Brunswick, NJ.

Vidutis, Richard, Historian. (2016). Missouri SHPO Consultation Letter. DR-4250-MO [Missouri Ozark Floods], Bowers Mill Bridge, Bowers Mill Township, Lawrence County, MO FEMA NHPA compliance submission-Project PA-07-MO-4250-RPA-0212, June 10.

Wilkerson, W. D. (2010). "Losing Ground. The Cultural Landscapes in Plaquemines Parish." In *Culture after the Hurricanes. Rhetoric and Reinvention on the Gulf Coast,* edited by M. B. Hackler, 139–165. Jackson: University Press of Mississippi.

Wofford, Lee Anne. (2014). Deputy SHPO, Historic Preservation Division Director. Personal communication.

PART 4

The Role of Higher Education in Leading Evidence-based Practice

CHAPTER 14

"But Where Are the People?" Grappling with Teaching New Approaches to Our Relationship with Place and the Past

Michelle Jolly, Melinda Milligan, Margaret Purser, and Laura Alice Watt

Teaching together was an idea the four of us had been kicking around for several years. Four professors from four different departments—anthropology, environmental studies, history, and sociology—with a common focus on communities' sense of place, history, and identity as expressed through cultural heritage. In part because of this shared interest, we each felt a bit like outliers in our own disciplines and were drawn toward collaborating across the usual institutional boundaries. So, when our Dean offered a small amount of seed money to develop cross-disciplinary team-taught courses, we jumped at the chance to work together, to develop a course that would encourage our students to think differently about the past and its connection to place and community.

Why us? While none of us are "typical" public historians or heritage practitioners, we each bring a unique relationship to the traditions of heritage studies: a historical anthropologist using material culture and community-based mapping to give voice to local community priorities in the context of official cultural heritage policy; an environmental historian borrowing landscape theory from cultural geography to analyze the ways in which landscape preservation efforts actually change what is being preserved; a historian interested in broadening the number of voices and perspectives involved in representing the ways in which we talk—and teach—about the past; and a sociologist versed in place attachment studying the relationships of historic preservation and gentrification. Heritage is a topic we each study in one form or another, and over time we had each become intrigued by the connections—or the lack thereof—between the scholarship of social sciences and the kinds of heritage practices we encountered in a variety of both United States and international communities. Yet, none of our departments' course offerings reflected anything of these topics.

Hence, we decided to co-develop a course that explored the ways in which people use places to tell stories about the past and about themselves. Deceptively simple-sounding, this fundamental human process has taken on new and potent significance in a world grappling with schisms over the reality of global warming and climate change, deteriorating natural and built environments, increasingly globalized and diasporic human populations, and deeply contested definitions of and rights to heritage and identity. While these are vast, international processes, they play out at very localized and everyday scales, in our neighborhoods, communities, and the surrounding region.

The result became an upper-division undergraduate course titled "Shared Places, Contested Pasts: Historical Memory and Historic Preservation," which we have now offered twice, three years apart. In developing and revising the course material, the four of us have decided that the transformation of heritage practice into a broader, more human-centered approach requires, first, a transformation in thinking. Practitioners and consumers alike can benefit from a conversation about what we are trying to conserve: What is cultural heritage? Who makes choices about what to preserve? Why is preservation done the way it is? How might different priorities, cultural practices, or paradigms change what and how we preserve? How are the meanings of fundamental concepts like "authenticity" and "significance" changing over time and in response to different cultural practices? In short, what are the underlying ideas and assumptions that shape preservation practices?

These are fundamentally social scientific questions, concerned with how humans create meaning, in this case, around place and past. They are not, as Robert Russell (2014) points out, the kinds of questions typically explored within the confines of a historic environment graduate degree program, where the focus is primarily on training students to use the legal tools and processes involved in preservation practice. But they are questions appropriate to a university classroom, nevertheless. Put another way, we wanted to engage students in an investigation of people-centered place and preservation theory in a course that would be collaborative, multi-disciplinary, and multi-vocal from the start.

In tackling this co-teaching challenge, we four have grappled with a number of the issues raised in this volume, and we believe that our experiences with this course can help shed some light onto the ways in which we collectively need to re-think training in heritage studies. It is not enough to expect heritage professionals to absorb social science literature, nor can we disregard academic theory as belonging only to the ivory tower. A critically informed and deeply applied approach is needed, and preparing our students for this kind of integrated conversation about heritage is itself a challenge—in part because many undergraduates do not yet have a strong sense of their own disciplines, much less of the perspectives of others. Yet, we found that the key lies in asking students to *think* differently, not just implement a new methodology or technique. They need to learn not only the logic of social science but also to see it working in practice, in an integrated, interdisciplinary fashion—which, in large part, turns out to rest in changing their habits of mind, teaching them to worry less about finding answers and more about asking questions. And we believe there is a larger lesson for heritage scholars and practitioners alike.

The Challenge before Us in Heritage Education

"How should we train students in historic environment degree programs to implement human-centered theory in the practice of conserving the historic environment?" (Wells and Stiefel, 2016). This urgent question emerges from a transformation that has been taking place, not only in the field of historic preservation, but in a variety of cultural heritage fields concerned with preserving places for aesthetic and historical reasons. Partly in response to David Lowenthal's *The Past is A Foreign Country* (1985), the focus has shifted from a fabric-centered to a human-centered approach to conservation. However, the changing perspective among heritage scholars has not moved as easily to common practice, which continues to be somewhat bound by the traditional constraints of preservation law and practices developed primarily in response to filling out bureaucratic forms. Scholars and practitioners, such as those in this volume, continue to struggle with questions of "how human-centered conservation theory can and should change practice" (Wells and Stiefel, 2016).

In that context, we must consider the question of heritage education, not only for those students who are practitioners-in-training, but also for those who become social scientists as well as the (future) members of communities, and thus the consumers of cultural heritage conservation. To the extent that heritage practitioners do not, and increasingly will not, simply control meanings associated with historical "fabric," but facilitate "the gathering and interpretation of meanings from people as well as empowering communities to recognize, treat, and interpret their built heritage and cultural landscapes" (Wells and Stiefel, 2016), they must learn to collaborate with other stakeholders concerned with heritage conservation. This includes practitioners from a variety of contexts, academic social scientists, and community members. So, the questions must be framed more broadly: How should we train undergraduate and graduate students to think about human relationships to the past through place, to consider how we go about conserving these places and their multiple meanings to different groups of people, and to recognize the value of collaboration among various stakeholders in the important process of conserving cultural heritage? How can we use the classroom to engage both future heritage practitioners *and* future heritage consumers (donors, visitors, users, and community partners) in a conversation about place, past, identity, and preservation that can lay the groundwork for future collaboration? How might such classroom conversations foster the implementation of human-centered theory in the practice of conserving the historic environment?

These sorts of questions demand that we recognize the changed context in which experts interested in cultural heritage (whether practitioners or academics) increasingly operate. Interest in human-centered theories raises questions about standing—who has standing in the discussion about what we preserve and how we preserve it? Traditionally, heritage practitioners, wielding the policies and guidelines laid out in a plethora of legal frameworks, have claimed the primary expertise in such discussions. Familiar with federal, state, and municipal-level laws and procedures, they have been both the midwives and the gatekeepers to the process of heritage preservation. Inspired by Lowenthal's *The Past is a Foreign Country* and the many similar critiques that have followed it, some in heritage research have argued against this hierarchy of experts, downplaying "orthodox practices as overly reliant on expert rule and positivistic, top-down processes while advocating for a more values-centered, ground-up approach to practice that empowers more stakeholders" (Avrami, Mason, and Torre, 2000; Carman and Sørensen, 2009; Gibson and Pendlebury, 2009; Green, 1998; Harrison, 2013; Lixinski, 2015; Low, 1994; Smith, 2006; Waterton and Smith, 2010; Winter, 2013). Much of this discussion was happening across a very broad international policy context, with UNESCO's World Heritage List serving as both a context for developing new, integrative approaches, and also as a focus of critique by those seeking even broader community-based and collaborative approaches. Examples would include statements such as the "Nara + 20: On Heritage Practices, Cultural Values, And The Concept Of Authenticity" that radically reframed the role of communities in heritage conservation by acknowledging the inevitable "evolution of cultural values," and the process of change in heritage management (Japan ICOMOS National Committee, 2014). Discussions expanded in U.S. government policy publications as well, including the National Park Service's CRM Bulletin, renamed "CRM: The Journal of Heritage Stewardship" in 2003 and published for the subsequent eight years, specifically to "broaden the intellectual foundation of the management of cultural resources" (National Park Service, 2015). As this literature expanded, many scholars and practitioners alike began to argue that practitioners needed to be re-educated, taught to adopt new modes of thinking about preservation, and trained to use social science methodology to incorporate more stakeholders and modify their practice.

The extent to which heritage consumers are recognized as having standing in these conversations is unclear. On the one hand, individual property holders are empowered by the National Historic Preservation Act (NHPA) to join the conversation about preservation if their property meets the requirements. On the other hand, even in more human-centered theory, practitioners and social scientists still generally control the conversation about preservation, who participates in it, and how that conversation takes place. However, even a brief survey of current American popular discourse reveals a multitude of debates about the present framed in terms of the past: whether or not to display the Confederate flag; the historical antecedents for individual property rights over collective ones in Western public lands; personal opinions of the "founding fathers" about everything from Constitutional originalism to the separation of church and state; the rights of African-Americans to restitution for slavery. When examined at state or local levels, this list could be expanded nearly infinitely. Some heritage professionals have embraced this new role for society's collective memory, and have begun to define a framework for heritage interpretation that serves as a platform for civic engagement (Little and Shackel, 2014).

In such contexts, questions about standing, as well as the roles and responsibilities of experts, come to the fore once again. But they also reinforce the need for educational programs that are aimed at creating an intellectually enfranchised public that can actively engage in a discussion about the meaning of its shared or contested pasts. Yet, for social scientists to demand a change from fabric-centered to human-centered practices, and a retraining of heritage practitioners accordingly, is—as has already been made clear—not simple or realistic to implement at the present time. For one thing, while practitioners (and their bosses) may recognize the limitations of current practice, challenging existing law and policy from within is a process that moves exceedingly slowly, if at all. Local-scale modifications of practice, in places where practitioners have successfully contested the existing regulations, constitute a piecemeal approach to change and rarely result in broader revisions of the law (Morgan, Morgan, and Barrett, 2006). Human-centered theory might transform how we practice preservation—but not without changes to the law and mandated procedures. It is easy to dismiss such ideas as "pie in the sky." Moreover, practitioners are already too few in number and overworked trying to preserve the places and stories about the past that are already in the queue. To ask them to learn social science methodologies and apply them to their work oversimplifies both the nature of heritage practice and social science methodologies, which experts spend years learning to use.

But there is a larger problem than (simple or not-so simple) practicality. Social scientists whose work is in, or intersects with, heritage studies are themselves figuring out which methodologies are most useful for gathering and interpreting meanings from people and engaging communities in recognizing, interpreting, and preserving their built heritage and cultural landscapes. It turns out that the familiar methodologies that social scientists (in fields such as anthropology, archaeology, sociology, history, and environmental studies) have used in the study of place and past do not necessarily adapt easily to new ideas of human-centered preservation. As we change our thinking about place, past, identity, community, and preservation, so the methodologies change and adapt. This process of adaptation makes training practitioners to use "the" methodologies a challenging proposition, as the methods themselves are something of a moving target. Perhaps even more importantly, it means that the current learning curve is steep for both heritage practitioners and a wide range of social scientists trying to work in this arena.

Much of the new thinking and new practice emphasizes the importance of collaboration. This is also something we are learning how to do across the entire professional spectrum of heritage research. Neither academics nor heritage practitioners are necessarily very good at it, particularly when collaboration involves engaging in sometimes-difficult conversations with multiple stakeholders regarding questions of place, past, and preservation. But the fact that we have to do it opens up a broader approach to how we encourage the implementation of human-centered theory in the practice of conserving the historic environment. Specifically, perhaps we need to focus on collaboration even more than we already do.

In particular, social scientists and heritage practitioners could work *together* to implement more social science in preservation practice. The labor required for this transformation is clearly more than either profession can bear alone. And the benefits are mutual. Social scientists and heritage practitioners might both learn how to collaborate more effectively with community members. Perhaps even more importantly, the resulting work might mean that community members—the broad range of heritage "consumers," including not only stakeholders in specific decisions but also donors, visitors, volunteers, and users of cultural heritage sites—might come to see both heritage practitioners and social scientists as collaborative partners in the broader project of conserving significant places and telling meaningful stories about the past.

This brings us back to the "Shared Places, Contested Pasts" course that the four of us taught, first in the Spring of 2012 and again in Spring 2015, as one possible solution to the problem. Our interdisciplinary teaching experience suggests ways in which we can use the classroom to engage both future heritage practitioners *and* future heritage consumers in conversation about place, past, identity, and preservation, which can lay the groundwork for future collaboration, and how such classroom conversations might foster the implementation of human-centered theory in the practice of conserving the historic environment.

"Shared Places, Contested Pasts"

Sonoma State University is a medium-sized public university, part of the California State University system. Primarily an undergraduate institution—although it has some strong graduate programs, including History and one of the oldest Cultural Resources Management (CRM) programs in the country—Sonoma State fosters an atmosphere of small faculty-led classes and encourages faculty to connect their scholarship with the classroom as well as with surrounding communities. Academic departments are also small, so faculty members often forge intellectual connections across department lines. Even given this context, though, our class, spanning four separate departments, is unique.

We have now taught this course, "Shared Places/Contested Pasts: Historical Memory and Historic Preservation," twice to about 150 total students. These students came from many majors—primarily anthropology, environmental studies and planning, history, and sociology—but also others, including undeclared students. The students also ranged in class level from freshman to senior and included ten to fifteen percent graduate students from CRM and History in each class. Of these students, some took the class because they were in training to become cultural heritage practitioners or hoped to do this work after graduation. Others took it because they had taken a course from one of the professors before or found the topic interesting in relation to their major. And a fair number took the course simply because it was an elective class with open seats. So, students' prior knowledge and expectations regarding the course content varied widely.

Though they formed a small minority of the enrolled students, we felt that including the CRM students, in particular, would give us an opportunity to begin to diversify that program's curriculum in important ways. Two successive program reviews (in 2008 and 2013) had resulted in significant input from local professionals, government agencies, and program alumni now working in the field, all indicating a strong need for graduates with skills in community-based project development, stakeholder consultation, and a broader interdisciplinary background. A new graduate field school in Heritage Management had been added to the curriculum in 2009, focused on community-based research methods. Including CRM students in the "Shared Places" course experiment allowed us to continue broadening the curriculum in advance of new faculty hires and a complete curriculum revision, now underway in 2017.

Our goal, in each iteration of "Shared Places/Contested Pasts," was to lead a class of students on an intellectual journey, an investigation of the questions that underlie cultural heritage conservation, and to engage them in the hands-on investigation of how local communities preserve their cultural heritage and, thus, tell stories about their past. What we discovered, however, was that developing and teaching this course was its own intellectual journey, a microcosm of the experience cultural heritage professionals and scholars are grappling with. The class, both for us and for the students, modeled the conundrum that cultural heritage practitioners also face of operating in the liminal space between asking the new questions and knowing how to answer them. Working with our students, helping them shift their thinking from a focus on the products of preservation (fabric-centered) to the *process* of preservation (people-centered), pushed us to think harder about how professionals (both practitioners and scholars) are engaged in this same transition—and to grapple with some of the ways in which we all need to collaborate to make this transition together.

We started with the premise that in order to learn about how place, past, community, and preservation intersect, students would need to combine theory and practice. So, led by the team of faculty members from a variety of social science disciplines, students engaged in a multi-disciplinary study of social scientific theory about place, past, and community through readings, lectures, discussions, and written assignments. At the same time, over the course of the semester, students worked in multi-disciplinary teams to study several sites in local communities to observe how cultural heritage practitioners and city planners had used historic sites, neighborhoods, and landscapes to tell stories about the past and about their community in the present. Throughout the course, we sought to both model and encourage collaboration, interdisciplinarity, and attention to multi-vocality.

Theory: Multi-Disciplinary Social Science Content

To begin, we wanted our students to be well-grounded in multi-disciplinary social scientific theory about place, past, and heritage management. The broader conversation about how communities link their sense of place and the past now weaves through a wide variety of disciplinary literatures, demanding an interdisciplinary approach. However, our understanding of how to convey this conversation had to change significantly over the two iterations of the course as we discovered the challenges students have in engaging with multiple disciplinary perspectives.

This part of the course structure was quite conventional, and on the face of it might seem like the most straightforward component of the course, the most familiar to students—you do the reading, you come to class for lecture, you take notes, and you write papers about what you learned. The only added dimension was to have this material presented by four different faculty from four different disciplinary perspectives (history, sociology, anthropology, and environmental studies). Certainly, when we first taught the course, we did not foresee any particular difficulties with this presentation of the content. From our perspective, what we saw were strongly convergent discussions about key issues affecting this shared field and relating directly to practice. These included the potent ideological role of historical narratives and narrative construction, the challenges to professional notions of accuracy and authenticity created by community collaboration approaches, the move towards more community-based and future-oriented practices of stewardship and sustainability in the management of significant places and resources, and the ethical considerations raised when professionals find themselves negotiating between contested historical narratives and claims to place, or confronted with demands to privilege the stories people like over the facts the record reveals.

However, we underestimated the challenges this multi-disciplinary, theory-based course posed to students. Students from different departments struggled with the multi-disciplinary nature of the content, which meant that some significant part of the course readings and lectures inevitably felt alien to a large part of the class. In addition, they struggled to place themselves as any kind of active participants in the larger conversation. They mostly did not see themselves as "historians," "anthropologists," or "sociologists," but even more importantly, they often could not see the different readings and case studies as part of any larger, developing discussion of ideas at all—many students perceived each article as a unique, stand-alone statement.

Once we realized this, we took steps to address it, building more explicit discussion of discipline-based perspectives into lectures. We clarified how the different disciplines relate to and support (or not) one another around questions of place, past, and community. We also built in a clearer explanation of how our own research, which we presented to the students as case studies, draws on interdisciplinary insights. In short, we tried to be as transparent as possible about disciplinary ways of knowing in order to support students who were unused to seeing this structure that underlies the ways of thinking they learn. Rather than assume that students could read any kind of social science article with facility, we learned that they need support in teasing out the structure of the articles, being able to recognize important points, and being able to connect them to each other.

Practice: Site Observation Assignment

Being exposed to social scientific thinking—even through examples of how other scholars approach questions of place, past, and community identity—is not enough to change students' thinking or teach them how to use these modes of thought in their own work. For that, they must use the concepts they are learning in applied situations. But in this four-unit, interdisciplinary elective course, there was no way to teach students a comprehensive set of social scientific field methods, nor could we send them out to do archaeological digs, photo analysis, focus groups, or other research that might allow them to study places and people's relationship to them directly. These discipline-specific social science skills would be taught in methods classes in the students' majors or maybe only later in graduate school. Instead, we worked with students to develop a toolkit of social science techniques and habits of mind that they could use to look at sites where people have been engaged in place-making and story-telling in a community, evaluate their work, and thereby see the intentionality and structure through which communities tell stories. In other words, they would apply social scientific thinking and observational skills, learned through their theoretical reading and case studies, to an analysis of the ways in which practitioners in local communities are already telling stories about place and past—who is telling those stories? How are they being told? Which stories are included or, sometimes more importantly, excluded? How have cultural heritage professionals and city planners tried to use historic sites, neighborhoods, or landscapes to tell stories about the past and about their community in the present? How can we use the construction of these sites to find clues about community identity? These questions required students to ask people-centered questions about place and to apply the theoretical approaches they learned in class to the "fabric" they could find locally.

For this assignment, students were put into interdisciplinary teams of four and asked to choose a named municipality within sixty driving minutes of the university. Each team member was responsible for doing background research on that town or small city and then visiting four sites—a museum, historic park, neighborhood, and "natural" park or open space—conducting site observations, taking notes, and reporting back to their team. The site observations, for which we provided very detailed guidelines, asked students to observe the ways in which their chosen place represented its past in relationship to its community. For example, students might visit a local museum to examine which exhibits and artifacts were included, what stories were told, and how, or to what degree, these exhibits represented the community. This meant recognizing that a museum exhibit is not just a collection of artifacts but an intentional effort to tell a story—that what is included or excluded, how it is displayed, captioned, and so on all have significance. At the end of the semester, each team combined their individual observations to create a group presentation about how their particular community uses heritage, in the forms of both the built and natural environments, to tell stories about the past.

We expected students would be excited to be asked to do "real" research. Indeed, students are often quick to say that they wish their classes included more hands-on, real-world applications of knowledge. In practice, students found this kind of research daunting. There were practical challenges—most communities were at such distance as to require students to drive to visit sites, which sometimes meant they had to share cars, dragoon a friend into accompanying them, and/or take time off from work or sports. But the larger challenge was students' uncertainty about how to do this kind of observation: "The observation process for this class was unlike anything I have done in my other classes," remarked one student in our end-of-semester course evaluations. Another wrote, "I had trouble in regards to extracting stories from the built environment. I literally felt that I would have no idea what to look for."

Finding What to Look for: Bringing Theory and Practice Together

Supporting students through the site observations assignment was a challenge. On the one hand, we increased the amount of guidance we provided to students, giving them specific items to look for and framing each site type as well as we could. On the other hand, the problem was much bigger than clarifying the instructions. Drawing on their theoretical reading, students needed to recognize that places—buildings, parks, neighborhoods—tell stories that have been created by people for particular purposes and specific audiences. These stories are reflected in what geographer Peirce Lewis calls our "unintended autobiographies"—the built environment, the landscape, the choice of museum exhibits and site interpretations—and consequently they can be "read" by a careful observer (Lewis, 1979). This understanding is key to people-centered heritage study. And it proved to be extremely difficult for students to grasp.

First, students expected to see "fabric," not stories, in their community surroundings. They were primed, by previous experience, to see landscape features, storefronts, and street signs as "natural" parts of the landscape, not placed there intentionally. The idea that their surrounding environment was not simply "there," but actually represented people's ideas or aspirations, proved difficult to grasp—particularly in neighborhoods, which they tended to regard as simple accretions of daily life, and nature parks, where awareness of the managed nature of the landscape was almost entirely absent.

Second, students struggled with the fact that the community site studies they were assigned required them to look, not just for a story, but for evidence of *more than one* story about the past being told at a given local museum, historic site, park, or neighborhood. Nearly all of their previous academic experience had led them to expect a single authoritative narrative about "the truth of what happened," historically—THE history of a community. Students had a hard time grasping that museum exhibits, parks, and neighborhoods had "authors" at all, much less that there might have been multiple community perspectives included and/or excluded in the creation of such a place.

Third, when students were able to see how different perspectives were included or excluded, they perceived these differences for some groups more readily than others. For example, students were quick to point out ways in which museum exhibits, historic parks, and online histories of their community excluded Native Americans and, often, Spanish and Mexican settlers. But they were less able to recognize the absence of other groups (e.g. women) or a focus on particular time periods (e.g. 1870–1930) to the exclusion of others. This is one of the things we are still working on—how do you get students to see holes in the fabric, or hear voices that are not there? This is not only a key element of a people-centered approach, but it is also a particularly important concept for "heritage consumers" to be able to participate fully in any broader society discussion of the past and present, rather than presuming that there is only one story to know, or one perspective that is "right."

This assumption of a single authoritative narrative also colored many students' perception of the collaborative and interdisciplinary nature of the course. For example, from the professors' point of view, one of the best aspects of the course was the opportunity for all of us to be in the classroom together and teach together. Although one of us took the lead lecturing on each day, we were all there for every class, chimed in on discussions, and helped manage the classroom during small group work. To us, this looked like an opportunity to model collaboration and interdisciplinary discussion for the students—just the sort of work we want them to be able to do. In practice, it turned out that this leadership style looked less like collaboration and more like chaos to the students. They found it confusing—hard to see leadership and authority.

This messy, collaborative approach was—to some extent—meant to include the students as well. The students were conducting real research in interdisciplinary teams, not reproducing some project or standard paper done by many before them. So, we made it clear that the class itself was an ongoing discussion, a work in progress—yet, for some students, this approach seemed more threatening than exciting. After all, for students accustomed to classes in which the goal is to learn information and spit it back in an exam, a course in which there are no right answers and little concrete "information" may seem both pointless and deeply anxiety-provoking. Interestingly, this experience may sound familiar to heritage practitioners whose offers to collaborate with community members may be perceived not as openness to participation, but as incompetence. To help our students address this problem, we worked to make goals more clear and also encouraged students to see the class through, instead of dropping the course in frustration. Our experience is that students who make it to the "pay-off"—the ones whose collaborative, interdisciplinary teams present the fruits of their theoretical and practical work to each other—finally understand how theory and practice can come together to transform their understanding of place, past, and community.

Course Outcomes: Developing Heritage Practitioners and Consumers

How successful was the course in encouraging students to use social scientific thinking in the practice of cultural heritage conservation, whether as practitioners or as consumers? Students in the course who were already preparing to be CRM practitioners reported using what they learned fruitfully in their theses and internships, often taking lessons from the class directly into the field. For example, during and after the most recent iteration of the course, several CRM graduate students worked with one of our co-professors to set up a community mapping project to help local residents directly identify their own heritage and stories. We also have had some students come out of the class deciding to become cultural heritage practitioners. Notably, one student who took the first iteration of our course as a freshman—struggled with it, and won through—is now completing an MA thesis in History examining the ways in which a nearby conservation group is restructuring "the story" of a recently-acquired Sonoma County ranch to better conform with the group's own goals, overwriting the ranch owners' personal perspectives on the land in favor of a more standard wilderness narrative. He is currently applying to Ph.D. programs.

Finally, most students came out of the class not as future practitioners, of course, but as future *consumers* of cultural heritage—as visitors, donors, and/or community members. As our practice moves increasingly toward community-based heritage projects in which locals are deeply involved, it behooves us to encourage community members themselves to develop people-centered thinking about cultural heritage conservation. Many of these students said the course had dramatically changed the way they think; as one put it, "Most people these days simply are not interested in the history of where they are; they think it has little to no bearing on their current lives.... In fact, I've learned it is the exact opposite—it has everything to do with it. The events of the past molded and carved the area into what it is today, along with people's perceptions of it."

In and Beyond the Classroom: Social Sciences "Habits of Mind"

Writing this chapter together has brought the four of us back to an examination of what we taught and learned in "Shared Places, Contested Pasts." We have parsed piles of student course evaluations, old lecture notes, and handwritten scrawls in the margins of past syllabi containing cryptic messages about what to do differently next time. We have talked for hours about how what we saw during this experience parallels so much of the current discussions we all see in our four respective fields—and how the points of intersection amongst those myriad discussions are becoming more numerous, persistent, and nuanced.

From those discussions, we have identified four core aspects of what might be called "habits of mind" shared across many social sciences that can inform efforts to infuse historic preservation with a more people-centered theory and practice. As already discussed, these are not "methods" per se. It is unreasonable to expect busy practitioners to learn complex methodologies that take years to master, especially when those methods themselves are being transformed by the challenges created by a people-centered heritage framework. In fact, the assertion of a significant divide between mutually exclusive categories of "scholars" and "practitioners" appears more and more problematic in the face of this mutually transformative shift from fabric-centered to people-centered heritage. Many practitioners are developing increasingly sophisticated means of modifying practice, especially on a local scale, even when they cannot easily change the policy frameworks within which that practice occurs. Moreover, they are writing about those efforts, creating a broad dialogue on innovative programs, best practices, and policy critiques. Scholarship is changing in much the same way. New ideas and new interdisciplinary collaborations challenge old assumptions and create new venues for applying theoretical frameworks; for example, a new movement in the traditional fields of natural resources-focused conservation and land management strongly emphasizes public-private partnerships and other forms of community collaboration across many Western public lands (Charnley, Sheridan, and Nabham, 2015).

What we learned from teaching our students how to grapple with this process is that simultaneously asking new questions *while* figuring out how to answer them requires learning how to think differently, both about what you are doing and about why you are doing it. We have defined four related components of these habits of mind as particularly relevant to creating a more people-centered heritage practice.

Developing an Observational Stance That Is Critical, Reflexive, and Questioning

A fundamental assertion in social sciences is that knowledge is constructed and that a key aspect of what we are doing when we conduct our research is looking for that construction. This definitely applies to knowledge about the past, about places, and about the connections between the two. Conventional historic preservation practice catalogs places whose significance is evaluated by the careful documentation of historical facts. Asking questions about these facts, who they represent, and how individual places fit into any larger social context shifts the basis for evaluation from exclusively external, aesthetic or authoritative criteria to more inclusive, socially imbedded ones. This is not to say that the value of factual research and verification goes away. But this kind of stance changes what our facts and evidence are used for, and by whom.

Employing a Narrativist Analytical Framework

If knowledge is constructed, then it has an author—or more accurately, many authors—and a history structured as a conversation between and amongst them over time in a given place. This means not only learning to expect that there is a story but also to recognize that there is more than one. Learning to see the multi-vocality of community storytelling, and especially looking for the absence of some voices and some stories from the more public arenas of collective historical storytelling becomes part of the rationale for the "doing" of heritage practice. A significant part of our job becomes our ability to reflect back to a community the ways in which its narratives are authored, making their constructed nature more visible, and so more open to discussion.

Seeing Community as a Process

Communities clearly do not tell "a" story. Not only are there many versions of a community's narrative about its many pasts, but none of these stories are fixed. Instead, the contested voices, editorializing, and alternative storylines form an integral part of any community's ongoing process of defining its identity through its relationships to both past and place. This process of "imagining" community is messy, often contentious, and articulated through inherently differential relationships of power (Adell et al., 2015; Neal and Walton, 2008). Heritage practice can and should be part of that process—but not based narrowly on our professional authority, where we risk becoming just one more story staking a claim to some singular "truth" about "what happened." Instead, we are increasingly drawn into this ongoing dialogue, and the possible roles we will play there are still emerging. This is the forefront of transformation in the field.

Defining Practice as Collaborative, Comparative, and Situated

This link between shifting to a more people-centered heritage practice and learning to be genuinely collaborative with other practitioners, other disciplines, and community constituencies alike lies at the heart of what connects theory to practice. Places defined as connecting the past and the present become sites for broadly collective reflection and evolving discussion, rather than fixed monuments defined by the authority of experts. But expertise is still needed. In the communities where we work, heritage practice helps to structure the collaborative process by comparing different sites and differing narratives, engaging in the dialogue as an active participant. But understanding that these discussions are situated in specific communities does not have to mean either a tyranny of the local or that scholars and practitioners alike cease to articulate our own broader syntheses. That is exactly what is creating this richly cross-referenced literature increasingly shared across so many heritage-related fields.

Making these habits of mind explicit and intentional, and inculcating these amongst ourselves, our students, and our community partners—rather than teaching a suite of fixed methodologies—imbues heritage practice with a social sciences perspective that allows theory and method alike to continue to evolve. The reality is that we are in the midst of making this transformation and are ourselves being changed by the process.

References

Adell, N., Bendix, R. F., Bortolotto, C., and Tauschek, M., eds. (2015). "Between Imagined Communities and Communities of Practice: Participation, Territory and the Making of Heritage." *Göttingen Studies in Cultural Property*, Vol. 8. Universitätsverlag Göttingen.

Avrami, E., Mason, R., & de Torre, M. L. (2000). *Values and Heritage Conservation*. Los Angeles: Getty Conservation Institute.

Carman, J., & Sørensen, M. L. S. (2009). "Heritage Studies: An Outline." In M. L. S. Sørensen & J. Carman (Eds.), *Heritage Studies: Methods and Approaches* (pp. 11–28). London and New York: Routledge.

Charnley, S., Sheridan, T. E., and Nabhan, G. P., eds. (2015). *Stitching the West Back Together: Conservation of Working Landscapes*. Chicago, IL: University of Chicago Press.

Gibson, L., & Pendlebury, J., eds. (2009). *Valuing Historic Environments*. Surrey and Burlington: Ashgate Publishing.

Green, H. L. (1998). "The Social Construction of Historical Significance." In M. A. Tomlan (Ed.), *Preservation of What, for Whom? A Critical Look at Historical Significance* (pp. 85–94). Ithaca, NY: National Council for Preservation Education.

Harrison, R. (2013). *Heritage: Critical Approaches*. New York: Routledge.

Japan ICOMOS National Committee. (2014). "Nara + 20: On Heritage Practices, Cultural Values, and The Concept Of Authenticity." Stable www.japan-icomos.org/pdf/nara20_final_eng.pdf. Accessed January 29, 2017.

Lewis, P. (1979). "Axioms for Reading the Landscape: Some Guides to the American Scene." In W. Donald Meining (Ed.), *The Interpretation of Ordinary Landscapes: Geographic Essays* (pp. 11–32). New York: Oxford University Press.

Little, B., & Shackel, P. (2014). *Archaeology, Heritage and Civic Engagement: Working Toward the Public Good*. Walnut Creek, CA: Left Coast Press.

Lixinski, L. (2015). "Between Orthodoxy and Heterodoxy: The Troubled Relationships between Heritage Studies and Heritage Law." *International Journal of Heritage Studies*, 21(3), 203–214.

Low, S. M. (1994). "Cultural Conservation of Place." In M. Hufford (Ed.), *Conserving Culture: A New Discourse on Heritage* (pp. 66–77). Chicago, IL: University of Illinois Press.

Lowenthal, D. (1985). *The Past is a Foreign Country*. Cambridge and New York: Cambridge University Press.

Morgan, D., Morgan, N., & Barrett, B. (2006). "Finding a Place for the Commonplace: Hurricane Katrina, Communities, and Preservation Law." *American Anthropologist*, 108(4), 706–718. doi:10.1525/aa.2006.108.4.706.

National Park Service. (2015). "CRM: The Journal of Heritage Stewardship." U.S. National Park Service, last modified May 1, (2015). https://home1.nps.gov/CRMJournal/index.html

Neal, S., & Walters, S. (2008). "Rural Be/Longing and Rural Social Organizations: Conviviality and Community-Making in the English Countryside." *Sociology*, 42(2), 279–297.

Russell, R. (2014). "First Pete and then Repeat? Fundamental Differences in Intention between Undergraduate and Graduate Preservation Programs in the United States." In B. L. Stiefel & J. C. Wells (Eds.), *Preservation Education: Sharing Best Practices and Finding Common Ground*. Lebanon, NH: University Press of New England.

Smith, L. (2006). *Uses of Heritage*. London and New York: Routledge.

United States National Park Service. "CRM: The Journal of Heritage Stewardship." Stable www.nps.gov/crmjournal/. Accessed January 29, 2017.

Waterton, E., & Smith, L. (2010). "The Recognition and Misrecognition of Community Heritage." *International Journal of Heritage Studies*, 16(1), 4–15.

Wells, J. (2015). "Making a Case for Historic Place Conservation Based on People's Values." *Forum Journal of the National Trust for Historic Preservation*, 29(3), 44–62.

Wells, J. C., & Stiefel, B. L. (2016). Call for Papers for Making the Past Less Foreign Using Evidence Based on the Human Aspects of Heritage Conservation to Change Practice.

Winter, T. (2013). "Clarifying the Critical in Critical Heritage Studies." *International Journal of Heritage Studies*, 19(6), 532–545.

CHAPTER 15

"The Places My Granddad Built"

Using Popular Interest in Genealogy as a Pedagogical Segue to Historic Preservation

Barry L. Stiefel

For several years, I have wondered how best to respond to the demographic changes I observe among the students in my historic preservation courses. The challenge is related, I believe, both to majority-minority population shifts and the ever-evolving collective heritage of North America. Thus, I began experimenting with a variation of the self-discovery learning pedagogical method— an approach I call, "What is *Your* Heritage and the State of Its Preservation?" This process of inquiry originated from my days as a preservation student, when I took it upon myself to ascertain the relationship of my ancestry and its heritage to history, in general, as well as the state of condition/ preservation of important places, material culture, and intangible traditions. So, there is also a public history component to this approach. As David Lowenthal observes in his 2015 revision of *The Past is a Foreign Country*:

> …today's public is encouraged to privilege its own view of the past. Postmodernists preach that historians like all of us are partial and selective; we should dismiss academics all the more for claiming to be above the fray. All past views are biased. This is not altogether distressing; however defective, all pasts are equally deserving of attention. Your past, my past, and so-and-so's past all have the populist merit of being *someone's* past [emphasis original]. In this sense, the collective past is a collage, the crazy quilt of humanity's myriad individual memories…. Since all pasts are constructed to be self-serving, the more avowedly self-interested they are the more honest and insightful their narrators.
>
> (Lowenthal 2015, 14–15)

My response to this observation is a question: might people in general, whether professional practitioners or amateurs, become better advocates for preservation if they have investigated the state of preservation of their own heritage? By engaging in such an experience, can a person develop greater empathy for others whose heritage is imperiled, as they would not want such negative treatment of their own, as an extension of Lowenthal's concept of "self-serving"? Based on the projects produced by my students, this approach reflects their interest and values related to the past and contemporary historic built environment, providing an intriguing snapshot each semester of how young adults are defining their collective heritage and our national identity. It is the young professional demographic that will facilitate the gathering of heritage and shape the interpretation of its significance as well as empower communities to recognize, treat, and interpret their historic built environments and cultural landscapes, because they will be the policymakers and practitioners of tomorrow. "The Places My Granddad Built" is the title of one student project that delved into these issues (Glanton 2014). Indeed, as this student—Kaitlin Glanton—argued in her thesis, "[t]he places in which we make our homes play a vital role in shaping who we are. This is why studying and preserving them for future generations is so important, so that they may also benefit" (Glanton 2014, 56).

Self-Discovery Learning and Family History

Jerome Bruner, an educational psychologist, was the first to articulate and investigate the self-discovery learning method in the late 1950s and early 1960s. In summary, discovery learning is a constructivist learning theory that proposes one can learn well from an inquiry-based process, which seeks to solve problems from drawing on past experiences and existing knowledge to discover facts or new truths. Learning development takes place when the student explores their world through interaction with objects or places, grapples with controversies or questions, and/or tests hypotheses or conducts experiments. The premise is that some individuals may be able to learn better, or improve their ability to retain information, concepts, or knowledge by discovering information on their own, in contrast to a traditional transmissionist pedagogical approach, where the student observes a lecture or demonstration from an educator (Bruner 1961). The developmental psychologist, Jean Piaget, who also studied discovery learning, analogized that learners are not simple empty vessels to be filled with information but active creators of knowledge (Piaget 1973). The activity of knowledge creation reinforces cognition of information, resulting in both greater understanding for the person and higher retention.

More often than not, individuals conduct genealogical research and family history on their own volition—it is a self-discovery learning process. Purist genealogy is often more biologically focused with respect to heredity, in contrast to a family history that concentrates on the socio-cultural aspects of heritage. There is popular interest in learning about ones' pedigree, extended family, as well as the stories associated with ancestors. People may take a seminar or two on research methods techniques, such as how and where to find vital records and other primary sources, but the goal of the learning experience is to gain more knowledge about ones' past, with the discovery of information often taking place alone after improved researching skills have been obtained. Examples of this include the PBS documentary series *Finding Your Roots*, starring Harvard University professor and American historian, Henry Louis Gates, Jr. In the series, Gates and his associates research the genealogy and family history of celebrity guest stars, and episodes are often presented so that viewers can become inspired to conduct their own inquiry, independently, and gain some skills to conduct their own work. The most significant example in this respect was the special episode in 2007 on the American talk show host, Oprah Winfrey, in *Finding Oprah's Roots: Finding Your Own*, which included tips on how to investigate African-American heritage, much of it being applicable to non-African-Americans as well (Winfrey and Gates 2007). Within *Finding Oprah's Roots* are several advertisements and product placements of the genealogical and vital records database *Ancestry.com*, an official sponsor of the *Finding Your Roots* television program, and their parent organization, the

Church of Jesus Christ of Latter-day Saints ("All LDS Members, Including Youth, Can Now Get Free Access to FamilySearch Partner Websites" 2014).

As a preservationist and one who teaches the topic to others, I was most drawn to the stories about Oprah's family members and specific places, including the freedom house, her grandfather Elmore Winfrey rebuilt in McCool, Mississippi, in 1966; the Buffalo Rosenwald School in Attala County, Mississippi developed by her great-grandmother Amanda Presley Winters in the 1920s; as well as the land her ancestor Constantine Winfrey purchased in 1876, which housed a school for colored children beginning in 1906 (Winfrey and Gates 2007). During these segments, the National Register of Historic Places eligibility criteria ran through my head due to their historical significance to American history, and not because of the association that would come through their celebrity descendant. The freedom house and schools were of great significance on a local level to America's history, where the Civil Rights Movement and experiences of African-Americans in the New South took place. Family history research and historic preservation education could be used to enhance each other. Indeed, this is a very similar approach to the program, *Teaching with Historic Places*, co-developed by the National Park Service and the National Trust for Historic Places, though in this instance there is no agenda in investigating places related to one's personal past ("Teaching with Historic Places" 2014). On the flip side, other institutions, such as the Smithsonian, have offered programs like *Researching Your Genealogy: A Journey of Self-Discovery*, but with nothing relating the genealogy to historic places (Colletta 2012).

Within the What is *Your* Heritage and the State of Its Preservation class, which serves as a capstone, the student writes a lengthy in-depth research paper on the state of preservation of heritage sites, material objects, or traditions associated with their family's history. So far, I have taught the capstone (called Senior Seminar) three times, for the classes of 2014, 2016, and 2018. The assignment uses genealogical research methods in an unconventional way by elevating the assessment of ancestors beyond the typical names, dates, and generational succession so commonly found on family trees. The students have to ask themselves profound questions to guide their inquiry, such as "Where (as in a specific spot) did my ancestors come from?"; "What was life like for them?"; and "What cultural traditions were important for them?" In this way, people, whether a specific individual or a group, became connected and contextualized within time, place, and society. Moreover, the student has to synthesize the knowledge, skills, and experiences acquired in past classes, including architectural history, researching historic properties, preservation planning, cultural landscape analysis, and materials conservation.[1]

There are pros and cons to the self-discovery learning method, which became evident within the course. Proponents of self-discovery learning claim that the approach encourages active engagement, promotes motivation, promotes autonomy, responsibility, independence, the development of creative problem-solving skills, and a tailored learning experience ("Discovery Learning (Bruner)" 2007–2016). Some of these benefits were articulated by the students in the anonymous course-instructor evaluations at the end of the semester, which is shared below, along with their criticisms. However, it should be emphasized that the comments here do not represent all students that took the class. According to the blind courses-instructor evaluation, which is conducted online and outside of the classroom by the College of Charleston's administration, statistical data reveals that only eight of seventeen students (forty-seven percent) in the Class of 2014 provided feedback, and in 2016, sixteen of twenty-five students (sixty-four percent) (2018 data unavailable). Other colleagues in the program also teach Senior Seminar, with other topics. The average graduating senior class from the College of Charleston's Historic Preservation & Community Planning program is thirty, with an average enrollment of 120–130 students combined for all four undergraduate years (there is a separate graduate degree program too). The College of Charleston does not have a penalty system if a student chooses not to respond to the course-instructor evaluation, so participation is voluntary, not too different from the popularly known Rate My Professors.com website.[2] Thus, those students who participate in course-evaluations are frequently motived outliers, who are either enthusiastically for or against the course, or the professor. In the second year of its instruction, students' interest increase by forty-two percent, which is an intriguing growth in enrollment, possibly due to the course subject matter.

Positive feedback from anonymous course-instructor evaluations by the Class of 2014 ["Individual Report for Barry Stiefel (HPCP 415-01: Senior Seminar)" 2015]:

- I loved the topic of my HPCP [Historic Preservation & Community Planning] senior seminar. I could not have thought of a better way to sum up my time as a HPCP major by studying my family heritage and the state of its preservation.

- He [Dr. Stiefel] always asks challenging and probing questions during seminar which encourages students to think critically and develop their own answers regarding certain topics.

- I thought it was great how Stiefel was able to select the readings for the course and pull them together to tie into how we were writing our thesis. It really helped to understand what he was trying to get us to think about and consider while writing our papers. His enthusiasm for heritage, culture and value made the course more stimulating as well.

- The course was unlike any other HPCP course I have been required to take. I am really glad that I have gotten the chance to take the time to see and write about my family's heritage. I would suggest that he choose this topic again for when his teaching the HPCP Senior Seminar.

Positive feedback from anonymous course-instructor evaluations by the Class of 2016 ["Individual Report for Barry Stiefel (HPCP 415-01: Senior Seminar)" 2016]:

- I felt like the senior thesis led by Dr. Stiefel helped me to see how I have grown in the HPCP major and as a student during my time at the College. Through this project I was able to apply so many things that I had picked up from courses along the way and write a thesis that I was proud of and that will be relevant for me for years to come.

- A great way to end the Historic Preservation major.

- Dr. Stiefel has a unique teaching style and I believe he is a great professor who is extremely knowledgeable, especially in his line of work. He is very passionate about this course and I can see why I just think this is a year-long class and not a semester, especially with this specific topic.

Thus, we see that some students found the experience of the assignment to be a positive capstone exercise, and that similar comments not only appear more than once but also multiple years. Critics of self-discovery learning claim that there are pitfalls and shortcomings to the teaching approach, such as cognitive overload, potential misconceptions, and failure in the instructor's ability to detect problems and misconceptions. These comments were reflected in the course-instructor evaluations too.

THE PLACES MY GRANDDAD BUILT

Negative feedback from anonymous course-instructor evaluations by the Class of 2014 ["Individual Report for Barry Stiefel (HPCP 415-01: Senior Seminar)" 2015]:

- The reading assignments had nothing to do with my thesis. I think we should assign our own readings as part of the research we do for the thesis. I had plenty to read on top of the very long documents he assigned.

- I loved choosing my own topic on my thesis than doing the genealogy assignment. I think students should be allowed to choose their own topics, so I'm glad that he let some of us change it [to a non-family history assignment].

- He wasn't helpful at all during the semester. I felt like I was on my own to write this long paper, which I had never done before. I was looking for more guidance and direction, none of which I got from Stiefel.

Negative feedback from anonymous course-instructor evaluations by the Class of 2016 ["Individual Report for Barry Stiefel (HPCP 415-01: Senior Seminar)" 2016]:

- I felt that there could have been more guidance with what was expected in terms of the scope of what was in senior papers—I think this was a source of confusion for much of the class.

- I personally was excited about the big project until I started research on the suggested websites like Ancestry.com where it was almost impossible for me to find useful information. Research outside of that was so and so, honestly there are not a lot of scholarly sources out there that pertain to such a touchy, personal topic like Our Heritage and the State of its Preservation.

- Honestly, I don't feel like I learned much from this course other than some new information about my family. The paper topic pertains to students who have something unique in their family like an heirloom, tradition, or family custom. It was extremely difficult to write 36 pages on something that wasn't there. I had to dig emotionally to write about why I didn't have a tradition, heirloom, passed down custom, or tangible artifact to share on the state of its preservation. I mean we all have a heritage whether it's being preserved or not, but this topic is linked more to people who have that something to write about.

- I found out a lot about my family, which was great, but I'm not sure how much it helped me develop my knowledge in historic preservation as a whole.

- I almost feel like this course could be two semesters long, or at least split into two distinct sections. The first half focusing on the reading assigned by Dr. Stiefel and learning about the process of writing a thesis and preserving culture, and the second half concentrating only on research and writing of the paper.

As noted, the pedagogy is imperfect, with differentiation coming from the personality, experiences, and motivation of the student—especially when we consider that some of the anonymous student comments contradicted each other. Moreover, similar negative feedback not only appears more than once but also in multiple years despite my attempts to address these issues the second time the course was taught. Lastly, there was additional feedback regarding the pedagogy as a capstone experience

293

from the Historic Preservation & Community Planning program's exit interviews. Relevant comments from anonymous program exit interviews by the Class of 2014 ("Historic Preservation and Community Planning Confidential Exit Interview Form, Spring" 2014):

- It made me understand the broader scope of historic preservation and the importance of research.

- This course really was a synthesis of my HPCP study at the College. I applied all of my knowledge from previous classes into the course and writing this paper.

- Very useful. One of the only classes that really introduced me to the heritage aspect of preservation.

- This was a good way to synthesize what was learned in previous classes, but I know I would have produced a more cohesive, successful paper if this process took a[n] entire year, opposed to just a semester.

- The topic of "What is the state of your heritage preservation?" should be a [degree] major requirement. This class allows us to look past the buildings and @ the family/personal preservation efforts.

Relevant comment from anonymous program exit interviews from the Class of 2016 ("Historic Preservation and Community Planning Confidential Exit Interview Form, Spring" 2016):

- I really enjoyed using the different ways of research, I have learned in order to collect info for and write my senior paper.

On the exit interview form, the students reflected on their entire four years at the College of Charleston, and some volunteered the following comments on the course, though they did not have to, as shown here. The comments from the exit interview, when provided, are informative in that the course content and pedagogical approach were successful as a capstone experience—covering the bulk of skills acquired from the curriculum and synthesizing them in a coherent and practical way. The course is only offered within one semester, and I agree with the suggestion that a full academic year to work on the project would produce a more cohesive project, but this is an external institutional constraint.

A miniature version of this assignment was also conducted in the Introduction to Historic Preservation class, which I use as a teaser for attracting undecided students to declare Historic Preservation & Community Planning as their major. Unfortunately, the students from the introduction class provide little feedback to work with regarding if this was a successful assignment in their decision-making process to declare this subject to be their major, for there are five additional assignments. None of the experiences of each assignment was commented on individually, just all of them together as a whole. Obtaining more input from students on this is difficult due to the structured regulations my institution has regarding the anonymous course evaluation process by students and the prompted question, which was simply to comment on the assignments. Nonetheless, it serves as a useful exercise for introducing beginning students on the research methods for purposes of investigating people and their history associated with specific places, and for these reasons I am continuing with the smaller assignment version in the introductory class. However, a comment from the graduation class of 2016, for the Senior Seminar that year, stated: "Dr. Stiefel showed enthusiasm for the

THE PLACES MY GRANDDAD BUILT

subject and I enjoyed learning about his process during a similar assignment" ["Individual Report for Barry Stiefel (HPCP 415-01: Senior Seminar)" 2016], which leads me to assume that this student took Introduction to Historic Preservation taught by me in a previous academic year.

Preservation Innovation Before and [Hopefully] After Graduation

An unanticipated result of the seminar What is *Your* Heritage and the State of its Preservation were the number of non-traditional theses topics that many students selected for their research, especially, considering that they had come from a traditionalist curriculum based in the interdisciplinary professions of architectural history, archaeology, landscape architecture, public history, and urban planning, reflecting the educational backgrounds of the faculty and cross-listed opportunities with other departments. Not all students completed a thesis by the end of the semester (some dropped the course or failed to complete it for various reasons, but these numbers were not unusual in comparison to other Senior Seminar topics taught by colleagues), but of those that did in 2014, they produced the following papers:

- The City We Built: A Story of Persecution, Perseverance, and Preservation [in New York], by Andrew Brenner

- Italian Immigration and Assimilation in Somerville in Comparison to Boston's North End, by Derek Filosi

- Cultivating A Heritage: The Gee Family's Impact on a Historic Town [in Mississippi], by Lela Gee-Boswell

- Untitled [theme on a German-American family's traditions and places of significance], by Anna Krueger*

- Preserving a Legacy for Future Generations [in North Carolina], by EmmaLee Kunze

- The Underlying Cornerstone of Architectural and Urban Development in North Carolina: As Told from a[n African American] Genealogical Perspective, by Tyler Lavone Person

- Untitled [theme on a Guatemalan immigrant family to South Carolina and their traditions], by Kimberly Palomo*

- Cultural Heritage and the Significance of Place: The History of a Family's Relationship to the American Landscape, by Corinne Rhea

- The Preservation of an Important Past: [The Oliver Wolcott House of Litchfield, Connecticut], by Kelsey Simpson

- Spencer Family Heritage, by Josh Spencer

Those theses with an asterisk (*) delved into what would be considered unconventional preservation issues, at least with respect to what is commonly practiced in the United States. Their interest lay more in the realm of intangible heritage preservation, as defined by the UNESCO Convention for the Safeguarding of the Intangible Cultural Heritage of 2003, which is intriguing considering that the United States has not ratified this convention, thus it is infrequently practiced or used in this country. At most, the Convention for the Safeguarding of the Intangible Cultural Heritage of 2003 is a footnote in many American historic preservation higher education curriculums.

Following graduation in 2014, five additional students continued with their research and writing to publish an edited volume of their papers under my editorship, titled *What is Your Heritage and the State of its Preservation?: Essays on Family History Exploration from the Field*, which was published later that year (Stiefel 2014):

> Chapter 1: A Selected History of the Clarkson-James Family: 1732–1915, by Blanding Lee Clarkson
>
> Chapter 2: Family History Through the Creation of Quilts, by Emily Floyd*
>
> Chapter 3: The Places My Granddad Built, by Kaitlin Glanton
>
> Chapter 4: A Marine Corps Heritage, by Dannielle Nadine Hobbs*
>
> Chapter 5: From Normandy to Charleston, by Michael C. Patnaude
>
> Chapter 6: From Jerusalem to Stono Ferry, South Carolina: Discoveries on the Katz-Stiefel Family, by Barry L. Stiefel

I've contributed the sixth chapter, *From Jerusalem to Stono Ferry, South Carolina*, which was a paper I wrote as a student during my fourth year of higher education—the same place in life as the students—but it was not for a thesis assignment. These students had a profound impact because this book became a supplementary textbook for the class of 2016, who could use these examples as hypothetical models. Two of the five published chapters by the students focused on unconventional preservation topics. Emily Floyd's *Family History Through the Creation of Quilts,* studied the important matrilineal social and cultural ties passed across generations through the craft of quilt making in rural West Virginia, with an analysis of the preservation infrastructure (or the lack thereof) and the public interest for it. *A Marine Corps Heritage* by Dannielle Nadine Hobbs makes an interesting study of family tradition, vernacular places, and preservation related to the military, as well as how the women of her family have been involved with this (Figure 15.1).

During the 2016 course, Susan Kammeraad-Campbell from Storyboard America approached us about collaborating and assisting the students in their thesis development, which added an interesting new twist. "Storyboard is a library-based national initiative being developed and tested in South Carolina and Ohio through radio broadcasts, podcasts, and anthologies." The objective is "to help people think more deeply about themselves, [and] about their own stories" (Kammeraad-Campbell and Kirk 2015). Delving into family stories about historic places, material objects, and intangible traditions was part of what the students were investigating anyway, and so a two-part workshop was developed that assisted students to better articulate how oral history could be used to give better meaning to what they were researching. The experience was especially valuable for some students to better conceptualize and articulate the heritage(s) they were exploring in their papers, which for 2016 were:

- Building Upon Lost Heritage, by Brooke Butler*
- The Bridghams: What They Meant to America and the Connection We Share Living Near the Ocean, by Clauson Coward

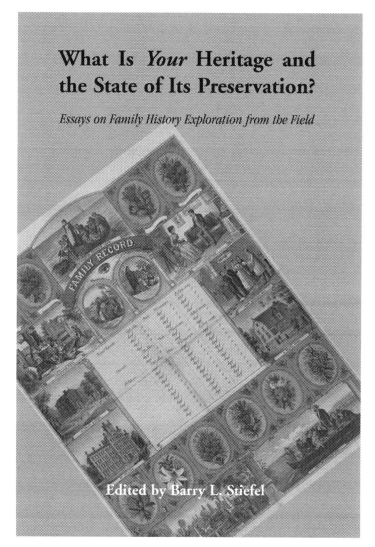

Figure 15.1 Cover of *What is Your Heritage and the State of its Preservation?: Essays on Family History Exploration from the Field*, edited by Barry L. Stiefel with contributing chapters from students in the 2014 class. From the author.

- A Heritage Forgotten and Found: The Journey in Finding my Spanish Heritage, by John Darby
- The City That Shaped Me, by Carson Demont
- (Re)Framing the Esterline Name: Preserving the Unpreserved, by Nathaniel Esterline*
- What is Your Heritage and the State of its Preservation?, by Gabrielle Harfst
- Interpreting Col. Grover Heiman as a Geographer: Heritage as a Vessel for One's Own Identity, by Christian Hughes

THE PLACES MY GRANDDAD BUILT

- The Story Behind It: How Stories and Recognizance Shape Family Heritage, by Amanda Grace Hunter*

- *"This Ain't a Surfin Movie"*, by Priscila Interiano-Ledbetter*

- Reinventing the State of Preservation: Live for Life, by McKenna Kornman*

- My Family's Impact on New England, by Paige Lavigne

- My Henderson Family Heritage: Our Transition from Four Legs to Four Wheels and Automobiles, by Zachary Liollio*

- Duty-Honor-Country: Preserving the life of a Traveling Soldier, by Sterling Lombard

- *No Room For Heartache*, by Hugh Kevin Skelley*

- A Legacy of Photography, by Andrew Staton*

- From the Mountains to the Sea, and Back Again: The Story of My Grandparents, by Benjamin Thomas

What became apparent within the Class of 2016's papers were the different ways students explored the affiliation of their heritage identity. This may have been due to the workshop exercises given by Kammeraad-Campbell from Storyboard America, which some students commented on as being influential in their decision-making process. However, the heritage identity(ies) of the students did not all go the same way. Several, such by Clauson Coward, Sterling Lombard, Paige Lavigne, among others, explored what it meant to them to be part of a homogenous American milieu. Others, such as by Interiano-Ledbetter and Darby, focused on a hybrid ethnic identity, specifically what it respectively meant to be a Guatemalan-American or American of Majorcan descent, regardless if that the student themselves was the one to have undergone the immigration (Interiano-Ledbetter) or a distant ancestor from the eighteenth century (Darby). In each case, the heritage affiliation was what the student found to be meaningful through their own self-discovery process, though occasional coaching and advising was provided to foster critical thinking and analysis. Again, many of the students zeroed in on more traditional topics, such as buildings and landscapes, but others explored different aspects of material culture and intangible traditions too. Liollio studied the long family tradition of his ancestor's work on vehicles, beginning with horse-drawn wagons, followed by railroad vehicles, and then automobiles; with a case study of a 1930 Model A Ford that was maintained within the family into the student's lifetime. The students were not just interested in the tangible material objects but also the intangible customs of traditional craftsmanship and stewardship. Liollio provided an example of this not only showing the historic and cultural significance of the vehicles he studied but also as part of his final presentation, filmed himself machining a piston from a raw piece of aluminum that could serve as a replacement part for an automotive engine.

For the Class of 2016, we also produced a post-seminar publication, *What is Your Heritage and the State of its Preservation?: Volume 2 Collaborations with Storyboard America*, which I also edited and Kammeraad-Campbell provided a Foreword, with the following chapters:

Chapter 1: A Southern Textile Heritage in the South Carolina Upstate, by Meagan Pickens

Chapter 2: Where I'm From: Finding Myself through Memories Made in the Middle of Nowhere Virginia, by Kaylee Lass

THE PLACES MY GRANDDAD BUILT

Chapter 3: My Big Fat Italian Heritage, by Christa Kearns*

Chapter 4: As American as Apple Pie: What it takes to be an American Citizen, Kyra Rooney*

Chapter 5: Rubel Jewelers: Preservation of a Family Business, by Evan Rubel*

Chapter 6: And The Beat Goes On: Preserving Music Through Family Heritage, by Katherine Schofield*

Chapter 7: From Obelenus to O'Bell: A Case Study of Lithuanian Heritage Transplanted to America, by Marian Mazzone

The seventh chapter, by Mazzone, was actually a colleague-faculty contribution. Since I had contributed a chapter in this capacity in 2014, I decided to continue this tradition. Mazzone's chapter offered a profound contrast to the students since she undertook this project voluntarily, and not as a course-assignment that was part of degree completion requirement. While Mazzone is the Chair of the Art & Architectural History Department at the College of Charleston, and her scholarship focuses on modern and contemporary, she was able to provide profound insights regarding the historical research that is done related to preservation:

> I am a trained researcher, and know how to find information. Most people do not have the experience or the time to do the work I have had to invest to find even a bare outline of John Obelenus' life [her ancestor]. I am left with the knowledge of how little we know of the lives of members of our own family that took place only a hundred years ago, much less the lives of people from other times and places.

(Mazzone 2016, 241)

Where Mazzone's observations become exceptionally noticeable among the students is when we review Kaylee Lass's chapter *Where I'm From: Finding Myself through Memories Made in the Middle of Nowhere* from 2016, and *A Selected History of the Clarkson-James Family: 1732–1915*, by Blanding Lee Clarkson, from 2014. Coincidentally, both students had very important family histories related to slavery, an unavoidable topic in the American South when assessing historic places from the nineteenth century and earlier. During the early nineteenth century, Clarkson's ancestor, William Clarkson (1761–1825) lived at 18 Bull Street in Charleston, South Carolina, a National Historic Landmark known as the Blacklock House (coincidentally, next door to the College of Charleston's Historic Preservation & Community Planning program facility, at 12 Bull Street). During the early nineteenth century, this land was largely loosely developed, at the edge of the city, with his ancestors owning much of the property. Approximately a block away from 18 Bull Street is where Denmark Vesey (1767–1822) resided, a freed person of color who is most remembered for attempting to initiate a violent slave uprising, which was intercepted by local authorities and brutally crushed before it could begin. Lass's ancestors lived in Southampton County, Virginia, also during the Antebellum period, an agrarian plantation landscape where the labor force was also heavily dependent on slavery. Her ancestor, Major Thomas Ridley II (1778–18??), was a plantation owner and commander of the militia that encountered Nat Turner (1800–1831) and his followers on their revolt in August 1831. Three of Ridley's personal slaves were tried, and two executed, in addition to other slaves and freed people of color. Significant parts of the landscapes that the Turner revolt took place on was land owned by Ridley.

THE PLACES MY GRANDDAD BUILT

What struck me most was the students' interest in investigating their respective ancestral involvement with these horrific instances in history, as well as the need to preserve these places. Clarkson was not able to find much detailed information, as could be expected from Mazzone's observations. He was not able to ascertain how his ancestor, William Clarkson, knew Vesey; but at the very least they were acquaintances considering their proximity to one another during the 1810s and 1820s. The living descendant Clarkson believes that it

> is no stretch of historical fancy to imagine that some of William Clarkson's enslaved Africans, either at his plantation in Middleburg or his private home at 18 Bull Street, were the same individuals that Denmark Vessey [sic] plotted freedom and revolt with.

> (Clarkson 2014, 17)

Lass had found more about her director ancestor's relationship with slaves and the Nat Turner revolt, and readily admitted: "The dark side of my heritage is undeniable in the institution of slavery. It is not something I am proud of, but I cannot change the past and thus it must not be ignored" (Lass 2016, 63). I was moved by the way Clarkson and Lass addressed the difficult family histories of their respective pasts, advocating for the preservation of these sites of conscience, especially considering that their ancestors were culpable accomplices to what took place. They chose to be honest in their self-discovery learning process, when during a moment alone in research they could have easily turned the page and looked the other way, focusing instead on another rosier time in their history.

While Clarkson and Lass would be defined as Caucasian Americans, as well as the majority of the students in the classes for both 2014 and 2016, there were some with the minority group ancestry, including Latin American, African-American, and Native American. When the seminar met, students had unique opportunities to share their findings and discuss sensitive issues, such as slavery and oppression. As of yet, I have not seen students at odds with one another, though historically their ancestors would have been on opposing sides of contentious issues, such as slave ownership. The sins of the ancestral forefathers and foremothers were not redirected onto the living descendants, which is an important step when dealing with issues of reconciliation at heritage sites of conscience, along with honesty.

The other students also had their own amazing stories, where some delved into writing about it well, and others not. The students with extensive information on their heritage often had the problem of too much information—reflecting the shortcoming of self-discovery learning—and had to make tough decisions regarding what their focus would be on for purposes of completing the assignment in a timely manner so that they could graduate. In both years, there were students who found they were descended from well-known people in the history, including European nobility, signers of the Declaration of Independence or Constitution, war heroes, immigrants who came across on the Mayflower, and so forth. Other students were more attracted to the history of common people, either out of interest or because this research was more manageable for the assignment. The experiment of using a genealogical approach to historic preservation allowed us to chart the claims of journalist Steve Olson, from *Mapping Human History*:

> People like to trace their ancestry to famous figures. In Japan many families trace their lineage to the ninth-century emperor Seiwa. Many French believe they are descended from Charlemagne. Such claims are typically impossible to prove, and many genealogists dismiss them as fantasies.

300

However, these claims are almost certainly true. The exponential growth in number of our ancestors going back in time connects us tightly to the past.... Being descended from someone doesn't necessarily mean that you have any DNA from that person.... The amount of DNA each of us gets from any one of our 1,024 ancestors ten generations back is minuscule – and we might not get any DNA from that person, given the way the chromosomes rearrange themselves every generation.

(Olson 2002, 47)

Which, goes back to why this pedagogical exercise is not purist genealogy. Yes, ancestral research takes place, but the biological aspects are immaterial. It is the social connections and networks through time are what matters, and material cultural artifacts often serve as vehicles for transmission across generations.

The biological aspect loses importance when we consider that people are adopted all the time, and the adoptee often adopts the cultural heritage and traditions of those that have adopted them, and may even inherit tangible artifacts or places, as well as intangible traditions. Therefore, an adoptee can investigate the non-genetic lineage of the heritage(s) they identify with. Thinking critically about what is taking place for the preservation of one's heritage(s) is the purpose of this self-discovery learning exercise. While my biological parents raised me, as an exercise I researched the pedigree of my intellectual heritage, being academic historic preservation. My doctorate in Historic Preservation from Tulane University (completed 2008) was conducted under co-chairs Colin M. MacLachlan from the Department of History and Eugene D. Cizek of the Preservation Studies Program. I investigated Cizek's educational forbearers since I associated with this side most. His doctorate was in Environmental Social Psychology, also from Tulane University, completed in 1978 under Bernard Lemann (1906–2000). Cizek's dissertation topic was on *Faubourg Marigny: A Proposal for Environmental Conservation*, which included the preservation of the built environment (Cizek 1978). Lemann was also a professor of architecture at Tulane University and a pioneer in New Orleans's preservation movement during the mid-twentieth century (Smith 2012). His doctorate, completed in 1936 from Harvard University, was on *Honore Daumier: The Origins and Evolution of his Art* (Lemann 1936), which surprisingly was a biographical art history dissertation, with no emphasis on the built environment or preservation. Lemann studied under Paul J. Sachs (1878–1965), a pioneer in the museum studies field at Harvard University, where he both obtained his education and worked for much of his academic career. His doctorate, however, was an honorary one conferred by Harvard and thus the line ends there. Sachs was also a member of the infamous multinational banking firm, Goldman Sachs (Alexander 1997). From this investigation, I was intrigued to learn the origins of my intellectual forbearers, and that the roots grew out of art history and museum studies. As Kammeraad-Campbell concluded in her Foreword in the second volume of *What Is Your Heritage and the State of It's Preservation*:

Often when we think of preservation we think of buildings and artifacts, about shoring up shifting foundations, repointing bricks, and slowing the forces that cause decay – sun, moisture, wind, and neglect. But ultimately it is not the bricks and clapboards that will endure – built structures and artifacts have a life; their true meaning is in their use, not in their endurance. Stories are durable. Stories endure. Write yours.

(Kammeraad-Campbell 2016, xi).

Self-Discovery Genealogy for Enhancing the Value of Preservation Education

An irony behind my proposed approach of using popular interest in genealogy as a pedagogical segue for preservation education is that, like the genealogical research methodology just described, this has also been a self-discovery learning process. As far as I am aware there has been little published that explores the topical or educational overlap between genealogical investigation and the preservation of places, and thus, I have been working in isolation. While I can recognize the potential benefits that come from learning on one's own, as argued by Bruner, in this instance, the isolation has been a hindrance. Just like Bruner and other scholars of education, they interacted and debated the merits of self-discovery learning as an intellectual community. Thus, one objective of this chapter is also to encourage other preservation educators to consider similar approaches in their teaching that utilizes popular genealogy, to facilitate intellectual discourse. Otherwise, this self-discovery pedagogical exploration ends with a schizophrenic-like monologue. The following is my experience, though I highly recommend anyone who is willing to explore this path forge a new route of his or her own because the element of self-discovery is an underlying vital part.

My experience of combining genealogy and preservation began with two converging interests while an undergraduate and graduate student. As an undergraduate student, I majored in Environmental Policy and minored in Anthropology because I was profoundly interested in the dynamic cultural relationship of people with their environments. At this time, my paternal grandmother had passed away and at a family gathering following the funeral, I was given a copy of the family history a cousin of mine compiled on this part of the family, which instilled in me a curiosity regarding other parts. Within a matter of days after returning home from this event, I encountered others researching some of our shared family segments and specifically from my patrilineage learned about ancestors dating back to the eighteenth century—adding approximately 200 years more beyond what I had known previously. This was when the metaphorical genealogical "bug" bit me, and through my own endeavors eventually researched this part of the family back to the early seventeenth/late sixteenth century through archives in Germany. However, at this moment, genealogy simply remained a scholarly hobby for me.

After completing my undergraduate studies, I began a Master of Urban Planning and specialized in environmental planning. Through a course in my first semester, I became reintroduced to historic preservation (initially exposed to it as a high school elective) and became interested in the practice as a means for fostering urban sustainability through the adaptive reuse of buildings and other aspects of the historic built environment. At this moment, cultural heritage was important to me but I had not-yet mentally made the connection as an intrinsic part of sustainability. Thus, I dual enrolled in the historic preservation program at another institution nearby, where I took evening classes for a Graduate Certificate. Shortly before the Spring break of my first year, I encountered a discounted airfare sale to Frankfurt-am-Main, and spontaneously bought the ticket since Hesse, Germany is where my forefathers came from: one was to visit the archives to learn more about them and the other reason was to experience the places they lived since no family members had resided there since World War II.

On the edge of the village in rural Hesse where my forefathers came from I encountered an eighteenth-century fachwerk-style barn with a bilingual inscription in German and the extinct dialect of Western Yiddish, which translates as "This barn was built by Isaak Katz and Rewecka his house wife in anno 1779." After having recently done research, I knew that "Isaak Katz and

Rewecka his house wife" were my great-great-great-great-great-great-grandparents (X6), and that since circa 1810, the family surname had been changed from "Katz" to "Stiefel" due to Napoleonic-influenced reforms. I am also one of the few living lineal descendants of Isaak Katz and Rewecka. To my dismay, the barn was not in the best of shape, for there was a gaping hole in the façade where the current farmer loads hay into the loft. I was emotionally overwhelmed by what lay in front of me. First, the ancient barn that was the only material culture connection I had ever had to anything in my family's history prior to their immigration from Europe to North America. The immigrant ancestor, my great-grandfather, Sol Stiefel, was the sixth of eleven children, and had brought no material inheritance with him to the United States when he came as a teenager. The other was that the current owner of the only monument to my ancestors from this part of the world was mistreating it. An urging desire to fix this discretion to the barn overtook me. This was my epiphany as to why historic preservation was important: not only to fix what I felt was the poor treatment of my heritage but to also help others who were in a similar situation because I could sincerely empathize with them. Because of this moment, I re-shifted my career to a historic preservation focus where I am also educating others on the importance of preserving. Unfortunately, due to my limited means, I have been unable to do anything for that barn in rural Hesse, which has meant so much to me. However, as I continued my historic preservation education and career path, I eventually learned that other practitioners and amateurs were similarly motivated and with better results (Figures 15.2–15.4).

Figure 15.2 Fachwerk-style barn built by the author's patrilineal ancestors in 1779, outside of Rauschenberg, Hesse, Germany. From the personal collection of the author.

Figure 15.3 Close-up of the German inscription on the barn that translates as "This barn was built by Isaak Katz and Rewecka his house wife in anno 1779." In the upper left corner, can be seen part of the hole in the façade. From the personal collection of the author.

Figure 15.4 Close-up of the Yiddish inscription on the barn that translates as "This barn was built by Isaak Katz and Rewecka his house wife in anno 1779." In the upper right corner, can be seen part of the hole in the façade. From the personal collection of the author.

Precedents and Future Directions for Preserving Family Heritage Sites

Rarely discussed within American historic preservation history is how often descendants and relatives of significant people are involved in the preservation of buildings and places of importance. An early Charleston example was the restoration of the Heyward-Washington House, which opened as the city's first house museum in 1931. The Heyward-Washington House is significant in American history as the home of Thomas Heyward Jr., a signer of the Declaration of Independence. In 1791, George Washington also spent a week there while visiting the city. The Heyward-Washington House is owned by the Charleston Museum, a property and organization that American writer Edwin DuBose Heyward was well acquainted with through personal involvement. Indeed, the neighborhood environs of the Heyward-Washington House served as the setting for the novel and play *Porgy*, and opera *Porgy and Bess* (Weyeneth 2000).

Another instance of family involvement was in the evaluation of colonial-era historic houses of worship by the National Park Service during the 1930s and 1940s, which included the church tower ruins of Jamestown, Virginia; Gloria Dei of Philadelphia, Pennsylvania; St. Paul's Church of Eastchester, New York, and Touro Synagogue of Newport, Rhode Island; among others (Sprinkle 2014). In the case of Touro Synagogue, it received substantial support and backing from Arthur Hays Sulzberger, *New York Times* publisher between 1935 and 1961, whose mother's lineage, the Hays family, used the building as their place of worship during the second half of the eighteenth century (Stiefel and Goodwin 2009). The designation of Touro Synagogue as a National Historic Site is largely due to Sulzberger's personal interest in the site. Moreover, Sulzberger's attention to Touro Synagogue came more than a century after Abraham Touro of Boston, son of Isaac Touro, the congregation's first spiritual leader, paid for a caretaker to take care of the synagogue, in addition to bequeathing $10,000 to the congregation in the form of a trust for the building's continued upkeep. Rhode Island's General Assembly and Newport's town council oversaw this trust. The money went toward extensive restoration work and maintenance on the synagogue between 1827 and 1829. The impetus of the project was the nostalgia of Abraham Touro. His brother Judah Touro of New Orleans followed suit with his own donations for preservation and maintenance in 1854 (Lewis 1975).

Thus, in multiple settings, family ties with the desire to preserve places that our forefathers and foremothers built and used resonate. The article "The Importance of Preserving Austin's Historical Homes" in magazine *Austin Way* covers Libby Sartain of Austin, Texas, who, with her architect-husband, purchased and restored in 2015 the home, built by her great-great-great grand-father in 1857 (Smith 2015). The common thread in each instance—the College of Charleston students, Edwin DuBose Heyward, Arthur Hays Sulzberger, the Touro brothers, Libby Sartain, as well as myself as a student—was that we were all just beginning to be exposed to the field of historic preservation, whether it was for professional or amateur purposes. Indeed, after lengthy searching I was unable to uncover a documented case study of a well-experienced preservationist formally going back to study or evaluate the places, buildings, or other important aspects related to their heritage. The evidence of this investigation suggests that those who have undergone an experience of exploring the state of preservation of the heritage they identify with may go on to become advocates for preservation at large. However, despite the long history of such self-discovery for purposes of preservation, both the preservation movement and associated educational programs have yet to capitalize on this as a promotional agenda for fostering advocacy and broader public interest. Using the self-discovery genealogical approach to investigate places, material culture, and intangible traditions within the preservation education curriculum may be a way to bring about the positive change.

Notes

1   Besides the course description on the syllabus, this text also appears in the student-produced publication from the class, Barry L. Stiefel, ed. *What Is Your Heritage and the State of Its Preservation?: Essays on Family History Exploration from the Field* (Berwyn Heights, MD: Heritage Books, Inc. 2014), back cover.

2   As of this moment the Senior Seminar on "What is *Your* Heritage and the State of its Preservation" (HPCP 415) has not appeared on RateMyProfessors.com. See "Barry Stiefel at the College of Charleston", www. ratemyprofessors.com/ShowRatings.jsp?tid=1356862, (24 May 2016).

References

Alexander, Edward Porter (1997). *The Museum in America: Innovators and Pioneers*. Walnut Creek, CA: AltaMira Press.

"All LDS Members, Including Youth, Can Now Get Free Access to FamilySearch Partner Websites", (2014). *FamilySearch*, https://familysearch.org/blog/en/create-free-account-familysearch-partners/, 3 February 2016.

Bruner, Jerome S. (1961). *The Process of Education*. Cambridge, MA: Harvard University Press.

Cizek, Eugene D. (1978). *Faubourg Marigny: A Proposal for Environmental Conservation* (Doctoral dissertation. Tulane University, 1978).

Clarkson, Blanding Lee (2014). "A Selected History of the Clarkson-James Family: 1732–1915", in *What is Your Heritage and the State of its Preservation?: Essay on Family History Exploration from the Field*. Berwyn Heights, MD: Heritage Books, Inc., 1–27.

Colletta, John (2012). "Researching Your Genealogy: A Journey of Self-Discovery All-Day Seminar", *Smithsonian Associates*, http://smithsonianassociates.org/ticketing/tickets/reserve.aspx?ID=224485, 23 May 2016.

"Discovery Learning (Bruner)", (2007–2016). *Learning-Theories.com: Knowledge Base and Webliography*, www.learning-theories.com/discovery-learning-bruner.html, 3 February 2016.

Glanton, Kaitlin (2014). "The Places My Granddad Built", in *What is Your Heritage and the State of its Preservation?: Essay on Family History Exploration from the Field*, Barry L. Stiefel, ed. Berwyn Heights, MD: Heritage Books, Inc., 54–83.

"Historic Preservation and Community Planning Confidential Exit Interview Form, Spring", (2014). College of Charleston. Located with the Administrative Assistant at the Historic Preservation & Community Planning Program office, 12 Bull Street, Charleston, South Carolina, 29424, USA.

"Historic Preservation and Community Planning Confidential Exit Interview Form, Spring", (2016). College of Charleston. Located with the Administrative Assistant at the Historic Preservation & Community Planning Program office, 12 Bull Street, Charleston, South Carolina, 29424, USA.

"Individual Report for Barry Stiefel (HPCP 415-01: Senior Seminar)", (2015). *College of Charleston Course-Instructor Evaluations (Spring 2014)*.

"Individual Report for Barry Stiefel (HPCP 415-01: Senior Seminar)", (2016). *College of Charleston Course-Instructor Evaluations (Spring 2016)*.

Kammeraad-Campbell, Susan (2016). "Foreword", in *What is Your Heritage and the State of its Preservation?: Volume 2, Collaborations with Storyboard America*. Berwyn Heights, MD: Heritage Books, Inc., viii–xi.

Kammeraad-Campbell, Susan and Kirk, James (2015). "About Storyboard", *Storyboard America*, www.storyboardamerica.com/about.html, 24 May 2016.

Lass, Kaylee (2016). "Where I'm From: Finding Myself through Memories Made in the Middle of Nowhere", in *What is Your Heritage and the State of its Preservation?: Volume 2, Collaborations with Storyboard America*. Berwyn Heights, MD: Heritage Books, Inc., 43–82.

Lemann, Bernard (1936). *Honore Daumier: The Origins and Evolution of his Art* (Doctoral dissertation. Harvard University, 1936).

Lewis, Theodore (1975). "History of Touro Synagogue," *Bulletin of the Newport Historical Society*, Vol. 48, 295.

Lowenthal, David (2015). *The Past is a Foreign Country: Revisited*. Cambridge, UK: Cambridge University Press.

Mazzone, Marian (2016). "From Obelenus to O'Bell: A Case Study of Lithuanian Heritage Transplanted to America", in *What is Your Heritage and the State of Its Preservation?: Volume 2, Collaborations with Storyboard America*. Berwyn Heights, MD: Heritage Books, Inc., 222–44.

Olson, Steve (2002). *Mapping Human History: Discovering the Past through Our Genes*. Boston: Houghton Mifflin.

Piaget, Jean (1973). *To Understand Is to Invent: The Future of Education*. New York: Grossman Publishers.

Smith, Claiborne (2015). "Austin's Historical Homes", *Austin Way*, http://austinway.com/preserving-historic-homes-and-buildings-in-austin, 10 March 2016.

Smith, Jazmin (2012). "Bernard Lemann papers, 1936–1981 | Louisiana Research Collection", *Tulane University*, http://specialcollections.tulane.edu/archon/?p=collections/findingaid&id=103&q=&rootcontentid=128501

Sprinkle, John H. (2014). *Crafting Preservation Criteria: The National Register of Historic Places and American Historic Preservation*. New York: Routledge.

Stiefel, Barry L., ed. (2014). *What is Your Heritage and the State of Its Preservation?: Essays on Family History Exploration from the Field*. Berwyn Heights, MD: Heritage Books, Inc.

Stiefel, Barry L. and Goodwin, George (2009). "Three New World Synagogues: Symbols of Toleration, Pride, and Continuity", *Jewish Historical Society of British Columbia: The Scribe,* Vol. 29, 27–44.

"Teaching with Historic Places", (2014). *National Park Service*, www.nps.gov/nr/twhp/about.htm, 3 February 2016.

Weyeneth, Robert R. (2000). *Historic Preservation for a Living City: Historic Charleston Foundation, 1947–1997*. Columbia: University of South Carolina Press.

Winfrey, Oprah and Gates, Jr., Henry L. (2007). *Finding Oprah's Roots: Finding Your Own*. Arlington, VA: PBS Home Video.

CHAPTER 16

Resistance to Research

Diagnosis and Treatment of a Disciplinary Ailment

Ned Kaufman

There are many reasons why evidence-based research in the social sciences is making little headway in the preservation world. Crossing the border between research and practice is always difficult, and the addition of a disciplinary boundary raises the hurdle. Perhaps, too, the social scientists are not always doing the research that would be most useful to practitioners. But the malady I call Resistance to Research is an affliction rooted deeper, in the very structures of the preservation discipline.

Before continuing, I should clarify what I mean by research. I do not mean investigations into architectural or landscape history, or into the chemistry of adhesives or the statics of structures. These studies concern the things on which preservation works, but they do not (except in matters of detail) determine what preservation seeks to do or how. They have little bearing on whether or not we should have a National Register of Historic Places, or tax credits, or programs to address climate change, or on whether local landmark regulations are on the whole too strict or not strict enough, or whether testimony from the public that "We have always lived in this place and like it as it is" should or should not be considered relevant. They tell us little about how well existing policies accomplish their objectives, what unintended impacts they might have, or what options might be preferable. By research, I mean the kinds of investigations that do help answer these and similar questions: research that bears on the policies beneath the preservation enterprise, the assumptions that drive them, the forces that shape them, their impact on the world. Whenever I refer to Resistance to Research, I shall mean specifically this kind of research.

Three structural obstacles, then, stand in the way of research:

1. *The highly-formalized nature of preservation practice.* Theory aside, nearly all preservation work is circumscribed by requirements which are rigidly defined by law and regulation and are therefore highly resistant to change. Since these requirements can be (and always have been) met without the aid of social science research, there is no need to carry out new research and no point in absorbing it. Research is literally useless.

2. *The lack of institutional capacity to absorb new knowledge.* Even if the preservation field found compelling reasons to take on new information, it couldn't do so: it doesn't have the organizational components that would make it possible.

3. *The lack of a clear sense of purpose.* The preservation field (at least so it seems to me) is deeply uncertain about its own goals and methods. One hopes that this lack of direction signals a moment of creative ferment from which a strengthened sense of purpose will arise. Meanwhile, it paralyzes any possible effort to construct an effective research agenda.

There has been a minor revival of interest recently in the question of preservation education, and this has produced some valuable studies—valuable not least of all because they open up the question of preservation research. My own understanding of this issue is derived mainly from my experiences in the field, which, in the spirit of disclosing one's sources, I should therefore summarize. They include, briefly, a PhD in architectural history, followed by some years of graduate teaching (and research) in liberal arts departments; more years as a full-time professor in a preservation program located within an architecture school; a few years as a museum curator; a decade or so as a preservation program officer in a non-profit organization based in New York; a few years as founding co-director of another non-profit preservation program; several years as founder and co-director of another graduate preservation program in another architecture school; nearly a decade as designer and director of the research and training programs at a large architecture firm; fifteen years or so as an adjunct professor, mostly in preservation programs but also in liberal arts departments; nearly fifteen years as a preservation consultant (free-lancer is a more accurate description), working mostly for government agencies but also for non-profits, foundations, schools, and even a developer or two; and some hard-to-count number of years as an independent researcher, investigating and writing about what I (rather than my employers or clients) think is important. Strung back to back these stints would add up to more than a working lifetime: some have overlapped. Together they form the primary sources for my diagnosis of the ailment that I have called Resistance to Research. And for my conviction that the only way to cure it is to remove the structural obstacles I have named earlier and will now describe.

Why is the formalization of practice an impediment to research? Consider what it is that preservationists do. For the most part, they are paid to manage, monitor, exploit, or circumvent four basic programs: local landmark and historic district regulation, national and state registers of historic places, environmental and preservation statutes concerning development, and tax credits for rehabilitation of old or historic buildings.[1] These are all government programs, which means that a strikingly large proportion of what preservationists do is laid out for them by legislation, regulation, and case law. And when one considers that most of what is contained in these four program areas can be traced back ultimately to a single law—the National Historic Preservation Act of 1966—one begins to appreciate how narrow indeed is the scope for personal judgment, experimentation, or for that matter, research. Preservationists can investigate all they want, but at the end of the day, they *must* work to the legal guidelines. "Preservationists are not paid to think," as Jack Elliott recalls being lectured by a state official in chapter 4 of this book.

While Elliott writes from the perspective of a public servant, the control exercised by law and regulation extends throughout the discipline. It sets the agenda for the non-profit civic and advocacy groups whose job is to support and monitor the officials. It defines the playing field for the private-sector consultants whose job is to help clients manage compliance, exploit tax credits, or circumvent regulation. It even shapes the work of the academics, because their job is to turn out next year's crop of practice-ready preservationists, each prepared to apply the rules upon graduation. As they have wrapped themselves around every branch of the discipline, the rules have choked off avenues for research: not just for pure academic research but also for the kind of practical, applied research that happens when smart practitioners try out new approaches. The rules bind everyone and come from every direction. The National Trust for Historic Preservation requires that all "documents or plans for preservation work" supported by its Preservation Fund grants "*must conform to the Secretary of the Interior's Standards for the Treatment of Historic Properties.*" Rhode Island's Certified Local Government Grants program (the state's biggest source of grant funding) requires all projects to "provide for the identification and evaluation, planning and protection, and public awareness of properties and sites *listed in or considered eligible for listing in the National Register of Historic Places.*" Rules like these (and there are many) insulate accepted ideas from the challenge of new ones: history, historic buildings, and the proper treatment of historic buildings are all just what the rules say they are. Thus, the rules ensure that the discipline will learn only what it already knows. In such a world there is no need for research: practitioners might as well read Jane Austen or paddle a canoe as study the latest findings in community sociology, ecology, or environmental psychology, because none of them can be put to use in their work. It is all equally irrelevant if not equally enjoyable.

What the discipline already knows, unfortunately, is somewhat out of date. It's been a full half-century since preservation's legal and conceptual structures were set in place in the mid-1960s, and almost forty years since the tax credits were added at the end of the 1970s. Since then, the world has been turned practically upside down, yet the preservation system has hardly changed. As a result, the two have moved steadily further out of focus with each other, until today the profession seems at times hardly to be in contact with reality. Climate change, large-scale global migration, urban collapse, rising poverty, and soaring economic inequality preoccupy all mindful Americans; just as pertinently they define the current realities within which heritage is either preserved or lost. Yet, preservation has little to say on any of these pressing subjects. How can it when they don't fit into the discipline's world picture, as it was etched into legal bronze fifty years ago? The isolation achieved by the American preservation field is truly impressive, encompassing not just the contemporary reality outside its domain but even much current thinking within it: for example, the matter of intangible cultural heritage, which has made an important place for itself in global preservation thinking, yet still finds no place in American practice. Resistance to Research is deep and broad.

Why haven't preservationists pushed back? One reason, I think, is that practitioners (and their academic colleagues) have learned to fear change. Beyond fears of personal retribution, there is a widespread collective terror that efforts to update the system will only open it to attack: demanding more and better preservation might, therefore, leave us with less and worse. Another reason is structural. Generating credible proposals for change requires resources of time, money, and effort in excess of what's needed to get through the discipline's daily workload as set by legislation and programmatic requirements. Such surplus resources simply do not exist. Decades of government budget cuts, financial crashes, and economic redistribution have left public agencies stripped bare, non-profits fighting for survival, and consultants competing for an ever narrower range of work. There is no excess of anything. In effect, the entire discipline is working tightly to specification: a very efficient plan from a certain perspective, but one that's not likely to stimulate new knowledge or ideas. One might put it differently and say that the discipline is working to rule, in the sense of an industrial labor action: that is, it is doing the bare minimum required of it under contract. This is not happening because practitioners are drawing the line on long hours or low pay or bad working conditions. It is happening because, after doing what's required of them, they don't have resources left over for doing what isn't—namely research. The government departments are lucky if they can get through their statutory requirements. The non-profits are consumed with fundraising and cannot risk putting assets into potentially unproductive lines of work. The private-sector consultants get paid for doing only what the market demands, which is what the existing rules specify. As for the academics...well, we are coming to them. But the bottom line is that the discipline's rigid dependence on rules, enforced by lack of resources for experimentation, makes policy-related research largely pointless, or at best an unaffordable luxury.

Which brings us to the second of our three structural obstacles, the discipline's inadequate capacity for research. Supposing it were wanted, where could the field generate policy-related research? These days, research in policy-dependent disciplines generally comes from three types of organization: think-tanks, university departments, and university research centers. Let us look at each in turn. First, the think-tanks, which churn out much of the policy research that gets political traction and also whip up public discussion of them. Preservation has no think-tank, nor does any general-purpose tank consistently put resources into it. As for special-purpose tanks, the closest approximation is the National Trust's Preservation Green Lab, which does fine work but can hardly be expected to carry the burden alone.

After think-tanks come the universities, and here the picture is more complicated. With about sixty university-based programs granting professional certificates or degrees, the field's capacity to train practitioners, at any rate, seems adequate. But the universities' role in research is another story. In many policy-related fields, traditional teaching departments have been supplemented in recent decades by research centers or institutes. The mission of these entities is explicitly and single-mindedly to generate research. They offer the inducements of dedicated fund-raising machines and also tempt many faculty members with the promise of transcending the disciplinary boundaries imposed by their departments. The good news is that several heritage research centers have sprung up in recent years: at the University of Maryland, the University of Massachusetts Amherst, Montclair State University (New Jersey), and Texas A&M University. All claim to work across disciplinary boundaries. Yet, their capacity for policy-relevant research is at best slender. Most focus on well-established areas of practice; some centralize without apparently expanding the functions of existing departments; some have purely local missions; a few struggle for survival. Not one lists policy development or analysis as a research goal. Preservation's research capacity with regard to university-based centers, in short, is no greater than its command of think-tank resources.

Which brings us back to the academic preservation departments themselves. One might expect these to generate a steady stream of policy research and analysis (especially considering how policy-dependent the discipline is), yet, in fact, they produce very little. Whether they *could* produce more is the question. It's not obvious how to estimate their theoretical research capacity (understanding that we are not rating individuals but the discipline itself), but we might attempt it through a sequence of approximations. We begin, then, by counting the departments which grant graduate degrees (as distinct from undergraduate degrees or professional certificates), as these are the departments most likely to care about whether their faculty does research. There are thirty-seven such departments. Next, we count the graduate-degree-granting departments which are located within Research-1 universities, as these are the universities which consistently expect faculty to do research and support it: now we are down to twenty-four departments. And, here, we arrive at a measure we can begin to compare with other policy-related disciplines: for example, urban planning, which has fifty such departments, or anthropology, which has at least sixty-five. Next, we must consider the question of what is called, ominously, the terminal degree. While many urban planning and anthropology departments offer doctorates, only a handful of preservation programs get beyond the master's degree level. Since it is mainly at the doctoral level that students are asked to carry out (and faculty to supervise) sustained research, it can be doubted whether most master's-level

RESISTANCE TO RESEARCH

programs—even at Research-I universities—are really set up to support a significant research effort. Though we are not finished with our analysis, preservation's potential research footprint is already looking dangerously light.

We come now to a crucial question: how many faculty members in these twenty-four departments hold full-time appointments in preservation? This is a more significant number than total faculty, because some departments borrow faculty from other departments and disciplines; and because nearly all rely heavily on adjunct faculty (or more correctly, contingent academic labor) to carry their teaching burden. Both groups enrich the classroom experience, yet they don't necessarily add to preservation's research effort. Of the two, the adjunct faculty are by far the more consequential. The total number of adjuncts is hard to estimate, since neither the National Council on Preservation Education nor anyone else tracks this critically important number. But I would guess that adjuncts account nationally for perhaps three-fourths of total preservation faculty and cover an equivalent proportion of the teaching load.[2] Whatever their precise number turns out to be, it's clear enough that the reproduction of the discipline from year to year and generation to generation depends heavily on them. In an ideal world, they would provide a powerful engine for research. Yet, most universities bar them from seeking research funding; some flatly forbid them from doing research (this being supposedly a prerogative of the full-time faculty). These are, to put it mildly, pretty severe disincentives, but there are more. Those adjuncts who persist, carving time out from busy professional and teaching schedules (and the teaching is scandalously underpaid) to do research and write it up and get it published and present it at conferences find that they must generally pay for the entire process themselves. They also find that, lacking the kinds of institutional support which full-time faculty take for granted, many policy-relevant research avenues are closed off. While some nonetheless manage to produce important research, it is prudent for purposes of estimating institutional capacity to subtract adjuncts (and borrowed faculty) from the count.

That leaves the full-time preservation faculty. How many are there? Again, no one seems to know. But I suspect the mean per department lies well below three, and few if any programs can boast more than five.[3] If this is the case, then the number of potentially research-ready preservation faculty members located at Research-I universities might come to about fifty, and surely under sixty, in total. From this number, we have to subtract faculty members who serve as program directors (and are therefore occupied with administration), those whose training and fields of specialization have little policy relevance, those whose heavy teaching loads virtually forbid research, those who are purely practitioners, and finally, those who prefer to devote their time to other university activities. We are left with the equivalent of perhaps as few as ten, and almost certainly no more than fifteen, full-time preservation faculty members nationally who at any given time are in a position to undertake significant policy-relevant research.

This is a shocking number. Admittedly, it's just a guess (for the reasons already given). And one can certainly find reasons to ignore it. After all, several contributors to this very volume have managed to do research despite not being affiliated with Research-I universities (I myself am unaffiliated with any university). And some of the most useful recent writings on preservation have come from practitioners whose academic affiliations (if any) are distinctly secondary.[4] But to gauge the discipline's research capacity, we would have to set these exceptions against others found on the opposite side: for example, quite large departments which produce little or no policy-related research.

Perhaps the actual numbers will turn out to be a little better than I have suggested, or perhaps (heaven help us), a little worse. But the precise number is hardly the point: we are not talking about specific individuals but rather about a metric with which to grasp the discipline's capacity (or, as it

RESISTANCE TO RESEARCH

turns out, its incapacity) for serious research. And as it happens, other institutional factors depress it even further. Such as it is, preservation's research capacity might be barely adequate if the higher-ups (I mean the program directors, department chairs, and deans) pushed for the full use of it. But they don't. I doubt if there is one anywhere in the country who measures the success of a preservation program by its output of policy-relevant research. Even where research (or at least publication) is expected, anecdotal evidence suggests that at some institutions tenure and promotion standards are used to enforce conformity with established themes and subjects, stifling the wayward assistant professor whose undisciplined head-scratchings might otherwise lead to provocative new lines of research. Even if they wanted to, few administrators are in a position to provide meaningful support for policy-relevant preservation research. At the highest level (the deans), preservation is nearly everywhere a low priority. At the lowest level (the program directors), the highest priorities are to fill the classrooms each year and cover the curriculum. In an alternate universe (one where the course of study focused on anticipating the problems of the future and developing strategies to meet them), the curriculum itself might become a sparkplug for policy-relevant research, but in actuality the curriculum (as I've already suggested) is basically a technical training regimen which neither requires nor benefits much from policy-relevant research.[5]

To some extent, these problems can be explained as the growing pains of a discipline locked into a master's degree curriculum two sizes too small. There's a strong case to be made that in today's world three or four semesters (or even five) are not enough to train a preservationist. On the other side, there are strong cases to be made that in today's world graduates in a low-earning field can't handle any more student debt; and that the standard university PhD model may not be the best answer anyway. What about continuing education, or lifelong learning as it is now called? A good idea for sure, but it won't solve the research problem (neither, for that matter, will PhD programs if they emphasize architectural history, theory, or materials conservation).

In sum, then, while preservation's sixty or so university programs look from the outside remarkably like the sort of genuine university departments one might expect to generate a healthy stream of research, they are not. They are, in fact, hardly more than teaching mills which do little to make up for the lack of think-tanks or strong research centers. All in all, preservation's research capacity is perilously low: too low to sustain it in a complex and competitive policy environment.

Supposing preservationists wanted to do research; supposing they *could* do research: how would they know what to investigate? This question brings us to the last of our structural obstacles, the discipline's lack of direction. Again, information on this point is anecdotal: that said, my impression is that there is considerable frustration within the field. This is coming from students; it is also coming from seasoned professionals. There is a perception that the established ways are not working as well as they ought to, and perhaps used to. The old assumptions are looking threadbare. Quite a few preservationists, then, are convinced that *something* should change, and that the change should be more than a mere nip and tuck. But they are frustrated by the resistance they encounter within their agencies or professional associations or academic departments even to discussing the problem. That said, I don't think anyone is entirely confident of what exactly should change, or how. There is a diffuse mood of dissatisfaction but no clear path out of it.

One might expect such a condition to stimulate a lively ferment of research. But in fact, it is deeply discouraging. Without a sense of disciplinary direction there is no possibility of putting together a robust research agenda; and without such an agenda the prospects for a meaningful accumulation of research are dim. This would be so even if the other obstacles were swept away. The best we can hope for in the current situation is an idiosyncratic assortment of individual research plans, with no individual having the resources to make her or his plan stick and the field as a whole being unable to make good use of any. In such a situation, all lines of investigation will look equally intriguing, but they will also be equally irrelevant and will remain, most probably, equally ignored. The preservation field will have to rediscover a sense of purpose before it can mount a serious research effort.

For what it's worth, my own view of the way forward is to reorient preservation practice towards the pressing social, economic, and environmental challenges of our own time—just as those who created the conceptual structures of the 1960s responded to the challenges of theirs. As to what those challenges are, I would guess that many Americans would agree at least provisionally on the list I offered earlier—climate change, poverty, economic inequality, immigration, diversity, and urban decline—though they might include others and their views on each might differ. Defining the challenges merits a discussion in itself. But whatever they turn out to be, the principle is to make preservation effective at protecting heritage from the troubles they unleash—and, just as important, at deploying our national and global stock of heritage to help relieve or mitigate those troubles.

This is my view. Others will differ. I don't know what most of my colleagues might propose because the field is not talking enough—not widely, deeply, or openly enough—about its own malaise or about the tremendous possibilities for renewal which the present moment affords. There are indeed signs that a discipline-wide debate may be breaking through the hard crust of conformity to rules and regulations: it should be encouraged, for the questions are pressing. What is preservation for? What problems are germane to it? What kinds of solutions are valid? What values ought to guide the work? Preservation's very identity and future hang on the answers.

There is another question, and on it hangs the future of preservation research: what new knowledge will be useful to a refocused and re-energized discipline? My proposal generates its own research agenda: it is one which draws heavily on the social and environmental sciences for what they can tell us about the interactions between heritage and enviro-socio-economic conditions. But other proposals will generate quite different agendas. When the discipline once again knows what it is for, what it is trying to do, how it relates to society and the economy and the environment, a serviceable research plan will emerge. But not before.

Of course, the important thing is not the future of preservation research but of preservation itself. And so, one must ask one more question: where is the lever for change, the lever that can spring an immobilized discipline from its moorings and get it moving again? Where is the lever that can pry a conventionalized practice wide open? It lies, I think, in the first of the structural obstacles I described: it is the law, and the regulations, and the programmatic guidelines. It is the programs themselves. These are responsible for channeling the work that preservationists do and the thoughts they are allowed to think. The law is the lever that can push preservation onto a new track. Changing it—and with it, the policies and programs and precedents that flow from it—is indeed the only thing that will allow preservationists to turn in new and different directions.

The moral for those who want to encourage real preservation research—research which gets its teeth into reality—is simple. Rather than arranging conferences and publications and other well-intentioned efforts to promote cross-disciplinary dialogue, they should focus their efforts on changing the law and revamping the apparatus that hangs from it. Not only because the law and the apparatus are not working well but also because changing them is the only way to change what preservationists are allowed to do. And until that happens, all hypotheses, all proposals, all speculations, all research findings will remain mere flights of fancy. That said, a tremendous debate is needed to establish how the existing rules and programs should change. And, of course, to build up the head of steam needed to accomplish the change.

RESISTANCE TO RESEARCH

When that debate happens, the obstacles will fall and Resistance to Research will begin to crumble, as evanescent as a vague memory of a troubling dream.

Notes

1 A fifth area might be defined to include government funded documentation programs, mainly HABS (Historic American Building Survey), HAER (Historic American Engineering Record), and HALS (Historic American Landscapes Survey). As the work of these programs neither has, nor is intended to have, any practical impact on the survival of the things they document I have not included them in my accounting.

2 Jeremy Wells has compiled data on 27 master's-level programs based on their websites, as of 2011. For the 25 programs for which he was able to extract information on both full-time and adjunct faculty, adjuncts accounted for just over 67 percent of the total. However, this number is probably a lower bound; first, because full-time faculty may be over counted in Wells's list (see note 3); and second, because (as Wells acknowledges) the information on university websites is frequently out-of-date and unreliable—and (as I can personally attest) nowhere more so than in what relates to adjunct faculty. Jeremy C. Wells, "A Critical Analysis of Master's Programs in Historic Preservation," *AIA Preservation Architect Newsletter* (online), Spring 2011, Table 3.

3 Based on the programs' own websites, Jeremy Wells suggests that for 27 masters-level programs in 2011 the average number of "tenured or tenure track-faculty" was three, with some programs having as many as seven or eight. But these numbers do not distinguish between faculty with full-time appointments *in preservation* and those with appointments elsewhere in the university. They may also be too generous in counting emeritus faculty, contingent faculty whose status is disguised by titles like Instructor, and others (like Professors of Practice) whose university commitments are less than full-time. In early 2017, I rechecked the statistics for five programs with high numbers (at least five) of tenured or tenure-track faculty. In Wells's account, these five programs totalled 35 full-time faculty; in mine, no more than 15. The difference in these five programs alone is enough to reduce the average from three to just under 2.5 per program. Jeremy C. Wells, "A Critical Analysis of Master's Programs in Historic Preservation," *AIA Preservation Architect Newsletter* (online), Spring 2011, Table 3.

4 For example, see Jean Carroon, (*Sustainable Preservation: Greening Existing Buildings,* Hoboken, John Wiley and Sons, 2010); any of Thomas F. King's many books (for example, *Places That Count: Traditional Cultural Properties in Cultural Resource Management*, Walnut Creek, CA, AltaMira Press, 2003; or *Our Unprotected Heritage: Whitewashing the Destruction of our Cultural and Natural Environment*, Walnut Creek, CA, Left Coast Press, 2009); or Preservation Green Lab, National Trust for Historic Preservation (*The Role of District Energy in Greening Existing Neighborhoods*, 2010, in partnership with the University of Oregon's Center for Sustainable Business Practices); or John H. Sprinkle, Jr. (*Crafting Preservation Criteria: The National Register of Historic Places and American Historic Preservation*, New York and London, Routledge, 2014).

5 I am far from the only observer to criticize the graduate preservation curriculum. As Robert Russell observes, the atmosphere in most graduate preservation programs is "at best indifferent to thinking and at at times overtly hostile to intellectual activity." Robert Russell, "First Pete and then Repeat? Fundamental Differences in Intention between Undergraduate and Graduate Preservation Programs in the United States," in Barry L. Stiefel and Jeremy C. Wells (eds.), *Preservation Education: Sharing Best Practices and Finding Common Ground*, Lebanon, NH (University Press of New England), 2014, p. 49.

Conclusion

A Human-Centered Way Forward

Jeremy C. Wells and Barry L. Stiefel

This book, while addressing how to make the professional care of old places more responsive to human needs, has covered a broad range of topics focusing on gathering and using evidence to implement a human-centered built heritage conservation practice. To be sure, higher education has a fundamental role to play in this endeavor, but to date has neglected its responsibility, preferring to treat the professional care of old places as a periphery endeavor to the primary aims of architecture and planning. As Ned Kaufman relates in Chapter 16, none of the content discussed in this book is relevant until higher education begins to promote and facilitate research in human-centered heritage conservation. If staffing these small programs remains difficult, with neither full-time faculty unencumbered by administrative responsibilities, nor access to resources for research, the future remains very dim indeed.

But implementing a human-centered approach to the professional care of old places is not just the responsibility of higher education, it is also the responsibility of practitioners, and arguably, society as a whole. If the meanings and benefits of heritage conservation continue to be defined by those inside the system who already have power, this endeavor will continue to have little relevance to the public. The key concept here is the broad engagement of as many stakeholders and actors as possible, lay and expert, inside the discipline of heritage conservation and outside of it, and including both Western and non-Western perspectives. In the United States, we need to do better than the benchmark of 1966 when academics fed public sentiment through the narrow straw of pedantic aesthetics and art history that established the National Historic Preservation Act (Rains & Henderson, 1966). Indeed, as David Lowenthal argues in *The Past Is a Foreign Country: Revisited* (2015, 421),

> [t]he end result of indiscriminate preservation would be a stultifying museumized world, in which nothing ever made or done was allowed to perish. Failure to winnow is madness. Yet, heritage is such a scared cow that few dare call for its culling. Italy is so stuffed with treasure that only a fraction of it is adequately cared for, let alone accessible. Things are much the same the world over. Everyone knows this, yet no steward publicly affirms it

Therefore, what would the professional care of old places look like if it could more fully encapsulate the meanings and values of the public instead of conservation for the sake of preserving buildings in and of itself? This question is not only new territory but also challenges the power of people who are part of the system of heritage. But, if we accept this challenge there are some potential ways forward.

Several clear themes emerge from the chapters of this book that provide both clues for the essential characteristics of human-centered heritage conservation and ways to move this vision into practice. These themes include the nature of empirical evidence and transcendence, giving practitioners space (and permission) to think, the need for environmental psychology to be part of the discussion, practice frameworks, the "shadow" that prevents change to practice, isolation, and the lack of

Can Empiricism Be Reconciled with Transcendence?

Jack Elliot (Chapter 4) made several observations that position empiricism as antithetical to a transcendental experience of heritage, and, on the surface, this seems entirely reasonable. His argument is that empiricism is too reductive and eliminates the depth of meaning, voiding the essential nature of a transcendental experience. Empiricism, as it has been classically presented (see Tainter & Lucas, 1983), requires direct observation via the senses and discards many meanings and feelings because they are not objective and thus definitely qualifies Elliott's argument. If we view empiricism in this way, then the phenomenological experience of being in historic places cannot be understood, much less described, because such an experience cannot be reduced to objective descriptions of color, measurement, or temperature, for instance. But this assumes that there is only one, narrow definition of empiricism rooted in positivism. David Seamon (1982, 123) makes the argument against this positivistic definition of empiricism and claims that phenomenology, which is rooted in transcendental experiences, is instead "radically empirical" and "relies on all kinds of evidence, inner or outer, less or more tangible." Indeed, while phenomenologists clearly reject a positivistic definition of empiricism (Ihde, 2012, 75), they embrace the practice of phenomenology, which is focused on understanding the lived experience, as radically empirical (Ihde, 2012, 16; Pollio, Henley, & Thompson, 1997, ix; Rosenthal & Bourgeois, 1980; Wild, 1942).

But what does it mean for a description of an experience to be "radically" empirical? An anthropological perspective can be useful in answering this question by elucidating the difference between *etic* and *emic* perspectives as used in ethnographies. An *etic* perspective of culture is positivistic and often quantitative while an *emic* perspective is qualitative; or, in a different sense, *etic* descriptions of culture must be objective and reproducible and are from the perspective of an external observer of culture, involving measurement, while *emic* descriptions focus on meanings and nuances that cannot be reduced to numbers, requiring one to become part of, or integrated into a culture to better understand cultural meanings as a member of the culture. Clifford Geertz (1973) provides a well-known example of the differences between the *etic* and *emic* perspectives by describing someone's wink. It is possible to measure the number of winks and the length of time that an eye is closed to produce positivistic data. Or, one could simply ask the winker why she closed one eye to produce qualitative data. Only the *emic* perspective can tell us *why* she winked—perhaps due to an eye irritation or maybe to convey a message to someone. In this sense, the *etic* perspective is empirical in a positivistic way while the *emic* perspective is empirical in a radical way. It is not possible to reduce an *emic* description into known quanta of meaning units divorced from the fundamental nature of the experience; the number of meanings is not important, but rather understanding the meanings is essential. This distinction is the idea behind the concept of "radicalness," which focuses on the fundamental nature of experience that can involve an infinite number of meanings.

Thus, empirical evidence need not be equated with Cartesian science, positivism, or quantification. Instead, it can be qualitative as well with an infinitely profound depth of meaning. The essential argument of this book is that empirical evidence, which is based on observation and experience, is needed to balance the overemphasis of rationalistic theory that is so prevalent in built heritage conservation practice as expressed through doctrine, rules, and regulations. If we make a claim, for instance, as in item 9 of the US-based Secretary of the Interior's Standards, that an intervention shall differentiate the old and the new, it needs to be supported by evidence. Not coincidentally, we do not actually know how

CONCLUSION

people perceive "old" and "new" building fabric nor how people can be convinced that an intervention is "compatible." This example is emblematic of a rationalistic theory that has no (known) evidence to substantiate its use. Rationalistic preservation/conservation theory is rife with such examples that contribute to the isolation of professional heritage conservation practice from normal human experience.

Giving Practitioners a Space (and Permission) to Think

Perhaps, the most provocative element of Jack Elliott's essay (Chapter 4), in this book, is a description of how, when he was working in a state historic preservation office, his manager scolded his efforts to better serve the public's interests with the directive that "Preservationists are not paid to think!" This comment ought to be chilling to every professional charged with the care of old places because it reinforces the fact that there is no real space for these practitioners working in areas of planning and compliance to think about and improve upon their practice. So much of the work of preservation/conservation planning and compliance is dictated by rules and regulations that there are too few opportunities to think outside the box and question the elements of decades-old ordinances, statutes, or regulations. To be sure, this sort of change lies within the realm of politics, but the fact remains that those individuals who are best prepared to address the challenges of preservation/conservation practice in the twenty-first century (practitioners) are also the same people who are muzzled by their employers. This effectively guarantees the ossification of the field.

There are no studies or data regarding the degree to which conservation/preservation practitioners are told to not think or inhibited in some way by their employers, so these accounts are anecdotal. But the increasing frequency of these stories begins to look very much like a pattern. When the first editor served on the board of the National Alliance for Preservation Commissions (NAPC; US-based), he frequently heard of these kinds of accounts from members, who work as preservation planners in local municipalities. When he organized conferences and invited practitioners, they told him that they cannot have their names associated with their government employers. He even had one woman fold her name badge over to hide her employer's identity. These people are genuinely afraid to question compliance-based activities of built heritage conservation, much less offer ways to make the system more responsive to public needs. Where can they speak freely? Where is the safe place to discuss how practice can better serve the public? The answer is that the most logical place for these discussions is with organizations that support the work of practitioners. But, with only one exception, these organizations do not appear to be opening a safe place for practitioners to think. Presently, academia only has the concept of "tenure" within the heritage preservation field as a means of protecting freedom of speech pertaining to criticisms within the profession, and as previously noted, these positions are few and in decline.

The NAPC ought to be able to provide a forum for preservation planners to engage in critical debates and explorations, but in our experience (including serving on the board of the organization), their activities tend to reinforce existing preservation/conservation doctrine and fail to question, in meaningful ways, the elements of preservation ordinances that do not work in the public interest. This is not to deprecate the role of the NAPC, which is essential in helping local historic preservation commissions serve their regulatory role in a way that minimizes the legal liability of municipalities, but there appears to be a reluctance to question or discuss aspects of changing regulatory frameworks that depart from established doctrine. Similarly, the American Cultural Resources Association (ACRA) supports practitioners who work in environmental compliance (e.g., NHPA Section 106, NEPA's EIS) and their annual conference features innovative work in the areas of interpretation involving the public in archaeological work. However, like NAPC, ACRA fails to directly address

319

CONCLUSION

the rules and regulations upon which the majority of its member's livelihoods are based. Technically, the National Conference of State Historic Preservation Officers (NCSHPO), which supports professionals who work in state historic preservation offices, cannot critically debate the existence of or the implementation of rules and regulations because it runs counter to its mission "as delegates of the Secretary of the Interior pursuant to the National Historic Preservation Act of 1966, as amended (NHPA) (16 USC 470)." This contrasts with the National Association of Tribal Historic Preservation Officers (NATHPO) where its "overarching purpose is to support the preservation, maintenance and revitalization of the culture and traditions of Native peoples of the United States". While the mission of NATHPO is conducted through the respective tribal bureaucracies of tribal historic preservation offices, there is a more human-centric focus within its purview that includes the "preserv[ing] and rejuvenat[ion[of the unique cultural traditions and practices of their tribal communities" (NATHPO, 2017), in addition to conventional structures and archaeological sites.

The prioritization of material objects over community needs does not seem particularly different in the United Kingdom. The Association of Local Government Archaeological Officers (ALGAO) does not have an annual conference and exists primarily to educate practitioners in established doctrines, rules, and regulations and advocate for "historic environment services." While the Chartered Institute for Archeologists (CIFA) does have an annual conference, like ALGAO, it primarily exists to promote existing standards and encourage the employment of archaeologists. The Institute for Historic Building Conservation (IHBC) primarily focuses on the conservation of building fabric and less on holistic aspects of planning for the conservation of places and landscapes and also shares most of the same operational goals as ALGAO and CIFA; it is also very active in certifying architectural conservators and educational programs. ALGAO, CIFA, and IHBC all provide very useful services to their members, upholding high standards in education and promoting the heritage conservation sector to provide employment and consultancy opportunities. But none of these organizations have taken a critical stance against the orthodox doctrine, rules, and regulations that dictate many of their members' activities.

Canada has the Canadian Association of Heritage Professionals that "represent[s] the interests of professional practitioners in many related fields of heritage conservation." Like NCSHPO, it too fails to take a critical stance on existing doctrine, rules, and regulations because doing so would run counter to its mission to assure that a heritage professional "conforms to accepted technical and ethical standards and works in accordance with the regulations and guidelines of the person's specialty heritage field and the jurisdictions of practice." This analysis is not meant to be exhaustive, but this pattern repeats across Australia and European countries as well with NGOs that represent the interests of practitioners focusing on educational and practice standards that reinforce rather than challenge the status quo. In sum, these organizations appear neither interested nor able to create a safe place where practitioners can "think" and in doing so, challenge existing notions of how the conservation of the built environment and cultural landscapes ought to be achieved, especially, where these activities overlap with the regulatory environment. Perhaps this result should not be so surprising because these organizations also exist to generate employment and consultancy opportunities for their members, and so challenging the very field in which this advocacy occurs could jeopardize this part of their mission. To be sure, organizations that advocate for heritage practitioners will be reluctant to bite the hand (i.e., rules and regulations) that feeds it, so to speak.

Academic conferences, such as the Association for Critical Heritage Studies, and many of the scientific committees of ICOMOS, do provide space for practitioners to think, and more importantly, to speak about their experiences in an environment that is much more open to critical approaches.

320

CONCLUSION

(A counter-argument for ICOMOS is that it also tends to reinforce the *status quo* rather than invite alternative perspectives, however.) But, perhaps not so surprisingly, heritage practitioners rarely attend these conferences, and their voice is often not represented, much less heard. Many of these academic conferences take positions against practitioners that can be perceived as less than welcoming, further decreasing the chance of practitioners taking advantage of this venue as a space to think.

This leaves NGOs that are general advocates for heritage conservation. In the United States, the National Trust for Historic Preservation is leading an effort to broadly engage the public and practitioners in defining "people-based preservation," which is contingent on exploring ways that practice can change. This approach was readily apparent at the Trust's conference in Houston, Texas in November of 2016 where many practitioners participated in a roundtable discussion of the future of people-centered preservation. The first author joined this discussion, which produced many useful ideas, although (at least from his perspective), not many addressed the regulatory environment directly. But the consensus from the group was that a people-centered direction was very much a way to move forward and that the regulatory environment often impedes this goal. This is in contrast to the second author, who has worked with the Community Built Association where the approach is on "collaboration[s] between professionals and community volunteers to design, organize and create community projects that reshape public spaces." This includes historic preservation projects, but also "murals, playgrounds, parks, public gardens, [and] sculptures" (Community Built Association, 2017). Therefore, "[c]ommunity-based historic preservation aims to preserve and express local identity and heritage" (Melcher, Stiefel, & Faurest, 2017) in addition to other aspects of the built environment, as needed. In other words, there are NGOs that use evidence to engage in human-centered built environment initiatives for the purpose of improving quality of life, but where historic preservation practice is simply one of the multiple tools utilized, instead of the only or primary. While the editors have not performed an exhaustive survey of all heritage advocacy NGOs across the globe that are addressing practice, it is likely that there are other, similar examples as well.

Whither Environmental Psychology?

A primary aim of this book is to explore ways in which social science-based evidence can be used to influence heritage conservation practice. Evidence for the public perception of heritage and the use of heritage is abundant from the field of critical heritage studies (e.g., Gibson, 2009; Harrison, 2013; Jones, 2009; Milholland, 2010; Pichler, 2012; Ross, 2010; Smith, 2009; Smith & Campbell, 2015; Sommer, 2009; Waterton & Smith, 2010; Watson, 2015), but the vast majority of this scholarship comes primarily from the disciplines of anthropology, public history, and folklore. Environmental psychology is largely absent, with a few exceptions (e.g., Levi, 2005; Lewicka, 2008; Wells & Baldwin, 2012), even though there are many claims for how the conservation of old places is related to the sense of place, identity, and emotional attachment, all of which are areas that this field of research is designed to address. Moreover, while anthropologists readily acknowledge the potential for the applied aspects of their work, such as the Society for Applied Anthropology (SfAA), there are fewer examples from environmental psychology, although the Environmental Design Research Association (EDRA) does provide an explicitly applied outlet for research conducted by environmental psychologists. The problem is that most environmental psychologists, unlike anthropologists, do not seem to have a particular interest in the conservation of old places.

This book, therefore, is unusual in that it contains studies using methodological approaches from environmental psychology to address heritage conservation practice (You-Kyong Ahn, Chapter 5;

321

CONCLUSION

Annamarie Bliss, Chapter 6; Suzanne Bott, Chapter 2) in balance with more traditional, ethnographic approaches (Jolly, Milligan, Purser, and Watt, Chapter 14; Taplin, Scheld and Low, Chapter 7; Stephanie Ryberg-Webster, Chapter 10). The editors believe that environmental psychology needs to play a more prominent role, among the other social science methodological approaches, if we are to better understand the interaction of people with place. There is no reason, however, that other social scientists or practitioners cannot readily adapt methods from environmental psychology, such as photoelicitation, which have proven to be powerful in this way that they can access the way people feel about and perceive places (Harper, 2003; Hughes, 2012).

Critical heritage studies (or any study of old places) need not imply or demand any adherence to a particular discipline or ontological or epistemological frame. The methodologies and methods used to answer research questions, including those that arise from practice, should be chosen based on their ability to answer a research question rather than fealty to a particular discipline. This goal, however, demands that researchers and practitioners who address the conservation of old places need to both be open to, and receive training in, a wider variety of methodological approaches than is done currently. Continuing education incentives should also be considered part of the metaphorical toolbox of techniques to bring about lasting positive change so that scholars and practitioners can be updated on current trends and be engaged in dialogue with one another.

Converting Evidence into Practice: Frameworks for Guidance

Assuming that evidence for conservation practice becomes more abundant in the future, how do we then use this evidence to influence practice? Scholarship on this question is largely silent, although community-based participatory research may offer a model, especially, given that it has been used with community-based archaeology and natural resource conservation (Wells, 2015). Rather than relying on practitioner expertise to guide the heritage conservation process, practitioners become expert facilitators. In this model, the task of the practitioner is to gather and understand the meanings of stakeholders in a way that minimizes power differentials between the participants. Practitioners, therefore, cannot come to the table with *a priori* assumptions but rather need to have an open mind toward considering meanings and values that may differ or conflict with those found in orthodox built heritage conservation practice. The overall process moves from the traditional, expert-driven top-down process to a stakeholder-driven bottom-up approach.

The key concept in the expert as facilitator model is one of the balance between many meanings and values regarding a place or a structure, and a willingness to always consider the context in the overall decision-making process. In some cases, such as where a heritage object is particularly rare and contains significant art/historical value, orthodox conservation values can play a larger role. The value of old places, however, is increasingly viewed as quite ordinary and commonplace (Harrison, 2013), which makes this approach unnecessary in most cases, and the meanings of most stakeholders (especially civil experts), even if they differ from orthodox conservation values, can be allowed to predominate. How this looks in practice, however, greatly needs exploration.

A useful example of how a grassroots approach to the care of old places might work is exemplified in the National Trust for Historic Preservation's Main Street program, which was originally created in the late 1970s to revitalize historic downtowns. The Main Street Approach relies, almost exclusively, on the work of tens of volunteers and one paid, "Main Street manager" (essentially, an executive director). These volunteers are community stakeholders and, most importantly, civil experts—typically residents and business owners—who have a long-term vested interest in

CONCLUSION

revitalizing their downtown. Although influenced by orthodox preservation/conservation approaches, evidence indicates that the way in which Main Street volunteers conserve their downtowns often differs dramatically from orthodox doctrine (Wells, 2010). The authors are not aware of a better example of community stakeholders empowering themselves in the preservation/conservation and design aspects of their historic downtown, including the use of grant funds to incentivize the design that adheres to the stakeholders' values and not the values of orthodox conservation doctrine (Wells, 2017).

The "Shadow" Obscuring the Reality of Built Heritage Conservation Practice

Evidence comes in many forms, and while much of this book focuses on the use of the social sciences to gather evidence to influence heritage conservation practice, Richard Hutching's chapter (3) explored the "dark side" of cultural resource management using the perspectives of critical theory and colonialism. The essence of Hutching's argument is that the bureaucracy of the state that controls the meanings of heritage matters more than the actual meanings people have for tangible and intangible heritage. In other words, the system of heritage conservation consumes the rationale for why we engage in conservation in the first place. Instead of real discourse on the meanings and uses of heritage, we have a system that places primacy on efficiency, predictability, calculability/quantification, control, and dehumanization.

Hutching's observations are not entirely novel, but rather originate from several decades of critical approaches to heritage that have revealed:

- The authorized heritage discourse (AHD), which defines heritage conservation as an activity that delegitimizes debates about heritage, ossifies practice, places the convention expert in the role of moral guide, ignores conflict, and gives power to the state (and its actors) while disempowering communities (Smith, 2006).

- The realization that the orthodox doctrines of heritage are a product of Modernism and its attempt to produce a rationalistic way to objectify the meanings associated with buildings, places, and landscapes, at the same time that it rejects any possibility of reviving elements of past traditions and building practices (Semes, 2009).

- Built heritage conservation has traditionally, and in some ways continues to be, an elitist endeavor that overemphasizes discourses from rich, White, males while disempowering people who are already marginalized (Graham, Ashworth, & Tunbridge, 2000; Kaufman, 2009; King, 2009; Nanda et al., 2001; Schofield, 2009).

- Unmanaged heritage tourism increasingly is destroying intangible as well as tangible heritage along with indigenous communities (Breglia, 2006).

- Orthodox heritage conservation practice has become "an instrument of top-down social engineering on a global scale" (Silberman, 2016).

- Orthodox doctrine, rules/regulations, and practice all use heritage values and meanings that are not shared or understood by stakeholders or the public at large and ignore the ordinary, everyday places that people value the most (Schofield, 2009, 2014).

CONCLUSION

- The values of orthodox conservation doctrine and practice rely on pseudoscientific tautologies in which current practice has been justified through past practice (Muñoz Viñas, 2005). Rather than resting on scientific principles, the values of orthodox conservation practitioners are "just another set of cultural values" that are reinforced through expert rule and hegemonic discourses (Waterton, Smith, & Campbell, 2006).

- Heritage is about people, not things (Filippucci, 2009); objects do not have values, people do (Appelbaum, 2007). The separation of heritage into "tangible" and "intangible" elements is artificial: all heritage is intangible because it is "constructed from cultural meanings" (Smith, 2006, 56).

- Authenticity is a sociocultural and experiential construct; there is no such thing as a "truly" or objective authentic state of an object (Cane, 2009). Once the past has happened, there is no possibility of going back and objectively re-establishing the state of an object at some point in time; each attempt at intervening in the life of a building, place, or landscape always creates a new, future reality (Lowenthal, 1985).

These observations are just the tip of the proverbial iceberg as a growing and critical reaction again orthodox heritage conservation practice continually grows on a day-by-day basis.

While realizing that the critique of orthodox conservation practice is both complex and nuanced, the current state of the field is perhaps best compared to the post-modern turn made by many disciplines in the 1970s and 1980s, including planning's communicative turn that moved important elements of practice away from rationalism toward discursive theory (Fischler, 2000). What makes built heritage conservation unique, and continues to delay its transition to a contemporary world, is its overreliance on rules and regulations to achieve its aims, thereby bypassing the need to be more responsive to the public (Hutchings & La Salle, 2015; Wells & Lixinski, 2016). Indeed, on the complete opposite side of the spectrum, as Stiefel explores in Chapter 15, occasionally evidence can be personal and localized, even coming from one's own family history.

The Professional Care of Old Places Is Still an Island

As Stephanie Ryberg-Webster found in Chapter 10, "preservation operates largely in its own silo" independently from other disciplines and fields that address the built environment. Professionals outside of historic preservation believe that the field "narrowly focuses on architecture, strictly adheres to stringent rules, relies on experts to define significant history, and offers limited benefits beyond tax credit financing." The isolation of built heritage conservation practice is arguably due to its overreliance on rules, laws, and regulations to control people's behavior (Wells & Lixinski, 2016). Or, in cruder terms, there are far too many "sticks" and too few "carrots"; we punish people for inappropriate heritage behavior rather than rewarding "good" behavior. (Note that this oversimplification ignores the fact that we need better evidence for what "good" heritage behavior is.) The practitioners of built heritage conservation are too often called heritage or preservation "police" (Emerick, 2009; Fisher, 2007; Holtorf, 2007; Talmage, 2010). This characterization should not be surprising considering that heritage professionals are out of touch with the values of most stakeholders (Hayden, 1995, 47; Hobson, 2004, 13; King, 2009, 78, 100; Lowenthal, 1985; Smith, 2006). This situation is not likely to change anytime soon because the regulatory environment is incapable of accommodating dissenting views (Gibson & Pendlebury, 2009, 9); indeed, from the perspective of the state, heritage

CONCLUSION

is conflict-free (Smith & Waterton, 2012, 166) although there is ample evidence that the meanings of heritage are *born of conflict* (Breglia, 2006). For built heritage conservation practice to be more relevant to a greater part of society, we need a better understanding of how the meanings of heritage form values and the overall process of moving from conflict to consensus. Otherwise, practice will remain in its illusory island of tranquility, isolated from the real world and the relationship of heritage with human flourishing and conflict.

Within higher education, historic preservation and architectural conservation programs are often isolated from other academic programs with few opportunities to collaborate with colleagues within the same school or department, much less across the university (Wells & Stiefel, 2014). This isolation is due in part to the rather unique genesis of practice associated with the care of old places. As a field of practice and study, built heritage conservation was born from the laws created by politicians and the resulting administrative rules created by government bureaucracy. (It shares this origin with the field of environmental or natural resource conservation.) Built heritage conservation practice is, therefore, infused with the perspective of state control, hegemonic discourse, and colonialism (Hutchings & La Salle, 2015) and its practitioners are often taught using this discourse (Wells & Stiefel, 2014). In sum, rather than relying on evidence or even reason to defend the practice, built heritage conservation practice is simply justified through the law. In turn, this law is based on tautological doctrine wherein practice is justified through past practice (Muñoz Viñas, 2005). In this milieu, it can be difficult to engage colleagues from other fields and disciplines in discussions, much less collaboration, because of the restricted nature of discourse. This can change to some extent but built heritage conservation programs in the United States, Canada, and many places in Europe are taught on this traditional platform of tautological doctrines and law.

It is little wonder then, that the field associated with the professional care of old places is very small compared to other areas of research and practice, fragmented, and lacks institutional support for the work of practitioners. (In other words, there is no organization that speaks on behalf of professionals and researchers whose object of attention is old places.) In sum, it is not a particularly attractive or interesting area to explore change or discuss ways that practice can benefit people without separating the practice from the law and orthodox doctrine. With few exceptions, higher education is not leading an effort to expand the contemporary relevance of the professional care of old places to society; instead, this change is coming from the allied fields of archaeology and museum studies largely through the work of people associated with critical heritage studies. With the exception of efforts at ICOMOS (1993) that, as of the writing of this chapter, are more than twenty years old, there has been no attempt to define built heritage conservation curricula through multidisciplinary collaboration that involves a wide variety of stakeholders, including practitioners and the public (Wells & Stiefel, 2014). The efforts to develop conservation curricula are, therefore, very weak or altogether absent and fail to address the relationships between other areas of research and practice. Built heritage conservation/historic preservation programs need to build better bridges with their built environment and especially social science and environmental conservation colleagues.

The separation of built heritage conservation from environmental conservation, especially in the United States and Canada, is further evidence of the way in which heritage conservation practice creates an artificial divide between culture and nature, when in reality they are a continuum (Dyer, 2007). A shift in built heritage conservation practice, moving toward a holistic view of the environment and embracing cultural landscape approaches (Alanen & Melnick, 2000; Davenport & Anderson, 2005; Gibson, 2009; Goetcheus, 2008a, 2008b; Longstreth, 2008; Lozny, 2006), is long

CONCLUSION

due. It is also a potential solution to this isolation as is working with colleagues from the social sciences and built environment studies. Heritage conservation needs to learn from work in the social sciences (Stephenson & Mascia, 2009; Stewart, Williams, & Kruger, 2013), arts and humanities, and environment/behavior research (Demsky & Mack, 2008) that seeks a better understanding of the relationship people have with the place and how this information can provide evidence for changing practice. We no longer need islands of practice, but rather should seek to create a continent of collaboration.

The central argument here is that the way in which built heritage conservation is isolated from its peers severely hampers the potential for multidisciplinary and transdisciplinary collaboration, which has the potential to produce evidence that could change practice in a way that better supports human flourishing. The overreliance of law and orthodox doctrine used in conservation practice alienates not only the public but potential collaborators as well. And, perhaps most importantly, we must be open to evidence, produced from this collaboration that invalidates existing rules, laws, and regulations as well as orthodox conservation doctrine.

Where Are the Non-Western and International Perspectives?

The co-editors of this book are very much aware of the voices that have been omitted from this discussion. Significant parts of the globe—specifically, Latin America, Africa, Asia, and the Middle East—are not present. In addition, while Richard Hutching's chapter (Chapter 3) does explore heritage conservation from an indigenous, North American perspective, most of the voices here are the predominant ones that have always participated in this discussion. This omission is anything but intentional; in the preparation of this book, the co-authors reached out to academics and practitioners in these geographical areas but failed to garner contributions. Perhaps this is a failure in the mode of outreach or there is insufficient interest, or this result could be due to any number of possible factors, including language barriers. This result is not unique; for instance, the field of critical heritage studies also largely features an Australian/European perspective, and its studies are mostly written in English, even though it claims an emancipatory approach to its endeavors.

Thus, the problem of a lack of wider engagement, which is far from unique, is quite evident in this book and it needs to be addressed on multiple levels by multiple actors. For instance, the predominant language—English—in which critical discourse is disseminated needs to be broadened to other languages. Spanish, French, Portuguese, Mandarin, Japanese, and Arabic are examples of languages in which much of this critical discourse appears to be minimal or altogether absent. But the fact remains that, with the exception of English, Spanish and Portuguese, the co-editors of this book have limited faculties for engaging with publications (or people) in these languages. This problem begs the question of how a world congress on human-centered conservation of built heritage and cultural landscapes might manifest. UNESCO would seem to be a logical vehicle for such an endeavor, and indeed, this organization has been quite active in promoting intangible heritage, but often within a Western framework of objective identification, listing, and quantification of benefits. But, let us ask this question from the perspective of global stakeholders: what would a grassroots world congress on human-centered conservation of built heritage and cultural landscapes look like? Are there any examples or models from which we can draw? To date, there are no ready answers to these questions, but they need to be asked with increasing frequency and of more stakeholders.

To be sure, there is an increasing amount of useful scholarship on the intangible heritage of non-Western peoples. Typically, this research exposes the colonialist tendencies to impose

CONCLUSION

Western conservation doctrine on non-Western peoples (e.g., Andrews & Buggey, 2008; Breglia, 2006; Milholland, 2010; Orbasli, 2007; Ross, 2010; Silva & Chapagain, 2013). While it is beyond the scope of this chapter to perform a complete literature review on this scholarship, there is ample evidence to indicate that the way in which built heritage conservation is practiced in a Western context is often incompatible with different cultural belief systems. To impose a fabric-based practice (as opposed to a human-based one) in this context is unethical and colonialist as Richard Hutching advocates in Chapter 3; as such, practice does indeed destroy cultures. Rather than conserving heritage, orthodox heritage conservation in this example is a destroyer of heritage. The creation of Tribal Historic Preservation Offices in the United States provides an intriguing example of an attempt to foster rather than destroy culture within a country where traditional heritage preservation approaches are more exclusively focused on built environment material culture.

Therefore, we need a better understanding of what the care of old places means in different cultural contexts from both professional and lay perspectives. In some ways, this is easier to conceptualize if we realize that the orthodox, Western, practice of built heritage conservation is an example of a cultural practice itself, reflective of a narrow range of socioeconomic values (Waterton et al., 2006) and is not, in and of itself, objectively "better" than other versions of reality. What if heritage conservation could be re-conceptualized as an activity that does not impose value systems, but rather is a framework for understanding and negotiating meanings and values? The theme, in this book, of social science mediated evidence (including community-participatory-based techniques) to inform practice offers a potential way to actualize this idea.

Conclusion

This book began with the question of how a human-centered focus on the professional care of old places can and should change practice through the gathering and use of evidence. The use of evidence to change practice has a long history of success in both medicine and architectural design, and it certainly can be employed much more extensively in heritage conservation than it has to date. Human-centered conservation implies that the act of conserving must be predicated on understanding people's motivations, behaviors, meanings, and values. Thus, conservation practice becomes centered on the gathering of evidence to understand these factors.

"Evidence" comes in many forms, but again, if we are addressing evidence that intersects with people, there is a strong argument to be made that applied methods from the social sciences are not only useful, but perhaps ought to form a core set of tools for how practitioners engage in their work. We need to overcome conceptual barriers, including a general unfamiliarity with what the social sciences are, among both academics and practitioners who work in the conservation of the historic environment. Contingent on this activity is a new vocabulary that needs to be created around human-centered conservation using words, concepts, and methods that are more easily understood by people who are not social scientists. If the net result of these efforts is to make most people's eyes glaze over when they hear the phrase, "social sciences", then we have failed in our endeavor to make heritage conservation more responsive to people's needs.

But heritage conservation is not alone in this issue. Much can be learned from those working in environmental conservation who use applied social science research methods to understand people's intrinsic motivators and then to base practice on influencing these motivating factors. Global environmental conservation advocates, such as the World Wildlife Foundation and Conservation

327

CONCLUSION

International, are trying to bridge the meaning divide between non-Western stakeholders and social scientists in their advocacy efforts. Surely, we can learn something useful from their efforts in how evidence impacts conservation practice.

Those of us who work in built heritage conservation like to say that our work is the "management of change." But, we need to start thinking of a change in terms of our own field as well. The future of the conservation of built heritage and cultural landscapes is, therefore, dependent on *managing how we change our own discipline*. Few would argue that the ultimate aim of conservation should be to arrest the change; in a similar fashion, the actors of heritage conservation need to embrace disciplinary change as an activity central to the practice. In doing so, they might realize that the ultimate aim of our work is to benefit people by adapting, dynamically, to human needs.

References

Alanen, A. R., & Melnick, R. Z. (2000). Why cultural landscape preservation? In A. R. Alanen & R. Melnick (Eds.), *Preserving cultural landscapes in America* (pp. 1–21). Baltimore: Johns Hopkins University Press.

Andrews, T. D., & Buggey, S. (2008). Authenticity in aboriginal cultural landscapes. *Association for Preservation Technology Bulletin, 39*(2/3), 63–71.

Appelbaum, B. (2007). *Conservation treatment methodology*. Boston: Butterworth-Heinemann.

Breglia, L. (2006). *Monumental ambivalence: The politics of heritage*. Austin: University of Texas Press.

Cane, S. (2009). Why do we conserve? Developing understanding of conservation as a cultural construct. In A. Richmond & A. Bracker (Eds.), *Conservation: Principles, dilemmas and uncomfortable truths* (pp. 163–176). Amsterdam; Boston: Butterworth-Heinemann.

Community Built Association. (2017). About Us, http://communitybuilt.org/about/, 27 February.

Davenport, M. A., & Anderson, D. H. (2005). Getting from sense of place to place-based management: An interpretive investigation of place meanings and perceptions of landscape change. *Society and Natural Resources, 18,* 625–641.

Demsky, K., & Mack, L. (2008). Environmental design research (EDR): The field of study and guide to the literature. *Journal of Architectural and Planning Research, 25*(4), 271–275.

Dyer, A. (2007). Inspiration, enchantment and a sense of wonder … can a new paradigm in education bring nature and culture together again? In P. Howard & T. Papagiannēs (Eds.), *Natural heritage: At the interface of nature and culture* (pp. 86–97). London: Routledge.

Emerick, K. (2009). Archaeology and the cultural heritage management 'toolkit': The example of a community heritage project at Cawood, North Yorkshire. In E. Waterton & L. Smith (Eds.), *Taking archaeology out of heritage* (pp. 91–116). Newcastle-upon-Tyne: Cambridge Scholars Press.

Filippucci, P. (2009). Heritage and methodology: A view from social anthropology. In M. L. S. Sørensen & J. Carman (Eds.), *Heritage studies: Methods and approaches* (pp. 319–325). New York: Routledge.

Fischler, R. (2000). Communicative planning theory: A Foucauldian assessment. *Journal of Planning Education, 19*(4), 358–368.

Fisher, M. (2007, December 7). State vs. Church: March of the preservation police. *Washington Post*.

Geertz, C. (1973). *The interpretation of cultures: Selected essays* (pp. ix, 470). New York: Basic Books.

Gibson, L. (2009). Cultural landscapes and identity. In J. Pendlebury (Ed.), *Valuing historic environments* (pp. 67–92). Surrey and Burlington: Ashgate Publishing.

Gibson, L., & Pendlebury, J. (2009). Introduction: Valuing historic environments. In *Valuing historic environments* (pp. 1–16). Surrey and Burlington: Ashgate Publishing.

Goetcheus, C. (2008a). Landscape preservation education in the United States: Status in 2007. *Preservation Education and Research, 1,* 15–28.

CONCLUSION

Goetcheus, C. (2008b). What's next for historic landscape preservation? In E. MacDonald (Ed.), *Exploring the boundaries of historic landscape preservation*; proceedings of the twenty-ninth annual meeting of the alliance for historic landscape preservation, 2007, Athens, Georgia (pp. 192–201). Clemson, SC: Clemson University.

Graham, B., Ashworth, G. J., & Tunbridge, J. E. (2000). *A geography of heritage: Power, culture and economy.* London: Arnold Publishers.

Harper, D. (2003). Reimagining visual methods: Galileo to Neuromancer. In N. K. Denzin & Y. S. Lincoln (Eds.), *Collecting and interpreting qualitative materials* (pp. 176–198). Thousand Oaks, CA: San Publications.

Harrison, R. (2013). *Heritage: Critical approaches.* New York: Routledge.

Hayden, D. (1995). *The power of place.* Cambridge, MA: M.I.T. Press.

Hobson, E. (2004). Conservation and planning: Changing values in policy and practice (pp. 56–78). London: Spon Press.

Holtorf, C. (2007). What does not move any hearts—Why should it be saved? The denkmalpflege diskussion in Germany. *International Journal of Cultural Property, 13*, 33–55.

Hughes, J. (2012). *SAGE visual methods.* London: SAGE.

Hutchings, R., & La Salle, M. (2015). Archaeology as disaster capitalism. *International Journal of Historical Archaeology, 19*, 699–720.

ICOMOS. (1993). *Guidelines for education and training in the conservation of monuments, ensembles and sites.* Paris: ICOMOS.

Ihde, D. (2012). *Experimental phenomenology: Multistabilities.* Albany: State University of New York Press.

Jones, S. (2009). Experiencing authenticity at heritage sites: Some implications for heritage management and conservation. *Conservation and Management of Archaeological Sites, 11*(2), 133–147.

Kaufman, N. (2009). *Place, race, and story: Essays on the past and future of historic preservation.* New York: Routledge.

King, T. F. (2009). *Our unprotected heritage: Whitewashing the destruction of our cultural and natural resources.* Walnut Creek, CA: Left Coast Press.

Levi, D. J. (2005). Does history matter? Perceptions and attitudes toward fake historic architecture and historic preservation. *Journal of Architectural and Planning Research, 22*(2), 149–159.

Lewicka, M. (2008). Place attachment, place identity, and place memory: Restoring the forgotten city past. *Journal of Environmental Psychology, 28*, 209–231.

Longstreth, R. W. (2008). Introduction: The challenges of cultural landscape for preservation. In R. W. Longstreth (Ed.), *Cultural landscapes: Balancing nature and heritage in preservation practice* (pp. 1–20). Minneapolis: University of Minnesota Press.

Lowenthal, D. (1985). *The past is a foreign country.* Cambridge, UK: Cambridge University Press.

Lowenthal, D. (2015). *The past is a foreign country: Revisited.* Cambridge, UK: Cambridge University Press.

Lozny, L. R. (2006). Place, historical ecology and cultural landscape: New directions for culture resource management. In *Landscapes under pressure* (pp. 15–26). New York: Springer.

Melcher, K., Faurest, K., & Stiefel, B., (Eds.). (2017). Introduction: Defining community-built. In *Community-Built: Art, Construction, Preservation and Place.* New York: Routledge

Milholland, S. (2010). In the eyes of the beholder: Understanding and resolving incompatible ideologies and languages in US environmental and cultural laws in relationship to Navajo sacred lands. *American Indian Culture and Research Journal, 34*(2), 103–124.

Muñoz Viñas, S. (2005). *Contemporary theory of conservation.* Amsterdam: Elsevier.

Nanda, R., Burke, F., Burman, P. A. T. I., Kohler, N., Mileti, D. S., Roemich, H., ... Sörlin, S. (2001). Group report: Values and society. In N. S. Baer (Ed.), *Rational decision-making in the preservation of cultural property* (pp. 61–80). Berlin: Dahlem University Press.

NATHPO. (2017, February 23). What is the National Association of Tribal Historic Preservation Officers (NATHPO)?, *About NATHPO.* www.nathpo.org/aboutnathpo.htm

CONCLUSION

Orbasli, A. (2007). Training conservation professionals in the middle east. *Built Environment, 33*(3), 307–322.

Pichler, A. (2012). The dynamics of heritage choice and heritage regimes in the "making of Old Havana". In R. F. Bendix, A. Eggert, & A. Peselmann (Eds.), *Heritage regimes and the state* (pp. 39–59). Göttingen: Göttingen University.

Pollio, H. R., Henley, T. B., & Thompson, C. J. (1997). *The phenomenology of everyday life*. Cambridge: Cambridge University Press.

Rains, A., & Henderson, L. G. (1966). *With heritage so rich*. New York: Random House.

Rosenthal, S. B., & Bourgeois, P. L. (1980). *Pragmatism and phenomenology: A philosophic encounter*. Amsterdam: Grüner.

Ross, A. (2010). Defining cultural heritage at Gummingurru, Queensland, Australia. In C. Phillips & H. Allen (Eds.), *Bridging the divide: Indigenous communities and archaeology into the 21st century* (pp. 107–128). Walnut Creek, CA: Left Coast Press.

Schofield, J. (2009). Being autocentric: Towards symmetry in heritage management practices. In L. Gibson & J. Pendlebury (Eds.), *Valuing historic environments* (pp. 93–113). Surrey and Burlington: Ashgate Publishing.

Schofield, J. (2014). *Who needs experts? Counter-mapping cultural heritage*. Farnham: Ashgate.

Seamon, D. (1982). The phenomenological contribution to environmental psychology. *Journal of Environmental Psychology, 2*, 119–140.

Semes, S. W. (2009). *The future of the past: A conservation ethic for architecture, urbanism, and historic preservation*. New York and London: W.W. Norton & Company.

Silberman, N. (2016). Changing visions of heritage value: What role should the expert play? *Ethnologies, 36*(1–2 (special issue on Intangible cultural heritage)).

Silva, K. D., & Chapagain, N. K. (2013). *Asian heritage management: Contexts, concerns, and prospects*. New York: Routledge.

Smith, L. (2006). *Uses of heritage*. London and New York: Routledge.

Smith, L. (2009). Deference and humility: The social values of the country house. In L. Gibson & J. Pendlebury (Eds.), *Valuing historic environments* (pp. 33–50). Burlington, VT: Ashgate.

Smith, L., & Campbell, G. (2015). The elephant in the room: Heritage affect, and emotion. In W. Logan, M. N. Craith, & U. Kockel (Eds.), *A companion to heritage studies* (pp. 443–460). Chichester: Wiley-Blackwell.

Smith, L., & Waterton, E. (2012). Constrained by commonsense: The authorized heritage discourse in contemporary debates. In R. Skates, C. McDavid, & J. Carman (Eds.), *The oxford handbook of public archaeology*. Oxford: Oxford University Press.

Sommer, U. (2009). Methods used to investigate the use of the past in the formation of regional identities. In M. L. S. Sørensen & J. Carman (Eds.), *Heritage studies: Methods and approaches* (pp. 103–120). Routledge.

Stephenson, S. L., & Mascia, M. B. (2009). *Putting people on the map: An approach to integrating social data in conservation planning*. Washington, DC: Society for Conservation Biology.

Stewart, W. P., Williams, D. R., & Kruger, L. E. (2013). *The emergence of place-based conservation: Place-based conservation: Perspectives from the social sciences*. New York: Springer.

Tainter, J. A., & Lucas, G. J. (1983). Epistemology of the significance concept. *American Antiquity, 48*(4), 707–719.

Talmage, V. (2010). Lessons for land conservation. *Forum Journal, 25*(1), 11–17.

Waterton, E., & Smith, L. (2010). The recognition and misrecognition of community heritage. *International Journal of Heritage Studies, 16*(1), 4–15.

Waterton, E., Smith, L., & Campbell, G. (2006). The utility of discourse analysis to heritage studies: The Burra Charter and social inclusion. *International Journal of Heritage Studies, 12*(4), 339–355.

Watson, S. (2015). Emotions in the history museum. In A. Whitcomb & K. Message (Eds.), *The international handbook of museum studies: Museum theory* (pp. 283–301). New York: Wiley-Blackwell.

Wells, J. C. (2010). Our history is not false: Perspectives from the revitalisation culture. *International Journal of Heritage Studies, 16*(6), 464–485.

CONCLUSION

Wells, J. C. (2015). In stakeholders we trust: Changing the ontological and epistemological orientation of built heritage assessment through participatory action research. In B. Szmygin (Ed.), *How to assess built heritage? Assumptions, methodologies, examples of heritage assessment systems.* Florence and Lublin: Romualdo Del Bianco Foundatione and Lublin University of Technology.

Wells, J. C. (2017). The Main Street approach to community design. In K. Melcher, B. Stiefel, & K. Faurest (Eds.), *Community-built: Art, construction, preservation, and place* (pp. 172–189). New York: Routledge.

Wells, J. C., & Baldwin, E. D. (2012). Historic preservation, significance, and age value: A comparative phenomenology of historic Charleston and the nearby new-urbanist community of I'On. *Journal of Environmental Psychology, 32*(4), 384–400.

Wells, J. C., & Lixinski, L. (2016). Heritage values and legal rules: Identification and treatment of the historic environment via an adaptive regulatory framework (part 1). *Journal of Cultural Heritage Management and Sustainable Development, 6*(3), 345–364.

Wells, J. C., & Stiefel, B. L. (2014). Conclusion: Common problems and potential solutions. In B. L. Stiefel & J. C. Wells (Eds.), *Preservation education: Sharing best practices and finding common ground.* Hanover: University Press of New England.

Wild, J. (1942). On the nature and aims of phenomenology. *Philosophy and Phenomenological Research, 3*(1), 85–95.

APPENDIX A

The Palmer House Charter

Principles for Integrating Environmental Design and Behavior Research into Built Heritage Conservation Practice

This document was drafted at a day-long intensive organized by the Environmental Design Research Association's Historic Environment Knowledge Network at the EDRA42 meeting in Chicago in May 2011.

Definitions:

Environment-Behavior Research: The use of a wide variety of social science research methodologies to understand how people value and behave in certain natural, cultural, and designed environments. Environment-behavior studies look at how environments change or influence human behavior as well as how people value and perceive environments.

Participatory Research: Research that seeks to equalize the power differential between the "researcher" and the "subject" such that the researcher becomes a "facilitator" and the "subjects" are transformed into "co-researchers." In most traditions, it is up to the participants to define what is valid knowledge, what should be researched (e.g., the topic and research question), and how data are gathered and analyzed. When the explicit goals include the empowerment and emancipation of communities to achieve social justice, the term "participatory action research" is used.

EDRA: The Environmental Design Research Association is an international, interdisciplinary organization whose purpose is to advance and disseminate environmental design research toward improving understanding of the interrelationships between people and their built and natural surroundings. EDRA's goal is to facilitate the creation of environments that are responsive to human needs (http://edra.org).

Historic Environment Network: EDRA's Historic Environment Network was created in 2008 to connect scholars and practitioners with an interest in research that addresses the intersection of environmental perception and valuation with built heritage and cultural landscapes (https://www.edra.org/group/HE).

Communities of Practice: Any social structure of order, such as institutions, practitioners, cultural groups, and communities, in which common concerns or interests are shared. Communities of practice can consist of trained, educated experts or everyday people with disparate professional and educational backgrounds.

APPENDIX A: THE PALMER HOUSE CHARTER

1. Assumptions

1.1 This document has been created for members of EDRA, preservation/conservation professionals and policymakers, environmental design professionals/researchers, community members, and the public at large.

1.2 Built heritage conservation should benefit people.

1.3 Built heritage conservation practice should be substantiated with empirical evidence.

1.4 Social science research methods should play a central role in identification and treatment of the historic environment using the values, perceptions, and experiences of most stakeholders.

1.5 Applied social science research can provide empirical evidence to substantiate practice.

1.6 Orthodox preservation/conservation doctrine and practice focuses on fabric, not people.

1.7 Orthodox practice tends to overemphasize the values of experts and sideline the values of most stakeholders.

1.8 Orthodox practice is difficult to change because it is sustained through fixed legal and doctrinal frameworks.

1.9 Spirit of place, sense of place, and place attachment are integral concepts of historical authenticity.

1.10 Historical authenticity is multidimensional.

1.11 Because the meaning of tangible heritage cannot exist independently of human interpretation, then all heritage is, at some level, "intangible."

1.12 Participatory research techniques are important in equalizing the power differential between the "researcher" and the "subject."

1.13 Cultural heritage is a human right.

1.14 The ideas, concepts, and goals in this document are not meant to replace orthodox, fabric-centered preservation/conservation theory and doctrine, but rather to form another perspective that should be balanced with traditional theory and practice.

2. Goals

2.1 Cultural heritage should be used to empower communities and foster social justice.

2.2 Where feasible, all relevant communities of practice should be treated as equals in the stewardship of the historic environment.

2.3 Where feasible, the practitioner/researcher should function as a facilitator between community members and experts in how a broad range of values are used in the identification and treatment of the historic environment.

2.4 The natural and cultural environments should be conceived as a continuum and not a dichotomy.

2.5 Critical heritage studies theory should inform built heritage conservation policy and practice.

2.6 Environment-behavior and participatory research should be used to help identify historic places, conserve these resources' historical authenticity, and define heritage conservation performance.

2.7 Environment-behavior and participatory research should be used to produce better, empirically based arguments for the conservation of the historic environment.

2.8 The role of place and environment in significance and authenticity should be emphasized.

2.9 The relationship between cultural heritage and spirit of place/place attachment should be explored.

2.10 The role of place attachment and the impulse to preserve/conserve should be explored.

APPENDIX A: THE PALMER HOUSE CHARTER

2.11 The emotional and physical benefits of the conservation of the historic environment (quality of life) should be better understood and articulated.

2.12 Policy and practice should change to recognize that the values associated with the historic environment are dynamic.

3. Examples of applied historic environment research

3.1 Identifying places that communities believe are "historic" but don't conform to orthodox art/historical values.

3.2 How to treat historic buildings and landscapes in a way that maintains desired sociocultural meanings and values.

3.3 Understanding the everyday person's experience of the historic environment.

3.4 Balancing expert and most stakeholder values.

3.5 Understanding the polyvocality of historical authenticity.

3.6 Understanding the embodied relationship between the physical age of place and emotional attachment.

3.7 Exploring multicultural and extra-Western perspectives of the historic environment.

3.8 Informing historical significance with stakeholders' values.

3.9 Empirically based design review standards.

3.10 How to create arguments to conserve the historic environment based on quality of life and sense of place.

3.11 Ways to effectively communicate with most stakeholders using their meanings rather than the meanings of experts.

4. Methodological approaches

4.1 Qualitative and quantitative approaches are equally valid, depending on the context.

4.2 Where feasible, a methodology and associated methods should be chosen based on their fit for a given research question, and not based on the particular discipline of the researcher.

4.3 Interdisciplinary research techniques are, therefore, available from a wide range of disciplines, such as:

• Anthropology	• Interior design
• Archaeology	• Planning
• Sociology	• Natural resource conservation
• Psychology	• Geography
• Philosophy	• Public history
• Parks, recreation, and tourism management	• Historic preservation
• Architecture	• Heritage studies
• Landscape architecture	• Community development

4.4 Any relevant individual or mix of qualitative and quantitative methodologies can be considered, such as ethnography, grounded theory, phenomenologies, participatory research, content analysis, historical (interpretive research), correlational (survey) research, and experimental research.

APPENDIX A: THE PALMER HOUSE CHARTER

5. Responsibilities

5.1 The EDRA Historic Environment Network will:

    5.1.1 Promote environment-behavior and participatory research in built heritage conservation practice.

    5.1.2 Work with the EDRA board to better integrate built heritage conservation practice into EDRA's activities.

    5.1.3 Investigate ways to promote the ideas in this document to other built environment disciplines, such as architecture, landscape architecture, planning, interior design, and environmental conservation.

    5.1.4 Play a leading role in pioneering collaborative opportunities with practitioners and researchers.

    5.1.5 Work with built environment educational accreditation programs to promote environment-behavior and participatory research that addresses the historic environment.

5.2 Practitioners and researchers who employ environment-behavior and participatory methodologies should seek opportunities to engage in collaborative partnerships with built heritage conservation practitioners.

Participants Who Helped Draft This Document at the EDRA 42 Session in Chicago, IL

Organizer

Jeremy Wells, University of Maryland, College Park

Presenters

You-Kyong Ahn, Calvin College

April Allen, Michigan State University

Cari Goetcheus, Clemson University

Michael Holleran, University of Texas School of Architecture

Paul Kapp, University of Illinois at Urbana-Champaign

Sara Kocher, Sara Kocher Consulting

Christopher Koziol, University of Colorado, Denver

Daniel Levi, Cal Poly

Jennifer Minner, University of Texas School of Architecture

Bryan Orthel, Washington State University

Audience

Maria Cristina Dias Lay, Federal University of Rio Grande do Sul (Brazil)

Wei Zhao, University of Illinois at Urbana-Champaign

336

Biographies of Editors and Contributing Authors

Barry L. Stiefel is an associate professor at the College of Charleston's Historic Preservation and Community Planning Program. Stiefel's research interests are in how the sum of local preservation efforts affects regional, national, and multi-national policies within the field of cultural resource management and heritage conservation. He has authored and/or edited numerous articles and books, including *Community-Built: Art, Construction, Preservation, and Place* (co-edited with Katherine Melcher and Kristin Faurest, Routledge, 2017); and *Sustainable Heritage: Merging Environmental Conservation and Historic Preservation* (co-authored with Amalia Leifeste, Routledge, 2018).

Jeremy C. Wells is an assistant professor in the Historic Preservation Program at the University of Maryland, College Park and a Fulbright scholar. His research explores ways to make built heritage conservation practice more responsive to people through the use of applied social science research methods from environmental psychology, humanistic geography, anthropology, and community development/public health. Wells is a member of the Environmental Design Research Association's (EDRA's) board and past Chair. At EDRA, he created the Historic Environment Knowledge Network to engage academics and practitioners in addressing the person/place and environment/behavior aspects of heritage conservation. Wells runs the heritagestudies.org website that explores how to evolve heritage conservation practice using the critical heritage studies theory to better balance meanings and power between experts and most stakeholders.

You Kyong Ahn received a Ph.D. in Architecture and Historic Preservation from Texas A&M University in 2007. Her area of interest is to continue the integrity of historic buildings and neighborhoods through the human-centered preservation method. She was an assistant professor and director of the pre-architecture program of Art and Art History Department at Calvin College during 2007–2015.

AnnaMarie Bliss is a Ph.D. candidate in Architecture at the University of Illinois at Urbana-Champaign. She holds a professional Master of Architecture degree from Kansas State University. In practice, she works as a historic preservation designer focusing on historic governmental properties and downtown revitalizations. Her dissertation work examines human perceptual interactions at the thresholds of contemporary additions to tourist-historic architecture in Barcelona, Spain. Additionally, her recent studies include examining the efficacy of using images and social media as a means for research in historic preservation and architectural design. She is a P.E.O. Scholar, the highest honor for women in doctoral studies. Her work has been distinguished in architectural studies by being awarded the American Institute of Architects of Kansas Student Honor Award and Alpha Rho Chi Medal of Honor. She currently teaches graduate history and theory of architecture courses and undergraduate design studios at the University of Illinois.

BIOGRAPHIES OF EDITORS AND CONTRIBUTING AUTHORS

Suzanne Elizabeth Bott is a research associate at the Arizona State Museum at the University of Arizona in Tucson. She is a historic preservation planner, reconstruction and redevelopment specialist, and resource conservationist. She received a doctorate from Colorado State University in Human Dimensions of Natural Resource Management in 2000, a Masters in Planning and Community Development, and Bachelors in Geography and Environmental Conservation from the University of Colorado. Her research interests are in the phenomenology of finding meaning in place, and work centers on preserving and celebrating places of meaning around the world. She worked in Iraq for the U.S. government for three years during Operation Iraqi Freedom and served as a Cultural Heritage Advisor in Mosul from 2008 to 2010.

Jack D. Elliott, Jr. has lived most of his life on the site of the extinct town of Palo Alto, Mississippi where his family has resided since 1846. His personal experience of history and place resulted in a strong interest in the historical geography of his area and in the sacramentality of place, which has been reinforced by work in the Holy Land since 1977. He was employed for 25 years (1985–2010) as a historical archaeologist with the Mississippi Department of Archives and History. While working there he began to reflect and write upon the nature of the experience of historic places while coming to realize that the institutionalization of this for preservation purposes in the form of bureaucracies and regulations has often proved to be detrimental to an openness to understanding. He has taught as an adjunct at the Meridian campus of Mississippi State University since 1988.

Richard A. Engelhardt was the UNESCO Regional Advisor for Culture in Asia and the Pacific from 1994 to 2008, based in Bangkok, where he headed UNESCO's culture sector programs for the Asia-Pacific region. He was educated in history, archaeology, and anthropology of the Asia-Pacific region at Yale and Harvard universities. Following his graduation, he joined the United Nations where, for 30 years, he directed heritage conservation and culture development projects throughout the Asia and the Indo-Pacific region on behalf of UNESCO. In this capacity, Engelhardt has pioneered many regional initiatives in the fields of culture, heritage and creativity, including the UNESCO Asia-Pacific Heritage Conservation Awards. As the Head of the UNESCO Office in Cambodia, Engelhardt launched and directed the international safeguarding campaign for Angkor during the 1990s. In recognition of his services in the preservation of the Angkor monuments, H.M. King Norodom Sihanouk awarded Engelhardt the prestigious title of Commandeur de l'Ordre Royal du Cambodge.

Kimberli Fitzgerald is a Senior Historic Planner for the City of Salem, Oregon. For Salem, she has also staffed the Historic Landmarks Commission and Public Art Commission. She holds Masters in City Planning degree from the University of Pennsylvania and a B.A. in Political Science and Government from Linfield College.

Ted Grevstad-Nordbrock is an assistant professor in Community and Regional Planning at Iowa State University with over twenty-five years of professional experience in historic preservation, including twelve with the Michigan State Historic Preservation Office (SHPO). He completed his Ph.D. in Geography from Michigan State University, with a Dissertation entitled, "An Analysis of diverse Gentrification Processes and Their Relationship to Historic Preservation Activity in Three Chicago Neighborhoods." In his current position he manages ISU's Preservation and Cultural Heritage program and the ISU-US Department of State Cultural Heritage Documentation Project.

Richard M. Hutchings is a social scientist specializing in critical development and heritage studies. Concerned with late modern heritage stewardship, the bulk of his work involves a critical analysis

BIOGRAPHIES OF EDITORS AND CONTRIBUTING AUTHORS

of the institution and practice of heritage management (also known as resource management), particularly archaeology and cultural resource management. Dr. Hutchings is a founding director of the Institute for Critical Heritage and Tourism, British Columbia, Canada, and author of the book *Maritime Heritage in Crisis: Indigenous Landscapes and Global Ecological Breakdown* (Routledge).

Michelle Jolly is a professor of history at Sonoma State University. She teaches courses in 19th century U.S. history, U.S. women's history, and California and the West, as well as a core course in SSU's Cultural Resources Management Program. She has directed a community-based research project on the oral history of the women's movement in Sonoma County. From 2002 to 2012, she served as a content coordinator for six Teaching American History Programs, working with teachers and faculty to improve history content knowledge in K-12 classrooms. Beginning in 2012, she took the lead on the creation of a Sophomore Year Experience program at SSU, including a second-year core course called "How to Think Like a Social Scientist." Currently, she is developing a project on women, softball, and community in the mid-twentieth century California Central Valley.

Ned Kaufman is a founder of Place Matters and of Pratt Institute's graduate program in Historic Preservation. He is the author of *Place, Race, and Story* (Routledge) as well as studies ranging from Victorian Gothic to the management of public lands and historic sites.

Setha Low is currently the Professor of Environmental Psychology, Geography, Anthropology, and Women's Studies, and Director of the Public Space Research Group at The Graduate Center, City University of New York where she teach courses and trains Ph.D. students in the anthropology of space and place, urban anthropology, the anthropology of the body, and cultural values in historic preservation. Her most recent book is *Spatializing Culture* (2017).

Tom Mayes has written and spoken widely about why old places matter to people, as well as preservation easements, shipwreck protection, historic house museums, the Americans with Disabilities Act, and preservation of public policy. For many years, he taught historic preservation law at the University of Maryland Graduate Program in Historic Preservation. In 2013, Tom received the National Endowment for the Arts Rome Prize in Historic Preservation, and wrote a series of essays titled Why Old Places Matter.

Melinda Milligan is a professor of sociology at Sonoma State University. She specializes in the sociology and social psychology of the built environment with an emphasis on historic preservation. Her past research has focused on place attachment, nostalgia, organizational change and death, the architectural design process, and the New Urbanism. She teaches courses on public space, organizational ethnography, urban sociology, social interaction, and emotions. Currently, she is completing a book on the everyday experiences of preservation from the perspectives of both homeowners renovating historic houses and the preservation professionals they encounter. In addition, she is the president of the Society for the Study of Symbolic Interaction (2018–2019).

Jennifer Minner is an Assistant Professor in the Department of City and Regional Planning at Cornell University. Dr. Minner's experience includes planning, research, and community mapping projects related to historic preservation, land use and sustainability, community economic development, and institutional research and higher education assessment. She is a past president and a founding board member of the MidTexMod chapter of Docomomo U.S. She was the chair and heritage commissioner on the City of Olympia, Washington Heritage Commission and served on the Ithaca Landmarks

BIOGRAPHIES OF EDITORS AND CONTRIBUTING AUTHORS

Preservation Commission. Dr. Minner received a B.A. in cultural anthropology from the University of Washington, a Masters in Urban and Regional Planning from Portland State University, and a Ph.D. in community and regional planning from the University of Texas at Austin.

Heather A. Peters is a research anthropologist, specializing in China, with a special focus on the ethnic diversity of Yunnan Province. She obtained her Ph.D. from Yale University. From 1997 to 2015, she served as a Senior Consultant in the Culture Unit of UNESCO Bangkok. She develops, oversees, and coordinates cultural projects covering issues ranging from the protection and development of World Heritage sites to the prevention of trafficking and unsafe migration of young ethnic minority women and men from Yunnan, China to Thailand, as well as the creation of culturally and linguistically appropriate HIV/AIDS, trafficking and drug prevention materials. Specifically, she has worked on projects aimed at integrating preservation and development of World Heritage sites in the Old Town of Lijiang in Yunnan province and the Hani Rice Terraces in Honghe, Yunnan, seeking to harmonize the perceived conflict between preservation and economic development (especially tourism). Recently, she has focused on the importance of Intangible Cultural Heritage (ICH) to communities today, the rights of indigenous peoples and communities at World Heritage sites, and the role of culture in development.

Margaret Purser is a professor of anthropology at Sonoma State University. She is a past chair of the SSU Anthropology Department, and teaches courses in archaeology, cultural landscape studies, and contemporary heritage management studies. She has worked on community-based research projects on Nevada ranching, Sierra Nevada gold mining, maritime landscapes in the Sacramento River Delta, and coffee and sugar plantations in Pacific coastal Guatemala. From 2000 to 2010, she worked on the nomination of the nineteenth century Pacific port town of Levuka, Fiji, to the UNESCO World Heritage List. Her current project is called the "Santa Rosa Neighborhood Heritage Mapping Project," which is creating an online interactive map of that city's many diverse and vibrant neighborhoods designed to help celebrate the sesquicentennial celebrations in 2018.

Stephanie Ryberg-Webster is an Associate Professor of Urban Studies in the Levin College of Urban Affairs at Cleveland State University, where she also directs the Master of Urban Planning and Development program. Her research explores the complex intersections of historic preservation and urban development, including preservation in shrinking/legacy cities, synergies and tensions between preservation and community development, federal and state historic rehabilitation tax credits, and the preservation of Cleveland's African-American heritage. Dr. Ryberg-Webster's current work explores the 1970s-era history of historic preservation in Cleveland, as urban disinvestment escalated. Dr. Ryberg-Webster teaches courses in urban planning, historic preservation, urban design, and contemporary urban issues. She earned a Ph.D. from the University of Pennsylvania, a Master of Historic Preservation from the University of Maryland, and a Bachelor of Urban Planning from the University of Cincinnati.

Suzanne Scheld, Ph.D. is a cultural anthropologist at California State University, Northridge. She has a background in urban anthropology and an interest in social hierarchies, history, and the politics of public space in the U.S. and in West Africa. Dr. Scheld has extensive training and experience conducting applied and theoretic ethnographic research. She teaches undergraduate and graduate courses in Urban Anthropology, Globalization, Space and Place, and Gender and Anthropology. She is currently the chair of the Department of Anthropology and the Coordinator of the Interdisciplinary Studies of Africa Minor's

340

BIOGRAPHIES OF EDITORS AND CONTRIBUTING AUTHORS

Program at CSUN, and the president-elect of the Society for National, Transnational/Global Anthropology (SUNTA), a section of the American Anthropological Association.

Dana H. Taplin is an environmental psychologist with a background in urban planning, has an interest in the history, design, uses, and meanings of public space. Dr. Taplin has conducted research on rail trails, urban parks, schoolyard playgrounds, and heritage landscapes. His work investigates how the histories of public spaces figure in their present day uses and meanings and how different stakeholders struggle to define authentic interpretations of historical significance. Dr. Taplin has collaborated with the other authors for over twenty years in the field research and on conference talks and writings, including an earlier book, Rethinking Urban Parks.

Richard Vidutis has worked as a contract consultant on projects throughout the United States in the fields of Ethnography/Folklife, Museum Programming & Planning, and History (Cultural Resources Management, and Historic Preservation) for private firms, and state and federal agencies, for example, FEMA, National Park Service, Library of Congress Folklife Center, Michigan State University, Maryland Historical Society, and Florida Folklife Program. Mr. Vidutis specializes in ethnographic studies and history of urban and rural landscapes with a strong emphasis on ethnic cultures in the United States. In recent years, his focus has come to include heritage preservation in post-disaster landscapes following Hurricanes Katrina and Sandy and flooding in Missouri's Ozarks. Along with a Ph.D. from the Folklore Institute, Indiana University, Mr. Vidutis has also studied archiving at Wayne State University, and museum preservation & conservation at the Ford Museum. His educational background includes scholarships to Adam Mickiewicz University, Poznan, Vilnius University, and Helsinki University.

Montira Horayangura Unakul received her AB in Economics and East Asian Studies from Harvard University and MArch-MCP from the University of California, Berkeley and was trained in heritage conservation at ICCROM. She was awarded a Yenching Fellowship to Peking University, the Raymond L Prize in Community Design and meritorious commendations for service to various institutions in Thailand. She has worked with UNESCO since 2001, where she has conceptualized and managed projects in World Heritage, built heritage conservation, museums, cultural tourism, community-based heritage management, heritage education, intercultural dialogue, and peace education. She currently serves on the advisory boards of the Siamese Heritage Trust, the International Association for the Study of Traditional Environments, and the Southeast Asian Regional Centre for Archaeology and Fine Arts. She lectures and publishes extensively on cultural heritage issues.

Laura Alice Watt is a professor of environmental history and policy in the Department of Geography, Environment, and Planning at Sonoma State University. She also serves as a Graduate Coordinator for SSU's Cultural Resources Management Masters program. Her research interests focus on the ways in which protection of ecological and historic landscapes affects the interactions of people and place over time. Her book, *The Paradox of Preservation: Wilderness and Working Landscapes at Point Reyes National Seashore*, was published by the University of California Press in 2017. She is currently starting a new project researching the environmental history of the Rocky Mountain Biological Laboratory, established on the site of an old silver mining town at Gothic, Colorado. She is also an avid photographer and sailor.

Index

Note: Boldface page numbers refer to tables & italic page numbers refer to figures. Page numbers followed by "n" refer to endnotes.

Abraham Lincoln and Soldiers Home National Monument 47
Abrams, J. 68, 69, 78
ACHS *see* Association for Critical Heritage Studies (ACHS)
ACRA *see* American Cultural Resources Association (ACRA)
ADB *see* Asian Development Bank (ADB)
Advance Mortgage Corporation of Detroit 188
Advisory Council on Historic Preservation 23, 195
age value 15
AHD *see* authorized heritage discourse (AHD)
Ahn, You Kyong 20–1
Akasofu, S. 81
Alabama, traditional cultural property 263
Alanen, A. R. 260
Alaska, traditional cultural property 263, 264
ALGAO *see* Association of Local Government Archaeological Officers (ALGAO)
Alliance for New York State Parks 21–2, 147
"Alliance to Revitalize Jones Beach" 147
American Cultural Resources Association (ACRA) 260, 319–20
American Folklife Center 256–7
Andrea, R. 171
Annual Report on the Economic Impact of the Federal Historic Tax Credit for FY 2015 190
Appleton, J. 50
Archaeological Theory and the Politics of Cultural Heritage (Smith) 84
Archibald, R. R. 92, 95
architectural features 21, 104, 122; building materials 119–20; demographic backgrounds 111–12; East

Hills participants on 112, 115, 121; entrances and porches 118–19; focus group design 106, 111, *111*; heritage value of 105; integrity of 122; meaning of 104; quantitative survey 106; reciprocal relationship 104, 105; survey design and implementation 107, **108–9**, 109, *110*; undesired building fronts *119*; vernacular 105–6, 121–2; in Wealthy Heights 107–10, 112, **113–14**, 115, **116–18**, 120–1; *see also* East Hills; Heritage Hill; Wealthy Heights
architectural preservation theories 130–1
architectural tourism 21, 134, 160–1
archival research 1, 36
Armstrong, G. T. 8
Asia-Pacific region, heritage management in 241–4, *243*; community teams 242; LEAP concept 241–2; tourism industry 242, 243
Asian Academy for Heritage Management 248, 249
Asian Development Bank (ADB) 236
asset-building approach 200
Association for Critical Heritage Studies (ACHS) 4, 16–17, 34, 37, 39–40, 320
Association of Local Government Archaeological Officers (ALGAO) 320
Austen, J. 311
Austin Oaks Subdivision 169–70
authenticity 37, 50, 276, 324; discourse in heritage studies 130; in tourism 131–2
authorized heritage discourse (AHD) 36, 40, 41, 70, 323
Avrami, E. 15

343

INDEX

Bagnall, G. 36
Baldini, U. 13
Bamiyan Valley of Afghanistan 59–60, *60*
Banfield, Edward C. 214–15
Barcelona Turisme 132
Barth, R. 69
Barzun, J. 97
Beaux-Arts ground plan 146
Beijing, preservation policies in 130
Benjamin Franklin Ghost House 60
Berger, P. 69
Bernard, H. R. 10
Bliss, Anna Marie 21
Bly, R. 69
Boardwalk Restaurant 146, 152
Bohr, N. 91
Boito, C. 8, 9, 13, 42
Bokova, I. 235
Booher, D. 162
Borden Grid 75, *76*
Bott, S. E. 20
Brandi, C. 13
Bringing Buildings Back (Mallach) 200
Brown, D. 207
Brown, L. S. 60
Bruner, J. 290, 302
Buckley, K. 17
Budapest Declaration on World Heritage 237
Buddha 59, *60–1*
built heritage conservation 1–2, 16, 18, 327, 333; changing
    system of 13–14; practice 36, 323–5; research and 12–13;
    rules and regulations 13; separation from environmental
    conservation 325–6
Bulger, P. 258
Bureau of Land Management 96
bureaucracies 68, 76, 77
Burra Charter 9, 13, 237

calculability, McDonaldization of heritage stewardship and
    75–6
California, traditional cultural property 262
Campbell, G. 36, 37
Canadian Association of Heritage Professionals 320
Cantril, H. 131
Carbonara, G. 13, 42
care of old places 2–3; human-centered 19–26, 324–7;
    professional 18–19
Caro, R. 145, 153
Carter, T. 258
catagenesis 83
CED *see* community and economic development (CED)

Cederholm, E. A. 133
Central Mall 146, 151, 152
Certified Local Government (CLG) 214–15, 230
Chamber of Commerce 215, 217
Chambers, R. 236
Charleston Renaissance 93
Chartered Institute for Archeologists (CIFA) 320
Chicago 178, 191n5; decentralization of population 178;
    gentrification process 178–9; Lincoln Park 179–80
Chicago Daily Tribune 182
Chicago Reader 188
Chicago Tribune 179, 184
Christianity, relic preservation and 8
CHS *see* critical heritage studies (CHS)
CIFA *see* Chartered Institute for Archeologists (CIFA)
"circles of social control" 69, *70*
citizen involvement program 214
City Council and Planning Commission 222, 231
Cizek, E. D. 301
Clarkson, W. 299, 300
CLC *see* Cleveland Landmarks Commission (CLC)
Cleveland 196, 199; community development corporations
    204–5; community economic development perspectives
    202; historic preservation in 200–2
Cleveland Landmarks Commission (CLC) 196, 201
Cleveland Restoration Society (CRS) 196, 201, 204
CLG *see* Certified Local Government (CLG)
"collaborative learning and co-management" 162
collaborative rationality 162
collective shadow 68–9
College of Charleston's Historic Preservation & Community
    Planning program 291–2
Colorado, traditional cultural property 261, 264
communicative action theory 162
communities of practice 333
community and economic development (CED) 195, *199*,
    199–200; built environment 203; historic preservation in
    Cleveland 200–2, 204–5; practitioners 23
community as process 285–6
community-based heritage conservation 249, 250
Community Built Association 321
Community Development Department 202, 221
community heritage, in community (re)building 205
community tours 22, 160, 172 *see also* heritage tours
Conkey, M. 93
*Conservation of Culture: Folklorists and the Public Sector,
    The* 257
conservation/preservation practitioners 319–21
Constantine 8
"The Contributions of Historic Preservation to Housing and
    Economic Development" 190

INDEX

control, McDonaldization of heritage stewardship and 77

Convention Concerning the Protection of the World Cultural and Natural Heritage (1972) 234, 236

Convention for the Protection of the Architectural Heritage of Europe (1985) 237

Convention for the Safeguarding of the Intangible Cultural Heritage (ICH) 238, 248

Convention on the Protection and Promotion of the Diversity of Cultural Expressions 238

conventional expert 2, 5, 14

Cooper, G. 154

Coughenour, C. 59

course outcomes, cultural heritage conservation 284

Coward, C. 298

critical geography 162, 168

critical heritage studies (CHS) 3, 14–15, 255, 322; ACHS manifesto 39–40; definition 34; heritage studies *vs.* 35; historic environment advocacy organizations 41; manifesto 37–9; Marxist reference 38; as nascent field 19; origin of 15–16; to practitioner 37–40; qualitative case studies and 16; research 34; scholars 5, 33–4; scholarship 16–17

CRM *see* Cultural Resources Management (CRM)

"CRM: The Journal of Heritage Stewardship" 278

CRS *see* Cleveland Restoration Society (CRS)

Cultural Conservation: The Protection of Cultural Heritage 257

cultural heritage 276; community involvement 235, 236; management 233, 234; protection of 235; tangible and intangible 259–60

cultural heritage conservation 13; challenges 234–5; communities and stakeholders 235–6, 239; mainstream practice of 239; Nara Document on Authenticity 237; participation of communities 238; World Heritage Convention 236, 238

"Cultural Heritage Management and Tourism: Models for Co-operation among Stakeholders" 241–2

Cultural Resource Laws & Practice 18

Cultural Resources Management (CRM) 18, 19–20, 67, 96–7; archaeology and 84n2; definition 72; as dehumanizing system 78; disaster 74; efficiency 73–4; foundations of 256; historic preservation and 255–6, 268–70; ideologies 72–3; programs 279, 280; and regulatory compliance 24; standard operating procedures of 260–1

Cultural Survival and Revival in the Buddhist Sangha Project 247

CyArk 59

cynical pessimism 81

Datel, R. 93

de Botton, A. 63

De Certeau, M. 144

Death and the Life of Great American Cities, The 168

Declaration of Amsterdam (1975) 237

Delaware, traditional cultural property 262–3

Demers, D. 33

democratizing preservation 207

demolition 200, 204, 206, 228–9

Department of Housing and Urban Development 209

Detroit Shoreway Community Development Organization (DSCDO) 204

disaster ethnography 264–5, *265, 266*

DOCOMOMO-US 172n1

Domenech i Montaner, Lluis 32, 131

domestic historic preservation tours 161

Dorson, R. 259

DSCDO *see* Detroit Shoreway Community Development Organization (DSCDO)

Dubois, A. 171

Dupont, W. 47, 48

East Austin: annual tours in 168; gentrification 171; *see also* Jane's Walk tours

East Hills 111–12, 115, 121, 124n7, 124n9 *see also* architectural features

East Hills Council of Neighbors 106, 109

ecological risk assessments, with homicide 79–80

economic and community development goals 195–6

economic benefits, trade-offs and 197, 203–5

Economic Development Administration (EDA) 209

EDA *see* Economic Development Administration (EDA)

education and outreach program 216, 219, 222, 229

efficiency, McDonaldization of heritage stewardship and 73–5

Eiseley, L. 89

Eliade, M. 93

Elliott, J. 13, 20, 310, 318, 319

embodied space 144

Emerick, K. 4, 5, 17

emic perspective of culture 318

empiricism 9–10, 318

engagement and empowerment opportunities 197–8

Engelhardt, R. 23

environment-behavior research 333

Environmental Design Research Association (EDRA) 11–12, 321, 333

environmental psychology 321–2

equity preservation agenda 207

ethnographic research methods 17, 21

ethnography 256–9, 269 *see also* disaster ethnography

etic perspective of culture 318

Eutropia 8

"Every Kid in a Park" program 62

345

INDEX

evidence 6–12; care of old places and 12; definition 7; empiricism and 9–10; gathering 22; National Register 9; orthodox conservation practice 8

evidence-based design 11

evidence-based medicine 11

evidence for conservation practice 322, 327

exit interview form 294

fabric and human-centered approaches 17–18

fachwerk-style barn 302, *303–4*

Fairmount neighborhood 215

fast-food industry 68

Faubourg Marigny: A Proposal for Environmental Conservation 301

Federal Emergency Management Administration (FEMA) 255, 264, 265, *266*, 267

Feintuch, B. 257

FEMA *see* Federal Emergency Management Administration (FEMA)

Ferguson, J. 235

financial incentives 22, 216, 219, 221, 230

Finding Oprah's Roots: Finding Your Own 290–1

Finding Your Roots 290, 291

Fitch, R. 154

Fitzgerald, K. 23

Florence Charter on Historic Gardens (1982) 237

Floyd, E. 296

Flyvbjerg, B. 163

focus groups 53

"Folklife and the Public Sector: Assessment and Prognosis" 257

Ford Foundation 235

Ford, O'Neil 166

Forester, J. 162

"formal" rationality 67–8

Foucault, M. 163

Fredheim, L. H. 15

French Legation 171

full-time preservation faculty 313

Garrod, B. 134

Gates, H.J. 290

Gaudi, A. 131

Geertz, C. 318

genealogical research methods 290, 291

gentrification 168–9, 178; historic preservation's role in 188–91; in Lincoln Park 179–80

Getty research project 15

Gibson, L. 14

Giddens, A. 80

Glanton, K. 290

Goldberger, P. 143, 145

government inefficiency 74–5

graduate preservation programs 316n5

Grand Rapids 106

Great Hall 134, *135*, 138

Grevstad-Nordbrock, T. 22–3

Grille Borden 75, *76*

grounded theory research 49

Grouse Creek Cultural Study: Integrating Folklife and Historic Preservation Field Research, The 257–8

Gruen, P. 160–1

Guam 262

Guide to the Principles of the Conservation of Historic Buildings 9

Guiding Principles (SPAB) 9

Habermas, J. 162

Habitat's projects 106

"habits of mind" 284–5

Halbwachs, M. 104

Hale, S. 69

Hamlet 91

Harper, P 240

Harrison, R. 36

Harvard Community Services Center 204

Harvey, R. 147

Heisenberg, W. 91

Helena Augusta 8

HemisFair '68 Official Souvenir Guidebook 164

HemisFair '68 tour 159, 164, *165*, 171; Confluence Theater 166; Federal Pavilion 166; modernism 167; Texas Pavilion 167; tour guides 166; Tower of the Americas 167

HemisFair Park Redevelopment Corporation (HPARC) 164, 166

heritage 35, 36; conservation practice 36–7; cultural landscapes and 1; manifest 2; as political tool 38; social science research methods 39

heritage conservation 19, 317, 327; community-based 249; with development goals 244–5; educational programs 60, 63; globalized norms of 246; interest of 2; management theory and 248; meanings associated with 4; as practice in conflict 4–6; practitioners 4, 5; valorizing traditional modes of 245–8; younger generations 248–9

heritage education 276–9

Heritage Hill 106; community members of 109; photographic images 112; population of 124n9; *see also* architectural features

Heritage Hill Association 109

heritage management 239–41, 249

Heritage Organizations 215, 217

heritage preservation practitioners 24, 277, 278–9, 295

346

INDEX

heritage resources, measurement tools for 20

heritage studies 36, 130, 275

heritage tours 22, 159, 160, 198, 221, 227, 323; applied social science and 162–3; collaborative rationality 162–3; communicative action theory 162; HemisFair '68 tour 164, *165*, 166–8; Jane's Walk tours 168–71, *169, 170*; limitations of 172; phronetic social sciences 163

Heyward, E. D. 304, 305

Heyward, T. 304

Heyward-Washington House 304–5

higher education 24, 317; in evidence-based practice 25; historic preservation and architectural conservation programs 326

historic architecture 47, 130, 178, 203

historic buildings 197, 203, 215, 219

historic district 103, 104, 107, **108–9**

historic entry 137, *138*

historic environment graduate degree program 276

Historic Environment Knowledge Network 12

Historic Environment Network 333

Historic Landmark Commission (HLC) 214–15, 217; blog 229; education and outreach subcommittee 229; historic preservation plan 214–15, 227, 228, 231, 232; photo contest 229; public participation 232; robust awards program 230; Salem Heritage Neighborhood Program 230; surveys and interviews methodology 221–2; technical advisory committee 215, 219; *see also* Salem

historic neighborhoods 22, 23, 195–6, 201–4

historic preservation 23, 89, 177, 197; in Charleston 93; in Cleveland 200–2; current realities of 57–63, *58–62*; evocations of transcendence 92–3; gentrification 178–9; human-centered approaches to 144; intellectual provincialism 94; Kronborg Castle 91–2; National Register of Historic Places 181–2; Preservation Chicago 188–9; programs 22; recommendations to 189–90; in revaluing neighborhoods 188; "significant" properties 96; symbolization 91, 95–6, 98; in United States 122–3; *see also* Lincoln Park

Historic Preservation & Community Planning program 294

historic preservation movement 20, 90, 94

historic preservation plan 214–15, 227, 228, 231, 232

Historic Preservation Round-Table 216, *216*

historic property owners 217, 227–8; survey methodology and results 219–21, **220**

Historic Sites Act of 1935 96

historical value 15

HLC *see* Historic Landmark Commission (HLC)

Hobbs, D, N. 296

Hoi An 242, 244

Holtzman, R. N. 184

home tours 161

Homebuilders Association 215

"Homeowners' Manuals" series 246–7

Homer-Dixon, T. 82, 83

Honore Daumier: The Origins and Evolution of his Art (Leeman) 301

Hough neighborhood 199

Housing Authority Act of 1937 170

Housing Policy Debate 190

Howard Johnson's 152

Howard, P. 6

HPARC *see* HemisFair Park Redevelopment Corporation (HPARC)

Hufford, M. 257

Hull, R. B. IV. 51

human-centered conservation practice 14–18, 20

human-centered theory 278, 279

human-centric heritage preservation/conservation practices 19, 317

human experience, holistic nature of 90

human history 90

Hurley, A. 161

Hurricane Katrina 264, *265–7*, 269

Hurricane Sandy 264, *265*

Hutchings, R. 20, 323, 326

ICCROM 248

ICOMOS *see* International Council on Monuments and Sites (ICOMOS)

IDA *see* Institute for Digital Archaeology (IDA)

Idaho, TCP nominations 262, 263

Idea of the Holy, The (Otto) 93

identity of places 50

IHBC *see* Institute for Historic Building Conservation (IHBC)

Image of the City (Lynch) 130

"The Importance of Preserving Austin's Historical Homes" 305

Indiana, traditional cultural property 261

individual-related domains 53

industrial legacy 201

inner-city neighborhoods 199

Innes, J. 162

"insignificant architecture" 267

Institute for Digital Archaeology (IDA) 59

Institute for Historic Building Conservation (IHBC) 320

Institute of Texan Cultures 167, 168

institutionalization 70

Interagency Archeological Salvage Program 256

Interior's Standards for Rehabilitation 221

internalization 70, 84n4

International Council on Monuments and Sites (ICOMOS) 4, 63, 236–7, 250n4, 264, 270n3, 320, 325

INDEX

International Journal of Historical Archaeology 72
Interpreting Our Heritage (Tilden) 98
Investment Tax Credit 182
Iraqi Institute for the Conservation of Antiquities and Heritage 58
Ittleson, W. H. 131

Jabbour, A. 257
Jackson, J. B. 51–2
Jacobs, J. 168
Jane's Walk tours *169*, 171; geography of segregation 168–9; history of public housing 170; racial integration 169–70
Jefferson, T. 7, 8
Jeorges, B. 153, 154
John D. Rockefeller's Standard Oil Company 201
Johnson, L. B. 164, 169
Johnson, S. 167
Jolly, M. 24
Jones Beach 21, 143, 155; bodily sensation 150; built environment of 144; corporate sponsorship opportunities 147; demographic composition 148–9; design vocabulary of public beaches 145–6; ethnographic assessment 149; international sensation 145; memories of 150–2; modernism and 146; park user perspectives 149–50; public memories 152–4; Public Research Group 147; as public space 154–5; research methodology 148; restaurant service 146
"Jones Beach Revitalization Plan" 147
Jones, S. 40
Jung, Carl G. 67, 68

Kalke Farmstead 268
Kammeraad-Campbell, S. 296, 298–9, 301
Katz, I. 302, 303
Kaufman, N. 5, 25, 161, 317
Kemmis, S. 236
Khalaf, M. 15
Kinahan, K. 198, 200
King, T. 18, 40, 72, 74, 79–81, 84n1, 258, 269
Kitson, J. 161
Kronborg Castle 91–2

Lahr, M. 190, 198
landscape perception 52
Lang, J. 130, 131
Lao PDR 243, 245
Lass, K. 299, 300
Lavigne, P. 298
Lazarus, R. 82
Lefebvre, H. 104, 145
Lemann, B. 301

Lertzman, K. 71
LGBTQ groups 21, 143
Liang Hong 60
Lichbach, M. 10
Lijiang, tourism industry 243
Likert scale 219, 221
Lincoln Park 178, **180–1**, 190–1, 191n1; gentrification in 179–80; physical upgrading in 184–8, *185, 186–7*; redevelopment activity in 188; revitalizing 182–4
Lipe, W. 15
Listokin, B. 198
Listokin, D. 190, 198
Local Effort and Community Preservation in Asia and the Pacific (LEAP) program 241–2, 244
local municipality's preservation program 23; addressing issues 222–7, **223–6**; assessing current conditions 214–15; citizen involvement program 214; final goals and implementation 227–8; historic property owners survey methodology/results 219–21, **220**; lessons for other communities 231–2; planning model 214; progress toward completing the goals 228–31; public outreach process 215–18; *see also* Historic Landmark Commission (HLC)
Lombard, S. 298
Long Island, historic preservation group on 146
Longenecker, J. 73
Loomis, O. 257
Louisiana, traditional cultural property 261–2
Low, S. 144
Lowenthal, D. 15, 25, 34, 35, 97, 145, 255, 289, 317
Lusignan, P. 260
Lynch, K. 130

McDonaldization of heritage stewardship 20, 71, 73, 83–4; calculability 75–6; control 77; cultural resource management 72–3; efficiency 73–5; irrationality of rationality 78; meeting the shadow 83; modernity 80–1; predictability 76; resource management 71–2; scientific stewardship 79; shadow 68–71; thesis 67, 68; wicked heritage problems 82
McGhee, F. 170
McGuire, R. 72, 73
Machiavelli, N. 163
McTaggert, R. 236
Maine, traditional cultural property 263
Making Social Science Matter (Flyvbjerg) 163
Mallach, A. 200
manifesto, for nascent organization 37–8
Manifesto of the Society for the Protection of Ancient Buildings 13
Mann, T. 89

INDEX

Mapping Human History (Olson) 300–1
Marx, K. 37, 38
Mason, R. 14, 15, 36, 145, 207
Mayes, T. 18
Mazzone, M. 299, 300
meaning in places 45
Meeks, S. 207
Melnick, R. Z. 260
memories 150–1
Merrell, P. 79–80
Milligan, M. 24
Mills, C. W. 84n3
Minner, J. 22, 207
Minnesota, traditional cultural property 263, 264
Missions Initiative 62
Modern Movement 159
modernism 131, 159
modernisme architecture 132–3
modernity 81; responses to *80*
Moghaddam, F. 79, 80
Monticello 7, 8
Morris, W. 13
Moses, R. 143, 146, 147, 152, 153, 172
Mosul Museum 58, 59
Muir, J. 93
multi-disciplinary social scientific theory 280–1
Munoz Vinas, S. 1, 9, 13
Murtagh, W. J. 95
muse sculptures 135, *137*

Nam Ha Ecotourism Project 244–5
NAPC *see* National Alliance for Preservation Commissions (NAPC)
Nara Document on Authenticity (1994) 132, 237, 238
narrativist analytical framework 285
Nasar, J. 130, 141
NATHPO *see* National Association of Tribal Historic Preservation Officers (NATHPO)
National Alliance for Preservation Commissions (NAPC) 319
National Association of Tribal Historic Preservation Officers (NATHPO) 320
National Commission on Neighborhoods 188, 189
National Conference of State Historic Preservation Officers (NCSHPO) 320
National Council for Preservation Education 41, 313
National Forest Service 96
National Historic Preservation Act (NHPA) 12, 93, 96, 177, 255, 257, 278, 320
National Park Service 13, 47, 62, 96, 255, 256, 291, 305
National Preservation Conference 18
National Register 97, 181, 183, 184, 190, 259, 262

National Register Historic Districts 217
National Register of Historic Places 9, 103, 146, 178, 181–3, 191, 256, 291, 309
National Trust for Historic Places 291
National Trust for Historic Preservation (NTHP) 18, 63, 207, 311, 321
National Trust for Historic Preservation's Main Street program 322
National Trust's Preservation Green Lab 312
NCSHPO *see* National Conference of State Historic Preservation Officers (NCSHPO)
neighborhood resources feedback **223–4**
New York Times 188
Nietzsche, F. 163
Nimrud 58, *58*
nondiscussables 69, 70–1
Norberg-Schulz, C. 92
NTHP *see* National Trust for Historic Preservation (NTHP)

Oelschlaeger, M. 81
Office of the UNESCO Regional Advisor for Culture in Asia and the Pacific (RACAP) 234, 241, 244, 246, 249
"Old Neighborhood Gets a People Lift: There Goes the Neighborhood… Revitalized!" 184
Old Town Triangle 179
Olson, S. 300
1972 Convention Concerning the Protection of the World Cultural and Natural Heritage 236
One Space, Many Places: Folklife and Land Use in New Jersey's Pinelands National Reserve (Hufford) 257
Operational Guidelines of the World Heritage Convention (2005) 238, 240
oral history 268
Oregon State Historic Preservation Office 215, 228–9
Oregon's Land Conservation and Development Commission goal 214
Orfeó Català 133
orthodox conservation doctrine 9, 323–4
Otto, R. 93
Our Unprotected Heritage: Whitewashing the Destruction of Our Cultural and Natural Environment (King) 18, 84

Palau de la Música Catalana 132, 134, 137, 139, 140
Palmer House Charter 12, 333–6
Palo Alto 92
Pannekoek, F. 40
participant-led photo-elicitation 134, 137
participatory research 333
Participatory Rural Appraisal (PRA) approach 236
Past is a Foreign Country, The (Lowenthal) 15–16, 25, 36, 255, 277, 289, 317

INDEX

Pendlebury, J. 1, 14, 130
people-based preservation 321
People, Building Neighborhoods 188, 189
people-centered heritage practice 24, 286
perceived stimuli 131
perceiving process 131
Perception: A transactional approach 131
perceptions of meaning 45, 48
perceptions of phenomena 131
Percy, W. 90
Periodic Reporting process 238
Peters, H. 23
Philippot, P. 13, 42
photo-elicitation 21, 129; glass wall 138, *139*; Great Hall 134, *135*, 138; muse sculptures 135, *137*; participant-led 134, 137; researcher-led 134, 138; as social sciences research method 133; stained glass lantern, women of music 135, *136*; trencadís columns, parlor 135, *136*; types of 134
photographs, sociocultural meanings and 133–4
phronesis 163
phronetic social sciences *see* phronesis
Piaget, J. 290
pietas 98
place attachment 50
place-centered heritage conservation 2
place, characteristics of 51
place experiences 51
Place to Remember: Using History to Build Community, A (Archibald) 92
placelessness 50
Planning in the Face of Power 162
policy-related research 312–13
post-processual archaeological theory 16
Power Broker, The (Caro) 145
power elite 84n3
PRA approach *see* Participatory Rural Appraisal (PRA) approach
pragmatic acceptance 80
predictability, McDonaldization of heritage stewardship and 76
Preservation Chicago 188–9
preservation/conservation doctrine 10
"Preservation for People: A Vision for the Future" 18
"Preservation for Tomorrow" conference (1972) *183*
preservation of the distinguished 103
preservation of the undistinguished 103
preservation profession 196, 199, 206, 207, 311–12
preservation research 314–16
preservation theory 41–2
preservation's research capacity 314

"Principles for Integrating Environmental Design and Behavior Research into Built Heritage Conservation Practice" 12
Principles of Repair 9
Project Mosul 59
psychometrics, sense of place 46; case study 48–9; current realities of historic preservation 57–63, *58–62*; development of 49–50; focus groups 52–3, **54**; perceptions of sense of place 50–2; psychometric measurement tools 49; reliability analysis 55, **55**; "shiver effect" 47–8; survey outcomes and implications 56; survey testing and data analysis 53, **55**, 55–6, 57; tangible and intangible resources 46; use of measurement tools 52
public history 35
public housing 159–60, 170
public outreach and education program 227
public outreach process 215–18, 227, 232
Public Research Group (CUNY) 21, 147
Public Space Strategy (2014) 106
Purser, M. 24
Pyu Ancient Cities 241

radical engagement 81
Radical Preservation 90–1, 98
"Radical Preservation: Toward a New and More Ancient Paradigm" 90
radicalness 318
rationalism 10
rationalistic preservation/conservation theory 318–19
RBS *see* River Basin Surveys (RBS)
Reconnaissance Level Survey (RLS) 230
Recreation Experience Preference (REP) model 52
Regional Plan Association's (1929) 154
"Rehabilitation Is Key to Lincoln Park Plan" 182
Rekrei 59
relationships 50
researcher-led photo-elicitation 134, 138
Researching Your Genealogy: A Journey of Self-Discovery 291
Resistance to Research 309–10
Resolution of the International Symposium on the Conservation of Smaller Historic Towns (1975) 23
resource management 20, 71–2, 78; conformity 69; modernity 80; rationality 67; shadow 78–9
resourcism 81–2
Revenue Act of 1978 182
Rhode Island's Certified Local Government Grants program 311
Rhodes, C. 71
Ricoeur, P. 92–3
Ridley, T. 299
Riegl, A. 15, 42

350

INDEX

Ritzer, G. 67, 68, 75, 77
River Basin Surveys (RBS) 256
RLS *see* Reconnaissance Level Survey (RLS)
Rogers, J. L. 258
Rogers, R. 81–2
Round Table Workshop 219
Rowntree, L. 93
Ruskin, J. 8, 13, 42, 144, 145, 150
Russell, R. 276, 316n5
Ryberg-Webster, S. 23, 198, 200, 324

SACHP *see* State Advisory Committee on Historic
    Preservation (SACHP)
Sachs, P. J. 301
Sagan, C. 6, 18
Salem 219; demolition of local landmark 229; heritage
    all-star designation 231; heritage sites 219; historic
    preservation plan 214–15, 227, 228, 231, 232; *see also*
    Historic Landmark Commission (HLC)
Salem Area Comprehensive Plan 215
Salem Heritage Neighborhood Program 230, 232
"Salem History Matters" 229
San Antonio Conservation Society 164, 167–8
sangha communities 247–8
Sarason, S. 3
Schofield, J. 36
SDGs *see* Sustainable Development Goals (SDGs)
Seamon, D. 318
Secretary of the Interior's Standards for Preservation
    Planning 105
Section 502 257
SEED *see* South East Economic Development (SEED)
self-discovery learning method 290, 305; critics of 292–3;
    for preservation education 302–3, *303–4*; pros and cons
    to 291
"self-serving" 289–90
sense of place 45; perceptions of 50–2; psychometrics to
    measure 49–50; *see also* psychometrics, sense of place
setting domains 53
SfAA *see* Society for Applied Anthropology (SfAA)
shadow 68–71
"Shared Places, Contested Pasts: Historical Memory and
    Historic Preservation" 276, 279–80, 284
Sheffield Historic District 182, 184, 185, 188, 191
"shiver effect" 47–8
SHPOs *see* State Historic Preservation Offices (SHPOs)
"significant architecture" 262
Silberman, N. 40
Sinkin, W. 166, 172
site observation assignment 281–2; supporting students
    through 282–4

Smith, L. 2, 4, 5, 35–7, 77
Smithsonian Institution 256
social history 161–2, 168
social science approach 24
social scientists 40, 278–9
Society for Applied Anthropology (SfAA) 321
sociocultural meanings, photographs and 133–4
South East Economic Development (SEED) 106
spirit of place 51
SPSS *see* Statistical Package for the Social Sciences (SPSS)
stained glass lantern, women of music 135, *136*
Standards and Guidelines for the Conservation of Historic
    Places 9
Stapp, D. 73
State Advisory Committee on Historic Preservation
    (SACHP) 213
State Historic Preservation Offices (SHPOs) 256, 260
State Register of Historic Places 146
Statesman Journal 217
Statistical Package for the Social Sciences (SPSS) 55
Steele, F. 50
Stevenson, K. H. 96
Stevenson, R. L. 69
Stiefel, B. 25, 78, 292–4
stimulated perception 131
Storyboard America 296, 298
Strange Case of Dr. Jekyll and Mr. Hyde, The (Stevenson) 69
Streets of Dreams 159
Sulzberger, A. H. 305
Surveymonkey 219, 221
Sustainable Development Goals (SDGs) 235
sustained optimism 80, 81–2

TAC *see* technical advisory committee (TAC)
Taplin, D. H. 21–2
TAT *see* Thematic Apperception Testing (TAT)
tax credits 190, 198, 202–4
Tax Reform Act of 1976 181–2
Teaching with Historic Places 291
technical advisory committee (TAC) 215–17, 219, 222
Temple of Mrn 59
Tennessee-Tombigbee Waterway 257
Texas Historical Commission 168
Thematic Apperception Testing (TAT) 52
Thompson, F. 166
Tilden, F. 98
Torre, Marta de la 15
tourism 130; architectural 21, 134, 160–1; Asia-Pacific
    region 242, 243; authenticity in 131–2; Lijiang 243
Touro, A. 305
Touro, J. 305

INDEX

Touro Synagogue 305
trade-offs, economic benefits and 203–5
Traditional Cultural Property (TCP) projects 24,
256, 258, 260–1, 269; conceptualizing 262;
indigenous 263; no preference for 262; nominations
261–2; non-indigenous 263–4; not accepted
262–3
transactional perception 131
transactionalism 131
transcendence 92, 94
Travel Salem 215, 217
trencadís columns, parlor 135, *136*
Tresoldi, E. 60
Tretter, E. 168, 169
Tribal Historic Preservation Offices 327
Triumphal Arch 59
Trump, D. 147, 152
Trump Organization 143
Trump project 147, 152
Tuan, Y.-F. 35, 50
Turner, N. 299
Tusquets, O. 133
Twitter 133
2003 Convention 238, 239
2005 Convention 238
typology, of preservation features 107, 109, *110*

Unakul, M. 23
UNESCO Bangkok 246
UNESCO General Conference 236
UNESCO International Safeguarding Campaigns 237
UNESCO World Heritage site 8–9, 26n2, 277
United Nations Conference on Human Environment
(1972) 236
United Nations Educational, Scientific and Cultural
Organization (UNESCO) 24, 139, 233–4, 236–8, 240,
249, 250n2, 326
United States: heritage education 34–5, 276–9; historic
preservation 4–5, 41; "preservation planning"
10–11
#Unite4Heritage program 58
Upside of Down, The (Homer-Dixon) 82
urban development 163, 195
Urban Forest Plan (2009) 106
urban planning 162, 195, 206, 249, 312, 340
urban preservation: built environment 203; community and
economic development 195, *199*, 199–202; community
(re)building 205; construction 204; economic and
community development goals 195–6; economic benefits
and trade-offs 197, 203–5; heritage tourism 198; physical
improvements 197; poverty 199, 201, 204; professional

silos 197; renovation 204; tax credit investments 198;
view from preservationists 197–9, *198*
urban walking 144
U.S. Army Corps of Engineers 96
U.S. National Park Service 9
USAID 235
Uses of Heritage (Smith) 39

values-based preservation practice 14, 17, 198
Vanishing Treasures program 62
Venice Charter 9, 13, 236–7
Venturi, R. 60
Vidutis, R. 24
Vigo, G. 51
Vincent, M. 59
Viollet-le-Duc, E. 8, 42, 130–2, 144
Visser, T. 41
Visual Preference SurveyTM 52
Voegelin, E. 20, 90, 98

Wagner, C. 167
Walker, M. 72, 73
Walter, E.V. 91
Wang, N. 131
Wapner, S. 131
"Warriors Project" 62
Washington, G. 304
Waterton, E. 36
Watt, Laura A. 24
WB *see* World Bank (WB)
Wealthy Heights 106, 123, 123n4; architectural features in
107–10, 112, **113–14**, 115, **116–18**, 120–1; community
members of 109, 110; focus group 106–7; preservation
features of 121; residential buildings in *107*; typologies
109, *110*; web survey 106; *see also* architectural features
Weber, M. 67
Weber's theory of rationalization 67
Wells, J. 78, 316n2
Wells, J. C. 19, 236
Werner, H. 131
West Bathhouse "Neo-Collegiate Gothic WPA Art Deco"
145, 146
Western Science Based-Management Systems (WSBMS)
71, 78
*What is Your Heritage and the State of its Preservation?:
Essays on Family History Exploration from the Field*
(Stiefel) 295–6, *297*, 298–9, 301
WHS *see* World Heritage Sites (WHS)
"Why Do Old Places Matter" 18
wicked heritage problems 82
Winfrey, O. 290

INDEX

Winner, L. 153, 154
Winter, T. 5, 17, 37, 40
wire mesh structure 60, *61–2*
Witcomb, A. 5, 17
With Heritage So Rich 93–4
Wonjo, C. T. 198
Woolgar, S. 154
World Bank (WB) 236
World Heritage 23–4
World Heritage Committee 238
World Heritage Convention 132, 236, 238, 239, 244, 246
World Heritage Sites (WHS) 130, 238, 240, 248, 340
World Heritage Town *243*

World Wildlife Foundation and Conservation International 327–8
WSBMS *see* Western Science Based-Management Systems (WSBMS)

Yamato Declaration on Integrated Approaches for Safeguarding Tangible and Intangible Cultural Heritage (2004) 238
Yellowstone National Park 244, 251n9

Zeisel, J. 133
Zhang Xinyu 60
Zweig, C. 68, 69, 78, 83

Printed in the United States
by Baker & Taylor Publisher Services